THE RINEHART READER

Third Edition

Jean Wyrick
Colorado State University

Beverly J. Slaughter
Brevard Community College

THOMSON
WADSWORTH

Australia Canada Mexico Singapore Spain United Kingdom United States

The Rinehart Reader, Third Edition

Jean Wyrick and Beverly J. Slaughter

Publisher: *Earl McPeek*
Acquisitions Editor: *Julie McBurney*
Product Manager: *Laura Brennan*
Developmental Editor: *Camille Adkins*
Project Editor: *Dee Salisbury, Laura Miley*
Art Director: *Vicki Whistler*
Production Manager: *Kathleen Ferguson*
Cover image and detailed part openers: Henri Matisse, *Geraniums,* 1915. Oil on canvas, 59.37 cm. X 48.58 cm. Courtesy of the Fogg Art Museum, Harvard University Art Museumss. Request from the Collection of Maurice Wertheim, Class of 1906. © 1997 Succession H. Matisse, Paris/Artists Rights Society (ARS) NY.

Printed in Canada
9 10 11 12 13   07 06 05 04 03

For more information contact Wadsworth, 25 Thomson Place, Boston, MA 02210 USA, or you can visit our Internet site at http://www.wadsworth.com

ISBN: 0-1550-5512-7

Library of Congress Catalog Card Number: 98-070446

PREFACE

To some students the term "classic" suggests a certain accumulation of dust. This classic collection should dispose of that notion once and for all. The selections in *The Rinehart Reader* are classics in the sense of being established works by many of our best writers, works that instructors have turned to as models of eloquence and power again and again. But they are certainly not dusty. They are works that will challenge, inform, and stimulate student writers. In short, they are selections that fit Ezra Pound's wonderful definition of literature as "news that stays news."

Within that standard of quality, the selections provide ample variety. They range across the generations from the eighteenth century to the present. They vary in style and tone, from light hearted to elegant. They include multiple selections by several writers that illustrate the scope of individual style. And they range in method and intent across the traditional rhetorical categories.

In this third edition we were given the opportunity to offer some exciting new selections, based on information provided by teachers and students who had used the first two editions. We are pleased to include such diverse writers as Stuart Chase, Malcolm X, Gretel Ehrlich, and Mary Gordon. In several cases we chose to present new selections by authors who appeared in the earlier editions; thus the splendid styles of writers such as Maya Angelou, Annie Dillard, Russell Baker, Maxine Hong Kingston, Norman Cousins, and Lewis Thomas continue to be represented in this edition. Those who have taught from this textbook will be pleased to see that they may still introduce to their students the power of Alice Walker, Richard Rodriguez, E. B. White, Jessica Mitford, Martin Luther King, Jr., Mark Twain, and other favorites. Overall, readers will find nineteen new essays added to the fifty-eight most appreciated by users of earlier editions.

Users of the third edition will also discover an entirely new feature: the introduction of literature to *The Rinehart Reader*. Poets such as Robert Frost, Gwendolyn Brooks, Robert Hayden, and Sylvia Plath are included, along with fiction writers such as Edgar Allan Poe, Kate Chopin, Katherine Ann Porter, and Ernest Hemingway. Each rhetorical section now contains a poem and short story chosen not only to complement the strategy under discussion but also to encourage class discussion that will, in turn, stimulate fresh, imaginative writing assignments. An occasional literary assignment among the essays also shows students that the rhetorical techniques explained in this text—use of examples, comparison and contrast, cause and effect, argument, and so on—are "thinking" and organizational strategies effectively used by all sorts of writers for a variety of purposes.

Previous users of this book will also note that the second chapter, "The Writing Process," has been substantially revised to help students throughout the stages of invention, planning, and drafting. This chapter also emphasizes the recursive nature of revision throughout the writing process, as well as guiding students through a final revision procedure near the completion of their assignment.

For new readers, here is an overview of the text's features and some suggestions for their use: *The Rinehart Reader* opens with a unique two-part section. The first chapter, "Why Read?", offers a rationale for critical reading, followed by note-taking techniques that are then demonstrated in detail in an annotated essay. Following this introduction are works by eight distinguished authors on the subject of reading. These essays offer a variety of comments on reading—its importance in both our personal and public lives.

The second chapter, "The Writing Process," presents a clear, concise guide through the stages of composing an essay. Seven essays on the subject of writing follow, five by authors experienced in teaching writing. Several essays in this section also offer a personal or inspirational look at what writing means to some of its finest practitioners.

This comprehensive introduction gives students more on the subject of critical reading and the writing process than do most other college readers. For many courses, it can eliminate the need for supplementary texts. After completing the first two chapters, students will have an understanding of the reading-writing processes and will be ready for the classic essays that follow.

The essays themselves are grouped by chapter in the traditional rhetorical sequence, from narration to argumentation. Each chapter has a separate introduction that defines the rhetorical mode, shows how and when it is commonly used, and characterizes it through brief examples, many from the essays in this text. The introduction then provides students with step-by-step guidelines for developing that particular strategy in their own writing.

Each reading selection is preceded by a brief biography and photograph of the author. A set of five review questions—at least one of them a potential writing assignment—follows the reading. An additional set of writing assignments concludes each chapter. These final assignments refer to the specific readings, thus supporting what is, after all, the main purpose of the reader—to use classic essays as working models and prompts for student writing.

Reference features include a glossary of rhetorical and literary terms, a list of authors represented by more than one essay, an annotated table of contents, and an alternate thematic table of contents. An excellent instructor's manual, prepared by Anne Machin Norris, is also available at no additional charge.

We hope this brief description has clarified what the third edition of *The Rinehart Reader* is and what it isn't. We have not attempted to create a reader with a "gimmick" or one with unusual or peripheral selections. What *The Rinehart Reader* does provide is ample material on reading and the writing process, the rhetorical organization that most instructors prefer, and an excellent selection of readings that have demonstrated their value both as literature and as models of effective writing. Our intention is to give you what you need and expect from a traditional reader, developed to the very highest editorial standards. We would be lax in pursuing that goal if we failed to invite your comments and suggestions. Please direct them, along with any requests for information or sample materials, to the English Editor; Wadsworth; 25 Thomson Place; Boston, MA 02210.

ACKNOWLEDGMENTS

WE would like to thank the many helpful people at Wadsworth for their work on this edition. We acknowledge former English Executive Editor Michael Rosenberg's support during the early stages of writing the text, and we appreciate the continuing confidence of English Editor Julie McBurney during its completion. As always, our deepest appreciation to Senior Developmental Editor Camille Adkins, whose expertise guided this edition with insight and good humor. Very special thanks to Laura Miley, our current Project Editor, for all her excellent help on this edition. We are also grateful to Dee Salisbury, former Project Editor; Kathleen Ferguson, Senior Production Manager; Vicki Whistler, Art Director; Cheri Throop, Photo and Permissions Researcher; Teresa Chartos, Copy Editor; Jessica Claffey, Editorial Assistant; and Anne Machin Norris, who wrote the accompanying Instructor's Manual. Nancy Land and the Publications Development Company continue to do a fine job with great care and attention to detail.

We are also indebted to the following colleagues who reviewed the text for this edition and helped us with our final selection of readings: Robert G. Collmer, Baylor University; Richard Conway, Lamar Community College; Michael Felker, South Plains College; Jane Longdon, Community College of Allegheny County; William Nix, Pearl River Community College; and Mary Lee Strode, State Technical Institute at Memphis.

Last, we express our gratitude to our families for their patience and understanding during the development of this edition.

To the Student

How do writers write? George Simenon would churn out whole novels in eleven-day frenzies, with a complete medical examination before and after. Flaubert would sit smoking a pipe from noon till four in the morning, often completing no more than a sentence. Proust wrote lying in bed. Hemingway wrote standing up. The lives and habits of writers offer endless anecdotes, but no useful rules.

Yet there are clearly problems and techniques that all writers share. This book is organized to reveal them. It groups diverse works according to essential rhetorical forms, allowing you to see, for example, how both Alice Walker and Richard Selzer develop a narration, how both Thomas Jefferson and Rachel Carson construct and close an argument. From such comparisons common elements emerge—not rules per se, but strategies, structures, methods, and tools.

These strategies may not be readily apparent in the essays themselves. In fact, the better the writing, the less exposed are its methods, the less obvious is the hard work that produced it. We may breeze through a piece by Thurber, but Thurber certainly didn't. Try stopping in the middle of one of his sentences. Then ask yourself how you would complete the sentence, the paragraph, or the entire essay. Suddenly, it's no breeze.

In this respect, the first chapters of the book are vital. They will show you how to read critically, think like a writer, and practice as you go. The same is true for the introductions to the mode and strategy that begin each chapter in Part 2. As you read the selections in each chapter, you should refer to the chapter's introduction often. Doing so will help you understand specific strategies of development you are studying. These introductions will also help you focus on the specific technique being considered. In the writing assignments that follow the selections, you will be asked to practice certain methods of organization and development.

Of course, any essay is more than just a neat stack of rhetorical techniques. This book offers a wealth of ideas, styles, voices, facts, punchlines, images, and philosophies, all of which are resources for your own writing. You can greatly expand these resources by using the book's Thematic Table of Contents for additional comparative readings and the list of multiple selections to examine the range of a single author's style. The Annotated Table of Contents is useful for the browser.

We hope that this book will be a part of a lively, informative course and a source of good reading long after graduation. We always enjoy hearing from students and teachers who use our texts. Any comments, questions, or suggestions may be sent to the English Editor; Wadsworth; 25 Thomson Place; Boston, MA 02210.

ABOUT THE TITLE OF THIS BOOK

Stanley M. Rinehart, Jr. (1897–1969), was a distinguished book publisher. In 1929, he, his brother Frederick, and editor John Farrar founded the publishing house of Farrar & Rinehart, which later became (in 1946) Rinehart & Company, and then (in 1960) Holt, Rinehart and Winston. As president of Rinehart & Company, Stanley Rinehart published such works as Norman Mailer's *The Naked and the Dead,* the "Nero Wolfe" detective novels of Rex Stout, and Rinehart Editions, a series of quality paperback editions of classic literature. The firm began its college department in 1934 and soon became a major publisher in the field, specializing in the humanities and social sciences. Today, Wadsworth carries on this same tradition of excellence through such noteworthy volumes as *The Rinehart Reader.*

CONTENTS

Chapter Four

Description   178

Chapter Five

Process   238

Chapter Six

Definition   288

Chapter Seven

Illustration   341

ANNOTATED CONTENTS

PART TWO

Essays for Reading and Analysis

Chapter Four

Description   178

[§] Denotes poetry
[*] Denotes short story

Chapter Five

Process   238

§ Denotes poetry
* Denotes short story

---

§ Denotes poetry
* Denotes short story

---

§ Denotes poetry
* Denotes short story

Chapter Eight
Comparison and Contrast   394

Chapter Nine
Division and Classification   443

§ Denotes poetry
* Denotes short story

[§] Denotes poetry
[*] Denotes short story

Chapter Eleven

Persuasion and Argument   *555*

§ Denotes poetry
* Denotes short story

---

§ Denotes poetry
* Denotes short story

Thematic Contents

IV. Race and Cultural Identity

V. Education

VI. Women's Issues

VII. Health and Medicine

Authors Represented by Multiple Works

PART ONE

Reading and Writing Essays

CHAPTER ONE

Why Read? How Can Reading These Essays Help Me?

Almost no student or professional ends a day without having read or written something: he or she has, in fact, most likely done both. Students read textbooks, research articles, study outlines, and lab manuals and must write tests, essays, term papers, critiques, summaries, reports, and, eventually, letters of application. Professionals of all kinds face proposals, memos, committee minutes, reports, evaluations, computer printouts, and business letters. Because so much of life's important business (both personal and professional) is conducted by reading and writing, you can improve your chances of success if you improve your reading and writing skills now.

Reading and writing are intertwined skills; if you improve one, the other will also profit. Consequently, close study of the essays in this text should help you become a better writer in several ways.

First, you'll get to see what good writing looks like. Discovering the various ways that admired authors such as Mark Twain, George Orwell, and Maya Angelou organized and developed their material should give you some new ideas about selecting your own strategies, arranging your ideas, and clarifying your explanatory details. Familiarizing yourself with the effective stylistic devices and diction of great writers may also stimulate you to use language in ways you've never tried before. And while no one expects you to sound like James Thurber or Virginia Woolf at this point, why not study the best while you're working on your own prose style?

Second, reading and discussing the prose of others should make you more aware of the writing process itself. Each writer represented in this book faced a series of problems similar to those you face when you write; each had to make decisions regarding organization, development, coherence, sentence style, tone, and so forth, just as you do. By asking questions (Why did Ellen Goodman begin the essay this way? Why did Lewis Thomas compare this to that?), you will begin to see how the writer constructed the essay—and that knowledge in turn can help you build your essay.

Third, exposure to some of the interesting opinions and arguments expressed in this collection may help you discover some new insights of your own, ideas you may wish to write about now and think about for years.

Finally, discussing the ideas and rhetorical choices of these authors should also help you become more sensitive to the importance of revision. All good writers revise, and most revise as they write as well as between drafts. Reading the excellent prose in this text should encourage you to write and revise for readers, not just for yourself. As you revise, ask yourself questions such as: Can my reader see this as clearly as I could see Richard Selzer's patient in "The Discus Thrower" (Chapter 3)? Is my conclusion as emphatic as E. B. White's in "Once More to the Lake" (Chapter 4)? Do I need to add details to make my prose as vivid as Jessica Mitford's in "The American Way of Death" (Chapter 5)?

Thus, by becoming a critical reader of the essays in this text, you can improve the content, clarity, organization, and style of your own writing.

How to Become a Critical Reader

To become a critical reader, you need to understand not only the content but also the composition of the essay under study. Try practicing the process outlined below; while this process calls for a thorough reading, some rereading, marking of the text, and note taking, the benefits to you as both reader and writer will be worth the extra time.

I. Stage One: Prereading

Before you begin the essay, consider these questions.

1. *Who is the author?* Is he or she an authority on this subject? What expectations do you have about his or her opinions? The author's reputation, previous works, occupation, political stance, or philosophy may help you prepare for the ideas ahead. (In this text, always read the biographical headnotes.) For instance, it may be helpful to know, before you begin her piece on the funeral industry, that Jessica Mitford was a well-known investigative reporter or that Margaret Mead, writing on superstitions, was a world-famous anthropologist.

2. *Who was the original audience?* Writers expand, delete, and shape their material according to the needs and attitudes of their readers. Martin Luther King, Jr., for instance, had to calm as well as inspire the audience listening to his "I Have a Dream" speech (Chapter 11). Seeing how other writers addressed their audiences will help you learn this skill yourself.

3. *Where and when was this essay published?* A selection from a scientific journal may have more credibility than one in a popular magazine, and it may demand more concentration from its readers, too. The date of

publication might explain some of the unfamiliar references or slightly archaic language. In older essays, such as George Orwell's classic "Politics and the English Language" (Chapter 10), you may find some examples from the 1940s that are still relevant today.

4. *What is the title?* Titles often announce the essay's subject matter ("The Jeaning of America," "College Pressures," "On Self-Respect") or even state the writer's attitude toward the subject ("How Books Helped Shape My Life," "Mankind's Better Moments," "Why Don't We Complain?") or tell what the essay will do ("Two Ways of Looking at the River," "Grant and Lee: A Study in Contrasts," "Once More to the Lake"). Titles also often set the tone of the essay, and they frequently act like barkers outside of circus tents: they try to grab your attention and encourage you to go in. Studying the titles of professional essays can help you name your own work in an engaging way.

II. STAGE TWO: READING FOR PURPOSE AND PRIMARY STRATEGY

1. First, read the essay through without marking anything. Then jot down a sentence or two summarizing your general impression. Consider what you think the author was trying to do *(purpose)* and how well he or she succeeded (a typical response might be "argued for a new work-study program—unconvincing, boring—too many confusing statistics").

2. Next, identify the *primary strategy of development.* Is the essay written in the form of a narrative or a description? An argument? An expository essay primarily developed by examples, process analysis, definition, comparison/contrast, causal analysis, or classification? Did the author select the best strategy for his or her purpose? Why or why not? For instance, would Maya Angelou have been more persuasive in an editorial on the value of role models than in the narrative of "Sister Flowers" (Chapter 3)? Would Jessica Mitford in "The American Way of Death" (Chapter 5) have been more effective if she had merely argued against embalming rather than allowing readers to see the process?

III. STAGE THREE: ESSAY ANALYSIS

Once you have a clear overview of the essay's purpose and form, go back to the beginning of the selection and make notes on the essay's content, organization, and style. These notes will help show you how the author put his or her essay together, and they will also prepare you to discuss the essay in class. (A sample essay marked according to the advice below appears on pp. 8–11 for you to use as a model.)

1. Look again at the *title* and at the *introduction.* Did they draw you into the essay? Did they set the appropriate tone?

2.   Frequently, writers of expository and argumentative essays will present their main point *(thesis)* early in the essay; the thesis may be stated plainly in one or more sentences or it may be implied. Once you've located the main point, underline the sentence (or note the area in which it is most strongly implied) and write the word "thesis" or a capital "T" in the margin so that you can find it easily.

3.   As you read through the essay again, you may discover important statements that support the thesis. These statements are sometimes found in *topic sentences,* which often occur near the beginning or at the end of body paragraphs. So that you can quickly find each of these supporting points later, underline and number each one and place a key word or a short phrase in the margin by each number. (Hint: writers often use subheadings to announce a new point; watch for these and also for any italicized or underlined words.) Writing down these key words and ideas will also help you remember the *content* of the essay. You may also find it useful to underline or put a star by important or especially effective statements, to put a question mark by those passages you think are weak, exaggerated, or untrue. Also, use the margins to jot down brief responses, raise questions, or make note of new ideas (or possible essay topics). Don't be afraid to talk back or argue with the author. These markings and notes will help you assess the essay's effectiveness in your final evaluation.

4.   Each time you discover one of the essay's key points, ask yourself how the author *develops* that idea. For instance, does he or she try to support or prove the point by providing examples, statistics, or testimony; by comparing or contrasting it to something else; or by describing, classifying, or defining the subject? A writer can choose one method of development or any combination, but each major point in an essay should be presented clearly and logically with some sort of evidence. Underdeveloped ideas or ones supported only by generalizations, obviously biased sources, or emotional outpourings are not ultimately convincing.

5.   As you move through the essay, you will probably run across some words you don't know. Often, you can guess the meanings of these words from their context, the surrounding words and ideas. If, however, you find some unfamiliar words essential to the author's main points, you may wish to circle these, consult your dictionary, and jot down their definition or a familiar synonym in the margin.

6.   Look closely at the essay's *conclusion*. Does it emphasize the author's thesis without being boring or repetitive? Does it call for action or suggest a solution? A good conclusion offers a pleasing sense of closure; readers should not feel they just stepped off the edge of a cliff.

7.   Consider the essay's *tone*, the writer's *voice*. Is it ironic, sarcastic, serious, informal, humorous, or something else? An inappropriate tone can undercut an author's intended effect on the reader. For instance, a flippant, overly informal tone may offend the reader who takes seriously the subject in

question; a sarcastic tone may signal a writer who's too angry to be logical. On the other hand, a coolly rational tone can be convincing, and sometimes humor can be persuasive in a way that nothing else can. Creating the right tone is important.

8. The author's *style* is important, too. Does he or she use figurative language (for example, similes, metaphors, personification) in an arresting way? Literary allusions? Specialized diction? Does he or she use any sentence patterns that are especially effective? Repetition of words or phrases? Writers use a variety of stylistic devices to make their prose vivid and memorable; you may want to study some of the devices you find so that you can try using them in your own essays.

9. To help you structure your own essay, you may find it useful to note how the writer moved from one point to the next. Bracketing the *transition devices* that link the paragraphs or the ideas within paragraphs can make you aware of the ways a good writer subtly creates a smooth, easy-to-follow flow of thought. (You won't have time to do this throughout the entire essay, but you might try marking a few paragraphs.)

10. Once you have completed the steps above, you're ready to make your final evaluation of the essay. Review your notes and markings; they should help you quickly locate the important parts of the essay and your impressions of those parts. Is the essay's thesis supported by enough logically developed, persuasive points? Is each point as clear, convincing, and well stated as it should be? Is the essay organized effectively? What strengths and weaknesses did you find after this critical reading? Has your original evaluation changed? If so, write a new assessment of the essay. Add any other comments you want to remember about this piece of writing.

Finally, after this critical reading of the essay, have you discovered any new ideas, strategies, or techniques you wish to incorporate into *your* writing?

Following is an essay marked and annotated according to the steps just discussed.

TELEVISION AND THE AMERICAN FAMILY

Marie Winn

Title announces subject   (1936–   )

Marie Winn is the author of twelve books for or
about children and many articles for such publications as *The New York Times Magazine* and
The Village Voice. An influential book, *Children
Without Childhood* (1983), grew from her article,
"What Became of Childhood Innocence?" and
illustrates the changes in attitudes toward children since the 1960s. Her 1985 book, *Unplug-
ging the Plug-In Drug* continues a discussion
begun in 1978 with the publication of her well-
known study *The Plug-In Drug: Television, Children and the Family,* from which this excerpt is
taken. Winn currently writes nature books,
including *Red-Tails in Love: A Wildlife Drama
in Central Park* (1998).

*Author is widely published
on children*

*General audience of
readers concerned about
television's relationship to
family*

over 13 years ago. Dated?

1   Home and family life have changed in important
ways since the advent of television. The peer group
has become television-oriented, and much of the
time children spend together is occupied by television viewing. Culture generally has been transformed by television. Therefore it is improper to
assign to television the subsidiary role its many
apologists (too often members of the television industry) insist it plays. Television is not merely one
of a number of important influences upon today's
child. Through the changes it has made in family
life, television emerges as *the* important influence
in children's lives today.

*Introduction sets up T.V. as
most important influence*

The Quality of Family Life

2   [Television's] contribution to [family life] has been
an equivocal one. For while it has, indeed, kept the

*Having more than one
outcome*

members of the family from dispersing, it has not served to bring them *together*. <u>By its domination of the time families spend together, it destroys the special quality that distinguishes one family from another, a quality that depends to a great extent on what a family *does*, what special rituals, games, recurrent jokes, familiar songs, and shared activities it accumulates.</u>

Thesis: T.V.'s domination of family time destroys "specialness"

3   "Like the sorcerer of old," writes Urie Bronfenbrenner,* "the television set casts its magic spell, freezing speech and action, turning the living into silent statues so long as the enchantment lasts. <u>The primary danger of the television screen lies not so much in the behavior it produces—although there is danger there—as in the behavior it prevents:</u> the talks, the games, the family festivities and arguments through which much of the child's learning takes place and through which his character is formed. Turning on the television set can turn off the process that transforms children into people."

Supporting testimony from a professional

4   Yet <u>parents have accepted a [television]-dominated [family life] so completely that they cannot see how the medium is involved in whatever problems they might be having.</u> A first-grade teacher reports:

1. Acceptance by parents

5   "I have one child in the group who's an only child. I wanted to find out more about her family life because this little girl was quite isolated from the group, didn't make friends, so I talked to her mother. Well, they don't have time to do anything in the evening, the mother said. The parents come home after picking up the child at the babysitter's. Then the mother fixes dinner while the child watches TV. Then they have dinner and the child goes to bed. I said to this mother, 'Well, couldn't she help you fix dinner? That would be a nice time for the two of you to talk,' and the mother said, 'Oh, but I'd hate to have her miss 'Zoom.' It's such a good program!'"

Quotation: shows T.V. replacing mother-daughter conversation

6   <u>Even when families make efforts to control television, too often its very presence counterbalances the positive features of family life.</u> A writer and mother of two boys aged 3 and 7 described

2. Even "controlled" T.V. disrupts family life

---

* Bronfenbrenner was a professor in the Department of Human Development at Cornell University.

her family's television schedule in *The New York Times*:

> We were in the midst of a full-scale War. Every day was a new battle and every program was a major skirmish. We agreed it was a bad scene all around and were ready to enter diplomatic negotiations. . . . In principle we have agreed on $2\frac{1}{2}$ hours of TV a day, "Sesame Street," "Electric Company" (with dinner gobbled up in between) and two half-hour shows between 7 and 8:30 which enables the grown-ups to eat in peace and prevents the two boys from destroying one another. Their pre-bedtime choice is dreadful, because, as Josh recently admitted, "There's nothing much on I really like." So . . . it's "What's My Line" or "To Tell the Truth." . . . Clearly there is a need for first-rate children's shows at this time. . . .

More quoted testimony—another parent—shows that watching is all-important

7   Consider the ["family life"] described here: Presumably the father comes home from work during the "Sesame Street"–"Electric Company" stint. The children are either watching television, gobbling their dinner, or both. While the parents eat their dinner in peaceful privacy, the children watch another hour of television. Then there is only a half-hour left before bedtime, just enough time for baths, getting pajamas on, brushing teeth, and so on. The children's evening is regimented with an almost military precision. They watch their favorite programs, and when there is "nothing much on I really like," they watch whatever else is on—because *watching* is the important thing. Their mother does not see anything amiss with watching programs just for the sake of watching; she only wishes there were some first-rate children's shows on at those times.

And mother?

?

3. Better shows not the solution

8   Without conjuring up memories of the Victorian era with family games and long, leisurely meals, and large families, the question arises: isn't there a better family life available than this dismal, mechanized arrangement of children watching television for however long is allowed them, evening after evening?

Contrast to pre-television era

9   Of course, families today still do *special* things together at times: go camping in the summer, go to

4. T.V. diminishes ordinary life

the zoo on a nice Sunday, take various trips and expeditions. But their *ordinary* daily life together is diminished—that sitting around at the dinner table, that spontaneous taking up of an activity, those little games invented by children on the spur of the moment when there is nothing else to do, the scribbling, the chatting, and even the quarreling, all the things that form the fabric of a family, that define a childhood. Instead, the children have their regular schedule of television programs and bedtime, and the parents have their peaceful dinner together.

Gives examples of what's missed

5. T.V. keeps peace but prevents family growth

10   The author of the article in the *Times* notes that "keeping a family sane means mediating between the needs of both children and adults." But surely the needs of adults are being better met than the needs of the children, who are effectively shunted away and rendered untroublesome, while their parents enjoy a life as undemanding as that of any childless couple. In reality, it is those very demands that young children make upon a family that lead to growth, and it is the way parents accede to those demands that builds the relationships upon which the future of the family depends. If the family does not accumulate its backlog of shared experiences, shared *everyday* experiences that occur and recur and change and develop, then it is not likely to survive as anything other than a caretaking institution.

Exaggerated?

Conclusion: calls for shared experiences & gives warning

First impression: Winn wants us to see that television is destroying the quality of family life. Several persuasive points show how T.V. replaces family activity, talking.

Primary Strategy: causal analysis—the effects of T.V. on kids and family are clearly presented.

Final Evaluation: Even though some of the shows mentioned are long-gone, her main point is convincing. It's not just violent T.V. that hurts kids—it's the time spent watching instead of interacting with parents as a family. I agree—when I think of good times with my family, we were doing things together, not watching T.V. (Possible essay topic: the importance of last summer's family camping trip.)

Other Notes

1. Organization and development: good use of personal and professional testimony and real examples to support points. Should she have addressed times when the family watches together?

2. Style/Voice—Winn is serious, straightforward, concerned. Note good use of question in ¶ 8. Uses italics for emphasis—too often? Easy to read—no jargon.

WRITERS ON READING

In the following section, eight writers praise the diverse pleasures and benefits of reading. Some of these authors, such as Richard Wright and Eudora Welty, describe their first experiences with books; others, such as Judith Viorst, Lance Morrow, and Robert MacNeil, explain how reading has influenced their lives in numerous ways and at various times. Donald Murray suggests ways to best profit from one's reading, and Wendell Berry argues for the absolute necessity of reading skills in today's society. Certainly, most of these authors would agree with book lover and editor Clifton Fadiman, who once wrote that when you study a classic, "you do not see more in the book than you did before; you see more in *you* than was there before." According to these writers, the art of reading is possibly the most essential part of your education not only because it aids you in becoming a better writer, but also because it helps you thrive in a changing world.

READING AS A READER

Donald Murray
(1924–   )

≋≋≋⟶

Donald Murray has earned a national reputation for his life's work of teaching others how to write. He has been a professor of English (he is now professor emeritus of English) at the University of New Hampshire, a reporter for the *Boston Globe,* a contributing editor to *Time* magazine, and a feature writer for a variety of other magazines. He was awarded the Pulitzer Prize for editorial writing and is the author of many writing textbooks, including *The Craft of Revision* (1991) and *Crafting a Life* (1995). In "Reading as a Reader," first published as a part of *Read to Write* (1986), he describes a useful process for reading both to understand what is going on in the world and to discover the craft writers use to convey information.

1   A nightmare. You are shoved into a huge room that has dozens of doors and windows along every wall. You go to an open door and see a party you want to join. The door slams shut. You can't open it. You run to a window across the room and see a street in a city you've never visited. There are stores, restaurants, a jazz band playing, and a crowd of shoppers laughing and talking with each other in a strange language. Suddenly shutters slam shut and you can't see anything but darkness.

2   You step to a door where a man and a woman sit in comfortable chairs by a fireplace. They are talking to each other, but most of all you notice the way they listen. It would be wonderful to be listened to that way. They spot you, smile, and invite you to join them. The door shuts. Out another door is space and a spacewalker tumbles down, twists around, and starts to point. That door shuts. You start moving from window to door, catching a glimpse of surf rippling along an endless beach, a large book that seems to have important instructions, what looks like a movie but is far more real than that,

Donald Murray (© Courtesy Donald Murray)

and a formula that lies upon a laboratory table. Each door, each window slams shut. You move faster from door to window to door. You can see through each, but you can't escape the empty room. In a window, you see a newspaper with large headlines you can't understand; through a door someone beckons you to join a committee examining an accounting balance sheet; two couples dance a poem and wave as if they'd like to know you; a computer screen fills with green marks that don't make sense to you. Each window and every door shuts and you are left alone in the empty room.

3   That is the world of the person who can't read. Messages are delivered that can't be understood, opportunities are available that can't be taken, and, worst of all, there is a terrible loneliness, for the nonreader is isolated from the past, from what happens out of sight or off camera, from joining—and influencing—the members of those groups interested in business, the environment, religion, politics, sports, engineering, theatre, travel, art, music, and science, who communicate with each other by writing and reading.

4   The student in any field—medicine, public safety, language study, computer technology, environmental studies, sociology, biochemistry, political science, engineering, history, hotel management, law, business—finds it is essential to be an effective reader. Reading is increasingly important in a complex, global, technical society. We depend on the communication of an enormous amount of information and, in such a world, information, even more than money, means power. We may read books, memos, newspapers, or we may read a computer screen or printout, but read we must if we are to understand and participate in our world, to know and to influence what is going on. We also read to write, to learn the craft that not only allows us to receive information but also to discover what we know and share it.

IF YOU HAVE TROUBLE READING

5   Everybody has trouble reading. We all face texts that are incomprehensible to us. In some cases the material is extremely difficult; in some cases the author's style is difficult, and in many cases the writing is bad—we can't make the meaning come clear because there is no clear meaning. We cannot, of course, know whether the writer has anything of importance to say to us until we figure out what the writer has said. If we are reading just for recreation, then we can toss aside a book that is too difficult or has a style we don't enjoy. But on the job, as citizens, and in following our hobbies we have to read a lot of difficult writing and a lot of bad writing. Some of the worst writing unfortunately occurs in textbooks that students have to read to learn a subject or pass a course, or both. We all need to know what to do when we have trouble reading.

The Reader's Attitude

6   Our attitude about reading usually controls how we read as much as our attitude about writing, doing math, playing a sport, or having friends controls our

effectiveness in those areas. If we approach a text believing that we are not readers, or that we can't read, that attitude may make it more difficult for us to understand the challenging text.

7   In some cases the attitude we have simply may not be appropriate. Most students who get to college can read moderately well, regardless of what teachers and newspapers say. What we have to do is to build on the skills we already have. Our attitude should be that we are in college to learn, and learning means being able to read a broad variety of texts more effectively. You are taking this course to learn how to read with greater skill and to learn how reading can help improve your writing.

8   Don't worry too much about television and film making your generation nonreaders. The myths about the past only make us guilty and they are often just myths. In the good old days when I was growing up, you were a wimp if you read, and I was a secret reader. Most people I knew did very little reading. But if you are to be educated—to make use of information from many fields and times and authorities—then you will have to improve your reading.

9   The best way is simply to read more. You learn to ride a bicycle by hopping aboard and pedaling until you get up enough speed. Reading is, at the beginning, a skill that takes frequent practice.

10   Also remember that the writer has some responsibility to go halfway or more to the reader. Writing that is hard to read is occasionally the product of a complicated and important mind; however, it is more likely the product of an arrogant and pretentious mind. Do not blame yourself for a writer's irresponsibility.

11   It is not helpful to feel inadequate, stupid, whipped by a text before you begin. It *is* helpful to have command of a variety of strategies which may help you decipher a text.

READING FOR EXPERIENCE

12   Humans are the animals that can live more lives than a cat, and many of them are lived through reading. As we read we go back and forth in time, pass across oceans and barriers of language, religion, and culture.

13   Yes, for many readers, reading is an escape. I used to hide the fact that I read to escape or, if discovered, apologize for fleeing to the make-believe world of adventure stories or mysteries as other people escape by reading science fiction, westerns, or romance novels—even though President Kennedy never apologized for using spy stories to escape the realities of international affairs, nor did President Eisenhower hide his affection for westerns. And, after my daughter Lee died suddenly when she was only twenty, I learned an important lesson—one of many. Although I had been a lifetime compulsive reader, for weeks I could not read and, when I began to read again, it was only mystery and spy stories with a strong story line that could hold my interest. I escaped and I had good reason to escape, no apologies needed. Since then I keep a piece of escape reading nearby all the time, and when I travel or can't sleep or

start thinking too compulsively about what can't be thought about, I escape into a story.

14   We should not, however, forget that reading for escape from our world may also mean that we escape into other worlds. Reading is the enemy of ignorance, provincialism, and parochialism.

15   It is important that we read our way out of our own world, our own times, our own skin and live the lives of other people to find out how they feel and think. The ability to distance ourselves from ourselves and become someone else is a significant way to learn.

16   We may read biography or autobiography and escape into another person's life. We can, through reading, escape into the mind of a philosopher, observe with a scientist, study with a scholar, analyze with a critic, and live through a novel or a play. Reading powerful texts provides us with experience that rivals real experience in our memory, and may, in fact, influence us more than what we learn from our actual living.

Learning to Be Uncritical

17 To read for experience we have to learn to suppress our critical faculties for the moment and enter into the story, allowing the author to carry us along so that we absorb the world the writer has created for us. It usually helps to read fast and let the language, the flow, the energy of the text carry us along.

18   Reading for experience is usually an emotional as well as an intellectual activity, and in many cases all our senses are involved. We see the world of the writer, smell it, taste it, touch it. In some cases it becomes more real to us than ordinary living, the way a dream has its own special intensity. We have to learn how not to fight the text, but to give ourselves up to it, and not worry too much if we miss something here or there. We shouldn't stop to argue with the text, but to listen to the text in this first reading. Later we may want to read the text again differently, critically, more slowly. And certainly we will want to stand back from the experience we have had, the way we stand back from a party, a game, or a job, and put the experience into context, evaluate it, judge it, try to figure out what we learned from it. But first we have to have the experience.

READING FOR INFORMATION

19 When we read for information we experience the text in a different way. Depending on the information we seek, we may not want to enter into the story, and we do not much care how the writing is written, as long as the writing does not get in the way of the information we need. Our newspapers know we want information on stocks and football standings, and so they give us this information in the form of tables and listings. That writing is hardly "written" at all. Other times we need information that is hidden in a normal text of sentences and paragraphs. In that case we have to mine the text and extract the

information we need. In this kind of reading we may choose to stand apart from the text, not to be involved in but simply to make use of what is said.

Scanning

20 To extract information from a text we need to scan, swooping over the text, looking for any clues that may help us find where the information is. We may turn first to an index or table of contents to see if it will tell us where the information we need is placed. In the case of an academic article we may read the abstract, a summary paragraph usually printed in small type at the beginning of the article to serve information gatherers and save them time.

Watching for Road Signs

21 If we think the text has the information we need, we should run through it, paying attention to chapter headings, crossheads (such as the one above, "Watching for Road Signs"), illustrations, diagrams, or other signals designed to help us get to the information we need. When we confront the text itself we should look for key words that will tell us that the information may be nearby. For example, if we are looking for information on the low salaries of women office workers, we may look for such words as "secretaries," "file clerks," "typists," "receptionists," "salaries," "wages," "compensation," "sexism," "prejudice," "women," "girls," "office workers," and so on. We can run through many pages of type easily, stopping only when we see something that tells us the information may be nearby.

Making Notes

22 In reading for information we usually have a notebook or note cards handy so that we can put down the information we find. If the information is to be quoted directly, we should put quotation marks around it so that we know when we come to use it that the note is precisely as the author presented it. If we are to put the information in our own words it's helpful to do that immediately. It's also important to note the context in which the information was presented. The context for the information on office workers might be a feminist political statement, a report by a male scholar, a study by a union that wants to organize office workers, a statement by a corporation, or a survey by a government agency. It is most important that the note include the precise reference so that it can be included in the text and so that you and your reader can go back and find the information. This means the title of the publication, the author, and all of the details about the publication itself.

READING FOR UNDERSTANDING

23 Our most important reading occurs when we read to comprehend everything that a text has to teach us. We read for the experience of the text and we read

for the information we can mine from it—and more. Reading stocks our mind with information and connections between pieces of information—theories, ideas, concepts, principles—that grow and change as we grow and change, experiencing, integrating all that we take in from living and thinking. We read to learn, to stimulate our minds, and so we have to learn to read well enough to make intellectual use of a great variety of texts, including many which are not easy to read. Some of them are difficult because the subject matter is difficult and the author has not been able to—or is writing for a specialized audience and feels no need to—simplify it for a general reader. Other books are difficult because the author does not write well but still has brought together information and ideas that are significant.

24   All our lives we will be reading texts that are difficult for us to read. We will learn about a subject, read intensely in that area, get to know significant but difficult authors, and find it relatively easy to read what was once difficult; but, at the same time, we will continue to be learners, reading in new areas, and meeting new and challenging authors.

25   This process of lifelong education has become true for many people who have not considered themselves intellectuals or who did not imagine they would continue to learn—or have to continue to learn—after graduation. We live, however, in a society in which change seems to be the only constant. People advised me, for example, not to leave jobs with companies that no longer exist. Some security. The best security is an education that teaches you how to learn so you can adapt to the inevitable changes life will bring. Guess who laughed at writing on a word processor and found himself using one a few weeks later?

26   We all have difficult friends who are worth the effort, and you will have difficult authors to read whose articles, stories, poems, manuals, monographs, plays, and books—fiction and nonfiction—are worth the effort. We have to learn strategies for dealing with these texts. We do not need to use these strategies all the time, but we do need to have them on hand when we cannot understand what we are reading and so cannot even tell if the text is worth reading.

Who Are You?

27 The first step toward understanding is to know what you bring to the text as a reader. If a police officer, black or white, is assigned to a neighborhood, he or she must first know what prejudices, what stereotypes, what beliefs, what fears he or she wears with the badge. Each of us looks at the same neighborhood with significant differences, depending on our experience and our background. The same thing is true of a reader.

28 Expert readers know what they don't know and what they know as they approach a text. They know that their prejudices, preconceptions, personal background, and experiences affect the way they read the text. We all come to a book with a complicated inventory of information, ideas, and opinions that combine to make the text our own. We have begun to realize it is important to

understand this. Every text is different for every reader. That doesn't mean that we can't agree on what the text says, because we can, in discussion, usually work out a common understanding. It does mean that we often get to that understanding in very different ways. And it certainly can include the fact that we may disagree about what the text says.

29   The text is not separate from the reader. As the reader reads the text becomes what is read. If you see, for example, a group of teenagers with different colored skins fighting, what each observer sees is powerfully colored, pun intended, by the observer's own background. Often there is not just one truth, but many truths. And we see through our own eyes, our own experiences, our own knowledge.

Who's the Author?

30 Once you know who you are—at least who you are in relation to this subject— then it may help to know who the writer is. Usually there are short biographies or an identifying sentence that tells who the writer is and what is the writer's authority to write this piece: "Norbert Morrison, now a Congressman from Iowa, has been practicing cannibalism since his Freshman year in college." If you think that the background of the author is vital to your understanding of the piece, then you can use the standard reference books, such as *Who's Who* and *Current Biography,* in the library to discover what you need to know about the writer.

What's the Form?

31 It may help to understand the piece we are reading if we know the genre or form in which it is written. This sounds obvious, but notice how many people use the term "novel," which means a fictional story, a work of the imagination, to describe nonfiction books of history or biography which are supposed to be based on documentable facts. It may help you understand the piece you are reading if you know it is a profile, a short biography written by someone other than the subject, or an autobiographical essay in which the person is writing about himself or herself. Part of form is purpose. In an argument the author wants to persuade us, but in a personal essay about the same subject the author may simply want to entertain. In a news story about the same subject, the writer may simply want to deliver objective fact.

What's the Context?

32 It helps to know the context or the nature of the world in which the piece was written. Pieces that were written during the Vietnam War, when there was both strong opposition to the war and powerful support for the war, may be confusing to a young reader who did not experience the pressure from both sides.

33   The reader should know the point of view of the publication in which an article is published. Some political magazines, for example, have a conservative

point of view. Others are liberal. The reader needs to know that context. It may help, for example, to know that the discussion of a nuclear plant is written in a context of concern for human safety, for the environment, or for the economy.

Reading the Front Matter

34 Clues to questions of the writer's authority and the context of the book or article may be found by reading the notes about authors in a magazine or the material published on the dust jacket of a book or on a title page. It is often a good idea, for example, to see where the book was published. It may be significant to know that a book about Vietnam was published first in France, a nation that suffered its Vietnam ahead of ours. It also may be important to know if the book was written in 1958, before we got deeply involved, in 1968, when we were heavily involved, or in 1978, when the war was over. The table of contents, the preface, bibliographical notes at the end, and the index are all clues that may help us unlock the meaning of the book.

Reading Uncritically

35 The more difficult the text, the more important it is that we read it *uncritically* first. This doesn't seem to make sense until you realize that if the subject matter, the form of the writing, and the author's style are all strange to the reader, then the reader may bog down in paying too close attention to each specific piece of information, each sentence, each word. If we pay too close attention the first time around, we have no idea of the whole, no feeling for the meaning or the purpose of the piece of writing. If we read it fast, uncritically, we will miss a lot, and at times even feel as if we were in a foreign country where we can't understand what anyone is saying. But we do pick up more than we know and get a feeling for the piece of writing. Once we have an overall view of the territory we can go back and, working within that overall vision, pay close attention to the details that will give us a true understanding of the text. Remember the first time you went to a big game; you had to try to absorb the crowd, the teams, the whole atmosphere of what was going on. You probably didn't pay too much attention to the details of the game. But when you become a fan you understand the larger context and can focus your attention on a revealing detail, such as how a player moves away from the main action of the game. Reading uncritically is the first step toward reading critically.

Reading Carefully

36 When a text deserves close attention, then we keep repeating the pattern of looking from larger context to smaller and back. We need to know what each word means in context, and that cannot be known simply by knowing the meaning of each word. Most words have many meanings. Those meanings change, depending on all the other meanings into which they are built.

37   This diagram may help:

BOOK
   CHAPTER
      SECTION
         PARAGRAPH
            SENTENCE
               PHRASE
                  WORD

38   It looks complicated, and it is. Reading is one of the most sophisticated, intellectual acts we perform. But remember that you bring an enormous background of experience to this task. Even if you are not a person who considers yourself a reader, you are reading other people all the time. You read your parents and your roommate, your teachers and your friends, and the strangers you meet on the street or in a bar. You read the place in which they exist—who sits behind the desk or comes around and sits beside you in a chair during an interview. You read dress—formal or casual—and whether it is appropriate to the situation and the person. We are often amused at the Freshman who tries to look middle-aged, and at the middle-aged professor who tries to look like a Freshman. You read what the person says and how he or she says it: "You look as if you're new around here, can I help you?" You read body language: the hands on hips or the arms folded across the chest, or the hand extended palm out for a shake. You come to a text bringing all these intellectual skills with you so you can apply them to written language.

39   The diagram shows what you already do, reading the detail (the hesitant step, the avoiding eye, the move that brings the person too close to you) and fitting it into a generalization (this guy doesn't trust people like me) that, in turn, causes you to read meaning into what seemed like insignificant details a moment before. The reader moves back and forth from concept to word and word to concept, with increasing understanding.

40   Some of the tricks of the careful reader's trade are the following:

Underline.   It may help to understand the text if you underline key words, facts, phrases, sentences, and, on occasion, paragraphs. The purpose of underlining, however, is to help you identify the points of greatest significance and make them clear by pulling them out of the text. We have all seen inexperienced students highlighting or underlining almost every word of the text, a sure clue that they do not understand the text and are learning little from it.

Marginal Comments.   Reading is a private encounter between writer and reader. Writing in the margins allows the reader to talk back—or write back—to the writer. It is a helpful way for the reader to make the text his or her own. These comments can be abrupt, quick, or extensive, sometimes even extending to a card or a piece of paper that is taped to the page. In the margin the reader agrees and disagrees, extends the text and connects it with the reader's own experience, questions the text on the basis of the reader's experience, makes connections with other experiences, other evidence, other pieces of writing. You should train yourself to become more than a passive reader, to enter into the act of making meaning with the writer.

Connecting. It's often helpful to use arrows or circles or squares or lines or numbers to connect significant facts, words, or lines in a text. Sometimes you can see the importance of a word that is repeated in a text in this way, or actually draw the map of the piece right over the text, revealing how a meaning has been woven through the text.

Outlining. The skill of outlining may be even more important to a reader than a writer. If you outline—in whatever form is comfortable to you—what is being said in the text, you will strip the text down to its essentials, and you may be able to see the meaning that lies under the text and then be able to understand what the writer was doing in the text.

Precis. This is an old-fashioned device that is extremely helpful in understanding a text. I grumped at Miss Leavitt—no Ms. in those days—who made us precis, precis, precis our way through the eleventh grade, and groaned again when I saw my English teacher for the twelfth grade—you guessed it: Miss Leavitt. I precised my way through the twelfth grade. But it taught me to read with a piercing eye, tracking down meaning and helping to teach me to write concise, disciplined prose.

41　　To write a precis, say in a few paragraphs—preferably one paragraph— what is said in an entire article, chapter, or book, using your own words. The effort of compression squeezes out the nonessentials and forces you to discover the central meaning of the text.

42　　Some of the key elements in the text that reveal meaning include:

43　　1. *Title.* The title attempts to tell the reader what follows in a way that will attract the reader. Often it gives away the point of view or the tone of the piece of writing. I find titles extremely helpful as a way of planning writing. They often tell me how I feel as well as how I think about the subject, establish a point of view, and even set up limits for the piece of writing. The title of this book, for example, helped me focus on the fact that this text is designed to help the student read to improve the student's own writing.

44　　2. *The lead.* The lead is a journalistic term for the introduction or beginning of a piece of writing. A formal introduction too often announces what will be in the writing, so that the piece of writing itself becomes repetitive, an expansion of what has already been said. The lead—the first sentence, the first paragraph, the first page of the text—attempts to lead the reader into the text. It is quick and direct, but it establishes the subject, the limits of the subject, and the tone of the piece. Good writers usually will not proceed until they have the lead right. I may write 50 or 60 leads to an article before I get one that is right. You will be wise to pay attention to leads, both as a reader and as a writer.

45 3. *The ending*. The ending is the reverse of the lead. It is the last line, the last paragraph, the last page, and it is vital, for the ending is what the reader remembers best about a piece of writing. In the formal conclusion there is usually too much repetition. It has been said, and is said again in the same way with the same evidence. Skillful writers conclude by implication, not so much summarizing as giving the reader a quotation, an anecdote, a piece of evidence that draws the piece to a close in the reader's mind. Again, a young writer should pay close attention to how effective endings are written, and the reader should pay close attention, because in the ending the author gives away what he or she thinks has been said. The end is the writer's destination, the point toward which the writer has been writing.

46 4. *Turning points*. The reader should look for turning points in the text. They are like marks blazed on a tree on a mountain trail, and more. They not only point the reader to where the reader should go, but they also quickly summarize where they think the reader has been. If you spot the turning points and understand what the writer believes has been said and intends to say next, you will begin to see how the piece is working.

47 5. *Documentation*. One of the most revealing elements in the text is the evidence the writer uses to persuade the reader to believe what is being said. The evidence is crucial, and it should be questioned by the reader. Remember that evidence is not only formal, footnoted, scholarly documentation, but the anecdotes, analogies, and metaphors the writer uses to connect the text to the reader's own experience.

48 6. *Voice*. The element more than any other that makes us read on, makes us believe—or disbelieve—the text, makes us think and care, is the writer's voice. When we read we listen to the text, and what we hear influences us. We should look closely at how the writer uses language to understand what the writer is saying. We should be aware of the denotation of words, the precise meaning; and the connotation, what they mean in context. We can, for example, use the word bread to mean food, and by changing the context have it mean money. To hear the voice—and the meaning—it is often essential to read aloud.

49 7. *Key words*. Every piece of writing has key words. We must try to see what they are and to make sure we understand them. Those words often carry a huge weight of meaning, and we must attempt to understand what meanings they have in the text. A journalist writing about freedom of the press in this country uses freedom to mean protection *from* government interference, but a Russian may use the word freedom to argue for freedom *by* government interference, a concept we find very hard to understand.

50 When we understand what the text says, then we can stand back and judge the entire text, evaluating what was said and how it was said.

READING FOR APPRECIATION

51 Another way to approach a text is for appreciation. Of course, to appreciate a text it must be experienced and understood but then the reader, knowing what is said, can consider *how* it is said.

52 You all have experience as critics in many fields. For example, think how you relate to "your" music. You listen to the latest in a particular tradition, usually understanding how that tradition has evolved and how it relates to other musical traditions. You notice how the songs that are popular today are different from yesterday. You notice what they say and how they say it. You study, often unconsciously, how the music itself is changing, and you not only evaluate a particular piece of music, but performers as well. You see them in a tradition and you see how they relate to each other. And you know that the more familiar you become with a kind of music, a particular song, a type of performer, or a particular performer, the better you understand and appreciate what is going on.

53 This is what readers do, and it is so much a part of what writers do that we will discuss much of this in greater detail before the end of the chapter. Experienced readers heighten the quality of their experience by an interest in esthetics, the "how" in writing.

Listening for the How

54 Readers who want to appreciate reading are good listeners. They listen for the music in the writing, the rise and fall of the voice of the writer, the rhythm, the pace, and the change in pace, the intensity. To hear the music it is a good idea to read aloud, and read with some feeling, letting yourself enter into the text, act out the text so you can hear the writer speaking. Expert readers hear what they are reading as much as or more than they see it.

55 Sometimes a difficult text will come clear if it is read aloud. And, of course, the opposite can be true. Reading a text aloud can make the text self-destruct. The out-loud reading can reveal just how badly the writer writes.

Knowing the Tradition

56 As in music, each tradition of writing—poetry, fiction, nonfiction, drama—has its own historical flow. And so do the subgroups under each tradition. Nonfiction prose, for example, has divisions such as argument, whose roots pass back through the Romans to the ancient Greeks; and modern reportage isn't really so modern, it goes back at least to Addison, Steele, Thomas Paine, and others in the eighteenth century. The personal new journalism of the recent past was really a cyclical movement in which writers and editors relearned the lessons of earlier periods, when personalized journalism was popular. English professors spend a lifetime studying literary traditions, how they evolved, and how they are changing. You don't have to do that to appreciate writing. But the

more you know about the history of a form in which you are interested, the deeper your appreciation will be.

Knowing What You Like and Knowing What There Is to Like

57 The great defense of ignorance is, "I don't know anything about painting (literature, plays, movies, music), but I know what I like." You should know what you like and don't like, but you should also grow in your appreciation of what you are hearing, reading, and seeing. You should start with the assumption that what is in front of you has been done on purpose. That doesn't mean that you will like it. The cook may have very carefully prepared liver. You may not appreciate the craft and art of the chef, but you should at least taste it.

58 Tasting it in the arts means more than looking. It means making an attempt to understand what the artist or writer or composer was doing, and why. Don't have unrealistic expectations for a piece of writing. Each piece of work should be seen in its own tradition, for reading and the other arts are not just emotional experiences. They are esthetic experiences in which the emotion and the intellect combine. They are not accidental; they are purposeful. If you make a lifetime habit of trying to understand, you will find many more things that will give you appreciation—satisfaction, fulfillment, and joy. And, of course, you will find many things that you do not like, no matter what effort you make. I like liver, no reason you should.

59 You should know what you like but that knowing should keep growing, building on what you already appreciate. I like classical chamber music today. I came to it through an appreciation of small jazz combos. My understanding of what small jazz groups were trying to do allowed me to appreciate quintets, quartets, and trios, and the pleasing combat between the players. The more we know and appreciate, the more we see to know and appreciate. It keeps us forever young. Reading opens doors and windows so that we can decide what we want to learn and explore.

READING TO WRITE AND WRITING TO READ

60 Think of what you do as you read. It is an interesting and complex act. You look at the symbols on the page—the letters, the words—and take in what the writer has written. You experience the text, but that experience is mixed at the same time with all the other experiences you have had. The author's experience, and your experience, mix together as hot and cold water mix as they come out of the shower head. The text you are "reading" is no longer the author's text but a new text that has been composed by you as you read it.

61 We write as we read, and this experience of composing a text from our reading obviously helps us learn to write. We see the material that is around us. We see how each person shapes that material. Some of you may read in this book a text you have read a few years ago, or in high school, and find that you are a different reader now. Of course. We change and grow with our experiences in living, in writing, and in reading. And we learn not passively from a

text that is given to us, but actively, interacting with the text, studying it as some people study the Bible, the Torah, or the Koran, putting into the text what we can and getting out of the text what we are able to receive.

62   We also read as we write. The text we expect to write is not the text we write. We pour our experience with life and language through that tap, and it is mixed with the evolving text. The words we choose limit and shape our meaning. The phrases and sentences with which we hook our words together carry us in directions we did not expect to go. The denotation—the precise meaning of the words—and the connotation—the meanings that hover around the words—teach us as we write.

63   The text on our page moves us forward toward meaning in the same way that speech does. We all need to talk things out with a friend, a counselor, a member of the clergy, sometimes a stranger. We need to talk, not so much to get advice, but to hear what we have to say about a crisis in our life, or a decision we have to make. What we say gives discipline and form and meaning to those thoughts and feelings that are vague until we speak. We write a text through speaking, and we read it through hearing.

64   What appears on the page has to be read quickly as it is written, the way a football player has to read the defense while attempting to run through it. The text is in motion; it is changing as we do it. And that's something that the writer finds exciting. Too many of us have the idea that you are supposed to know what you have to say before you say it. If that were true few writers would write. We write to find out what we have to say, to read a text that is changing as we read it. We read what we have just written, and that influences what is being written and continually changes what may be written. Eventually we rewrite and revise and edit to clarify the meaning that we are reading.

65   Readers are writers whether they know it or not. And writers are always readers. There is no reasonable separation between the acts of reading and writing. Each activity is twin to the other, providing us with information and a disciplined way of finding meaning in that information, with the special bonus of being able to share that meaning with others, who, like you in reading my text, will compose your own text from it. I can no more control what you will find in your head in reading my words than I can control who my daughters may marry.

66   Write to learn how to read, and read to learn how to write.

Eudora Welty (© Nancy Crampton)

A Sweet Devouring

Eudora Welty
(1909–   )

Born in Jackson, Mississippi, Eudora Welty is a highly respected writer of fiction. Most of her work focuses on life in the South, particularly Mississippi, and captures the essence of place through vivid descriptions and lyrical speech that is so unique to her landscapes. After graduating with a B.A. in English from the University of Wisconsin in 1929, she briefly attended Columbia University's School of Business. In 1932, she returned to Jackson, where she worked for local newspapers, a radio station, and the Works Progress Administration as a junior publicity agent. In the 1930s, she published short stories in magazines and literary journals, including the *Southern Review* and the *Atlantic Monthly*. In 1972, she was awarded the Pulitzer Prize for *The Optimist's Daughter*. Her series of Harvard lectures, *One Writer's Beginnings* (1983), provides many insights into her growth as a writer. In "A Sweet Devouring," first published in *The Eye of the Story* (1977), Welty describes the pleasures of reading she discovered as a young girl.

1   OUR library in those days was a big rotunda lined with shelves. A copy of *V.V.'s Eyes* seemed to follow you wherever you went, even after you'd read it. I didn't know what I liked, I just knew what there was a lot of. After *Randy's Spring* there came *Randy's Summer*, *Randy's Fall* and *Randy's Winter*. True, I didn't care very much myself for her spring, but it didn't occur to me that I might not care for her summer, and then her summer didn't prejudice me against her fall, and I still had hopes as I moved on to her winter. I was disappointed in her

whole year, as it turned out, but a thing like that didn't keep me from want-ing to read every word of it. The pleasures of reading itself—who doesn't remember?—were like those of a Christmas cake, a sweet devouring. The "Randy Books" failed chiefly in being so soon over. Four Seasons doesn't make a series.

2   All that summer I used to put on a second petticoat (our librarian wouldn't let you past the front door if she could see through you), ride my bicycle up the hill and "through the Capitol" (shortcut) to the library with my two read books in the basket (two was the limit you could take out at one time when you were a child and also as long as you lived), and tiptoe in ("Silence") and exchange them for two more in two minutes. Selection was no object. I coasted the two new books home, jumped out of my petticoat, read (I sup-pose I ate and bathed and answered questions put to me), then in all hope put my petticoat back on and rode those two books back to the library to get my next two.

3   The librarian was the lady in town who wanted to be it. She called me by my full name and said, "Does your mother know where you are? You know good and well the fixed rule of this library: *Nobody is going to come running back here with any book on the same day they took it out.* Get both those things out of here and don't come back till tomorrow. And I can practically see through you."

4   My great-aunt in Virginia, who understood better about needing more to read than you *could* read, sent me a book so big it had to be read on the floor—a bound volume of six or eight issues of *St. Nicholas* from a previous year. In the very first pages a series began: *The Lucky Stone* by Abbie Farwell Brown. The illustrations were right down my alley: a heroine so poor she was ragged, a witch with an extremely pointed hat, a rich, crusty old gentleman in—better than a wheelchair—a runaway carriage; and I set to. I gobbled up installment after installment through the whole luxurious book, through the last one, and then came the words, turning me to *un*lucky stone: "To be con-cluded." The book had come to an end and *The Lucky Stone* wasn't finished! The witch had it! I couldn't believe this infidelity from my aunt. I still had my secret childhood feeling that if you hunted long enough in a book's pages, you could find what you were looking for, and long after I knew books better than that, I used to hunt again for the end of *The Lucky Stone*. It never occurred to me that the story had an existence anywhere else outside the pages of that sin-gle green-bound book. The last chapter was just something I would have to do without. Polly Pepper could do it. And then suddenly I tried something—I read it again, as much as I had of it. I was in love with books at least partly for what they looked like; I loved the printed page.

5   In my little circle books were almost never given for Christmas, they cost too much. But the year before, I'd been given a book and got a shock. It was from the same classmate who told me there was no Santa Claus. She gave me a book, all right—*Poems by Another Little Girl.* It looked like a real book, was printed like a real book—but it was *by her.* Homemade poems? Illusion-dispelling was her favorite game. She was in such a hurry, she had such a pile to

get rid of—her mother's electric runabout was stacked to the bud vases with copies—that she hadn't even time to say "Merry Christmas!" With only the same raucous laugh with which she had told me, "Been filling my own stocking for years!" she shot me her book, receiving my Japanese pencil box with a moonlight scene on the lid and a sharpened pencil inside, jumped back into the car and was sped away by her mother. I stood right where they had left me, on the curb in my Little Nurse's uniform, and read that book, and I had no better way to prove when I got through than I had when I started that this was not a real book. But of course it wasn't. The printed page is not absolutely everything.

6   Then this Christmas was coming, and my grandfather in Ohio sent along in his box of presents an envelope with money in it for me to buy myself the book I wanted.

7   I went to Kress's. Not everybody knew Kress's sold books, but children just before Christmas know everything Kress's ever sold or will sell. My father had showed us the mirror he was giving my mother to hang above her desk, and Kress's is where my brother and I went to reproduce that by buying a mirror together to give her ourselves, and where our little brother then made us take him and he bought her one his size for fifteen cents. Kress's had also its version of the Series Books, called, exactly like another series, "The Camp Fire Girls," beginning with *The Camp Fire Girls in the Woods.*

8   I believe they were ten cents each and I had a dollar. But they weren't all that easy to buy, because the series stuck, and to buy some of it was like breaking into a loaf of French bread. Then after you got home, each single book was as hard to open as a box stuck in its varnish, and when it gave way it popped like a firecracker. The covers once prized apart would never close; those books once open stayed open and lay on their back helplessly fluttering their leaves like a turned-over June bug. They were as light as a matchbox. They were printed on yellowed paper with corners that crumbled, if you pinched on them too hard, like old graham crackers, and they smelled like attic trunks, caramelized glue, their own confinement with one another and, over all, the Kress's smell—bandanas, peanuts and sandalwood from the incense counter. Even without reading them I loved them. It was hard, that year, that Christmas is a day you can't read.

9   What could have happened to those books?—but I can tell you about the leading character. His name was Mr. Holmes. He was not a Camp Fire Girl: he wanted to catch one. Through every book of the series he gave chase. He pursued Bessie and Zara—those were the Camp Fire Girls—and kept scooping them up in his touring car, while they just as regularly got away from him. Once Bessie escaped from the second floor of a strange inn by climbing down a gutter pipe. Once she escaped by driving away from Mr. Holmes in his own automobile, which she had learned to drive by watching him. What Mr. Holmes wanted with them—either Bessie or Zara would do—didn't give me pause; I was too young to be a Camp Fire Girl; I was just keeping up. I wasn't alarmed by Mr. Holmes—when I cared for a chill, I knew to go to Dr. Fu Manchu, who had his own series in the library. I wasn't fascinated either. There

was one thing I wanted from those books, and that was for me to have ten to read at one blow.

10   Who in the world wrote those books? I knew all the time they were the false "Camp Fire Girls" and the ones in the library were the authorized. But book reviewers sometimes say of a book that if anyone else had written it, it might not have been this good, and I found it out as a child—their warning is justified. This was a proven case, although a case of the true not being as good as the false. In the true series the characters were either totally different or missing (Mr. Holmes was missing), and there was too much time given to teamwork. The Kress's Campers, besides getting into a more reliable kind of trouble than the Carnegie Campers, had adventures that even they themselves weren't aware of: the pages were in wrong. There were transposed pages, repeated pages, and whole sections in upside down. There was no way of telling if there was anything missing. But if you know your way in the woods at all, you could enjoy yourself tracking it down. I read the library "Camp Fire Girls," since that's what they were there for, but though they could be read by poorer light they were not as good.

11   And yet, in a way, the false Campers were no better either. I wonder whether I felt some flaw at the heart of things or whether I was just tired of not having any taste; but it seemed to me when I had finished that the last nine of those books weren't as good as the first one. And the same went for all Series Books. As long as they are keeping a series going, I was afraid, nothing can really happen. The whole thing is one grand prevention. For my greed, I might have unwittingly dealt with myself in the same way Maria Edgeworth dealt with the one who put her all into the purple jar—I had received word it was just colored water.

12   And then I went again to the home shelves and my lucky hand reached and found Mark Twain—twenty-four volumes, not a series, and good all the way through.

DISCOVERING BOOKS

Richard Wright
(1908–1960)

Richard Wright was born on a cotton plantation near
Natchez, Mississippi, to a sharecropper and a school-
teacher. When he was five, his father deserted the family, and five years later, his mother suffered the first of
a series of strokes that left her partially paralyzed.
Wright was sent to live with his grandmother. He
dropped out of school after completing ninth grade,
worked a variety of odd jobs, and eventually made his
way first to Memphis, then to Chicago, and finally to
New York City. He also worked for the Works Progress
Administration Federal Writers' Project in Chicago and
in New York as a writer of guidebooks and as the
director of the Federal Negro Theater. In 1938, he published his first book, *Uncle Tom's Children: Four
Novellas,* but gained national recognition with his next
book, *Native Son* (1940). In 1944, Wright officially left
the Communist Party. In 1945, he published his autobiography *Black Boy.* Two years later, he and his family
moved to Paris, where he continued to write many
books, including *The Outsider* (1953), *Savage Holiday*
(1954), *White Man, Listen!* (1957), and *The Long
Dream* (1958). Another book, *The Man Who Lived
Underground,* was published posthumously in 1971. In
"Discovering Books," Wright explains why he saw
reading as an essential part of preparing himself to
become a writer.

Richard Wright (Corbis-Bettmann)

1   ONE morning I arrived early at work and went into the bank lobby where the Negro porter was mopping. I stood at a counter and picked up the Memphis *Commercial Appeal* and began my free reading of the press. I came finally to the editorial page and saw an article dealing with one H. L. Mencken. I knew by hearsay that he was the editor of the *American Mercury*, but aside from that I knew nothing about him. The article was a furious denunciation of Mencken, concluding with one, hot, short sentence: Mencken is a fool.

2   I wondered what on earth this Mencken had done to call down upon him the scorn of the South. The only people I had ever heard denounced in the South were Negroes, and this man was not a Negro. Then what ideas did Mencken hold that made a newspaper like the *Commercial Appeal* castigate him publicly? Undoubtedly he must be advocating ideas that the South did not like. Were there, then, people other than Negroes who criticized the South? I knew that during the Civil War the South had hated northern whites, but I had not encountered such hate during my life. Knowing no more of Mencken than I did at that moment, I felt a vague sympathy for him. Had not the South, which had assigned me the role of a nonman, cast at him its hardest words?

3   Now, how could I find out about this Mencken? There was a huge library near the riverfront, but I knew that Negroes were not allowed to patronize its shelves any more than they were the parks and playgrounds of the city. I had gone into the library several times to get books for the white men on the job. Which of them would now help me to get books? And how could I read them without causing concern to the white men with whom I worked? I had so far been successful in hiding my thoughts and feelings from them, but I knew that I would create hostility if I went about this business of reading in a clumsy way.

4   I weighed the personalities of the men on the job. There was Don, a Jew; but I distrusted him. His position was not much better than mine and I knew that he was uneasy and insecure; he had always treated me in an offhand, bantering way that barely concealed his contempt. I was afraid to ask him to help me to get books; his frantic desire to demonstrate a racial solidarity with the whites against Negroes might make him betray me.

5   Then how about the boss? No, he was a Baptist and I had the suspicion that he would not be quite able to comprehend why a black boy would want to read Mencken. There were other white men on the job whose attitudes showed clearly that they were Kluxers or sympathizers, and they were out of the question.

6   There remained only one man whose attitude did not fit into an anti-Negro category, for I had heard the white men refer to him as a "Pope lover." He was an Irish Catholic and was hated by the white Southerners. I knew that he read books, because I had got him volumes from the library several times. Since he, too, was an object of hatred, I felt that he might refuse me but would hardly betray me. I hesitated, weighing and balancing the imponderable realities.

7   One morning I paused before the Catholic fellow's desk.

8   "I want to ask you a favor," I whispered to him.

9   "What is it?"

10   "I want to read. I can't get books from the library. I wonder if you'd let me use your card?"

11   He looked at me suspiciously.

12   "My card is full most of the time," he said.

13   "I see," I said and waited, posing my question silently.

14   "You're not trying to get me into trouble, are you, boy?" he asked, staring at me.

15   "Oh, no, sir."

16   "What book do you want?"

17   "A book by H. L. Mencken."

18   "Which one?"

19   "I don't know. Has he written more than one?"

20   "He has written several."

21   "I didn't know that."

22   "What makes you want to read Mencken?"

23   "Oh, I just saw his name in the newspaper," I said.

24   "It's good of you to want to read," he said. "But you ought to read the right things."

25   I said nothing. Would he want to supervise my reading?

26   "Let me think," he said. "I'll figure out something."

27   I turned from him and he called me back. He stared at me quizzically.

28   "Richard, don't mention this to the other white men," he said.

29   "I understand," I said. "I won't say a word."

30   A few days later he called me to him.

31   "I've got a card in my wife's name," he said. "Here's mine."

32   "Thank you, sir."

33   "Do you think you can manage it?"

34   "I'll manage fine," I said.

35   "If they suspect you, you'll get in trouble," he said.

36   "I'll write the same kind of notes to the library that you wrote when you sent me for books," I told him. "I'll sign your name."

37   He laughed.

38   "Go ahead. Let me see what you get," he said.

39   That afternoon I addressed myself to forging a note. Now, what were the names of books written by H. L. Mencken? I did not know any of them. I finally wrote what I thought would be a foolproof note: *Dear Madam: Will you please let this nigger boy*—I used the word "nigger" to make the librarian feel that I could not possibly be the author of the note—*have some books by H. L. Mencken?* I forged the white man's name.

40   I entered the library as I had always done when on errands for whites, but I felt that I would somehow slip up and betray myself. I doffed my hat, stood a respectful distance from the desk, looked as unbookish as possible, and waited for the white patrons to be taken care of. When the desk was clear of people, I still waited. The white librarian looked at me.

41   "What do you want, boy?"

42   As though I did not possess the power of speech, I stepped forward and simply handed her the forged note, not parting my lips.

43   "What books by Mencken does he want?" she asked.

44   "I don't know, ma'am," I said, avoiding her eyes.

45   "Who gave you this card?"

46   "Mr. Falk," I said.

47   "Where is he?"

48   "He's at work, at the M—— Optical Company," I said. "I've been in here for him before."

49   "I remember," the woman said. "But he never wrote notes like this."

50   Oh, God, she's suspicious. Perhaps she would not let me have the books? If she had turned her back at that moment, I would have ducked out the door and never gone back. Then I thought of a bold idea.

51   "You can call him up, ma'am," I said, my heart pounding.

52   "You're not using these books, are you?" she asked pointedly.

53   "Oh, no, ma'am. I can't read."

54   "I don't know what he wants by Mencken," she said under her breath.

55   I knew now that I had won; she was thinking of other things and the race question had gone out of her mind. She went to the shelves. Once or twice she looked over her shoulder at me, as though she was still doubtful. Finally she came forward with two books in her hand.

56   "I'm sending him two books," she said. "But tell Mr. Falk to come in next time, or send me the names of the books he wants. I don't know what he wants to read."

57   I said nothing. She stamped the card and handed me the books. Not daring to glance at them, I went out of the library, fearing that the woman would call me back for further questioning. A block away from the library I opened one of the books and read a title: *A Book of Prefaces*. I was nearing my nineteenth birthday and I did not know how to pronounce the word *preface*. I thumbed the pages and saw strange words and strange names. I shook my head, disappointed. I looked at the other book; it was called *Prejudices*. I knew what that word meant; I had heard it all my life. And right off I was on guard against Mencken's books. Why would a man want to call a book *Prejudices*? The word was so stained with all my memories of racial hate that I could not conceive of anybody using it for a title. Perhaps I had made a mistake about Mencken? A man who had prejudices must be wrong.

58   When I showed the books to Mr. Falk, he looked at me and frowned.

59   "That librarian might telephone you," I warned him.

60   "That's all right," he said. "But when you're through reading those books, I want you to tell me what you get out of them."

61   That night in my rented room, while letting the hot water run over my can of pork and beans in the sink, I opened *A Book of Prefaces* and began to read. I was jarred and shocked by the style, the clear, clean, sweeping sentences. Why did he write like that? And how did one write like that? I pictured the man as a raging demon, slashing with his pen, consumed with hate,

denouncing everything American, extolling everything European or German, laughing at the weaknesses of people, mocking God, authority. What was this? I stood up, trying to realize what reality lay behind the meaning of the words. . . . Yes, this man was fighting, fighting with words. He was using words as a weapon, using them as one would use a club. Could words be weapons? Well, yes, for here they were. Then, maybe, perhaps, I could use them as a weapon? No. It frightened me. I read on and what amazed me was not what he said, but how on earth anybody had the courage to say it.

62   Occasionally I glanced up to reassure myself that I was alone in the room. Who were these men about whom Mencken was talking so passionately? Who was Anatole France? Joseph Conrad? Sinclair Lewis, Sherwood Anderson, Dostoevski, George Moore, Gustave Flaubert, Maupassant, Tolstoy, Frank Harris, Mark Twain, Thomas Hardy, Arnold Bennett, Stephen Crane, Zola, Norris, Gorky, Bergson, Ibsen, Balzac, Bernard Shaw, Dumas, Poe, Thomas Mann, O. Henry, Dreiser, H. G. Wells, Gogol, T. S. Eliot, Gide, Baudelaire, Edgar Lee Masters, Stendhal, Turgenev, Huneker, Nietzsche, and scores of others? Were these men real? Did they exist or had they existed? And how did one pronounce their names?

63   I ran across many words whose meanings I did not know, and I either looked them up in a dictionary or, before I had a chance to do that, encountered the word in a context that made its meaning clear. But what strange world was this? I concluded the book with the conviction that I had somehow overlooked something terribly important in life. I had once tried to write, had once revelled in feeling, had let my crude imagination roam, but the impulse to dream had been slowly beaten out of me by experience. Now it surged up again and I hungered for books, new ways of looking and seeing. It was not a matter of believing or disbelieving what I read, but of feeling something new, or being affected by something that made the look of the world different.

64   As dawn broke I ate my pork and beans, feeling dopey, sleepy. I went to work, but the mood of the book would not die; it lingered, coloring everything I saw, heard, did. I now felt that I knew what the white men were feeling. Merely because I had read a book that had spoken of how they lived and thought, I identified myself with that book. I felt vaguely guilty. Would I, filled with bookish notions, act in a manner that would make the whites dislike me?

65   I forged more notes and my trips to the library became more frequent. Reading grew into a passion. My first serious novel was Sinclair Lewis's *Main Street*. It made me see my boss, Mr. Gerald, and identify him as an American type. I would smile when I saw him lugging his golf bags into the office. I had always felt a vast distance separating me from the boss, and now I felt closer to him, though still distant. I felt now that I knew him, that I could feel the very limits of his narrow life. And this had happened because I had read a novel about a mythical man called George F. Babbitt.

66   The plots and stories in the novels did not interest me so much as the point of view revealed. I gave myself over to each novel without reserve, without trying to criticize it; it was enough for me to see and feel something different. And

for me, everything was something different. Reading was like a drug, a dope. The novels created moods in which I lived for days. But I could not conquer my sense of guilt, my feeling that the white men around me knew that I was changing, that I had begun to regard them differently.

67   Whenever I brought a book to the job, I wrapped it in newspaper—a habit that was to persist for years in other cities and under other circumstances. But some of the white men pried into my packages when I was absent and they questioned me.

68   "Boy, what are you reading those books for?"

69   "Oh, I don't know, sir,"

70   "That's deep stuff you're reading, boy."

71   "I'm just killing time, sir."

72   "You'll addle your brains if you don't watch out."

73   I read Dreiser's *Jennie Gerhardt* and *Sister Carrie* and they revived in me a vivid sense of my mother's suffering; I was overwhelmed, I grew silent, wondering about the life around me. It would have been impossible for me to have told anyone what I derived from these novels, for it was nothing less than a sense of life itself. All my life had shaped me for the realism, the naturalism of the modern novel, and I could not read enough of them.

74   Steeped in new moods and ideas, I bought a ream of paper and tried to write; but nothing would come, or what did come was flat beyond telling. I discovered that more than desire and feeling were necessary to write and I dropped the idea. Yet I still wondered how it was possible to know people sufficiently to write about them? Could I ever learn about life and people? To me, with my vast ignorance, my Jim Crow station in life, it seemed a task impossible of achievement. I now knew what being a Negro meant. I could endure the hunger. I had learned to live with hate. But to feel that there were feelings denied me, that the very breath of life itself was beyond my reach, that more than anything else hurt, wounded me. I had a new hunger.

75   In buoying me up, reading also cast me down, made me see what was possible, what I had missed. My tension returned, new, terrible, bitter, surging, almost too great to be contained. I no longer *felt* that the world about me was hostile, killing; I *knew* it. A million times I asked myself what I could do to save myself, and there were no answers. I seemed forever condemned, ringed by walls.

76   I did not discuss my reading with Mr. Falk, who had lent me his library card; it would have meant talking about myself and that would have been too painful. I smiled each day, fighting desperately to maintain my old behavior, to keep my disposition seemingly sunny. But some of the white men discerned that I had begun to brood.

77   "Wake up there, boy!" Mr. Olin said one day.

78   "Sir!" I answered for the lack of a better word.

79   "You act like you've stolen something," he said.

80   I laughed in the way I knew he expected me to laugh, but I resolved to be more conscious of myself, to watch my every act, to guard and hide the new knowledge that was dawning within me.

81   If I went north, would it be possible for me to build a new life then? But how could a man build a life upon vague, unformed yearnings? I wanted to write and I did not even know the English language. I bought English grammars and found them dull. I felt that I was getting a better sense of the language from novels than grammars. I read hard, discarding a writer as soon as I felt that I had grasped his point of view. At night the printed page stood before my eyes in sleep.

82   Mrs. Moss, my landlady, asked me one Sunday morning:

83   "Son, what is this you keep on reading?"

84   "Oh, nothing. Just novels."

85   "What you get out of 'em?"

86   "I'm just killing time," I said.

87   "I hope you know your own mind," she said in a tone which implied that she doubted if I had a mind.

88   I knew of no Negroes who read the books I liked and I wondered if any Negroes ever thought of them. I knew that there were Negro doctors, lawyers, newspapermen, but I never saw any of them. When I read a Negro newspaper I never caught the faintest echo of my preoccupation in its pages. I felt trapped and occasionally, for a few days, I would stop reading. But a vague hunger would come over me for books, books that opened up new avenues of feeling and seeing, and again I would forge another note to the white librarian. Again I would read and wonder as only the naive and unlettered can read and wonder, feeling that I carried a secret, criminal burden about with me each day.

89   That winter my mother and brother came and we set up housekeeping, buying furniture on the installment plan, being cheated and yet knowing no way to avoid it. I began to eat warm food and to my surprise found the regular meals enabled me to read faster. I may have lived through many illnesses and survived them, never suspecting that I was ill. My brother obtained a job and we began to save toward the trip north, plotting our time, setting tentative dates for departure. I told none of the white men on the job that I was planning to go north; I knew that the moment they felt I was thinking of the North they would change toward me. It would have made them feel that I did not like the life I was living, and because my life was completely conditioned by what they said or did, it would have been tantamount to challenging them.

90   I could calculate my chances for life in the South as a Negro fairly clearly now.

91   I could fight the southern whites by organizing with other Negroes, as my grandfather had done. But I knew that I could never win that way; there were many whites and there were but few blacks. They were strong and we were weak. Outright black rebellion could never win. If I fought openly I would die and I did not want to die. News of lynchings were frequent.

92   I could submit and live the life of a genial slave, but that was impossible. All of my life had shaped me to live by my own feelings and thoughts. I could make up to Bess and marry her and inherit the house. But that, too, would be the life of a slave; if I did that, I would crush to death something within me,

and I would hate myself as much as I knew the whites already hated those who had submitted. Neither could I ever willingly present myself to be kicked, as Shorty had done. I would rather have died than do that.

93   I could drain off my restlessness by fighting with Shorty and Harrison. I had seen many Negroes solve the problem of being black by transferring their hatred of themselves to others with a black skin and fighting them. I would have to be cold to do that, and I was not cold and I could never be.

94   I could, of course, forget what I had read, thrust the whites out of my mind, forget them; and find release from anxiety and longing in sex and alcohol. But the memory of how my father had conducted himself made that course repugnant. If I did not want others to violate my life, how could I voluntarily violate it myself?

95   I had no hope whatever of being a professional man. Not only had I been so conditioned that I did not desire it, but the fulfillment of such an ambition was beyond my capabilities. Well-to-do Negroes lived in a world that was almost as alien to me as the world inhabited by whites.

96   What, then, was there? I held my life in my mind, in my consciousness each day, feeling at times that I would stumble and drop it, spill it forever. My reading had created a vast sense of distance between me and the world in which I lived and tried to make a living, and that sense of distance was increasing each day. My days and nights were one long, quiet, continuously contained dream of terror, tension, and anxiety. I wondered how long I could bear it.

Judith Viorst (© 1991 by Jill Krementz)

How Books Helped Shape My Life

Judith Viorst
(1936–   )

Born in Newark, New Jersey, Judith Viorst is an essayist, poet, columnist, and contributing editor to *Red-
book* magazine. Her poetic monologues written for the
CBS special "Annie, the Woman in the Life of a Man"
won her an Emmy Award in 1970. She has published
collections of both poetry and prose, including *It's
Hard to Be Hip Over Thirty, and Other Tragedies of
Married Life* (1970); *Yes, Married: A Saga of Love and
Complaint* (1972); *Necessary Losses* (1987); *Forever
Fifty* (1989); *Earrings!* (1990); *Murdering Mr. Monti*
(1994); and her most recent work, *Imperfect Control:
Our Lifelong Struggles with Power and Surrender*
(1998). "How Books Helped Shape My Life" was first
published in 1960 in *Redbook* magazine. In the essay,
she discusses the impact fictional heroines had on her
emotional and intellectual development.

1 In books I've read since I was young I've searched for heroines who could
serve as ideals, as models, as possibilities—some reflecting the secret self that
dwelled inside me, others pointing to whole new ways that a woman (if only
she dared!) might try to be. The person that I am today was shaped by Nancy
Drew; by Jo March, Jane Eyre and Heathcliff's soul mate Cathy; and by other
fictional females whose attractiveness or character or audacity for a time were
the standards by which I measured myself.

2 I return to some of these books to see if I still understand the powerful
hold that these heroines once had on me. I still understand.

3 Consider teen-aged Nancy Drew—beautiful, blond-haired, blue-eyed girl
detective—who had the most terrific life that I as a ten-year-old could ever
imagine. Motherless (in other words, quite free of maternal controls), she
lived with her handsome indulgent lawyer father in a large brick house set
back from the street with a winding tree-lined driveway on the outside and a

faithful, nonintrusive housekeeper Hannah cooking yummy meals on the inside. She also had a boy friend, a convertible, nice clothes and two close girl friends—not as perfect as she, but then it seemed to me that no one could possibly be as perfect as Nancy Drew, who in dozens and dozens of books *(The Hidden Staircase, The Whispering Statue, The Clue in the Diary, The Clue of the Tapping Heels)* was resourceful and brave and intelligent as she went around solving mysteries left and right, while remaining kind to the elderly and invariably polite and absolutely completely delightfully feminine.

4   I mean, what else *was* there?

5   I soon found out what else when I encountered the four March sisters of *Little Women,* a sentimental, old-fashioned book about girls growing up in Civil War time in New England. About spoiled, vain, pretty Amy. And sickly, saintly Beth. And womanly, decent Meg. And about—most important of all—gawky, bookworm Jo. Dear Jo, who wasn't as flawless as the golden Nancy Drew but who showed me that girls like her—like *us*—could be heroines. Even if we weren't much to look at. Even if we were clumsy and socially gauche. And even if the transition into young womanhood often appeared to our dubious eye to be difficult and scary and even unwelcome.

6   Jo got stains on her dress and laughed when she shouldn't and lost her temper and didn't display tact or patience or restraint. Jo brought a touch of irreverence to the cultural constraints of the world she lived in. And yet her instincts were good and her heart was pure and her headstrong ways led always to virtue. And furthermore Jo—as I yearned to be—was a writer!

7   In the book the years go by, Beth dies, Meg and Amy marry and Jo—her fierce heart somewhat tamed—is alone. "'An old maid, that's what I'm to be. A literary spinster, with a pen for a spouse, a family of stories for children, and twenty years hence a morsel of fame, perhaps!' . . . Jo sighed, as if the prospect was not inviting."

8   This worried young reader concurred—not inviting at all!

9   And so I was happy to read of Jo's nice suitor, Mr. Bhaer, not handsome or rich or young or important or witty, but possessed of kindness and dignity and enough intelligence to understand that even a girl who wasn't especially pretty, who had no dazzling charms and who wanted to write might make a wonderful wife. And a wonderful mother. And live happily ever after.

10   What a relief!

11   What Jo and Nancy shared was active participation in life—they went out and *did*; they weren't simply done to—and they taught and promised me (at a time when mommies stayed home and there was no Women's Movement) that a girl could go out and do and still get a man. Jo added the notion that brusque, ungainly girls could go out and do and still get a man. And Jane of *Jane Eyre,* whose author once said, "I will show you a heroine as small and as plain as myself," added the further idea that such women were able to "feel just as men feel" and were capable of being just as passionate.

12   Orphaned Jane, a governess at stately Thornfield Hall, was a no-nonsense lady, cool and self-contained, whose lonely, painful childhood had ingrained in her an impressive firmness of character, an unwillingness to charm or curry

favor and a sense of herself as the equal of any man. Said Jane to Mr. Rochester, the brooding, haughty, haunted master of Thornfield: "Do you think I am an automaton?—a machine without feelings? Do you think, because I am poor, obscure, plain, and little, I am soulless and heartless? You think wrong—I have as much soul as you, and full as much heart!"

13   I loved it that such hot fires burned inside so plain a Jane. I loved her for her unabashed intensity. And I loved her for being so pure that when she learned of Mr. Rochester's lunatic wife, she sacrificed romance for honor and left him immediately.

14   For I think it's important to note that Nancy and Jo and Jane, despite their independence, were basically as good as girls can be: honest, generous, kind, sincere, reliable, respectable, possessed of absolute integrity. They didn't defy convention. They didn't challenge the rules. They did what was right, although it might cause them pain. And their virtue was always rewarded—look at Jane, rich and married at last to her Mr. Rochester. Oh, how I identified with Jane!

15   But then I read *Wuthering Heights,* a novel of soul-consuming love on the Yorkshire moors, and Catherine Earnshaw totally captured me. And she captured me, not in spite of her dangerous, dark and violent spirit, but *because* of it.

16   Cathy was as wild as the moors. She lied and connived and deceived. She was insolent, selfish, manipulative and cruel. And by marrying meek, weak Edgar instead of Heathcliff, her destiny, she betrayed a love she described in throbbing, unforgettable prose as . . . elemental:

17   "My love for Healthcliff resembles the eternal rocks beneath—a source of little visible delight, but necessary. Nelly, I *am* Healthcliff—he's always, always in my mind—not as a pleasure, any more than I am always a pleasure to myself—but as my own being. . . . "

18   Now who, at the age of 16, could resist such quivering intensity? Who would settle for less than elemental? Must we untamed creatures of passion— I'd muse as I lay awake in my red flannel nightie—submit ourselves to conventional morality? Or could I actually choose not to be a good girl?

19   Cathy Earnshaw told me that I could. And so did Lady Brett, of *The Sun Also Rises.*

20   Brett Ashley was to me, at 18, free, modern, woman incarnate, and she dangled alluring new concepts before my eyes:

21   The value of style: "She wore a slipover jersey sweater and a tweed skirt, and her hair was brushed back like a boy's. She started all that."

22   The glamour of having a dark and tortured past: "Finally, when he got really bad, he used to tell her he'd kill her. . . . She hasn't had an absolutely happy life."

23   The excitement of nonconformity: "I've always done just what I wanted."

24   The importance of (understated) grace under pressure: "Brett was rather good. She's always rather good."

25   And the thrill of unrepressed sexuality: "Brett's had affairs with men before. She tells me all about everything."

26   Brett married lovelessly and drank too much and drifted too much and had an irresponsible fling with a bullfighter. But she also had class—and her

own morality. She set her bullfighter free—"I'd have lived with him if I hadn't seen it was bad for him." And even though she was broke, she lied and "told him I had scads of it. . . . I couldn't take his money, you know."

27   Brett's wasn't the kind of morality that my mother was teaching me in suburban New Jersey. But maybe I wasn't meant for suburban life. Maybe—I would muse as I carefully lined my eyes with blue liner—maybe I'm meant for something more . . . emancipated.

28   I carried Brett's image with me when, after college, I lived for a while in Greenwich Village, in New York. But I couldn't achieve her desperate gallantry. And it struck me that Brett was too lonely and sad, and that Cathy had died too young (and that Scarlett O'Hara got Tara but lost her Rhett), and that maybe I ought to forget about unconventionality if the price was going to be so painfully high. Although I enjoyed my Village fling, I had no wish to live anguishedly ever after. I needed a heroine who, like me, wanted just a small taste of the wild before settling down into happy domesticity.

29   I found her in *War and Peace*. Her name was Natasha.

30   Natasha, the leading lady of this epic of Russian society during Napoleon's time, was "poetic . . . charming . . . overflowing with life," an enchanting girl whose sweet eagerness and passionate impulsivity were tempered by historic and private tragedies. Betrothed to the handsome and excellent Prince Andrew, she fell in love with a heel named Anatole, and when she was warned that this foolish and dangerous passion would lead to her ruin, "I'll go to my ruin . . . ," she said, "as soon as possible."

31   It ended badly with Anatole. Natasha tried suicide. Prince Andrew died. Natasha turned pale, thin, subdued. But unlike Brett and Cathy, her breach with convention was mended and, at long last, she married Pierre—a decent, substantial, loving man, the kind of man all our mothers want us to marry.

32   In marriage Natasha grew stouter and "the old fire very rarely kindled in her face now." She became an exemplary mother, an ideal wife. "She felt that her unity with her husband was maintained not by the poetic feelings that had attracted him to her but by something else—indefinite but firm as the bond between her own body and soul."

33   It sounded—if not elemental and doomed—awfully nice.

34   I identified with Natasha when, the following year, I married and left Greenwich Village. I too was ready for domesticity. And yet . . . her husband and children became "the subject which wholly engrossed Natasha's attention." She had lost herself—and I didn't want to lose me. What I needed next was a heroine who could reconcile all the warring wants of my nature—for fire and quiet, independence and oneness, ambition and love, and marriage and family.

35   But such reconciling heroines, in novels and real life, may not yet exist.

36   Nevertheless Natasha and Jane and Jo, Cathy, Nancy and Brett—each spoke to my heart and stirred me powerfully. On my journey into young womanhood I was fortunate to have them as my companions. They were, they will always remain, a part of me.

A HOMEMADE EDUCATION

Malcolm X

(1925–1965)

Malcolm X was born Malcolm Little in Omaha,
Nebraska, the son of a Baptist minister who was mur-
dered for his political beliefs. After his mother's mental
breakdown following her husband's death, Malcolm X
dropped out of high school and began associating with
street criminals and drug addicts. During the time he
spent in prison from 1946 to 1952, he learned to read,
studied the Black Muslim religion and the teachings of
Elijah Muhammad, and became an advocate of racial
separatism. Later, he rejected Muhammad's views and
began working toward a vision of worldwide racial
unity and equality. He was assassinated in 1965 as he
addressed a rally in Harlem. His writings include *The
Autobiography of Malcolm X* (1965), *Malcolm X
Talks to Young People* (1969), and *Malcolm X on
Afro-American Unity* (1970)—the latter two published
posthumously. "A Homemade Education" is taken
from his *Autobiography* and tells the story of how he
improved his abilities to read and write.

1   IT was because of my letters that I happened to stumble upon starting to acquire some kind of a homemade education.

2   I became increasingly frustrated at not being able to express what I
wanted to convey in letters that I wrote, especially those to Mr. Elijah Muhammad. In the street, I had been the most articulate hustler out there—I had com-
manded attention when I said something. But now, trying to write simple
English, I not only wasn't articulate, I wasn't even functional. How would I
sound writing in slang, the way I would *say* it, something such as, "Look,
daddy, let me pull your coat about a cat: Elijah Muhammad—"

Malcolm X (UPI/Corbis-Bettmann)

3 Many who today hear me somewhere in person, or on television, or those who read something I've said, will think I went to school far beyond the eighth grade. This impression is due entirely to my prison studies.

4 It had really begun back in the Charlestown Prison, when Bimbi[1] first made me feel envy of his stock of knowledge. Bimbi had always taken charge of any conversations he was in, and I had tried to emulate him. But every book I picked up had few sentences which didn't contain anywhere from one to nearly all of the words that might as well have been in Chinese. When I just skipped those words, of course, I really ended up with little idea of what the book said. So I had come to the Norfolk Prison Colony still going through only book-reading motions. Pretty soon, I would have quit even these motions, unless I had received the motivation that I did.

5 I saw that the best thing I could do was get hold of a dictionary—to study, to learn some words. I was lucky enough to reason also that I should try to improve my penmanship. It was sad. I couldn't even write in a straight line. It was both ideas together that moved me to request a dictionary along with some tablets and pencils from the Norfolk Prison Colony school.

6 I spent two days just riffling uncertainly through the dictionary's pages. I'd never realized so many words existed! I didn't know *which* words I needed to learn. Finally, just to start some kind of action, I began copying.

7 In my slow painstaking, ragged handwriting, I copied into my tablet everything printed on that first page, down to the punctuation marks.

8 I believe it took me a day. Then, aloud, I read back, to myself, everything I'd written on the tablet. Over and over, aloud, to myself, I read my own handwriting.

9 I woke up the next morning, thinking about those words—immensely proud to realize that not only had I written so much at one time, but I'd written words that I never knew were in the world. Moreover, with a little effort, I also could remember what many of these words meant. I reviewed the words whose meanings I didn't remember. Funny thing, from the dictionary first page right now, that "aardvark" springs to my mind. The dictionary had a picture of it, a long-tailed, long-eared, burrowing African mammal, which lives off termites caught by sticking out its tongue as an anteater does for ants.

10 I was so fascinated that I went on—I copied the dictionary's next page. And the same experience came when I studied that. With every succeeding page, I also learned of people and places and events from history. Actually the dictionary is like a miniature encyclopedia. Finally the dictionary's A section had filled a whole tablet—and I went on into the B's. That was the way I started copying what eventually became the entire dictionary. It went a lot faster after so much practice helped me to pick up handwriting speed. Between what I wrote in my tablet, and writing letters, during the rest of my time in prison I would guess I wrote a million words.

---

[1] A fellow inmate.

11   I suppose it was inevitable that as my word-base broadened, I could for the first time pick up a book and read and now begin to understand what the book was saying. Anyone who has read a great deal can imagine the new world that opened. Let me tell you something: from then until I left that prison, in every free moment I had, if I was not reading in the library, I was reading on my bunk. You couldn't have gotten me out of books with a wedge. Between Mr. Muhammad's teachings, my correspondence, my visitors . . . and my reading of books, months passed without my even thinking about being imprisoned. In fact, up to then, I never had been so truly free in my life.

WORDSTRUCK

Robert MacNeil

(1931–   )

~~~~~~~~

Best known for his news program "The MacNeil/
Lehrer News Hour" on PBS, Robert MacNeil began his
broadcasting career in Montreal, Canada, in the early
1950s. He also worked as a national and foreign correspondent for NBC, and in 1974 received an Emmy
Award for his coverage of the Senate Watergate hearings. Now retired from the News Hour, his broadcasting experience is evident in his book *The People
Machine: The Influence of Television on American Politics* (1968) and in his autobiography *The Right Place
at the Right Time* (1982). In "Wordstruck," which is
from his second autobiography of the same title
(1989), MacNeil reveals his love of literature and discusses the power of words to nourish the reader.

1   Nova Scotia lies one time zone closer to England than most of North
America, but in the days of my childhood it was spiritually closer still. Psychologically, the province I grew up in was still in large measure a British colony.
Halifax society was conditioned by the presence of generations of well-born,
sometimes aristocratic, British officers and showed it. The higher up the social
pecking order in that small but cosmopolitan seaport town, the more people
identified with England. We looked to England for the real juice of our patriotism, our ideals of dress and manners, codes of honour, military dash, and
styles of drill, marmalade and gin, pipe tobacco and tweed. We drew spiritual
values from the Church of England and humour from *Punch*. It was natural,
therefore, that from that fountainhead of everything wise and wonderful came
the books that shaped my imagination. When the magic of words first en-
snared me, they were words for the most part written in England and intended
for English ears: nursery rhymes, Beatrix Potter, *Winnie-the-Pooh, Peter Pan,
The Water Babies,* and *The Wind in the Willows.*

2   Obviously I must have been steeped in British middle-class idiom. After
all, Canadian boys didn't say *Oh, bother!* when something annoyed them, or

Robert MacNeil (© by Kate Kunz, Courtesy of MacNeil/Lehrer News Hour)

wear *Wellingtons* or *mackintoshes,* as Christopher Robin did, yet I knew them well. They became as familiar as the rubber boots and raincoats we wore. In spite of all this concentrated exposure to English writing, I didn't pick up and use such expressions. They accumulated in a reserve store, a second vocabulary; my dictionary of vicarious literary experience.

3   What did consciously affect me was the literary landscape. I was, and remain today, highly susceptible to the physical setting described in books. Starting with the Milne stories, part of me began inhabiting or wishing to be in the places they depicted, both the landscape and the emotional climate.

4   With a few exceptional moments, my life was unclouded and serene. There was the row over the taxi window. At the age of five I was sitting on the curb throwing stones into the street. A taxi passed and one of my stones broke a window. The taxi stopped, the driver grabbed me and marched me up to the house. My mother reacted so strongly that he began pleading with her, "No, don't beat him. It's all right! It was just an accident."

5   Nothing like that ever happened to Christopher Robin. Nobody threw sand in his eyes, which happened once to me, followed by an agonizing session of having them flushed out with boric acid. Nobody required him to eat everything on the plate—the liver or the scrambled egg which had long gone cold and clammy—down to the last bite, because of the starving Chinese or my moral character. The emotional climate was irresistible, I suppose, because Christopher Robin seemed to be totally in command of his world, as I manifestly was not of mine. He seemed, from a child's perspective, free from arbitrary orders. He decided when to put on his Wellingtons and when to visit his friends. He seemed to live to please himself as long as he bore the tedium of being polite to his elders.

6   The backdrop to the serenity of this emotional landscape was a physical world which also drew me strongly. It was something else first experienced in these books. The land in a book is a magic land: the author may tell you that it is ugly and barren, devastated by storms or wars, but it will fascinate me as real landscapes often cannot. The mere fact that they form the setting for a story that draws you in, for characters you identify with, casts an enchantment over that place. So it was with the meadow, the woods, the brooks inhabited by Winnie-the-Pooh, Rabbit, Owl, Kanga, and Tigger.

7   This was my first experience of being drawn into the spell cast by a storyteller whose words spin gossamer bonds that tie your heart and hopes to him. It was the discovery that words make another place, a place to escape to with your spirit alone. Every child entranced by reading stumbles on that blissful experience sooner or later.

8   For this Canadian child in the thirties there was something more at work. Somehow the idea was planted in me that the English landscape had a spiritual legitimacy that our Canadian landscape did not, because it was always the English landscape we read about. England was where stories were set, where people had adventures; England became the land of story books for me.

9   English woods, meadows, lanes, and villages stirred feelings that ours did not, as did the words for features of the English landscape not encountered

in Canada: *commons, dells, dingles, downs, moors, fells, tarns, burns,* and *becks*—the words were heavy with the promise of adventure.

10   That played subtly into other Anglophile influences working on me and I grew up putting a special value on things English. The forces drawing me there were irresistible, like a strong elastic band pulling me to the British Isles.

11   Lots of Americans feel that. For Canadians of my generation struggling, and often losing the struggle, for a national and psychic identity, England became more real than our own world, because of the books we lived in from childhood. It has taken another generation to throw off the vestiges of that psychic colonialism I grew up with, although there are a few shreds of it still left in the Canadian psyche. The seeds of my personal struggle, my personal strain of the virus, must have been planted by the words of Milne, Stevenson, Dickens, and Barrie.

12   In the garden of the small apartment house we lived in was a very big tree. One day, filled with visions of hollow trees that people could enter, even live in, I attacked the trunk of this tree. The power of imagination or wishful thinking was so strong that it by-passed any sense of physical reality. I actually believed I could cut rooms inside the tree; or, if I made a little effort, a staircase would magically appear. I would ascend the tree into an enchanted storybook world. Under my puny hatchet, the tree suffered no more than a few nicks and I retired very disappointed. I must have been thinking of Owl's tree with its curved steps in the Hundred Acre Wood or the hollow-tree entrances to the homes of the Lost Boys in *Peter Pan.*

13   That book made a strong impression at the age of four or five. *Peter Pan* was the first story that actually frightened me a little, just enough fear to make it pleasurable. The snatching of the Lost Boys by the pirates was a moment I could laugh off only when Captain Hook got it from the crocodile which had swallowed the alarm clock, but it left a shadow of anxiety. As for Peter, I never shared his desire not to grow up. I was less moved by the pathetic need to have his shadow sewn back on than by the hard-to-define attractions I felt for Wendy, who did the sewing.

14   Wendy jumped into my psyche as though there had been a template for her already cut out: the sister I did not have; a subtle blend of comforting maternalism and other vaguely intuited but desirable feminine attributes.

15   (No sister, but by now I had a brother, Hugh, almost four years younger. He arrived home just before the Christmas on which we had one of the last trees with real lighted candles on the tips of its branches, as memorable for its warm wax smell as for the sight.)

16   In *Peter Pan* I do not recall being consciously aware of the language, just the stories and the characters. What surprises me now is to find how facetious Barrie's style is, full of coy nudges and arch asides, which, if I had ever noticed them, were forgotten. Even more surprising is the level of the language:

Next comes Nibs, the gay and debonair, followed by Slightly, who cuts whistles out of the trees and dances ecstatically to his own tunes.

17   *Debonair* and *ecstatically* are not nowadays considered vocabulary for children under ten. But then that is true of many of the books considered appropriate to read to us fifty years ago, and probably even truer fifty years before that.

18   Certainly, *Robinson Crusoe* and *Gulliver's Travels,* written for adults, make no concessions to twentieth-century children. This is Gulliver's scene setting for the naval attack by Blefuscu on Lilliput:

> . . . upon this notice of an intended invasion, I avoided appearing on that side of the coast, for fear of being discovered by some of the enemy's ships, who had received no intelligence of me, all intercourse between the two empires having been strictly forbidden during the war, upon pain of death, and an embargo laid by our Emperor upon all vessels whatsoever.

19   What happened when I heard words I did not understand? I may have asked occasionally, but I remember clearly never wanting to interrupt the story. Either I got the drift from the context or ignored the words I did not know until some later time. That is how I find myself dealing with foreign languages: asking for translations of some words, guessing at others, remembering, forgetting, but, in net terms, the word command growing by the day.

20   Archaic language did not put me off. The stories had such compelling narrative ideas—Crusoe marooned alone, Gulliver in a land of people six inches tall—that I listened past the older words, listened harder. When I was aware of them they gave the stories a pleasant flavour, a little additional mystery, part of the atmosphere, like the illustrations of period costumes and weapons. It did not discourage me that Robin Hood said *methinks* and *sooth.*

> "Ah, Little John, methinks care for thine own appetite hath a share in that speech, as well as care for me. But in sooth I care not to dine alone. I would have a stranger guest, some abbot or bishop or baron, who would pay us for our hospitality. I will not dine till a guest be found, and I leave it to you three to find him."

21   In the *Just So Stories* and *The Jungle Books,* which we read in the same years, Kipling pushed his language right in front of me; I couldn't ignore it, the exotic Indian words, like *Bandarlog* and *dhak* tree, that seemed to have a taste as well as a sound; the strong names for the characters like Tabaqui the jackal, Nag the cobra, and Rikki-Tikki-Tavi, the mongoose. There were also his rhetorical devices, borrowed from the oral storytellers, repetitions like *the great grey-green, greasy Limpopo River, all set about with fever trees.* They are funny to a child and they grow hypnotic like magic incantations. The repetitions, the sing-song rhythms, and the exotic vocabulary were so suggestive that I imagined I could smell things like the perfumed smoke from the dung fire or the mysterious odour of sandalwood.

22   Kipling would make me sense a world totally beyond my experience: the heat, the dust, the smells, the clamour, the cries and noises of men and animals.

The dark natural forces, like the snakes, were never sentimentalized but in Kipling's hands became both more menacing and yet more tolerable because you were permitted to know their thoughts, too.

> Nag waved to and fro, and then Rikki-Tikki heard him drinking from the biggest water jar that was used to fill the bath. "That is good," said the snake. "Now, when Karait was killed, the big man had a stick. He may have that stick still, but when he comes to bathe in the morning he will not have a stick. I shall wait here till he comes." . . . Nag coiled himself down, coil by coil, round the bulge at the bottom of the water jar, and Rikki-Tikki stayed still as death.

23   Robinson Crusoe was my first full-blooded adult hero and his story enthralled me. I did not know until I got to college and heard about Defoe's place in the social history of England that what I absorbed so avidly was really an exemplar of right values—a model for the emerging British middle class—God-fearing, devout, honest, hard-working, sober, and obsessively protective of property. Something quite bourgeois in me must have responded, because I felt a deepening satisfaction and security as the poor devil retrieved each useful tool or cask of gunpowder from his wrecked ship.

24   Crusoe was another fictional character instantly congenial to me. I knew that I could cope with being the lone survivor of such a disaster. Crusoe made his isolation so cosy that I envied his being alone to fend for himself so cheerfully.

25   All these stories were laying down little lessons in psychology, as well as language, and this material was not being laid down in an empty place. New pieces triggered responses from material that was already there, for example, the pleasure it gave me as Crusoe provisioned his cave.

26   *Laid down* is a term with many associations—the keel of a ship to be built; fruits preserved for the winter; wine laid down to age. It is the term they use in sound and videotape editing when one track or sequence has been recorded and others will be added and mixed together.

27   It must be with words as it is with music. Music heard early in life lays down a rich bed of memories against which you evaluate and absorb music encountered later. Each layer adds to the richness of your musical experience; it ingrains expectations that will govern your taste for future music and perhaps change your feelings about music you already know. Certain harmonic patterns embed themselves in your consciousness and create yearnings for repetition, so that you can relive that pleasurable disturbance of the soul. Gradually, your head becomes an unimaginably large juke box, with instantaneous recall and cross-referencing, far more sophisticated than anything man-made.

28   It is so with words and word patterns. They accumulate in layers, and as the layers thicken they govern all use and appreciation of language thenceforth. Like music, the patterns of melody, rhythm, and quality of voice become templates against which we judge the sweetness and justness of new patterns and rhythms; and the patterns laid down in our memories create expectations and hungers for fulfillment again. It is the same for the bookish person and for

the illiterate. Each has a mind programmed with language—from prayers, hymns, verses, jokes, patriotic texts, proverbs, folk sayings, clichés, stories, movies, radio, and television.

29   I picture each of those layers of experience and language gradually accumulating and thickening to form a kind of living matrix, nourishing like a placenta, serving as a mini-thesaurus or dictionary of quotations, yet more retrievable and interactive and richer because it is so one's own, steeped in emotional colour and personal associations.

Lance Morrow (Courtesy of Lance Morrow, Boston University)

THE BEST REFUGE FOR INSOMNIACS

Lance Morrow
(1939–   )

A Harvard graduate, Lance Morrow is best known for his work at *Time* magazine, a career that has spanned over thirty years. Winner of the National Magazine Award in 1981, he has also written *America: A Rediscovery* (1987), *Fishing in the Tiber* (1989), and *The Chief: A Memoir of Fathers and Sons* (1984), which chronicles his relationship with his father Hugh Morrow, former *Saturday Evening Post* writer. His most recent works include *The Heart: A Memoir,* Vol. 1 (1995) and *Mad Genius: The Odyssey, Pursuit, and Capture of the Unabomber Suspect* (1996), which he coauthored. "The Best Refuge for Insomniacs" first appeared in *Time* in 1991. In the essay, Morrow discusses the importance of books in providing comfort, companionship, and stability to readers.

---

1   I know a woman whose son died by drowning on the night of his high school graduation. She told me she got through the weeks and months afterward by reading and rereading the works of Willa Cather. The calm and clarity of Cather's prose stabilized the woman and helped her through the time.

2   We have rafts that we cling to in bad weather—consolations, little solidarities, numbers we dial, people we wake up in the middle of the night.

3   Somehow it is not much fun to wake up the television set. The medium is a microwave: it makes reality taste wrong. Television transforms the world into a bright dust of electrons, noisy and occasionally toxic. Turn on the set and lingering dreams float out to mingle with CNN. Dreams are not an electronic medium.

4   During the war in the gulf, the escapist magician made urgent reality inescapable. Television became spookier than usual in its metaphysical way: the instant global connection that is informative and hypnotic and jumpy all at once—immediate and unreal. The sacramental anchormen dispensed their unctions and alarms. During the war, I found shelter in books in the middle of the night. They are cozier. The global electronic collective, the knife of the

news, could wait until the sun came up. The mind prefers to be private in its sleepless stretches.

5   Read what? I am not talking exactly about reading to escape. Nor about reading to edify and impress oneself. *Paradise Lost* is not much help at 3 in the morning, except of course as a heavy sleeping potion. I mean the kind of reading one does to keep sane, to touch other intelligences, to absorb a little grace. In Vietnam the soldiers said, "He is a man you can walk down the road with." They meant, a man you can trust when the road is very dangerous. Every reader knows there are certain books you can go down the road with.

6   Everyone has his or her own list—each list no doubt is peculiar, idiosyncratic. The books you keep for the middle of the night serve a deeply personal purpose, one of companionship. Your connection with them is a mystery of affinities. Each mind has its night weather, its topographies. I like certain books about fly fishing, for example, especially Norman Maclean's brilliant *A River Runs Through It*, which, like fishing itself, sometimes makes sudden, taut connections to divinity.

7   One man rereads the adventures of Sherlock Holmes. He cherishes their world, the fogs and bobbies, the rational wrapped in an ambient madness, the inexplicable each time yielding its secret in a concluding sunburst, a sharp clarity.

8   Television news, when it flies in raw and ragged, can be lacerating. The medium destroys sequence. Reading restores to the mind a stabilization of linear prose, a bit of the architecture of thought. First one sentence, then another, building paragraphs, whole pages, chapters, books, until eventually something like an attention span returns and perhaps a steadier regard for cause and effect. War (and television) shatters. Reading, thoughts reconstruct. The mind in reading is active, not passive-depressive.

9   There is no point in being too reverent about books. *Mein Kampf* was—is—a book. Still, some books have the virtue of being processed through an intelligence. Writers make universes. To enter that creation gives the reader some intellectual dignity and a higher sense of his possibilities. The dignity encourages relief and acceptance. The universe may be the splendid, twittish neverland of P. G. Wodehouse (escape maybe, but a steadying one) or Anthony Trollope's order, or Tolkien's. I know a married couple who got though a tragic time by reading Dickens to each other every night. Years ago, recovering from a heart operation, I read Shelby Foote's three-volume history of the American Civil War—a universe indeed, the fullest, most instructive tragedy of American history, all of the New World's Homer and Shakespeare enacted in four years. People find the books they need.

10   I like writers who have struggled with a dark side and persevered: Samuel Johnson, for example; his distinction and his majestic sanity both achieved the hard way. He emerged very human and funny and with astonishing resources of kindness. I have been reading Henry James' letters in the middle of the night. If James' novels are sometimes tiresome, his letters, which he produced in amazing quantity, are endlessly intelligent and alive. To a friend named Grace Norton, who was much afflicted, he wrote, "Remember that every life is

a special problem which is not yours but another's and content yourself with the terrible algebra of your own . . . We all live together, and those of us who love and know, live so most." He told her, "Even if we don't reach the sun, we shall at least have been up in a balloon."

11   Odd that 19th century writers should write a prose that seems so stabilizing in the late 20th. Ralph Waldo Emerson is good to have beside the bed between 3 and 6 in the morning. So is the book of *Job*. Poetry: Wallace Stevens for his strange visual clarities, Robert Frost for his sly moral clarities, Walt Whitman for his spaciousness and energy. Some early Hemingway. I read the memoirs of Nadezhda Mandelstam *(Hope Against Hope; Hope Abandoned)*, the widow of Osip Mandelstam, a Soviet poet destroyed by Stalin. I look at *The Wind in the Willows* out of admiration for Mr. Toad and for what he has to teach about folly and resilience.

12   The contemplation of anything intelligent—it need not be writing—helps the mind through the black hours. Mozart, for example; music like bright ice water, or, say, the memory of the serene Palladian lines of Jefferson's Monticello. These things realign the mind and teach it not to be petty. All honest thought is a form of prayer. I read Samuel Johnson ("Despair is criminal") and go back to sleep.

Wendell Berry (Thomas Victor)

IN DEFENSE OF LITERACY

Wendell Berry
(1934–   )

Born in Henry County, Kentucky, Wendell Berry is a
prolific poet, novelist, and essayist. He received his B.A.
and M.A. from the University of Kentucky, where he
later became a professor of English. His writings, which
often deal with the preservation of nature, the value of
manual labor, and the simple joys of the simple life,
have appeared in national literary publications and popular periodicals. He has published two collections of
short stories—*Fidelity: Five Stories* (1992) and *Watch
with M: And Six Other Stories of the Yet-Remembered
Ptolemy Proudfoot and His Wife, Miss Minnie, nee
Quinch* (1994)—and two collections of poetry, *Entries:
Poems* (1994) and *The Farm* (1995). Most recent works
include *Another Turn of the Crank: Essays* (1996);
Harlan Hubbard: Life and Work (1998); and *A Tim-
bered Choir: The Sabbath Poems, 1979–1997* (1998).
In "In Defense of Literacy," which first appeared in
Continuous Harmony (1972), Berry argues for the
study of literature as a defense against the assault of
"prepared public language" that addresses only the
"practical" and "immediate" concerns of humankind.

1      $\mathbf{I}$N a country in which everybody goes to school, it may seem absurd to offer
a defense of literacy, and yet I believe that such a defense is in order, and that
the absurdity lies not in the defense, but in the necessity for it. The published
illiteracies of the certified educated are on the increase. And the universities
seem bent upon ratifying this state of things by declaring the acceptability, in
their graduates, of adequate—that is to say, of mediocre—writing skills.

2   The schools, then, are following the general subservience to the "practical,"
as that term has been defined for us according to the benefit of corporations. By

"practicality" most users of the term now mean whatever will most predictably and most quickly make a profit. Teachers of English and literature have either submitted, or are expected to submit, along with teachers of the more "practical" disciplines, to the doctrine that the purpose of education is the mass production of producers and consumers. This has forced our profession into a predicament that we will finally have to recognize as a perversion. As if awed by the ascendency of the "practical" in our society, many of us secretly fear, and some of us are apparently ready to say, that if a student is not going to become a teacher of his language, he has no need to master it.

3   In other words, to keep pace with the specialization—and the dignity according to specialization—in other disciplines, we have begun to look upon and to teach our language and literature as specialties. But whereas specialization is of the nature of the applied sciences, it is a perversion of the disciplines of language and literature. When we understand and teach these as specialties, we submit willy-nilly to the assumption of the "practical men" of business, and also apparently of eduction, that literacy is no more than an ornament: when one has become an efficient integer of the economy, *then* it is permissible, even desirable, to be able to talk about the latest novels. After all, the disciples of "practicality" may someday find themselves stuck in conversation with an English teacher.

4   I may have oversimplified that line of thinking, but not much. There are two flaws in it. One is that, among the self-styled "practical men," the practical is synonymous with the immediate. The long-term effects of their values and their acts lie outside the boundaries of their interest. For such people a strip mine ceases to exist as soon as the coal has been extracted. Short-term practicality is long-term idiocy.

5   The other flaw is that language and literature are always *about* something else, and we have no way to predict or control what they may be about. They are about the world. We will understand the world, and preserve ourselves and our values in it, only insofar as we have a language that is alert and responsive to it, and careful of it. I mean that literally. When we give our plows such brand names as "Sod Blaster," we are imposing on their use conceptual limits which raise the likelihood that they will be used destructively. When we speak of man's "war against nature," or of a "peace offensive," we are accepting the limitations of a metaphor that suggests and even proposes violent solutions. When students ask for the right of "participatory input" at the meetings of a faculty organization, they are thinking of democratic process, but they are *speaking* of a convocation of robots, and are thus devaluing the very traditions that they invoke.

6   Ignorance of books and the lack of a critical consciousness of language were safe enough in primitive societies with coherent oral traditions. In our society, which exists in an atmosphere of prepared, public language—language that is either written or being read—illiteracy is both a personal and a public danger. Think how constantly "the average American" is surrounded by premeditated language, in newspapers, and magazines, on signs and billboards, on TV and radio. He is forever being asked to buy or believe somebody else's line of goods. The line of goods is being sold, moreover, by men who are trained to make him buy it or believe it, whether or not he needs it or understands it or knows its value or wants it. This sort of selling is an honored profession among

us. Parents who grow hysterical at the thought that their son might not cut his hair are *glad* to have him taught, and later employed, to lie about the quality of an automobile or the ability of a candidate.

7   What is our defense against this sort of language—this language-as-weapon? There is only one. We must know a better language. We must speak, and teach our children to speak, a language precise and articulate and lively enough to tell the truth about the world as we know it. And to do this we must know something of the roots and resources of our language, we must know its literature. The only defense against the worst is a knowledge of the best. By their ignorance people enfranchise their exploiters.

8   But to appreciate fully the necessity for the best sort of literacy we must consider not just the environment of prepared language in which most of us now pass most of our lives, but also the utter transience of most of this language, which is meant to be merely glanced at, or heard only once, or read once and thrown away. Such language is by definition, and often by calculation, not memorable; it is language meant to be replaced by what will immediately follow it, like that of shallow conversation between strangers. It cannot be pondered or effectively criticized. For those reasons, an unmixed diet of it is destructive of the informed, resilient, critical intelligence that the best of our traditions have sought to create and to maintain—an intelligence that Jefferson held to be indispensable to the health and longevity of freedom. Such intelligence does not grow by bloating upon the ephemeral information and misinformation of the public media. It grows by returning again and again to the landmarks of its cultural birthright, the works that have proved worthy of devoted attention.

9   "Read not the Times. Read the Eternities," Thoreau said. Ezra Pound wrote that "literature is news that STAYS news." In his lovely poem, "The Island," Edwin Muir spoke of man's inescapable cultural boundaries and of his consequent responsibility for his own sources and renewals:

> Men are made of what is made,
> The meat, the drink, the life, the corn,
> Laid up by them, in them reborn.
> And self-begotten cycles close
> About our way; indigenous art
> And simple spells make unafraid
> The haunted labyrinths of the heart. . . .

10   These men spoke of a truth that no society can afford to shirk for long: we are dependent, for understanding, and for consolation and hope, upon what we learn of ourselves from songs and stories. This has always been so, and it will not change.

11   I am saying, then, that literacy—the mastery of language and the knowledge of books—is not an ornament, but a necessity. It is impractical only by the standards of quick profit and easy power. Longer perspective will show that it alone can preserve in us the possibility of an accurate judgment of ourselves, and the possibilities of correction and renewal. Without it, we are adrift in the present, in the wreckage of yesterday, in the nightmare of tomorrow.

CHAPTER TWO

THE WRITING PROCESS

The writing process too often begins with the prospective "author" staring blankly at an empty sheet of paper, wondering where to start. Undoubtedly, every student has, at one time, been in that position. Even for many professionals, writing is not always easy. The symptoms of "writer's woes" are often the same for everyone: groping for an idea, perhaps finding a few thoughts but drawing a blank after a few sentences, struggling with words, fighting frustration.

No, writing is not a job entered into lightly, but it is a job that is possible to master and even enjoy. Even though no one has invented a foolproof formula for good writing, there are some ways to approach writing to make the task less of a struggle. The trick is in knowing the "phases" of the writing process and progressing toward your writing goal through those phases. Once you master the process of writing, you will find yourself staring less frequently at that empty sheet of paper.

The four phases of the writing process are planning, shaping, drafting, and revising. In the *planning* (or *prewriting*) phase, you will identify your assignment's purpose and audience, gather your thoughts, collect other information if needed, and determine your main focus. In the next phase, you will begin to form your clear stance and *shape* your ideas into a logical structure. This, in turn, leads to the *drafting* phase, the actual development of your essay's ideas on paper. *Revision* takes place during each phase of the entire writing process and plays an important role near the end of the process as well, as you rethink and carefully refine the ideas and language in your last draft. It takes practice, practice, and more practice, but you will discover that each time you move through the phases of writing, the process becomes easier. You will also discover your own version of the writing-process phases and ultimately find that all writing will be easier. Remember, you will need the skill of writing in every walk of life, not just the academic one. You may have résumés, business letters, memos, proposals, and other tasks ahead of you, so the more time you spend in honing your skills, the more those skills can work for you—now and in the future.

PHASE ONE: PLANNING

Planning your essay simply means thinking about what you have to say and how you want to say it. You might begin this phase by identifying the purpose of the writing. In writing a business letter, define the reason behind it. In answering an exam question, determine exactly what is being asked. In writing a letter to your best friend, think about what you have to say. The same principle is applied to writing an essay: first, determine the purpose of the writing.

For much of your college writing, you will be given assignments of some sort. In planning an essay to address such an assignment, start by making sure you understand precisely what you are being asked to do. If you have questions, do not hesitate to ask for clarification. Remember, before you *can* write, you must know *why* you're writing.

Once you understand just what the assignment is and what it asks of you, you can decide on an approach to the topic. Are you being asked to express personal feelings or attitudes? Is your goal to explain, define, describe, or persuade? All of these are important considerations in this prewriting phase.

When your purpose is clear, you will find it easier to set the boundaries that will lead to shaping your material. One of the elements to consider is your *audience*. Although it may seem so, writing is not a solitary action. Whatever you put down on paper must be addressed to someone, and that person's knowledge, needs, and attitudes will influence what you write and how you write it. Even diary entries are addressed to "Dear Diary," that pseudonym for the writer's other self. You should tailor your subject, your word choice, your tone, and your support to the audience you are addressing.

Consider a discussion, for instance, on the need for better health insurance for people over age sixty-five. The audience being addressed would greatly influence the treatment of the subject. The content and emphasis of the topic would certainly be different for an audience of teenagers, for whom age sixty-five may seem an eternity away, than for people in their forties, who envision requiring coverage for their own eventual health needs or who now have relatives needing better coverage. Treatment of the topic would be still different if the discussion were addressed to people who are now over sixty-five and are presently needing better health-insurance coverage.

Many of your college essays will be addressed to a *general* audience. A general audience expects information and language that is clear and easily understood, not the jargon of a specific technical field or social group. Since your audience will most often be college-level, intelligent people who are interested in current issues and events, approach your subject with those characteristics in mind. On occasion, though, you might address a *specific* audience—such as clergy, doctors, attorneys, musicians, engineers, or scientists. With this group, you can use terminology unique to the profession, language that members of a specific audience would readily understand but a general audience might not. In other words, write on a level that corresponds to the characteristics that describe your reader. However, no matter who will receive the writing, your goal should be the same—to convince the reader that what you have to say is reasonable, intelligent, valid, and worthy of consideration.

Depending on the subject you are writing about, you may find that your own personal knowledge is not enough. When that is the case, gather the information you will need to support your ideas. Remember that you, the writer, should strive for clear and complete communication, and if that means researching a topic to provide sufficient and precise information or to enhance your own knowledge, do it. You will present yourself as a more credible source, and your reader will more readily accept your ideas.

WHAT DO I WRITE ABOUT?

As a writer, your objective is to present clear, concise information to your reader. That job will be easier if the scope of your project is reasonable. Therefore, the first step in deciding what to write about is narrowing the subject into a workable topic. It would be impossible, for instance, to write a 500-word paper describing how the AIDS virus has affected the American health arena. However, you might explore the effect that the virus has had on one segment of the population, say preschool-aged hemophiliacs, and the acceptance of these children in the classroom. With a narrowed topic, you will be able to discuss intelligently the important aspects of your subject and truly enlighten your reader, not confuse him or her with vague generalities caused by attempting to discuss a complex subject in too little space.

The best way to narrow your subject to a workable topic is to see what topic ideas fall within the limits of the assignment you are addressing. For instance, if your assignment is an essay of 1,000 words, your subjects might be narrowed to topics like these:

Subject:	Recent Supreme Court Decisions
Possible Topic:	Your local district's reaction to a ruling regulating the sale of "kiddie porn" magazines in convenience stores
Subject:	New Trends in Education
Possible Topic:	The impact of year-round classes in the public schools

WHAT DO I HAVE TO SAY?

All right, you've decided on a topic. Now what? What are you going to say about it? One of the best ways to discover what you have to say is through *brainstorming*. In brainstorming, you start by listing everything you can think of about your topic. Jot down words, phrases, sentences—anything and everything that comes to mind about the topic. Don't worry about relevance or grammar—just write.

If you were going to write about the impact of year-round schooling, you might start with a list of the effects of such a plan:

- flexible school/vacation schedules
- greater student success in music courses
- greater student success in foreign language courses
- scheduling problems for teachers who want to take summer courses
- better use of school equipment
- higher school attendance
- retention of knowledge
- higher test scores
- better use of school facilities
- fewer mischievous acts such as vandalism
- fewer criminal acts such as theft
- less student boredom
- greater opportunity for remediation
- greater opportunity for enhancement programs
- greater variety in curricula
- disrupted family vacations
- disrupted family summer schedules (with other children NOT in such a program)
- costly renovation to school not usually used during summer (e.g., air conditioning)
- increased supply costs
- increased need for building maintenance
- increased energy costs

Give yourself ten minutes to brainstorm. Remember, the object is not necessarily to compose or to organize—you will move into that phase later—but to get some ideas down on paper.

Once you have something in front of you, you can begin to group those ideas into related clusters:

- flexible school/vacation schedule
- greater success in music courses (because of continuity of study)
- greater success in foreign language courses (because of continuity of study)
- better use of school equipment
- better use of school facilities
- greater retention of knowledge

advantages to
year-round school

- less vandalism
- less theft
- more activities/less boredom
- greater opportunity for remediation
- greater opportunity for cultural enrichment/enhancement
- greater variety in curricula

} advantages to year-round school

- scheduling problems for teachers who want to take summer classes
- disrupted family vacations
- costly renovations
- increased supply costs
- increased need for building maintenance
- increased energy costs

} disadvantages to year-round school

Clusters, then, are created when you group your ideas together around some common topic. As you cluster the effects of year-round schools, you may find that some items can fit into more than one cluster. That's fine. You might also find that some items do not fit very well with the common topic you have established. That's fine, too, because now is a good time to reexamine your list—adding items, deleting items, creating new clusters. You should also see that your ideas are taking on a rough organizational "shape" created by the clusters. For example, these clusters of advantages and disadvantages can be even further refined:

- greater student success in foreign language and music courses
- greater opportunity for remediation or enhancement programs
- retention of knowledge
- higher test scores

} advantages for children

- variety in curricula
- greater student success overall
- more activities/less boredom

} advantages for teachers

- better use of facilities
- better use of equipment
- less vandalism/theft

} advantages for school districts

- scheduling problems for teachers in their continuing education
- possible need to redesign units to fit new scheduling

} disadvantages for teachers

- increased energy costs
- increased supply costs
- increased need for facilities maintenance
- costly renovation to schools not usually used during summer (e.g., air conditioning)

} disadvantages for school districts

- disrupted family vacations
- disrupted family schedules with other children NOT in year-round school (plans for summer camp or after-school care)

} disadvantages to children and families

Another way to narrow your subject and discover a method of rhetorical development at the same time is by asking yourself a series of questions about the topic. You will not be able to answer each question for every topic, of course, but if you can answer most of the questions beside the name of the pattern (or patterns) below, you may find not only a topic to write about but also one or more methods of rhetorical development to use in structuring your essay.

Narration:	What happened? When did it happen? Where did it happen? To whom did it happen?
Description:	What does it look, smell, sound, or feel like? That is, identify aspects such as size, shape, texture, and the like. How can it be characterized?
Exemplification:	What are some examples of it? What details typify it?
Process:	How did it happen? How does it work? How is it made?
Cause and Effect:	Why did it happen? What caused it? What are the results?

Division and Classification:	What are its parts?
	Can its parts be separated, grouped, or sub-divided?
	Do its parts fit into a logical order?
	Can its parts be categorized?
	Into what categories can the parts be arranged?
Definition:	What is it?
	Are there other things like it?
	How does it resemble the other things?
	How does it differ from the other things?
	What are its unique characteristics?
Comparison and Contrast:	How is it similar to other things?
	How is it different from other things?

The benefit of using these questions is not only in obtaining a workable topic but also in discovering a preliminary method of organizing those ideas according to the rhetorical modes discussed later in this text.

CREATING A "WORKING THESIS"

Once you have discovered what there is to say about a topic, you can decide how you want to say it. Your ideas will need a focus, a concentration, a *thesis*. Your thesis will be the central or main idea of your essay. It will tell your reader what point you plan to make about your topic.

As you look at the clusters examining the impact of year-round schooling, notice the organizational shape that is emerging. Since you noted both advantages and disadvantages of the system, you might start this part of the planning phase by deciding which aspect is stronger or which one you feel better equipped to write about. Here is a possibility: you notice that your list of advantages far outnumbers the list of disadvantages, so you decide to concentrate on the advantages. Now you discover it is possible to express your ideas in a sentence—a "working thesis"—that explains your assessment of the system:

Year-round classes present many advantages to public schools.

Notice the path your ideas have taken:

Subject:	Trends in Education
Possible Topic:	The impact of year-round classes in public schools
Thesis:	Year-round classes present many advantages to public schools.

The subject was narrowed to a more specific topic that, in turn, was narrowed still further to a more specific structure, the thesis.

Your thesis sentence will be the focal point of your essay, so you should take care in developing it. Consider these principles for a good thesis sentence:

1. *Structure:* The thesis must be presented as a declarative sentence— not as a fragmented idea or as a question. Questions may be used to introduce your topic, but the thesis should be viewed as an answer to a question, not as a question itself.

2. *Content:* Your thesis is best expressed as an opinion, a judgment, something that will be supported. Remember, your goal is to present an idea to your reader and then show why your idea is valid, why it should be accepted. The thesis should be expressed as an idea that your reader *could* disagree with.

3. *Style:* The thesis statement is not a declaration of purpose, an announcement of intent, or a title for your work.

Declaration of Purpose: In this paper I intend to show that year-round schooling can benefit everyone involved.

Announcement: This paper will explore the advantages of year-round schooling.

Title: Year-Round Schools—A Better Way to Learn

Notice that while each of these examples gives only a hint of what you intend to discuss in the essay, the thesis clearly shows the reader the central point you intend to make about your subject.

Remember, too, that any thesis you write at this point is a *working thesis.* That is, it's a thesis that will help you start thinking and writing, but it's not cast in stone. *Revision occurs in every stage of the writing process,* so you may find that your ideas and even your thesis may change as you plan, shape, and draft. Use the working thesis to help you think and unify your ideas.

You may find in some types of writing a thesis that is not stated explicitly but instead is strongly implied. For example, Toni Morrison does not state an explicit thesis in "A Slow Walk of Trees," but her main idea is clear: if African-Americans are to improve their status and condition, *they* must do it themselves without seeking help from or succumbing to hindrances imposed by others. Here, the *sense* of the thesis is present so the reader understands Morrison's focus and direction. Note, also, that a thesis is generally used in essay writing. On occasion, you may be asked to write an objective *report* that stresses the presentation of solid, factual information. You will still need some central idea to structure the writing, but you will find that your purpose is to relate facts rather than to support (or validate) an idea. In such writing, your focus may be expressed as a declaration of purpose: "This report will outline the university's budget proposal for the new computer center."

PHASE TWO: SHAPING

Once you have progressed through the planning phase of writing an essay, you will probably notice that your ideas are now loosely structured. Your essay is heading in a specific direction. It is taking shape.

In essence, you have already taken your first step into the next phase of writing: shaping your work. Here you will develop a definite form for your work, molded by the elements you will use to support your thesis. One method of shaping an essay is through outlining. You probably noticed that as you clustered your ideas in the planning stage, you actually created an informal outline.

Another method of organization uses a thesis *plan,* or "essay map." A plan suggests to the reader exactly how the thesis will be supported and to the writer exactly which elements need to be fully developed. As you look over your clusters on year-round classes, you see that the advantages you listed primarily affect the students, the teachers, and the school districts' budgets. Thus, your plan might look like this:

> Plan: A year-round calendar would promote children's learning, increase teachers' effectiveness, and improve school districts' financial problems.

The plan above suggests the structure of the essay's body very much as an outline would. It gives the reader a glimpse of the topics you have chosen to use to support the thesis. Each benefit of the year-round plan would be explored separately.

It is also in the shaping phase that you can begin to look more closely at the rhetorical development you will use for the essay. Ideas can be formulated or reformulated to adhere to specific strategies (definition, classification, exemplification, and others). In many ways, you will see that the shaping phase is a transitional phase, preparing you for the next phase of structuring and revising your essay.

PHASE THREE: DRAFTING

Now that you are satisfied with your working thesis and plan for your essay, it is time to begin drafting, the actual structuring and developing of your thoughts in essay form. The following discussion will help you create and revise the various parts of your essay. You may find that some sections or sentences in your essay will flow easily but that others will take repeated tries to get right; you may find that you need several drafts to correct organizational glitches. You might even write yourself into a different thesis position and need to replan. Don't be discouraged: remember that revision—"rethinking"—occurs throughout the writing process.

STRUCTURING THE ESSAY

An essay's structure consists of three parts: the introduction, the body, and the conclusion. You will see that your writing is already loosely fitting into these basic parts. So one way to structure your essay is to take each part and refine it piece by piece. Of course, if you work better by looking at the whole, by all means approach this phase in that manner.

The *introduction* literally introduces your reader to your topic and to the position you will take in discussing it. Generally consisting of one or two paragraphs, the introduction sets the stage for your essay, so it is in the introduction that you must get your reader's attention, engage your reader's interest, and make your reader curious enough to read on.

A good introduction usually starts with one or two *lead* or *introductory* sentences or paragraphs. These "leads" are used to get the reader's initial attention and to work your way into your topic. A lead may appear in the form of a question (or series of questions), a definition, an anecdote, a quotation, or even a construction resembling the thesis itself. From the lead you can work into the presentation of your thesis.

Judith Viorst, for example, in her essay "Friends, Good Friends, and Such Good Friends" (Chapter 9), uses three lead paragraphs to introduce her ideas about friendship. She introduces her topic with ideas she once had about friendship and then moves toward her thesis (and loosely structured plan) expressed in paragraph 3:

> . . . I once would have said that a friend is a friend all the way, but now I believe that's a narrow point of view. For the friendships I have and the friendships I see are conducted at many levels of intensity, serve many different functions, meet many different needs and range from those as all-the-way as the friendship of soul sisters . . . to that of the most nonchalant and casual playmates.

The *body* of the essay, or middle section, is the "meat" of the work. Here your thesis is supported, expanded, explored. Here you present your reader with all the facts, details, statistics, examples, and descriptions needed to prove your thesis valid. Notice how Viorst develops her essay on the multiple types and facets of friendships. She takes the controlling idea and starts by organizing friends into types or "varieties." Then she discusses each variety according to the criteria of her thesis plan: the intensity of the relationship, the function of the relationship, and the needs met by the relationship.

As you examine and develop the body of your own essay, notice that the most prominent examples of the different rhetorical strategies appear here. Organizing the body of your essay is as important as structuring the essay as a whole.

Consider your paragraphs. Most paragraphs you use for support will be *unified* around a clear *topic sentence*. The topic sentence works very much like the thesis, but it governs the paragraph instead of the essay as the thesis does. When a paragraph is unified, all the material used as support is relevant to the topic sentence. Include nothing that does not directly relate to the topic sentence. Whether the topic sentence appears at the beginning, middle, or end of the paragraph, its inclusion in the paragraph is vital, whether it is explicitly stated or strongly implied.

Another important consideration for your body paragraphs is their *development*. In order for a paragraph to be well developed, you must use as much relevant detail or specific information as necessary to be convincing. Examples should be clear; reasons should be logical; evidence should be persuasive. Remember, it is your duty to explain and support any general statement you make in a manner appropriate for your audience and your purpose in the writing.

Richard Rodriguez begins the first body paragraph of his essay about affirmative action, "None of This Is Fair" (Chapter 11), with a clear, focused topic sentence: "For me opportunities have been extravagant." He goes on to give concrete examples of those extravagant opportunities, citing "fellowships, summer research grants, teaching assistantships" along with invitations to conferences, offers of teaching positions, and travel opportunities. Each sentence pertains to the topic-sentence idea—extravagant opportunities. Skimpy, underdeveloped, vague, or overly general body paragraphs are not effective, so devote much of your energy to ensuring adequate development of your major points.

The reader should also sense *coherence* in (and between) the paragraph bodies. There should be a sense of smoothness or fluency as the reader moves from sentence to sentence, thought to thought, with appropriate connections acting as bridges. Repetition of key words, synonyms and pronouns standing in for key words, and transitional words and phrases may also be used to smooth the flow from one body paragraph to another. For example:

1. Use synonyms and pronouns to avoid monotonous repetition of key words. William Golding's "Thinking as a Hobby" (Chapter 9) provides a good example of this method:

. . . Some time later I learned about these (statuettes). . . they symbolized . . . the whole of life. The naked lady was the (Venus of Milo) (She) was (Love) . . . (She) was just busy being beautiful. The (leopard) was (Nature) and (he) was being natural. The naked, muscular (gentleman) was . . . Rodin's (Thinker) an (image) of pure thought. . . .

2. Use transitional words to show relationships between clauses and between paragraphs.

Addition: and
                      in addition
                      also
                      furthermore

Contrast:	however
	but
	on the contrary
	still
	nevertheless
Comparison:	likewise
	similarly
	in the same way
Cause/Effect:	as a result
	hence
	otherwise
	therefore
	thus
	then
	consequently
Concession:	even though
	although
	of course
Time:	after
	until
	at length
	immediately
	following
	thereafter
	meantime
	soon
Example/Illustration:	for example
	in fact
	for instance
	in other words
	to illustrate
	indeed
	specifically

Note how Alice Walker shows the passage of time in this paragraph from "Beauty: When the Other Dancer Is the Self" (Chapter 3):

After months of torture at my school, my parents decide to send me back to our old community, to my old school. I live with my grandparents and the teacher they board. But there is no room for Phoebe, my cat. By the time my grandparents decide there *is* room, and I ask for my cat, she cannot be found. Miss Yarborough, the boarding teacher, takes me under her wing, and begins to teach me to play the piano. (But soon) she marries an African—a "prince," she says—and is whisked away to his continent.

3.   Use parallel grammatical structures in successive sentences to emphasize the relationship of the sentences to a single idea in the paragraph. Look at one paragraph taken from Martin Luther King's speech "I Have a Dream" (Chapter 11):

> . . . We have also come to this hallowed spot to remind America of the fierce urgency of *now*. This is no time to engage in the luxury of cooling off or to take the tranquilizing drugs of gradualism. *Now* is the time to make real the promises of democracy. *Now* is the time to rise from the dark and desolate valley of segregation to the sunlit path of racial justice. *Now* is the time to open the doors of opportunity to all of God's children. *Now* is the time to lift our nation from the quicksands of racial injustice to the solid rock of brotherhood.

Repetition of key words, synonyms and pronouns standing in for key words, and transition words and phrases may also be used to smooth the flow from one body paragraph to another.

Your essay's *conclusion* should be as carefully planned as its introduction and body paragraphs. Keep in mind that the conclusion is the last part your audience reads; thus, it is the part that should reinforce your major ideas and give the reader a sense of completeness.

Your conclusion may take one of several forms:

1.   *A restatement of the thesis.*

Notice how Judith Viorst uses this technique in "How Books Helped Shape My Life" (Chapter 1):

Thesis:

> The person that I am today was shaped by Nancy Drew; by Jo March, Jane Eyre and Heathcliff's soul mate Cathy; and by other fictional females whose attractiveness or character or audacity for a time were the standards by which I measured myself.

Conclusion:

> Nevertheless Natasha and Jane and Jo, Cathy, Nancy and Brett—each one spoke to my heart and stirred me powerfully. On my journey into young womanhood I was fortunate to have them as my companions. They were, they will always remain, a part of me.

2.   *A quotation that sums up or emphasizes your thesis.*

Barbara Tuchman ends "'This Is the End of the World': The Black Death" (Chapter 10) with a quotation from St. John:

. . . those who survived "repented not of the work of their hands. . . . Neither repented they of their murders, nor of their sorceries, nor of their fornication, nor of their thefts."

3. *A brief summary of the main points of your essay.*

John Ciardi uses this method in "What Is Happiness?" (Chapter 6) when he sums up the central points of the essay with the last paragraph:

> By all means let the happiness-market sell us minor satisfactions and even minor follies so long as we keep them in scale and buy them out of spiritual change. I am no customer for either puritanism or asceticism. But drop any real spiritual capital at those bazaars, and what you come home to will be your own poorhouse.

4. *A one- or two-sentence clincher that gives a sense of suspense, irony, surprise, or humor to the end of the essay.*

Consider Brent Staples' "Black Men and Public Space" (Chapter 7). The essay relates incidents the author has had "as a night walker in an urban landscape." He speaks of the perception white people—especially white women—have of black men, particularly at night. Describing himself as "a softy who is scarcely able to take a knife to a raw chicken—let alone hold one to a person's throat—," he was "surprised, embarrassed, and dismayed" that a woman coincidentally walking the same dark street as he found him "indistinguishable from the muggers who occasionally seeped into the area from the surrounding ghetto." After several illustrations of similar experiences, Staples concludes the essay this way:

> And on late-evening constitutionals I employ what has proved to be an excellent tension-reducing measure: I whistle melodies from Beethoven and Vivaldi and the more popular classical composers. . . . Virtually everybody seems to sense that a mugger wouldn't be warbling bright, sunny selections from Vivaldi's *Four Seasons*. It is my equivalent of the cowbell that hikers wear when they know they are in bear country.

Your conclusion should *not* take on these characteristics:

1. a tone inconsistent with the rest of the essay
2. an introduction of new material
3. an apology for your writing style (I've tried to explain this idea as best I can . . .), for your lack of expertise (Of course, I'm not an expert on the subject . . .), or for the stance you've taken in the essay (These are only my opinions, mind you . . .)
4. a flat or exact restatement of the thesis

PHASE FOUR: REVISING

Revising your essay is an essential part of the writing process. You have probably been revising your essay from the start—discovering and exploring new ideas as you clarified your purpose and position. You may have found that one area of your writing sparked an idea that suggested a better treatment or wording of something you expressed earlier, so you revised that earlier part. Or perhaps as you were writing, you discovered an additional idea pertinent to the topic, an idea that needed to be expressed (but one you somehow overlooked). In many ways, large and small, revision has been a part of your writing process all along. Rethinking, reshaping, reconsidering, and reconstructing all take place *within* each phase of the writing process—they make up important parts of the entire process.

Let's suppose that you have completed a draft that you feel is close to the finished product. Try putting the essay away for a while—a day or two, or even a few hours—to give yourself a cooling-off period. After you have been away from your prose, you will find it is much easier to evaluate its clarity, organization, development, coherence, and style. After you return to your essay, don't try to evaluate all of its parts in one quick reading. Trying to evaluate everything, from organization to punctuation, will overload and frustrate you. Instead of trying to revise at one fell swoop, break the process into smaller, more mangeable steps. Here is one possible order for doing this and some questions to ask yourself:

1. *Review purpose, thesis, and audience.*

    Have I fulfilled the objectives of my assignment? Does my essay reflect my clearly understood purpose? Is my thesis a specifically worded statement of my main point? Have I addressed my audience's needs and expectations?

2. *Review ideas and their development.*

    Do all my supporting ideas directly relate to my thesis? Are they explained clearly and persuasively? Are they developed with enough detail? Have I omitted any pertinent points? Do I need to delete any irrelevant material?

3. *Review organization.*

    Have I selected the best strategy to address my purpose? Are my ideas presented in a logical, coherent order, or should I rearrange them? Are my paragraphs clearly focused? Do they flow smoothly? Does my introduction draw my reader into my thesis? Does my conclusion end my essay effectively?

4. *Review clarity and style.*

    Are all my sentences clear, concise, and pleasing? Are my words accurate and precise? Could I replace bland, vague, or convoluted language with vivid, specific words? Is my tone appropriate for my subject and my audience? Is my "voice" authentic rather than pretentious or phony?

5. *Review mechanics.*

Have I searched for and destroyed all errors in grammar and punctuation? Spelling? Confused words (affect/effect)? Typographical errors?

Overall, ask yourself these last questions: Will my reader feel a sense of satisfaction at the end of my essay, believing that the subject has been discussed thoroughly and fairly? Has this essay been effectively written and revised so that I am proud of this piece of writing?

WRITERS ON WRITING

You may never have stopped to consider how or why writers write, but now, as you are beginning a composition course, is a good time to look at writing from a professional's viewpoint. The seven writers included in this section will share with you the "writing wisdom" they have discovered over the years. Joan Didion, for example, tries to explain why she writes, and Jacqueline Berke outlines the characteristics she believes all good writing displays. Veteran teacher-writers Peter Elbow, Sheridan Baker, and Donald Murray offer multiple suggestions for getting started and for clarifying ideas. As you read these writers and the others included here, think about your attitude toward writing while you ponder the questions these professionals ask: Why do I write? How do I write? How can I improve my writing?

Joan Didion (© Tom Sobolik/Black Star)

WHY I WRITE

Joan Didion
(1934–   )

Novelist, essayist, journalist, and screenwriter, Joan Didion was born in Sacramento, California, where her family has lived for five generations. A graduate of the University of California at Berkeley, Didion spent a few years in New York as a feature editor for *Vogue*. In 1964, she returned to California, where she now resides. Her work includes several novels—*River Run* (1963), *Play It As It Lays* (1971), *A Book of Common Prayer* (1977), and *Democracy* (1984)—and several essay collections, including *Slouching Toward Bethlehem* (1969), *The White Album* (1978), *Salvador* (1983), and *Miami* (1987). With her husband, John Gregory Dunne, Didion has collaborated on several screenplays—*A Star Is Born* (1976), *True Confessions* (1981), and, most recently, *Up Close and Personal* (1996). Her latest books are *After Henry* (1992), a collection of essays, and *The Last Thing He Wanted* (1996), a novel. Didion's writing blends fiction, autobiography, and personal commentary on contemporary American culture. Didion admits that she "stole" the title of "Why I Write" from George Orwell, and, as he did, she explores the motivations and purposes behind the act of writing.

1   OF course I stole the title for this talk, from George Orwell. One reason I
stole it was that I like the sound of the words: *Why I Write*. There you have

three short unambiguous words that share a sound, and the sound they share is this:

I

I

I

2   In many ways writing is the act of saying *I*, of imposing oneself upon other people, of saying *listen to me, see it my way, change your mind*. It's an aggressive, even a hostile act. You can disguise its aggressiveness all you want with veils of subordinate clauses and qualifiers and tentative subjunctives, with ellipses and evasions—with the whole manner of intimating rather than claiming, of alluding rather than stating—but there's no getting around the fact that setting words on paper is the tactic of a secret bully, an invasion, an imposition of the writer's sensibility on the reader's most private space.

3   I stole the title not only because the words sounded right but because they seemed to sum up, in a no-nonsense way, all I have to tell you. Like many writers I have only this one "subject," this one "area": the act of writing. I can bring you no reports from any other front. I may have other interests: I am "interested," for example, in marine biology, but I don't flatter myself that you would come out to hear me talk about it. I am not a scholar. I am not in the least an intellectual, which is not to say that when I hear the word "intellectual" I reach for my gun, but only to say that I do not think in abstracts. During the years when I was an undergraduate at Berkeley I tried, with a kind of hopeless late-adolescent energy, to buy some temporary visa into the world of ideas, to forge for myself a mind that could deal with the abstract.

4   In short I tried to think. I failed. My attention veered inexorably back to the specific, to the tangible, to what was generally considered, by everyone I knew then and for that matter have known since, the peripheral. I would try to contemplate the Hegelian dialectic and would find myself concentrating instead on a flowering pear tree outside my window and the particular way the petals fell on my floor. I would try to read linguistic theory and would find myself wondering instead if the lights were on in the bevatron up the hill. When I say that I was wondering if the lights were on in the bevatron you might immediately suspect, if you deal in ideas at all, that I was registering the bevatron as a political symbol, thinking in shorthand about the military-industrial complex and its role in the university community, but you would be wrong. I was only wondering if the lights were on in the bevatron, and how they looked. A physical fact.

5   I had trouble graduating from Berkeley, not because of this inability to deal with ideas—I was majoring in English, and I could locate the house-and-garden imagery in "The Portrait of a Lady" as well as the next person, "imagery" being by definition the kind of specific that got my attention—but simply because I had neglected to take a course in Milton. For reasons which now sound baroque I needed a degree by the end of that summer, and the English department finally agreed, if I would come down from Sacramento every Friday and talk about the cosmology of "Paradise Lost," to certify me proficient in Milton. I did this. Some Fridays I took the Greyhound bus, other Fridays I caught the Southern Pacific's City of San Francisco on the last leg of its

transcontinental trip. I can no longer tell you whether Milton put the sun or the earth at the center of his universe in "Paradise Lost," the central question of at least one century and a topic about which I wrote 10,000 words that summer, but I can still recall the exact rancidity of the butter in the City of San Francisco's dining car, and the way the tinted windows on the Greyhound bus cast the oil refineries around Carquinez Straits into a grayed and obscurely sinister light. In short my attention was always on the periphery, on what I could see and taste and touch, on the butter, and the Greyhound bus. During those years I was traveling on what I knew to be a very shaky passport, forged papers: I knew that I was no legitimate resident in any world of ideas. I knew I couldn't think. All I knew then was what I couldn't do. All I knew then was what I wasn't, and it took me some years to discover what I was.

6   Which was a writer.

7   By which I mean not a "good" writer or a "bad" writer but simply a writer, a person whose most absorbed and passionate hours are spent arranging words on pieces of paper. Had my credentials been in order I would never have become a writer. Had I been blessed with even limited access to my own mind there would have been no reason to write. I write entirely to find out what I'm thinking, what I'm looking at, what I see and what it means. What I want and what I fear. Why did the oil refineries around Carquinez Straits seem sinister to me in the summer of 1956? Why have the night lights in the bevatron burned in my mind for twenty years? *What is going on in these pictures in my mind?*

8   When I talk about pictures in my mind I am talking, quite specifically, about images that shimmer around the edges. There used to be an illustration in every elementary psychology book showing a cat drawn by a patient in varying stages of schizophrenia. This cat had a shimmer around it. You could see the molecular structure breaking down at the very edges of the cat: the cat became the background and the background the cat, everything interacting, exchanging ions. People on hallucinogens describe the same perception of objects. I'm not a schizophrenic, nor do I take hallucinogens, but certain images do shimmer for me. Look hard enough, and you can't miss the shimmer. It's there. You can't think too much about these pictures that shimmer. You just lie low and let them develop. You stay quiet. You don't talk to many people and you keep your nervous system from shorting out and you try to locate the cat in the shimmer, the grammar in the picture.

9   Just as I meant "shimmer" literally I mean "grammar" literally. Grammar is a piano I play by ear, since I seem to have been out of school the year the rules were mentioned. All I know about grammar is its infinite power. To shift the structure of a sentence alters the meaning of that sentence, as definitely and inflexibly as the position of a camera alters the meaning of the object photographed. Many people know about camera angles now, but not so many know about sentences. The arrangement of the words matters, and the arrangement you want can be found in the picture in your mind. The picture dictates the arrangement. The picture dictates whether this will be a sentence with or without clauses, a sentence that ends hard or a dying-fall sentence, long or short, active or passive. The picture tells you how to arrange the words

and the arrangement of the words tells you, or tells me, what's going on in the picture. *Nota bene:*

10   It tells you.

11   You don't tell it.

12   Let me show you what I mean by pictures in the mind. I began "Play It As It Lays" just as I have begun each of my novels, with no notion of "character" or "plot" or even "incident." I had only two pictures in my mind, more about which later, and a technical intention, which was to write a novel so elliptical and fast that it would be over before you noticed it, a novel so fast that it would scarcely exist on the page at all. About the pictures: the first was of white space. Empty space. This was clearly the picture that dictated the narrative intention of the book—a book in which anything that happened would happen off the page, a "white" book to which the reader would have to bring his or her own bad dreams—and yet this picture told me no "story," suggested no situation. The second picture did. This second picture was of something actually witnessed. A young woman with long hair and a short white halter dress walks through the casino at the Riviera in Las Vegas at one in the morning. She crosses the casino alone and picks up a house telephone. I watch her because I have heard her paged, and recognize her name: she is a minor actress I see around Los Angeles from time to time, in places like Jax and once in a gynecologist's office in the Beverly Hills Clinic, but have never met. I know nothing about her. Who is paging her? Why is she here to be paged? How exactly did she come to this? It was precisely this moment in Las Vegas that made "Play It As It Lays" begin to tell itself to me, but the moment appears in the novel only obliquely, in a chapter which begins:

13   "Maria made a list of things she would never do. She would never: walk through the Sands or Caesar's alone after midnight. She would never: ball at a party, do S-M unless she wanted to, borrow furs from Abe Lipsey, deal. She would never: carry a Yorkshire in Beverly Hills."

14   That is the beginning of the chapter and that is also the end of the chapter, which may suggest what I meant by "white space."

15   I recall having a number of pictures in my mind when I began the novel I just finished, "A Book of Common Prayer." As a matter of fact one of these pictures was of that bevatron I mentioned, although I would be hard put to tell you a story in which nuclear energy figures. Another was a newspaper photograph of a hijacked 707 burning on the desert in the Middle East. Another was the night view from a room in which I once spent a week with paratyphoid, a hotel room on the Colombian coast. My husband and I seemed to be on the Colombian coast representing the United States of America at a film festival (I recall invoking the name "Jack Valenti" a lot, as if its reiteration could make me well), and it was a bad place to have fever, not only because my indisposition offended our hosts but because every night in this hotel the generator failed. The lights went out. The elevator stopped. My husband would go to the event of the evening and make excuses for me and I would stay alone in this hotel room, in the dark. I remember standing at the window trying to call

Bogotá (the telephone seemed to work on the same principle as the generator) and watching the night wind come up and wondering what I was doing eleven degrees off the equator with a fever of 103. The view from that window definitely figures in "A Book of Common Prayer," as does the burning 707, and yet none of these pictures told me the story I needed.

16   The picture that did, the picture that shimmered and made these other images coalesce, was the Panama airport at 6 A.M. I was in this airport only once, on a plane to Bogotá that stopped for an hour to refuel, but the way it looked that morning remained superimposed on everything I saw until the day I finished "A Book of Common Prayer." I lived in that airport for several years. I can still feel the hot air when I step off the plane, can see the heat already rising off the tarmac at 6 A.M. I can feel my skirt damp and wrinkled on my legs. I can feel the asphalt stick to my sandals. I remember the big tail of a Pan American plane floating motionless down at the end of the tarmac. I remember the sound of a slot machine in the waiting room. I could tell you that I remember a particular woman in the airport, an American woman, a *norteamericana,* a thin *norteamericana* about 40 who bore a big square emerald in lieu of a wedding ring, but there was no such woman there.

17   I put this woman in the airport later. I made this woman up, just as I later made up a country to put the airport in, and a family to run the country. This woman in the airport is neither catching a plane nor meeting one. She is ordering tea in the airport coffee shop. In fact she is not simply "ordering" tea but insisting that the water be boiled, in front of her, for twenty minutes. Why is this woman in this airport? Why is she going nowhere, where has she been? Where did she get that big emerald? What derangement, of disassociation, makes her believe that her will to see the water boiled can possibly prevail?

18   "She had been going to one airport or another for four months, one could see it, looking at the visas on her passport. All those airports where Charlotte Douglas's passport had been stamped would have looked alike. Sometimes the sign on the tower would say 'Bienvenidos' and sometimes the sign on the tower would say 'Bienvenue,' some places were wet and hot and others dry and hot, but at each of these airports the pastel concrete walls would rust and stain and the swamp off the runway would be littered with the fuselages of cannibalized Fairchild F-227's and the water would need boiling.

19   "I knew why Charlotte went to the airport even if Victor did not.

20   "I knew about airports."

21   These lines appear about halfway through "A Book of Common Prayer," but I wrote them during the second week I worked on the book, long before I had any idea where Charlotte Douglas had been or why she went to airports. Until I wrote these lines I had no character called "Victor" in mind: the necessity for mentioning a name, and the name "Victor," occurred to me as I wrote the sentence. *I knew why Charlotte went to the airport* sounded incomplete. *I knew why Charlotte went to the airport even if Victor did not* carried a little more narrative drive. Most important of all, until I wrote these lines I did not know who "I" was, who was telling the story. I had intended

until that moment that the "I" be no more than the voice of the author, a 19th-century omniscient narrator. But there it was:

22   "I knew why Charlotte went to the airport even if Victor did not.

23   "I knew about airports."

24   This "I" was the voice of no author in my house. This "I" was someone who not only knew why Charlotte went to the airport but also knew someone called "Victor." Who was Victor? Who was this narrator? Why was this narrator telling me this story? Let me tell you one thing about why writers write: had I known the answer to any of these questions I would never have needed to write a novel.

LIFE AT CLOSE RANGE

Gretel Ehrlich
(1946–   )

A graduate of Bennington College and UCLA Film
School, Gretel Ehrlich began her career as a filmmaker.
A trip to Wyoming to film a documentary, however,
resulted in a personal transformation. The open range
provided a dramatic change for her, prompting a period
of self-discovery. Her life is intertwined now with her
Wyoming ranch, riding, ranching, and writing. Her
essays have appeared in the *New York Times,* the
Atlantic, Harper's, and *Sierra,* and she has published a
novel, *Heart Mountain* (1988); poetry, *To Touch the
Water* (1981); short stories, *Wyoming Stories* (1986)
and *Drinking Dry Clouds* (1991); and a collection of
essays, *The Solace of Open Spaces* (1986). Gretel
Ehrlich's recent work includes *Writing Down the River:
Into the Heart of the Grand Canyon* (1998), *The Horse
Whisperer: The Making of a Legend* (1998), and *Questions of Heaven* (1998). In "Life at Close Range,"
Ehrlich explains the influence of the range and its open
spaces on her writing and on her "ways of knowing."

1   It's June and soon we'll be moving cattle to the high mountain pastures. Already the first slanting rains have come—black arrows that come back up as
green grass. At this time of year it can still snow, but ducks and shorebirds stop
over on our little lake to rest before going on to the Arctic or Canada. As soon
as the mountain meltwater comes down, I go to work irrigating 125 acres of
hay meadows and on the way, because I always carry binoculars, I keep track
of what's on the pond: godwits, terns, mallards, teal, sora rails, snipes, and
phalaropes. Coyotes come to drink early in the morning, vying with bald and
golden eagles for a prairie dog on the way. It's not only what I do see as I set irrigation water, but what I don't see in the way of animals and birds that
counts—those hidden ones like bears, mountain lions, badgers, ermine, and
snakes who I know are here too, but I can't always see.

Gretel Ehrlich (Courtesy of Beacon Press, Boston. Photo by Eika Aoshima)

2   A writer's imagination must be like that: filled not just with literal truths, but with the unseen, the unknown whose shy presence is felt. What's underneath the lake water, the sod-bound fields, the lid of my skull, I wonder?

3   Yesterday lightning ignited a ridge above our ranch and, as quickly, a boisterous rain squall put it out. Then the hail came, dancing, blanching the land. The isolated ranch my husband and I inhabit often seems otherworldly: mist spills on us sweeping everything from sight, then on rising, the green-breasted earth steams. Last night the moon was so bright a moth inside the house beat against the window, trying to get out, and in the morning, at almost the same place, I found a blue luna moth, big as my hand, trying to get in. A writer's life must be like those moths, beating down obstructions to get at truths.

4   Sometimes when strangers ask what I do, I say I write, but around here, they think I said "ride." I do both of course, because most ranchwork is done on horseback. Writing is thought of as being cerebral work, while ranching, which takes up a good deal of my time, is mostly physical. But I couldn't write if I didn't ride and I'd find fourteen-hour days in the saddle quite tedious if I didn't have writing to come home to. In fact, I often write—notepad balanced on saddlehorn—gathering cattle, and when I'm in my writing room, a separate building on a hill with a view of the sorting corrals, I often get up mid-sentence to fix a panel of fence or change an irrigation dam, or put a stray horse away. This whole business of dividing body and mind is ludicrous. After all, the breath that starts the song of a poem, or the symphony of a novel—the same breath that lifts me into the saddle—starts in the body, and at the same time, enlivens the mind.

5   Our ranch is thirty miles from the nearest grocery store, eighty miles from a movie theater, a hundred and fifty miles from an airport, yet I feel as if I were at the center of things, "in media res." Our ranch, and the entire ecosystem in which it lies, is my laboratory. Wherever I am on it, whatever I'm doing, I'm always thinking, remembering, feeling, observing, absorbing, and listening—to wasps eating ants, to the eddies of wind above oceans of pines, to the pond ducks fighting at breeding time, to the whir of nighthawks driving down. But it's a curious laboratory, one in which I don't do experiments on nature, but nature experiments with me. I'm a land steward, but it's the land that tells me what's right and what's wrong, and I have to learn to listen.

6   If you live in a place—any place, city or country—long enough and deeply enough you can learn anything, the dynamics and interconnections that exist in every community, be it plant, human, or animal—you can learn what a writer needs to know. Here, as anywhere, the search for ways of knowing is a great discipline, an ultimate freedom in which you will find the entire world opens to you. When I began writing full time, I asked a well-known essayist his advice and he said, "Write from the heart," which was another way of saying, you must see through to the heart of things.

7   These days I do that by getting down on my hands and knees—literally and figuratively—and inspecting life at close range. From monitoring grass plants, soil quality, insects, and animals, as well as the health of entire watersheds, I've learned to scrutinize and savor the constructs of language, the

points at which ideas, ethics, and sensations meet or collide, the way the tone of a piece of writing—like muscle tone, or the ecotone of a landscape—moves smoothly or drops out from under my pen. From diving into the midst of other lives, in nature and in the human realm, working as nurturer, student, midwife, I've stumbled on the liberating sense of equality that exists everywhere and have been able to dismiss with great conviction the idiotic idea of human dominance over nature, and know it to be physically and intellectually absurd. With equality comes a sense of the holiness—sacred or secular—of every animate and inanimate thing.

8   Writing, like being a good hand with a horse, requires wakefulness and a willingness to surrender. I try to burn away preconception and let what is actually here come in. Any act of writing is a meditation on existence. It implies stopping, breathing in and out. "Do not write more clearly than you can think," the physicist Niels Bohr said. The truth is hard; no false décor allowed.

9   Riding out across a six-thousand-acre mountain pasture becomes an ambulation of mind. The body of the horse carries me into imagery, and memory, and, like the wind, I try to hone what has registered in me as a precision, making every word count, every word a tiny truth in itself. Roping a calf, I have to think ahead as the coil spins out, but at the same time, stay agile, flexible, alive in the present so that I can take my dallies with speed and care and not lose a thumb. Both jobs—writing and cowboying—take up the whole mind and heart. Weather pushes me the way I push at internal barriers and, after a decade or so, both jobs work together like mortar and pestle, the one pulverizing the other into clarity.

10   There is no knowing what makes a writer, what ingredients have contributed. Was it the stories my very urban (and urbane) grandfather told me over and over? Was it the frustration of being almost silent during my young life which fed the need to communicate, albeit on my own terms? Was it my inordinate love of animals and books—the one love growing alongside the other that led me to this isolated, animal-rich place where the play of the mind and heart could take a far reach? It seems that any list of ingredients will do except deadness, frivolity, the refusal to enter silence and loneliness and listen to what is inside. A writer makes a pact with loneliness. It is her, or his, beach on which waves of desire, wild mind, speculation break. In my work, in my life, I am always moving toward and away from aloneness. To write is to refuse to cover up the rawness of being alive, of facing death.

11   Early in my life, maybe from reading D. H. Lawrence, I dedicated myself to "living fully," which included reading, keeping my standards high. To write and not read the best that has been written (and only the best; there's not time for anything less) is foolish. It's like a gardener putting in seeds where there is no ground. It is in the context of our ordinary, everyday lives that seeds germinate. In the larger sense, place ultimately becomes a mirror of mind.

12   In his notebooks, Henry James wrote: "The law of the artist is the terrible law of fructification, of fertilization, the law of acceptance of all experience, of all suffering, of all life, all suggestion and sensation and illumination." Looking out the windows of my writing room at this moment, I see an elk carrying

mist on his shoulders, drifting out of a canyon; a duck diving for food; a mead-owlark alighting on a fence post, tilting his head back and singing after a June rain.

13   A good hand on a ranch requires vigilance, acute powers of observation, readiness to anticipate what might go wrong or what's coming next, a taste for recklessness, intuitive skills, patience, and what cowboys look for when they buy a horse: a lot of heart. Aspiring to those qualities as a rancher, I can only hope my writing will benefit as well.

Peter Elbow (Courtesy of Peter Elbow)

FREEWRITING

Peter Elbow
(1935–   )

New York City native Peter Elbow was educated at
Williams College, Brandeis, Oxford, and Harvard. He
has taught at several colleges and universities, including
Franconia, the University of Massachusetts at Amherst,
MIT, Wesleyan, and SUNY at Stony Brook. He is well
known for his books and essays on the teaching of
writing, including *Writing without Teachers* (1973),
Writing with Power (1981), *Embracing Contraries:
Explorations in Learning and Teaching* (1986), and
Sharing and Responding (1989). In "Freewriting,"
Elbow offers suggestions to help writers discover ideas
and improve their writing.

1   THE most effective way I know to improve your writing is to do freewriting
exercises regularly. At least three times a week. They are sometimes called
"automatic writing," "babbling," or "jabbering" exercises. The idea is simply
to write for ten minutes (later on, perhaps fifteen or twenty). Don't stop for
anything. Go quickly without rushing. Never stop to look back, to cross something out, to wonder how to spell something, to wonder what word or thought
to use, or to think about what you are doing. If you can't think of a word or a
spelling, just use a squiggle or else write, "I can't think of it." Just put down
something. The easiest thing is just to put down whatever is in your mind. If
you get stuck it's fine to write "I can't think what to say, I can't think what to
say" as many times as you want; or repeat the last word you wrote over and
over again; or anything else. The only requirement is that you *never* stop.

2   What happens to a freewriting exercise is important. It must be a piece of
writing which, even if someone reads it, doesn't send any ripples back to you.
It is like writing something and putting it in a bottle in the sea. The teacherless
class helps your writing by providing maximum feedback. Freewritings help
you by providing no feedback at all. When I assign one, I invite the writer to let
me read it, but also tell him to keep it if he prefers. I read it quickly and make

no comments at all and I do not speak with him about it. The main thing is that a freewriting must never be evaluated in any way; in fact there must be no discussion or comment at all.

3   Here is an example of a fairly coherent exercise (sometimes they are very coherent, which is fine):

> I think I'll write what's on my mind, but the only thing on my mind right now is what to write for ten minutes. I've never done this before and I'm not prepared in any way—the sky is cloudy today, how's that? now I'm afraid I won't be able to think of what to write when I get to the end of the sentence—well, here I am at the end of the sentence—here I am again, again, again, again, at least I'm still writing—Now I ask is there some reason to be happy that I'm still writing—ah yes! Here comes the question again—What am I getting out of this? What point is there in it? It's almost obscene to always ask it but I seem to question everything that way and I was gonna say something else pertaining to that but I got so busy writing down the first part that I forgot what I was leading into. This is kind of fun oh don't stop writing—cars and trucks speeding by somewhere out the window, pens clittering across peoples' papers. The sky is still cloudy—is it symbolic that I should be mentioning it? Huh? I dunno. Maybe I should try colors, blue, red, dirty words—wait a minute—no can't do that, orange, yellow, arm tired, green pink violet magenta lavender red brown black green—now that I can't think of any more colors—just about done—relief? maybe.

4   Freewriting may seem crazy but actually it makes simple sense. Think of the difference between speaking and writing. Writing has the advantage of permitting more editing. But that's its downfall too. Almost everybody interposes a massive and complicated series of editings between the time words start to be born into consciousness and when they finally come off the end of the pencil or typewriter onto the page. This is partly because schooling makes us obsessed with the "mistakes" we make in writing. Many people are constantly thinking about spelling and grammar as they try to write. I am always thinking about the awkwardness, wordiness, and general mushiness of my natural verbal product as I try to write down words.

5   But it's not just "mistakes" or "bad writing" we edit as we write. We also edit unacceptable thoughts and feelings, as we do in speaking. In writing there is more time to do it so the editing is heavier: when speaking, there's someone right there waiting for a reply and he'll get bored and think we're crazy if we don't come out with *something*. Most of the time in speaking, we settle for the catch-as-catch-can way in which the words tumble out. In writing, however, there's a chance to try to get them right. But the opportunity to get them right is a terrible burden: you can work for two hours trying to get a paragraph "right" and discover it's not right at all. And then give up.

6   Editing, *in itself*, is not the problem. Editing is usually necessary if we want to end up with something satisfactory. The problem is that editing goes on *at the same time* as producing. The editor is, as it were, constantly looking over the shoulder of the producer and constantly fiddling with what he's doing

while he's in the middle of trying to do it. No wonder the producer gets nervous, jumpy, inhibited, and finally can't be coherent. It's an unnecessary burden to try to think of words and also worry at the same time whether they're the right words.

7   The main thing about freewriting is that it is *nonediting*. It is an exercise in bringing together the process of producing words and putting them down on the page. Practiced regularly, it undoes the ingrained habit of editing at the same time you are trying to produce. It will make writing less blocked because words will come more easily. You will use up more paper, but chew up fewer pencils.

8   Next time you write, notice how often you stop yourself from writing down something you were going to write down. Or else cross it out after it's written. "Naturally," you say, "it wasn't any good." But think for a moment about the occasions when you spoke well. Seldom was it because you first got the beginning just right. Usually it was a matter of a halting or even garbled beginning, but you kept going and your speech finally became coherent and even powerful. There is a lesson here for writing: trying to get the beginning just right is a formula for failure—and probably a secret tactic to make yourself give up writing. Make some words, whatever they are, and then grab hold of that line and reel in as hard as you can. Afterwards you can throw away lousy beginnings and make new ones. This is the quickest way to get into good writing.

9   The habit of compulsive, premature editing doesn't just make writing hard. It also makes writing dead. Your voice is damped out by all the interruptions, changes, and hesitations between the consciousness and the page. In your natural way of producing words there is a sound, a texture, a rhythm—a voice—which is the main source of power in your writing. I don't know how it works, but this voice is the force that will make a reader listen to you, the energy that drives the meanings through his thick skull. Maybe you don't *like* your voice; maybe people have made fun of it. But it's the only voice you've got. It's your only source of power. You better get back into it, no matter what you think of it. If you keep writing in it, it may change into something you like better. But if you abandon it, you'll likely never have a voice and never be heard.

Sheridan Baker (Courtesy of Sheridan Baker)

WHAT SHALL I WRITE?

Sheridan Baker
(1918–   )

Author of two textbooks on writing, Sheridan Baker is
a respected editor of literary works and an educator,
having spent much of his career as professor of English
at the University of Michigan. His *The Practical Stylist*
(1962) and *The Complete Stylist* (1976) are considered
textbook classics for college and university students. He
is also known for editing the works of the eighteenth-
century English novelist Henry Fielding. In this excerpt
from *The Practical Stylist,* Baker gives advice about two
of the most important steps in the writing process: finding a subject to write about and creating a thesis that
will interest both the writer and the reader.

---

1   FIRST you need a subject, and then you need a thesis. Yes, but *what shall I
write?* That is the question, persisting from the first Christmas thank-you letter down to this very night. Here you are, an assignment due and the paper as
blank as your mind. The Christmas letter may give us a clue. Your mother
probably told you, as mine did, to write about what you had been doing.
Almost anything would do—Cub Scouts, Brownies, the birthday party,
skating—so long as you had been doing it. As you wrote, it grew interesting
all over again. Finding a mature subject is no different: look for something
you have experienced, or thought about. The more it matters to you, the
more you can make it matter to your readers. It might be skiing. It might be
clothes. It might be roommates, wives, husbands, the Peloponnesian War,
running for office, a personal discovery of racial tensions, an experience on
the job. But do not tackle a big philosophical abstraction, like Freedom, or a
big subject, like the Supreme Court. They are too vast; your time and space
and knowledge, all too small. You would probably manage no more than a
collection of platitudes. Start rather with something specific, like apartment-
hunting, and let the ideas of freedom and justice and responsibility arise from
there. An abstract idea is a poor beginning. To be sure, as you move ahead
through your course in writing, you will work more directly with ideas, with

problems posed by literature, with questions in the great civilizing debate about what we are doing in this strange world and universe. But again, look for something within your concern. The best subjects lie nearest at hand, and nearest the heart.

2   Suppose we start with Adulthood. That is certainly something close enough to all of us in prospect or achievement. It will illustrate conveniently how to generalize from personal experience, and how to narrow a subject down to manageable size. Your first impulse will be to describe your first real-ization that you were grown up, say, a recent test of responsibility: drugs, theft, speeding, sex. Written as autobiography, in the first person, "I," it would doubtless be interesting, even amusing or heartrending, as are most things human. But it would remain merely personal, a kind of confession, or hymn of self-praise. It would probably lack an important ingredient of intellectual ma-turity. You would still be working in that bright, self-centered spotlight of con-sciousness in which we live before we really begin to grow up and beyond which many of us never learn to step—where the child assumes that all his ex-periences are unique. If you shift from "me" to "the adult," however, you will be actually stepping into the perspective of maturity: acknowledging that oth-ers have gone through exactly the same thing, that your particular experiences have illustrated once again the general dilemma of responsibility versus the group of some perilous threshold to adulthood. So you will write not "I was afraid to say anything" but:

> The teen-ager fears going against the group more than death itself. When the speedometer hits 100, silence is the rule, though terror is screaming in every throat.

3   By *generalizing* your private feelings, you change your subject into a thesis by asserting something about it, by finding publicly valid reasons for your pri-vate convictions. You simply assume you are normal and fairly representative, and you then generalize with confidence, transposing your particular experi-ences, your particular thoughts and reactions, into statements about the gen-eral ways of the world. You might want to sharpen your statement a little more, as you turn your subject into a thesis, asserting something like: "The teen-ager's thrilling high-speed ride, if survived, can be a sobering lesson in the dy-namics of the group and adult responsibility." Put your proposition into one sentence. This will get you focused. And now you are ready to begin.

WHERE ESSAYS FAIL

4   You can usually blame a bad essay on a bad beginning. If your essay falls apart, it probably has no primary idea to hold it together. "What's the big idea?" we used to ask. The phrase will serve as a reminder that you must find the "big idea" behind your several smaller thoughts and musing before you start to write. In the beginning was the *logos*, says the Bible—the idea, the plan, caught in a flash as if in a single word. Find your *logos*, and you are ready to round out your essay and set it spinning.

5   The big idea behind our ride in the speeding car was that in adolescence, especially, the group can have a deadly influence on the individual. If you had not focused your big idea in a thesis, you might have begun by picking up thoughts at random, something like this:

> Everyone thinks he is a good driver. There are more accidents caused by young drivers than any other group. Driver education is a good beginning, but further practice is very necessary. People who object to driver education do not realize that modern society, with its suburban pattern of growth, is built around the automobile. The car becomes a way of life and a status symbol. When teenagers go too fast they are probably only copying their own parents, without any sense of responsibility.

6   A little reconsideration, aimed at a good thesis-sentence, could turn this into a reasonably good opening paragraph, with your thesis, your big idea, asserted at the end to focus your reader's attention:

> Modern society is built on the automobile. Children play with tiny cars; teenagers long to take out the car alone. Soon they are testing their skills at higher and higher speeds, especially with a group of friends along. One final test at extreme speeds usually suffices. It is usually a sobering experience, if survived, and can open one's eyes to the deadly dynamics of the group and the emerging sense of an adult responsibility for oneself and others.

7   Thus the central idea, or thesis, is your essay's life and spirit. If your thesis is sufficiently clear, it may tell you immediately how to organize your supporting material. But if you do not find a thesis, your essay will be a tour through the miscellaneous. Essays replete with scaffolds and catwalks—"We have just seen this; now let us turn to this"—are essays in which the inherent idea is weak or nonexistent. A purely expository and descriptive essay, one simply about "Cats," for instance, will have to rely on outer scaffolding alone (some orderly progression from Persia to Siam) since it really has no idea at all. It is all subject, all cats, instead of being based on an idea *about* cats, with a thesis *about* cats.

THE ARGUMENTATIVE EDGE

Find Your Thesis

8   The *about*-ness puts an argumentative edge on the subject. When you have something to say *about* cats, you have found your underlying idea. You have something to defend, something to fight about: not just "Cats," but "The cat is really a person's best friend." Now the hackles of all dog people are rising, and you have an argument on your hands. You have something to prove. You have a thesis.

9   "What's the big idea, Mac?" Let the impudence in that time-honored demand remind you that the most dynamic thesis is a kind of affront to somebody. No one will be very much interested in listening to you expound the

thesis "The dog is a person's best friend." Everyone knows that already. Even the dog lovers will be uninterested, convinced they know better than you. But the cat. . . .

10 So it is with any unpopular idea. The more unpopular the viewpoint and the stronger the push against convention, the stronger the thesis and the more energetic the essay. Compare the energy in "Democracy is good" with that in "Communism is good," for instance. The first is filled with platitudes, the second with plutonium. By the same token, if you can find the real energy in "Democracy is good," if you can get down through the sand to where the roots and water are, you will have a real essay, because the opposition against which you generate your energy is the heaviest in the world: boredom. Probably the most energetic thesis of all, the greatest inner organizer, is some tired old truth that you cause to spurt with new life, making the old ground green again.

11 To find a thesis and to put it into one sentence is to narrow and define your subject to a workable size. Under "Cats" you must deal with all felinity from the jungle up, carefully partitioning the eons and areas, the tigers and tabbies, the sizes and shapes. The minute you proclaim the cat the friend of humanity, you have pared away whole categories and chapters, and need only think up the arguments sufficient to overwhelm the opposition. So, put an argumentative edge on your subject—and you will have found your thesis.

12 Simple exposition, to be sure, has its uses. You may want to tell someone how to build a doghouse, how to can asparagus, how to follow the outlines of relativity, or even how to write an essay. Performing a few exercises in simple exposition will no doubt sharpen your insight into the problems of finding orderly sequences, of considering how best to lead your readers through the hoops of writing clearly and accurately. It will also illustrate how much finer and surer an argument is.

13 You will see that picking an argument immediately simplifies the problems so troublesome in straight exposition: the defining, the partitioning, the narrowing of the subject. Not that you must be constantly pugnacious or aggressive. I have overstated my point to make it stick. Actually, you can put an argumentative edge on the flattest of expository subjects. "How to build a doghouse" might become "Building a doghouse is a thorough introduction to the building trades, including architecture and mechanical engineering." "Canning asparagus" might become "An asparagus patch is a course in economics." "Relativity" might become "Relativity is not so inscrutable as many suppose." Literary subjects take an argumentative edge almost by nature. You simply assert what the essential point of a poem or play seems to be: "*Hamlet* is essentially about a world that has lost its values." You assume that your readers are in search of clarity, that you have a loyal opposition consisting of the interested but uninformed. You have given your subject its edge; you have limited and organized it at a single stroke. Pick an *argument,* then, and you will automatically be defining and narrowing your subject, and all the partitions you don't need will fold up. Instead of dealing with things, subjects, and pieces of subjects, you will be dealing with an idea and its consequences.

Sharpen Your Thesis

14 Come out with your subject pointed. Take a stand, make a judgment of value, make a *thesis*. Be reasonable, but don't be timid. It is helpful to think of your thesis, your main idea, as a debating question—"Resolved: Welfare payments must go"—taking out the "Resolved" when you actually write your thesis down. But your resolution will be even stronger, your essay clearer and tighter, if you can sharpen your thesis even further—"Resolved: Welfare payments must go because—." Fill in that blank, and your worries are practically over. The main idea is to put your whole argument into one sentence.

15 Try, for instance: "Welfare payments must go because they are making people irresponsible." I don't know at all if that is true, and neither will you until you write your way into it, considering probabilities and alternatives and objections, and especially the underlying assumptions. In fact, no one, no master sociologist or future historian, can tell absolutely if it is true, so multiplex are the causes in human affairs, so endless and tangled the consequences. The basic assumption—that irresponsibility is growing—might be entirely false. No one, I repeat, can tell absolutely. But by the same token, your guess may be as good as another's. At any rate, you are ready to write. You have found your *logos*.

16 Now put your well-pointed thesis-sentence on a scrap of paper to keep from drifting off target. But you will want to dress it for the public, to burnish it and make it comely. Suppose you try:

> Welfare payments, perhaps more than anything else, are eroding personal initiative.

But is this fully true? Perhaps you had better try something like:

> Despite their immediate benefits, welfare payments may actually be eroding personal initiative and depriving society of needed workers.

This is your full thesis; write that down on a scrap of paper too.

Jacqueline Berke (Courtesy of Jacqueline Berke. Photo by Eric Wegman Studio)

THE QUALITIES OF GOOD WRITING

Jacqueline Berke

⟨ornament⟩

Author of the highly regarded writing text *Twenty Questions for the Writer* (1972), Jacqueline Berke teaches graduate courses in composition at Drew University. In 1986, she was selected as the university's Scholar/Teacher of the Year. Her *"The Diary of Anne Frank:* Widely Acclaimed but Doubly Betrayed," which was presented to the Modern Language Association in 1991, presents a perspective on the famous work in what Berke calls "a more realistic way than the dramatic reputation suggests." In "The Qualities of Good Writing," she presents the components that are necessary for effective writing.

1 EVEN before you set out, you come prepared by instinct and intuition to make certain judgments about what is "good." Take the following familiar sentence, for example: "I know not what course others may take, but as for me, give me liberty or give me death." Do you suppose this thought of Patrick Henry's would have come ringing down through the centuries if he had expressed this sentiment not in one tight, rhythmical sentence but as follows?

> It would be difficult, if not impossible, to predict on the basis of my limited information as to the predilections of the public, what the citizenry at large will regard as action commensurate with the present provocation, but after arduous consideration I personally feel so intensely and irrevocably committed to the position of social, political, and economic independence, that rather than submit to foreign and despotic control which is anathema to me, I will make the ultimate sacrifice of which humanity is capable—under the aegis of personal honor, ideological conviction, and existential commitment, I will sacrifice my own mortal existence.

2   How does this rambling, high-flown paraphrase measure up to the bold "Give me liberty or give me death"? Who will deny that something is "happening" in Patrick Henry's rousing challenge that not only fails to happen in the paraphrase but is actually negated there? Would you bear with this long-winded, pompous speaker to the end? If you were to judge this statement strictly on its rhetoric (its choice and arrangement of words), you might aptly call it more boring than brave. Perhaps a plainer version will work better:

> Liberty is a very important thing for a person to have. Most people—at least the people I've talked to or that other people have told me about—know this and therefore are very anxious to preserve their liberty. Of course I can't be absolutely sure about what other folks are going to do in this present crisis, what with all these threats and everything, but I've made up my mind that I'm going to fight because liberty is really a very important thing to me; at least that's the way I feel about it.

3   This flat, "homely" prose, weighted down with what the French author Gustave Flaubert called "fatty deposits," is grammatical enough. As in the pompous paraphrase, every verb agrees with its subjects, every comma is in its proper place; nonetheless it lacks the qualities that make a statement—of one sentence or one hundred pages—pungent, vital, moving, and memorable.

4   Let us isolate these qualities and describe them briefly.

ECONOMY

5 The first quality of good writing is *economy.* In an appropriately slender volume entitled *The Elements of Style,* authors William Strunk Jr. and E. B. White state the case for economy concisely:

> A sentence should contain no unnecessary words, for the same reason that a drawing should have no unnecessary lines and a machine no unnecessary parts. This requires not that the writer make all his sentences short or that he avoid all detail . . . but that every word tell.

6   In other words, economical writing is *efficient* and *aesthetically satisfying.* While it makes a minimum demand on the energy and patience of readers, it returns to them a maximum of sharply compressed meaning. This is one of your basic responsibilities as a writer: to inflict no unnecessary words on your reader—just as a dentist inflicts no unnecessary pain, a lawyer no unnecessary risk. Economical writing avoids strain and at the same time promotes pleasure by producing a sense of form and right proportion, a sense of words that fit the ideas they embody. Economical writing contains no "deadwood" to dull the reader's attention, not an extra, useless phrase to clog the free flow of ideas, one following swiftly and clearly upon another.

SIMPLICITY

7   Another basic quality of good writing is *simplicity*. Here again this does not require that you make all your sentences primer-like or that you reduce complexities to the bare bone, but rather that you avoid embellishment and embroidery. A natural, unpretentious style is best. It signifies sincerity, for one thing: when people say what they *really mean,* they tend to say it with disarming simplicity. But paradoxically, simplicity or naturalness does not come naturally. By the time we are old enough to write, most of us have grown so self-conscious that we stiffen, sometimes to the point of rigidity, when we are called upon to make a statement in speech or in writing. It is easy to offer the kindly advice "Be yourself" but many people do not feel like themselves when they take a pencil in hand or sit down at a typewriter. During the early days of the Second World War, when air raids were feared in New York City and blackouts were instituted, an anonymous writer—probably a young civil service worker at City Hall—produced and distributed the following poster:

> *Illumination*
> *Is Required*
> *to be*
> *Extinguished*
> *on These Premises*
> *After Nightfall*

8   What this meant, of course, was simply "Lights Out After Dark." But apparently that direct imperative—clear and to the point—did not sound "official" enough, so the writer resorted to long Latinate words and involved syntax (note the awkward passives "*Is* Required" and "*to be* Extinguished") to establish a tone of dignity and authority. In contrast, how beautifully simple are the words of the translators of the King James Version of the Bible, who felt no need for flourish, flamboyance, or grandiloquence. The Lord did not loftily or bombastically proclaim that universal illumination was required to be instantaneously installed. Simply but majestically "God said, Let there be light: and there was light. . . . And God called the light Day, and the darkness He called Night."

9   Most memorable declarations have been spare and direct. The French author Andre Maurois noted that Abraham Lincoln and John F. Kennedy seemed to "speak to each other across the span of a century," for both men embodied noble themes in eloquently simple terms. Said Lincoln in his second Inaugural Address. "With malice toward none, with charity for all, with firmness in the right as God gives us to see the right, let us strive on to finish the work we are in. . . . " One hundred years later President Kennedy made his Inaugural dedication: "With a good conscience our only sure reward, with history the final judge of our deeds, let us go forth to lead the land we love. . . . "

CLARITY

10 A third fundamental element of good writing is *clarity*. Some people question whether it is always possible to be clear. After all, certain ideas are inherently complicated and inescapably difficult. True enough. But the responsible writer recognizes that writing should not add to the complications nor increase the difficulty: it should not set up an additional roadblock to understanding. If writers understand their own ideas and want to convey them to others, they are obliged to render those ideas in clear, orderly, readable, understandable prose—else why bother writing in the first place? Actually, obscure writers are usually confused themselves, uncertain of what they want to say or what they mean; they have not yet completed that process of thinking through and reasoning into the heart of the subject.

11 Whatever the topic, whatever the occasion, expository writing should be readable, informative, and, wherever possible, engaging. At its best it may even be poetic.

12 Even in technical writing, where the range of styles is necessarily limited, you must always be aware of "the reader over your shoulder." Take topics such as how to follow postal regulations for overseas mail, how to change oil in an engine, or how to produce aspirin from salicylic acid. Here are technical descriptions that defy a memorable turn of phrase. Such writing is of necessity cut and dried, dispassionate, and bloodless. But it need not be tedious or confusing to readers who want to find out about mailing letters, changing oil, or making aspirin. Readers who are looking for such information should have reasonably easy access to it. Written instructions should be clear, spare, direct, and, most of all, *human:* No matter how technical the subject, all writing is done *for* human beings *by* human beings. Writing, like language itself, is a strictly human enterprise. Machines may stamp letters, measure oil, and convert acids, but only human beings talk and write about these procedures so that other human beings may better understand them. It is always appropriate, therefore, to be human in the way you write.

RHETORICAL STANCE

13 Part of this humanity must stem from your sense of who your readers are. You must assume a "rhetorical stance." Indeed this is a fundamental principle of rhetoric: *nothing should ever be written in a vacuum*. You should identify your audience, hypothetical or real, so that you may speak to them in an appropriate voice. A student, for example, should never "just write," without visualizing a definite group of readers—fellow students, perhaps, or the educated community at large (intelligent nonspecialists). Without such definite readers in mind, you cannot assume a suitable and appropriate relationship to your material, your purpose, and your audience. A proper rhetorical stance, in other words, requires that you have an active sense of the following:

1. Who you are as a writer
2. Who your readers are
3. Why you are addressing them and on what occasion
4. Your relationship to your subject matter
5. How you want your readers to relate to the subject matter

"Courtship" Devices

14 In addition to a rhetorical stance, a writer should draw upon those personal and aesthetic effects that enhance a statement without distorting it and that delight—or at least sustain—a reader's attention. "One's case," said Aristotle, "should, in justice, be fought on the strength of the facts alone." This would be ideal: mind speaking to mind. The truth is, however, that people do not react soley on rational grounds, or, to quote Aristotle in a more cynical mood, "External matters do count much, because of the sorry nature of the audience." Facing reality then, you should try to "woo" the reader through a kind of "courtship." You should try, as Carl Rogers reminds us, to break down the natural barriers and fears that separate people, whether their encounters are face to face or on the printed page.

15 You must personalize your relationship with the reader by using those rhetorical devices that enable you to emerge from the page as a human being, with a distinctive voice and, in a broad sense, a personality. When the writer and reader come together, the occasion should be special, marked by a common purpose and an element of pleasure.

16 Rhetoric provides a rich storehouse of courting devices, and we shall consider these in Part Three. For example, the pleasant rhythm of a balanced antithesis is evident in President Kennedy's immortal statement, ". . . ask not what your country can do for you; ask what you can do for your country." The lilting suspense of a periodic sentence (one that suspends its subject or predication until the end) appears in Edward Gibbon's delightful account of how he came to write the famous *Decline and Fall of the Roman Empire:*

> It was at Rome, on the 15th of October 1764, as I sat musing amidst the ruins of the Capitol, while the barefooted friars were singing vespers in the temple of Jupiter, that the idea of writing the decline and fall of the city first started to my mind.

17 Simeon Potter, a modern scholar, has observed that the word picture Gibbon draws, although brief, is "artistically perfect":

> The rhythm is stately and entirely satisfying. The reader is held in suspense to the end. Had he wished, and had he been less of an artist, Gibbon might have said exactly the same things in a different way, arranging them in their logical and grammatical order: "The idea of writing the decline and fall of the city first started to my mind as I sat musing amidst the ruins of the Capitol at Rome on the 15th of

October 1764, while the barefooted friars were singing vespers in the temple of Jupiter." What has happened? It is not merely that a periodic sentence has been re-expressed as a loose one. The emphasis is now all wrong and the magnificent cadence of the original is quite marred. All is still grammatically correct, but "proper words" are no longer in "proper places." The passage has quite lost its harmonious rhythm.

18   In addition, then, to economy, simplicity, and clarity—the foundation of sound, dependable rhetoric—include this marvelous dimension of "harmonious rhythm," of proper words in proper places. If you are sensitive to these strategies, you will delight as well as inform your reader, and in delighting, reinforce your statement.

STYLE

William Zinsser
(1922–   )

 ⁓⁓⁓

Author of the highly acclaimed book *On Writing Well: An Informal Guide to Writing Nonfiction* (1976), William Zinsser was educated at Princeton and worked for *Life* and *Look* magazines as well as the *New York Herald Tribune*. In 1970, Zinsser joined the faculty at Yale University and created the first nonfiction writing course ever offered at the university. His *On Writing Well* is based not only on his own experiences as a writer, but also on his observations of his students' writing processes. He has written several books, including *Pop Goes America* (1966), *Writing with a Word Processor* (1982), *Paths of Resistance: The Art and Craft of the Political Novel* (1989), and *Worlds of Childhood: The Art and Craft of Writing for Children* (1990). In the following excerpt from *On Writing Well*, Zinsser advises writers to resist trying to write in an overblown style, but to instead "believe in your own identity."

1   So much for early warnings about the bloated monsters that lie in ambush for the writer trying to put together a clean English sentence.

2   "But," you may say, "if I eliminate everything you think is clutter and if I strip every sentence to its barest bones, will there be anything left of me?" The question is a fair one and the fear entirely natural. Simplicity carried to its extreme might seem to point to a style little more sophisticated than "Dick likes Jane" and "See Spot run."

3   I'll answer the question first on the level of carpentry. Then I'll get to the larger issue of who the writer is and how to preserve his or her identity.

William Zinsser (© Nancy Crampton)

4   Few people realize how badly they write. Nobody has shown them how much excess or murkiness has crept into their style and how it obstructs what they are trying to say. If you give me an eight-page article and I tell you to cut it to four, you'll howl and say it can't be done. Then you'll go home and do it, and it will be much better. After that comes the hard part: cutting it to three.

5   The point is that you have to strip your writing down before you can build it back up. You must know what the essential tools are and what job they were designed to do. If I may labor the metaphor of carpentry, it's first necessary to be able to saw wood neatly and to drive nails. Later you can bevel the edges or add elegant finials, if that's your taste. But you can never forget that you are practicing a craft that's based on certain principles. If the nails are weak, your house will collapse. If your verbs are weak and your syntax is rickety, your sentences will fall apart.

6   I'll admit that various nonfiction writers, like Tom Wolfe and Norman Mailer, have built some remarkable houses. But these are writers who spent years learning their craft, and when at last they raised their fanciful turrets and hanging gardens, to the surprise of all of us who never dreamed of such ornamentation, they knew what they were doing. Nobody becomes Tom Wolfe overnight, not even Tom Wolfe.

7   First, then, learn to hammer the nails, and if what you build is sturdy and serviceable, take satisfaction in its plain strength.

8   But you will be impatient to find a "style"—to embellish the plain words so that readers will recognize you as someone special. You will reach for gaudy similes and tinseled adjectives, as if "style" were something you could buy in a style store at the mall and drape onto your words in bright decorator colors. (Decorator colors are the colors that decorators come in.) There is no style store; style is organic to the person doing the writing, as much a part of him as his hair, or, if he is bald, his lack of it. Trying to add style is like adding a toupee. At first glance the formerly bald man looks young and even handsome. But at second glance—and with a toupee there's always a second glance—he doesn't look quite right. The problem is not that he doesn't look well groomed; he does, and we can only admire the wigmaker's skill. The point is that he doesn't look like himself.

9   This is the problem of writers who set out deliberately to garnish their prose. You lose whatever it is that makes you unique. The reader will notice if you are putting on airs. He wants the person who is talking to him to sound genuine. Therefore a fundamental rule is: Be yourself.

10   No rule, however, is harder to follow. It requires writers to do two things which by their metabolism are impossible. They must relax and they must have confidence.

11   Telling a writer to relax is like telling a man to relax while being prodded for a possible hernia, and as for confidence, see how stiffly he sits, glaring at the screen that awaits his words. See how often he gets up to look for something to eat. A writer will do anything to avoid the act of writing. I can testify from my newspaper days that the number of trips to the water cooler per reporter-hour far exceeds the body's need for fluids.

12   What can be done to put the writer out of these miseries? Unfortunately, no cure has been found. I can only offer the consoling thought that you are not alone. Some days will go better than others; some will go so badly that you'll despair of ever writing again. We have all had many of these days and will have many more.

13   Still, it would be nice to keep the bad days to a minimum, which brings me back to the matter of trying to relax.

14   Assume that you are the writer sitting down to write. You think your article must be of a certain length or it won't seem important. You think how august it will look in print. You think of all the people who will read it. You think that it must have the solid weight of authority. You think that its style must dazzle. No wonder you tighten; you are so busy thinking of your awesome responsibility to the finished article that you can't even start. Yet you vow to be worthy of the task, and, casting about for grand phrases that wouldn't occur to you if you weren't trying so hard to make an impression, you plunge in.

15   Paragraph 1 is a disaster—a tissue of ponderous generalities that seem to have come out of a machine. No *person* could have written them. Paragraph 2 isn't much better. But Paragraph 3 begins to have a somewhat human quality, and by Paragraph 4 you begin to sound like yourself. You've started to relax. It's amazing how often an editor can just throw away the first three or four paragraphs of an article, or even the first few pages, and start with the paragraph where the writer begins to sound like himself. Not only are those first paragraphs hopelessly impersonal and ornate; they don't say anything. They are a self-conscious attempt at a fancy introduction, and none is necessary.

16   Writers are obviously at their most natural when they write in the first person. Writing is a personal transaction between two people, conducted on paper, and the transaction will go well to the extent that it retains its humanity. Therefore I urge people to write in the first person: to use "I" and "me" and "we" and "us." They put up a fight.

17   "Who am I to say what *I* think?" they ask. "Or what *I* feel?"

18   "Who are you *not* to say what you think?" I reply. "There's only one you. Nobody else thinks or feels in exactly the same way."

19   "But no one cares about my opinions," they say. "It would make me feel conspicuous."

20   "They'll care if you tell them something interesting," I say, "and tell them in words that come naturally."

21   Nevertheless, getting writers to use "I" is seldom easy. They think they must earn the right to reveal their emotions or their thoughts. Or that it's egotistical. Or that it's undignified—a fear that hobbles the academic world. Hence the professorial use of "one" ("One finds oneself not wholly in accord with Dr. Maltby's view of the human condition") and of the impersonal "it is" ("It is to be hoped that Professor Felt's monograph will find the wider audience it most assuredly deserves"). I don't want to meet "one"—he's a boring guy. I want a professor with a passion for his subject to tell me why it fascinates *him*.

22   I realize that there are vast regions of writing where "I" isn't allowed. Newspapers don't want "I" in their news stories; many magazines don't want

it in their articles; businesses and institutions don't want it in the reports they send so profusely into the American home; colleges don't want "I" in their term papers or dissertations; and English teachers discourage any first-person pronoun except the literary "we" ("We see in Melville's symbolic use of the white whale. . ."). Many of those prohibitions are valid. Newspaper articles should consist of news, reported objectively. I also sympathize with teachers who don't want to give students an easy escape into opinion—"I think Hamlet was stupid"—before the students have grappled with the discipline of assessing a work on its merits and on external sources. "I" can be a self-indulgence and a cop-out.

23   Still, we have become a society fearful of revealing who we are. We have bred a national language of impersonality. The institutions that seek our support by sending us their brochures sound remarkably alike, though surely all of them—hospitals, schools, libraries, museums, zoos— were founded and are still sustained by men and women with different dreams and visions. Where are these people? It's hard to glimpse them among all the passive sentences that say "initiatives were undertaken" and "priorities have been identified."

24   Even when "I" is not permitted, it's still possible to convey a sense of I-ness. James Reston doesn't use "I" in his columns; yet I have a good idea of what kind of person he is, and I could say the same of many other essayists and reporters. Good writers are visible just behind their words. If you aren't allowed to use "I," at least think "I" while you write, or write the first draft in the first person and then take the "I's" out. It will warm up your impersonal style.

25   Style, of course, is tied to the psyche, and writing has deep psychological roots. The reasons why we express ourselves as we do, or fail to express ourselves because of "writer's block," are partly buried in the subconscious mind. There are as many kinds of writer's block as there are kinds of writers, and I have no intention of trying to untangle them. This is a short book, and my name isn't Sigmund Freud.

26   But I've noticed a new reason for avoiding "I" that runs deeper than what is not allowed or what is undignified. Americans are suddenly unwilling to go out on a limb. A generation ago our leaders told us where they stood and what they believed. Today they perform strenuous verbal feats to escape this fate. Watch them wriggle through TV interviews without committing themselves. I remember President Ford assuring a group of visiting businessmen that his fiscal policies would work. He said: "We see nothing but increasingly brighter clouds every month." I took this to mean that the clouds were still fairly dark. Ford's sentence was just misty enough to say nothing and still sedate his constituents.

27   Later administrations brought no relief. Defense Secretary Caspar Weinberger, assessing a Polish crisis in 1984, said: "There's continuing ground for serious concern and the situation remains serious. The longer it remains serious, the more ground there is for serious concern." President Bush, questioned about his stand on assault rifles in 1989, said: "There are various groups that think you can ban certain kinds of guns. I am not in that mode. I am in the mode of being deeply concerned."

28   But my all-time champ is Elliot Richardson, who held four major cabinet positions in the 1970s—attorney general and secretary of defense, commerce and HEW. It's hard to know where to begin picking from his vast trove of equivocal statements, but consider this one: "And yet, on balance, affirmative action has, I think, been a qualified success." A 13-word sentence with five hedging words. I give it first prize as the most wishy-washy sentence in recent public discourse, though a close rival would be Richardson's analysis of how to ease boredom among assembly-line workers: "And so, at last, I come to the one firm conviction that I mentioned at the beginning: it is that the subject is too new for final judgments."

29   That's a firm conviction? Leaders who bob and weave like aging boxers don't inspire confidence—or deserve it. The same thing is true of writers. Sell yourself, and your subject will exert its own appeal. Believe in your own identity and your own opinions. Proceed with confidence, generating it by willpower. Writing is an act of ego, and you might as well admit it. Use its energy to keep yourself going.

THE MAKER'S EYE:
REVISING YOUR OWN MANUSCRIPTS

Donald Murray
(1924–   )

Donald Murray has earned a national reputation for his life's work of teaching others how to write. He has been a professor of English (he is now professor emeritus of English) at the University of New Hampshire, a reporter for the *Boston Globe,* a contributing editor to *Time* magazine, and a feature writer for a variety of other magazines. He was awarded the Pulitzer Prize for editorial writing and is the author of many writing textbooks, including *The Craft of Revision* (1991) and *Crafting a Life* (1995). In "The Maker's Eye," Murray shows that revising is an integral part of the writing process.

Donald Murray
(University of Wyoming)

1   WHEN students complete a first draft, they consider the job of writing done—and their teachers too often agree. When professional writers complete a first draft, they usually feel that they are at the start of the writing process. When a draft is completed, the job of writing can begin.

2   That difference in attitude is the difference between amateur and professional, inexperience and experience, journeyman and craftsman. Peter F. Drucker, the prolific business writer, calls his first draft "the zero draft"—after that he can start counting. Most writers share the feeling that the first draft, and all of those which follow, are opportunities to discover what they have to say and how best they can say it.

3   To produce a progression of drafts, each of which says more and says it more clearly, the writer has to develop a special kind of reading skill. In school we are taught to decode what appears on the page as finished writing. Writers, however, face a different category of possibility and responsibility when they read their own drafts. To them the words on the page are never finished. Each can be changed and rearranged, can set off a chain reaction of confusion or

clarified meaning. This is a different kind of reading which is possibly more difficult and certainly more exciting.

4   Writers must learn to be their own best enemy. They must accept the criticism of others and be suspicious of it; they must accept the praise of others and be even more suspicious of it. Writers cannot depend on others. They must detach themselves from their own pages so that they can apply both their caring and their craft to their own work.

5   Such detachment is not easy. Science fiction writer Ray Bradbury supposedly puts each manuscript away for a year to the day and then rereads it as a stranger. Not many writers have the discipline or the time to do this. We must read when our judgment may be at its worst, when we are close to the euphoric moment of creation.

6   Then the writer, counsels novelist Nancy Hale, "should be critical of everything that seems to him most delightful in his style. He should exorcise what he most admires, because he wouldn't thus admire it if he weren't . . . in a sense protecting it from criticism." John Ciardi, the poet, adds, "The last act of the writing must be to become one's own reader. It is, I suppose, a schizophrenic process, to begin passionately and to end critically, to begin hot and to end cold; and, more important, to be passion-hot and critic-cold at the same time."

7   Most people think that the principal problem is that writers are too proud of what they have written. Actually, a greater problem for most professional writers is one shared by the majority of students. They are overly critical, think everything is dreadful, tear up page after page, never complete a draft, see the task as hopeless.

8   The writer must learn to read critically but constructively, to cut what is bad, to reveal what is good. Eleanor Estes, the children's book author, explains: "The writer must survey his work critically, coolly, as though he were a stranger to it. He must be willing to prune, expertly and hard-heartedly. At the end of each revision, a manuscript may look . . . worked over, torn apart, pinned together, added to, deleted from, words changed and words changed back. Yet the book must maintain its original freshness and spontaneity."

9   Most readers underestimate the amount of rewriting it usually takes to produce spontaneous reading. This is a great disadvantage to the student writer, who sees only a finished product and never watches the craftsman who takes the necessary step back, studies the work carefully, returns to the task, steps back, returns, steps back, again and again. Anthony Burgess, one of the most prolific writers in the English-speaking world, admits, "I might revise a page twenty times." Roald Dahl, the popular children's writer, states, "By the time I'm nearing the end of a story, the first part will have been reread and altered and corrected at least 150 times. . . . Good writing is essentially rewriting. I am positive of this."

10   Rewriting isn't virtuous. It isn't something that ought to be done. It is simply something that most writers find they have to do to discover what they have to say and how to say it. It is a condition of the writer's life.

11   There are, however, a few writers who do little formal rewriting, primarily because they have the capacity and experience to create and review a large number of invisible drafts in their minds before they approach the page. And some writers slowly produce finished pages, performing all the tasks of revision simultaneously, page by page, rather than draft by draft. But it is still possible to see the sequence followed by most writers most of the time in rereading their own work.

12   Most writers scan their drafts first, reading as quickly as possible to catch the larger problems of subject and form, then move in closer and closer as they read and write, reread and rewrite.

13   The first thing writers look for in their drafts is *information*. They know that a good piece of writing is built from specific, accurate, and interesting information. The writer must have an abundance of information from which to construct a readable piece of writing.

14   Next writers look for *meaning* in the information. The specifics must build to a pattern of significance. Each piece of specific information must carry the reader toward meaning.

15   Writers reading their own drafts are aware of *audience*. They put themselves in the reader's situation and make sure that they deliver information which a reader wants to know or needs to know in a manner which is easily digested. Writers try to be sure that they anticipate and answer the questions a critical reader will ask when reading the piece of writing.

16   Writers make sure that the *form* is appropriate to the subject and the audience. Form, or genre, is the vehicle which carries meaning to the reader, but form cannot be selected until the writer has adequate information to discover its significance and an audience which needs or wants that meaning.

17   Once writers are sure the form is appropriate, they must then look at the *structure*, the order of what they have written. Good writing is built on a solid framework of logic, argument, narrative, or motivation which runs through the entire piece of writing and holds it together. This is the time when many writers find it most effective to outline as a way of visualizing the hidden spine by which the piece of writing is supported.

18   The element on which writers may spend a majority of their time is *development*. Each section of a piece of writing must be adequately developed. It must give readers enough information so that they are satisfied. How much information is enough? That's as difficult as asking how much garlic belongs in a salad. It must be done to taste, but most beginning writers underdevelop, underestimating the reader's hunger for information.

19   As writers solve development problems, they often have to consider questions of *dimension*. There must be a pleasing and effective proportion among all the parts of the piece of writing. There is a continual process of subtracting and adding to keep the piece of writing in balance.

20   Finally, writers have to listen to their own voices. *Voice* is the force which drives a piece of writing forward. It is an expression of the writer's authority and concern. It is what is between the words on the page, what glues the piece

of writing together. A good piece of writing is always marked by a consistent, individual voice.

21   As writers read and reread, write and rewrite, they move closer and closer to the page until they are doing line-by-line editing. Writers read their own pages with infinite care. Each sentence, each line, each clause, each phrase, each word, each mark of punctuation, each section of white space between the type has to contribute to the clarification of meaning.

22   Slowly the writer moves from word to word, looking through language to see the subject. As a word is changed, cut, or added, as a construction is re-arranged, all the words used before that moment and all those that follow that moment must be considered and reconsidered.

23   Writers often read aloud at this stage of the editing process, muttering or whispering to themselves, calling on the ear's experience with language. Does this sound right—or that? Writers edit, shifting back and forth from eye to page to ear to page. I find I must do this careful editing in short runs, no more than fifteen or twenty minutes at a stretch, or I become too kind with myself. I begin to see what I hope is on the page, not what actually is on the page.

24   This sounds tedious if you haven't done it, but actually it is fun. Making something right is immensely satisfying, for writers begin to learn what they are writing about by writing. Language leads them to meaning, and there is the joy of discovery, of understanding, of making meaning clear as the writer employs the technical skills of language.

25   Words have double meanings, even triple and quadruple meanings. Each word has its own potential for connotation and denotation. And when writers rub one word against the other, they are often rewarded with a sudden insight, an unexpected clarification.

26   The maker's eye moves back and forth from word to phrase to sentence to paragraph to sentence to phrase to word. The maker's eye sees the need for variety and balance, for a firmer structure, for a more appropriate form. It peers into the interior of the paragraph, looking for coherence, unity, and emphasis, which make meaning clear.

27   I learned something about this process when my first bifocals were prescribed. I had ordered a larger section of the reading portion of the glass because of my work, but even so, I could not contain my eyes within this new limit of vision. And I still find myself taking off my glasses and bending my nose towards the page, for my eyes unconsciously flick back and forth across the page, back to another page, forward to still another, as I try to see each evolving line in relation to every other line.

28   When does this process end? Most writers agree with the great Russian writer Tolstoy, who said, "I scarcely ever reread my published writings; if by chance I come across a page, it always strikes me: all this must be rewritten; this is how I should have written it."

29   The maker's eye is never satisfied, for each word has the potential to ignite new meaning. This article has been twice written all the way through the writing process, and it was published four years ago. Now it is to be republished in

a book. The editors made a few small suggestions, and then I read it with my maker's eye. Now it has been re-edited, re-revised, re-read, re-re-edited, for each piece of writing to the writer is full of potential and alternatives.

30   A piece of writing is never finished. It is delivered to a deadline, torn out of the typewriter on demand, sent off with a sense of accomplishment and shame and pride and frustration. If only there were a couple more days, time for just another run at it, perhaps then. . . .

PART TWO

ESSAYS FOR
READING AND ANALYSIS

CHAPTER THREE

NARRATION

NARRATION is the simple act of telling a story, recounting an event, or relaying an incident. It is one of the most natural methods we have of communicating ideas. Narration can take the form of a story told to ignite a child's imagination, of an anecdote relayed to amuse friends, or perhaps of an incident presented to illustrate a point. Histories of cultures and civilizations have been passed down to generations through oral narratives.

When we read (or hear) a narrative, we know that what will unfold will be a series of events (what happens) in someone's life (to whom it happens) at some time (when it happens) somewhere (where it happens). We might also discover why whatever happens happens. These elements—what happens, to whom it happens, when it happens, where it happens, and perhaps why it happens—are the basic elements upon which a narrative is built. Thus, the narrative can be defined as a series of events presented in a logical and meaningful sequence.

For example, in Maya Angelou's "Sister Flowers," a chapter from her first autobiography, *I Know Why the Caged Bird Sings*, Angelou recalls a time in her childhood when she was made to feel special and respected. She unfolds the sequence of events by introducing the woman who would have a profound influence on her, "the lady who threw me my first life line."

Another example is Langston Hughes' "Salvation." Taken from his 1940 autobiography, *The Big Sea*, the selection recounts the events that led to the author's fraudulent salvation at a revival meeting. He begins the narrative by telling when the revival meeting takes place (he was 13), where it takes place (at his Aunt Reed's church), and, of course, who is involved (the children).

Because the narrative is a natural rhetorical structure, it is frequently used in combination with other structures. Minutes of a business meeting often appear as narrative incidents. A history essay on the men and women who fought in Operation Desert Storm could be introduced with a brief story about one soldier. Using narration with other rhetorical structures, such as definition (Chapter Six) or illustration (Chapter Seven), can add to the richness of the discussion and can also clarify difficult issues or principles by presenting them in terms with which the reader can easily identify.

WRITING THE NARRATIVE ESSAY

Remember that the key to writing a good narrative is arranging your material into a sequence of events that is logical, clear, and effective. The following tips will help you in preparing a narrative:

1. *Concentrate on what's important.*

Always keep your purpose in mind and avoid spending too much space on elements that, though interesting, are secondary to your purpose. For example, if you are writing a narrative that illustrates the virtue of honesty, it may not be necessary to include elaborate details about the narrative's setting.

2. *Use details to create a vivid picture.*

Regardless of the narrative's purpose, you should create a scene so vivid that the reader will grasp the lesson, know the character, or understand the experience. The use of well-placed, colorful language in your writing will do much to evoke a feeling or mood, produce a mental picture, or induce a particular emotion. As you choose your words, be aware of their connotation and denotation. Colorful words can easily become emotionally charged words containing positive or negative associations. Certainly, you may choose to use such words deliberately for one reason or another; just remember to keep your audience in mind, and make sure that your language is appropriate for your reader.

3. *Keep the narrative perspective consistent.*

Obviously, your narrative will need a "voice" or narrator to tell it. A first-person narrator will recount the events in personal terms, using first-person pronouns (I, we, us). A third-person narrator may also be used, referring to characters as he, she, or they. Whatever the case, be sure to maintain a consistent voice throughout the narration.

Once you have established the narrative perspective or the voice, maintain the "character" of that perspective. If your narrator is a tough, rough-and-tumble kind of guy, his language should reflect that personality trait. Don't have him speaking the language of "the street" in some places and switch to that of an intellectual sophisticate in others.

4. *Select an appropriate and logical time sequence.*

The time ordering of your narrative should enhance its purpose. You may use straight chronology (relating the events as they happen) or retrospective—flashback—(momentarily leaving the present to reach into a time before the main action of the narrative) to develop the writing. Whatever sequencing technique you use, though, should complement the overall effect and purpose of the narrative.

5. *Create and maintain smoothness in the narrative.*

A sense of coherence is as important in narrative writing as it is in any other kind of writing. You should, however, avoid juvenile connections of excessive coordinations—that is, stringing your sentences together with *and* or *and then.* Instead, vary your sentence structures and use synonyms and pronouns to add freshness to your writing. Deliberate, but careful (and sparse), repetition can also create emphasis.

Without question, writing a good narrative takes practice, but the time spent in honing the skill is well worth your effort.

Langston Hughes (© J. Sommer Collection/Archive Photos)

SALVATION

Langston Hughes
(1902–1967)

James Mercer Langston Hughes' love of poetry
began at his high school in Cleveland, Ohio. In
his English classes, he read the poetry of Carl
Sandburg and Edgar Lee Masters and published
several poems in the school's literary magazine.
He attended Columbia University until 1921,
when he left school to work and travel. By then
he was determined to become a writer. While he
was working in Washington, D.C., he asked
poet Vachel Lindsay to read some of his poems.
Deeply impressed with the pieces, Lindsay
helped Hughes to publish his work. His career
was launched with the publication of *The Weary
Blues* (1926). In 1929, Hughes was awarded a
bachelor's degree from Lincoln University. Later,
he settled in New York and became a prominent
figure in the Harlem Renaissance, which
included such literary notables as Countée
Cullen, Zora Neale Hurston, Claude McKay,
and Jean Toomer. In 1956, he penned his second
autobiographical work, *I Wonder As I Wander.*
Hughes also wrote newspaper columns for the
Chicago Defender and the *New York Post.*
Although his writings include novels, plays, and
newspaper columns, he is best known for his
innovative poetry that introduced the patterns of
African-American dialect and the rhythms of
jazz. In "Salvation," which is from his first autobiographical work *The Big Sea* (1940), Hughes
demonstrates his gift for humor and his insight
into the human experience.

1   I was saved from sin when I was going on thirteen. But not really saved. It happened like this. There was a big revival at my Auntie Reed's church. Every night for weeks there had been much preaching, singing, praying, and shouting, and some very hardened sinners had been brought to Christ, and the membership of the church had grown by leaps and bounds. Then just before the revival ended, they held a special meeting for children, "to bring the young lambs to the fold." My aunt spoke of it for days ahead. That night I was escorted to the front row and placed on the mourners' bench with all the other young sinners, who had not yet been brought to Jesus.

2   My aunt told me that when you were saved you saw a light, and something happened to you inside! And Jesus came into your life! And God was with you from then on! She said you could see and hear and feel Jesus in your soul. I believed her. I had heard a great many old people say the same thing and it seemed to me they ought to know. So I sat there calmly in the hot, crowded church, waiting for Jesus to come to me.

3   The preacher preached a wonderful rhythmical sermon, all moans and shouts and lonely cries and dire pictures of hell, and then he sang a song about the ninety and nine safe in the fold, but one little lamb was left out in the cold. Then he said: "Won't you come? Won't you come to Jesus? Young lambs, won't you come?" And he held out his arms to all us young sinners there on the mourners' bench. And the little girls cried. And some of them jumped up and went to Jesus right away. But most of us just sat there.

4   A great many old people came and knelt around us and prayed, old women with jet-black faces and braided hair, old men with work-gnarled hands. And the church sang a song about the lower lights are burning, some poor sinners to be saved. And the whole building rocked with prayer and song.

5   Still I kept waiting to *see* Jesus.

6   Finally all the young people had gone to the altar and were saved, but one boy and me. He was a rounder's son named Westley. Westley and I were surrounded by sisters and deacons praying. It was very hot in the church, and getting late now. Finally Westley said to me in a whisper: "God damn! I'm tired o' sitting here. Let's get up and be saved." So he got up and was saved.

7   Then I was left all alone on the mourners' bench. My aunt came and knelt at my knees and cried, while prayers and song swirled all around me in the little church. The whole congregation prayed for me alone, in a mighty wail of moans and voices. And I kept waiting serenely for Jesus, waiting, waiting—but he didn't come. I wanted to see him, but nothing happened to me. Nothing! I wanted something to happen to me, but nothing happened.

8   I heard the songs and the minister saying: "Why don't you come? My dear child, why don't you come to Jesus? Jesus is waiting for you. He wants you. Why don't you come? Sister Reed, what is this child's name?"

9   "Langston," my aunt sobbed.

10   "Langston, why don't you come? Why don't you come and be saved? Oh, Lamb of God! Why don't you come?"

11   Now it was really getting late. I began to be ashamed of myself, holding everything up so long. I began to wonder what God thought about Westley, who certainly hadn't seen Jesus either, but who was now sitting proudly on the platform, swinging his knickerbockered legs and grinning down at me, surrounded by deacons and old women on their knees praying. God had not struck Westley dead for taking his name in vain or for lying in the temple. So I decided that maybe to save further trouble, I'd better lie, too, and say that Jesus had come, and get up and be saved.

12   So I got up.

13   Suddenly the whole room broke into a sea of shouting, as they saw me rise. Waves of rejoicing swept the place. Women leaped in the air. My aunt threw her arms around me. The minister took me by the hand and led me to the platform.

14   When things quieted down, in a hushed silence, punctuated by a few ecstatic "Amens," all the new young lambs were blessed in the name of God. Then joyous singing filled the room.

15   That night, for the last time in my life but one—for I was a big boy twelve years old—I cried. I cried, in bed alone, and couldn't stop. I buried my head under the quilts, but my aunt heard me. She woke up and told my uncle I was crying because the Holy Ghost had come into my life, and because I had seen Jesus. But I was really crying because I couldn't bear to tell her that I had lied, that I had deceived everybody in the church, that I hadn't seen Jesus, and that now I didn't believe there was a Jesus any more, since he didn't come to help me.

restate thesis

TOPICS FOR WRITING AND DISCUSSION

1. While he is at the revival meeting, Hughes experiences pressure to "be saved" from many different sources. List these sources and explain how Hughes reacts to each. Which source finally convinces him to get up and join the ranks of those who have attained salvation? *preacher, deacons, old people → Aunt*

2. What did Hughes' aunt tell him about the experience of being saved? How did her description compare to Hughes' observations and feelings while he was at the service? *she would see Jesus, but Hughes didn't*

3. Narratives frequently use dialogue (directly recorded conversation). Hughes uses dialogue sparingly, only occasionally interspersing a comment with his own observations of the scene. Which individuals speak directly? What effect does Hughes' use of dialogue have? How does the dialogue suggest the essay's thesis? *Aunt & preacher*

4. How does Hughes use imagery and figurative language to heighten the sense of conflict he feels? Notice, for example, that the entire congregation breaks "into a sea of shouting" as Hughes finally rises and walks toward the altar. *hot, pressure, crying*

5. Write a narrative describing a conflict you faced, the pressures brought to bear on your decision, and the choice you made. As did Hughes, try to use dialogue and strong imagery.

Richard Selzer (© Nancy Crampton)

THE DISCUS THROWER

Richard Selzer
(1928–   )

The son of a family doctor, Richard Selzer himself
earned an M.D. from Albany Medical College. His
experiences as a surgeon are the inspiration for his
essays and short stories, including his *Rituals of
Surgery* (1974), a collection of short stories. He has
published short stories and essays in magazines such as
Redbook, Esquire, and *Harper's,* and has collected
them in *Mortal Lessons* (1977), *Confessions of a Knife*
(1979), *Letters to a Young Doctor* (1982), and *Taking
the World in for Repairs* (1986). After contracting
Legionnaire's disease in 1991, he documented his
recovery in *Raising the Dead: A Doctor's Encounter
with His Own Mortality* (1994). His latest work is *The
Doctor Stories* (1998). "The Discus Thrower" draws
on his experience as a physician and provides thoughtful insight into the human resistance to death.

1   I spy on my patients. Ought not a doctor to observe his patients by any means
and from any stance, that he might the more fully assemble evidence? So I stand
in the doorways of hospital rooms and gaze. Oh, it is not all that furtive an act.
Those in bed need only look up to discover me. But they never do.

2   From the doorway of Room 542 the man in the bed seems deeply tanned.
Blue eyes and close-cropped white hair give him the appearance of vigor and
good health. But I know that his skin is not brown from the sun. It is rusted,
rather, in the last stage of containing the vile repose within. And the blue eyes
are frosted, looking inward like the windows of a snowbound cottage. This
man is blind. This man is also legless—the right leg missing from midthigh
down, the left from just below the knee. It gives him the look of a bonsai, roots
and branches pruned into the dwarfed facsimile of a great tree.

3   Propped on pillows, he cups his right thigh in both hands. Now and then he shakes his head as though acknowledging the intensity of his suffering. In all of this he makes no sound. Is he mute as well as blind?

4   The room in which he dwells is empty of all possessions—no get-well cards, small, private caches of food, day-old flowers, slippers, all the usual kickshaws of the sickroom. There is only the bed, a chair, a nightstand, and a tray on wheels that can be swung across his lap for meals.

5   "What time is it?" he asks.

6   "Three o'clock."

7   "Morning or afternoon?"

8   "Afternoon."

9   He is silent. There is nothing else he wants to know.

10   "How are you?" I say.

11   "Who is it?" he asks.

12   "It's the doctor. How do you feel?"

13   He does not answer right away.

14   "Feel?" he says.

15   "I hope you feel better," I say.

16   I press the button at the side of the bed.

17   "Down you go," I say.

18   "Yes, down," he says.

19   He falls back upon the bed awkwardly. His stumps, unweighted by legs and feet, rise in the air, presenting themselves. I unwrap the bandages from the stumps, and begin to cut away the black scabs and the dead, glazed fat with scissors and forceps. A shard of white bone comes loose. I pick it away. I wash the wounds with disinfectant and redress the stumps. All this while, he does not speak. What is he thinking behind those lids that do not blink? Is he remembering a time when he was whole? Does he dream of feet? Of when his body was not a rotting log?

20   He lies solid and inert. In spite of everything, he remains impressive, as though he were a sailor standing athwart a slanting deck.

21   "Anything more I can do for you?" I ask.

22   For a long moment he is silent.

23   "Yes," he says at last and without the least irony. "You can bring me a pair of shoes."

24   In the corridor, the head nurse is waiting for me.

25   "We have to do something about him," she says. "Every morning he orders scrambled eggs for breakfast, and, instead of eating them, he picks up the plate and throws it against the wall."

26   "Throws his plate?"

27   "Nasty. That's what he is. No wonder his family doesn't come to visit. They probably can't stand him any more than we can."

28   She is waiting for me to do something.

29   "Well?"

30   "We'll see," I say.

31   The next morning I am waiting in the corridor when the kitchen delivers his breakfast. I watch the aide place the tray on the stand and swing it across his lap. She presses the button to raise the head of the bed. Then she leaves.

32   In time the man reaches to find the rim of the tray, then on to find the dome of the covered dish. He lifts off the cover and places it on the stand. He fingers across the plate until he probes the eggs. He lifts the plate in both hands, sets it on the palm of his right hand, centers it, balances it. He hefts it up and down slightly, getting the feel of it. Abruptly, he draws back his right arm as far as he can.

33   There is the crack of the plate breaking against the wall at the foot of his bed and the small wet sound of the scrambled eggs dropping to the floor.

34   And then he laughs. It is a sound you have never heard. It is something new under the sun. It could cure cancer.

35   Out in the corridor, the eyes of the head nurse narrow.

36   "Laughed, did he?"

37   She writes something down on her clipboard.

38   A second aide arrives, brings a second breakfast tray, puts it on the night-stand, out of his reach. She looks over at me shaking her head and making her mouth go. I see that we are to be accomplices.

39   "I've got to feed you," she says to the man.

40   "Oh, no you don't," the man says.

41   "Oh, yes I do," the aide says, "after the way you just did. Nurse says so."

42   "Get me my shoes," the man says.

43   "Here's oatmeal," the aide says. "Open." And she touches the spoon to his lower lip.

44   "I ordered scrambled eggs," says the man.

45   "That's right," the aide says.

46   I step forward.

47   "Is there anything I can do?" I say.

48   "Who are you?" the man asks.

49   In the evening I go once more to that ward to make my rounds. The head nurse reports to me that Room 542 is deceased. She has discovered this quite by accident, she says. No, there had been no sound. Nothing. It's a blessing, she says.

50   I go into his room, a spy looking for secrets. He is still there in his bed. His face is relaxed, grave, dignified. After a while, I turn to leave. My gaze sweeps the wall at the foot of the bed, and I see the place where it has been repeatedly washed, where the wall looks very clean and very white.

TOPICS FOR WRITING AND DISCUSSION

1.   Describe the attitude of this patient toward his situation. Why is he called "the discus thrower"? Why is such a name ironic? Why does he repeatedly call for his shoes?

2. What is Selzer's attitude toward this patient? How does his view of this man compare to that of the head nurse? What was Selzer's point in narrating this patient's last days?

3. Analyze several of the many metaphors and similes that appear in this essay. What does each one add to the vividness of the descriptions? What does dialogue add to our understanding of the people in these scenes?

4. Selzer's subtitle for this essay was "Do Not Go Gentle," a reference to a well-known poem by Dylan Thomas. In the poem, Thomas addresses his dying father and urges him to fight against death, to rage against "the dying of the light." Why do you think Selzer wanted his readers to think about the Thomas poem as they read his essay?

5. Write an essay narrating a time you spent with a sick person, making clear that patient's response to his or her illness. Did your observation of this person's attitude change you in any way? Consider using figurative language and dialogue to make clear your story of the patient and your feelings.

SISTER FLOWERS

Maya Angelou
(1928–   )

Maya Angelou was born Marguerite Johnson in St.
Louis but grew up in the rural community of Stamps,
Arkansas. An acclaimed poet, actress, singer, and playwright, she is perhaps best known for her autobiographical memoirs: *I Know Why the Caged Bird Sings*
(1970), *Gather Together in My Name* (1974), *Singin'
and Swingin' and Gettin' Merry Like Christmas*
(1976), *The Heart of a Woman* (1981), and *Wouldn't
Take Nothing for My Journey Now* (1993). Her many
talents have led to her appointments by President Ford
to the Bicentennial Commission and by President
Carter to the National Commission on the Observance
of International Women's Year. Notably, Angelou was
requested to write a poem for the 1993 inauguration of
President Clinton; she read her poem "On the Pulse of
Morning" during that ceremony. *Phenomenal Woman*
(1995) is her most recent book of poetry and *Even the
Stars Look Lonesome* (1997) is her recent book. The
essay that follows, "Sister Flowers," is an excerpt from
her first autobiographical work, *I Know Why the
Caged Bird Sings*. In it, Angelou recalls a special person who made a difference in her life—a woman who
gave her respect.

1   For nearly a year, I sopped around the house, the Store, the school and the
church, like an old biscuit, dirty and inedible. Then I met, or rather got to
know, the lady who threw me my first life line.

2   Mrs. Bertha Flowers was the aristocrat of Black Stamps. She had the grace
of control to appear warm in the coldest weather, and on the Arkansas summer days it seemed she had a private breeze which swirled around, cooling her.

Maya Angelou reading at President Clinton's first inauguration in January 1993.
(© Consolidated News/Archive Newsphotos Archive Photos)

She was thin without the taut look of wiry people, and her printed voile dresses and flowered hats were as right for her as denim overalls for a farmer. She was our side's answer to the richest white woman in town.

3   Her skin was a rich black that would have peeled like a plum if snagged, but then no one would have thought of getting close enough to Mrs. Flowers to ruffle her dress, let alone snag her skin. She didn't encourage familiarity. She wore gloves too.

4   I don't think I ever saw Mrs. Flowers laugh, but she smiled often. A slow widening of her thin black lips to show even, small white teeth, then the slow effortless closing. When she chose to smile on me, I always wanted to thank her. The action was so graceful and inclusively benign.

5   She was one of the few gentlewomen I have ever known, and has remained throughout my life the measure of what a human being can be.

6   Momma had a strange relationship with her. Most often when she passed on the road in front of the Store, she spoke to Momma in that soft yet carrying voice, "Good day, Mrs. Henderson." Momma responded with "How you, Sister Flowers?"

7   Mrs. Flowers didn't belong to our church, nor was she Momma's familiar. Why on earth did she insist on calling her Sister Flowers? Shame made me want to hide my face. Mrs. Flowers deserved better than to be called Sister. Then, Momma left out the verb. Why not ask, "How *are* you, *Mrs.* Flowers?" With the unbalanced passion of the young, I hated her for showing her ignorance to Mrs. Flowers. It didn't occur to me for many years that they were as alike as sisters, separated only by formal education.

8   Although I was upset, neither of the women was in the least shaken by what I thought an unceremonious greeting. Mrs. Flowers would continue her easy gait up the hill to her little bungalow, and Momma kept on shelling peas or doing whatever had brought her to the front porch.

9   Occasionally, though, Mrs. Flowers would drift off the road and down to the Store and Momma would say to me, "Sister, you go on and play." As she left I would hear the beginning of an intimate conversation. Momma persistently using the wrong verb, or none at all.

10   "Brother and Sister Wilcox is sho'ly the meanest—" "Is," Momma? "Is"? Oh, please, not "is," Momma, for two or more. But they talked, and from the side of the building where I waited for the ground to open up and swallow me, I heard the soft-voiced Mrs. Flowers and the textured voice of my grandmother merging and melting. They were interrupted from time to time by giggles that must have come from Mrs. Flowers (Momma never giggled in her life). Then she was gone.

11   She appealed to me because she was like people I had never met personally. Like women in English novels who walked the moors (whatever they were) with their loyal dogs racing at a respectful distance. Like the women who sat in front of roaring fireplaces, drinking tea incessantly from silver trays full of scones and crumpets. Women who walked over the "heath" and read morocco-bound books and had two last names divided by a hyphen. It would be safe to say that she made me proud to be Negro, just by being herself.

12   She acted just as refined as whitefolks in the movies and books and she was more beautiful, for none of them could have come near that warm color without looking gray by comparison.

13   I was fortunate that I never saw her in the company of po-whitefolks. For since they tend to think of their whiteness as an evenizer, I'm certain that I would have had to hear her spoken to commonly as Bertha, and my image of her would have been shattered like the unmendable Humpty-Dumpty.

14   One summer afternoon, sweet-milk fresh in my memory, she stopped at the Store to buy provisions. Another Negro woman of her health and age would have been expected to carry the paper sacks home in one hand, but Momma said, "Sister Flowers, I'll send Bailey* up to your house with these things."

15   She smiled that slow dragging smile, "Thank you, Mrs. Henderson. I'd prefer Marguerite, though." My name was beautiful when she said it. "I've been meaning to talk to her, anyway." They gave each other age-group looks.

16   Momma said, "Well, that's all right then. Sister, go and change your dress. You going to Sister Flowers's."

17   The chifforobe was a maze. What on earth did one put on to go to Mrs. Flowers's house? I knew I shouldn't put on a Sunday dress. It might be sacrilegious. Certainly not a house dress, since I was already wearing a fresh one. I chose a school dress, naturally. It was formal without suggesting that going to Mrs. Flowers's house was equivalent to attending church.

18   I trusted myself back into the Store.

19   "Now, don't you look nice." I had chosen the right thing, for once. . . .

20   There was a little path beside the rocky road, and Mrs. Flowers walked in front swinging her arms and picking her way over the stones.

21   She said, without turning her head, to me, "I hear you're doing very good school work, Marguerite, but that it's all written. The teachers report that they have trouble getting you to talk in class." We passed the triangular farm on our left and the path widened to allow us to walk together. I hung back in the separate unasked and unanswerable questions.

22   "Come and walk along with me, Marguerite." I couldn't have refused even if I wanted to. She pronounced my name so nicely. Or more correctly, she spoke each word with such clarity that I was certain a foreigner who didn't understand English could have understood her.

23   "Now no one is going to make you talk—possibly no one can. But bear in mind, language is man's way of communicating with his fellow man and it is language alone which separates him from the lower animals." That was a totally new idea to me, and I would need time to think about it.

24   "Your grandmother says you read a lot. Every chance you get. That's good, but not good enough. Words mean more than what is set down on paper. It takes the human voice to infuse them with the shades of deeper meaning."

25   I memorized the part about the human voice infusing words. It seemed so valid and poetic.

---

* Angelou's brother.

26   She said she was going to give me some books and that I not only must read them, I must read them aloud. She suggested that I try to make a sentence sound in as many different ways as possible.

27   "I'll accept no excuse if you return a book to me that has been badly handled." My imagination boggled at the punishment I would deserve if in fact I did abuse a book of Mrs. Flowers's. Death would be too kind and brief.

28   The odors in the house surprised me. Somehow I had never connected Mrs. Flowers with food or eating or any other common experience of common people. There must have been an outhouse, too, but my mind never recorded it.

29   The sweet scent of vanilla had met us as she opened the door.

30   "I made tea cookies this morning. You see, I had planned to invite you for cookies and lemonade so we could have this little chat. The lemonade is in the icebox."

31   It followed that Mrs. Flowers would have ice on an ordinary day, when most families in our town bought ice late on Saturdays only a few times during the summer to be used in the wooden ice-cream freezers.

32   She took the bags from me and disappeared through the kitchen door. I looked around the room that I had never in my wildest fantasies imagined I would see. Browned photographs leered or threatened from the walls and the white, freshly done curtains pushed against themselves and against the wind. I wanted to gobble up the room entire and take it to Bailey, who would help me analyze and enjoy it.

33   "Have a seat, Marguerite. Over there by the table." She carried a platter covered with a tea towel. Although she warned that she hadn't tried her hand at baking sweets for some time, I was certain that like everything else about her the cookies would be perfect.

34   They were flat round wafers, slightly browned on the edges and butter-yellow in the center. With the cold lemonade they were sufficient for childhood's lifelong diet. Remembering my manners, I took nice little lady-like bites off the edges. She said she had made them expressly for me and that she had a few in the kitchen that I could take home to my brother. So I jammed one whole cake in my mouth and the rough crumbs scratched the insides of my jaws, and if I hadn't had to swallow, it would have been a dream come true.

35   As I ate she began the first of what we later called "my lessons in living." She said that I must always be intolerant of ignorance but understanding of illiteracy. That some people, unable to go to school, were more educated and even more intelligent than college professors. She encouraged me to listen carefully to what country people called mother wit. That in those homely sayings was couched the collective wisdom of generations.

36   When I finished the cookies she brushed off the table and brought a thick, small book from the bookcase. I had read *A Tale of Two Cities* and found it up to my standards as a romantic novel. She opened the first page and I heard poetry for the first time in my life.

37   "It was the best of times and the worst of times . . ." Her voice slid in and curved down through and over the words. She was nearly singing. I wanted to

look at the pages. Were they the same that I had read? Or were there notes, music, lined on the pages, as in a hymn book? Her sounds began cascading gently. I knew from listening to a thousand preachers that she was nearing the end of her reading, and I hadn't really heard, heard to understand, a single word.

38   "How do you like that?"

39   It occurred to me that she expected a response. The sweet vanilla flavor was still on my tongue and her reading was a wonder in my ears. I had to speak.

40   I said, "Yes, ma'am." It was the least I could do, but it was the most also.

41   "There's one more thing. Take this book of poems and memorize one for me. Next time you pay me a visit, I want you to recite."

42   I have tried often to search behind the sophistication of years for the enchantment I so easily found in those gifts. The essence escapes but its aura remains. To be allowed, no, invited, into the private lives of strangers, and to share their joys and fears, was a chance to exchange the Southern bitter wormwood for a cup of mead with Beowulf or a hot cup of tea and milk with Oliver Twist. When I said aloud, "It is a far, far better thing that I do, than I have ever done . . ." tears of love filled my eyes at my selflessness.

43   On that first day, I ran down the hill and into the road (few cars ever came along it) and had the good sense to stop running before I reached the Store.

44   I was liked, and what a difference it made. I was respected not as Mrs. Henderson's grandchild or Bailey's sister but for just being Marguerite Johnson.

45   Childhood's logic never asks to be proved (all conclusions are absolute). I didn't question why Mrs. Flowers had singled me out for attention, nor did it occur to me that Momma might have asked her to give me a little talking to. All I cared about was that she had made tea cookies for *me* and read to *me* from her favorite book. It was enough to prove that she liked me.

TOPICS FOR WRITING AND DISCUSSION

1. What is Angelou's main purpose in this narrative? What does she want to show about Sister Flowers' effect on her?

2. Does Angelou use enough specific details to make her narrative believable? Her descriptions vivid? Her characters realistic? Cite two or three examples of descriptive language you find particularly effective.

3. Why does Angelou use dialogue in paragraphs 37–41 instead of just describing the scene?

4. Why does Angelou include paragraphs 42–45 at the end of her essay? What conclusions does the adult Angelou draw?

5. Can you think of a similar situation in your life in which an older, respected person effected a positive change in your character? How might you construct a narrative essay to tell your story?

38 Who Saw Murder Didn't Call the Police

Martin Gansberg
(1920–1995)

Martin Gansberg began his career as a copy boy in 1942 at the *New York Times*. Over the next forty years, until his retirement from the *Times* in 1985, he held a variety of positions, including reporter, copy editor, and editorial assistant. He also wrote for such magazines as *Diplomat, Catholic Digest,* and *Facts*. The following essay, "38 Who Saw Murder Didn't Call the Police," is his coverage of the murder of Kitty Genovese in 1964. It is a widely acclaimed portrait of citizens who witnessed a crime but "didn't want to get involved."

1   F OR more than half an hour 38 respectable, law-abiding citizens in Queens watched a killer stalk and stab a woman in three separate attacks in Kew Gardens.

2   Twice the sound of their voices and the sudden glow of their bedroom lights interrupted him and frightened him off. Each time he returned, sought her out and stabbed her again. Not one person telephoned the police during the assault; one witness called after the woman was dead.

3   That was two weeks ago today. But Assistant Chief Inspector Frederick M. Lussen, in charge of the borough's detectives and a veteran of 25 years of homicide investigations, is still shocked.

4   He can give a matter-of-fact recitation of many murders. But the Kew Gardens slaying baffles him—not because it is a murder, but because the "good people" failed to call the police.

5   "As we have reconstructed the crime," he said, "the assailant had three chances to kill this woman during a 35-minute period. He returned twice to complete the job. If we had been called when he first attacked, the woman might not be dead now."

6   This is what the police say happened beginning at 3:20 A.M. in the staid, middle-class, tree-lined Austin Street area:

Martin Gansberg (NYT Pictures)

7 Twenty-eight-year-old Catherine Genovese, who was called Kitty by almost everyone in the neighborhood, was returning home after her job as manager of a bar in Hollis. She parked her red Fiat in a lot adjacent to the Kew Gardens Long Island Rail Road Station, facing Mowbray Place. Like many residents of the neighborhood, she had parked there day after day since her arrival from Connecticut a year ago, although the railroad frowns on the practice.

8 She turned off the lights of her car, locked the door and started to walk the 100 feet to the entrance of her apartment at 82–70 Austin Street, which is in a Tudor building, with stores on the first floor and apartments on the second.

9 The entrance to the apartment is in the rear of the building because the front is rented to retail stores. At night the quiet neighborhood is shrouded in the slumbering darkness that marks most residential areas.

10 Miss Genovese noticed a man at the far end of the lot, near a seven-story apartment house at 82–40 Austin Street. She halted. Then, nervously, she headed up Austin Street toward Lefferts Boulevard, where there is a call box to the 102nd Police Precinct in nearby Richmond Hill.

"He Stabbed Me"

11 She got as far as a street light in front of a bookstore before the man grabbed her. She screamed. Lights went on in the 10-story apartment house at 82–67 Austin Street, which faces the bookstore. Windows slid open and voices punctuated the early-morning stillness.

12 Miss Genovese screamed: "Oh, my God, he stabbed me! Please help me! Please help me!"

13 From one of the upper windows in the apartment house, a man called down: "Let that girl alone!"

14 The assailant looked up at him, shrugged and walked down Austin Street toward a white sedan parked a short distance away. Miss Genovese struggled to her feet.

15 Lights went out. The killer returned to Miss Genovese, now trying to make her way around the side of the building by the parking lot to get to her apartment. The assailant stabbed her again.

16 "I'm dying!" she shrieked. "I'm dying!"

A City Bus Passed

17 Windows were opened again, and lights went on in many apartments. The assailant got into his car and drove away. Miss Genovese staggered to her feet. A city bus, Q-10, the Lefferts Boulevard line to Kennedy International Airport, passed. It was 3:35 A.M.

18 The assailant returned. By then, Miss Genovese had crawled to the back of the building, where the freshly painted brown doors to the apartment house held out hope of safety. The killer tried the first door; she wasn't there. At the

second door, 82–62 Austin Street, he saw her slumped on the floor at the foot of the stairs. He stabbed her a third time—fatally.

19   It was 3:50 by the time the police received their first call, from a man who was a neighbor of Miss Genovese. In two minutes they were at the scene. The neighbor, a 70-year-old woman and another woman were the only persons on the street. Nobody else came forward.

20   The man explained that he had called the police after much deliberation. He had phoned a friend in Nassau County for advice and then he had crossed the roof of the building to the apartment of the elderly woman to get her to make the call.

21   "I didn't want to get involved," he sheepishly told the police.

Suspect Is Arrested

22 Six days later, the police arrested Winston Moseley, a 29-year-old business-machine operator, and charged him with homicide. Moseley had no previous record. He is married, has two children and owns a home at 133–19 Sutter Avenue, South Ozone Park, Queens. On Wednesday, a court committed him to Kings County Hospital for psychiatric observation.

23   When questioned by the police, Moseley also said that he had slain Mrs. Annie May Johnson, 24, of 146–12 133rd Avenue, Jamaica, on Feb. 29 and Barbara Kralik, 15, of 174–17 140th Avenue, Springfield Gardens, last July. In the Kralik case, the police are holding Alvin L. Mitchell, who is said to have confessed that slaying.

24   The police stressed how simple it would have been to have gotten in touch with them. "A phone call," said one of the detectives, "would have done it." The police may be reached by dialing "O" for operator or SPring 7-3100. . . .

25   Today witnesses from the neighborhood, which is made up of one-family homes in the $35,000 to $60,000 range with the exception of the two apartment houses near the railroad station, find it difficult to explain why they didn't call the police. . . .

26   A housewife, knowingly if quite casually, said, "We thought it was a lover's quarrel." A husband and wife both said, "Frankly, we were afraid." They seemed aware of the fact that events might have been different. A distraught woman, wiping her hands in her apron, said, "I didn't want my husband to get involved."

27   One couple, now willing to talk about that night, said they heard the first screams. The husband looked thoughtfully at the bookstore where the killer first grabbed Miss Genovese.

28   "We went to the window to see what was happening," he said, "but the light from our bedroom made it difficult to see the street." The wife, still apprehensive, added: "I put out the light and we were able to see better."

29   Asked why they hadn't called the police, she shrugged and replied: "I don't know."

30   A man peeked out from a slight opening in the doorway to his apartment and rattled off an account of the killer's second attack. Why hadn't he called

the police at the time? "I was tired," he said without emotion. "I went back to bed."

31   It was 4:25 A.M. when the ambulance arrived to take the body of Miss Genovese. It drove off. "Then," a solemn police detective said, "the people came out."

TOPICS FOR WRITING AND DISCUSSION

1. How does Gansberg realistically recreate the murder scene? Cite some examples of details that help readers see the people and events of this narrative.

2. Does Gansberg remain consistently objective in his reporting? What was Gansberg's purpose in telling this story the way he did?

3. Evaluate the first and last paragraphs of this narrative. What effect is Gansberg trying to achieve? Is he successful? What does his use of dialogue add to this story?

4. This selection originally appeared in a newspaper. In what ways does this news story differ from an essay? Do you think this story would have been as powerful had it been written as an editorial?

5. Have you ever been a victim of or a witness to a crime? Write a narrative that describes the crime and your reaction to it. If you were the victim, did others come to your aid? If you were a bystander, did you become involved? Do you, in retrospect, believe you made the right decision? Consider directing your essay to others who may someday find themselves in your position.

Alice Walker (Jeff Reinking/Picture Group)

BEAUTY: WHEN THE OTHER DANCER IS THE SELF

Alice Walker
(1944–   )

Alice Walker was the youngest of the eight children born to Willie Lee and Minnie Grant Walker. The Walkers worked as sharecroppers in Georgia, and the author's early years inform both her fiction and nonfiction. Following her graduation from Sarah Lawrence College in New York, Walker worked for civil rights, teaching in Head Start programs and registering black voters. A poet, essayist, and scholar, she has achieved recognition for her work as editor of an anthology of Zora Neale Hurston's writings (*I Love Myself When I Am Laughing*, 1979) and as a contributing editor to *Ms.* magazine. She is best known for her fiction, particularly her novel *The Color Purple*, which won the Pulitzer Prize in 1982 and was later made into a popular film. Walker's novel, *The Temple of My Familiar*, was published in 1989, and in 1991 she published a collection of poetry, *Her Blue Body Everything We Know: Earthling Poems, 1965–1990. Possessing the Secret of Joy*, a novel, was published in 1992. Walker has also published several collections of articles, journal entries, essays, and poems: *In Search of Our Mothers' Gardens* (1983), from which this selection is taken; *The Same River Twice* (1996); and *Anything We Love Can Be Saved* (1997).

1   IT is a bright summer day in 1947. My father, a fat, funny man with beautiful eyes and a subversive wit, is trying to decide which of his eight children he will take with him to the county fair. My mother, of course, will not go. She is

knocked out from getting most of us ready: I hold my neck stiff against the pressure of her knuckles as she hastily completes the braiding and then beribboning of my hair.

2   My father is the driver for the rich old white lady up the road. Her name is Miss Mey. She owns all the land for miles around, as well as the house in which we live. All I remember about her is that she once offered to pay my mother thirty-five cents for cleaning her house, raking up piles of her magnolia leaves, and washing her family's clothes, and that my mother—she of no money, eight children, and a chronic earache—refused it. But I do not think of this in 1947. I am two and a half years old. I want to go everywhere my daddy goes. I am excited at the prospect of riding in a car. Someone has told me fairs are fun. That there is room in the car for only three of us doesn't faze me at all. Whirling happily in my starchy frock, showing off my biscuit-polished patent-leather shoes and lavender socks, tossing my head in a way that makes my ribbons bounce, I stand, hands on hips, before my father. "Take me, Daddy," I say with assurance: "I'm the prettiest!"

3   Later, it does not surprise me to find myself in Miss Mey's shiny black car, sharing the back seat with the other lucky ones. Does not surprise me that I thoroughly enjoy the fair. At home that night I tell the unlucky ones all I can remember about the merry-go-round, the man who eats live chickens, and the teddy bears, until they say: that's enough, baby Alice. Shut up now, and go to sleep.

4   It is Easter Sunday, 1950. I am dressed in a green, flocked, scalloped-hem dress (handmade by my adoring sister, Ruth) that has its own smooth satin petticoat and tiny hot-pink roses tucked into each scallop. My shoes, new T-strap patent leather, again highly biscuit-polished. I am six years old and have learned one of the longest Easter speeches to be heard that day, totally unlike the speech I said when I was two: "Easter lilies / pure and white / blossom in / the morning light." When I rise to give my speech I do so on a great wave of love and pride and expectation. People in the church stop rustling their new crinolines. They seem to hold their breath. I can tell they admire my dress, but it is my spirit, bordering on sassiness (womanishness), they secretly applaud.

5   "That girl's a little *mess*," they whisper to each other, pleased.

6   Naturally I say my speech without stammer or pause, unlike those who stutter, stammer, or, worst of all, forget. This is before the word "beautiful" exists in people's vocabulary, but "Oh, isn't she the *cutest* thing!" frequently floats my way. "And got so much sense!" they gratefully add . . . for which thoughtful addition I thank them to this day.

7   *It was great fun being cute. But then, one day, it ended.*

8   I am eight years old and a tomboy. I have a cowboy hat, cowboy boots, checkered shirt and pants, all red. My playmates are my brothers, two and four years older than I. Their colors are black and green, the only difference in the way we are dressed. On Saturday nights we all go to the picture show, even my

mother; Westerns are her favorite kind of movie. Back home, "on the ranch," we pretend we are Tom Mix, Hopalong Cassidy, Lash LaRue (we've even named one of our dogs Lash LaRue); we chase each other for hours rustling cattle, being outlaws, delivering damsels from distress. Then my parents decide to buy my brothers guns. These are not "real" guns. They shoot "BBs," copper pellets my brothers say will kill birds. Because I am a girl, I do not get a gun. Instantly I am relegated to the position of Indian. Now there appears a great distance between us. They shoot and shoot at everything with their new guns. I try to keep up with my bow and arrows.

9   One day while I am standing on top of our makeshift "garage"—pieces of tin nailed across some poles—holding my bow and arrow and looking out toward the fields, I feel an incredible blow in my right eye. I look down just in time to see my brother lower his gun.

10   Both brothers rush to my side. My eye stings, and I cover it with my hand. "If you tell," they say, "we will get a whipping. You don't want that to happen, do you?" I do not. "Here is a piece of wire," says the older brother, picking it up from the roof; "say you stepped on one end of it and the other flew up and hit you." The pain is beginning to start. "Yes," I say. "Yes, I will say that is what happened." If I do not say this is what happened, I know my brothers will find ways to make me wish I had. But now I will say anything that gets me to my mother.

11   Confronted by our parents we stick to the lie agreed upon. They place me on a bench on the porch and I close my left eye while they examine the right. There is a tree growing from underneath the porch that climbs past the railing to the roof. It is the last thing my right eye sees. I watch as its trunk, its branches, and then its leaves are blotted out by the rising blood.

12   I am in shock. First there is intense fever, which my father tries to break using lily leaves bound around my head. Then there are chills: my mother tries to get me to eat soup. Eventually, I do not know how, my parents learn what has happened. A week after the "accident" they take me to see a doctor. "Why did you wait so long to come?" he asks, looking into my eye and shaking his head. "Eyes are sympathetic," he says. "If one is blind, the other will likely become blind too."

13   This comment of the doctor's terrifies me. But it is really how I look that bothers me most. Where the BB pellet struck there is a glob of whitish scar tissue, a hideous cataract, on my eye. Now when I stare at people—a favorite pastime, up to now—they will stare back. Not at the "cute" little girl, but at her scar. For six years I do not stare at anyone, because I do not raise my head.

14   Years later, in the throes of a mid-life crisis, I ask my mother and sister whether I changed after the "accident." "No," they say, puzzled. "What do you mean?"

15   *What do I mean?*

16   I am eight, and, for the first time, doing poorly in school, where I have been something of a whiz since I was four. We have just moved to the place where the "accident" occurred. We do not know any of the people around us

because this is a different county. The only time I see the friends I knew is when we go back to our old church. The new school is the former state penitentiary. It is a large stone building, cold and drafty, crammed to overflowing with boisterous, ill-disciplined children. On the third floor there is a huge circular imprint of some partition that has been torn out.

17 "What used to be here?" I ask a sullen girl next to me on our way past it to lunch.

18 "The electric chair," says she.

19 At night I have nightmares about the electric chair, and about all the people reputedly "fried" in it. I am afraid of the school, where all the students seem to be budding criminals.

20 "What's the matter with your eye?" they ask, critically.

21 When I don't answer (I cannot decide whether it was an "accident" or not), they shove me, insist on a fight.

22 My brother, the one who created the story about the wire, comes to my rescue. But then brags so much about "protecting" me, I become sick.

23 After months of torture at the school, my parents decide to send me back to our old community, to my old school. I live with my grandparents and the teacher they board. But there is no room for Phoebe, my cat. By the time my grandparents decide there *is* room, and I ask for my cat, she cannot be found. Miss Yarborough, the boarding teacher, takes me under her wing, and begins to teach me to play the piano. But soon she marries an African—a "prince," she says—and is whisked away to his continent.

24 At my old school there is at least one teacher who loves me. She is the teacher who "knew me before I was born" and bought my first baby clothes. It is she who makes life bearable. It is her presence that finally helps me turn on the one child at the school who continually calls me "one-eyed bitch." One day I simply grab him by his coat and beat him until I am satisfied. It is my teacher who tells me my mother is ill.

25 My mother is lying in bed in the middle of the day, something I have never seen. She is in too much pain to speak. She has an abscess in her ear. I stand looking down on her, knowing that if she dies, I cannot live. She is being treated with warm oils and hot bricks held against her cheek. Finally a doctor comes. But I must go back to my grandparents' house. The weeks pass but I am hardly aware of it. All I know is that my mother might die, my father is not so jolly, my brothers still have their guns, and I am the one sent away from home.

26 "You did not change," they say.

27 *Did I imagine the anguish of never looking up?*

28 I am twelve. When relatives come to visit I hide in my room. My cousin Brenda, just my age, whose father works in the post office and whose mother is a nurse, comes to find me. "Hello," she says. And then she asks, looking at my recent school picture, which I did not want taken, and on which the "glob," as I think of it, is clearly visible. "You still can't see out of that eye?"

29 "No," I say, and flop back on the bed over my book.

30   That night, as I do almost every night, I abuse my eye. I rant and rave at it, in front of the mirror. I plead with it to clear up before morning. I tell it I hate and despise it. I do not pray for sight. I pray for beauty.

31   "You did not change," they say.

32   I am fourteen and baby-sitting for my brother Bill, who lives in Boston. He is my favorite brother and there is a strong bond between us. Understanding my feelings of shame and ugliness he and his wife take me to a local hospital, where the "glob" is removed by a doctor named O. Henry. There is still a small bluish crater where the scar tissue was, but the ugly white stuff is gone. Almost immediately I become a different person from the girl who does not raise her head. Or so I think. Now that I've raised my head I win the boyfriend of my dreams. Now that I've raised my head I have plenty of friends. Now that I've raised my head classwork comes from my lips as faultlessly as Easter speeches did, and I leave high school as valedictorian, most popular student, and *queen,* hardly believing my luck. Ironically, the girl who was voted most beautiful in our class (and was) was later shot twice through the chest by a male companion, using a "real" gun, while she was pregnant. But that's another story in itself. Or is it?

33   "You did not change," they say.

34   It is now thirty years since the "accident." A beautiful journalist comes to visit and to interview me. She is going to write a cover story for her magazine that focuses on my latest book. "Decide how you want to look on the cover," she says. "Glamorous, or whatever."

35   Never mind "glamorous," it is the "whatever" that I hear. Suddenly all I can think of is whether I will get enough sleep the night before the photography session: if I don't, my eye will be tired and wander, as blind eyes will.

36   At night in bed with my lover I think up reasons why I should not appear on the cover of a magazine. "My meanest critics will say I've sold out," I say. "My family will now realize I write scandalous books."

37   "But what's the real reason you don't want to do this?" he asks.

38   "Because in all probability," I say in a rush, "my eye won't be straight."

39   "It will be straight enough," he says. Then, "Besides, I thought you'd made your peace with that."

40   And I suddenly remember that I have.

41   *I remember:*

42   I am talking to my brother Jimmy, asking if he remembers anything unusual about the day I was shot. He does not know I consider that day the last time my father, with his sweet home remedy of cool lily leaves, chose me, and that I suffered and raged inside because of this. "Well," he says, "all I remember is standing by the side of the highway with Daddy, trying to flag down a car. A white man stopped, but when Daddy said he needed somebody to take his little girl to the doctor, he drove off."

43   *I remember:*

44   I am in the desert for the first time. I fall totally in love with it. I am so overwhelmed by its beauty, I confront for the first time, consciously, the meaning of the doctor's words years ago: "Eyes are sympathetic. If one is blind, the other

will likely become blind too." I realize I have dashed about the world madly, looking at that, storing up images against the fading of the light. *But I might have missed seeing the desert!* The shock of that possibility—and gratitude for over twenty-five years of sight—sends me literally to my knees. Poem after poem comes—which is perhaps how poets pray.

On Sight

I am so thankful I have seen
The Desert
And the creatures in the desert
And the desert Itself.

The desert has its own moon
Which I have seen
With my own eye.

There is no flag on it.

Trees of the desert have arms
All of which are always up
That is because the moon is up
The sun is up
Also the sky
The stars
Clouds
None with flags.

If there *were* flags, I doubt
the trees would point.
Would you?

45   *But mostly, I remember this:*

46   I am twenty-seven, and my baby daughter is almost three. Since her birth, I have worried about her discovery that her mother's eyes are different from other people's. Will she be embarrassed? I think. What will she say? Every day she watches a television program called "Big Blue Marble." It begins with a picture of the earth as it appears from the moon. It is bluish, a little battered-looking, but full of light, with whitish clouds swirling around it. Every time I see it I weep with love, as if it is a picture of Grandma's house. One day when I am putting Rebecca down for her nap, she suddenly focuses on my eye. Something inside me cringes, gets ready to try to protect myself. All children are cruel about physical differences, I know from experience, and that they don't always mean to be is another matter. I assume Rebecca will be the same.

47   But no-o-o-o. She studies my face intently as we stand, her inside and me outside her crib. She even holds my face maternally between her dimpled little hands. Then, looking every bit as serious and lawyerlike as her father, she

says, as if it may just possibly have slipped my attention: "Mommy, there's a *world* in your eye." (As in, "Don't be alarmed, or do anything crazy.") And then, gently, but with great interest: "Mommy, where did you *get* that world in your eye?"

48   For the most part, the pain left then. (So what, if my brothers grew up to buy even more powerful pellet guns for their sons and to carry real guns themselves. So what, if a young "Morehouse man" once nearly fell off the steps of Trevos Arnett Library because he thought my eyes were blue.) Crying and laughing I ran to the bathroom, while Rebecca mumbled and sang herself off to sleep. Yes indeed, I realized, looking into the mirror. There *was* a world in my eye. And I saw that it was possible to love it: that in fact, for all it had taught me of shame and anger and inner vision, I *did* love it. Even to see it drifting out of orbit in boredom, or rolling up out of fatigue, not to mention floating back at attention in excitement (bearing witness, a friend has called it), deeply suitable to my personality, and even characteristic of me.

49   That night I dream I am dancing to Stevie Wonder's song "Always" (the name of the song is really "As," but I hear it as "Always"). As I dance, whirling and joyous, happier than I've ever been in my life, another bright-faced dancer joins me. We dance and kiss each other and hold each other through the night. The other dancer has obviously come through all right, as I have done. She is beautiful, whole and free. And she is also me.

Topics for Writing and Discussion

1. In this essay, Walker uses a series of short narratives to describe the path she took as she moved toward realizing her own worth. List the narratives, noting particularly the people who are central to each story. How does each person cause Walker to question or to affirm herself?

2. Near the end of the essay, Walker's daughter Rebecca says, "Mommy, there's a *world* in your eye." What does she mean? What meanings does Walker derive from her daughter's comment? How does this episode suggest the thesis of the essay?

3. A common structure for a narrative essay is straight chronological order, but Walker tells her story with many sudden jumps backward and forward in time. Identify these flashbacks and leaps ahead and explain how they affect the essay's meaning. Notice especially how this complicated time structure relates to the concluding paragraphs in which Walker introduces a final series of memories with the repeated phrase, "I remember."

4. Read the last paragraphs carefully and discuss how they help to explain the relationship of the title to Walker's thesis.

5. Write a narrative essay focusing on a frightening event in your childhood. You may want to experiment with Walker's technique of moving back and forth from far past, to present, to more recent past, and back to present. Be sure to provide clear transitions, as Walker does, to show how the parts of your essay are related.

Maxine Hong Kingston (© Nancy Crampton)

CHINESE-AMERICAN SILENCE
(FROM *THE WOMAN WARRIOR*)

Maxine Hong Kingston
(1940–   )

Born in Stockton, California, to recently immigrated
Chinese parents, Maxine Hong Kingston had to negoti-
ate between two vastly different worlds. *The Woman
Warrior: Memoirs of a Girlhood Among Ghosts* (1976)
is a partly autobiographical collection of essays that
focuses on her attempt to understand her female Chinese ancestors and their role in creating her own identity. It won the National Book Critics Award for
nonfiction. *China Man* (1980), which won the American Book Award and was nominated for the Pulitzer
Prize, is a continuation of that endeavor to examine
heritage and its role in shaping the character of succeeding generations. A resident of Hawaii since 1967,
Kingston received the honor of being named a Living
Treasure of Hawaii (1980). Recent work includes
Tripmaster Monkey: His Fake Book (1989) and
Hawa 'I One Summer (1998). "Chinese-American
Silence," from *The Woman Warrior,* examines the diffi-
culties of balancing one's identity as a person influ-
enced by two very different cultures.

1   LONG ago in China, knot-makers tied string into buttons and frogs, and
rope into bell pulls. There was one knot so complicated that it blinded the
knot-maker. Finally an emperor outlawed this cruel knot, and the nobles could
not order it anymore. If I had lived in China, I would have been an outlaw
knot-maker.

2   Maybe that's why my mother cut my tongue. She pushed my tongue up
and sliced the frenum. Or maybe she snipped it with a pair of nail scissors. I
don't remember her doing it, only her telling me about it, but all during

childhood I felt sorry for the baby whose mother waited with scissors or knife in hand for it to cry—and then, when its mouth was wide open like a baby bird's, cut. The Chinese say "a ready tongue is an evil."

3   I used to curl my tongue in front of the mirror and tauten my frenum into a white line, itself as thin as a razor blade. I saw no scars in my mouth. I thought perhaps I had had two frena, and she had cut one. I made other children open their mouths so I could compare theirs to mine. I saw perfect pink membranes stretching into precise edges that looked easy enough to cut. Sometimes I felt very proud that my mother committed such a powerful act upon me. At other times I was terrified—the first thing my mother did when she saw me was to cut my tongue.

4   "Why did you do that to me, Mother?"

5   "I told you."

6   "Tell me again."

7   "I cut it so that you would not be tongue-tied. Your tongue would be able to move in any language. You'll be able to speak languages that are completely different from one another. You'll be able to pronounce anything. Your frenum looked too tight to do those things, so I cut it."

8   "But isn't 'a ready tongue an evil'?"

9   "Things are different in this ghost country."

10   "Did it hurt me? Did I cry and bleed?"

11   "I don't remember. Probably."

12   She didn't cut the other children's. When I asked cousins and other Chinese children whether their mothers had cut their tongues loose, they said, "What?"

13   "Why didn't you cut my brothers' and sisters' tongues?"

14   "They didn't need it."

15   "Why not? Were theirs longer than mine?"

16   "Why don't you quit blabbering and get to work?"

17   If my mother was not lying she should have cut more, scraped away the rest of the frenum skin, because I have a terrible time talking. Or she should not have cut at all, tampering with my speech. When I went to kindergarten and had to speak English for the first time, I became silent. A dumbness—a shame—still cracks my voice in two, even when I want to say "hello" casually, or ask an easy question in front of the check-out counter, or ask directions of a bus driver. I stand frozen, or I hold up the line with the complete, grammatical sentence that comes squeaking out at impossible length. "What did you say?" says the cab driver, or "Speak up," so I have to perform again, only weaker the second time. A telephone call makes my throat bleed and takes up that day's courage. It spoils my day with self-disgust when I hear my broken voice come skittering out into the open. It makes people wince to hear it. I'm getting better, though. Recently I asked the postman for special-issue stamps; I've waited since childhood for postmen to give me some of their own accord. I am making progress, a little every day.

18   My silence was thickest—total—during the three years that I covered my school paintings with black paint. I painted layers of black over houses and

flowers and suns, and when I drew on the blackboard, I put a layer of chalk on top. I was making a stage curtain, and it was the moment before the curtain parted or rose. The teachers called my parents to school, and I saw they had been saving my pictures, curling and cracking, all alike and black. The teachers pointed to the pictures and looked serious, talked seriously too, but my parents did not understand English. ("The parents and teachers of criminals were executed," said my father.) My parents took the pictures home. I spread them out (so black and full of possibilities) and pretended the curtains were swinging open, flying up, one after another, sunlight underneath, mighty operas.

19   During the first silent year I spoke to no one at school, did not ask before going to the lavatory, and flunked kindergarten. My sister also said nothing for three years, silent in the playground and silent at lunch. There were other quiet Chinese girls not of our family, but most of them got over it sooner than we did. I enjoyed the silence. At first it did not occur to me I was supposed to talk or to pass kindergarten. I talked at home and to one or two of the Chinese kids in class. I made motions and even made some jokes. I drank out of a toy saucer when the water spilled out of the cup, and everybody laughed, pointing at me, so I did it some more. I didn't know that Americans don't drink out of saucers.

20   I liked the Negro students (Black Ghosts)* best because they laughed the loudest and talked to me as if I were a daring talker too. One of the Negro girls had her mother coil braids over her ears Shanghai-style like mine; we were Shanghai twins except that she was covered with black like my paintings. Two Negro kids enrolled in Chinese school, and the teachers gave them Chinese names. Some Negro kids walked me to school and home, protecting me from the Japanese kids, who hit me and chased me and stuck gum in my ears. The Japanese kids were noisy and tough. They appeared one day in kindergarten, released from concentration camp, which was a tic-tac-toe mark, like barbed wire, on the map.

21   It was when I found out I had to talk that school became a misery, that the silence became a misery. I did not speak and felt bad each time that I did not speak. I read aloud in first grade, though, and heard the barest whisper with little squeaks come out of my throat. "Louder," said the teacher, who scared the voice away again. The other Chinese girls did not talk either, so I knew the silence had to do with being a Chinese girl.

22   Reading out loud was easier than speaking because we did not have to make up what to say, but I stopped often, and the teacher would think I'd gone quiet again. I could not understand "I." The Chinese "I" has seven strokes, intricacies. How could the American "I," assuredly wearing a hat like the Chinese, have only three strokes, the middle so straight? Was it out of politeness that this writer left off strokes the way a Chinese has to write her own name small and crooked? No, it was not politeness; "I" is a capital and "you" is lower-case. I stared at that middle line and waited so long for its black center

---

* Kingston's family referred to non-Chinese people as "ghosts."

to resolve into tight strokes and dots that I forgot to pronounce it. The other troublesome word was "here," no strong consonant to hang on to, and so flat, when "here" is two mountainous ideographs. The teacher, who had already told me every day how to read "I" and "here," put me in the low corner under the stairs again, where the noisy boys usually sat.

23   When my second grade class did a play, the whole class went to the auditorium except the Chinese girls. The teacher, lovely and Hawaiian, should have understood about us, but instead left us behind in the classroom. Our voices were too soft or nonexistent, and our parents never signed the permission slips anyway. They never signed anything unnecessary. We opened the door a crack and peeked out, but closed it again quickly. One of us (not me) won every spelling bee, though.

24   I remember telling the Hawaiian teacher, "We Chinese can't sing 'land where our fathers died.'" She argued with me about politics, while I meant because of curses. But how can I have that memory when I couldn't talk? My mother says that we, like the ghosts, have no memories.

25   After American school, we picked up our cigar boxes, in which we had arranged books, brushes, and an inkbox neatly, and went to Chinese school, from 5:00 to 7:30 P.M. There we chanted together, voices rising and falling, loud and soft, some boys shouting, everybody reading together, reciting together and not alone with one voice. When we had a memorization test, the teacher let each of us come to his desk and say the lesson to him privately, while the rest of the class practiced copying or tracing. Most of the teachers were men. The boys who were so well behaved in the American school played tricks on them and talked back to them. The girls were not mute. They screamed and yelled during recess, when there were no rules; they had fist-fights. Nobody was afraid of children hurting themselves or of children hurting school property. The glass doors to the red and green balconies with the gold joy symbols were left wide open so that we could run out and climb the fire escapes. We played capture-the-flag in the auditorium, where Sun Yat-sen and Chiang Kai-shek's pictures hung at the back of the stage, the Chinese flag on their left and the American flag on their right. We climbed the teak ceremonial chairs and made flying leaps off the stage. One flag headquarters was behind the glass door and the other on stage right. Our feet drummed on the hollow stage. During recess the teachers locked themselves up in their office with the shelves of books, copybooks, inks from China. They drank tea and warmed their hands at a stove. There was no play supervision. At recess we had the school to ourselves, and also we could roam as far as we could go— downtown, Chinatown stores, home—as long as we returned before the bell rang.

26   At exactly 7:30 the teacher again picked up the brass bell that sat on his desk and swung it over our heads, while we charged down the stairs, our cheering magnified in the stairwell. Nobody had to line up.

27   Not all of the children who were silent at American school found voice at Chinese school. One new teacher said each of us had to get up and recite in front of the class, who was to listen. My sister and I had memorized the lesson

perfectly. We said it to each other at home, one chanting, one listening. The teacher called on my sister to recite first. It was the first time a teacher had called on the second-born to go first. My sister was scared. She glanced at me and looked away; I looked down at my desk. I hoped that she could do it because if she could, then I would have to. She opened her mouth and a voice came out that wasn't a whisper, but it wasn't a proper voice either. I hoped that she would not cry, fear breaking up her voice like twigs underfoot. She sounded as if she were trying to sing though weeping and strangling. She did not pause or stop to end the embarrassment. She kept going until she said the last word, and then she sat down. When it was my turn, the same voice came out, a crippled animal running on broken legs. You could hear splinters in my voice, bones rubbing jagged against one another. I was loud, though. I was glad I didn't whisper. There was one little girl who whispered.

28   You can't entrust your voice to the Chinese, either; they want to capture your voice for their own use. They want to fix up your tongue to speak for them. "How much less can you sell it for?" we have to say. Talk the Sales Ghosts down. Make them take a loss.

29   We were working at the laundry when a delivery boy came from the Rexall drugstore around the corner. He had a pale blue box of pills, but nobody was sick. Reading the label we saw that it belonged to another Chinese family, Crazy Mary's family. "Not ours," said my father. He pointed out the name to the Delivery Ghost, who took the pills back. My mother muttered for an hour, and then her anger boiled over. "That ghost! That dead ghost! How dare he come to the wrong house?" She could not concentrate on her marking and pressing. "A mistake! Huh!" I was getting angry myself. She fumed. She made her press crash and hiss. "Revenge. We've got to avenge this wrong on our future, on our health, and on our lives. Nobody's going to sicken my children and get away with it." We brothers and sisters did not look at one another. She would do something awful, something embarrassing. She'd already been hinting that during the next eclipse we slam pot lids together to scare the frog from swallowing the moon. (The word for "eclipse" is *frog-swallowing-the-moon*.) When we had not banged lids at the last eclipse and the shadow kept receding anyway, she'd said, "The villagers must be banging and clanging very loudly back home in China."

30   ("On the other side of the world, they aren't having an eclipse, Mama. That's just a shadow the earth makes when it comes between the moon and the sun."

31   "You're always believing what those Ghost Teachers tell you. Look at the size of the jaws!")

32   "Aha!" she yelled. "You! The biggest." She was pointing at me. "You go to the drugstore."

33   "What do you want me to buy, Mother?" I said.

34   "Buy nothing. Don't bring one cent. Go and make them stop the curse."

35   "I don't want to go. I don't know how to do that. There are no such things as curses. They'll think I'm crazy."

36   "If you don't go, I'm holding you responsible for bringing a plague on this family."

37   "What am I supposed to do when I get there?" I said, sullen, trapped. "Do I say, 'Your delivery boy made a wrong delivery'?"

38   "They know he made a wrong delivery. I want you to make them rectify their crime."

39   I felt sick already. She'd make me swing stinky censers around the counter, at the druggist, at the customers. Throw dog blood on the druggist. I couldn't stand her plans.

40   "You get reparation candy," she said. "You say, 'You have tainted my house with sick medicine and must remove the curse with sweetness.' He'll understand."

41   "He didn't do it on purpose. And no, he won't, Mother. They don't understand stuff like that. I won't be able to say it right. He'll call us beggars."

42   "You just translate." She searched me to make sure I wasn't hiding any money. I was sneaky and bad enough to buy the candy and come back pretending it was a free gift.

43   "Mymotherseztagimmesomecandy," I said to the druggist. Be cute and small. No one hurts the cute and small.

44   "What? Speak up. Speak English," he said, big in his white druggist coat.

45   "Tatatagimme somecandy."

46   The druggist leaned way over the counter and frowned. "Some free candy," I said. "Sample candy."

47   "We don't give sample candy, young lady," he said.

48   "My mother said you have to give us candy. She said that is the way the Chinese do it."

49   "What?"

50   "That is the way the Chinese do it."

51   "Do what?"

52   "Do things." I felt the weight and immensity of things impossible to explain to the druggist.

53   "Can I give you some money?" he asked.

54   "No, we want candy."

55   He reached into a jar and gave me a handful of lollipops. He gave us candy all year round, year after year, every time we went into the drugstore. When different druggists or clerks waited on us, they also gave us candy. They had talked us over. They gave us Halloween candy in December, Christmas candy around Valentine's day, candy hearts at Easter, and Easter eggs at Halloween. "See?" said our mother. "They understand. You kids just aren't very brave." But I knew they did not understand. They thought we were beggars without a home who lived in back of the laundry. They felt sorry for us. I did not eat their candy. I did not go inside the drugstore or walk past it unless my parents forced me to. Whenever we had a prescription filled, the druggist put candy in the medicine bag. This is what Chinese druggists normally do, except they give raisins. My mother thought she taught the Druggist Ghosts a lesson in good manners (which is the same word as "traditions").

56   My mouth went permanently crooked with effort, turned down on the left side and straight on the right. How strange that the emigrant villagers are

shouters, hollering face to face. My father asks, "Why is it I can hear Chinese from blocks away? Is it that I understand the language? Or is it they talk loud?" They turn the radio up full blast to hear the operas, which do not seem to hurt their ears. And they yell over the singers and wail over the drums, everybody talking at once, big arm gestures, spit flying. You can see the disgust on American faces looking at women like that. It isn't just the loudness. It is the way Chinese sounds, chingchong ugly, to American ears, not beautiful like Japanese sayonara words with the consonants and vowels as regular as Italian. We make guttural peasant noise and have Ton Duc Thang names you can't remember. And the Chinese can't hear Americans at all; the language is too soft and western music unhearable. I've watched a Chinese audience laugh, visit, talk-story, and holler during a piano recital, as if the musician could not hear them. A Chinese-American, somebody's son, was playing Chopin, which has no punctuation, no cymbals, no gongs. Chinese piano music is five black keys. Normal Chinese women's voices are strong and bossy. We American-Chinese girls had to whisper to make ourselves American-feminine. Apparently we whispered even more softly than the Americans. Once a year the teachers referred my sister and me to speech therapy, but our voices would straighten out, unpredictably normal, for the therapists. Some of us gave up, shook our heads, and said nothing, not one word. Some of us could not even shake our heads. At times shaking my head no is more self-assertion than I can manage. Most of us eventually found some voice, however faltering. We invented an American-feminine speaking personality.

TOPICS FOR WRITING AND DISCUSSION

1. What is Kingston's main purpose in telling these stories about her childhood? Why does she have, as an adult, "a terrible time talking"?
2. How does the opening story about her mother's cutting of her tongue introduce the problem she describes in her essay?
3. What does the story of the druggist convey about Kingston's feelings about being a Chinese-American child?
4. What does Kingston's use of dialogue and run-together words add to the effectiveness of the story at the drugstore?
5. Although Kingston's silence is directly related to her situation of having to function within two disparate cultures, nearly everyone has experienced feelings of isolation or has been in an uncomfortable environment. Write about such an experience, using vivid details and dialogue to make your feelings clear to your reader.

Robert Frost reading at John F. Kennedy's inauguration. (UPI/Corbis-Bettmann)

"Out, Out—"

Robert Frost
(1874–1963)

Though born in San Francisco, Robert Frost was
known as the quintessential New Englander. He
attended both Dartmouth College and Harvard, but
graduated from neither. In 1900, Frost inherited a farm
in Derry, New Hampshire, from his grandfather. There
he spent the next twelve years farming, teaching
English at Pinkerton Academy, and writing poetry
(which was mostly ignored). In 1912, he sold the farm
and moved his family to England, where he continued
to farm and to write. It was in England that his first
two volumes of poetry, *A Boy's Will* (1913) and *North
of Boston* (1914), were published and were well
received. In 1915, the family returned to the United
States, settling on a farm near Franconia, New Hampshire. After the American publication of his first two
works, Frost began to receive recognition in the United
States. Great acclaim quickly followed. He was
awarded four Pulitzer Prizes, and in 1961, he read
"The Gift Outright" at the inauguration of President
John F. Kennedy. In this poem *"Out, Out—"* Frost tells
the story of a boy's accident on a New England farm.

The buzz saw snarled and rattled in the yard
And made dust and dropped stove-length sticks of wood,
Sweet-scented stuff when the breeze drew across it.
And from these those that lifted eyes could count
5 Five mountain ranges one behind the other
Under the sunset far into Vermont.

And the saw snarled and rattled, snarled and rattled,
As it ran light, or had to bear a load.
And nothing happened: day was all but done.
10 Call it a day, I wish they might have said
To please the boy by giving him the half hour
That a boy counts so much when saved from work.
His sister stood beside them in her apron
To tell them "Supper." At the word, the saw,
15 As if to prove saws knew what supper meant,
Leaped out at the boy's hand, or seemed to leap—
He must have given the hand. However it was,
Neither refused the meeting. But the hand!
The boy's first outcry was a rueful laugh,
20 As he swung toward them holding up the hand,
Half in appeal, but half as if to keep
The life from spilling. Then the boy saw all—
Since he was old enough to know, big boy
Doing a man's work, though a child at heart—
25 He saw all spoiled. "Don't let him cut my hand off—
The doctor, when he comes. Don't let him, sister!"
So. But the hand was gone already.
The doctor put him in the dark of ether.
He lay and puffed his lips out with his breath.
30 And then—the watcher at his pulse took fright.
No one believed. They listened at his heart.
Little—less—nothing!—and that ended it.
No more to build on there. And they, since they
Were not the one dead, turned to their affairs.

TOPICS FOR WRITING AND DISCUSSION

1. In this poem, Frost tells about a tragic event on a New England farm. Summarize the story in a few sentences as if you were a bystander reporting the accident to local authorities.

2. The title of the poem is an allusion, that is, a reference to familiar literature or history. In this case, Frost quotes part of a well-known line from Shakespeare's *Macbeth* (act 5, scene 5):

> Out, out brief candle!
> Life's but a walking shadow, a poor player
> That struts and frets his hour upon the stage
> And then is heard no more.

How does the title's allusion help clarify Frost's view of life's fragility and uncertainty at such a tragic time?

3. How does Frost use details and repetition in the poem's first nine lines to create a sense of an ordinary day, one in which those present might assume

that nothing will go wrong? Pay special attention to Frost's sentence construction and his use of "and." Despite the ordinariness of the day, how does Frost characterize the saw?

4. Note the tone of the last two lines in this poem. Who are "they" that he refers to? What is their attitude? Is this a sentimental, realistic, or insensitive response? Why does Frost end the poem on this note?

5. Accidents may happen when we least expect them. Narrate the story of an accident you witnessed, making clear your attitude toward the event. Is your attitude toward life's misfortune the same as that expressed in Shakespeare's lines or do you draw other conclusions?

Edgar Allan Poe (Corbis-Bettmann)

THE CASK OF AMONTILLADO

Edgar Allan Poe
(1809–1849)

The son of traveling actors, Edgar Poe was born in
Boston. Within a year of his birth, his alcoholic father
deserted the family, and before he was three, his mother
died of tuberculosis. He was adopted by the prosperous
merchant John Allan of Richmond, Virginia, and eventually took his adoptive father's surname as his middle
name. Poe was educated in Virginia and England, served
two years in the army, and attended West Point. After
his expulsion from the academy, John Allan disowned
Poe, completely disinheriting him. Left to support himself, Poe turned to writing as a profession. In 1833 his
story "Ms. Found in a Bottle" won a fifty-dollar prize,
and he obtained a position at the *Southern Literary
Messenger.* By 1835 he was editor of the *Messenger* but
was fired two years later. Despite his instability, Poe was
widely admired for his detective stories ("Murders in the
Rue Morgue") and tales of psychological terror ("The
Tell-Tale Heart"), his romantic poetry ("The Raven"),
and his influential literary criticism. Poe's last years were
plagued with poverty, illness, drug and alcohol abuse,
and depression over the death of his young wife. The
circumstances by which Poe died in 1849 remain a mystery. The 1846 story that follows, "The Cask of Amontillado," is considered one of Poe's best tales of terror.

1   THE thousand injuries of Fortunato I had borne as I best could, but when he
ventured upon insult I vowed revenge. You, who so well know the nature of my
soul, will not suppose, however, that I gave utterance to a threat. *At length* I

would be avenged; this was a point definitely settled—but the very definitiveness with which it was resolved precluded the idea of risk. I must not only punish but punish with impunity. A wrong is unredressed when retribution overtakes its redresser. It is equally unredressed when the avenger fails to make himself felt as such to him who has done the wrong.

2   It must be understood that neither by word nor deed had I given Fortunato cause to doubt my good will. I continued, as was my wont, to smile in his face, and he did not perceive that my smile *now* was at the thought of his immolation.

3   He had a weak point—this Fortunato—although in other regards he was a man to be respected and even feared. He prided himself on his connoisseurship in wine. Few Italians have the true virtuoso spirit. For the most part their enthusiasm is adopted to suit the time and opportunity, to practise imposture upon the British and Austrian *millionaires*. In painting and gemmary, Fortunato, like his countrymen, was a quack, but in the matter of old wines he was sincere. In this respect I did not differ from him materially;—I was skillful in the Italian vintages myself, and bought largely whenever I could.

4   It was about dusk, one evening during the supreme madness of the carnival season, that I encountered my friend. He accosted me with excessive warmth, for he had been drinking much. The man wore motley. He had on a tight-fitting parti-striped dress, and his head was surmounted by the conical cap and bells. I was so pleased to see him that I thought I should never have done wringing his hand.

5   I said to him—"My dear Fortunato, you are luckily met. How remarkably well you are looking to-day. But I have received a pipe of what passes for Amontillado,[1] and I have my doubts."

6   "How?" said he. "Amontillado? A pipe? Impossible! And in the middle of the carnival!"

7   "I have my doubts," I replied; "and I was silly enough to pay the full Amontillado price without consulting you in the matter. You were not to be found, and I was fearful of losing a bargain."

8   "Amontillado!"

9   "I have my doubts."

10   "Amontillado!"

11   "And I must satisfy them."

12   "Amontillado!"

13   "As you are engaged, I am on my way to Luchresi. If any one has a critical turn it is he. He will tell me ———"

14   "Luchresi cannot tell Amontillado from Sherry."

15   "And yet some fools will have it that his taste is a match for your own."

16   "Come, let us go."

17   "Whither?"

---

[1] A Spanish sherry.

18   "To your vaults."

19   "My friend, no; I will not impose upon your good nature. I perceive you have an engagement. Luchresi ————"

20   "I have no engagement;—come."

21   "My friend, no. It is not the engagement, but the severe cold with which I perceive you are afflicted. The vaults are insufferably damp. They are encrusted with nitre."

22   "Let us go, nevertheless. The cold is merely nothing. Amontillado! You have been imposed upon. And as for Luchresi, he cannot distinguish Sherry from Amontillado."

23   Thus speaking, Fortunato possessed himself of my arm; and putting on a mask of black silk and drawing a *roquelaire*[2] closely about my person, I suffered him to hurry me to my palazzo.

24   There were not attendants at home; they had absconded to make merry in honor of the time. I had told them that I should not return until the morning, and had given them explicit orders not to stir from the house. These orders were sufficient, I well knew, to insure their immediate disappearance, one and all, as soon as my back was turned.

25   I took from their sconces two flambeaux, and giving one to Fortunato, bowed him through several suites of rooms to the archway that led into the vaults. I passed down a long and winding staircase, requesting him to be cautious as he followed. We came at length to the foot of the descent, and stood together upon the damp ground of the catacombs of the Montresors.

26   The gait of my friend was unsteady, and the bells upon his cap jingled as he strode.

27   "The pipe," he said.

28   "It is farther on," said I; "but observe the white web-work which gleams from these cavern walls."

29   He turned towards me, and looked into my eyes with two filmy orbs that distilled the rheum of intoxication.

30   "Nitre?" he asked at length.

31   "Nitre," I replied. "How long have you had that cough?"

32   "Ugh! ugh! ugh!—ugh! ugh! ugh!—ugh! ugh! ugh!—ugh! ugh! ugh!—ugh! ugh! ugh!"

33   My poor friend found it impossible to reply for many minutes.

34   "It is nothing," he said at last.

35   "Come," I said, with decision, "we will go back; your health is precious. You are rich, respected, admired, beloved; you are happy, as once I was. You are a man to be missed. For me it is no matter. We will back; you will be ill, and I cannot be responsible. Besides, there is Luchresi ————"

36   "Enough," he said; "the cough is a mere nothing; it will not kill me. I shall not die of a cough."

---

[2] A cloak.

37   "True—true," I replied; "and, indeed, I had no intention of alarming you unnecessarily—but you should use all proper caution. A draught of this Medoc[3] will defend us from the damps."

38   Here I knocked off the neck of a bottle which I drew from a long row of its fellows that lay upon the mould.

39   "Drink," I said, presenting him the wine.

40   He raised it to his lips with a leer. He paused and nodded to me familiarly, while his bells jingled.

41   "I drink," he said, "to the buried that repose around us."

42   "And I to your long life."

43   He again took my arm, and we proceeded.

44   "These vaults," he said, "are extensive."

45   "The Montresors," I replied, "were a great and numerous family."

46   "I forget your arms."

47   "A huge human foot d'or, in a field azure; the foot crushes a serpent rampant whose fangs are imbedded in the heel."

48   "And the motto?"

49   *"Nemo me impune lacessit.*[4]

50   "Good!" he said.

51   The wine sparkled in his eyes and the bells jingled. My own fancy grew warm with the Medoc. We had passed through long walls of piled skeletons, with casks and puncheons intermingling, into the inmost recesses of the catacombs. I paused again, and this time I made bold to seize Fortunato by an arm above the elbow.

52   "The nitre!" I said; "see, it increases. It hangs like moss upon the vaults. We are below the river's bed. The drops of moisture trickle among the bones. Come, we will go back ere it is too late. Your cough————"

53   "It is nothing," he said; "let us go on. But first, another draught of the Medoc."

54   I broke and reached him a flagon of De Grave. He emptied it at a breath. His eyes flashed with a fierce light. He laughed and threw the bottle upwards with a gesticulation I did not understand.

55   I looked at him in surprise. He repeated the movement—a grotesque one.

56   "You do not comprehend?" he said.

57   "Not I," I replied.

58   "Then you are not of the brotherhood."

59   "How?"

60   "You are not of the masons."

61   "Yes, yes," I said; "yes, yes."

62   "You? Impossible! A mason?"

63   "A mason," I replied.

---

[3] A French wine.

[4] No one attacks me without punishment.

64   "A sign," he said, "a sign."

65   "It is this," I answered, producing from beneath the folds of my *roquelaire* a trowel.

66   "You jest," he exclaimed, recoiling a few paces. "But let us proceed to the Amontillado."

67   "Be it so," I said, replacing the tool beneath the cloak and again offering him my arm. He leaned upon it heavily. We continued our route in search of the Amontillado. We passed through a range of low arches, descended, passed on, and descending again, arrived at a deep crypt, in which the foulness of the air caused our flambeaux rather to glow than flame.

68   At the most remote end of the crypt there appeared another less spacious. Its walls had been lined with human remains, piled to the vault overhead, in the fashion of the great catacombs of Paris. Three sides of this interior crypt were still ornamented in this manner. From the fourth side the bones had been thrown down, and lay promiscuously upon the earth, forming at one point a mound of some size. Within the wall thus exposed by the displacing of the bones, we perceived a still interior crypt or recess, in depth about four feet, in width three, in height six or seven. It seemed to have been constructed for no especial use within itself, but formed merely the interval between two of the colossal supports of the roof of the catacombs, and was backed by one of their circumscribing walls of solid granite.

69   It was in vain that Fortunato, unlifting his dull torch, endeavored to pry into the depth of the recess. Its termination the feeble light did not enable us to see.

70   "Proceed," I said; "herein is the Amontillado. As for Luchresi————"

71   "He is an ignoramus," interrupted my friend, as he stepped unsteadily forward, while I followed immediately at his heels. In an instant he had reached the extremity of the niche, and finding his progress arrested by the rock, stood stupidly bewildered. A moment more and I had fettered him to the granite. In its surface were two iron staples, distant from each other about two feet, horizontally. From one of these depended a short chain, from the other a padlock. Throwing the links about his waist, it was but the work of a few seconds to secure it. He was too much astounded to resist. Withdrawing the key I stepped back from the recess.

72   "Pass your hand," I said, "over the wall; you cannot help feeling the nitre. Indeed, it is *very* damp. Once more let me *implore* you to return. No? Then I must positively leave you. But I must first render you all the little attentions in my power."

73   "The Amontillado!" ejaculated my friend, not yet recovered from his astonishment.

74   "True," I replied; "the Amontillado."

75   As I said these words I busied myself among the pile of bones of which I have before spoken. Throwing them aside, I soon uncovered a quantity of building stone and mortar. With these materials and with the aid of my trowel, I began vigorously to wall up the entrance of the niche.

76   I had scarcely laid the first tier of the masonry when I discovered that the intoxication of Fortunato had in a great measure worn off. The earliest indication I had of this was a low moaning cry from the depth of the recess. It was *not* the cry of a drunken man. There was a long and obstinate silence. I laid the second tier, and the third, and the fourth; and then I heard the furious vibrations of the chain. The noise lasted for several minutes, during which, that I might hearken to it with the more satisfaction, I ceased my labors and sat down upon the bones. When at last the clanking subsided, I resumed the trowel, and finished without interruption the fifth, the sixth, and the seventh tier. The wall was now nearly upon a level with my breast. I again paused, and holding the flambeaux over the mason-work, threw a few feeble rays upon the figure within.

77   A succession of loud and shrill screams, bursting suddenly from the throat of the chained form, seemed to thrust me violently back. For a brief moment I hesitated, I trembled. Unsheathing my rapier, I began to grope with it about the recess; but the thought of an instant reassured me. I placed my hand upon the solid fabric of the catacombs, and felt satisfied. I reapproached the wall; I replied to the yells of him who clamoured. I re-echoed, I aided, I surpassed them in volume and in strength. I did this, and the clamourer grew still.

78   It was now midnight, and my task was drawing to a close. I had completed the eighth, the ninth and the tenth tier. I had finished a portion of the last and the eleventh; there remained but a single stone to be fitted and plastered in. I struggled with its weight; I placed it partially in its destined position. But now there came from out the niche a low laugh that erected the hairs upon my head. It was succeeded by a sad voice, which I had difficulty in recognizing as that of the noble Fortunato. The voice said—

79   "Ha! ha! ha!—he! he! he!—a very good joke, indeed—an excellent jest. We will have many a rich laugh about it at the palazzo—he! he! he!—over our wine—he! he! he!"

80   "The Amontillado!" I said.

81   "He! he! he!—he! he! he!—yes, the Amontillado. But is it not getting late? Will not they be awaiting us at the palazzo, the Lady Fortunato and the rest? Let us be gone."

82   "Yes," I said, "let us be gone."

83   *"For the love of God, Montresor!"*

84   "Yes," I said, "for the love of God."

85   But to these words I hearkened in vain for a reply. I grew impatient. I called aloud—

86   "Fortunato!"

87   No answer. I called again—

88   "Fortunato!"

89   No answer. I called again—

90   "Fortunato!"

91   No answer still. I thrust a torch through the remaining aperture and let it fall within. There came forth in return only a jingling of the bells. My heart grew sick; it was the dampness of the catacombs that made it so. I hastened to

make an end of my labour. I forced the last stone into its position; I plastered it up. Against the new masonry I re-erected the old rampart of bones. For the half of a century no mortal has disturbed them. *In pace requiescat!*[5]

TOPICS FOR WRITING AND DISCUSSION

1. Who narrates this story, and what is his definition of successful revenge? In what two cases is a wrong "unredressed"?
2. Poe is famous for creating spooky settings in his stories of terror or the supernatural. Cite some examples of sensory details he uses to create a highly eerie underground scene.
3. Throughout the story, Montresor ironically plays on words. Explain the irony you see, for example, in the exchanges about Fortunato's cough (paragraphs 31–37) and the masons and the trowel (paragraphs 60–65). Do you see irony in Poe's choice of season for this story? In Fortunato's name, costume, and response to Montresor's coat of arms and family motto? What does such irony add to the story's atmosphere of terror?
4. Is this story told in chronological order or as a flashback? Why do you only discover this answer at the end of the story? Do you think Montresor has successfully achieved the kind of revenge he describes earlier in the story? Is *he* "resting in peace"? Readers disagree, so be prepared to defend your answer.
5. Have you ever sought revenge and had the guilt come back to haunt you? Narrate your story (humorously or seriously), showing your readers the futility or negative consequences of trying to "punish with impunity."

---

[5] May he rest in peace.

WRITING ASSIGNMENTS FOR CHAPTER THREE

NARRATION

1. In "Salvation," Langston Hughes narrates an incident in which he feels pressured to meet someone else's expectations. Think about a time in your life when you did *not* give in to peer or family pressure. Tell the story of your determination and show how you overcame the temptation to compromise your principles or better judgment.

2. In "The Discus Thrower," Richard Selzer narrates a series of descriptive episodes about his dying patient. These episodes appear almost as snapshots that together form a collage, a larger work that reveals the nature of the character Selzer is re-creating. Think of an event or complex episode in your life and imitate Selzer's technique by narrating three or more short scenes that together capture the essence of the time or person you are presenting. Consider, for example, some of the important or even traumatic episodes of your life: a graduation, a move, a marriage or divorce, a competition or sporting event, or a serious illness. Remember that the narrative as a whole should be clearly unified through the scenes you are creating for the reader.

3. In "Sister Flowers," Maya Angelou looks back at a childhood encounter that ultimately made a tremendous difference in her life. Recount a single episode from your youth that you now see as critically important in shaping the person you are today. Make your narrative as vivid as Angelou's by using clear, specific details that will help your readers see and understand the importance of the event and its characters.

4. In "38 Who Saw Murder Didn't Call the Police," Martin Gansberg reports what happened to Kitty Genovese, but, in reality, he has another more important purpose: he exposes what *didn't* happen as a result of people's fear of involvement. Become an investigative reporter yourself and write an essay exposing the real nature of some crime or injustice in your community. You might wish to read newspaper clippings or interview police officers or witnesses, if available. Or, if you prefer, take another look at a crime that made national news that you feel needs additional scrutiny or more publicity. Such a crime could be an older one (e.g., Lizzie Borden and her infamous axe) or a more recent one. Have a clear purpose to your reporting as Gansberg does.

5. Almost all of us, at one time or another, have enormously disliked or even felt ashamed of some part of our body. This problematic feature may have been something we were born with or perhaps it was a result of an illness or of an accident, as in the case of Alice Walker's eye. In "Beauty: When the Other Dancer Is the Self," Walker eloquently explains how she came to

terms with her problem, how she realized that she had "obviously come through all right." Narrate the story of how you (or perhaps a friend with a disability) came to a similar conclusion and accepted yourself, as did Walker, as someone who is "beautiful, whole and free." (If you wish, you might imagine as your audience someone who shares your problem and is looking to you for guidance.)

6. In "Chinese-American Silence," Maxine Hong Kingston offers stories from her childhood to show the consequences of living in two cultures. Narrate a personal event that shows a specific influence of your racial, ethnic, or cultural heritage on your life. Does your story show feelings of conflict or resolution? Does it show embarrassment, frustration, pride, joy, or something else?

7. Alice Walker's essay and Robert Frost's poem "'Out, Out—'" tell about tragic accidents. Write an essay that focuses on the flip side of such an event—an accident that produced happy or satisfying results, positive fall-out, or repercussions that you might not have enjoyed otherwise. Did this event change your view of life's possibilities in any way?

8. Edgar Allan Poe is considered the nineteenth-century American master of the macabre. Write a narrative in which you imitate (or parody) his style by creating either a character or setting in today's world that frightens your readers. Which sensory details work best for your narrative?

CHAPTER FOUR

DESCRIPTION

The sun lay on the grass and warmed it, and in the shade under the grass the insects moved, ants and ant lions to set traps for them, grasshoppers to jump into the
air and flick their yellow wings for a second, sow bugs like little armadillos, plodding restlessly on many tender feet. And over the grass at the roadside a land turtle
crawled, turning aside for nothing, dragging his high-domed shell over the grass.
His hard legs and yellow-nailed feet threshed slowly through the grass, not really
walking, but boosting and dragging his shell along. The barley beards slid off his
shell, and the clover burrs fell on him and rolled to the ground. His horny beak
was partly open, and his fierce, humorous eyes, under brows like fingernails, stared
straight ahead.

The passage from John Steinbeck's *The Grapes of Wrath* illustrates a rhetorical structure called *description*. Description is used to tell how something
looks, smells, sounds, feels, tastes, or behaves. It presents an impression or it
indicates a mood, helping readers to visualize or understand ideas or concepts.
In short, description relies on specific details sequenced carefully to produce
a *dominant impression*. Steinbeck's well-known description of a turtle crossing
a highway, "turning aside for nothing," presents a clear picture of determination, a slow but fierce tenacity.

Description is seldom used as an independent form of writing. Instead, it
is often combined with other rhetorical strategies to illustrate a point or to
make an abstract idea more understandable. For example, Annie Dillard in
"An American Childhood" creates an affectionate picture of her mother by
using descriptive narration:

Mother's energy and intelligence suited her for a greater role in a larger arena—
mayor of New York, say—than the one she had. She followed American politics
closely; she had been known to vote for Democrats. She saw how things should be
run, but she had nothing to run but our household.

Virginia Woolf describes the frustrations a female writer of sixteenth-century
England might have encountered in "If Shakespeare Had Had a Sister":

. . . Imaginatively she is of the highest importance; practically she is completely insignificant. She pervades poetry from cover to cover; she is all but absent from history. She dominates the lives of kings and conquerors in fiction; in fact she was the slave of any boy whose parents forced a ring upon her finger. . . .

Woolf is clearly using description and contrast to explore the roles and pressures faced by women.

TYPES OF DESCRIPTION

Description can be classified as *objective* or *subjective,* though in your own writing you may use a combination of the two. Objective description is factual, unaffected by the feelings or beliefs of the writer. The words used to portray something or someone objectively are chosen for their denotations rather than their connotations. A science experiment, for example, might be presented in objective language. Tillie Olsen uses first objective details in "I Stand Here Ironing" to describe a mother's observation of the convalescent home to which her daughter has been sent:

> Oh it is a handsome place, green lawns and tall trees and fluted flower beds. High up on the balconies of each cottage the children stand, the girls in their red bows and white dresses, the boys in white suits and giant red ties. The parents stand below shrieking up to be heard and the children shriek down to be heard, and between them the invisible wall. . . .

A factual description may lead to a subjective, personal observation. Olsen's description of a manicured landscape and smartly dressed children also includes shrieking parents and children separated from each other by an "invisible wall." The contrast is sharp and vivid.

Subjective (or *impressionistic*) description, as the term implies, presents the impressions of the author. The words used are often suggestive and implicative. Subjective description relies on the creation of a dominant impression. The selection of details is crucial because the impression created is often the focal point of the writing. Notice the impression E. B. White creates as he describes a summer storm:

> . . . a thunderstorm came up. It was like the revival of an old melodrama that I had seen long ago with childish awe. The second-act climax of the drama of the electrical disturbance over a lake in America had not changed in any important respect. This was the big scene, still the big scene. The whole thing was so familiar, the first feeling of oppression and heat and a general air around camp of not wanting to go very far away. In mid-afternoon (it was all the same) a curious darkening of the sky, and a lull in everything that had made life tick; and then the way the boats suddenly swung the other way at their moorings with the coming of a breeze

out of the new quarter, and the premonitory rumble. Then the kettle drum, then the snare, then the bass drum and cymbals, then crackling light against the dark, and the gods grinning and licking their chops in the hills. Afterward the calm, the rain steadily rustling in the calm lake, the return of light and hope and spirits, and the campers running out in joy and relief to go swimming in the rain, their bright cries perpetuating the deathless joke about how they were getting simply drenched, and the children screaming with delight at the new sensation of bathing in the rain. . . .

White's language helps his readers experience the drama and delight of the afternoon.

Writing the Descriptive Essay

Though description is seldom used alone as a rhetorical structure, it is often used as a writing tool. The following tips should help you in preparing an essay whose main purpose is to use description in order to make a point, illustrate a concept, or clarify an idea.

1. *Determine the purpose of the description.*

Scientific papers, business reports, and proposals—formal writing—often use objective description. On the other hand, most personal or informal writing would probably benefit from subjective description. The key is to determine which is appropriate for conveying the purpose of the writing.

2. *Carefully select details that will create a dominant impression.*

Choose details that will focus the reader's attention on a particular impression or create for the reader a vivid general image; then, use more details to expand the impression or image. Avoid, however, description that is too "busy," that is, one that contains too many different images. Omit details that could detract from your impression. Your goal should be to communicate a specific mood or feeling and hold the reader's attention there, as E. B. White did in the storm passage from "Once More to the Lake."

3. *Use a logical spatial ordering of details.*

If your description is a visual one, you might order the details the same way the eye would most naturally view them. If you are describing a person, you might order your details from head to toe or vice versa, or you might begin with a dominant feature and work from there. A description of a room in a house might begin with items farthest away and work inward, from floor to ceiling, from ceiling to floor, from nearest to farthest, or from a focal point outward. Notice how N. Scott Momaday uses spatial ordering in "The Way to Rainy Mountain":

> Yellowstone, it seemed to me, was at the top of the world, a region of deep lakes and dark timber, canyons and waterfalls. . . . The skyline in all directions is close at hand, the high wall of the woods and deep cleavages of shade . . . Descending eastward, the highland meadows are a stairway to the plain. . . . Clusters of trees, and animals grazing far in the distance, cause the vision to reach away and wonder to build upon the mind. . . The sun follows a longer course in the day, and the sky is immense beyond all comparison. . . Farther down, in the land of the Crows and the Blackfeet, the plain is yellow. . . .

Momaday begins with a panoramic view of Yellowstone and then narrows the description as he moves down from the "top of the world" to the yellow plains. From this spatial ordering, it is easy to get a specific visual image.

4. *Use figurative language to create vivid images.*

Figures of speech such as similes, metaphors, personification, and oxymoron can be effective in creating images.

A *simile* is a figure of speech that compares two dissimilar items frequently to clarify an unclear, unknown, or abstract item or feeling. It is commonly expressed using the words *like* or *as*. When Virginia Woolf describes fiction (in "If Shakespeare Had Had a Sister") as being "like a spider's web, attached ever lightly perhaps, but still attached to life at all four corners," she uses simile. Likewise, John Steinbeck (in "The Turtle") uses simile to relate the turtle's encounter with a light truck. He says the front wheel of the vehicle "flipped the turtle like a tiddly-wink, spun it like a coin, and rolled it off the highway."

A figure of speech similar to a simile is a *metaphor*. Here, however, the comparison of dissimilar things is made without prepositions or connectives such as *like* or *as*. When Woolf examines the composite being created by the paradox of literature and reality, she describes the creation (women) as "an odd monster that one made up by reading the historians first and the poets afterwards—a worm winged like an eagle [note the simile]; the spirit of life and beauty in a kitchen chopping up suet." Woolf actually goes on to extend the metaphor by making the entire essay a comparison of the perception of women's abilities and the reality of their abilities.

The key to the effective use of similes and metaphors is avoiding overused expressions such as "blind as a bat" or "dead as a doornail." Also, you should avoid "mixing" more than one metaphor, for the image you create can be confusing: "The senators refuse to bite the bullet that is now an albatross around their necks."

Another figure of speech that writers use to create an impression is *personification*. In personification, human characteristics of actions, personality, speech, or emotion are given to nonhuman entities. N. Scott Momaday relates a Native-American legend that includes personification: ". . . The sisters were terrified; they ran, and the bear after them. They came to the stump of a great tree, and the tree spoke to them. It bade them climb upon it, . . ."

Still another device you might consider is *oxymoron,* the pairing of opposites to create an image or effect. For example, an uneasy quiet could be described as "deafening silence."

Simile, metaphor, personification, and oxymoron can be effective descriptive tools when used properly, but care should be taken to use fresh, vivid figures of speech in order to create fresh, vivid impressions.

THE TURTLE

John Steinbeck
(1902–1968)

John Steinbeck used his birthplace of Salinas,
California, as the setting for much of his fiction.
His literary reputation was established with his
fourth novel, *Tortilla Flat* (1935), a work that
portrays the lives of workers in Monterey, California. *Of Mice and Men* (1937) gained him
further recognition, and in 1939 he was
awarded the Pulitzer Prize for *The Grapes of
Wrath* (1939), confirming his as a powerful
voice in American literature. Other works
include *The Red Pony* (1933), *Cannery Row*
(1945), *East of Eden* (1952), and *The Winter of
Our Discontent* (1961). Steinbeck's work was
recognized by the world when he was awarded
the Nobel Prize for literature in 1962. In his
acceptance speech, he described the duty of the
writer "to celebrate man's proven capacity for
greatness to heart and spirit—for gallantry in
defeat—for courage, compassion, and love." His
work celebrates human dignity and condemns
any system that encourages exploitation and
brutality. "The Turtle," an excerpt from *The
Grapes of Wrath,* can be seen as an allegory that
illustrates the human capacity for courage and
persistence.

1   THE concrete highway was edged with a mat of tangled, broken, dry
grass, and the grass heads were heavy with oat beards to catch on
a dog's coat, and foxtails to tangle in a horse's fetlocks, and clover
burrs to fasten in sheep's wool; sleeping life waiting to be spread and

John Steinbeck (© Archive Photos/AM Stock)

dispersed, every seed armed with an appliance of dispersal, twisting darts and parachutes for the wind, little spears and balls of tiny thorns, and all waiting for animals and for the wind, for a man's trouser cuff or the hem of a woman's skirt, all passive but armed with appliances of activity, still, but each possessed of the anlage of movement.

2   The sun lay on the grass and warmed it, and in the shade under the grass the insects moved, ants and ant lions to set traps for them, grasshoppers to jump into the air and flick their yellow wings for a second, sow bugs like little armadillos, plodding restlessly on many tender feet. And over the grass at the roadside a land turtle crawled, turning aside for nothing, dragging his high-domed shell over the grass. His hard legs and yellow-nailed feet threshed slowly through the grass, not really walking, but boosting and dragging his shell along. The barley beards slid off his shell, and the clover burrs fell on him and rolled to the ground. His horny beak was partly open, and his fierce, humorous eyes, under brows like fingernails, stared straight ahead. He came over the grass leaving a beaten trail behind him, and the hill, which was the highway embankment, reared up ahead of him. For a moment he stopped, his head held high. He blinked and looked up and down. At last he started to climb the embankment. Front clawed feet reached forward but did not touch. The hind feet kicked his shell along, and it scraped on the grass, and on the gravel. As the embankment grew steeper and steeper, the more frantic were the efforts of the land turtle. Pushing hind legs strained and slipped, boosting the shell along, and the horny head protruded as far as the neck could stretch. Little by little the shell slid up the embankment until at last a parapet cut straight across its line of march, the shoulder of the road, a concrete wall four inches high. As though they worked independently the hind legs pushed the shell against the wall. The head upraised and peered over the wall to the broad smooth plain of cement. Now the hands, braced on top of the wall, strained and lifted, and the shell came slowly up and rested its front end on the wall. For a moment the turtle rested. A red ant ran into the shell, into the soft skin inside the shell, and suddenly head and legs snapped in, and the armored tail clamped in sideways. The red ant was crushed between body and legs. And one head of wild oats was clamped into the shell by a front leg. For a long moment the turtle lay still, and then the neck crept out and the old humorous frowning eyes looked about and the legs and tail came out. The back legs went to work, straining like elephant legs, and the shell tipped to an angle so that the front legs could not reach the level cement plain. But higher and higher the hind legs boosted it, until at last the center of balance was reached, the front tipped down, the front legs scratched at the pavement, and it was up. But the head of wild oats was held by its stem around the front legs.

3   Now the going was easy, and all the legs worked, and the shell boosted along, waggling from side to side. A sedan driven by a forty-year-old woman approached. She saw the turtle and swung to the right, off the highway, the wheels screamed and a cloud of dust boiled up. Two wheels lifted for a moment and then settled. The car skidded back onto the road, and went on, but more

slowly. The turtle had jerked into its shell, but now it hurried on, for the highway was burning hot.

4   And now a light truck approached, and as it came near, the driver saw the turtle and swerved to hit it. His front wheel struck the edge of the shell, flipped the turtle like a tiddly-wink, spun it like a coin, and rolled it off the highway. The truck went back to its course along the right side. Lying on its back, the turtle was tight in its shell for a long time. But at last its legs waved in the air, reaching for something to pull it over. Its front foot caught a piece of quartz and little by little the shell pulled over and flopped upright. The wild oat head fell out and three of the spearhead seeds stuck in the ground. And as the turtle crawled on down the embankment, its shell dragged dirt over the seeds. The turtle entered a dust road and jerked itself along, drawing a wavy shallow trench in the dust with its shell. The old humorous eyes looked ahead, and the horny beak opened a little. His yellow toe nails slipped a fraction in the dust.

TOPICS FOR WRITING AND DISCUSSION

1. Does Steinbeck use objective or subjective description in this selection? Support your answer with references to the text.

2. What dominant impression does Steinbeck create as he describes the turtle and its journey? Again, select some details and images that support your answer.

3. Choose three examples of vivid figurative language that appear in this selection. Explain why you think these particular similes or metaphors are the most powerful ones in the description. What do they do for the scene that ordinary language would not?

4. Why do you think Steinbeck included this scene in a novel about poor but enduring migrant workers in the Depression? What symbolic role might the description of the wild oats play in this story?

5. Describe objectively one creature or object in nature you can study closely, one that you can repeatedly observe in person or through a microscope, telescope, binoculars, or camera eye. Select a logical pattern of organization for your description, and avoid making your description bland by using numerous clear details rather than generalities. (Hint: You might find it helpful to read an essay that arose from a similar assignment, "Take This Fish and Look at It," on pp. 269–273.)

MARRYING ABSURD

Joan Didion
(1934–   )

Joan Didion (© AP/ Wide World Photos)

Novelist, essayist, journalist, and screenwriter, Joan Didion is a native Californian, descended from pioneers. Her great-great-great-grandmother was a survivor of the Donner party that crossed the mountains in 1846. Didion graduated from the University of California at Berkeley and, after graduation, worked for a few years in New York as a feature editor for *Vogue*. In 1964, she returned to California, where she now resides. Her work includes several novels—*River Run* (1963), *Play It As It Lays* (1971), *A Book of Common Prayer* (1977), and *Democracy* (1984); books of essays, *Slouching Toward Bethlehem* (1969) and *The White Album* (1978); a book-length essay, *Salvador* (1983); and *Miami* (1987), a work focusing on Cuban exiles in Florida. With her husband, John Gregory Dunne, Didion has collaborated on several screenplays—*A Star Is Born* (1976), *True Confessions* (1981), and, most recently, *Up Close and Personal* (1996). Her latest books are *After Henry* (1992), a collection of essays, and *The Last Thing He Wanted* (1996), a novel. Didion's writing blends fiction, autobiography, and personal commentary on contemporary American culture. "Marrying Absurd," which first appeared in the *Saturday Evening Post* in 1967 and was reprinted in *Slouching Toward Bethlehem* (1969), is an example of her keen and realistic description of life—this time, Las Vegas wedding styles.

1   To be married in Las Vegas, Clark County, Nevada, a bride must swear that she is eighteen or has parental permission and a bridegroom that he is twenty-one or has parental permission. Someone must put up five dollars for the license. (On Sundays and holidays, fifteen dollars. The Clark County Court-house issues marriage licenses at any time of the day or night except between

noon and one in the afternoon, between eight and nine in the evening, and be-tween four and five in the morning.) Nothing else is required. The State of Nevada, alone among these United States, demands neither a premarital blood test nor a waiting period before or after the issuance of a marriage license. Driving in across the Mojave from Los Angeles, one sees the signs way out on the desert, looming up from that moonscape of rattlesnakes and mesquite, even before the Las Vegas lights appear like a mirage on the horizon: "GETTING MARRIED? Free License Information First Strip Exit." Perhaps the Las Vegas wedding industry achieved its peak operational efficiency between 9:00 p.m. and midnight of August 26, 1965, an otherwise unremarkable Thursday which happened to be, by Presidential order, the last day on which anyone could im-prove his draft status merely by getting married. One hundred and seventy-one couples were pronounced man and wife in the name of Clark County and the State of Nevada that night, sixty-seven of them by a single justice of the peace, Mr. James A. Brennan. Mr. Brennan did one wedding at the Dunes and the other sixty-six in his office, and charged each couple eight dollars. One bride lent her veil to six others. "I got it down from five to three minutes," Mr. Bren-nan said later of his feat. "I could've married them *en masse,* but they're peo-ple, not cattle. People expect more when they get married."

2   What people who get married in Las Vegas actually do expect—what, in the largest sense, their "expectations" are—strikes one as a curious and self-contradictory business. Las Vegas is the most extreme and allegorical of Amer-ican settlements, bizarre and beautiful in its venality and in its devotion to immediate gratification, a place the tone of which is set by mobsters and call girls and ladies' room attendants with amyl nitrite poppers in their uniform pockets. Almost everyone notes that there is no "time" in Las Vegas, no night and no day and no past and no future (no Las Vegas casino, however, has taken the obliteration of the ordinary time sense quite so far as Harold's Club in Reno, which for a while issued, at odd intervals in the day and night, mimeographed "bulletins" carrying news from the world outside); neither is there any logical sense of where one is. One is standing on a highway in the middle of a vast hostile desert looking at an eighty-foot sign which blinks "STARDUST" or "CAESAR'S PALACE." Yes, but what does that explain? This geo-graphical implausibility reinforces the sense that what happens there has no connection with "real" life; Nevada cities like Reno and Carson are ranch towns, Western towns, places behind which there is some historical impera-tive. But Las Vegas seems to exist only in the eye of the beholder. All of which makes it an extraordinarily stimulating and interesting place, but an odd one in which to want to wear a candlelight satin Priscilla of Boston wedding dress with Chantilly lace insets, tapered sleeves and a detachable modified train.

3   And yet the Las Vegas wedding business seems to appeal to precisely that impulse. "Sincere and Dignified Since 1954," one wedding chapel advertises. There are nineteen such wedding chapels in Las Vegas, intensely competitive, each offering better, faster, and, by implication, more sincere services than the next: Our Photos Best Anywhere, Your Wedding on A Phonograph Record,

Candlelight with Your Ceremony, Honeymoon Accommodations, Free Transportation from Your Motel to Courthouse to Chapel and Return to Motel, Religious or Civil Ceremonies, Dressing Rooms, Flowers, Rings, Announcements, Witnesses Available, and Ample Parking. All of these services, like most others in Las Vegas (sauna baths, payroll-check cashing, chinchilla coats for sale or rent) are offered twenty-four hours a day, seven days a week, presumably on the premise that marriage, like craps, is a game to be played when the table seems hot.

4   But what strikes one most about the Strip chapels, with their wishing wells and stained-glass paper windows and their artificial bouvardia, is that so much of their business is by no means a matter of simple convenience, of late-night liaisons between show girls and baby Crosbys. Of course there is some of that. (One night about eleven o'clock in Las Vegas I watched a bride in an orange minidress and masses of flame-colored hair stumble from a Strip chapel on the arm of her bridegroom, who looked the part of the expendable nephew in movies like *Miami Syndicate.* "I gotta get the kids," the bride whimpered. "I gotta pick up the sitter, I gotta get to the midnight show." "What you gotta get," the bridegroom said, opening the door of a Cadillac Coupe de Ville and watching her crumple on the seat, "is sober.") But Las Vegas seems to offer something other than "convenience"; it is merchandising "niceness," the facsimile of proper ritual, to children who do not know how else to find it, how to make the arrangements, how to do it "right." All day and evening long on the Strip, one sees actual wedding parties, waiting under the harsh lights at a crosswalk, standing uneasily in the parking lot of the Frontier while the photographer hired by The Little Church of the West ("Wedding Place of the Stars") certifies the occasion, takes the picture: the bride in a veil and white satin pumps, the bridegroom usually in a white dinner jacket, and even an attendant or two, a sister or a best friend in hot-pink *peau de soie,* a flirtation veil, a carnation nosegay. "When I Fall in Love It Will Be Forever," the organist plays, and then a few bars of Lohengrin. The mother cries; the stepfather, awkward in his role, invites the chapel hostess to join them for a drink at the Sands. The hostess declines with a professional smile; she has already transferred her interest to the group waiting outside. One bride out, another in, and again the sign goes up on the chapel door: "One moment please—Wedding."

5   I sat next to one such wedding party in a Strip restaurant the last time I was in Las Vegas. The marriage had just taken place; the bride still wore her dress, the mother her corsage. A bored waiter poured out a few swallows of pink champagne ("on the house") for everyone but the bride, who was too young to be served. "You'll need something with more kick than that," the bride's father said with heavy jocularity to his new son-in-law; the ritual jokes about the wedding night had a certain Panglossian character, since the bride was clearly several months pregnant. Another round of pink champagne, this time not on the house, and the bride began to cry. "It was just as nice," she sobbed, "as I hoped and dreamed it would be."

TOPICS FOR WRITING AND DISCUSSION

1. What is the dominant impression Didion creates in her essay? How would you characterize Didion's tone? Is it playful or serious? Fascinated or critical? What does it reveal about her attitude toward her subject?

2. What does Didion find odd and contradictory about a wedding industry located in a town like Las Vegas? What does she mean when she says that Las Vegas' appeal as a wedding mecca is its skill of "merchandising niceness, the facsimile of proper ritual, [for] children who do not know how else to find it" (paragraph 4)?

3. Didion uses a wealth of details to create her description, including specific references to signs, services, chapels, clients, and personnel. What does this level of specificity add to your understanding of Didion's view? Cite three examples that you find particularly vivid, explaining what they add to the reader's understanding of this place.

4. Explain the appropriateness of the essay's title. What, exactly, is "absurd" about these weddings? How does Didion's concluding example emphasize her point of view?

5. Describe a place you know that has a clearly unusual or contradictory identity. Include many specific details to create the dominant impression you want your readers to understand.

THE WAY TO RAINY MOUNTAIN

N. Scott Momaday
(1934–   )

Noted author, scholar, teacher, and artist, N. Scott
Momaday often uses his Kiowa heritage as the basis for
his works. He was born in Lawton, Oklahoma, and
grew up on various reservations in the Southwest.
Momaday received his B.A. from the University of New
Mexico and both his M.A. and Ph.D. from Stanford
University. He is the author of *Owl in the Cedar Tree*
(1965); *The Journey of Tai-me*—published as *The Way
to Rainy Mountain* (1967); and *House Made of Dawn*
(1967), for which he won the Pulitzer Prize for fiction.
He has also published collections of poems, including
Angle of Geese and Other Poems (1974) and *The
Gourd Dancer* (1976). Also in 1976 he published *The
Names: A Memoir,* a re-creation of his family history
through his boyhood memories. In 1989, he published
The Ancient Child; in 1991, *In the Presence of the Sun;*
and in 1993, *Circle of Wonder: A Native American
Christmas Story.* His most recent book is *The Man
Made of Words* (1997), a collection of stories and
essays. In *The Way to Rainy Mountain,* Momaday
reflects on the migration of the Kiowa from the Yellowstone country to the Great Plains. The piece that follows is an excerpt from that book.

---

1 A single knoll rises out of the plain in Oklahoma, north and west of the Wi-
chita Range. For my people, the Kiowas, it is an old landmark, and they gave it
the name Rainy Mountain. The hardest weather in the world is there. Winter
brings blizzards, hot tornadic winds arise in the spring, and in summer the
prairie is an anvil's edge. The grass turns brittle and brown, and it cracks beneath your feet. There are green belts along the rivers and creeks, linear groves

N. Scott Momaday in his office at the University of Arizona, Tucson. (Arizona Daily Star*)*

of hickory and pecan, willow and witch hazel. At a distance in July or August the steaming foliage seems almost to writhe in fire. Great green and yellow grasshoppers are everywhere in the tall grass, popping up like corn to sting the flesh, and tortoises crawl about on the red earth, going nowhere in the plenty of time. Loneliness is an aspect of the land. All things in the plain are isolate; there is no confusion of objects in the eye, but *one* hill or *one* tree or *one* man. To look upon that landscape in the early morning, with the sun at your back, is to lose the sense of proportion. Your imagination comes to life, and this, you think, is where Creation was begun.

2 I returned to Rainy Mountain in July. My grandmother had died in the spring, and I wanted to be at her grave. She had lived to be very old and at last infirm. Her only living daughter was with her when she died, and I was told that in death her face was that of a child.

3 I like to think of her as a child. When she was born, the Kiowas were living the last great moment of their history. For more than a hundred years they had controlled the open range from the Smoky Hill River to the Red, from the head-waters of the Canadian to the fork of the Arkansas and Cimarron. In alliance with the Comanches, they had ruled the whole of the southern Plains. War was their sacred business, and they were among the finest horsemen the world has ever known. But warfare for the Kiowas was preeminently a matter of disposi-tion rather than of survival, and they never understood the grim, unrelenting advance of the U.S. Cavalry. When at last, divided and ill-provisioned, they were driven onto the Staked Plains in the cold rains of autumn, they fell into panic. In Palo Duro Canyon they abandoned their crucial stores to pillage and had nothing then but their lives. In order to save themselves, they surrendered to the soldiers at Fort Sill and were imprisoned in the old stone corral that now stands as a military museum. My grandmother was spared the humiliation of those high gray walls by eight or ten years, but she must have known from birth the affliction of defeat, the dark brooding of old warriors.

4 Her name was Aho, and she belonged to the last culture to evolve in North America. Her forebears came down from the high country in western Montana nearly three centuries ago. They were a mountain people, a mysteri-ous tribe of hunters whose language has never been positively classified in any major group. In the late seventeenth century they began a long migration to the south and east. It was a journey toward the dawn, and it led to a golden age. Along the way the Kiowas were befriended by the Crows, who gave them the culture and religion of the Plains. They acquired horses, and their ancient nomadic spirit was suddenly free of the ground. They acquired Tai-me, the sa-cred Sun Dance doll, from that moment the object and symbol of their wor-ship, and so shared in the divinity of the sun. Not least, they acquired the sense of destiny, therefore courage and pride. When they entered upon the southern Plains they had been transformed. No longer were they slaves to the simple necessity of survival; they were a lordly and dangerous society of fighters and thieves, hunters and priests of the sun. According to their origin myth, they en-tered the world through a hollow log. From one point of view, their migration was the fruit of an old prophecy, for indeed they emerged from a sunless world.

5   Although my grandmother lived out her long life in the shadow of Rainy Mountain, the immense landscape of the continental interior lay like memory in her blood. She could tell of the Crows, whom she had never seen, and of the Black Hills, where she had never been. I wanted to see in reality what she had seen more perfectly in the mind's eye, and traveled fifteen hundred miles to begin my pilgrimage.

6   Yellowstone, it seemed to me, was the top of the world, a region of deep lakes and dark timber, canyons and waterfalls. But, beautiful as it is, one might have the sense of confinement there. The skyline in all directions is close at hand, the high wall of the woods and deep cleavages of shade. There is a perfect freedom in the mountains, but it belongs to the eagle and the elk, the badger and the bear. The Kiowas reckoned their stature by the distance they could see, and they were bent and blind in the wilderness.

7   Descending eastward, the highland meadows are a stairway to the plain. In July the inland slope of the Rockies is luxuriant with flax and the buckwheat, stonecrop and larkspur. The earth unfolds and the limit of the land recedes. Clusters of trees, and animals grazing far in the distance, cause the vision to reach away and wonder to build upon the mind. The sun follows a longer course in the day, and the sky is immense beyond all comparison. The great billowing clouds that sail upon it are shadows that move upon the grain like water, dividing light. Farther down, in the land of the Crows and Blackfeet, the plain is yellow. Sweet clover takes hold of the hills and bends upon itself to cover and seal the soil. There the Kiowas paused on their way; they had come to the place where they must change their lives. The sun is at home on the plains. Precisely there does it have the certain character of a god. When the Kiowas came to the land of the Crows, they could see the dark lees of the hills at dawn across the Bighorn River, the profusion of light on the grain shelves, the oldest deity ranging after the solstices. Not yet would they veer southward to the caldron of the land that lay below; they must wean their blood from the northern winter and hold the mountains a while longer in their view. They bore Tai-me in procession to the east.

8   A dark mist lay over the Black Hills, and the land was like iron. At the top of a ridge I caught sight of Devil's Tower upthrust against the gray sky as if in the birth of time the core of the earth had broken through its crust and the motion of the world was begun. There are things in nature that engender an awful quiet in the heart of man; Devil's Tower is one of them. Two centuries ago, because they could not do otherwise, the Kiowas made a legend at the base of the rock. My grandmother said:

> Eight children were there at play, seven sisters and their brother. Suddenly the boy was struck dumb; he trembled and began to run upon his hands and feet. His fingers became claws, and his body was covered with fur. Directly there was a bear where the boy had been. The sisters were terrified; they ran, and the bear after them. They came to the stump of a great tree, and the tree spoke to them. It bade them climb upon it, and as they did so it began to rise into the air. The bear came to kill them, but they were just beyond its reach. It reared against the tree and

scored the bark all around with its claws. The seven sisters were borne into the sky, and they became the stars of the Big Dipper.

9   From that moment, and so long as the legend lives, the Kiowas have kinsmen in the night sky. Whatever they were in the mountains, they could be no more. However tenuous their well-being, however much they had suffered and would suffer again, they had found a way out of the wilderness.

My grandmother had a reverence for the sun, a holy regard that now is all but gone out of mankind. There was a wariness in her, and an ancient awe. She was a Christian in her later years, but she had come a long way about, and she never forgot her birthright. As a child she had been to the Sun Dances; she had taken part in those annual rites, and by them she had learned the restoration of her people in the presence of Tai-me. She was about seven when the last Kiowa Sun Dance was held in 1887 on the Washita River above Rainy Mountain Creek. The buffalo were gone. In order to consummate the ancient sacrifice—to impale the head of a buffalo bull upon the medicine tree—a delegation of old men journeyed into Texas, there to beg and barter for an animal from the Goodnight herd. She was ten when the Kiowas came together for the last time as a living Sun Dance culture. They could find no buffalo; they had to hang an old hide from the sacred tree. Before the dance could begin, a company of soldiers rode out from Fort Sill under orders to disperse the tribe. Forbidden without cause the essential act of their faith, having seen the wild herds slaughtered and left to rot upon the ground, the Kiowas backed away forever from the medicine tree. That was July 20, 1890, at the great bend of the Washita. My grandmother was there. Without bitterness, and for as long as she lived, she bore a vision of deicide.

10   Now that I can have her only in memory, I see my grandmother in the several postures that were peculiar to her: standing at the wood stove on a winter morning and turning meat in a great iron skillet; sitting at the south window, bent above her beadwork, and afterwards, when her vision failed, looking down for a long time into the fold of her hands; going out upon a cane, very slowly as she did when the weight of age came upon her; praying. I remember her most often at prayer. She made long, rambling prayers out of suffering and hope, having seen many things. I was never sure that I had the right to hear, so exclusive were they of all mere custom and company. The last time I saw her she prayed standing by the side of her bed at night, naked to the waist, the light of a kerosene lamp moving upon her dark skin. Her long, black hair, always drawn and braided in the day, lay upon her shoulders and against her breasts like a shawl. I do not speak Kiowa, and I never understood her prayers, but there was something inherently sad in the sound, some merest hesitation upon the syllables of sorrow. She began in a high and descending pitch, exhausting her breath to silence; then again and again—and always the same intensity of effort, of something that is, and is not, like urgency in the human voice. Transported so in the dancing light among the shadows of her room, she seemed beyond the reach of time. But that was illusion; I think I knew then that I should not see her again.

11   Houses are like sentinels in the plain, old keepers of the weather watch. There, in a very little while, wood takes on the appearance of great age. All colors wear soon away in the wind and rain, and then the wood is burned gray and the grain appears and the nails turn red with rust. The windowpanes are black and opaque; you imagine there is nothing within, and indeed there are many ghosts, bones given up to the land. They stand here and there against the sky, and you approach them for a longer time than you expect. They belong in the distance; it is their domain.

12   Once there was a lot of sound in my grandmother's house, a lot of coming and going, feasting and talk. The summers there were full of excitement and reunion. The Kiowas are a summer people; they abide the cold and keep to themselves, but when the season turns and the land becomes warm and vital they cannot hold still; an old love of going returns upon them. The aged visitors who came to my grandmother's house when I was a child were made of lean and leather, and they bore themselves upright. They wore great black hats and bright ample shirts that shook in the wind. They rubbed fat upon their hair and wound their braids with strips of colored cloth. Some of them painted their faces and carried the scars of old and cherished enmities. They were an old council of warlords, come to remind and be reminded of who they were. Their wives and daughters served them well. The women might indulge themselves; gossip was at once the mark and compensation of their servitude. They made loud and elaborate talk among themselves, full of jest and gesture, fright and false alarm. They went abroad in fringed and flowered shawls, bright beadwork and German silver. They were at home in the kitchen, and they prepared meals that were banquets.

13   There were frequent prayer meetings, and great nocturnal feasts. When I was a child I played with my cousins outside, where the lamplight fell upon the ground and the singing of the old people rose up around us and carried away into the darkness. There were a lot of good things to eat, a lot of laughter and surprise. And afterwards, when the quiet returned, I lay down with my grandmother and could hear the frogs away by the river and feel the motion of the air.

14   Now there is a funeral silence in the rooms, the endless wake of some final word. The walls have closed in upon my grandmother's house. When I returned to it in mourning, I saw for the first time in my life how small it was. It was late at night, and there was a white moon, nearly full. I sat for a long time on the stone steps by the kitchen door. From there I could see out across the land; I could see the long row of trees by the creek, the low light upon the rolling plains, and the stars of the Big Dipper. Once I looked at the moon and caught sight of a strange thing. A cricket had perched upon the handrail, only a few inches away from me. My line of vision was such that the creature filled the moon like a fossil. It had gone there, I thought, to live and die, for there, of all places, was its small definition made whole and eternal. A warm wind rose up and purled like the longing within me.

15   The next morning I awoke at dawn and went out on the dirt road to Rainy Mountain. It was already hot, and the grasshoppers began to fill the air. Still,

it was early in the morning, and the birds sang out of the shadows. The long yellow grass on the mountain shone in the bright light, and a scissortail hied above the land. There, where it ought to be, at the end of a long and legendary way, was my grandmother's grave. Here and there on the dark stones were ancestral names. Looking back once, I saw the mountain and came away.

TOPICS FOR WRITING AND DISCUSSION

1. Why does Momaday use his grandmother as the central figure of this essay? What does she represent to him in terms of his heritage?
2. For what purpose does the author take his readers on this trip to Rainy Mountain? To whom is this essay written?
3. Select three or four images that appeal to the reader's sense of sight, sound, smell, or touch. What do these images add to the descriptions of people or places?
4. How does Momaday structure his essay so that the reader realizes the end of both a literal and symbolic journey? What does Momaday mean when he describes his grandmother's grave "where it ought to be, at the end of a long and legendary way"?
5. Consider your own ethnic or cultural background. Is there one person or place that symbolizes your heritage for you? Write an essay describing this person or place, using distinctive detail (and historical information where necessary) to make your choice clear to readers who would appreciate knowing more about your culture.

E. B. White writing in his "office" boathouse at home in Brookline, Maine
(© 1988 by Jill Krementz)

ONCE MORE TO THE LAKE

E. B. White
(1899–1985)

Perhaps the finest essayist of his time, Elwyn Brooks
White was born in Mount Vernon, New York. He
attended Cornell University, where he studied with
William Strunk, author of *The Little Book,* the classic
textbook on writing. Years later, White revised it, and
renamed it *The Elements of Style* (1959). After graduating from Cornell, White joined the staff of *The New
Yorker* magazine. From 1938 to 1943 he wrote the
column "One Man's Meat" in *Harper's* magazine. He is
noted for his award-winning essays, his editorials, his
poetry, and his children's books, including the classics
Charlotte's Web and *Stuart Little* (1945). His essay
"Once More to the Lake" describes his memories of
vacations in Maine—both as a child and as a father
with his own child.

1   ONE summer, along about 1904, my father rented a camp on a lake in
Maine and took us all there for the month of August. We all got ringworm
from some kittens and had to rub Pond's Extract on our arms and legs night
and morning, and my father rolled over in a canoe with all his clothes on; but
outside of that the vacation was a success and from then on none of us ever
thought there was any place in the world like that lake in Maine. We returned
summer after summer—always on August 1 for one month. I have since become a salt-water man, but sometimes in summer there are days when the restlessness of the tides and the fearful cold of the sea water and the incessant
wind that blows across the afternoon and into the evening make me wish for
the placidity of a lake in the woods. A few weeks ago this feeling got so strong
I bought myself a couple of bass hooks and a spinner and returned to the lake
where we used to go, for a week's fishing and to revisit old haunts.

2   I took along my son, who had never had any fresh water up his nose and
who had seen lily pads only from train windows. On the journey over to the

lake I began to wonder what it would be like. I wondered how time would have marred this unique, this holy spot—the coves and streams, the hills that the sun set behind, the camps and the paths behind the camps. I was sure that the tarred road would have found it out, and I wondered in what other ways it would be desolated. It is strange how much you can remember about places like that once you allow your mind to return into the grooves that lead back. You remember one thing, and that suddenly reminds you of another thing. I guess I remembered clearest of all the early mornings, when the lake was cool and motionless, remembered how the bedroom smelled of the lumber it was made of and of the wet woods whose scent entered through the screen. The partitions in the camp were thin and did not extend clear to the top of the rooms, and as I was always the first up I would dress softly so as not to wake the others, and sneak out into the sweet outdoors and start out in the canoe, keeping close along the shore in the long shadows of the pines. I remembered being very careful never to rub my paddle against the gunwale for fear of disturbing the stillness of the cathedral.

3   The lake had never been what you would call a wild lake. There were cottages sprinkled around the shores, and it was in farming country although the shores of the lake were quite heavily wooded. Some of the cottages were owned by nearby farmers, and you would live at the shore and eat your meals at the farmhouse. That's what our family did. But although it wasn't wild, it was a fairly large and undisturbed lake and there were places in it that, to a child at least, seemed infinitely remote and primeval.

4   I was right about the tar: it led to within half a mile of the shore. But when I got back there, with my boy, and we settled into a camp near a farmhouse and into the kind of summertime I had known, I could tell that it was going to be pretty much the same as it had been before—I knew it, lying in bed the first morning, smelling the bedroom and hearing the boy sneak quietly out and go off along the shore in a boat. I began to sustain the illusion that he was I, and therefore, by simple transposition, that I was my father. This sensation persisted, kept cropping up all the time we were there. It was not an entirely new feeling, but in this setting it grew much stronger. I seemed to be living a dual existence. I would be in the middle of some simple act, I would be picking up a bait box or laying down a table fork, or I would be saying something, and suddenly it would be not I but my father who was saying the words or making the gesture. It gave me a creepy sensation.

5   We went fishing the first morning. I felt the same damp moss covering the worms in the bait can, and saw the dragonfly alight on the tip of my rod as it hovered a few inches from the surface of the water. It was the arrival of this fly that convinced me beyond any doubt that everything was as it always had been, that the years were a mirage and that there had been no years. The small waves were the same, chucking the rowboat under the chin as we fished at anchor, and the boat was the same boat, the same color green and the ribs broken in the same places, and under the floorboards the same fresh-water leavings and débris—the dead helgramite, the wisps of moss, the rusty discarded fishhook, the dried blood from yesterday's catch. We stared silently at

the tips of our rods, at the dragonflies that came and went. I lowered the tip of mine into the water, tentatively, pensively dislodging the fly, which darted two feet away, poised, darted two feet back, and came to rest again a little farther up the rod. There had been no years between the ducking of this dragonfly and the other one—the one that was part of memory. I looked at the boy, who was silently watching his fly, and it was my hands that held his rod, my eyes watching. I felt dizzy and didn't know which rod I was at the end of.

6   We caught two bass, hauling them in briskly as though they were mackerel, pulling them over the side of the boat in a businesslike manner without any landing net, and stunning them with a blow on the back of the head. When we got back for a swim before lunch, the lake was exactly where we had left it, the same number of inches from the dock, and there was only the merest suggestion of a breeze. This seemed an utterly enchanted sea, this lake you could leave to its own devices for a few hours and come back to, and find that it had not stirred, this constant and trustworthy body of water. In the shallows, the dark, water-soaked sticks and twigs, smooth and old, were undulating in clusters on the bottom against the clean ribbed sand, and the track of the mussel was plain. A school of minnows swam by, each minnow with its small individual shadow, doubling the attendance, so clear and sharp in the sunlight. Some of the other campers were in swimming, along the shore, one of them with a cake of soap, and the water felt thin and clear and unsubstantial. Over the years there had been this person with the cake of soap, this cultist, and here he was. There had been no years.

7   Up to the farmhouse to dinner through the teeming, dusty field, the road under our sneakers was only a two-track road. The middle track was missing, the one with the marks of the hooves and the splotches of dried, flaky manure. There had always been three tracks to choose from in choosing which track to walk in; now the choice was narrowed down to two. For a moment I missed terribly the middle alternative. But the way led past the tennis court, and something about the way it lay there in the sun reassured me; the tape had loosened along the backline, the alleys were green with plantains and other weeds, and the net (installed in June and removed in September) sagged in the dry noon, and the whole place steamed with midday heat and hunger and emptiness. There was a choice of pie for dessert, and one was blueberry and one was apple, and the waitresses were the same country girls, there having been no passage of time, only the illusion of it as in a dropped curtain—the waitresses were still fifteen; their hair had been washed, that was the only difference— they had been to the movies and seen the pretty girls with the clean hair.

8   Summertime, oh, summertime, pattern of life indelible, the fade-proof lake, the woods unshatterable, the pasture with the sweetfern and the juniper forever and ever, summer without end; this was the background, and the life along the shore was the design, their tiny docks with the flagpole and the American flag floating against the white clouds in the blue sky, the little paths over the roots of the trees leading from camp to camp and the paths leading back to the outhouses and the can of lime for sprinkling, and at the souvenir counters at the store the miniature birchbark canoes and the postcards that

showed things looking a little better than they looked. This was the American family at play, escaping the city heat, wondering whether the newcomers in the camp at the head of the cover were "common" or "nice," wondering whether it was true that the people who drove up for Sunday dinner at the farmhouse were turned away because there wasn't enough chicken.

9   It seemed to me, as I kept remembering all this, that those times and those summers had been infinitely precious and worth saving. There had been jollity and peace and goodness. The arriving (at the beginning of August) had been so big a business in itself, at the railway station the farm wagon drawn up, the first smell of the pine-laden air, the first glimpse of the smiling farmer, and the great importance of the trunks and your father's enormous authority in such matters, and the feel of the wagon under you for the long ten-mile haul, and at the top of the last long hill catching the first view of the lake after eleven months of not seeing this cherished body of water. The shouts and cries of the other campers when they saw you, and the trunks to be unpacked, to give up their rich burden. (Arriving was less exciting nowadays, when you sneaked up in your car and parked it under a tree near the camp and took out the bags and in five minutes it was all over, no fuss, no loud wonderful fuss about trunks.)

10   Peace and goodness and jollity. The only thing that was wrong now, really, was the sound of the place, an unfamiliar nervous sound of the outboard motors. This was the note that jarred, the one thing that would sometimes break the illusion and set the years moving. In those other summertimes all motors were inboard; and when they were at a little distance, the noise they made was a sedative, an ingredient of summer sleep. They were one-cylinder and two-cylinder engines, and some were make-and-break and some were jump-spark, but they all made a sleepy sound across the lake. The one-lungers throbbed and fluttered, and the twin-cylinder ones purred and purred, and that was a quiet sound, too. But now the campers all had outboards. In the daytime, in the hot mornings, these motors made a petulant, irritable sound; at night, in the still evening when the afterglow lit the water, they whined about one's ears like mosquitoes. My boy loved our rented outboard, and his great desire was to achieve single-handed mastery over it, and authority, and he soon learned the trick of choking it a little (but not too much), and the adjustment of the needle valve. Watching him I would remember the things you could do with the old one-cylinder engine with the heavy flywheel, how you could have it eating out of your hand if you got really close to it spiritually. Motorboats in those days didn't have clutches, and you would make a landing by shutting off the motor at the proper time and coasting in with a dead rudder. But there was a way of reversing them, if you learned the trick, by cutting the switch and putting it on again exactly on the final dying revolution of the flywheel, so that it would kick back against compression and begin reversing. Approaching a dock in a strong following breeze, it was difficult to slow up sufficiently by the ordinary coasting method, and if a boy felt he had complete mastery over his motor, he was tempted to keep it running beyond its time and then reverse it a few feet from the dock. It took a cool nerve, because if you threw the switch a twentieth of a second too soon you would catch the flywheel when it still had

speed enough to go up past center, and the boat would leap ahead, charging bull-fashion at the dock.

11   We had a good week at the camp. The bass were biting well and the sun shone endlessly, day after day. We would be tired at night and lie down in the accumulated heat of the little bedrooms after the long hot day and the breeze would stir almost imperceptibly outside and the smell of the swamp drift in through the rusty screens. Sleep would come easily and in the morning the red squirrel would be on the roof, tapping out his gay routine. I kept remembering everything, lying in bed in the mornings—the small steamboat that had a long rounded stern like the lip of a Ubangi, and how quietly she ran on the moonlight sails, when the older boys played their mandolins and the girls sang and we ate doughnuts dipped in sugar, and how sweet the music was on the water in the shining night, and what it had felt like to think about girls then. After breakfast we would go up to the store and the things were in the same place— the minnows in a bottle, the plugs and spinners disarranged and pawed over by the youngsters from the boys' camp, the Fig Newtons and the Beeman's gum. Outside, the road was tarred and cars stood in front of the store. Inside, all was just as it had always been, except there was more Coca-Cola, and not so much Moxie and root beer and birch beer and sarsaparilla. We would walk out with the bottle of pop apiece and sometimes the pop would backfire up our noses and hurt. We explored the streams, quietly, where the turtles slid off the sunny logs and dug their way into the soft bottom; and we lay on the town wharf and fed worms to the tame bass. Everywhere we went I had trouble making out which was I, the one walking at my side, the one walking in my pants.

12   One afternoon while we were there at that lake a thunderstorm came up. It was like the revival of an old melodrama that I had seen long ago with childish awe. The second-act climax of the drama of the electrical disturbance over a lake in America had not changed in any important respect. This was the big scene, still the big scene. The whole thing was so familiar, the first feeling of oppression and heat and a general air around camp of not wanting to go very far away. In mid-afternoon (it was all the same) a curious darkening of the sky, and a lull in everything that had made life tick; and then the way the boats suddenly swung the other way at their moorings with the coming of a breeze out of the new quarter, and the premonitory rumble. Then the kettle drum, then the snare, then the bass drum and cymbals, then crackling light against the dark, and the gods grinning and licking their chops in the hills. Afterward the calm, the rain steadily rustling in the calm lake, the return of light and hope and spirits, and the campers running out in joy and relief to go swimming in the rain, their bright cries perpetuating the deathless joke about how they were getting simply drenched, and the children screaming with delight at the new sensation of bathing in the rain, and the joke about getting drenched linking the generations in a strong indestructible chain. And the comedian who waded in carrying an umbrella.

13   When the others went swimming, my son said he was going in, too. He pulled his dripping trunks from the line where they had hung all through the

shower and wrung them out. Languidly, and with no thought of going in, I watched him, his hard little body, skinny and bare, saw him wince slightly as he pulled up around his vitals the small, soggy, icy garment. As he buckled the swollen belt, suddenly my groin felt the chill of death.

TOPICS FOR WRITING AND DISCUSSION

1. Make a list of six changes White observes when he takes his son to the lake. Then make a list of six things that have stayed the same. What do these differences and similarities suggest about the nature of his vacations at the lake as compared to his son's vacation?

2. White says that while he was at the lake he seemed to be living a "dual existence." What does he mean by this? How does his sense of the distortion of time relate to his "dual existence"?

3. Analyze the rhythm of the language in paragraph 8 (beginning "Summertime, oh, summertime"). What does the rhythm contribute to the images? What tone is created by the combination of rhythm and images?

4. The final paragraph describes White watching his son pull on a wet bathing suit and feeling in his own groin "the chill of death." Why does he feel this premonition? How is this image connected to the images in the rest of the essay? Has anything in the essay prepared the reader for the sense of mortality White describes in the conclusion?

5. Think of a favorite childhood vacation place and describe making a return visit now, bringing with you a younger brother, sister, son, daughter, or friend. The return visit may be either real or imagined, but be sure to describe the differences you observe and to comment on their significance both to you and to the person you have brought with you.

AN AMERICAN CHILDHOOD

Annie Dillard
(1945–   )

Born in Pittsburgh in 1945, Annie Dillard is both a
writer and a naturalist. She attended Hollins College in
Virginia, and there she kept a notebook in which she
wrote her observations of the nature and wildlife found
in the Roanoke Valley. Her journal entries became a
collection of essays entitled *Pilgrim at Tinker Creek*
(1974), which won the Pulitzer Prize for nonfiction.
Her *Encounters with Chinese Writers* (1984), another
essay collection, is based on her observations of the
Chinese when she was a U.S. cultural delegate to the
People's Republic of China and a member of the
National Commission of U.S.–China Relations. Dillard
has written two collections of narrative essays, *Holy
the Firm* (1977), a highly contemplative meditation on
the human spirit, and *Teaching a Stone to Talk* (1982).
She has also published a memoir, *An American Childhood* (1987); a book of poetry, *Tickets for a Prayer
Wheel* (1974); a book examining the act of writing, *A
Writer's Life* (1989); a historical novel set in the Pacific
Northwest, *The Living* (1992); and her most recent
work, *Mornings Like This: Found Poems* (1996),
another collection of poetry. The following essay is an
excerpt from her memoir by the same title. In it, Dillard presents an affectionate portrait of her mother and
her mother's legacy.

1   ONE Sunday afternoon Mother wandered through our kitchen, where Father was making a sandwich and listening to the ball game. The Pirates were
playing the New York Giants at Forbes Field. In those days, the Giants had a

Annie Dillard (© Nancy Crampton)

utility infielder named Wayne Terwilliger. Just as Mother passed through, the radio announcer cried—with undue drama—"Terwilliger bunts one!"

2   "Terwilliger bunts one?" Mother cried back, stopped short. She turned. "Is that English?"

3   "The player's name is Terwilliger," Father said. "He bunted."

4   "That's marvelous," Mother said. "'Terwilliger bunts one.' No wonder you listen to baseball. 'Terwilliger bunts one.'"

5   For the next seven or eight years, Mother made this surprising string of syllables her own. Testing a microphone, she repeated, "Terwilliger bunts one"; testing a pen or typewriter, she wrote it. If, as happened surprisingly often in the course of various improvised gags, she pretended to whisper something else in my ear, she actually whispered, "Terwilliger bunts one." Whenever someone used a French phrase, or a Latin one, she answered solemnly, "Terwilliger bunts one." If Mother had had, like Andrew Carnegie, the opportunity to cook up a motto for a coat of arms, hers would have read simply and tellingly, "Terwilliger bunts one." (Carnegie's was "Death to Privilege.")

6   She served us with other words and phrases. On a Florida trip, she repeated tremulously, "That . . . is a royal poinciana." I don't remember the tree; I remember the thrill in her voice. She pronounced it carefully, and spelled it. She also liked to say "portulaca."

7   The drama of the words "Tamiami Trail" stirred her, we learned on the same Florida trip. People built Tampa on one coast, and they built Miami on another. Then—the height of visionary ambition and folly—they piled a slow, tremendous road through the terrible Everglades to connect them. To build the road, men stood sunk in muck to their armpits. They fought off cottonmouth moccasins and six-foot alligators. They slept in boats, wet. They blasted muck with dynamite, cut jungle with machetes; they laid logs, dragged drilling machines, hauled dredges, heaped limestone. The road took fourteen years to build up by the shovelful, a Panama Canal in reverse, and cost hundreds of lives from tropical, mosquito-carried diseases. Then, capping it all, some genius thought of the word Tamiami: they called the road from Tampa to Miami, this very road under our spinning wheels, the Tamiami Trail. Some called it Alligator Alley. Anyone could drive over this road without a thought.

8   Hearing this, moved, I thought all the suffering of road building was worth it (it wasn't my suffering), now that we had this new thing to hang these new words on—Alligator Alley for those who liked things cute, and, for connoisseurs like Mother, for lovers of the human drama in all its boldness and terror, the Tamiami Trail.

9   Back home, Mother cut clips from reels of talk, as it were, and played them back at leisure. She noticed that many Pittsburghers confuse "leave" and "let." One kind relative brightened our morning by mentioning why she'd brought her son to visit: "He wanted to come with me, so I left him." Mother filled in Amy and me on locutions we missed. "I can't do it on Friday," her pretty sister told a crowded dinner party, "because Friday's the day I lay in the stores."

10   (All unconsciously, though, we ourselves used some pure Pittsburghisms. We said "tele pole," pronounced "telly pole," for that splintery sidewalk post

I loved to climb. We said "slippy"—the sidewalks are "slippy." We said, "That's all the farther I could go." And we said, as Pittsburghers do say, "This glass needs washed," or "The dog needs walked"—a usage our father eschewed; he knew it was not standard English, nor even comprehensible English, but he never let on.)

11   "Spell 'poinsettia,'" Mother would throw out at me, smiling with pleasure. "Spell 'sherbet.'" The idea was not to make us whizzes, but, quite the contrary, to remind us—and I, especially, needed reminding—that we didn't know it all just yet.

12   "There's a deer standing in the front hall," she told me one quiet evening in the country.

13   "Really?"

14   "No. I just wanted to tell you something once without your saying, 'I know.'"

15   Supermarkets in the middle 1950s began luring, or bothering, customers by giving out Top Value Stamps or Green Stamps. When, shopping with Mother, we got to the head of the checkout line, the checker, always a young man, asked, "Save stamps?"

16   "No," Mother replied genially, week after week, "I build model airplanes." I believe she originated this line. It took me years to determine where the joke lay.

17   Anyone who met her verbal challenges she adored. She had surgery on one of her eyes. On the operating table, just before she conked out, she appealed feelingly to the surgeon, saying, as she had been planning to say for weeks, "Will I be able to play the piano?" "Not on me," the surgeon said. "You won't pull that old one on me."

18   It was, indeed, an old one. The surgeon was supposed to answer, "Yes, my dear, brave woman, you will be able to play the piano after this operation," to which Mother intended to reply, "Oh, good, I've always wanted to play the piano." This pat scenario bored her; she loved having it interrupted. It must have galled her that usually her acquaintances were so predictably unalert; it must have galled her that, for the length of her life, she could surprise everyone so continually, so easily, when she had been the same all along. At any rate, she loved anyone who, as she put it, saw it coming, and called her on it.

19   She regarded the instructions on bureaucratic forms as straight lines. "Do you advocate the overthrow of the United States government by force or violence?" After some thought she wrote, "Force." She regarded children, even babies, as straight men. When Molly learned to crawl, Mother delighted in buying her gowns with drawstrings at the bottom, like Swee'pea's, because, as she explained energetically, you could easily step on the drawstring without the baby's noticing, so that she crawled and crawled and crawled and never got anywhere except into a small ball at the gown's top.

20   When we children were young, she mothered us tenderly and dependably; as we got older, she resumed her career of anarchism. She collared us into her

gags. If she answered the phone on a wrong number, she told the caller, "Just a minute," and dragged the receiver to Amy or me, saying, "Here, take this, your name is Cecile," or, worse, just, "It's for you." You had to think on your feet. But did you want to perform well as Cecile, or did you want to take pity on the wretched caller?

21   During a family trip to the Highland Park Zoo, Mother and I were alone for a minute. She approached a young couple holding hands on a bench by the seals, and addressed the young man in dripping tones: "Where have you been? Still got those baby-blue eyes; always did slay me. And this"—a swift nod at the dumbstruck young woman, who had removed her hand from the man's— "must be the one you were telling me about. She's not so bad, really, as you used to make out. But listen, you know how I miss you, you know where to reach me, same old place. And there's Ann over there—see how she's grown? See the blue eyes?"

22   And off she sashayed, taking me firmly by the hand, and leading us around briskly past the monkey house and away. She cocked an ear back, and both of us heard the desperate man begin, in a high-pitched wail, "I swear, I never saw her before in my life. . . ."

23   On a long, sloping beach by the ocean, she lay stretched out sunning with Father and friends, until the conversation gradually grew tedious, when without forethought she gave a little push with her heel and rolled away. People were stunned. She rolled deadpan and apparently effortlessly, arms and legs extended and tidy, down the beach to the distant water's edge, where she lay at ease just as she had been, but half in the surf, and well out of earshot.

24   She dearly loved to fluster people by throwing out a game's rules at whim—when she was getting bored, losing in a dull sort of way, and when everybody else was taking it too seriously. If you turned your back, she moved the checkers around on the board. When you got them all straightened out, she denied she'd touched them; the next time you turned your back, she lined them up on the rug or hid them under your chair. In a betting rummy game called Michigan, she routinely played out of turn, or called out a card she didn't hold, or counted backward, simply to amuse herself by causing an uproar and watching the rest of us do double takes and have fits. (Much later, when serious suitors came to call, Mother subjected them to this fast card game as a trial by ordeal; she used it as an intelligence test and a measure of spirit. If the poor man could stay a round without breaking down or running out, he got to marry one of us, if he still wanted to.)

25   She excelled at bridge, playing fast and boldly, but when the stakes were low and the hands dull, she bid slams for the devilment of it, or raised her opponents' suit to bug them, or showed her hand, or tossed her cards in a handful behind her back in a characteristic swift motion accompanied by a vibrantly innocent look. It drove our stolid father crazy. The hand was over before it began, and the guests were appalled. How do you score it, who deals now, what do you do with a crazy person who is having so much fun? Or they

were down seven, and the guests were appalled. "Pam!" "Dammit, Pam!" He groaned. What ails such people? What on earth possesses them? He rubbed his face.

26   She was an unstoppable force; she never let go. When we moved across town, she persuaded the U.S. Post Office to let her keep her old address—forever—because she'd had stationery printed. I don't know how she did it. Every new post office worker, over decades, needed to learn that although the Doaks' mail is addressed to here, it is delivered to there.

27   Mother's energy and intelligence suited her for a greater role in a larger arena—mayor of New York, say—than the one she had. She followed American politics closely; she had been known to vote for Democrats. She saw how things should be run, but she had nothing to run but our household. Even there, small minds bugged her; she was smarter than the people who designed the things she had to use all day for the length of her life.

28   "Look," she said. "Whoever designed this corkscrew never used one. Why would anyone sell it without trying it out?" So she invented a better one. She showed me a drawing of it. The spirit of American enterprise never faded in Mother. If capitalizing and tooling up had been as interesting as theorizing and thinking up, she would have fired up a new factory every week, and chaired several hundred corporations.

29   "It grieves me," she would say, "it grieves my heart," that the company that made one superior product packaged it poorly, or took the wrong tack in its advertising. She knew, as she held the thing mournfully in her two hands, that she'd never find another. She was right. We children wholly sympathized, and so did Father; what could she do, what could anyone do, about it? She was Samson in chains. She paced.

30   She didn't like the taste of stamps so she didn't lick stamps; she licked the corner of the envelope instead. She glued sandpaper to the sides of kitchen drawers, and under kitchen cabinets, so she always had a handy place to strike a match. She designed, and hounded workmen to build against all norms, doubly wide kitchen counters and elevated bathroom sinks. To splint a finger, she stuck it in a lightweight cigar tube. Conversely, to protect a pack of cigarettes, she carried it in a Band-Aid box. She drew plans for an over-the-finger toothbrush for babies, an oven rack that slid up and down, and—the family favorite—Lendalarm. Lendalarm was a beeper you attached to books (or tools) you loaned friends. After ten days, the beeper sounded. Only the rightful owner could silence it.

31   She repeatedly reminded us of P. T. Barnum's dictum: You could sell anything to anybody if you marketed it right. The adman who thought of making Americans believe they needed underarm deodorant was a visionary. So, too, was the hero who made a success of a new product, Ivory soap. The executives were horrified, Mother told me, that a cake of this stuff floated. Soap wasn't supposed to float. Anyone would be able to tell it was mostly whipped-up air. Then some inspired adman made a leap: Advertise that it floats. Flaunt it. The rest is history.

32   She respected the rare few who broke through to new ways. "Look," she'd say, "here's an intelligent apron." She called upon us to admire intelligent control knobs and intelligent pan handles, intelligent andirons and picture frames and knife sharpeners. She questioned everything, every pair of scissors, every knitting needle, gardening glove, tape dispenser. Hers was a restless mental vigor that just about ignited the dumb household objects with its force.

33   Torpid conformity was a kind of sin; it was stupidity itself, the mighty stream against which Mother would never cease to struggle. If you held no minority opinions, or if you failed to risk total ostracism for them daily, the world would be a better place without you.

34   Always I heard Mother's emotional voice asking Amy and me the same few questions: "Is that your own idea? Or somebody else's?" "*Giant* is a good movie," I pronounced to the family at dinner. "Oh, really?" Mother warmed to these occasions. She all but rolled up her sleeves. She knew I hadn't seen it. "Is that your considered opinion?"

35   She herself held many unpopular, even fantastic, positions. She was scathingly sarcastic about the McCarthy hearings while they took place, right on our living-room television; she frantically opposed Father's wait-and-see calm. "We don't know enough about it," he said. "I do," she said. "I know all I need to know."

36   She asserted, against all opposition, that people who lived in trailer parks were not bad but simply poor, and had as much right to settle on beautiful land, such as rural Ligonier, Pennsylvania, as did the oldest of families in the finest of hidden houses. Therefore, the people who owned trailer parks, and sought zoning changes to permit trailer parks, needed our help. Her profound belief that the country-club pool sweeper was a person, and that the department-store saleslady, the bus driver, telephone operator, and housepainter were people, and even in groups the steelworkers who carried pickets and the Christmas shoppers who clogged intersections were people—this was a conviction common enough in democratic Pittsburgh, but not altogether common among our friends' parents, or even, perhaps, among our parents' friends.

37   Opposition emboldened Mother, and she would take on anybody on any issue—the chairman of the board, at a cocktail party, on the current strike; she would fly at him in a flurry of passion, as a songbird selflessly attacks a big hawk.

38   "Eisenhower's going to win," I announced after school. She lowered her magazine and looked me in the eyes: "How do you know?" I was doomed. It was fatal to say, "Everyone says so." We all knew well what happened. "Do you consult this Everyone before you make your decisions? What if Everyone decided to round up all the Jews?" Mother knew there was no danger of cowing me. She simply tried to keep us all awake. And in fact it was always clear to Amy and me, and to Molly when she grew old enough to listen, that if our

classmates came to cruelty, just as much as if the neighborhood or the nation came to madness, we were expected to take, and would be each separately capable of taking, a stand.

Topics for Writing and Discussion

1. In this affectionate description, Dillard reveals her mother's character most clearly by showing her in action. Had she chosen to include a statement that summarized precisely the dominant impression her mother made, what would it say?

2. What is the effect of Dillard's beginning with the extended "Terwilliger bunts one" anecdote?

3. Although "An American Childhood" is primarily a portrait of her mother, the reader also learns a great deal about Dillard herself and her mother's impact on her. What legacies do you think helped form Dillard's character and personality? What evidence can you cite from the text to support your answer?

4. Her mother's influence also can be detected in Dillard's skill and playfulness with language. What are some of the best examples of her descriptive language in this essay?

5. Write a character sketch of one of your parents or another family member, using a number of specific anecdotes that illustrate a single character trait. Consider including dialogue that lets the character reveal his or her own idiosyncrasies. Remember, Dillard's mother was a complex and multifaceted woman. The picture Dillard paints is effective because it focuses on the most distinctive characteristic of her mother, not every feature.

IF SHAKESPEARE HAD HAD A SISTER

Virginia Woolf
(1882–1941)

Born in London, the daughter of respected biographer
and scholar Sir Leslie Stephen, Virginia Woolf was
informally educated and never attended a university.
However, her extraordinary inquisitiveness, keen mind,
and voracious appetite for reading and learning provided her with an ample education. As a teenager, she
began the habit of keeping a journal and matured into
a prolific essayist and novelist. In 1912, she married
author and publisher Leonard Woolf. She and her husband formed the "Bloomsbury Group" with her sister
Vanessa and brother-in-law, the art critic Clive Bell,
economist John Maynard Keynes, painter Roger Frye,
biographer Lytton Strachey, and novelist E. M. Forster.
The Bloomsbury Group, named after a section of London near the British Museum, committed themselves to
excellence in literature and art and rebelled against the
traditions of the Victorians.

Woolf's novels *To the Lighthouse* (1927) and
Orlando (1929) were well received and helped to
establish her as a major writer. Other novels include
Jacob's Room (1922), *Mrs. Dalloway* (1925), and
The Waves (1931). Although Woolf is best known for
her novels, she was also a distinguished literary and
social critic. Among her best-known nonfiction is *A
Room of One's Own* (1929), a collection of lectures
exploring the roles and pressures faced by women. "If
Shakespeare Had Had a Sister" is taken from that
work and describes the frustrations a female writer
might have encountered in Shakespeare's time.

Virginia Woolf (© 1935 Man Ray)

1   I T was disappointing not to have brought back in the evening some important statement, some authentic fact. Women are poorer than men because—this or that. Perhaps now it would be better to give up seeking for the truth, and receiving on one's head an avalanche of opinion hot as lava, discoloured as dishwater. It would be better to draw the curtains; to shut out distractions; to light the lamp; to narrow the enquiry and to ask the historian, who records not opinions but facts, to describe under what conditions women lived, not throughout the ages, but in England, say, in the time of Elizabeth.

2   For it is a perennial puzzle why no woman wrote a word of that extraordinary literature when every other man, it seemed, was capable of song or sonnet. What were the conditions in which women lived, I asked myself; for fiction, imaginative work that is, is not dropped like a pebble upon the ground, as science may be; fiction is like a spider's web, attached ever so lightly perhaps, but still attached to life at all four corners. Often the attachment is scarcely perceptible; Shakespeare's plays, for instance, seem to hang there complete by themselves. But when the web is pulled askew, hooked up at the edge, torn in the middle, one remembers that these webs are not spun in midair by incorporeal creatures, but are the work of suffering human beings, and are attached to grossly material things, like health and money and the houses we live in.

3   I went, therefore, to the shelf where the histories stand and took down one of the latest, Professor Trevelyan's *History of England.* Once more I looked up Women, found "position of," and turned to the pages indicated. "Wife-beating," I read, "was a recognised right of man, and was practised without shame by high as well as low. . . . Similarly," the historian goes on, "the daughter who refused to marry the gentleman of her parents' choice was liable to be locked up, beaten and flung about the room, without any shock being inflicted on public opinion. Marriage was not an affair of personal affection, but of family avarice, particularly in the 'chivalrous' upper classes. . . . Betrothal often took place while one or both of the parties was in the cradle, and marriage when they were scarcely out of the nurses' charge." That was about 1470, soon after Chaucer's time. The next reference to the position of women is some two hundred years later, in the time of the Stuarts. "It was still the exception for women of the upper and middle class to choose their own husbands, and when the husband had been assigned, he was lord and master, so far at least as law and custom could make him. Yet even so," Professor Trevelyan concludes, "neither Shakespeare's women nor those of authentic seventeenth-century memoirs, like the Verneys and the Hutchinsons, seem wanting in personality and character." Certainly, if we consider it, Cleopatra must have had a way with her; Lady Macbeth, one would suppose, had a will of her own; Rosalind, one might conclude, was an attractive girl. Professor Trevelyan is speaking no more than the truth when he remarks that Shakespeare's women do not seem wanting in personality and character. Not being a historian, one might go even further and say that women have burnt like beacons in all the works of all the poets from the beginning of time—Clytemnestra, Antigone,

Cleopatra, Lady Macbeth, Phèdre, Cressida, Rosalind, Desdemona, the Duchess of Malfi, among the dramatists; then among the prose writers: Millamant, Clarissa, Becky Sharp, Anna Karenina, Emma Bovary, Madame de Guermantes—the names flock to mind, nor do they recall women "lacking in personality and character." Indeed, if woman had no existence save in the fiction written by men, one would imagine her a person of the utmost importance; very various; heroic and mean; splendid and sordid; infinitely beautiful and hideous in the extreme; as great as a man, some think even greater. But this is woman in fiction. In fact, as Professor Trevelyan points out, she was locked up, beaten and flung about the room.

4   A very queer, composite being thus emerges. Imaginatively she is of the highest importance; practically she is completely insignificant. She pervades poetry from cover to cover; she is all but absent from history. She dominates the lives of kings and conquerors in fiction; in fact she was the slave of any boy whose parents forced a ring upon her finger. Some of the most inspired words, some of the most profound thoughts in literature fall from her lips; in real life she could hardly read, could scarcely spell, and was the property of her husband.

5   It was certainly an odd monster that one made up by reading the historians first and the poets afterwards—a worm winged like an eagle; the spirit of life and beauty in a kitchen chopping up suet. But these monsters, however amusing to the imagination, have no existence in fact. What one must do to bring her to life was to think poetically and prosaically at one and the same moment, thus keeping in touch with fact—that she is Mrs. Martin, aged thirty-six, dressed in blue, wearing a black hat and brown shoes; but not losing sight of fiction either—that she is a vessel in which all sorts of spirits and forces are coursing and flashing perpetually. The moment, however, that one tries this method with the Elizabethan woman, one branch of illumination fails; one is held up by the scarcity of facts. One knows nothing detailed, nothing perfectly true and substantial about her. History scarcely mentions her. And I turned to Professor Trevelyan again to see what history meant to him. I found by looking at his chapter headings that it meant—

6   "The Manor Court and the Methods of Open-field Agriculture . . . The Cistercians and Sheep-farming . . . The Crusades . . . The University . . . The House of Commons . . . The Hundred Years' War . . . The Wars of the Roses . . . The Renaissance Scholars . . . The Dissolution of the Monasteries . . . Agrarian and Religious Strife . . . The Origin of English Seapower . . . The Armada . . ." and so on. Occasionally an individual woman is mentioned, an Elizabeth, or a Mary; a queen or a great lady. But by no possible means could middle-class women with nothing but brains and character at their command have taken part in any one of the great movements which, brought together, constitute the historian's view of the past. Nor shall we find her in any collection of anecdotes. Aubrey hardly mentions her. She never writes her own life and scarcely keeps a diary; there are only a handful of her letters in existence. She left no plays or poems by which we can judge her. What one wants, I thought—and why does not some brilliant student at Newnham or Girton

supply it?—is a mass of information; at what age did she marry; how many children had she as a rule; what was her house like; had she a room to herself; did she do the cooking; would she be likely to have a servant? All these facts lie somewhere, presumably, in parish registers and account books; the life of the average Elizabethan woman must be scattered about somewhere, could one collect it and make a book of it. It would be ambitious beyond my daring, I thought, looking about the shelves for books that were not there, to suggest to the students of those famous colleges that they should re-write history, though I own that it often seems a little queer as it is, unreal, lopsided; but why should they not add a supplement to history? calling it, of course, by some inconspicuous name so that women might figure there without impropriety? For one often catches a glimpse of them in the lives of the great, whisking away into the background, concealing, I sometimes think, a wink, a laugh, perhaps a tear. And, after all, we have lives enough of Jane Austen; it scarcely seems necessary to consider again the influence of the tragedies of Joanna Baillie upon the poetry of Edgar Allan Poe; as for myself, I should not mind if the homes and haunts of Mary Russell Mitford were closed to the public for a century at least. But what I find deplorable, I continued, looking about the bookshelves again, is that nothing is known about women before the eighteenth century. I have no model in my mind to turn about this way and that. Here I am asking why women did not write poetry in the Elizabethan age, and I am not sure how they were educated; whether they were taught to write; whether they had sitting-rooms to themselves; how many women had children before they were twenty-one; what, in short, they did from eight in the morning till eight at night. They had no money evidently; according to Professor Trevelyan they were married whether they liked it or not before they were out of the nursery, at fifteen or sixteen very likely. It would have been extremely odd, even upon this showing, had one of them suddenly written the plays of Shakespeare, I concluded, and I thought of that old gentleman, who is dead now, but was a bishop, I think, who declared that it was impossible for any woman, past, present, or to come, to have the genius of Shakespeare. He wrote to the papers about it. He also told a lady who applied to him for information that cats do not as a matter of fact go to heaven, though they have, he added, souls of a sort. How much thinking those old gentlemen used to save one! How the borders of ignorance shrank back at their approach! Cats do not go to heaven. Women cannot write the plays of Shakespeare.

7   Be that as it may, I could not help thinking, as I looked at the works of Shakespeare on the shelf, that the bishop was right at least in this; it would have been impossible, completely and entirely, for any woman to have written the plays of Shakespeare in the age of Shakespeare. Let me imagine, since facts are so hard to come by, what would have happened had Shakespeare had a wonderfully gifted sister, called Judith, let us say. Shakespeare himself went, very probably—his mother was an heiress—to the grammar school, where he may have learnt Latin—Ovid, Virgil and Horace—and the elements of grammar and logic. He was, it is well known, a wild boy who poached rabbits, perhaps shot a deer, and had, rather sooner than he should have done, to marry a

woman in the neighbourhood, who bore him a child rather quicker than was right. That escapade sent him to seek his fortune in London. He had, it seemed, a taste for theatre; he began by holding horses at the stage door. Very soon he got work in the theatre, became a successful actor, and lived at the hub of the universe, meeting everybody, knowing everybody, practising his art on the boards, exercising his wits in the streets, and even getting access to the palace of the queen. Meanwhile his extraordinarily gifted sister, let us suppose, remained at home. She was as adventurous, as imaginative, as agog to see the world as he was. But she was not sent to school. She had no chance of learning grammar and logic, let alone of reading Horace and Virgil. She picked up a book now and then, one of her brother's perhaps, and read a few pages. But then her parents came in and told her to mend the stockings or mind the stew and not moon about with books and papers. They would have spoken sharply but kindly, for they were substantial people who knew the conditions of life for a woman and loved their daughter—indeed, more likely than not she was the apple of her father's eye. Perhaps she scribbled some pages up in an apple loft on the sly, but was careful to hide them or set fire to them. Soon, however, before she was out of her teens, she was to be betrothed to the son of a neighbouring wool-stapler. She cried out that marriage was hateful to her, and for that she was severely beaten by her father. Then he ceased to scold her. He begged her instead not to hurt him, not to shame him in this matter of her marriage. He would give her a chain of beads or a fine petticoat, he said; and there were tears in his eyes. How could she disobey him? How could she break his heart? The force of her own gift alone drove her to it. She made up a small parcel of her belongings, let herself down by a rope one summer's night and took the road to London. She was not seventeen. The birds that sang in the hedge were not more musical than she was. She had the quickest fancy, a gift like her brother's, for the tune of words. Like him, she had a taste for the theatre. She stood at the stage door; she wanted to act, she said. Men laughed in her face. The manager—a fat, loose-lipped man—guffawed. He bellowed something about poodles dancing and women acting—no woman, he said, could possibly be an actress. He hinted—you can imagine what. She could get no training in her craft. Could she even seek her dinner in a tavern or roam the streets at midnight? Yet her genius was for fiction and lusted to feed abundantly upon the lives of men and women and the study of their ways. At last—for she was very young, oddly like Shakespeare the poet in her face, with the same grey eyes and rounded brows—at last Nick Greene the actor-manager took pity on her; she found herself with child by that gentleman and so—who shall measure the heat and violence of the poet's heart when caught and tangled in a woman's body?—killed herself one winter's night and lies buried at some cross-roads where the omnibuses now stop outside the Elephant and Castle.

8   That, more or less, is how the story would run, I think, if a woman in Shakespeare's day had had Shakespeare's genius. But for my part, I agree with the deceased bishop, if such he was—it is unthinkable that any woman in Shakespeare's day should have had Shakespeare's genius. For genius like

Shakespeare's is not born among labouring, uneducated, servile people. It was not born in England among the Saxons and the Britons. It is not born today among the working classes. How, then, could it have been born among women whose work began, according to Professor Trevelyan, almost before they were out of the nursery, who were forced to it by their parents and held to it by all the power of law and custom? Yet genius of a sort must have existed among women as it must have existed among the working classes. Now and again an Emily Brontë or a Robert Burns blazes out and proves its presence. But certainly it never got itself on to paper. When, however, one reads of a witch being ducked, of a woman possessed by devils, of a wise woman selling herbs, or even of a very remarkable man who had a mother, then I think we are on the track of a lost novelist, a suppressed poet, of some mute and inglorious Jane Austen, some Emily Brontë who dashed her brains out on the moor or mopped and mowed about the highways crazed with the torture that her gift had put her to. Indeed, I would venture to guess that Anon, who wrote so many poems without signing them, was often a woman. It was a woman Edward Fitzgerald, I think, suggested who made the ballads and the folk-songs, crooning them to her children, beguiling her spinning with them, or the length of the winter's night.

9   This may be true or it may be false—who can say?—but what is true in it, so it seemed to me, reviewing the story of Shakespeare's sister as I had made it, is that any woman born with a great gift in the sixteenth century would certainly have gone crazed, shot herself, or ended her days in some lonely cottage outside the village, half witch, half wizard, feared and mocked at. For it needs little skill in psychology to be sure that a highly gifted girl who had tried to use her gift for poetry would have been so thwarted and hindered by other people, so tortured and pulled asunder by her own contrary instincts, that she must have lost her health and sanity to a certainty. No girl could have walked to London and stood at a stage door and forced her way into the presence of actor-managers without doing herself a violence and suffering an anguish which may have been irrational—for chastity may be a fetish invented by certain societies for unknown reasons—but were none the less inevitable. Chastity had then, it has even now, a religious importance in a woman's life, and has so wrapped itself round with nerves and instincts that to cut it free and bring it to the light of day demands courage of the rarest. To have lived a free life in London in the sixteenth century would have meant for a woman who was poet and playwright a nervous stress and dilemma which might well have killed her. Had she survived, whatever she had written would have been twisted and deformed, issuing from a strained and morbid imagination. And undoubtedly, I thought, looking at the shelf where there are no plays by women, her work would have gone unsigned. That refuge she would have sought certainly. It was the relic of the sense of chastity that dictated anonymity to women even so late as the nineteenth century. Currer Bell, George Eliot, George Sand, all the victims of inner strife as their writings prove, sought ineffectively to veil themselves by using the name of a man. Thus they did homage to the convention, which if not implanted by the other sex

was liberally encouraged by them (the chief glory of a woman is not to be talked of, said Pericles, himself a much-talked-of man), that publicity in women is detestable. Anonymity runs in their blood. The desire to be veiled still possesses them. They are not even now as concerned about the health of their fame as men are, and, speaking generally, will pass a tombstone or a sign-post without feeling an irresistible desire to cut their names on it, as Alf, Bert or Chas must do in obedience to their instinct, which murmurs if it sees a fine woman go by, or even a dog, *Ce chien est à moi*. And, of course, it may not be a dog, I thought, remembering Parliament Square, the Sieges Allee and other avenues; it may be a piece of land or a man with curly black hair. It is one of the great advantages of being a woman that one can pass even a very fine negress without wishing to make an Englishwoman of her.

10   That woman, then, who was born with a gift of poetry in the sixteenth century, was an unhappy woman, a woman at strife against herself. All the conditions of her life, all her own instincts, were hostile to the state of mind which is needed to set free whatever is in the brain. But what is the state of mind that is most propitious to the act of creation, I asked. Can one come by any notion of the state that furthers and makes possible that strange activity? Here I opened the volume containing the Tragedies of Shakespeare. What was Shakespeare's state of mind, for instance, when he wrote *Lear* and *Antony and Cleopatra*? It was certainly the state of mind most favourable to poetry that there has ever existed. But Shakespeare himself said nothing about it. We only know casually and by chance that he "never blotted a line." Nothing indeed was ever said by the artist himself about his state of mind until the eighteenth century perhaps. Rousseau perhaps began it. At any rate, by the nineteenth century self-consciousness had developed so far that it was the habit for men of letters to describe their minds in confessions and autobiographies. Their lives also were written, and their letters were printed after their deaths. Thus, though we do not know what Shakespeare went through when he wrote *Lear,* we do know what Carlyle went through when he wrote the *French Revolution;* what Flaubert went through when he wrote *Madame Bovary;* what Keats was going through when he tried to write poetry against the coming of death and the indifference of the world.

11   And one gathers from this enormous modern literature of confession and self-analysis that to write a work of genius is almost always a feat of prodigious difficulty. Everything is against the likelihood that it will come from the writer's mind whole and entire. Generally material circumstances are against it. Dogs will bark; people will interrupt; money must be made; health will break down. Further, accentuating all these difficulties and making them harder to bear is the world's notorious indifference. It does not ask people to write poems and novels and histories; it does not need them. It does not care whether Flaubert finds the right word or whether Carlyle scrupulously verifies this or that fact. Naturally, it will not pay for what it does not want. And so the writer, Keats, Flaubert, Carlyle, suffers, especially in the creative years of youth, every form of distraction and discouragement. A curse, a cry of agony rises from those books of analysis and confession. "Mighty poets in

their misery dead"—that is the burden of their song. If anything comes through in spite of all this, it is a miracle, and probably no book is born entire and uncrippled as it was conceived.

12 But for women, I thought, looking at the empty shelves, these difficulties were infinitely more formidable. In the first place, to have a room of her own, let alone a quiet room or a sound-proof room, was out of the question, unless her parents were exceptionally rich or very noble, even up to the beginning of the nineteenth century. Since her pin money, which depended on the good will of her father, was only enough to keep her clothed, she was debarred from such alleviations as came even to Keats or Tennyson or Carlyle, all poor men, from a walking tour, a little journey to France, from the separate lodging which, even if it were miserable enough, sheltered them from the claims and tyrannies of their families. Such material difficulties were formidable; but much worse were the immaterial. The indifference of the world which Keats and Flaubert and other men of genius have found so hard to bear was in her case not indifference but hostility. The world did not say to her as it said to them, Write if you choose; it makes no difference to me. The world said with a guffaw, Write? What's the good of your writing? Here the psychologists of Newnham and Girton might come to our help, I thought, looking again at the blank spaces on the shelves. For surely it is time that the effect of discouragement upon the mind of the artist should be measured, as I have seen a dairy company measure the effect of ordinary milk and Grade A milk upon the body of the rat. They set two rats in cages side by side, and of the two one was furtive, timid and small, and the other was glossy, bold and big. Now what food do we feed women as artists upon? I asked, remembering, I suppose, that dinner of prunes and custard. To answer that question I had only to open the evening paper and to read that Lord Birkenhead is of opinion—but really I am not going to trouble to copy out Lord Birkenhead's opinion upon the writing of women. What Dean Inge says I will leave in peace. The Harley Street specialist may be allowed to rouse the echoes of Harley Street with his vociferations without raising a hair on my head. I will quote, however, Mr. Oscar Browning, because Mr. Oscar Browning was a great figure in Cambridge at one time, and used to examine the students at Girton and Newnham. Mr. Oscar Browning was wont to declare "that the impression left on his mind, after looking over any set of examination papers, was that, irrespective of the marks he might give, the best woman was intellectually the inferior of the worst man." After saying that Mr. Browning went back to his rooms—and it is this sequel that endears him and makes him a human figure of some bulk and majesty—he went back to his rooms and found a stable-boy lying on the sofa—"a mere skeleton, his cheeks were cavernous and sallow, his teeth were black, and he did not appear to have the full use of his limbs. . . . 'That's Arthur' [said Mr. Browning]. 'He's a dear boy really and most highminded.'" The two pictures always seem to me to complete each other. And happily in this age of biography the two pictures often do complete each other, so that we are able to interpret the opinions of great men not only by what they say, but by what they do.

13   But though this is possible now, such opinions coming from the lips of important people must have been formidable enough even fifty years ago. Let us suppose that a father from the highest motives did not wish his daughter to leave home and become a writer, painter or scholar. "See what Mr. Oscar Browning says," he would say; and there was not only Mr. Oscar Browning; there was the *Saturday Review;* there was Mr. Greg—the "essentials of a woman's being," said Mr. Greg emphatically, "are that *they are supported by, and they minister to, men*"—there was an enormous body of masculine opinion to the effect that nothing could be expected of women intellectually. Even if her father did not read out loud these opinions, any girl could read them for herself; and the reading, even in the nineteenth century, must have lowered her vitality, and told profoundly upon her work. There would always have been that assertion—you cannot do this, you are incapable of doing that—to protest against, to overcome. Probably for a novelist this germ is no longer of much effect; for there have been women novelists of merit. But for painters it must still have some sting in it; and for musicians, I imagine, is even now active and poisonous in the extreme. The woman composer stands where the actress stood in the time of Shakespeare. Nick Greene, I thought, remembering the story I had made about Shakespeare's sister, said that a woman acting put him in mind of a dog dancing. Johnson repeated the phrase two hundred years later of women preaching. And here, I said, opening a book about music, we have the very words used again in this year of grace, 1928, of women who try to write music. "Of Mlle. Germaine Tailleferre one can only repeat Dr. Johnson's dictum concerning a woman preacher, transposed into terms of music. 'Sir, a woman's composing is like a dog's walking on his hind legs. It is not done well, but you are surprised to find it done at all.'" So accurately does history repeat itself.

14   Thus, I concluded, shutting Mr. Oscar Browning's life and pushing away the rest, it is fairly evident that even in the nineteenth century a woman was not encouraged to be an artist. On the contrary, she was snubbed, slapped, lectured and exhorted. Her mind must have been strained and her vitality lowered by the need of opposing this, of disproving that. For here again we come within range of that very interesting and obscure masculine complex which has had so much influence upon the woman's movement; that deep-seated desire, not so much that *she* shall be inferior as that *he* shall be superior, which plants him wherever one looks, not only in front of the arts, but barring the way to politics too, even when the risk to himself seems infinitesimal and the suppliant humble and devoted. Even Lady Bessborough, I remembered, with all her passion for politics, must humbly bow herself and write to Lord Granville Leveson-Gower: ". . . notwithstanding all my violence in politicks and talking so much on that subject, I perfectly agree with you that no woman has any business to meddle with that or any other serious business, further than giving her opinion (if she is ask'd)." And so she goes on to spend her enthusiasm where it meets with no obstacle whatsoever upon that immensely important subject, Lord Granville's maiden speech in the House of Commons. The spectacle is certainly a strange one, I thought. The history of men's opposition to women's emancipation is more interesting perhaps than the story of that emancipation itself. An amusing

book might be made of it if some young student at Girton or Newnham would collect examples and deduce a theory—but she would need thick gloves on her hands, and bars to protect her of solid gold.

15   But what is amusing now, I recollected, shutting Lady Bessborough, had to be taken in desperate earnest once. Opinions that one now pastes in a book labelled cock-a-doodle-dum and keeps for reading to select audiences on summer nights once drew tears, I can assure you. Among your grandmothers and great-grandmothers there were many that wept their eyes out. Florence Nightingale shrieked aloud in her agony. Moreover, it is all very well for you, who have got yourselves to college and enjoy sitting-rooms—or is it only bed-sitting-rooms?—of your own to say that genius should disregard such opinions; that genius should be above caring what is said of it. Unfortunately, it is precisely the men or women of genius who mind most what is said of them. Remember Keats. Remember the words he had cut on his tombstone. Think of Tennyson; think—but I need hardly multiply instances of the undeniable, if very unfortunate, fact that it is the nature of the artist to mind excessively what is said about him. Literature is strewn with the wreckage of men who have minded beyond reason the opinions of others.

16   And this susceptibility of theirs is doubly unfortunate, I thought, returning again to my original enquiry into what state of mind is most propitious for creative work, because the mind of an artist, in order to achieve the prodigious effort of freeing whole and entire the work that is in him, must be incandescent, like Shakespeare's mind, I conjectured, looking at the book which lay open at *Antony and Cleopatra*. There must be no obstacle in it, no foreign matter unconsumed.

17   For though we say that we know nothing about Shakespeare's state of mind, even as we say that, we are saying something about Shakespeare's state of mind. The reason perhaps why we know so little of Shakespeare—compared with Donne or Ben Jonson or Milton—is that his grudges and spites and antipathies are hidden from us. We are not held up by some "revelation" which reminds us of the writer. All desire to protest, to preach, to proclaim an injury, to pay off a score, to make the world the witness of some hardship or grievance was fired out of him and consumed. Therefore his poetry flows from him free and unimpeded. If ever a human being got his work expressed completely, it was Shakespeare. If ever a mind was incandescent, unimpeded, I thought, turning again to the bookcase, it was Shakespeare's mind.

TOPICS FOR WRITING AND DISCUSSION

1. In the larger essay from which this section is taken, Woolf says that in order to write, a woman must have a small independent income and "a room of one's own." In what ways does the example of Shakespeare's sister support that assertion? Why does Woolf think the sister would have failed to write immortal dramas as did her brother Shakespeare? Notice particularly the details of the Elizabethan woman's life as Woolf found it described in Trevelyan's *History of England*.

2. Woolf imagines various ways in which gifted women in the past expressed their talents. List several of the outlets she describes and explain whether you find her projections plausible. Do modern women with literary, artistic, and musical genius still resort to any of these outlets or do most of them find the same means of expression as do men with similar talents?

3. Notice the choice of words, the point of view, and the way Woolf addresses her audience. What tone is established? Formal? Informal? Pleading? Demanding? Sarcastic? Despairing? Hopeful? Or something else? Indicate specific passages to support your analysis.

4. What does Woolf mean when she says (near the end of the essay) that if a young woman were to write the history of men's opposition to women's emancipation "she would need thick gloves on her hands, and bars to protect her of solid gold"? What kind of protection would thick gloves offer? Why would the bars be made of gold?

5. Describe a woman you know personally (or one about whom you have read or studied) who has become successful in a previously male-dominated field. Some famous choices might include Amelia Earhart, Margaret Mead, Golda Meir, Sally Ride, or Sandra Day O'Connor. Focus your description on one outstanding quality that helped your choice succeed.

WE REAL COOL

Gwendolyn Brooks
(1917–   )

Born in Topeka, Kansas, Gwendolyn Brooks grew up on Chicago's South Side. In 1936, she graduated from Chicago's Wilson Junior College and has since received numerous honorary degrees. In 1950, she was awarded the Pulitzer Price for poetry for *Annie Allen,* becoming the first African-American writer to win the prize. In 1985, she was named Consultant in Poetry to the Library of Congress, again the first African-American to be named to that position. She is the author of many books of poetry, including *A Street in Bronzeville* (1945), *The Bean Eaters* (1960), *In the Mecca* (1968), *Riot* (1969), and *Beckonings* (1975). She has also written autobiographical collections, a novel (*Mad Martha,* 1953), and several children's books. Her brief poem "We Real Cool," set in a Chicago pool hall, originally appeared in *Selected Poems* (1959).

The Pool Players.
Seven at the Golden Shovel.

We real cool. We
Left school. We

Lurk late. We
Strike straight. We

5 Sing sin. We
Thin gin. We

Jazz June. We
Die soon.

Gwendolyn Brooks (© AP/Wide World Photos)

Topics for Writing and Discussion

1. Who are the "we" of this poem? Why doesn't Brooks write about "them"—that is, why do you think Brooks chooses to write from a first-person plural ("we") point of view?

2. Characterize the people described in this poem. How does Brooks, in only eight short lines, create a clear picture of them?

3. Why does Brooks use a series of short, parallel sentences in this poem? What does the rhyme and repetition of consonant sounds (called *alliteration*) contribute to the creation of setting and characters?

4. What effect do the last three words have on the reader? Summarize what you think Brooks was saying about such young people.

5. Brooks' poem was written some forty years ago. How does her description of these young people compare to today's dropouts or those who see themselves as "cool" gang members? Write a description of a person (or group) who, in your opinion, is trying to be "cool" but is headed for trouble.

Tillie Olsen (© 1978 Thomas Victor/AP/Wide World Photos)

I STAND HERE IRONING

Tillie Olsen
(1913–   )

Writer and political activist, Tillie Olsen was born and
raised in Omaha, Nebraska. She quit school in the
eleventh grade to help support her family, political
refugees of the 1905 Russian Revolution. At seventeen,
she joined the youth organization of the Communist
Party and wrote for the Young People's Socialist League.
She worked to organize Kansas City meat packers and
was jailed for handing out fliers to workers. In the
1930s, she wrote a number of newspaper articles and
essays on the plight of the poor during the Depression.
She also published some fiction in the *Partisan Review*,
but after her marriage, she found that raising four children and working at a variety of jobs left little time for
writing. In the 1950s, she returned to writing, and in
1961 she won the O. Henry Award for the best American short story, "Tell Me a Riddle." The success of the
collection by the same title allowed Olsen finally to publish *Yonnondio: From the Thirties* (1974), a novel she
began in 1934. In 1978, she published *Silences*, a volume of essays and lectures that explores how work and
family obligations affect women's creativity. Most recent
works include *Mother to Daughter, Daughter to
Mother: Mothers on Mothering: A Daybook and Reader*
(1984), and *Bright Web in the Darkness* (1997). "I
Stand Here Ironing," which is included in her short-
story collection *Tell Me a Riddle* (1961), describes the
experiences of a working-class mother.

1   I stand here ironing, and what you asked me moves tormented back and
forth with the iron.

2   "I wish you would manage the time to come in and talk with me about your daughter. I'm sure you can help me understand her. She's a youngster who needs help and whom I'm deeply interested in helping."

3   "Who needs help." . . . Even if I came, what good would it do? You think because I am her mother I have a key, or that in some way you could use me as a key? She has lived for nineteen years. There is all that life that has happened outside of me, beyond me.

4   And when is there time to remember, to sift, to weigh, to estimate, to total? I will start and there will be an interruption and I will have to gather it all together again. Or I will become engulfed with all I did or did not do, with what should have been and what cannot be helped.

5   She was a beautiful baby. The first and only one of our five that was beautiful at birth. You do not guess how new and uneasy her tenancy in her now-loveliness. You did not know her all those years she was thought homely, or see her poring over her baby pictures, making me tell her over and over how beautiful she had been—and would be, I would tell her—and was now, to the seeing eye. But the seeing eyes were few or nonexistent. Including mine.

6   I nursed her. They feel that's important nowadays. I nursed all the children, but with her, with all the fierce rigidity of first motherhood, I did like the books then said. Though her cries battered me to trembling and my breasts ached with swollenness, I waited till the clock decreed.

7   Why do I put that first? I do not even know if it matters, or if it explains anything.

8   She was a beautiful baby. She blew shining bubbles of sound. She loved motion, loved light, loved color and music and textures. She would lie on the floor in her blue overalls patting the surface so hard in ecstasy her hands and feet would blur. She was a miracle to me, but when she was eight months old I had to leave her daytimes with the woman downstairs to whom she was no miracle at all, for I worked or looked for work and for Emily's father, who "could no longer endure" (he wrote in his good-bye note) "sharing want with us."

9   I was nineteen. It was the pre-relief, pre-WPA world of the depression. I would start running as soon as I got off the streetcar, running up the stairs, the place smelling sour, and awake or asleep to startle awake, when she saw me she would break into a clogged weeping that could not be comforted, a weeping I can hear yet.

10   After a while I found a job hashing at night so I could be with her days, and it was better. But it came to where I had to bring her to his family and leave her.

11   It took a long time to raise the money for her fare back. Then she got chicken pox and I had to wait longer. When she finally came, I hardly knew her, walking quick and nervous like her father, looking like her father, thin, and dressed in a shoddy red that yellowed her skin and glared at the pockmarks. All the baby loveliness gone.

12   She was two. Old enough for nursery school they said, and I did not know then what I know now—the fatigue of the long day, and the lacerations of group life in the kinds of nurseries that are only parking places for children.

13   Except that it would have made no difference if I had known. It was the only place there was. It was the only way we could be together, the only way I could hold a job.

14   And even without knowing, I knew. I knew the teacher that was evil because all these years it has curdled into my memory, the little boy hunched in the corner, her rasp, "why aren't you outside, because Alvin hits you? that's no reason, go out, scaredy." I knew Emily hated it even if she did not clutch and implore "—don't go Mommy" like the other children, mornings.

15   She always had a reason why we should stay home. Momma, you look sick. Momma, I feel sick. Momma, the teachers aren't there today, they're sick. Momma, we can't go, there was a fire there last night. Momma, it's a holiday today, no school, they told me.

16   But never a direct protest, never rebellion. I think of our others in their three-, four-year-oldness—the explosions, the tempers, the denunciations, the demands—and I feel suddenly ill. I put the iron down. What in me demanded that goodness in her? And what was the cost, the cost to her of such goodness?

17   The old man living in the back once said in his gentle way: "You should smile at Emily more when you look at her." What *was* in my face when I looked at her? I loved her. There were all the acts of love.

18   It was only with the others I remembered what he said, and it was the face of joy, and not of care or tightness or worry I turned to them—too late for Emily. She does not smile easily, let alone almost always as her brothers and sisters do. Her face is closed and sombre, but when she wants, how fluid. You must have seen it in her pantomimes, you spoke of her rare gift for comedy on the stage that rouses a laughter out of the audience so dear they applaud and applaud and do not want to let her go.

19   Where does it come from, that comedy? There was none of it in her when she came back to me that second time, after I had had to send her away again. She had a new daddy now to learn to love, and I think perhaps it was a better time.

20   Except when we left her alone nights, telling ourselves she was old enough.

21   "Can't you go some other time, Mommy, like tomorrow?" she would ask. "Will it be just a little while you'll be gone? Do you promise?"

22   The time we came back, the front door open, the clock on the floor in the hall. She rigid awake. "It wasn't just a little while. I didn't cry. Three times I called you, just three times, and then I ran downstairs to open the door so you could come faster. The clock talked loud. I threw it away, it scared me what it talked."

23   She said the clock talked loud again that night I went to the hospital to have Susan. She was delirious with the fever that comes before red measles, but she was fully conscious all the week I was gone and the week after we were home when she could not come near the new baby or me.

24   She did not get well. She stayed skeleton thin, not wanting to eat, and night after night she had nightmares. She would call for me, and I would rouse from exhaustion to sleepily call back: "You're all right, darling, go to sleep, it's just a dream," and if she still called, in a sterner voice, "now go to sleep, Emily,

there's nothing to hurt you." Twice, only twice, when I had to get up for Susan anyhow, I went in to sit with her.

25   Now when it is too late (as if she would let me hold and comfort her like I do the others) I get up and go to her at once at her moan or restless stirring. "Are you awake, Emily? Can I get you something?" And the answer is always the same: "No, I'm all right, go back to sleep, Mother."

26   They persuaded me at the clinic to send her away to a convalescent home in the country where "she can have the kind of food and care you can't manage for her, and you'll be free to concentrate on the new baby." They still send children to that place. I see pictures on the society page of sleek young women planning affairs to raise money for it, or dancing at the affairs, or decorating Easter eggs or filling Christmas stockings for the children.

27   They never have a picture of the children so I do not know if the girls still wear those gigantic red bows and the ravaged looks on the every other Sunday when parents can come to visit "unless otherwise notified"—as we were notified the first six weeks.

28   Oh it is a handsome place, green lawns and tall trees and fluted flower beds. High up on the balconies of each cottage the children stand, the girls in their red bows and white dresses, the boys in white suits and giant red ties. The parents stand below shrieking up to be heard and the children shriek down to be heard, and between them the invisible wall "Not To Be Contaminated by Parental Germs or Physical Affection."

29   There was a tiny girl who always stood hand in hand with Emily. Her parents never came. One visit she was gone. "They moved her to Rose Cottage" Emily shouted in explanation. "They don't like you to love anybody here."

30   She wrote once a week, the labored writing of a seven-year-old. "I am fine. How is the baby. If I write my leter nicly I will have a star. Love." There never was a star. We wrote every other day, letters she could never hold or keep but only hear read—once. "We simply do not have room for children to keep any personal possessions," they patiently explained when we pieced one Sunday's shrieking together to plead how much it would mean to Emily, who loved so to keep things, to be allowed to keep her letters and cards.

31   Each visit she looked frailer. "She isn't eating," they told us.

32   (They had runny eggs for breakfast or mush with lumps. Emily said later, I'd hold it in my mouth and not swallow. Nothing ever tasted good, just when they had chicken.)

33   It took us eight months to get her released home, and only the fact that she gained back so little of her seven lost pounds convinced the social worker.

34   I used to try to hold and love her after she came back, but her body would stay stiff, and after a while she'd push away. She ate little. Food sickened her, and I think much of life too. Oh she had physical lightness and brightness, twinkling by on skates, bouncing like a ball up and down up and down over the jump rope, skimming over the hill; but these were momentary.

35   She fretted about her appearance, thin and dark and foreign-looking at a time when every little girl was supposed to look or thought she should look a chubby blonde replica of Shirley Temple. The doorbell sometimes rang for her,

but no one seemed to come and play in the house or be a best friend. Maybe because we moved so much.

36 There was a boy she loved painfully through two school semesters. Months later she told me how she had taken pennies from my purse to buy him candy. "Licorice was his favorite and I brought him some every day, but he still liked Jennifer better'n me. Why, Mommy?" The kind of question for which there is no answer.

37 School was a worry to her. She was not glib or quick in a world where glibness and quickness were easily confused with ability to learn. To her overworked and exasperated teachers she was an overconscientious "slow learner" who kept trying to catch up and was absent entirely too often.

38 I let her be absent, though sometimes the illness was imaginary. How different from my now-strictness about attendance with the others. I wasn't working. We had a new baby, I was home anyhow. Sometimes, after Susan grew old enough, I would keep her home from school, too, to have them all together.

39 Mostly Emily had asthma, and her breathing, harsh and labored, would fill the house with a curiously tranquil sound. I would bring the two old dresser mirrors and her boxes of collections to her bed. She would select beads and single earrings, bottle tops and shells, dried flowers and pebbles, old postcards and scraps, all sorts of oddments; then she and Susan would play Kingdom, setting up landscapes and furniture, peopling them with action.

40 Those were the only times of peaceful companionship between her and Susan. I have edged away from it, that poisonous feeling between them, that terrible balancing of hurts and needs I had to do between the two, and did so badly, those earlier years.

41 Oh there are conflicts between the others too, each one human, needing, demanding, hurting, taking—but only between Emily and Susan, no, Emily toward Susan that corroding resentment. It seems so obvious on the surface, yet it is not obvious. Susan, the second child, Susan, golden- and curly-haired and chubby, quick and articulate and assured, everything in appearance and manner Emily was not; Susan, not able to resist Emily's precious things, losing or sometimes clumsily breaking them; Susan telling jokes and riddles to company for applause while Emily sat silent (to say to me later: that was *my* riddle, Mother, I told it to Susan); Susan, who for all the five years' difference in age was just a year behind Emily in developing physically.

42 I am glad for that slow physical development that widened the difference between her and her contemporaries, though she suffered over it. She was too vulnerable for that terrible world of youthful competition, of preening and parading, of constant measuring of yourself against every other, of envy, "If I had that copper hair," "If I had that skin. . . ." She tormented herself enough about not looking like the others, there was enough of the unsureness, the having to be conscious of words before you speak, the constant caring—what are they thinking of me? without having it all magnified by the merciless physical drives.

43 Ronnie is calling. He is wet and I change him. It is rare there is such a cry now. That time of motherhood is almost behind me when the ear is not one's

own but must always be racked and listening for the child cry, the child call. We sit for a while and I hold him, looking out over the city spread in charcoal with its soft aisles of light. "*Shoogily,*" he breathes and curls closer. I carry him back to bed, asleep. *Shoogily.* A funny word, a family word, inherited from Emily, invented by her to say: *comfort.*

44   In this and other ways she leaves her seal, I say aloud. And startle at my saying it. What do I mean? What did I start to gather together, to try and make coherent? I was at the terrible, growing years. War years. I do not remember them well. I was working, there were four smaller ones now, there was not time for her. She had to help be a mother, and housekeeper, and shopper. She had to set her seal. Mornings of crisis and near hysteria trying to get lunches packed, hair combed, coats and shoes found, everyone to school or Child Care on time, the baby ready for transportation. And always the paper scribbled on by a smaller one, the book looked at by Susan then mislaid, the homework not done. Running out to that huge school where she was one, she was lost, she was a drop; suffering over the unpreparedness, stammering and unsure in her classes.

45   There was so little time left at night after the kids were bedded down. She would struggle over books, always eating (it was in those years she developed her enormous appetite that is legendary in our family) and I would be ironing, or preparing food for the next day, or writing V-mail to Bill, or tending the baby. Sometimes, to make me laugh, or out of her despair, she would imitate happenings or types at school.

46   I think I said once: "Why don't you do something like this in the school amateur show?" One morning she phoned me at work, hardly understandable through the weeping: "Mother, I did it. I won, I won; they gave me first prize; they clapped and clapped and wouldn't let me go."

47   Now suddenly she was Somebody, and as imprisoned in her difference as she had been in anonymity.

48   She began to be asked to perform at other high schools, even in colleges, then at city and statewide affairs. The first one we went to, I only recognized her that first moment when thin, shy, she almost drowned herself into the curtains. Then: Was this Emily? The control, the command, the convulsing and deadly clowning, the spell, then the roaring, stamping audience, unwilling to let this rare and precious laughter out of their lives.

49   Afterwards: You ought to do something about her with a gift like that— but without money or knowing how, what does one do? We have left it all to her, and the gift has as often eddied inside, clogged and clotted, has been used and growing.

50   She is coming. She runs up the stairs two at a time with her light graceful step, and I know she is happy tonight. Whatever it was that occasioned your call did not happen today.

51   "Aren't you ever going to finish the ironing, Mother? Whistler painted his mother in a rocker. I'd have to paint mine standing over an ironing board." This is one of her communicative nights and she tells me everything and nothing as she fixes herself a plate of food out of the icebox.

52   She is so lovely. Why did you want me to come in at all? Why were you concerned? She will find her way.

53   She starts up the stairs to bed. "Don't get me up with the rest in the morning." "But I thought you were having midterms." "Oh, those," she comes back in, kisses me, and says quite lightly, "in a couple of years when we'll all be atom-dead they won't matter a bit."

54   She has said it before. She *believes* it. But because I have been dredging the past, and all that compounds a human being is so heavy and meaningful in me, I cannot endure it tonight.

55   I will never total it all. I will never come in to say: She was a child seldom smiled at. Her father left me before she was a year old. I had to work her first six years when there was work, or I sent her home and to his relatives. There were years she had care she hated. She was dark and thin and foreign-looking in a world where the prestige went to blondeness and curly hair and dimples, she was slow where glibness was prized. She was a child of anxious, not proud, love. We were poor and could not afford for her the soil of easy growth. I was a young mother, I was a distracted mother. There were the other children pushing up, demanding. Her younger sister seemed all that she was not. There were years she did not want me to touch her. She kept too much in herself, her life was such she had to keep too much in herself. My wisdom came too late. She has much to her and probably nothing will come of it. She is a child of her age, of depression, of war, of fear.

56   Let her be. So all that is in her will not bloom—but in how many does it? There is still enough left to live by. Only help her to know—help make it so there is cause for her to know—that she is more than this dress on the ironing board, helpless before the iron.

TOPICS FOR WRITING AND DISCUSSION

1.   Briefly characterize the two main characters in this story, Emily and her mother. What events were the most influential in shaping Emily's character?

2.   Are you more sympathetic to one character than another? Do you find the mother's explanations understandable considering the circumstances she faced, or is she merely rationalizing her choices?

3.   Who is talking to Emily's mother at the beginning of this story? Why does the mother decide she will never go in to discuss Emily with this person? Do you think her conclusions about Emily at the end of the story are accurate?

4.   Look closely at the images of ironing in this story, especially in paragraphs 1, 51, and 56. How does Olsen use ironing as a metaphor for the mother's thoughts? In addition, what does the mother mean in the final paragraph when she says she wants her daughter to realize that she's "more than this dress on the ironing board, helpless before the iron"?

5.   Write a description of the most interesting person you know; this person might be one of your friends, teachers, or perhaps a relative with a fascinating life story. You might focus your essay by showing how a particular set of circumstances or values shaped this person's life and character.

WRITING ASSIGNMENTS FOR CHAPTER FOUR

DESCRIPTION

1. In John Steinbeck's novel *The Grapes of Wrath,* from which "The Turtle" was taken, some readers see the slow, determined animal as a symbol of the beleaguered but enduring farm workers of the story. Try writing your own symbolic description of another animal, making clear to your readers through your use of language the character trait or type of person the animal represents.

2. In "The Way to Rainy Mountain," N. Scott Momaday describes a journey. Think of a journey you have taken, a trip in which you discovered something important about yourself or your family. Was it a pilgrimage of some sort, as Momaday describes his journey? A retracing of steps taken at an earlier time by you or an ancestor? A trip home or a new adventure? Focus on some significant part of your journey and describe what you saw and experienced, revealing its importance to the reader. (Perhaps your memory will be triggered by a scene of an important person, just as Momaday most vividly recalls a picture of his grandmother at her prayers.)

3. After E. B. White returned to his childhood vacation site with his son, he wrote about the experience (and his feelings of mortality) in the essay "Once More to the Lake." Think of an important place in your life (a room, a house, a hideaway) and describe it vividly so that your feelings toward the place are clear to your readers. You may wish, as did White, to use your last sentence to emphasize the deeper significance of the place you have chosen.

4. Go to a crowded location, one that is bustling with people and activities, such as your student center, a cafeteria, or a shopping mall. Record as many sensory details as you can in a twenty-minute period: what you see, hear, smell, and so on. Review your list later and use selected details to write a description of the place that presents a unified dominant impression. Make your description a vivid and convincing picture for someone who has never seen the place.

5. In "If Shakespeare Had Had a Sister," Virginia Woolf imagines a young Elizabethan woman who does not succeed as her male counterpart did. Describe a scene when, unlike Judith, you achieved a moment of great success and happiness. What goal had you accomplished? Why did you feel good about this accomplishment? Did you have to overcome any barriers to reach your goal?

6. In "An American Childhood," Annie Dillard reveals her mother's influence on her in several ways. Similarly, in "I Stand Here Ironing," Tillie Olsen's Emily may have developed the talent of making people laugh as a

response to her rather sad childhood. Describe one of your strongest character traits, using details and examples to illustrate this aspect of yourself. Did you "inherit" this trait from one of your parents or from someone else close to you? Or did you develop this trait in opposition to someone or something in your childhood?

7. Some rather unusual ceremonies are described in Joan Didion's essay "Marrying Absurd." Write an essay describing an important event, ceremony, or ritual you have witnessed or participated in. What was the significance of this event? Present a dominant impression to your readers by choosing details that communicate your attitude toward this event. Was it absurd, or something else entirely?

8. In "We Real Cool," Gwendolyn Brooks describes the dropouts of an earlier time. Using your descriptive skills, write a portrait of someone you know who has chosen a nontraditional path. How does this person differ from society's view of the "norm"? Is this choice a waste of potential or a statement of individuality? Include vivid details that reveal this person's personality and values.

CHAPTER FIVE

PROCESS

Whenever you tell how something works or how something happens or how something can be accomplished, you explain a *process*. If you were to purchase an unassembled file cabinet, you would probably need step-by-step instructions to show you how to assemble it. Similarly, if you wanted to know how diet and exercise are related to weight gain, weight loss, or weight maintenance, a nutritionist could demonstrate the relationship between calorie intake and physical activity to weight control by explaining the process of calorie burning. In both situations, you would get the information you want by observing carefully prescribed, sequenced steps or stages that lead to the desired end. Thus, in explaining a process, a writer must be able to describe clearly the steps or stages of the process and the order in which those steps or stages occur.

TYPES OF PROCESSES

There are two kinds of processes: directional and informative.

A *directional* process tells readers how to do or make something. It gives "how to" instructions. For instance, if you wanted to tell a friend how to get to your house for the weekend's big party, you would write clear, logical directions to your home. Or, if you wanted to tell someone how to assemble a bookcase, you would write clear, logically ordered, step-by-step directions that would guide your friend to the completion of the project. You can find examples of directional processes throughout your home and workplace: cookbooks (how to make chili), first-aid kits (how to treat a burn), telephone books (how to call person-to-person), car repair manuals (how to change the oil), copy machine instructions (how to reduce or enlarge a page of print). Most often, a directional process essay teaches the reader to create, fix, or do something, which explains why this kind of essay is also known as an *instructional* or *how to* process.

A second type of process is *informative*. Informative process differs from directional process in that the emphasis is not on completing a procedure or performing a task, but on understanding how or why a process works. Informative processes are not meant to be duplicated by the reader; the writer's aim is to inform through analysis rather than to give "how to" instructions. For instance, Carin Quinn's purpose in "The Jeaning of America" is not to tell readers how to make blue jeans but to reveal the steps in the creation of a uniquely American product. In "The American Way of Death," Jessica Mitford's intention is not for her readers to embalm their friends and relatives, but instead to enlighten her readers about a little-known but common procedure that she feels may not be necessary or desirable. Because an essay of this type often scrutinizes the parts of a process, it is sometimes referred to as *process analysis*.

ORGANIZING THE PROCESS ESSAY

Like other essays, the process essay—whether it is directional or informative—should consist of three parts: the introduction, the body, and the conclusion. The *introduction* is particularly important because it will contain the thesis statement or give the objective you wish to accomplish. You might also include any background information the reader may need to understand the process fully, a list of materials needed to complete the task, or any other details that will be needed to set the process in motion.

The *body* of the essay will develop the thesis or unfold the directions. Steps that contain many or complex details might be grouped together in stages in the process. Each stage should be sequenced in a logical, chronological order. As you construct the process essay, rely on the other rhetorical structures to help clarify steps: use description, narration, definition, or illustration to simplify complex principles or directions. Strive for a smooth writing style by using clear transitions. Numerical transitions (*first, second, third,* and so on) may be precise but can be boring. Try more creative sequencing techniques with transitions such as *begin by* (or, perhaps, verbal forms like *beginning with* or *to begin*), *continue by, go on to, when you have finished,* and so on.

Your *conclusion* may comment on the significance of the completed process or explain other important uses. Or, if appropriate, you might leave the reader with a thought or image that sums up or emphasizes the essay's purpose, as Jessica Mitford does in "The American Way of Death" when she concludes her satirical attack on the embalming process by describing a scene of a corpse holding an "open house" from 10 A.M. to 9 P.M. While your choice of conclusions may depend upon your purpose, don't abruptly stop your essay after the last step and don't end with a dry rewording of your thesis. Leave the reader with a feeling of having satisfactorily completed an interesting procedure.

WRITING THE PROCESS ESSAY

Whether you are constructing a directional or an informative process, consider the following advice to help you produce a clear essay:

1. *Present your process essay's objective or purpose in a thesis statement.*

In "The American Way of Death," Jessica Mitford explains the "purpose of embalming is to make the corpse presentable for viewing in a suitably costly container," and her essay goes on to explain the process of embalming and, at the same time, raises the question of the appropriateness of the practice. Carin Quinn first announces that blue jeans are an "American symbol," and her essay then shows how jeans became such a national tradition.

2. *Consider your audience.*

Are you addressing a novice or an expert? How much detail will your reader need to follow your directions or to understand your information? Do you need to describe any essential equipment or to define any technical terms? Remember that you are the specialist explaining a process to people who are interested but unfamiliar with its steps, stages, or parts.

3. *Explain each step clearly in sufficient detail and in logical order.*

Skipping a step in a process may mean that your readers cannot follow or complete the directions; fuzzy, unclear, or haphazard descriptions may mean that readers will misunderstand your instructions or will miss the point of your analysis. Notice that in "Attitude" Garrison Keillor carefully and methodically (and humorously) explains the steps involved in creating a good attitude on the baseball field. In "The American Way of Death," Jessica Mitford vividly moves through each stage of the embalming process, using an abundance of sensory details so that the reader clearly understands the entire process and Mitford's view of it. The steps in the process are ordered chronologically and are smoothly connected with transitional devices for easy comprehension.

4. *Maintain a consistent tense and point of view throughout the essay.*

Most often, directional process essays are written in the present tense and are directed at "you," a reader who wishes to follow the "how to" instructions. Informational essays may be written in the present or past tense and are generally presented from a third-person point of view (he, she, it, or they are doing something). If a writer is retelling a personal series of events, the first-person "I" may be used to present the information, as in Samuel H. Scudder's "Take This Fish and Look at It."

THE JEANING OF AMERICA—
AND THE WORLD

Carin Quinn

Essayist Carin Quinn received her master's degree in
American studies from California State University at
Los Angeles. The following essay, "The Jeaning of
America—and the World," first appeared in *American
Heritage* magazine in 1978. In it, Quinn looks at the
significance of blue jeans to the American way of life as
she explains their creation, history, and popularity.

1   THIS is the story of a sturdy American symbol which has now spread
throughout most of the world. The symbol is not the dollar. It is not even
Coca-Cola. It is a simple pair of pants called blue jeans, and what the pants
symbolize is what Alexis de Tocqueville called "a manly and legitimate passion
for equality. . . ." Blue jeans are favored equally by bureaucrats and cowboys;
bankers and deadbeats; fashion designers and beer drinkers. They draw no
distinctions and recognize no classes; they are merely American. Yet they are
sought after almost everywhere in the world—including Russia, where authorities recently broke up a teen-aged gang that was selling them on the black
market for two hundred dollars a pair. They have been around for a long time,
and it seems likely that they will outlive even the necktie.

2   This ubiquitous American symbol was the invention of a Bavarian-born
Jew. His name was Levi Strauss.

3   He was born in Bad Ocheim, Germany, in 1829, and during the European
political turmoil of 1848 decided to take his chances in New York, to which
his two brothers already had emigrated. Upon arrival, Levi soon found that his
two brothers had exaggerated their tales of an easy life in the land of the main
chance. They were landowners, they had told him; instead, he found them
pushing needles, thread, pots, pans, ribbons, yarn, scissors, and buttons to
housewives. For two years he was a lowly peddler, hauling some 180 pounds
of sundries door-to-door to eke out a marginal living. When a married sister in
San Francisco offered to pay his way West in 1850, he jumped at the opportunity, taking with him bolts of canvas he hoped to sell for tenting.

4   It was the wrong kind of canvas for that purpose, but while talking with a miner down from the mother lode, he learned that pants—sturdy pants that would stand up to the rigors of the digging—were almost impossible to find. Opportunity beckoned. On the spot, Strauss measured the man's girth and in-seam with a piece of string and, for six dollars in gold dust, had [the canvas] tailored into a pair of stiff but rugged pants. The miner was delighted with the result, word got around about "those pants of Levi's," and Strauss was in busi-ness. The company has been in business ever since.

5   When Strauss ran out of canvas, he wrote his two brothers to send more. He received instead a tough, brown cotton cloth made in Nîmes, France—called *serge de Nîmes* and swiftly shortened to "denim" (the word "jeans" de-rives from Gênes, the French word for Genoa, where a similar cloth was produced). Almost from the first, Strauss had his cloth dyed the distinctive in-digo that gave blue jeans their name, but it was not until the 1870s that he added the copper rivets which have long since become a company trademark. The rivets were the idea of a Virginia City, Nevada, tailor, Jacob W. Davis, who added them to pacify a mean-tempered miner called Alkali Ike. Alkali, the story goes, complained that the pockets of his jeans always tore when he stuffed them with ore samples and demanded that Davis do something about it. As a kind of joke, Davis took the pants to a blacksmith and had the pockets riveted; once again, the idea worked so well that word got around; in 1873 Strauss appropriated and patented the gimmick—and hired Davis as a regional manager.

6   By this time, Strauss had taken both his brothers and two brothers-in-law into the company and was ready for his third San Francisco store. Over the en-suing years the company prospered locally, and by the time of his death in 1902, Strauss had become a man of prominence in California. For three decades thereafter the business remained profitable though small, with sales largely confined to the working people of the West—cowboys, lumberjacks, railroad workers, and the like. Levi's jeans were first introduced to the East, apparently, during the dude-ranch craze of the 1930s, when vacationing East-erners returned and spread the word about the wonderful pants with rivets. Another boost came in World War II, when blue jeans were declared an essen-tial commodity and were sold only to people engaged in defense work. From a company with fifteen salespeople, two plants, and almost no business east of the Mississippi in 1946, the organization grew in thirty years to include a sales force of more than twenty-two thousand, with fifty plants and offices in thirty-five countries. Each year, more than 250,000,000 items of Levi's clothing are sold—including more than 83,000,000 pairs of riveted blue jeans. They have become, through marketing, word of mouth, and demonstrable reliability, the common pants of America. They can be purchased pre-washed, pre-faded, and pre-shrunk for the suitably proletarian look. They adapt themselves to any sort of idiosyncratic use; women slit them at the inseams and convert them into long skirts, men chop them off above the knees and turn them into something to be worn while challenging the surf. Decorations and ornamentations abound.

7   The pants have become a tradition, and along the way have acquired a history of their own—so much so that the company has opened a museum in San Francisco. There was, for example, the turn-of-the-century trainman who replaced a faulty coupling with a pair of jeans; the Wyoming man who used his jeans as a towrope to haul his car out of a ditch; the Californian who found several pairs in an abandoned mine, wore them, then discovered they were sixty-three years old and still as good as new and turned them over to the Smithsonian as a tribute to their toughness. And then there is the particularly terrifying story of the careless construction worker who dangled fifty-two stories above the street until rescued, his sole support the Levi's belt loop through which his rope was hooked.

Topics for Writing and Discussion

1. Why are blue jeans a symbol of the American way of life? What qualities do they represent that are uniquely American?
2. How did a series of errors and practical jokes contribute to the development of jeans? How does this process further reinforce blue jeans as an American symbol? As you answer this question, keep in mind frontier tall tales and folk heroes.
3. Quinn's use of parallel structure contributes to her lively writing style. Find examples of parallel structure and explain how Quinn's use of this pattern contributes to the pace and tone of the essay.
4. Quinn traces the history of blue jeans up to 1978 (the year the essay was first published). What details and examples would you include if you were to bring her essay up to date? How have jeans—and people's response to them—changed in the past decade?
5. Research a popular American product and write a general-interest essay about its creation and history, as Quinn did in "The Jeaning of America." For instance, consider the frisbee, the skateboard, the microwave, pantyhose, bow ties, air bags in cars, baseball caps, potato chips (the possibilities are numerous). Does your product reflect an American quality of some kind?

Jessica Mitford (© Archive Photos/Express Newspapers)

THE AMERICAN WAY OF DEATH

Jessica Mitford
(1917–1996)

Because of her exposés on American funeral directors,
obstetricians, and prison administrators, Jessica Mitford
was dubbed the "Queen of the Muckrakers." She was
from Batsford, Gloucestershire, England, the sixth of
seven children born to Lord and Lady Redesdale. Along
with her five sisters, she was schooled at home by her
mother. The eccentric activities of the family have been
the subject of several books, including Evelyn Waugh's
Brideshead Revisited. Known to her friends as "Decca,"
Mitford never shrank from the gruesome. Among her
best-known studies are *The American Way of Death*
(1963), her first major success; *The Trial of Dr. Spock*
(1969), which describes the trial of pediatrician Benjamin Spock for assisting Vietnam War draft resisters;
Kind and Usual Punishment: The Prison Business
(1973), an indictment of the American penal system;
Poison Penmanship: The Gentle Art of Muckraking
(1979); and *The American Way of Birth* (1992), a critique on the unnecessary expenses associated with child-
birth. She also wrote two autobiographies, *Daughters
and Rebels* (1960) and *A Fine Old Conflict* (1977), and
a novel, *Grace Had an English Heart* (1989). At the
time of her death, she was updating *The American Way
of Death*. In "The American Way of Death," an excerpt
from the 1963 edition of the book, Mitford skewers the
American funeral industry with her characteristic wit.

1   THE drama begins to unfold with the arrival of the corpse at the mortuary.
2   Alas, poor Yorick! How surprised he would be to see how his counterpart
of today is whisked off to a funeral parlor and is in short order sprayed, sliced,

pierced, pickled, trussed, trimmed, creamed, waxed, painted, roughed, and neatly dressed—transformed from a common corpse into a Beautiful Memory Picture. This process is known in the trade as embalming and restorative art, and is so universally employed in the United States and Canada that the funeral director does it routinely, without consulting corpse or kin. He regards as eccentric those few who are hardy enough to suggest that it might be dispensed with. Yet no law requires embalming, no religious doctrine commends it, nor is it dictated by considerations of health, sanitation, or even of personal daintiness. In no part of the world but in Northern America is it widely used. The purpose of embalming is to make the corpse presentable for viewing in a suitably costly container; and here too the funeral director routinely, without first consulting the family, prepares the body for public display.

3   Is all this legal? The processes to which a dead body may be subjected are after all to some extent circumscribed by law. In most states, for instance, the signature of next of kin must be obtained before an autopsy may be performed, before the deceased may be cremated, before the body may be turned over to a medical school for research purposes; or such provision must be made in the decedent's will. In the case of embalming, no such permission is required nor is it ever sought. A textbook, *The Principles and Practices of Embalming*, comments on this: "There is some question regarding the legality of much that is done within the preparation room." The author points out that it would be most unusual for a responsible member of a bereaved family to instruct the mortician, in so many words, to "*embalm*" the body of a deceased relative. The very term "embalming" is so seldom used that the mortician must rely upon custom in the matter. The author concludes that unless the family specifies otherwise, the act of entrusting the body to the care of a funeral establishment carries with it an implied permission to go ahead and embalm.

4   Embalming is indeed a most extraordinary procedure, and one must wonder at the docility of Americans who each year pay hundreds of millions of dollars for its perpetuation, blissfully ignorant of what it is all about, what is done, how it is done. Not one in ten thousand has any idea of what actually takes place. Books on the subject are extremely hard to come by. They are not to be found in most libraries or bookshops.

5   In an era when huge television audiences watch surgical operations in the comfort of their living rooms, when, thanks to the animated cartoon, the geography of the digestive system has become familiar territory even to the nursery school set, in a land where the satisfaction of curiosity about almost all matters is a national pastime, the secrecy surrounding embalming can, surely, hardly be attributed to the inherent gruesomeness of the subject. Custom in this regard has within this century suffered a complete reversal. In the early days of American embalming, when it was performed in the home of the deceased, it was almost mandatory for some relative to stay by the embalmer's side and witness the procedure. Today, family members who might wish to be in attendance would certainly be dissuaded by the funeral director. All others, except apprentices, are excluded by law from the preparation room.

6   A close look at what does actually take place may explain in large measure the undertaker's intractable reticence concerning a procedure that has become his major *raison d'être*. Is it possible he fears the public information about embalming might lead patrons to wonder if they really want this service? If the funeral men are loath to discuss the subject outside the trade, the reader may, understandably, be equally loath to go on reading at this point. For those who have the stomach for it, let us part the formaldehyde curtain. . . .

7   The body is first laid out in the undertaker's morgue—or rather, Mr. Jones is reposing in the preparation room—to be readied to bid the world farewell.

8   The preparation room in any of the better funeral establishments has the tiled and sterile look of a surgery, and indeed the embalmer-restorative artist who does his chores there is beginning to adopt the term "dermasurgeon" (appropriately corrupted by some mortician-writers as "demisurgeon") to describe his calling. His equipment, consisting of scalpels, scissors, augurs, forceps, clamps, needles, pumps, tubes, bowls and basins, is crudely imitative of the surgeon's, as is his technique, acquired in a nine- or twelve-month post-high-school course in an embalming school. He is supplied by an advanced chemical industry with a bewildering array of fluids, sprays, pastes, oils, powders, creams, to fix or soften tissue, shrink or distend it as needed, dry it here, restore the moisture there. There are cosmetics, waxes and paints to fill and cover features, even plaster of Paris to replace entire limbs. There are ingenious aids to prop and stabilize the cadaver: a Vari-Pose Head Rest, the Edwards Arm and Hand Positioner, the Repose Block (to support the shoulders during the embalming), and the Throop Foot Positioner, which resembles an old-fashioned stocks.

9   Mr. John H. Eckels, president of the Eckels College of Mortuary Science, thus describes the first part of the embalming procedure: "In the hands of a skilled practitioner, this work may be done in a comparatively short time and without mutilating the body other than by slight incision—so slight that it scarcely would cause serious inconvenience if made upon a living person. It is necessary to remove the blood, and doing this not only helps in the disinfecting, but removes the principal cause of disfigurements due to discoloration."

10   Another textbook discusses the all-important time element: "The earlier this is done, the better, for every hour that elapses between death and embalming will add to the problems and complications encountered. . . ." Just how soon should one get going on the embalming? The author tells us, "On the basis of such scanty information made available to this profession through its rudimentary and haphazard system of technical research, we must conclude that the best results are to be obtained if the subject is embalmed before life is completely extinct—that is, before cellular death has occurred. In the average case, this would mean within an hour after somatic death." For those who feel that there is something a little rudimentary, not to say haphazard, about this advice, a comforting thought is offered by another writer. Speaking of fears entertained in early days of premature burial, he points out, "One of the effects of embalming by chemical injection, however, has been to dispel fears of live

burial." How true; once blood is removed chances of live burial are indeed remote.

11   To return to Mr. Jones, the blood is drained out through the veins and replaced by embalming fluid pumped in through the arteries. As noted in *The Principles and Practices of Embalming,* "every operator has a favorite injection and drainage point—a fact which becomes a handicap only if he fails or refuses to forsake his favorites when conditions demand it." Typical favorites are the carotid artery, femoral artery, jugular vein, subclavian vein. There are various choices of embalming fluid. If Flextone is used, it will produce a "mild, flexible rigidity. The skin retains a velvety softness, the tissues are rubbery and pliable. Ideal for women and children." It may be blended with B. and G. Products Company's Lyf-Lyk tint, which is guaranteed to reproduce "nature's own skin texture . . . the velvety appearance of living tissue." Suntone comes in three separate tints: Suntan; Special Cosmetic Tint, a pink shade "especially indicated for young female subjects"; and Regular Cosmetic Tint, moderately pink.

12   About three to six gallons of a dyed and perfumed solution of formaldehyde, glycerin, borax, phenol, alcohol, and water is soon circulating through Mr. Jones, whose mouth has been sewn together with a "needle directed upward between the upper lip and gum and brought out through the left nostril," with the corners raised slightly "for a more pleasant expression." If he should be bucktoothed, his teeth are cleaned with Bon Ami and coated with colorless nail polish. His eyes, meanwhile, are closed with flesh-tinted eye caps and eye cement.

13   The next step is to have at Mr. Jones with a thing called a trocar. This is a long, hollow needle attached to a tube, It is jabbed into the abdomen, poked around the entrails and chest cavity, the contents of which are pumped out and replaced with "cavity fluid." This done, and the hole in the abdomen sewn up, Mr. Jones's face is heavily creamed (to protect the skin from burns which may be caused by leakage of the chemicals), and he is covered with a sheet and left unmolested for a while. But not for long—there is more, much more, in store for him. He has been embalmed, but not yet restored, and the best time to start the restorative work is eight to ten hours after embalming, when the tissues have become firm and dry.

14   The object of all this attention to the corpse, it must be remembered, is to make it presentable for viewing in an attitude of healthy repose. "Our customs require the presentation of our dead in the semblance of normality . . . unmarred by the ravages of illness, disease or mutilation," says Mr. J. Sheridan Mayer in his *Restorative Art.* This is rather a large order since few people die in the full bloom of health, unravaged by illness and unmarked by some disfigurement. The funeral industry is equal to the challenge: "In some cases the gruesome appearance of a mutilated or disease-ridden subject may be quite discouraging. The task of restoration may seem impossible and shake the confidence of the embalmer. This is the time for intestinal fortitude and determination. Once the formative work is begun and affected tissues are cleaned or removed, all doubt of success vanish. It is surprising and gratifying to discover the results which may be obtained."

15   The embalmer, having allowed an appropriate interval to elapse, returns to the attack, but now he brings into play the skill and equipment of sculptor and cosmetician. Is a hand missing? Casting one in plaster of Paris is a simple matter. "For replacement purposes, only a cast of the back of the hand is necessary; this is within the ability of the average operator and is quite adequate." If a lip or two, a nose or an ear should be missing, the embalmer has at hand a variety of restorative waxes with which to model replacements. Pores and skin texture are simulated by stippling with a little brush, and over this cosmetics are laid on. Head off? Decapitation cases are rather routinely handled. Ragged edges are trimmed, and head joined to torso with a series of splints, wires and sutures. It is a good idea to have a little something at the neck—a scarf or high collar—when time for viewing comes. Swollen mouth? Cut out tissue as needed from inside the lips. If too much is removed, the surface contour can easily be restored by padding with cotton. Swollen necks and cheeks are reduced by removing tissue through vertical incisions made down each side of the neck. "When the deceased is casketed, the pillow will hide the suture incisions . . . as an extra precaution against leakage, the suture may be painted with liquid sealer."

16   The opposite condition is more likely to present itself—that of emaciation. His hypodermic syringe now loaded with massage cream, the embalmer seeks out and fills the hollowed and sunken areas by injection. In this procedure the backs of the hands and fingers and the under-chin area should not be neglected.

17   Positioning the lips is a problem that recurrently challenges the ingenuity of the embalmer. Closed too tightly they tend to give a stern, even disapproving expression. Ideally, embalmers feel, the lips should give the impression of being ever so slightly parted, the upper lip protruding slightly for a more youthful appearance. This takes some engineering, however, as the lips tend to drift apart. Lip drift can sometimes be remedied by pushing one or two straight pins through the inner margin of the lower lip and then inserting them between the two front upper teeth. If Mr. Jones happens to have no teeth, the pins can just as easily be anchored in his Armstrong Face Former and Denture Replacer. Another method to maintain lip closure is to dislocate the lower jaw, which is then held in its new position by a wire run through holes which have been drilled through the upper and lower jaws at the midline. As the French are fond of saying, *il faut souffrir pour être belle.*[1]

18   If Mr. Jones has died of jaundice, the embalming fluid will very likely turn him green. Does this deter the embalmer? Not if he has intestinal fortitude. Masking pastes and cosmetics are heavily laid on, burial garments and casket interiors are color-correlated with particular care, and Jones is displayed beneath rose-colored lights. Friends will say, "How *well* he looks." Death by carbon monoxide, on the other hand, can be rather a good thing from the embalmer's viewpoint: "One advantage is the fact that this type of discoloration

---

[1] "One must suffer to be beautiful." [Editor's note.]

is an exaggerated form of a natural pink coloration." This is nice because the healthy glow is already present and needs but little attention.

19   The patching and filling completed, Mr. Jones is now shaved, washed and dressed. Cream-based cosmetic, available in pink, flesh, suntan, brunette, and blond, is applied to his hands and face, his hair is shampooed and combed (and, in the case of Mrs. Jones, set), his hands manicured. For the horny-handed son of toil special care must be taken; cream should be applied to remove ingrained grime, and the nails cleaned. "If he were not in the habit of having them manicured in life, trimming and shaping is advised for better appearance—never questioned by kin."

20   Jones is now ready for casketing (this is the present principle of the verb "to casket"). In this operation his right shoulder should be depressed slightly "to turn the body a bit to the right and soften the appearance of lying flat on the back." Positioning the hands is a matter of importance, and special rubber positioning blocks may be used. The hands should be cupped slightly for a more lifelike, relaxed appearance. Proper placement of the body requires a delicate sense of balance. It should lie as high as possible in the casket, yet not so high that the lid, when lowered, will hit the nose. On the other hand, we are cautioned, placing the body too low "creates the impression that the body is in a box."

21   Jones is next wheeled into the appointed slumber room where a few last touches may be added—his favorite pipe placed in his hand or, if he was a great reader, a book propped into position. (In the case of little Master Jones a Teddy bear may be clutched.) Here he will hold open house for a few days, visiting hours 10 A.M. to 9 P.M.

Topics for Writing and Discussion

1. What is Mitford's reason for explaining the embalming process? What is her attitude toward this procedure?
2. Does Mitford use enough sensory details to help you understand this process and her attitude toward it? Cite some of her most effective details that appeal to your sense of sight, smell, and touch.
3. Why does Mitford quote extensively from textbooks and trade journals used by funeral directors? What does Mitford's use of euphemisms such as "slumber room" and "dermasurgeon" add to her position?
4. How does Mitford's technique of using the hypothetical "Mr. Jones" add to the effectiveness of her argument? Why doesn't Mitford simply use the words "corpse" or "body" throughout her essay?
5. By supplying information about this process, does Mitford change your mind about its necessity or desirability? Not all readers respond positively to this essay; in fact, many find Mitford's comments upsetting or inappropriate. As you think about funerals or memorial services you have attended, write an essay that challenges or supports Mitford's point of view.

ATTITUDE

Garrison Keillor
(1942–   )

Born in Anoka, Minnesota, a suburb of Minneapolis,
Garrison Keillor began his broadcasting career in 1963
while a student at the University of Minnesota. He
worked as an announcer for a local radio station and
later joined Minnesota Public Radio in St. Paul as a
producer and announcer. In 1974, Keillor created "A
Prairie Home Companion," a variety program blending
storytelling, music, and humor, broadcast weekly on
National Public Radio, that is still enormously popular
today. The mythical town of Lake Wobegon, Minnesota, provides the setting for many of Keillor's stories
and sketches. His work also appears in print in such
periodicals as the *Atlantic Monthly* and *The New
Yorker.* His books include *Lake Wobegon Days* (1985),
Leaving Town (1987), *We Are Still Married* (1989),
WLT: A Radio Romance (1991), and *Wobegon Boy*
(1997). "Attitude" was published in a 1982 collection
of essays, *Happy to Be Here: Stories and Comic Pieces.*

1   LONG ago I passed the point in life when major-league ballplayers begin to
be younger than yourself. Now all of them are, except for a few aging trigenar-
ians and a couple of quadros who don't get around on the fastball as well as
they used to and who sit out the second games of doubleheaders. However, despite my age (thirty-nine), I am still active and have a lot of interests. One of
them is slow-pitch softball, a game that lets me go through the motions of
baseball without getting beaned or having to run too hard. I play on a pretty
casual team, one that drinks beer on the bench and substitutes freely. If a
player's wife or girlfriend wants to play, we give her a glove and send her out to
right field, no questions asked, and if she lets a pop fly drop six feet in front of
her, nobody agonizes over it.

Garrison Keillor (© Mario Ruiz / Picture Group)

2   Except me. This year. For the first time in my life, just as I am entering the dark twilight of my slow-pitch career, I find myself taking the game seriously. It isn't the bonehead play that bothers me especially—the pop fly that drops untouched, the slow roller juggled and the ball then heaved ten feet over the first baseman's head and into the next diamond, the routine singles that go through outfielders' legs for doubles and triples with gloves flung after them. No, it isn't our stone-glove fielding or pussyfoot base-running or limp-wristed hitting that give me fits, though these have put us on the short end of some mighty ridiculous scores this summer. It's our attitude.

3   Bottom of the ninth, down 18–3, two outs, a man on first and a woman on third, and our third baseman strikes out. *Strikes out!* In slow-pitch, not even your grandmother strikes out, but this guy does, and after his third strike—a wild swing at a ball that bounces on the plate—he topples over in the dirt and lies flat on his back, laughing. *Laughing!*

4   Same game, earlier. They have the bases loaded. A weak grounder is hit to-ward our second baseperson. The runners are running. She picks up the ball, and she looks at them. She looks at first, at second, at home. We yell, "Throw it! Throw it!" and she throws it, underhand, at the pitcher, who has turned and run to back up the catcher. The ball rolls across the third-base line and under the bench. Three runs score. The batter, a fatso, chugs into second. The other team hoots and hollers, and what does she do? She shrugs and smiles ("Oh, silly me"); after all, it's only a game. Like the aforementioned strikeout artist, she treats her error as a joke. They have forgiven themselves instantly, which is unforgivable. It is *we* who should forgive them, who can say, "It's all right, it's only a game." They are supposed to throw up their hands and kick the dirt and hang their heads, as if this boner, even if it is their sixteenth of the afternoon—*this* is the one that really and truly breaks their hearts.

5   That attitude sweetens the game for everyone. The sinner feels sweet re-morse. The fatso feels some sense of accomplishment; this is no bunch of rum-dums he forced into an error but a team with some class. We, the sinner's teammates, feel momentary anger at her—dumb! dumb play!—but then, see-ing her grief, we sympathize with her in our hearts (any one of us might have made that mistake or one worse), and we yell encouragement, including the shortstop, who, moments before, dropped an easy throw for a force at second. "That's all right! Come on! We got 'em!" we yell. "Shake it off! These turkeys can't hit!" This makes us all feel good, even though the turkeys now lead us by ten runs. We're getting clobbered, but we have a winning attitude.

6   Let me say this about attitude: Each player is responsible for his or her own attitude, and to a considerable degree you can *create* a good attitude by doing certain little things on the field. These are certain little things that ballplayers do in the Bigs, and we ought to be doing them in the Slows.

1.   When going up to bat, don't step right into the batter's box as if it were an elevator. The box is your turf, your stage. Take possession of it slowly and deliberately, starting with a lot of back-bending, knee-stretching, and torso-revolving in the on-deck circle. Then, approaching the box, stop outside it and

tap the dirt off your spikes with your bat. You don't have spikes, you have sneakers, of course, but the significance of the tapping is the same. Then, upon entering the box, spit on the ground. It's a way of saying, "This here is mine. This is where I get my hits."

2. Spit frequently. Spit at all crucial moments. Spit correctly. Spit should be *blown,* not ptuied weakly with the lips, which often results in dribble. Spitting should convey forcefulness of purpose, concentration, pride. Spit down, not in the direction of others. Spit in the glove and on the fingers, especially after making a real knucklehead play; it's a way of saying, "I dropped the ball because my glove was dry."

3. At bat and in the field, pick up dirt. Rub dirt in the fingers (especially after spitting on them). Toss dirt, as if testing the wind for velocity and direction. Smooth the dirt. Be involved with dirt. If no dirt is available (e.g., in the outfield), pluck tufts of grass. Fielders should be grooming their areas constantly between plays, flicking away tiny sticks and bits of gravel.

4. Take your time. Tie your laces. Confer with your teammates about possible situations that may arise and conceivable options in dealing with them. Extend the game. Three errors on three consecutive plays can be humiliating if the plays occur within the space of a couple of minutes, but if each error is separated from the next by extensive conferences on the mound, lace-tying, glove adjustments, and arguing close calls (if any), the effect on morale is minimized.

5. Talk. Not just an occasional "Let's get a hit now" but continuous rhythmic chatter, a flow of syllables: "Hey babe hey babe c'mon babe good stick now hey babe long tater take him downtown babe . . . hey good eye good eye."

Infield chatter is harder to maintain. Since the slow-pitch is required to be a soft underhand lob, infielders hesitate to say, "Smoke him babe hey low heat hey throw it on the black babe chuck it in there back him up babe no hit no hit." Say it anyway.

6. One final rule, perhaps the most important of all: When your team is up and has made the third out, the batter and the players who were left on base do not come back to the bench for their gloves. *They remain on the field, and their teammates bring their gloves out to them.* This requires some organization and discipline, but it pays off big in morale. It says, "Although we're getting our pants knocked off, still we must conserve our energy."

7   Imagine that you have bobbled two fly balls in this rout and now you have just tried to stretch a single into a double and have been easily thrown out sliding into second base, where the base runner ahead of you had stopped. It was the third out and a dumb play, and your opponents smirk at you as they run off the field. You are the goat, a lonely and tragic figure sitting in the dirt. You curse yourself, jerking your head sharply forward. You stand up and kick the base. How miserable! How degrading! Your utter shame, though brief, bears silent testimony to the worthiness of your teammates, whom you have let down, and they appreciate it. They call out to you now as they take the field,

and as the second baseman runs to his position he says, "Let's get 'em now," and tosses you your glove. Lowering your head, you trot slowly out to right. There you do some deep knee bends. You pick grass. You find a pebble and fling it into foul territory. As the first batter comes to the plate, you check the sun. You get set in your stance, poised to fly. Feet spread, hands on hips, you bend slightly at the waist and spit the expert spit of a veteran ballplayer—a player who has known the agony of defeat but who always bounces back, a player who has lost a stride on the base paths but can still make the big play.

8   This is *ball*, ladies and gentlemen. This is what it's all about.

TOPICS FOR WRITING AND DISCUSSION

1. What process is Keillor explaining in this essay? Is it directional or informative?
2. What is Keillor's purpose in writing this essay? Is his thesis confined to the playing of softball? How, according to this author, are attitude and performance related?
3. Describe the tone of this essay. How does Keillor produce this tone? What role do personal anecdotes play in this essay?
4. Why does Keillor take five paragraphs before introducing the steps in his process? Would the essay be more successful had he begun his list earlier? Why or why not?
5. Think of a time when you or someone you know did *not* conduct himself or herself with the right attitude during or following a difficult situation. Use this person's response to illustrate an essay showing others how to avoid the damage that can result from a negative or inappropriate attitude.

Martin Luther King, Jr. (© 1966 Ernst Haas / © 1966 Magnum Photos)

Nonviolent Resistance

Martin Luther King, Jr.
(1929–1968)

Martin Luther King, Jr., was born in Atlanta, Georgia. A product of the Atlanta public schools (where he skipped both the ninth and twelfth grades), he graduated from Morehouse College in 1948, just after he followed his father's example by being ordained as a Baptist minister. He was just 18. By 1951, he had earned a divinity degree from Crozer Theological Seminary in Pennsylvania, and in 1955 he received his doctorate in systematic theology from Boston University. That same year, he was called to be pastor of the Dexter Avenue Baptist Church in Montgomery, Alabama. King's rise to national prominence began in Montgomery, where he led a 382-day bus boycott that eventually led to the 1956 Supreme Court decision declaring the segregated bus system in Alabama unconstitutional. In 1957, King was elected president of the newly formed Southern Christian Leadership Conference (SCLC), which he founded with several African-American ministers. While holding this office, King continued to promote the abolishment of racial injustice through nonviolent resistance.

As a result of the efforts of the SCLC and Dr. King, President Kennedy proposed to Congress a far-reaching civil rights bill, and on August 28, 1964, King led the March on Washington, where he delivered his famous "I Have a Dream" speech. Congress later passed the Civil Rights Act of 1964, which prohibited discrimination in public places and demanded equal opportunity in education and employment. In 1964, King was awarded the Nobel Peace Prize (at 35, he was the youngest person ever to win the prize). His

organized march in Selma, Alabama, to protest the bla-
tant denial of African-Americans' voting rights contributed to Congressional passage of President
Johnson's landmark Voting Rights Act of 1965. While
in Memphis, Tennessee, to support the Poor People's
Campaign, he delivered his "I've Been to the Mountain-
top" speech. He was assassinated the next day while
standing on the balcony of his hotel room. The riots
that followed prompted Congress to enact the Civil
Rights Act of 1968, which banned discrimination in
the sale and renting of housing.

Widely acclaimed for his communication skills,
King's writings include the books *Stride Toward Free-
dom* (1958), *Why We Can't Wait* (1964), and *Where
Do We Go From Here: Chaos or Community* (1967).
His shorter pieces have been collected in *A Testament
of Hope* (1968) and *The Words of Martin Luther King,
Jr.* (1983), edited by his widow Coretta Scott King.
"Nonviolent Resistance," which first appeared in *Stride
Toward Freedom*, describes the processes oppressed
people follow as they confront their situation.

1   OPPRESSED people deal with their oppression in three characteristic ways.
One way is acquiescence: the oppressed resign themselves to their doom. They
tacitly adjust themselves to oppression, and thereby become conditioned to it.
In every movement toward freedom some of the oppressed prefer to remain
oppressed. Almost 2800 years ago Moses set out to lead the children of Israel
from the slavery of Egypt to the freedom of the promised land. He soon discovered that slaves do not always welcome their deliverers. They become
accustomed to being slaves. They would rather bear those ills they have, as
Shakespeare pointed out, than flee to others that they know not of. They prefer the "fleshpots of Egypt" to the ordeals of emancipation.

2   There is such a thing as the freedom of exhaustion. Some people are so
worn down by the yoke of oppression that they give up. A few years ago in the
slum areas of Atlanta, a Negro guitarist used to sing almost daily: "Ben down
so long that down don't bother me." This is the type of negative freedom and
resignation that often engulfs the life of the oppressed.

3   But this is not the way out. To accept passively an unjust system is to cooperate with that system; thereby the oppressed become as evil as the oppressor. Noncooperation with evil is as much a moral obligation as is cooperation with good. The oppressed must never allow the conscience of the oppressor to slumber. Religion reminds every man that he is his brother's keeper. To accept injustice or segregation passively is to say to the oppressor that his actions are morally right. It is a way of allowing his conscience to fall asleep. At this moment the oppressed fails to be his brother's keeper. So acquiescence—while often the easier way—is not the moral way. It is the way of the coward. The Negro cannot win the respect of his oppressor by acquiescing; he merely increases the oppressor's arrogance and contempt. Acquiescence is interpreted as proof of the Negro's inferiority. The Negro cannot win the respect of the white people of the South or the peoples of the world if he is willing to sell the future of his children for his personal and immediate comfort and safety.

4   A second way that oppressed people sometimes deal with oppression is to resort to physical violence and corroding hatred. Violence often brings about momentary results. Nations have frequently won their independence in battle. But in spite of temporary victories, violence never brings permanent peace. It solves no social problem; it merely creates new and more complicated ones.

5   Violence as a way of achieving racial justice is both impractical and immoral. It is impractical because it is a descending spiral ending in destruction for all. The old law of an eye for an eye leaves everybody blind. It is immoral because it seeks to humiliate the opponent rather than win his understanding; it seeks to annihilate rather than to convert. Violence is immoral because it thrives on hatred rather than love. It destroys community and makes brotherhood impossible. It leaves society in monologue rather than dialogue. Violence ends by defeating itself. It creates bitterness in the survivors and brutality in the destroyers. A voice echoes through time saying to every potential Peter, "Put up your sword." History is cluttered with the wreckage of nations that failed to follow his command.

6   If the American Negro and other victims of oppression succumb to the temptation of using violence in the struggle for freedom, future generations will be the recipients of a desolate night of bitterness, and our chief legacy to them will be an endless reign of meaningless chaos. Violence is not the way.

7   The third way open to oppressed people in their quest for freedom is the way of nonviolent resistance. Like the synthesis in Hegelian philosophy, the principle of nonviolent resistance seeks to reconcile the truths of two opposites—acquiescence and violence—while avoiding the extremes and immoralities of both. The nonviolent resister agrees with the person who acquiesces that one should not be physically aggressive toward his opponent; but he balances the equation by agreeing with the person of violence that evil must be resisted. He avoids the nonresistance of the former and the violent resistance of the latter. With nonviolent resistance, no individual or group need submit to any wrong, nor need anyone resort to violence in order to right a wrong.

8   It seems to me that this is the method that must guide the actions of the Negro in the present crisis in race relations. Through nonviolent resistance the Negro will be able to rise to the noble height of opposing the unjust system while loving the perpetrators of the system. The Negro must work passionately and unrelentingly for full stature as a citizen, but he must not use inferior methods to gain it. He must never come to terms with falsehood, malice, hate, or destruction.

9   Nonviolent resistance makes it possible for the Negro to remain in the South and struggle for his rights. The Negro's problem will not be solved by running away. He cannot listen to the glib suggestion of those who would urge him to migrate en masse to other sections of the country. By grasping his great opportunity in the South he can make a lasting contribution to the moral strength of the nation and set a sublime example of courage for generations yet unborn.

10   By nonviolent resistance, the Negro can also enlist all men of good will in his struggle for equality. The problem is not a purely racial one, with Negroes set against whites. In the end, it is not a struggle between people at all, but a tension between justice and injustice. Nonviolent resistance is not aimed against oppressors but against oppression. Under its banner consciences, not racial groups, are enlisted.

11   If the Negro is to achieve the goal of integration, he must organize himself into a militant and nonviolent mass movement. All three elements are indispensable. The movement for equality and justice can only be a success if it has both a mass and militant character; the barriers to be overcome require both. Nonviolence is an imperative in order to bring about ultimate community.

12   A mass movement of militant quality that is not at the same time committed to nonviolence tends to generate conflict, which in turn breeds anarchy. The support of the participants and the sympathy of the uncommitted are both inhibited by the threat that bloodshed will engulf the community. This reaction in turn encourages the opposition to threaten and resort to force. When, however, the mass movement repudiates violence while moving resolutely toward its goal, its opponents are revealed as the instigators and practitioners of violence if it occurs. Then public support is magnetically attracted to the advocates of nonviolence, while those who employ violence are literally disarmed by overwhelming sentiment against their stand.

13   Only through a nonviolent approach can the fears of the white community be mitigated. A guilt-ridden white minority lives in fear that if the Negro should ever attain power, he would act without restraint or pity to revenge the injustices and brutality of the years. It is something like a parent who continually mistreats a son. One day that parent raises his hand to strike the son, only to discover that the son is now as tall as he is. The parent is suddenly afraid—fearful that the son will use his new physical power to repay his parent for all the blows of the past.

14   The Negro, once a helpless child, has now grown up politically, culturally, and economically. Many white men fear retaliation. The job of the Negro is to

show them that they have nothing to fear, that the Negro understands and forgives and is ready to forget the past. He must convince the white man that all he seeks is justice, *for both himself and the white man.* A mass movement exercising nonviolence is an object lesson in power under discipline, a demonstration to the white community that if such a movement attained a degree of strength, it would use its power creatively and not vengefully.

15   Nonviolence can touch men where the law cannot reach them. When the law regulates behavior it plays an indirect part in molding public sentiment. The enforcement of the law is itself a form of peaceful persuasion. But the law needs help. The courts can order desegregation of the public schools. But what can be done to mitigate the fears, to disperse the hatred, violence, and irrationality gathered around school integration, to take the initiative out of the hands of racial demagogues, to release respect for the law? In the end, for laws to be obeyed, men must believe they are right.

16   Here nonviolence comes in as the ultimate form of persuasion. It is the method which seeks to implement the just law by appealing to the conscience of the great decent majority who through blindness, fear, pride, or irrationality have allowed their consciences to sleep.

17   The nonviolent resisters can summarize their message in the following simple terms: We will take direct action against injustice without waiting for other agencies to act. We will not obey unjust laws or submit to unjust practices. We will do this peacefully, openly, cheerfully because our aim is to persuade. We adopt the means of nonviolence because our end is a community at peace with itself. We will try to persuade with our words, but if our words fail, we will try to persuade with our acts. We will always be willing to talk and seek fair compromise, but we are ready to suffer when necessary and even risk our lives to become witnesses to the truth as we see it.

18   The way of nonviolence means a willingness to suffer and sacrifice. It may mean going to jail. If such is the case the resister must be willing to fill the jail houses of the South. It may even mean physical death. But if physical death is the price that a man must pay to free his children and his white brethren from a permanent death of the spirit, then nothing could be more redemptive.

TOPICS FOR WRITING AND DISCUSSION

1. What are the three ways oppressed people deal with their situation? How do the examples and the words King chooses to describe the first two processes let readers know that he opposes those choices?
2. Why does King believe that nonviolent resistance is the right method for black people to choose as they strive for freedom? What three elements must be part of the process of nonviolent resistance?
3. Who are King's intended readers? How does he appeal to those readers? How might other readers react to his proposals?
4. Read another selection in this text that focuses on questions of equal rights, such as "Discrimination" by Ralph Ellison, "Professions for Women" by

Virginia Woolf, or "I Have a Dream" also by King. Compare and contrast the ideas presented in your selection to those offered here on the subject of confronting oppression.

5. Research an important act of nonviolent resistance in America's struggles for equal rights, such as Rosa Parks' famous bus ride, the Freedom Riders' Mississippi sit-ins, or the suffragists' 1917 hunger strike. Recreate the stages of the event as they occurred for a reader who has heard of the episode but never knew exactly what happened.

More than Just a Shrine: Paying Homage to the Ghosts of Ellis Island

Mary Gordon
(1949–)

Novelist, poet, essayist, and short-story writer Mary Gordon was born in Long Island, New York, and educated at Barnard College and the University of Syracuse. Her work, which has received critical acclaim and popular success, includes *Final Payments* (1978), *The Company of Women* (1981), *Men and Angels* (1985), *The Other Side* (1989), *Temporary Shelter* (1990), *The Shadow of Man* (1996), and *Spending: A Utopian Divertimento* (1998). In 1997, she won first prize of the O. Henry Awards for "City Life." In the following essay, Gordon describes a trip to Ellis Island, where she imagines the immigration process undertaken by those desperate to enter America, including her own seventeen-year-old grandmother.

1 I once sat in a hotel in Bloomsbury trying to have breakfast alone. A Russian with a habit of compulsively licking his lips asked if he could join me. I was afraid to say no; I thought it might be bad for détente. He explained to me that he was a linguist, and that he always liked to talk to Americans to see if he could make any connection between their speech and their ethnic background. When I told him about my mixed ancestry—my mother is Irish and Italian, my father a Lithuanian Jew—he began jumping up and down in his seat, rubbing his hands together, and licking his lips even more frantically.

2 "Ah," he said, "so you are really somebody who comes from what is called the boiling pot of America." Yes, I told him, yes I was, but I quickly rose to leave. I thought it would be too hard to explain to him the relation of the boiling potters to the main course, and I wanted to get to the British Museum. I told him that the only thing I could think of that united people whose backgrounds, histories, and points of view were utterly diverse was that their people had landed at a place called Ellis Island.

Mary Gordon (AP/Wide World Photos)

3   I didn't tell him that Ellis Island was the only American landmark I'd ever visited. How could I describe to him the estrangement I'd always felt from the kind of traveler who visits shrines to America's past greatness, those rebuilt forts with muskets behind glass and sabers mounted on the walls and gift shops selling maple sugar candy in the shape of Indian headdresses, those reconstructed villages with tables set for fifty and the Paul Revere silver gleaming? All that Americana—Plymouth Rock, Gettysburg, Mount Vernon, Valley Forge—it all inhabits for me a zone of blurred abstraction with far less hold on my imagination than the Bastille or Hampton Court. I suppose I've always known that my uninterest in it contains a large component of the willed: I am American, and those places purport to be my history. But they are not mine.

4   Ellis Island is, though; it's the one place I can be sure my people are connected to. And so I made a journey there to find my history, like any Rotarian traveling in his Winnebago to Antietam to find his. I had become part of that humbling democracy of people looking in some site for a past that has grown unreal. The monument I traveled to was not, however, a tribute to some old glory. The minute I set foot upon the island I could feel all that it stood for: insecurity, obedience, anxiety, dehumanization, the terrified and careful deference of the displaced. I hadn't traveled to the Battery and boarded a ferry across from the Statue of Liberty to raise flags or breathe a richer, more triumphant air. I wanted to do homage to the ghosts.

5   I felt them everywhere, from the moment I disembarked and saw the building with its high-minded brick, its hopeful little lawn, its ornamental cornices. The place was derelict when I arrived; it had not functioned for more than thirty years—almost as long as the time it had operated at full capacity as a major immigration center. I was surprised to learn what a small part of history Ellis Island had occupied. The main building was constructed in 1892, then rebuilt between 1898 and 1900 after a fire. Most of the immigrants who arrived during the latter half of the nineteenth century, mainly northern and western Europeans, landed not at Ellis Island but on the western tip of the Battery at Castle Garden, which had opened as a receiving center for immigrants in 1855.

6   By the 1880s the facilities at Castle Garden had grown scandalously inadequate. Officials looked for an island on which to build a new immigration center because they thought that on an island immigrants could be more easily protected from swindlers and quickly transported to railroad terminals in New Jersey. Bedloe's Island was considered, but New Yorkers were aghast at the idea of a "Babel" ruining their beautiful new treasure, "Liberty Enlightening the World." The statue's sculptor, Frédéric Auguste Bartholdi, reacted to the prospect of immigrants landing near his masterpiece in horror; he called it a "monstrous plan." So much for Emma Lazarus.

7   Ellis Island was finally chosen because the citizens of New Jersey petitioned the federal government to remove from the island an old naval powder magazine that they thought dangerously close to the Jersey shore. The explosives were removed; no one wanted the island for anything. It was the perfect place to build an immigration center.

8   I thought about the island's history as I walked into the building and made my way to the room that was the center in my imagination of the Ellis Island experience: the Great Hall. It had been made real for me in the stark, accusing photographs of Louis Hine and others who took those pictures to make a point. It was in the Great Hall that everyone had waited—waiting, always, the great vocation of the dispossessed. The room was empty, except for me and a handful of other visitors and the park ranger who showed us around. I felt myself grow insignificant in that room, with its huge semicircular windows, its air, even in dereliction, of solid and official probity.

9   I walked in the deathlike expansiveness of the room's disuse and tried to think of what it might have been like, filled and swarming. More than sixteen million immigrants came through that room; approximately 250,000 were rejected. Not really a large proportion, but the implications for the rejected were dreadful. For some, there was nothing to go back to, or there was certain death; for others, who left as adventurers, to return would be to adopt in local memory the fool's role, and the failure's. No wonder that the island's history includes reports of three thousand suicides.

10   Sometimes immigrants could pass through Ellis Island in mere hours, though for some the process took days. The particulars of the experience in the Great Hall were often influenced by the political events and attitudes on the mainland. In the 1890s and the first years of the new century, when cheap labor was needed, the newly built receiving center took in its immigrants with comparatively little question. But as the century progressed, the economy worsened, eugenics became both scientifically respectable and popular, and World War I made American xenophobia seem rooted in fact.

11   Immigration acts were passed; newcomers had to prove, besides moral correctness and financial solvency, their ability to read. Quota laws came into effect, limiting the number of immigrants from southern and eastern Europe to less than 14 percent of the total quota. Intelligence tests were biased against all non-English-speaking persons and medical examinations became increasingly strict, until the machinery of immigration nearly collapsed under its own weight. The Second Quota Law of 1924 provided that all immigrants be inspected and issued visas at American consular offices in Europe, rendering the center almost obsolete.

12   On the day of my visit, my mind fastened upon the medical inspections, which had always seemed to me most emblematic of the ignominy and terror the immigrants endured. The medical inspectors, sometimes dressed in uniforms like soldiers, were particularly obsessed with a disease of the eyes called trachoma, which they checked for by flipping back the immigrants' top eyelids with a hook used for buttoning gloves—a method that sometimes resulted in the transmission of the disease to healthy people. Mothers feared that if their children cried too much, their red eyes would be mistaken for a symptom of the disease and the whole family would be sent home. Those immigrants suspected of some physical disability had initials chalked on their coats. I remembered the photographs I'd seen of people standing, dumbstruck and innocent

as cattle, with their manifest numbers hung around their necks and initials marked in chalk upon their coats: "E" for eye trouble, "K" for hernia, "L" for lameness, "X" for mental defects, "H" for heart disease.

13   I thought of my grandparents as I stood in the room; my seventeen-year-old grandmother, coming alone from Ireland in 1896, vouched for by a stranger who had found her a place as a domestic servant to some Irish who had done well. I tried to imagine the assault it all must have been for her; I've been to her hometown, a collection of farms with a main street—smaller than the athletic field of my local public school. She must have watched the New York skyline as the first- and second-class passengers were whisked off the gangplank with the most cursory of inspections while she was made to board a ferry to the new immigration center.

14   What could she have made of it—this buff-painted wooden structure with its towers and its blue slate roof, a place *Harper's Weekly* described as "a latter-day watering place hotel"? It would have been the first time she'd have heard people speaking something other than English. She would have mingled with people carrying baskets on their heads and eating foods unlike any she had ever seen—dark-eyed people, like the Sicilian she would marry ten years later, who came over with his family, responsible even then for his mother and sister. I don't know what they thought, my grandparents, for they were not expansive people, nor romantic; they didn't like to think of what they called "the hard times," and their trip across the ocean was the single adventurous act of lives devoted after landing to security, respectability, and fitting in.

15   What is the potency of Ellis Island for someone like me—an American, obviously, but one who has always felt that the country really belonged to the early settlers, that, as J. F. Powers wrote in "Morte D'Urban," it had been "handed down to them by the Pilgrims, George Washington and others, and that they were taking a risk in letting you live in it." I have never been the victim of overt discrimination; nothing I have wanted has been denied me because of the accidents of blood. But I suppose it is part of being an American to be engaged in a somewhat tiresome but always self-absorbing process of national definition. And in this process, I have found in traveling to Ellis Island an important piece of evidence that could remind me I was right to feel my differentness. Something had happened to my people on that island, a result of the eternal wrongheadedness of American protectionism and the predictabilities of simple greed. I came to the island, too, so I could tell the ghosts that I was one of them, and that I honored them—their stoicism, and their innocence, the fear that turned them inward, and their pride. I wanted to tell them that I liked them better than the Americans who made them pass through the Great Hall and stole their names and chalked their weaknesses in public on their clothing. And to tell the ghosts what I have always thought: that American history was a very classy party that was not much fun until they arrived, brought the good food, turned up the music, and taught everyone to dance.

Topics for Writing and Discussion

1. Why does Gordon visit Ellis Island but not other American landmarks? Why does she feel she is one of the "boiling potters" rather than part of the "main course" (paragraph 2)?

2. Once on the island, what process does Gordon imagine? Which details are particularly effective in creating a sense of "being there" for the reader? Why does she mention her grandparents?

3. What is Gordon's message for her immigrant "ghosts" at the end of her essay? Why does she want to pay them "homage"? What has she gained from her trip to Ellis Island?

4. What aspects of America does Gordon criticize in her essay? Do you agree with all her views? How would you defend your agreement or disagreement?

5. On Ellis Island, Gordon imagines her grandmother facing the difficulties of immigration. Do you know how any of your ancestors came to this country? Write an essay outlining the steps one of them took to settle in this country. (If you don't know details but have the approximate date and your ancestor's country of origin, consider researching a typical immigration process at that time. Imagine your relative's steps and reactions, as Gordon did.) What would you like to say to your "ghosts"?

TAKE THIS FISH AND LOOK AT IT

Samuel H. Scudder
(1837–1911)

Harvard-trained Samuel H. Scudder honed his acute observational skills under the tutelage of the well-known professor of natural history Louis Agassiz. Scudder's scholarly work includes a comprehensive catalogue of the scientific serials published between 1633 and 1876 in the natural and physical sciences as well as in mathematics. As a respected entomologist, he also made important contributions to the study of butterflies and Othopteran insects. In "Take This Fish and Look at It," Scudder reminds his readers of the importance of close, intense, and repeated observation.

1   IT was more than fifteen years ago that I entered the laboratory of Professor Agassiz, and told him I had enrolled my name in the Scientific School as a student of natural history. He asked me a few questions about my object in coming, my antecedents generally, the mode in which I afterwards proposed to use the knowledge I might acquire, and, finally, whether I wished to study any special branch. To the latter I replied that, while I wished to be well grounded in all departments of zoology, I purposed to devote myself specially to insects.

2   "When do you wish to begin?" he asked.

3   "Now," I replied.

4   This seemed to please him, and with an energetic "Very well!" he reached from a shelf a huge jar of specimens in yellow alcohol. "Take this fish," he said, "and look at it; we call it a haemulon; by and by I will ask you what you have seen."

5   With that he left me, but in a moment returned with explicit instructions as to the care of the object entrusted to me.

6   "No man is fit to be a naturalist," said he, "who does not know how to take care of specimens."

7   I was to keep the fish before me in a tin tray, and occasionally moisten the surface with alcohol from the jar, always taking care to replace the stopper

Samuel Scudder (Museum of Comparative Zoology, Harvard University, © President and Fellows of Harvard University)

tightly. Those were not the days of ground-glass stoppers and elegantly shaped exhibition jars; all the old students will recall the huge neckless glass bottles with their leaky, wax-besmeared corks, half eaten by insects, and begrimed with cellar dust. Entomology was a cleaner science than ichthyology, but the example of the Professor, who had unhesitatingly plunged to the bottom of the jar to produce the fish, was infectious; and though this alcohol had a "very ancient and fishlike smell," I really dared not show any aversion within these sacred precincts, and treated the alcohol as though it were pure water. Still I was conscious of a passing feeling of disappointment, for gazing at a fish did not commend itself to an ardent entomologist. My friends at home, too, were annoyed when they discovered that no amount of eau-de-Cologne would drown the perfume which haunted me like a shadow.

8   In ten minutes I had seen all that could be seen in that fish, and started in search of the Professor—who had, however, left the Museum; and when I returned, after lingering over some of the odd animals stored in the upper apartment, my specimen was dry all over. I dashed the fluid over the fish as if to resuscitate the beast from a fainting fit, and looked with anxiety for a return of the normal sloppy appearance. This little excitement over, nothing was to be done but to return to a steadfast gaze at my mute companion. Half an hour passed—an hour—another hour; the fish began to look loathsome. I turned it over and around; looked it in the face—ghastly; from behind, beneath, above, sideways, at three-quarters' view—just as ghastly. I was in despair; at an early hour I concluded that lunch was necessary; so, with infinite relief, the fish was carefully replaced in the jar, and for an hour I was free.

9   On my return, I learned that Professor Agassiz had been at the Museum, but had gone, and would not return for several hours. My fellow-students were too busy to be disturbed by continued conversation. Slowly I drew forth that hideous fish, and with a feeling of desperation again looked at it. I might not use a magnifying-glass; instruments of all kinds were interdicted. My two hands, my two eyes, and the fish: it seemed a most limited field. I pushed my finger down its throat to feel how sharp the teeth were. I began to count the scales in the different rows, until I was convinced that was nonsense. At last a happy thought struck me—I would draw the fish; and now with surprise I began to discover new features in the creature. Just then the Professor returned.

10   "That is right," said he; "a pencil is one of the best of eyes. I am glad to notice, too, that you keep your specimen wet, and your bottle corked."

11   With these encouraging words, he added: "Well, what is it like?"

12   He listened attentively to my brief rehearsal of the structure of parts whose names were still unknown to me: the fringed gill-arches and movable operculum; the pores of the head, fleshy lips and lidless eyes; the lateral line, the spinous fins and forked tail; the compressed and arched body. When I finished, he waited as if expecting more, and then, with an air of disappointment:

13   "You have not looked very carefully; why," he continued more earnestly, "you haven't even seen one of the most conspicuous features of the animal, which is as plainly before your eyes as the fish itself; look again, look again!" and he left me to my misery.

14　　I was piqued; I was mortified. Still more of that wretched fish! But now I set myself to my task with a will, and discovered one new thing after another, until I saw how just the Professor's criticism had been. The afternoon passed quickly; and when, towards its close, the Professor inquired:

15　　"Do you see it yet?"

16　　"No," I replied, "I am certain I do not, but I see how little I saw before."

17　　"That is next best," said he, earnestly, "but I won't hear you now; put away your fish and go home; perhaps you will be ready with a better answer in the morning. I will examine you before you look at the fish."

18　　This was disconcerting. Not only must I think of my fish all night, studying, without the object before me, what this unknown but most visible feature might be; but also, without reviewing my discoveries, I must give an exact account of them the next day. I had a bad memory; so I walked home by Charles River in a distracted state, with my two perplexities.

19　　The cordial greeting from the Professor the next morning was reassuring; here was a man who seemed to be quite as anxious as I that I should see for myself what he saw.

20　　"Do you perhaps mean," I asked, "that the fish has symmetrical sides with paired organs?"

21　　His thoroughly pleased "Of course! of course!" repaid the wakeful hours of the previous night. After he had discoursed most happily and enthusiastically—as he always did—upon the importance of this point, I ventured to ask what I should do next.

22　　"Oh, look at your fish!" he said, and left me again to my own devices. In a little more than an hour he returned, and heard my new catalogue.

23　　"That is good, that is good!" he repeated; "but that is not all; go on"; and so for three long days he placed that fish before my eyes, forbidding me to look at anything else, or to use any artificial aid. "Look, look, look," was his repeated injunction.

24　　This was the best entomological lesson I ever had—a lesson whose influence has extended to the details of every subsequent study; a legacy the Professor had left to me, as he has left it to so many others, of inestimable value, which we could not buy, with which we cannot part.

25　　A year afterward, some of us were amusing ourselves with chalking outlandish beasts on the Museum blackboard. We drew prancing starfishes; frogs in mortal combat; hydra-headed worms; stately crawfishes, standing on their tails, bearing aloft umbrellas; and grotesque fishes with gaping mouths and staring eyes. The Professor came in shortly after, and was as amused as any at our experiments. He looked at the fishes.

26　　"Haemulons, every one of them," he said; "Mr. _____ drew them."

27　　True; and to this day, if I attempt a fish, I can draw nothing but haemulons.

28　　The fourth day, a second fish of the same group was placed beside the first, and I was bidden to point out the resemblances and differences between the two; another and another followed, until the entire family lay before me, and a whole legion of jars covered the table and surrounding shelves; the odor had become a pleasant perfume; and even now, the sight of an old, six-inch worm-eaten cork brings fragrant memories.

29   The whole group of haemulons was thus brought in review; and, whether engaged upon the dissection of the internal organs, the preparation and examination of the bony framework, or the description of the various parts, Agassiz's training in the method of observing facts and their orderly arrangement was ever accompanied by the urgent exhortation not to be content with them.

30   "Facts are stupid things," he would say, "until brought into connection with some general law."

31   At the end of eight months, it was almost with reluctance that I left these friends and turned to insects; but what I had gained by this outside experience has been of greater value than years of later investigation in my favorite groups.

TOPICS FOR WRITING AND DISCUSSION

1.   What was Professor Agassiz's purpose in demanding that Scudder repeatedly look at the fish?

2.   Scudder claims that Professor Agassiz's process taught him a lesson "of inestimable value." What was this lesson? What does Agassiz mean when he says, "Facts are stupid things until brought into connection with some general law"?

3.   Why does Scudder use a narrative approach to tell about the process he learned from Agassiz? Why not simply present an essay that lists the steps one should take to become a good observer?

4.   Consider your own academic or professional life. How might the process of observation Scudder praises here be successfully applied to a subject you are studying? How might it be applied to the draft of an essay you are currently revising?

5.   Select and read an essay of your choice in this text—and then follow Professor Agassiz's good advice: look at it again. And again. Take notes on its purpose and craft after each reading. Write an essay that explains what you learned from this process. What did you see in later readings that you missed the first time through? How might your essay help other students improve their reading skills?

Robert Hayden (Pach/Corbis)

THOSE WINTER SUNDAYS

Robert Hayden
(1913–1980)

Born in Detroit, poet Robert Hayden was adopted by
working-class foster parents. He attended Detroit City
College (now called Wayne State University) and the
University of Michigan, where he studied with W. H.
Auden. He first received international recognition for
his work after winning the 1966 Grand Prize for Poetry
at the First World Festival of Negro Arts for *A Ballad
of Remembrance*. He taught at Fisk University from
1946 to 1968 and at the University of Michigan at Ann
Arbor from 1968 to 1980. In 1976, he was appointed
Consultant in Poetry at the Library of Congress. His
volumes of poetry include *Heart-Shape in the Dust*
(1940), *The Lion and the Archer* (1948), *Figures in
Time* (1955), *Middle Passage* (1962), *Selected Poems*
(1966), *Words in the Mourning Time* (1970), *Night
Blooming Cereus* (1972), and *American Journal*
(1978). "Those Winter Sundays" comes from *Angle of
Ascent* (1975) and presents a new understanding of
some old sacrifices.

Sundays too my father got up early
and put his clothes on in the blueblack cold,
then with cracked hands that ached
from labor in the weekday weather made
5 banked fires blaze. No one ever thanked him.

I'd wake and hear the cold splintering, breaking,
When the rooms were warm, he'd call,
and slowly I would rise and dress,
fearing the chronic angers of that house,

10 Speaking indifferently to him,
who had driven out the cold
and polished my good shoes as well.
What did I know, what did I know
of love's austere and lonely offices?

TOPICS FOR WRITING AND DISCUSSION

1. Who is speaking in this poem? What age would you guess this person to be now—child, adolescent, twenty-something, middle-aged adult, older adult? Why do you think so?

2. What process does the father repeat each day, even on Sundays? Why does the father have "cracked hands"?

3. How does the speaker treat his father? Why? How might you interpret his fear of the "chronic angers of that house"?

4. What do the last two lines say about the speaker's view of his father now? What exactly does he know now that he did not know before?

5. Can you think of a time when you came to a realization about a relative or friend's sacrifice for you, one that perhaps you had not fully comprehended when you were younger? What steps led to your realization or new view of this person?

THE LOTTERY

Shirley Jackson
(1919–1965)

Born in San Francisco, Shirley Jackson grew up in
Rochester, New York. She first attended college at the
University of Rochester and then at Syracuse University,
where she founded and edited the literary magazine, to
which she often contributed her own work. In 1948, she
received national attention when *The New Yorker* published "The Lottery," perhaps her best-known work.
Though she is often recognized for her chilling works
and characters with disturbing psychological problems—*The Road Through the Wall* (1948), *Hangsaman*
(1951), and *The Bird's Nest* (1954)—and those with
gothic themes—*The Haunting of Hill House* (1959) and
We Have Always Lived in the Castle (1962), Jackson
also humorously and affectionately chronicled the
adventures of raising her own family in *Life Among the
Savages* (1953) and *Raising Demons* (1957). Her last
book, *Come Along With Me* (1968), was published
posthumously by her husband, literary critic Stanley
Edgar Hyman. Her story "The Lottery" is a horrifying
fable of small-town conformity to tradition.

1 THE morning of June 27th was clear and sunny, with the fresh warmth of a
full-summer day; the flowers were blossoming profusely and the grass was
richly green. The people of the village began to gather in the square, between
the post office and the bank, around ten o'clock; in some towns there were so
many people that the lottery took two days and had to be started on June 26th,
but in this village, where there were only about three hundred people, the
whole lottery took less than two hours, so it could begin at ten o'clock in
the morning and still be through in time to allow the villagers to get home for
noon dinner.

Shirley Jackson (AP/Wide World Photos)

2   The children assembled first, of course. School was recently over for the summer, and the feeling of liberty sat uneasily on most of them; they tended to gather together quietly for a while before they broke into boisterous play, and their talk was still of the classroom and the teacher, of books and reprimands. Bobby Martin had already stuffed his pockets full of stones, and the other boys soon followed his example, selecting the smoothest and roundest stones; Bobby and Harry Jones and Dickie Delacroix—the villagers pronounced this name "Dellacroy"—eventually made a great pile of stones in one corner of the square and guarded it against the raids of the other boys. The girls stood aside, talking among themselves, looking over their shoulders at the boys, and the very small children rolled in the dust or clung to the hands of their older brothers or sisters.

3   Soon the men began to gather, surveying their own children, speaking of planting and rain, tractors and taxes. They stood together, away from the pile of stones in the corner, and their jokes were quiet and they smiled rather than laughed. The women, wearing faded house dresses and sweaters, came shortly after their menfolk. They greeted one another and exchanged bits of gossip as they went to join their husbands. Soon the women, standing by their husbands, began to call to their children, and the children came reluctantly, having to be called four or five times. Bobby Martin ducked under his mother's grasping hand and ran, laughing, back to the pile of stones. His father spoke up sharply, and Bobby came quickly and took his place between his father and his oldest brother.

4   The lottery was conducted—as were the square dances, the teen-age club, the Halloween program—by Mr. Summers, who had time and energy to devote to civic activities. He was a round-faced, jovial man and he ran the coal business, and people were sorry for him, because he had no children and his wife was a scold. When he arrived in the square, carrying the black wooden box, there was a murmur of conversation among the villagers, and he waved and called, "Little late today." The postmaster, Mr. Graves, followed him, carrying a three-legged stool, and the stool was put in the center of the square and Mr. Summers set the black box down on it. The villagers kept their distance, leaving a space between themselves and the stool, and when Mr. Summers said, "Some of you fellows want to give me a hand?" there was a hesitation before two men, Mr. Martin and his oldest son, Baxter, came forward to hold the box steady on the stool while Mr. Summers stirred up the papers inside it.

5   The original paraphernalia for the lottery had been lost long ago, and the black box now resting on the stool had been put into use even before Old Man Warner, the oldest man in town, was born. Mr. Summers spoke frequently to the villagers about making a new box, but no one liked to upset even as much tradition as was represented by the black box. There was a story that the present box had been made with some pieces of the box that had preceded it, the one that had been constructed when the first people settled down to make a village here. Every year, after the lottery, Mr. Summers began talking again about a new box, but every year the subject was allowed to fade off

without anything's being done. The black box grew shabbier each year; by now it was no longer completely black but splintered badly along one side to show the original wood color, and in some placed faded or stained.

6   Mr. Martin and his oldest son, Baxter, held the black box securely on the stool until Mr. Summers had stirred the papers thoroughly with his hand. Because so much of the ritual had been forgotten or discarded, Mr. Summers had been successful in having slips of paper substituted for the chips of wood that had been used for generations. Chips of wood, Mr. Summers had argued, had been all very well when the village was tiny, but now that the population was more than three hundred and likely to keep on growing, it was necessary to use something that would fit more easily into the black box. The night before the lottery, Mr. Summers and Mr. Graves made up the slips of paper and put them in the box, and it was then taken to the safe of Mr. Summers's coal company and locked up until Mr. Summers was ready to take it to the square next morning. The rest of the year, the box was put away, sometimes one place, sometimes another; it had spent one year in Mr. Graves's barn and another year underfoot in the post office, and sometimes it was set on a shelf in the Martin grocery and left there.

7   There was a great deal of fussing to be done before Mr. Summers declared the lottery open. There were the lists to make up—of heads of families, heads of households in each family, members of each household in each family. There was the proper swearing-in of Mr. Summers by the postmaster, as the official of the lottery; at one time, some people remembered, there had been a recital of some sort, performed by the official of the lottery, a perfunctory, tuneless chant that had been rattled off duly each year; some people believed that the official of the lottery used to stand just so when he said or sang it, other believed that he was supposed to walk among the people, but years and years ago this part of the ritual had been allowed to lapse. There had been, also, a ritual salute, which the official of the lottery had had to use in addressing each person who came up to draw from the box, but this also had changed with time, until now it was felt necessary only for the official to speak to each person approaching. Mr. Summers was very good at all this; in his clean white shirt and blue jeans, with one hand resting carelessly on the black box, he seemed very proper and important as he talked interminably to Mr. Graves and the Martins.

8   Just as Mr. Summers finally left off talking and turned to the assembled villagers, Mrs. Hutchinson came hurriedly along the path to the square, her sweater thrown over her shoulders, and slid into place in the back of the crowd. "Clean forgot what day it was," she said to Mrs. Delacroix, who stood next to her, and they both laughed softly. "Thought my old man was out back stacking wood," Mrs. Hutchinson went on, "and then I looked out the window and the kids was gone, and then I remembered it was the twenty-seventh and came a-running." She dried her hands on her apron, and Mrs. Delacroix said, "You're in time, though. They're still talking away up there."

9   Mrs. Hutchinson craned her neck to see through the crowd and found her husband and children standing near the front. She tapped Mrs. Delacroix on

the arm as a farewell and began to make her way through the crowd. The people separated good-humoredly to let her through; two or three people said, in voices just loud enough to be heard across the crowd, "Here comes your Missus, Hutchinson," and "Bill, she made it after all." Mrs. Hutchinson reached her husband, and Mr. Summers, who had been waiting, said cheerfully, "Thought we were going to have to get on without you, Tessie." Mrs. Hutchinson said, grinning, "Wouldn't have me leave m'dishes in the sink, now, would you, Joe?" and soft laughter ran through the crowd as the people stirred back into position after Mrs. Hutchinson's arrival.

10   "Well, now," Mr. Summers said soberly, "guess we better get started, get this over with, so's we can go back to work. Anybody ain't's here?"

11   "Dunbar," several people said, "Dunbar, Dunbar."

12   Mr. Summers consulted his list. "Clyde Dunbar," he said. "That's right. He's broke his leg, hasn't he? Who's drawing for him?"

13   "Me, I guess," a woman said, and Mr. Summers turned to look at her. "Wife draws for her husband," Mr. Summers said. "Don't you have a grown boy to do it for you, Janey?" Although Mr. Summers and everyone else in the village knew the answer perfectly well, it was the business of the official of the lottery to ask such questions formally. Mr. Summers waited with an expression of polite interest while Mrs. Dunbar answered.

14   "Horace's not but sixteen yet," Mrs. Dunbar said regretfully. "Guess I gotta fill in for the old man this year."

15   "Right," Mr. Summers said. He made a note on the list he was holding. Then he asked, "Watson boy drawing this year?"

16   A tall boy in the crowd raised his hand. "Here," he said. "I'm drawing for m'mother and me." He blinked his eyes nervously and ducked his head as several voices in the crowd said things like "Good fellow, Jack," and "Glad to see your mother's got a man to do it."

17   "Well," Mr. Summers said, "guess that's everyone. Old Man Warner make it?"

18   "Here," a voice said, and Mr. Summers nodded.

19   A sudden hush fell on the crowd as Mr. Summers cleared his throat and looked at the list. "All ready?" he called. "Now, I'll read the names—heads of families first—and the men come up and take a paper out of the box. Keep the paper folded in your hand without looking at it until everyone has had a turn. Everything clear?"

20   The people had done it so many times that they only half listened to the directions; most of them were quiet, wetting their lips, not looking around. Then Mr. Summers raised one hand high and said, "Adams." A man disengaged himself from the crowd and came forward. "Hi, Steve," Mr. Summers said, and Mr. Adams said, "Hi, Joe." They grinned at one another humorlessly and nervously. Then Mr. Adams reached into the black box and took out a folded paper. He held it firmly by one corner as he turned and went hastily back to his place in the crowd, where he stood a little apart from his family, not looking down at his hand.

21   "Allen," Mr. Summers said, "Anderson . . . Bentham."

22   "Seems like there's no time at all between lotteries any more," Mrs. Delacroix said to Mrs. Graves in the back row. "Seems like we got through with the last one only last week."

23   "Time sure goes fast," Mrs. Graves said.

24   "Clark . . . Delacroix."

25   "There goes my old man," Mrs. Delacroix said. She held her breath while her husband went forward.

26   "Dunbar," Mr. Summers said, and Mrs. Dunbar went steadily to the box while one of the women said, "Go on, Janey," and another said, "There she goes."

27   "We're next," Mrs. Graves said. She watched while Mr. Graves came around from the side of the box, greeted Mr. Summers gravely, and selected a slip of paper from the box. By now, all through the crowd there were men holding the small folded papers in their large hands, turning them over and over nervously. Mrs. Dunbar and her two sons stood together, Mrs. Dunbar holding the slip of paper.

28   "Harburt . . . Hutchinson."

29   "Get up there, Bill," Mrs. Hutchinson said, and the people near her laughed.

30   "Jones."

31   "They do say," Mr. Adams said to Old Man Warner, who stood next to him, "that over in the north village they're talking of giving up the lottery."

32   Old Man Warner snorted. "Pack of crazy fools," he said. "Listening to the young folks, nothing's good enough for *them*. Next thing you know, they'll be wanting to go back to living in caves, nobody work any more, live *that* way for a while. Used to be a saying about 'Lottery in June, corn be heavy soon.' First thing you know, we'd all be eating stewed chickweed and acorns. There's *always* been a lottery," he added petulantly. "Bad enough to see young Joe Summers up there joking with everybody."

33   "Some places have already quit lotteries," Mrs. Adams said.

34   "Nothing but trouble in *that*," Old Man Warner said stoutly. "Pack of young fools."

35   "Martin." And Bobby Martin watched his father go forward. "Overdyke . . . Percy."

36   "I wish they'd hurry," Mrs. Dunbar said to her older son. "I wish they'd hurry."

37   "They're almost through," her son said.

38   "You get ready to run tell Dad," Mrs. Dunbar said.

39   Mr. Summers called his own name and then stepped forward precisely and selected a slip from the box. Then he called, "Warner."

40   "Seventy-seventh year I been in the lottery," Old Man Warner said as he went through the crowd. "Seventy-seventh time."

41   "Watson." The tall boy came awkwardly through the crowd. Someone said, "Don't be nervous, Jack," and Mr. Summers said, "Take your time, son."

42   "Zanini."

43   After that, there was a long pause, a breathless pause, until Mr. Summers, holding his slip of paper in the air, said, "All right, fellows." For a minute, no one moved, and then all the slips of paper were opened. Suddenly, all the women began to speak at once, saying, "Who is it?" "Who's got it?" "Is it the Dunbars?" "Is it the Watsons?" Then the voices began to say, "It's Hutchinson. It's Bill," "Bill Hutchinson's got it."

44   "Go tell your father," Mrs. Dunbar said to her older son.

45   People began to look around to see the Hutchinsons. Bill Hutchinson was standing quiet, staring down at the paper in his hand. Suddenly, Tessie Hutchinson shouted to Mr. Summers, "You didn't give him time enough to take any paper he wanted. I saw you. It wasn't fair!"

46   "Be a good sport, Tessie," Mrs. Delacroix called, and Mrs. Graves said, "All of us took the same chance."

47   "Shut up, Tessie," Bill Hutchinson said.

48   "Well, everyone," Mr. Summers said, "that was done pretty fast, and now we've got to be hurrying a little more to get done in time." He consulted his next list. "Bill," he said, "you draw for the Hutchinson family. You got any other households in the Hutchinsons?"

49   "There's Don and Eva," Mrs. Hutchinson yelled. "Make *them* take their chance!"

50   "Daughters draw with their husbands' families, Tessie," Mr. Summers said gently. "You know that as well as anyone else."

51   "It wasn't *fair*," Tessie said.

52   "I guess not, Joe," Bill Hutchinson said regretfully. "My daughter draws with her husband's family, that's only fair. And I've got no other family except the kids."

53   "Then, as far as drawing for families is concerned, it's you," Mr. Summers said in explanation, "and as far as drawing for households is concerned, that's you, too. Right?"

54   "Right," Bill Hutchinson said.

55   "How many kids, Bill?" Mr. Summers asked formally.

56   "Three," Bill Hutchinson said, "There's Bill, Jr., and Nancy, and little Dave. And Tessie and me."

57   "All right, then," Mr. Summers said. "Harry, you got their tickets back?"

58   Mr. Graves nodded and held up the slips of paper. "Put them in the box, then," Mr. Summers directed. "Take Bill's and put it in."

59   "I think we ought to start over," Mrs. Hutchinson said, as quietly as she could. "I tell you it wasn't *fair*. You didn't give him time enough to choose. *Every*body saw that."

60   Mr. Graves had selected the five slips and put them in the box, and he dropped all the papers but those onto the ground, where the breeze caught them and lifted them off.

61   "Listen, everybody," Mrs. Hutchinson was saying to the people around her.

62   "Ready, Bill?" Mr. Summers asked, and Bill Hutchinson, with one quick glance around at his wife and children, nodded.

63   "Remember," Mr. Summers said, "take the slips and keep them folded until each person has taken one. Harry, you help little Dave." Mr. Graves took the hand of the little boy, who came willingly with him up to the box. "Take a paper out of the box, Davy," Mr. Summers said. Davy put his hand into the box and laughed. "Take just *one* paper," Mr. Summers said. "Harry, you hold it for him." Mr. Graves took the child's hand and removed the folded paper from the tight fist and held it while little Dave stood next to him and looked up at him wonderingly.

64   "Nancy next," Mr. Summers said. Nancy was twelve, and her school friends breathed heavily as she went forward, switching her skirt, and took a slip daintily from the box. "Bill, Jr.," Mr. Summers said, and Billy, his face red and his feet overlarge, nearly knocked the box over as he got a paper out. "Tessie," Mr. Summers said. She hesitated for a minute, looking around defiantly, and then set her lips and went up to the box. She snatched a paper out and held it behind her.

65   "Bill," Mr. Summers said, and Bill Hutchinson reached into the box and felt around, bringing his hand out at last with the slip of paper in it.

66   The crowd was quiet. A girl whispered, "I hope it's not Nancy," and the sound of the whisper reached the edges of the crowd.

67   "It's not the way it used to be," Old Man Warner said clearly. "People ain't the way they used to be."

68   "All right," Mr. Summers said. "Open the papers. Harry, you open little Dave's."

69   Mr. Graves opened the slip of paper and there was a general sigh through the crowd as he held it up and everyone could see that it was blank. Nancy and Bill, Jr., opened theirs at the same time, and both beamed and laughed, turning around to the crowd and holding their slips of paper above their heads.

70   "Tessie," Mr. Summers said. There was a pause, and then Mr. Summers looked at Bill Hutchinson, and Bill unfolded his paper and showed it. It was blank.

71   "It's Tessie," Mr. Summers said, and his voice was hushed. "Show us her paper Bill."

72   Bill Hutchinson went over to his wife and forced the slip of paper out of her hand. It had a black spot on it, the black spot Mr. Summers had made the night before with the heavy pencil in the coal-company office. Bill Hutchinson held it up, and there was a stir in the crowd.

73   "All right, folks," Mr. Summers said. "Let's finish quickly."

74   Although the villagers had forgotten the ritual and lost the original black box, they still remembered to use stones. The pile of stones the boys had made earlier was ready; there were stones on the ground with the blowing scraps of paper that had come out of the box. Mrs. Delacroix selected a stone so large she had to pick it up with both hands and turned to Mrs. Dunbar. "Come on," she said. "Hurry up."

75   Mrs. Dunbar had small stones in both hands, and she said, gasping for breath, "I can't run at all. You'll have to go ahead and I'll catch up with you."

76   The children had stones already, and someone gave little Davy Hutchinson a few pebbles.

77   Tessie Hutchinson was in the center of a cleared space by now, and she held her hands out desperately as the villagers moved in on her. "It isn't fair," she said. A stone hit her on the side of the head.

78   Old Man Warner was saying, "Come on, come on, everyone." Steve Adams was in the front of the crowd of villagers, with Mrs. Graves beside him.

79   "It isn't fair, it isn't right," Mrs. Hutchinson screamed, and then they were upon her.

Topics for Writing and Discussion

1.   What is the general attitude of the villagers toward this spring ritual? What is Mrs. Hutchinson's attitude before and then after the lottery?

2.   What is the purpose of this lottery? Does anyone in the story explain its exact purpose? Why does Jackson include several references to parts of the ritual that have been lost or forgotten?

3.   How might the black box itself, worn out and shabby, be symbolically associated with the tradition of the lottery? Why does Jackson include Old Man Warner's comments about the dangers of giving up the lottery? Are his responses convincing?

4.   What point do you think Jackson is making about certain kinds of rituals and traditions? About the unquestioning "nice" people who thoughtlessly follow them? About the possible connection between violence and irrational thinking that demands scapegoats?

5.   Are all rituals harmful? In contrast to Jackson's story, explain the steps in a ritual that you think works for the good of an identifiable group. Why is the ritual you chose worth repeating from generation to generation?

WRITING ASSIGNMENTS FOR CHAPTER FIVE

PROCESS

1. Write an essay describing the steps that led to an important discovery in your field of study or profession. Make clear, as Carin Quinn did in "The Jeaning of America," the lasting impact of this discovery on those in your discipline.

2. In "The American Way of Death," Jessica Mitford describes the custom of embalming. Select another American or family ritual, such as a wedding, a graduation, a twenty-first birthday party, Thanksgiving dinner, family reunion, or New Year's Eve, and describe the process as it occurs in your family or circle of friends. Make your attitude toward the process clear to the reader.

3. In "Attitude," humorist Garrison Keillor explains how to develop the proper frame of mind for slow-pitch baseball by going through a series of steps on the field. Write an essay for real or imagined teammates or friends that describes the acquisition of the proper attitude for participation in some group activity. Don't feel limited to a sport, however. You might, for instance, create the steps for adopting the right demeanor in the great art of mall walking, couch lounging, apartment renting, or library browsing. How does one create an aura of having the "right stuff" at the big job interview? On a blind date? Your essay might be humorous or serious, depending on your purpose and audience.

4. Select a problem on your campus and describe the steps you would urge your fellow students to take to resolve it. You may also wish to mention the responses that will not work, as Martin Luther King, Jr., did in his essay "Nonviolent Resistance." Your essay should be directed either to the person(s) in charge of the problem or to those you wish to participate in your solution.

5. In "More than Just a Shrine: Paying Homage to the Ghosts of Ellis Island," Mary Gordon discusses harsh immigration procedures from our past. Immigration to America today is still a highly controversial topic, with some arguing that we need stricter quotas and tougher laws. Others feel we should open our doors wider in the humanitarian spirit of Emma Lazarus' words inscribed on the Statue of Liberty. Research a current immigration policy as it affects a particular group. As you write about the steps in this procedure, make your opinion of this process clear to your reader. Is this a process that should be abandoned, changed, or maintained?

6. Professor Louis Agassiz did more for Samuel Scudder than merely teach him how to "Take This Fish and Look at It." Recall a time in your own life when a teacher, relative, or friend showed you a method of doing

something that taught you more than you expected to learn. Write about this experience in a way that presents your step-by-step discovery of the significance of your study. What did this experience teach you that was, to use Scudder's words, of "inestimable value"?

7. In "Those Winter Sundays," Robert Hayden describes a father's morning routine, a simple process undertaken with love for a child who only later appreciates its value. What seemingly commonplace rituals or routines took place in your home each day or week? What benefits did they provide, and for whom? Select one routine and describe its steps, making clear the larger significance that you now attach to it.

8. In "The Lottery," Shirley Jackson tells the story of villagers who participate in an irrational, violent ritual without questioning its purpose or logic. Have you ever broken away from a social custom you considered outdated, cruel, or immoral? Write an essay showing the steps you took to protest or abandon this practice.

CHAPTER SIX

DEFINITION

DEFINITION is a helpful strategy for analyzing, explaining, and illustrating concepts to show both their immediate and broader meanings. Take, for example, the word *friend*. A dictionary might define "friend" as a "companion," a "buddy," or an "ally." Each of these surely describes characteristics of a friend. However, to examine fully the notion of what a friend is, you may need to look further.

If you have ever faced an assignment where you were asked to "explain" or "discuss" a concept, you probably began the assignment with a definition. For example, in a literature course, you might have an assignment like this: "Explain Flannery O'Connor's concept of 'moment of grace.'" Or perhaps your sociology professor might ask you to "Discuss the question of ethics surrounding cloning." The best way to begin these assignments would be with a definition of "moment of grace" or of "cloning."

Typically, there are three kinds of definitions: formal, restrictive, and extended. The *formal* definition gives the "dictionary" meaning of a word (though some words may not actually be found in a dictionary). Formal definition has three parts: the *term* (the thing or idea itself), the *class* (the general class to which the word belongs), and the *differentiation* (how the thing or idea differs from other things in the same class). Here are some examples:

TERM	CLASS	DIFFERENTIATION
Haiku	A form of poetry	consisting of only 3 lines of 17 syllables in a pattern of 5, 7, and 5 syllables per line.
Strop	A flexible strip of leather	used to sharpen a razor.
Oratorio	A musical composition	for voices and orchestra, usually with a religious theme.

Another kind of definition is the *restrictive* definition, which defines a term by limiting it or putting "restrictions" on its meaning, thus allowing a writer to use the term in a specific manner for a particular discussion. For example, "moment of grace" is a term that specifically can be applied to discussions of O'Connor's fiction, for it was coined by the author herself. Many slang terms, jargon, and family "idiolects" are examples of restrictive definitions. Terms like "chill" (slang for calm down) or "cream puff" (real estate jargon for a meticulously maintained home) or a term that has special meaning for only your immediate family may be meaningless outside a particular context.

The third kind of definition is the one you are most likely to use—the *extended* definition. With this type, you can examine a term or concept deeply, analyzing it to make its meaning clearer to the reader. Often, the extended definition begins with a formal definition, may include restrictive definition, and then uses other rhetorical strategies to develop it. Generally speaking, the scope of your extended definition will be determined by the word or idea being defined, the purpose of the definition, and your audience.

Return to the assignment regarding O'Connor's concept of "moment of grace." You might begin your response with a formal definition:

"Moment of grace" is a spiritual act of accepting or rejecting the gift of salvation.

Then, you might restrict the definition:

"Moment of grace" is a concept created and frequently used by Southern writer Flannery O'Connor to identify the climax of her fictional works.

From this point you would probably explore the subject more fully (extending the definition) by providing examples of the "moment of grace" in several of the author's works, by describing typical scenes illustrating the "moment of grace," by analyzing the process by which the "moment of grace" occurs, by comparing or contrasting O'Connor's concept to the climactic scenes written by other writers, or by providing a narrative summary of the plot leading to the "moment of grace."

The essence of a successful definition is clarity. The purpose of a definition is to give your readers clearly presented, precise information that will allow them to understand better the term, principle, idea, or concept.

WRITING THE DEFINITION ESSAY

As you prepare your definition, consider the following suggestions to clarify your presentation:

1. *Use a synonym.*

Using other, more familiar words or phrases that have similar meanings may help clarify the concept you are defining. For example, in "What Is Happiness?" John Ciardi argues that happiness is neither "having" nor in "being" but in "becoming." In her definition essay, Joan Didion claims that people who have self-respect have "the courage of their mistakes."

2. *Use an example.*

Frequently, a term or abstract concept is best understood when the writer offers examples to illustrate its nature or use. Ralph Ellison's essay "Discrimination" presents several detailed scenes that show the racial prejudice his family encountered. In "Gobbledygook," Stuart Chase presents numerous examples to illustrate verbal clutter.

3. *Use a description.*

Sometimes it is helpful to describe what a term looks like, how its parts fit together, or how it functions or acts. In "New Superstitions for Old," for example, Margaret Mead describes one of the uses of superstitions as helping people deal with their feelings of helplessness in difficult situations. John Ciardi reminds us that happiness is always partial and that "effort is the gist of it."

4. *Use comparison or contrast.*

An idea or word may be made clearer by pointing out how it is similar to something else or by pointing out how it differs from another similar concept. Throughout his essay, Richard Rodriguez compares and contrasts symbols of American culture to those of Hispanic origins to show the benefits of a new Hispanic-American culture. And in her essay, Margaret Mead contrasts old and new superstitions as well as people's attitudes toward them.

5. *Use division and classification.*

On occasion it is useful to clarify a complex topic by discussing its types, kinds, classes, or categories. For instance, if you were writing a humorous essay defining "nerds," you might organize your discussion by categorizing the types of nerds you see on campus whose collective qualities contribute to the larger definition of the term.

6. *Use negation.*

Explaining what a word or idea is *not* often clarifies it for the reader. In "Gobbledygook," Stuart Chase frequently shows his readers "ungobbled" prose to illustrate the effectiveness of concise, straightforward writing. Margaret Mead tells her readers what superstition is and is not.

By using definition, you can clarify difficult or unfamiliar terms, ideas, or principles; analyze seemingly simple terms to expose deeper meanings; explain controversial concepts; or reveal new meanings. The strategy of definition may be incorporated in essays of all kinds, whenever readers would profit from a clearer understanding of the ideas under discussion.

WHAT IS HAPPINESS?

John Ciardi
(1916–1986)

After holding teaching positions at Harvard, Rutgers, and the University of Kansas, literary critic and poet John Ciardi left teaching in 1961 and devoted his professional career to writing. In addition to writing poetry, he wrote many critical essays on poetry and served as the poetry editor of the *Saturday Review* from 1956 to 1972. His poetry collections include *Homeward to America* (1940), *Other Skies* (1947), *Live Another Day* (1949), *From Time to Time* (1951), *As If: New and Selected Poems* (1955), *I Marry You: A Sheaf of Love Poems* (1958), *39 Poems* (1959), *In the Stone Works* (1961), *Person to Person* (1964), *The Strongest Everything* (1966), *An Alphabestiary* (1967), *Lives of X* (1971), *The Little That Is All* (1974), *For Instance* (1979), and *Selected Poems* (1984). Among many other works published posthumously is *Echoes: Poems Left Behind* (1989). Ciardi is also known for his translation of Dante's *The Inferno* (1954), *The Purgatorio* (1961), and *The Paradiso* (1970). In the essay that follows, Ciardi examines the nature of happiness, a word that "will not sit still for easy definition."

1   THE right to pursue happiness is issued to Americans with their birth certificates, but no one seems quite sure which way it ran. It may be we are issued a hunting license but offered no game. Jonathan Swift seemed to think so when he attacked the idea of happiness as "the possession of being well-deceived," the felicity of being "a fool among knaves." For Swift saw society as Vanity Fair, the land of false goals.

John Ciardi (© Archive Photos)

2   It is, of course, un-American to think in terms of fools and knaves. We do, however, seem to be dedicated to the idea of buying our way to happiness. We shall all have made it to Heaven when we possess enough.

3   And at the same time the forces of American commercialism are hugely dedicated to making us deliberately unhappy. Advertising is one of our major industries, and advertising exists not to satisfy desires but to create them—and to create them faster than any man's budget can satisfy them. For that matter, our whole economy is based on a dedicated insatiability. We are taught that to possess is to be happy, and then we are made to want. We are even told it is our duty to want. It was only a few years ago, to cite a single example, that car dealers across the country were flying banners that read "You Auto Buy Now." They were calling upon Americans, as an act approaching patriotism, to buy at once, with money they did not have, automobiles they did not really need, and which they would be required to grow tired of by the time the next year's models were released.

4   Or look at any of the women's magazines. There, as Bernard DeVoto once pointed out, advertising begins as poetry in the front pages and ends as pharmacopoeia and therapy in the back pages. The poetry of the front matter is the dream of perfect beauty. This is the baby skin that must be hers. These, the flawless teeth. This, the perfumed breath she must exhale. This, the sixteen-year-old figure she must display at forty, at fifty, at sixty, and forever.

5   Once past the vaguely uplifting fiction and feature articles, the reader finds the other face of the dream in the back matter. This is the harness into which Mother must strap herself in order to display that perfect figure. These, the chin straps she must sleep in. This is the salve that restores all, this is her laxative, these are the tablets that melt away fat, these are the hormones of perpetual youth, these are the stockings that hide varicose veins.

6   Obviously no half-sane person can be completely persuaded either by such poetry or by such pharmacopoeia and orthopedics. Yet someone is obviously trying to buy the dream as offered and spending billions every year in the attempt. Clearly the happiness-market is not running out of customers, but what is it trying to buy?

7   The idea "happiness," to be sure, will not sit still for easy definition: the best one can do is to try to set some extremes to the idea and then work in toward the middle. To think of happiness as acquisitive and competitive will do to set the materialistic extreme. To think of it as the idea one senses in, say, a holy man of India will do to set the spiritual extreme. That holy man's idea of happiness is in needing nothing from outside himself. In wanting nothing, he lacks nothing. He sits immobile, rapt in contemplation, free even of his own body. Or nearly free of it. If devout admirers bring him food he eats it; if not, he starves indifferently. Why be concerned? What is physical is an illusion to him. Contemplation is his joy and he achieves it through a fantastically demanding discipline, the accomplishment of which is itself a joy within him.

8   Is he a happy man? Perhaps his happiness is only another sort of illusion. But who can take it from him? And who will dare say it is more illusory than happiness on the installment plan?

9   But, perhaps because I am Western, I doubt such catatonic happiness, as I doubt the dreams of the happiness-market. What is certain is that his way of happiness would be torture to almost any Western man. Yet these extremes will still serve to frame the area within which all of us must find some sort of balance. Thoreau—a creature of both Eastern and Western thought—had his own firm sense of that balance. His aim was to save on the low levels in order to spend on the high.

10   Possession for its own sake or in competition with the rest of the neighborhood would have been Thoreau's idea of the low levels. The active discipline of heightening one's perception of what is enduring in nature would have been his idea of the high. What he saved from the low was time and effort he could spend on the high. Thoreau certainly disapproved of starvation, but he would put into feeding himself only as much effort as would keep him functioning for more important efforts.

11   Effort is the gist of it. There is no happiness except as we take on life-engaging difficulties. Short of the impossible, as Yeats put it, the satisfactions we get from a lifetime depend on how high we choose our difficulties. Robert Frost was thinking in something like the same terms when he spoke of "The pleasure of taking pains." The mortal flaw in the advertised version of happiness is in the fact that it purports to be effortless.

12   We demand difficulty even in our games. We demand it because without difficulty there can be no game. A game is a way of making something hard for the fun of it. The rules of the game are an arbitrary imposition of difficulty. When the spoilsport ruins the fun, he always does so by refusing to play by the rules. It is easier to win at chess if you are free, at your pleasure, to change the wholly arbitrary rules, but the fun is in winning within the rules. No difficulty, no fun.

13   The buyers and sellers at the happiness-market seem too often to have lost their sense of the pleasure of difficulty. Heaven knows what they are playing, but it seems a dull game. And the Indian holy man seems dull to us, I suppose, because he seems to be refusing to play anything at all. The Western weakness may be in the illusion that happiness can be bought. Perhaps the Eastern weakness is in the idea that there is such a thing as perfect (and therefore static) happiness.

14   Happiness is never more than partial. There are no pure states of mankind. Whatever else happiness may be, it is neither in having nor in being, but in becoming. What the Founding Fathers declared for us as an inherent right, we should do well to remember, was not happiness but the *pursuit* of happiness. What they might have underlined, could they have foreseen the happiness-market, is the cardinal fact that happiness is in the pursuit itself, in the meaningful pursuit of what is life-engaging and life-revealing, which is to say, in the idea of *becoming*. A nation is not measured by what it possesses or wants to possess, but by what it wants to become.

15   By all means let the happiness-market sell us minor satisfactions and even minor follies so long as we keep them in scale and buy them out of spiritual change. I am no customer for either puritanism or asceticism. But drop any

real spiritual capital at those bazaars, and what you come home to will be your own poorhouse.

TOPICS FOR WRITING AND DISCUSSION

1. In defining "happiness," Ciardi presents the conflicts between Eastern and Western perceptions. What emerges as his own definition of happiness? Does he believe happiness is fully attainable? Why or why not?

2. What methods (such as comparison, contrast, illustration) does Ciardi use to define "happiness"? Cite some examples.

3. Consider Ciardi's comments regarding the role of advertising and consumerism in prescribing what "happiness" should be for the American public. What other terms (beauty? success?) are defined for us by mass media advertising's exhortations to "buy!"? Choose two terms and explain how the media helps define them for us.

4. Ciardi's discussion of happiness suggests that some definitions may be culturally influenced. Consider various types of cultural or social groups (ethnic, racial, religious, political, economic, age, gender, and so on) that you know well. What other terms might be defined in very different ways by such groups? Choose one term and give a brief definition from the perspective of two cultures or social groups.

5. Present an extended definition of the term chosen for question 4 in an essay that might employ examples, description, comparison or contrast, division and classification, negation, or other techniques. Examine the term being defined from the perspective of one of the cultures chosen previously.

ON SELF-RESPECT

Joan Didion
(1934–   )

A fifth-generation Californian and descendant of pioneers, Joan Didion is a novelist, essayist, journalist, and screenwriter. After receiving a bachelor's degree from the University of California at Berkeley, Didion spent a few years in New York as a feature editor for *Vogue*. In 1964, she returned to California, where she continues to reside. Her work includes several novels—*River Run* (1963), *Play It As It Lays* (1971), *A Book of Common Prayer* (1977), and *Democracy* (1984)—and books of

Joan Didion (Tom Sobolik/Black Star)

essays, *Slouching Toward Bethlehem* (1969), *The White Album* (1978), *Salvador* (1983), and *Miami* (1987). With her husband, John Gregory Dunne, Didion has collaborated on several screenplays—*A Star Is Born* (1976), *True Confessions* (1981), and, most recently, *Up Close and Personal* (1996). Her latest books are *After Henry* (1992), a collection of essays, and *The Last Thing He Wanted* (1996), a novel. Didion's writing blends fiction, autobiography, and personal commentary on contemporary American culture. "On Self-Respect" is the author's reflection on an early failure and her consequent discovery of the meaning of self-respect.

1   ONCE, in a dry season, I wrote in large letters across two pages of a notebook that innocence ends when one is stripped of the delusion that one likes oneself. Although now, some years later, I marvel that a mind on the outs with itself should have nonetheless made painstaking record of its every tremor, I recall with embarrassing clarity the flavor of those particular ashes. It was a matter of misplaced self-respect.

2   I had not been elected to Phi Beta Kappa. This failure could scarcely have been more predictable or less ambiguous (I simply did not have the grades), but I was unnerved by it; I had somehow thought myself a kind of academic Raskolnikov, curiously exempt from the cause–effect relationships which hampered others. Although even the humorless nineteen-year-old that I was must have recognized that the situation lacked real tragic stature, the day that I did not make Phi Beta Kappa nonetheless marked the end of something, and innocence may well be the word for it. I lost the conviction that lights would always turn green for me, the pleasant certainty that those rather passive virtues which had won me approval as a child automatically guaranteed me not only Phi Beta Kappa keys but happiness, honor, and the love of a good man; lost a certain touching faith in the totem power of good manners, clean hair, and proven competence on the Stanford-Binet scale. To such doubtful amulets had my self-respect been pinned, and I faced myself that day with the nonplused apprehension of someone who has come across a vampire and has no crucifix at hand.

3   Although to be driven back upon oneself is an uneasy affair at best, rather like trying to cross a border with borrowed credentials, it seems to me now the one condition necessary to the beginnings of real self-respect. Most of our platitudes notwithstanding, self-deception remains the most difficult deception. The tricks that work on others count for nothing in that very well-lit back alley where one keeps assignations with oneself; no winning smiles will do here, no prettily drawn lists of good intentions. One shuffles flashily but in vain through one's marked cards—the kindness done for the wrong reason, the apparent triumph which involved no real effort, the seemingly heroic act into which one had been shamed. The dismal fact is that self-respect has nothing to do with the approval of others—who are, after all, deceived easily enough; has nothing to do with reputation, which, as Rhett Butler told Scarlett O'Hara, is something people with courage can do without.

4   To do without self-respect, on the other hand, is to be an unwilling audience of one to an interminable documentary that details one's failings, both real and imagined, with fresh footage spliced in for every screening. *There's the glass you broke in anger, there's the hurt on X's face; watch now, this next scene, the night Y came back from Houston, see how you muff this one.* To live without self-respect is to lie awake some night, beyond the reach of warm milk, phenobarbital, and the sleeping hand on the coverlet, counting up the sins of commission and omission, the trusts betrayed, the promises subtly broken, the gifts irrevocably wasted through sloth or cowardice or carelessness. However long we postpone it, we eventually lie down alone in that notoriously uncomfortable bed, the one we make ourselves. Whether or not we sleep in it depends, of course, on whether or not we respect ourselves.

5   To protest that some fairly improbable people, some people who *could not possibly respect themselves,* seem to sleep easily enough is to miss the point entirely, as surely as those people miss it who think that self-respect has

necessarily to do with not having safety pins in one's underwear. There is a common superstition that "self-respect" is a kind of charm against snakes, something that keeps those who have it locked in some unblighted Eden, out of strange beds, ambivalent conversations, and trouble in general. It does not at all. It has nothing to do with the face of things, but concerns instead a separate peace, a private reconciliation. Although the careless, suicidal Julian English in *Appointment in Samarra* and the careless, incurably dishonest Jordan Baker in *The Great Gatsby* seem equally improbable candidates for self-respect, Jordan Baker had it, Julian English did not. With that genius for accommodation more often seen in women than in men, Jordan took her own measure, made her own peace, avoided threats to that peace: "I hate careless people," she told Nick Carraway. "It takes two to make an accident."

6   Like Jordan Baker, people with self-respect have the courage of their mistakes. They know the price of things. If they choose to commit adultery, they do not then go running, in an access of bad conscience, to receive absolution from the wronged parties; nor do they complain unduly of the unfairness, the undeserved embarrassment, of being named corespondent. In brief, people with self-respect exhibit a certain toughness, a kind of moral nerve; they display what was once called *character*, a quality which, although approved in the abstract, sometimes loses ground to other, more instantly negotiable virtues. The measure of its slipping prestige is that one tends to think of it only in connection with homely children and United States senators who have been defeated, preferably in the primary, for reelection. Nonetheless, character—the willingness to accept responsibility for one's own life—is the source from which self-respect springs.

7   Self-respect is something that our grandparents, whether or not they had it, knew all about. They had instilled in them, young, a certain discipline, the sense that one lives by doing things one does not particularly want to do, by putting fears and doubts to one side, by weighing immediate comforts against the possibility of larger, even intangible, comforts. It seemed to the nineteenth century admirable, but not remarkable, that Chinese Gordon put on a clean white suit and held Khartoum against the Mahdi; it did not seem unjust that the way to free land in California involved death and difficulty and dirt. In a diary kept during the winter of 1846, an emigrating twelve-year-old named Narcissa Cornwall noted coolly: "Father was busy reading and did not notice that the house was being filled with strange Indians until Mother spoke about it." Even lacking any clue as to what Mother said, one can scarcely fail to be impressed by the entire incident: the father reading, the Indians filing in, the mother choosing the words that would not alarm, the child duly recording the event and noting further that those particular Indians were not, "fortunately for us," hostile. Indians were simply part of the *donnée*.

8   In one guise or another, Indians always are. Again, it is a question of recognizing that anything worth having has its price. People who respect themselves are willing to accept the risk that the Indians will be hostile, that the venture will go bankrupt, that the liaison may not turn out to be one in which

every day is a holiday because you're married to me. They are willing to invest something of themselves; they may not play at all, but when they do play, they know the odds.

9   That kind of self-respect is a discipline, a habit of mind that can never be faked but can be developed, trained, coaxed forth. It was once suggested to me that, as an antidote to crying, I put my head in a paper bag. As it happens, there is a sound physiological reason, something to do with oxygen, for doing exactly that, but the psychological effect alone is incalculable: it is difficult in the extreme to continue fancying oneself Cathy in *Wuthering Heights* with one's head in a Food Fair bag. There is a similar case for all the small disciplines, unimportant in themselves; imagine maintaining any kind of swoon, commiserative or carnal, in a cold shower.

10   But those small disciplines are available only insofar as they represent larger ones. To say that Waterloo was won on the playing fields of Eton is not to say that Napoleon might have been saved by a crash program in cricket; to give formal dinners in the rain forest would be pointless did not the candlelight flickering on the liana call forth deeper, stronger disciplines, values instilled long before. It is a kind of ritual, helping us to remember who and what we are. In order to remember it, one must have known it.

11   To have that sense of one's intrinsic worth which constitutes self-respect is potentially to have everything: the ability to discriminate, to love and to remain indifferent. To lack it is to be locked within oneself, paradoxically incapable of either love or indifference. If we do not respect ourselves, we are on the one hand forced to despise those who have so few resources as to consort with us, so little perception as to remain blind to our fatal weaknesses. On the other, we are peculiarly in thrall to everyone we see, curiously determined to live out—since our self-image is untenable—their false notions of us. We flatter ourselves by thinking this compulsion to please others an attractive trait: a gist for imaginative empathy, evidence of our willingness to give. Of *course* I will play Francesca to your Paolo, Helen Keller to anyone's Annie Sullivan: no expectation is too misplaced, no role too ludicrous. At the mercy of those we cannot but hold in contempt, we play roles doomed to failure before they are begun, each defeat generating fresh despair at the urgency of divining and meeting the next demand made upon us.

12   It is the phenomenon sometimes called "alienation from self." In its advanced stages, we no longer answer the telephone, because someone might want something; that we could say *no* without drowning in self-reproach is an idea alien to this game. Every encounter demands too much, tears the nerves, drains the will, and the specter of something as small as an unanswered letter arouses such disproportionate guilt that answering it becomes out of the question. To assign unanswered letters their proper weight, to free us from the expectations of others, to give us back to ourselves—there lies the great, the singular power of self-respect. Without it, one eventually discovers the final turn of the screw: one runs away to find oneself, and finds no one at home.

TOPICS FOR WRITING AND DISCUSSION

1. Why was Didion upset that she was not elected to Phi Beta Kappa? How did this failure initially change the way she looked at herself? What examples does she provide in paragraph 2 to explain her altered view of herself and her future?

2. At the beginning of paragraph 5, Didion anticipates an objection some readers might make to her comments on self-respect. Explain the protest Didion expects and her response to that protest. Do you find her ideas convincing? Why or why not?

3. Didion uses several different methods as she develops her definition. One particularly effective method is the use of examples. Beginning with paragraph 2, notice the pattern she follows for presenting examples. Do you find this pattern effective? Why?

4. Didion cites many authorities and makes many literary and historical allusions. What do these citations and allusions suggest about Didion's view of her audience? Would the essay be difficult to understand for the reader who did not recognize the sources or the meaning of the allusions?

5. Choose a concept such as honesty, loyalty, pride, bravery, or self-doubt, and write an essay that builds a definition of the concept through the use of anecdotes, examples, allusions, and references to authorities.

GOBBLEDYGOOK

Stuart Chase
(1888–1985)

Economist Stuart Chase is perhaps best known for his 1938 bestseller *The Tyranny of Words.* He was a long-time consultant to various government agencies, and the title of his 1932 book, *A New Deal,* provided the official label of the Roosevelt Administration. His other works include *The Proper Study of Mankind* (1948), *Roads to Agreement* (1951), *Power of Words* (1953), *Guides to Straight Thinking* (1956), *Some Things Worth Knowing* (1958), *The Most Probable World* (1968), and *Danger: Men Talking!* (1969). His fascination with the way we use—and misuse—language is evident in "Gobbledygook," a humorous essay with a clear message, excerpted from *Power of Words.*

1 SAID Franklin Roosevelt, in one of his early presidential speeches: "I see one-third of a nation ill-housed, ill-clad, ill-nourished." Translated into standard bureaucratic prose his statement would read:

> It is evident that a substantial number of persons within the Continental boundaries of the United States have inadequate financial resources with which to purchase the products of agricultural communities and industrial establishments. It would appear that for a considerable segment of the population, possibly as much as 33.3333* percent of the total, there are inadequate housing facilities, and an equally significant proportion is deprived of the proper types of clothing and nutriment.

---

* Not carried beyond four places. [Chase's note]

2　　　This rousing satire on gobbledygook—or talk among the bureaucrats—is adapted from a report* prepared by the Federal Security Agency in an attempt to break out of the verbal squirrel cage. "Gobbledygook" was coined by an exasperated Congressman, Maury Maverick of Texas, and means using two, or three, or ten words in the place of one, or using a five-syllable word where a single syllable would suffice. Maverick was censuring the forbidding prose of executive departments in Washington, but the term has now spread to windy and pretentious language in general.

3　　　"Gobbledygook" itself is a good example of the way a language grows. There was no word for the event before Maverick's invention; one had to say: "You know, that terrible, involved, polysyllabic language those government people use down in Washington." Now one word takes the place of a dozen.

4　　　A British member of Parliament, A. P. Herbert, also exasperated with bureaucratic jargon, translated Nelson's** immortal phrase, "England expects every man to do his duty":

> England anticipates that, as regards the current emergency, personnel will face up to the issues, and exercise appropriately the functions allocated to their respective occupational groups.

5　　　A New Zealand official made the following report after surveying a plot of ground for an athletic field:†

> It is obvious from the difference in elevation with relation to the short depth of the property that the contour is such as to preclude any reasonable development potential for active recreation.

Seems the plot was too steep.

6　　　An office manager sent this memo to his chief:

> Verbal contact with Mr. Blank regarding the attached notification of promotion has elicited the attached representation intimating that he prefers to decline the assignment.

Seems Mr. Blank didn't want the job.

> A doctor testified at an English trial that one of the parties was suffering from "circumorbital haematoma."

Seems the party had a black eye.

---

* This and succeeding quotations from F.S.A. report by special permission of the author, Milton Hall. [Chase's note]

** Horatio Nelson (1758–1805), English naval hero, victor over the French at Trafalgar. [Editor's note]

† This item and the next two are from the piece on gobbledygook by W. E. Farbstein, *New York Times,* March 29, 1953. [Chase's note]

In August 1952 the U.S. Department of Agriculture put out a pamphlet entitled: "Cultural and Pathogenic Variability in Single-Condial and Hyphaltip Iso-
lates of Hemlin-Thosporium Turcicum Pass."

Seems it was about corn leaf disease.

7   On reaching the top of the Finsteraarhorn in 1845, M. Dollfus-Ausset,
when he got his breath, exclaimed:

The soul communes in the infinite with those icy peaks which seem to have
their roots in the bowels of eternity.

Seems he enjoyed the view.

8   A government department announced:

Voucherable expenditures necessary to provide adequate dental treatment required as adjunct to medical treatment being rendered a pay patient in in-patient
status may be incurred as required at the expense of the Public Health Service.

Seems you can charge your dentist bill to the Public Health Service. Or can
you? . . .

Reducing the Gobble

9   As government and business offices grow larger, the need for doing something
about gobbledygook increases. Fortunately, the biggest office in the world is
working hard to reduce it. The Federal Security Agency in Washington,* with
nearly 100 million clients on its books, began analyzing its communication
lines some years ago, with gratifying results. Surveys find trouble in three main
areas: correspondence with clients about their social security problems, office
memos, official reports.

10   Clarity and brevity, as well as common humanity, are urgently needed in
this vast establishment which deals with disability, old age, and unemployment. The surveys found instead many cases of long-windedness, foggy meanings, clichés, and singsong phrases, and gross neglect of the reader's point of
view. Rather than talking to a real person, the writer was talking to himself.
"We often write like a man walking on stilts."

11   Here is a typical case of long-windedness:

Gobbledygook as found: "We are wondering if sufficient time has passed so
that you are in position to indicate whether favorable action may now be taken
on our recommendation for the reclassification of Mrs. Blank, junior clerk-
stenographer, CAF 2, to assistant clerk-stenographer, CAF 3?"
Suggested improvement: "Have you yet been able to act on our recommendation to reclassify Mrs. Blank?"

---

* Now the Department of Health, Education, and Welfare. [Chase's note]

Another case:

> Although the Central Efficiency Rating Committee recognizes that there are many desirable changes that could be made in the present efficiency rating system in order to make it more realistic and more workable than it now is, this committee is of the opinion that no further change should be made in the present system during the current year. Because of conditions prevailing throughout the country and the resultant turnover in personnel, and difficulty in administering the Federal programs, further mechanical improvement in the present rating system would require staff retraining and other administrative expense which would seem best withheld until the official termination of hostilities, and until restoration of regular operations.

12   The F.S.A. invites us to squeeze the gobbledygook out of this statement. Here is my attempt:

> The Central Efficiency Rating Committee recognizes that desirable changes could be made in the present system. We believe, however, that no change should be attempted until the war is over.

13   This cuts the statement from 111 to 30 words, about one-quarter of the original, but perhaps the reader can do still better. What of importance have I left out?

14   Sometimes in a book which I am reading for information—not for literary pleasure—I run a pencil through the surplus words. Often I can cut a section to half its length with an improvement in clarity. Magazines like *The Reader's Digest* have reduced this process to an art. Are long-windedness and obscurity a cultural lag from the days when writing was reserved for priests and cloistered scholars? The more words and the deeper the mystery, the greater their prestige and the firmer the hold on their jobs. And the better the candidate's chance today to have his doctoral thesis accepted.

15   The F.S.A. surveys found that a great deal of writing was obscure although not necessarily prolix. Here is a letter sent to more than 100,000 inquirers, a classic example of murky prose. To clarify it, one needs to *add* words, not cut them:

> In order to be fully insured, an individual must have earned $50 or more in covered employment for as many quarters of the coverage as half the calendar quarters elapsing between 1936 and the quarter in which he reaches age 65 or dies, whichever first occurs.

Probably no one without the technical jargon of the office could translate this; nevertheless, it was sent out to drive clients mad for seven years. One poor fellow wrote back: "I am no longer in covered employment. I have an outside job now."

16 Many words and phrases in officialese seem to come out automatically, as if from lower centers of the brain. In this standardized prose people never *get jobs,* they "secure employment"; *before* and *after* become "prior to" and "subsequent to"; one does not *do,* one "performs"; nobody *knows* a thing, he is "fully cognizant"; one never *says,* he "indicates." A great favorite at present is "implement."

17 Some charming boners occur in this talking-in-one's-sleep. For instance:

> The problem of extending coverage to all employees, regardless of size, is not as simple as surface appearances indicate.
>
> Though the proportions of all males and females in ages 16–45 are essentially the same . . .
>
> Dairy cattle, usually and commonly embraced in dairying . . .

18 In its manual to employees, the F.S.A. suggests the following:

Instead of	*Use*
give consideration to	consider
make inquiry regarding	inquire
is of the opinion	believes
comes into conflict with	conflicts
information which is of a confidential nature	confidential information

19 Professional or office gobbledygook often arises from using the passive rather than the active voice. Instead of looking you in the eye, as it were, and writing "This act requires . . ." the office worker looks out of the window and writes: "It is required by this statute that . . ." When the bureau chief says, "We expect Congress to cut your budget," the message is only too clear; but usually he says, "It is expected that the departmental budget estimates will be reduced by Congress."

> *Gobbled:* "All letters prepared for the signature of the Administrator will be single spaced."
>
> *Ungobbled:* "Single space all letters for the Administrator." (Thus cutting 13 words to 7.)

Only People Can Read

20 The F.S.A. surveys pick up the point . . . that human communication involves a listener as well as a speaker. Only people can read, though a lot of writing seems to be addressed to beings in outer space. To whom are you talking? The sender of the officialese message often forgets the chap on the other end of the line.

21 A woman with two small children wrote the F.S.A. asking what she should do about payments, as her husband had lost his memory. "If he never gets able

to work," she said, "and stays in an institution would I be able to draw any benefits? . . . I don't know how I am going to live and raise my children since he is disable to work. Please give me some information. . . ."

22   To this human appeal, she received a shattering blast of gobbledygook, beginning, "State unemployment compensation laws do not provide any benefits for sick or disabled individuals . . . in order to qualify an individual must have a certain number of quarters of coverage . . ." et cetera, et cetera. Certainly if the writer had been thinking about the poor woman he would not have dragged in unessential material about old-age insurance. If he had pictured a mother without means to care for her children, he would have told her where she might get help—from the local office which handles aid to dependent children, for instance.

23   Gobbledygook of this kind would largely evaporate if we thought of our messages as two way—in the above case, if we pictured ourselves talking on the doorstep of a shabby house to a woman with two children tugging at her skirts, who in her distress does not know which way to turn.

Results of the Survey

24   The F.S.A. survey showed that office documents could be cut 20 to 50 percent, with an improvement in clarity and a great saving to taxpayers in paper and payrolls.

25   A handbook was prepared and distributed to key officials.* They read it, thought about it, and presently began calling section meetings to discuss gobbledygook. More booklets were ordered, and the local output of documents began to improve. A Correspondence Review Section was established as a kind of laboratory to test murky messages. A supervisor could send up samples for analysis and suggestions. The handbook is now used for training new members; and many employees keep it on their desks along with the dictionary. Outside the Bureau some 25,000 copies have been sold (at 20 cents each) to individuals, governments, business firms, all over the world. It is now used officially in the Veterans Administration and in the Department of Agriculture.

26   The handbook makes clear the enormous amount of gobbledygook which automatically spreads in any large office, together with ways and means to keep it under control. I would guess that at least half of all the words circulating around the bureaus of the world are "irrelevant, incompetent, and immaterial"—to use a favorite legalism; or are just plain "unnecessary"—to ungobble it.

27   My favorite story of removing the gobble from gobbledygook concerns the Bureau of Standards at Washington. I have told it before but perhaps the reader will forgive the repetition. A New York plumber wrote the Bureau that he had found hydrochloric acid fine for cleaning drains, and was it harmless? Washington replied: "The efficacy of hydrochloric acid is indisputable, but the chlorine residue is incompatible with metallic permanence."

---

* By Milton Hall. [Chase's note]

28   The plumber wrote back that he was mighty glad the Bureau agreed with him. The Bureau replied with a note of alarm: "We cannot assume responsibility for the production of toxic and noxious residues with hydrochloric acid, and suggest that you use an alternate procedure." The plumber was happy to learn that the Bureau still agreed with him.

29   Whereupon Washington exploded: "Don't use hydrochloric acid; it eats hell out of the pipes!"

Topics for Writing and Discussion

1. What is "gobbledygook"? What are some of its main characteristics?
2. To explain this term, Chase relies primarily upon what strategy of definition? Cite some effective uses of this strategy.
3. What is one of the main reasons people produce gobbledygook? What are some suggested solutions?
4. How does the story at the essay's end sum up the purpose of this essay? Is it consistent with Chase's tone throughout the essay?
5. Chase's essay is over forty years old. Do you find his point outdated, or is gobbledygook still thriving in our world today? Browse through such material as insurance forms, credit card contracts, computer manuals, housing agreements, city ordinances, or even your college catalogue. Write an essay defining gobbledygook, using ample illustrations as Chase did.

Richard Rodriguez (© Robert Messick)

HISPANIC-AMERICAN CULTURE

Richard Rodriguez
(1944–   )

Born in San Francisco, the son of Mexican-American immigrants, Richard Rodriguez is a prolific writer who has published his work in numerous publications, including *Time, Harper's* and *Mother Jones*. He spoke only Spanish until he entered school at age five, and reacted so strongly to his early school experiences that for a while he refused to speak Spanish at home. He actually learned his parents' native language by studying Spanish in school as a foreign language. Rodriguez went on to study at Stanford University, Columbia University, the Warburg Institute in London, and the University of California at Berkeley, where he earned a Ph.D. in English literature. Among his writings are *Hunger of Memory: The Education of Richard Rodriguez* (1982), *Mexico's Children* (1990), and *Days of Obligation: An Argument with My Father* (1992). His most recent work, *Justice: A Question of Race*, was published in 1997. In "Hispanic-American Culture" Rodriguez invites readers to imagine a "marriage," a new, blended American culture.

1   WHAT is culture?

2   The immigrant shrugs. Latin American immigrants come to the United States with only the things they need in mind—not abstractions like culture. Money. They need dollars. They need food. Maybe they need to get out of the way of bullets.

3   Most of us who concern ourselves with Hispanic-American culture, as painters, musicians, writers—or as sons and daughters—are the children of immigrants. We have grown up on this side of the border, in the land of Elvis Presley and Thomas Edison; our lives are prescribed by the mall, by the DMV and the Chinese restaurant. Our imaginations yet vascillate between an Edenic

Latin America (the blue door)—which nevertheless betrayed our parents—and the repellent plate glass of a real American city—which has been good to us.

4   Hispanic-American culture is where the past meets the future. Hispanic-American culture is not an Hispanic milestone only, not simply a celebration at the crossroads. America transforms into pleasure what America cannot avoid. Is it any coincidence that at a time when Americans are troubled by the encroachment of the Mexican desert, Americans discover a chic in cactus, in the decorator colors of the Southwest? In sand?

5   Hispanic-American culture of the sort that is now showing (the teen movie, the rock song) may exist in an hourglass; may in fact be irrelevant to the epic. The U.S. Border Patrol works through the night to arrest the flow of illegal immigrants over the border, even as Americans wait in line to get into "La Bamba." Even as Americans vote to declare, once and for all, that English shall be the official language of the United States, Madonna starts recording in Spanish.

6   But then so is Bill Cosby's show irrelevant to the 10 o'clock news, where families huddle together in fear on porches, pointing at the body of the slain boy bagged in tarpoline. Which is not to say that Bill Cosby or Michael Jackson are irrelevant to the future or without neo-Platonic influence. Like players within the play, they prefigure, they resolve. They make black and white audiences aware of a bond that may not yet exist.

7   Before a national TV audience, Rita Moreno tells Geraldo Rivera that her dream as an actress is to play a character rather like herself: "I speak English perfectly well . . . I'm not dying from poverty . . . I want to play *that* kind of Hispanic woman, which is to say, an American citizen." This is an actress talking, these are show-biz pieties. But Moreno expresses as well the general Hispanic-American predicament. Hispanics want to belong to America without betraying the past.

8   Hispanics fear losing ground in any negotiation with the American city. We come from an expansive, an intimate culture that has been judged second-rate by the United States of America. For reasons of pride, therefore, as much as of affection, we are reluctant to give up our past. Hispanics often express a fear of "losing" culture. Our fame in the United States has been our resistance to assimilation.

9   The symbol of Hispanic culture has been the tongue of flame—Spanish. But the remarkable legacy Hispanics carry from Latin America is not language—an inflatable skin—but breath itself, capacity of soul, an inclination to live. The genius of Latin America is the habit of synthesis.

10   We assimilate. Just over the border there is the example of Mexico, the country from which the majority of U.S. Hispanics come. Mexico is mestizo—Indian and Spanish. Within a single family, Mexicans are light-skinned and dark. It is impossible for the Mexican to say, in the scheme of things, where the Indian begins and the Spaniard surrenders.

11   In culture as in blood, Latin America was formed by a rape that became a marriage. Due to the absorbing generosity of the Indian, European culture took on new soil. What Latin America knows is that people create one another

as they marry. In the music of Latin America you will hear the litany of blood-lines—the African drum, the German accordion, the cry from the minaret.

12   The United States stand as the opposing New World experiment. In North America the Indian and the European stood apace. Whereas Latin America was formed by a medieval Catholic dream of one world—of meltdown conversion—the United States was built up from Protestant individualism. The American melting pot washes away only embarrassment; it is the necessary initiation into public life. The American faith is that our national strength derives from separateness, from "diversity." The glamour of the United States is a carnival promise: You can lose weight, get rich as Rockefeller, tough up your roots, get a divorce.

13   Immigrants still come for the promise. But the United States wavers in its faith. As long as there was space enough, sky enough, as long as economic success validated individualism, loneliness was not too high a price to pay. (The cabin on the prairie or the Sony Walkman.)

14   As we near the end of the American century, two alternative cultures beckon the American imagination—both highly communal cultures—the Asian and the Latin American. The United States is a literal culture. Americans devour what we might otherwise fear to become. Sushi will make us corporate warriors. Combination Plate #3, smothered in mestizo gravy, will burn a hole in our hearts.

15   Latin America offers passion. Latin America has a life—I mean *life*—big clouds, unambiguous themes, death, birth, faith, that the United States, for all its quality of life, seems without now. Latin America offers communal riches: an undistressed leisure, a kitchen table, even a full sorrow. Such is the solitude of America, such is the urgency of American need, Americans reach right past a fledgling, homegrown Hispanic-American culture for the real thing—the darker bottle of Mexican beer; the denser novel of a Latin American master.

16   For a long time, Hispanics in the United States withheld from the United States our Latin American gift. We denied the value of assimilation. But as our presence is judged less foreign in America, we will produce a more generous art, less timid, less parochial. Carlos Santana, Luis Valdez, Linda Ronstadt—Hispanic Americans do not have a "pure" Latin American art to offer. Expect bastard themes, expect ironies, comic conclusions. For we live on this side of the border, where Kraft manufactures bricks of "Mexican style" Velveeta, and where Jack in the Box serves "Fajita Pita."

17   *The flame-red Chevy floats a song down the Pan American Highway: From a rolled-down window, the grizzled voice of Willie Nelson rises in disembodied harmony with the voice of Julio Iglesias. Gabby Hayes and Cisco are thus resolved.*

18   Expect marriage. We will change America even as we will be changed. We will disappear with you into a new miscegenation.

19   Along the border, real conflicts remain. But the ancient tear separating Europe from itself—the Catholic Mediterranean from the Protestant north—may yet heal itself in the New World. For generations, Latin America has been

the place—the bed—of a confluence of so many races and cultures that Protestant North America shuddered to imagine it.

20   Imagine it.

TOPICS FOR WRITING AND DISCUSSION

1. How does Rodriguez define Hispanic-American culture? In his view, what are the current conflicts between this culture and the general culture of the United States?

2. Does Rodriguez believe that cultures can remain pure? Why or why not? Do you think he believes that they should? What is the result of assimilation? Do you agree with his perspective?

3. Is it possible for an individual to be part of more than one culture? Write your own definition of culture, and then, using that definition as your guide, list the different cultures to which you may belong.

4. Rodriguez writes that Americans "reach right past a fledgling, home-grown Hispanic-American culture for the real thing—the darker bottle of Mexican beer; the denser novel of a Latin American master." Is this true of American attitudes toward other cultures assimilated within the United States? Describe one such culture whose "Americanized" branch may be ignored while its origins are romanticized or celebrated. Or describe a culture that, although "Americanized," receives a great deal of popular attention.

5. Review Rodriguez's forecast, "Expect marriage. We will change America even as we will be changed," and compare it to his earlier statement that "The American faith is that our national strength derives from separateness." Do you believe that some of the many ethnic and regional cultures that comprise America have remained largely separate? Have there already been cultures, now mostly assimilated, who have changed America even as they were changed? Choosing a specific cultural group as your focus, write an essay showing how this group has maintained—by choice or pressure—its "separateness" or how it has changed and, in turn, been changed through its assimilation.

NEW SUPERSTITIONS FOR OLD

Margaret Mead
(1901–1978)

Born in Philadelphia, Margaret Mead was an anthropologist who brought the work of cultural anthropology to public attention. She showed Americans the value of examining other cultures to understand better the complexities of being human. Mead received her undergraduate degree from Barnard College and later earned a Ph.D. from Columbia University, where she studied under Ruth Benedict and Franz Boas. Field research for her dissertation took her to the South Pacific and ultimately resulted in the book *Coming of Age in Samoa* (1928). In that work, she contrasts adolescence in Western and Samoan societies. Her later research took her to New Guinea, Bali, and many North American locations. Among her works are *Growing Up in New Guinea* (1930), *Sex and Temperament in Three Primitive Societies* (1935), *And Keep Your Powder Dry* (1942), and *Male and Female: A Study of Sexes in a Changing World* (1949). Her autobiography *Blackberry Winter* was published in 1972.

In 1926, Mead began a lifelong association with the American Museum of Natural History in New York City. A year after her death, she was posthumously awarded the Presidential Medal of Freedom. "New Superstitions for Old" appears in *A Way of Seeing* (1961). In the essay, Mead examines the concept of superstition and its roles in our lives.

Margaret Mead at the Museum of Natural History in New York City (© John Laundis/Black Star)

1   ONCE in a while there is a day when everything seems to run smoothly and even the riskiest venture comes out exactly right. You exclaim, "This is my lucky day!" Then as an afterthought you say, "Knock on wood!" Of course, you do not really believe that knocking on wood will ward off danger. Still, boasting about your own good luck gives you a slightly uneasy feeling—and you carry out the little protective ritual. If someone challenged you at that moment, you would probably say, "Oh, that's nothing. Just an old superstition."

2   But when you come to think about it, what is a superstition?

3   In the contemporary world most people treat old folk beliefs as superstitions—the belief, for instance, that there are lucky and unlucky days or numbers, that future events can be read from omens, that there are protective charms or that what happens can be influenced by casting spells. We have excluded magic from our current world view, for we know that natural events have natural causes.

4   In a religious context, where truths cannot be demonstrated, we accept them as a matter of faith. Superstitions, however, belong to the category of beliefs, practices and ways of thinking that have been discarded because they are inconsistent with scientific knowledge. It is easy to say that other people are superstitious because they believe what we regard to be untrue. "Superstition" used in that sense is a derogatory term for the beliefs of other people that we do not share. But there is more to it than that. For superstitions lead a kind of half life in a twilight world where, sometimes, we partly suspend our disbelief and act as if magic worked.

5   Actually, almost every day, even in the most sophisticated home, something is likely to happen that evokes the memory of some old folk belief. The salt spills. A knife falls to the floor. Your nose tickles. Then perhaps, with a slightly embarrassed smile, the person who spilled the salt tosses a pinch over his left shoulder. Or someone recites the old rhyme, "Knife falls, gentleman calls." Or as you rub your nose you think, That means a letter. I wonder who's writing? No one takes these small responses very seriously or gives them more than a passing thought. Sometimes people will preface one of these ritual acts—walking around instead of under a ladder or hastily closing an umbrella that has been opened inside a house—with such a remark as "I remember my great-aunt used to . . ." or "Germans used to say you ought not . . ." And then, having placed the belief at some distance away in time or space, they carry out the ritual.

6   Everyone also remembers a few of the observances of childhood—wishing on the first star; looking at the new moon over the right shoulder; avoiding the cracks in the sidewalk on the way to school while chanting, "Step on a crack, break your mother's back"; wishing on white horses, on loads of hay, on covered bridges, on red cars; saying quickly, "Bread-and-butter" when a post or a tree separated you from the friend you were walking with. The adult may not actually recite the formula "Star light, star bright . . ." and may not quite turn to look at the new moon, but his mood is tempered by a little of the old thrill that came when the observance was still freighted with magic.

7   Superstition can also be used with another meaning. When I discuss the religious beliefs of other peoples, especially primitive peoples, I am often asked, "Do they really have a religion, or is it all just superstition?" The point of contrast here is not between a scientific and a magical view of the world but between the clear, theologically defensible religious beliefs of members of civilized societies and what we regard as the false and childish views of the heathen who "bow down to wood and stone." Within the civilized religions, however, where membership includes believers who are educated and urbane and others who are ignorant and simple, one always finds traditions and practices that the more sophisticated will dismiss offhand as "just superstition" but that guide the steps of those who live by older ways. Mostly these are very ancient beliefs, some handed on from one religion to another and carried from country to country around the world.

8   Very commonly, people associate superstition with the past, with very old ways of thinking that have been supplanted by modern knowledge. But new superstitions are continually coming into being and flourishing in our society. Listening to mothers in the park in the 1930's, one heard them say, "Now, don't you run out into the sun, or Polio will get you." In the 1940's elderly people explained to one another in tones of resignation, "It was the Virus that got him down." And every year the cosmetics industry offers us new magic—cures for baldness, lotions that will give every woman radiant skin, hair coloring that will restore to the middle-aged the charm and romance of youth—results that are promised if we will just follow the simple directions. Families and individuals also have their cherished, private superstitions. You must leave by the back door when you are going on a journey, or you must wear a green dress when you are taking an examination. It is a kind of joke, of course, but it makes you feel safe.

9   These old half-beliefs and new half-beliefs reflect the keenness of our wish to have something come true or to prevent something bad from happening. We do not always recognize new superstitions for what they are, and we still follow the old ones because someone's faith long ago matches our contemporary hopes and fears. In the past people "knew" that a black cat crossing one's path was a bad omen, and they turned back home. Today we are fearful of taking a journey and would give anything to turn back—and then we notice a black cat running across the road in front of us.

10   Child psychologists recognize the value of the toy a child holds in his hand at bedtime. It is different from his thumb, with which he can close himself in from the rest of the world, and it is different from the real world, to which he is learning to relate himself. Psychologists call these toys—these furry animals and old, cozy baby blankets—"transitional objects"; that is, objects that help the child move back and forth between the exactions of everyday life and the world of wish and dream.

11   Superstitions have some of the qualities of these transitional objects. They help people pass between the areas of life where what happens has to be accepted without proof and the areas where sequences of events are explicable in

terms of cause and effect, based on knowledge. Bacteria and viruses that cause sickness have been identified; the cause of symptoms can be diagnosed and a rational course of treatment prescribed. Magical charms no longer are needed to treat the sick; modern medicine has brought the whole sequence of events into the secular world. But people often act as if this change had not taken place. Laymen still treat germs as if they were invisible, malign spirits, and physicians sometimes prescribe antibiotics as if they were magic substances.

12   Over time, more and more of life has become subject to the controls of knowledge. However, this is never a one-way process. Scientific investigation is continually increasing our knowledge. But if we are to make good use of this knowledge, we must not only rid our minds of old, superseded beliefs and fragments of magical practice, but also recognize new superstitions for what they are. Both are generated by our wishes, our fears and our feeling of helplessness in difficult situations.

13   Civilized peoples are not alone in having grasped the idea of superstitions—beliefs and practices that are superseded but that still may evoke compliance. The idea is one that is familiar to every people, however primitive, that I have ever known. Every society has a core of transcendent beliefs—beliefs about the nature of the universe, the world and man—that no one doubts or questions. Every society also has a fund of knowledge related to practical life—about the succession of day and night and of the seasons; about correct ways of planting seeds so that they will germinate and grow; about the process involved in making dyes or the steps necessary to remove the deadly poison from manioc roots so they become edible. Island peoples know how the winds shift and they know the star toward which they must point the prow of the canoe exactly so that as the sun rises they will see the first fringing palms on the shore toward which they are sailing.

14   This knowledge, based on repeated observations of reliable sequences, leads to ideas and hypotheses of the kind that underlie scientific thinking. And gradually as scientific knowledge, once developed without conscious plan, has become a great self-corrective system and the foundation for rational planning and action, old magical beliefs and observances have had to be discarded.

15   But it takes time for new ways of thinking to take hold, and often the transition is only partial. Older, more direct beliefs live on in the hearts and minds of elderly people. And they are learned by children who, generation after generation, start out life as hopefully and fearfully as their forebears did. Taking their first steps away from home, children use the old rituals and invent new ones to protect themselves against the strangeness of the world into which they are venturing.

16   So whatever has been rejected as no longer true, as limited, provincial and idolatrous, still leads a half life. People may say, "It's just a superstition," but they continue to invoke the ritual's protection or potency. In this transitional, twilight state such beliefs come to resemble dreaming. In the dream world a thing can be either good or bad; a cause can be an effect and an effect can be a cause. Do warts come from touching toads, or does touching a toad cure the

wart? Is sneezing a good omen or a bad omen? You can have it either way—or both ways at once. In the same sense, the half-acceptance and half-denial accorded superstitions give us the best of both worlds.

17   Superstitions are sometimes smiled at and sometimes frowned upon as observances characteristic of the old-fashioned, the unenlightened, children, peasants, servants, immigrants, foreigners or backwoods people. Nevertheless, they give all of us ways of moving back and forth among the different worlds in which we live—the sacred, the secular and the scientific. They allow us to keep a private world also, where, smiling a little, we can banish danger with a gesture and summon luck with a rhyme, make the sun shine in spite of storm clouds, force the stranger to do our bidding, keep an enemy at bay and straighten the paths of those we love.

TOPICS FOR WRITING AND DISCUSSION

1. In spite of our growing body of scientific knowledge, superstitions continue to play a role in our lives. How does Mead explain this apparently contradictory circumstance?
2. To develop her definition, Mead contrasts superstition with religion. After reading paragraphs 4 and 7 carefully, explain how she distinguishes superstition from religion. Note that *religion* has a different meaning in the two paragraphs.
3. Mead tells us both what superstition *is* and what it *is not*. Make a list of the things she says superstition is not and then analyze how she uses these negative examples to establish her definition.
4. Does Mead see superstitions as entirely positive? Entirely negative? Give examples from the essay to support your response.
5. Superstitions, according to Mead, help us move back and forth among the secular, scientific, and religious realms in which we live. Explain a superstition that you, your family, or a friend maintains. Define the belief or ritual in such a way that your readers understand clearly its origin, purpose, and effects.

DISCRIMINATION

Ralph Ellison
(1914–1994)

Born in Oklahoma City, Ralph Waldo Ellison was
named after Ralph Waldo Emerson, the nineteenth-
century poet and essayist. When Ellison attended
Tuskegee Institute, his intent was to pursue a career in
music. In 1936, he moved to New York City and met
author Richard Wright, who encouraged Ellison to pursue another interest—writing. Ellison soon became
associated with the Federal Writers' Project, publishing
short stories and articles in periodicals such as *New
Challenge* and *New Masses.* In 1952, he published his
novel *Invisible Man,* now regarded as a literary classic
and for which he received the National Book Award.
Unfortunately, Ellison never completed a second novel.
He also published two collections of social, political,
and critical essays titled *Shadow and Act* (1964) and
Going to the Territory (1986). Other collections were
published after his death: *The Collected Essays of
Ralph Ellison* (1995), *Conversations with Ralph Ellison*
(1995), and *Flying Home: And Other Stories* (1996).

"Discrimination" was written in 1989 as a part of
a *New York Times* supplement that focused on ethno-
centrism and racism.

1   IT got to you first at the age of six, and through your own curiosity. With
kindergarten completed and the first grade ahead, you were eagerly anticipating your first day of public school. For months you had been imagining your
new experience and the children, known and unknown, with whom you would
study and play. But the physical framework of your imagining, an elementary
school in the process of construction, lay close at hand on the block-square

Ralph Ellison (Woodfin Camp, Inc.)

site across the street from your home. For over a year you had watched it rise and spread in the air to become a handsome structure of brick and stone, then seen its broad encircling grounds arrayed with seesaws, swings, and baseball diamonds. You had imagined this picture-book setting as the scene of your new experience, and when enrollment day arrived, with its grounds astir with bright colors and voices of kids like yourself, it did, indeed, become the site of your very first lesson in public schooling—though not within its classrooms, as you had imagined, but well outside its walls. For while located within a fairly mixed neighborhood this new public school was exclusively for whites.

2   It was then you learned that you would attend a school located far to the south of your neighborhood, and that reaching it involved a journey which took you over, either directly or by way of a viaduct which arched head-spinning high above, a broad expanse of railroad tracks along which a constant traffic of freight-cars, switch engines, and passenger trains made it dangerous for a child to cross. And that once the tracks were safely negotiated you continued past warehouses, factories, and loading docks, and then through a notorious red-light district where black prostitutes in brightly colored housecoats and Mary Jane shoes supplied the fantasies and needs of a white clientele. Considering the fact that you couldn't attend school with white kids this made for a confusion that was further confounded by the giggling jokes which older boys whispered about the district's peculiar form of integration. For you it was a grown-up's mystery, but streets being no less schools than routes to schools, the district would soon add a few forbidden words to your vocabulary.

3   It took a bit of time to forget the sense of incongruity aroused by your having to walk *past* a school to get *to* a school, but soon you came to like your school, your teachers, and most of your schoolmates. Indeed, you soon enjoyed the long walks and anticipated the sights you might see, the adventures you might encounter, and the many things not taught in school that could be learned along the way. Your school was not nearly so fine as that which faced your home but it had its attractions. Among them its nearness to a park, now abandoned by whites, in which you picnicked and played. And there were the two tall cylindrical fire-escapes on either wing of its main building down which it was a joy to lie full-length and slide, spiraling down and around three stories to the ground—providing no outraged teacher was waiting to strap your legs once you sailed out of its chute like a shot off a fireman's shovel. Besides, in your childish way you were learning that it was better to take self-selected risks and pay the price than be denied the joy or pain of risk-taking by those who begrudged your existence.

4   Beginning when you were four or five you had known the joy of trips to the city's zoo, but one day you would ask your mother to take you there and have her sigh and explain that it was now against the law for Negro kids to view the animals. Had someone done something bad to the animals? No. Had someone tried to steal them or feed them poison? No. Could white kids still go? Yes! So why? Quit asking questions, it's the law and only because some white folks are out to turn this state into a part of the South.

5   This sudden and puzzling denial of a Saturday's pleasure was disappointing and so angered your mother that later, after the zoo was moved north of the city, she decided to do something about it. Thus one warm Saturday afternoon with you and your baby brother dressed in your best she took you on a long streetcar ride which ended at a strange lakeside park, in which you found a crowd of noisy white people. Having assumed that you were on your way to the integrated cemetery where at the age of three you had been horrified beyond all tears or forgetting when you saw your father's coffin placed in the ground, you were bewildered. But now as your mother herded you and your brother in to the park you discovered that you'd come to the zoo and were so delighted that soon you were laughing and babbling as excitedly as the kids around you.

6   Your mother was pleased and as you moved through the crowd of white parents and children she held your brother's hand and allowed as much time for staring at the cages of rare animals as either of you desired. But once your brother began to tire she herded you out of the park and toward the streetcar line. And then it happened.

7   Just as you reached the gate through which crowds of whites were coming and going you had a memorable lesson in the strange ways of segregated-democracy as instructed by a guard in civilian clothes. He was a white man dressed in a black suit and a white straw hat, and when he looked at the fashion in which your mother was dressed, then down to you and your brother, he stiffened, turned red in the face, and stared as though at something dangerous.

8   "Girl," he shouted, "where are your *white* folks!"

9   "*White* folks," your mother said, "What white folks? I don't *have* any white folks, I'm a Negro!"

10   "Now don't you get smart with me, colored gal," the white man said, "I mean where are the white folks you come *out* here with!"

11   "But I just told you that I didn't come here with any white people," your mother said, "I came here with my boys . . ."

12   "Then what are you doing in this park," the white man said.

13   And now when your mother answered you could hear the familiar sound of anger in her voice.

14   "I'm here," she said, "because I'm a *taxpayer,* and I thought it was about time that my boys have a look at those animals. And for that I didn't *need* any *white* folks to show me the way!"

15   "Well," the white man said, "*I'm* here to tell you that you're breaking the law! So now you'll have to leave. Both you and your chillun too. The rule says no niggers is allowed in the zoo. That's the law and I'm enforcing it!"

16   "Very well," your mother said, "we've seen the animals anyway and were on our way to the streetcar line when you stopped us."

17   "That's fine," the white man said, "and when that car comes you be sure that you get on it, you hear? You and your chillun too!"

18   So it was quite a day. You had enjoyed the animals with your baby brother and had another lesson in the sudden ways good times could be turned into bad when white people looked at your color instead of *you.* But

better still, you had learned something of your mother's courage and were proud that she had broken an unfair law and stood up for her right to do so. For while the white man kept staring until the streetcar arrived she ignored him and answered your brother's questions about the various animals. Then the car came with its crowd of white parents and children, and when you were entrained and rumbling home past the fine lawns and houses your mother gave way to a gale of laughter; in which, hesitantly at first, and then with assurance and pride, you joined. And from that day the incident became the source of a family joke that was sparked by accidents, faux pas, or obvious lies. Then one of you was sure to frown and say, "Well, I think you'll have to go now, both you and your chillun too!" And the family would laugh hilariously. Discrimination teaches one to discriminate between discriminators while countering absurdity with black (Negro? Afro-American? African-American?) comedy.

19   When you were eight you would move to one of the white sections through which you often passed on the way to your father's grave and your truly last trip to the zoo. For now your mother was the custodian of several apartments located in a building which housed on its street floor a drug store, a tailor shop, a Piggly Wiggly market, and a branch post office. Built on a downward slope, the building had at its rear a long driveway which led from the side street past an empty lot to a group of garages in which the apartments' tenants stored their cars. Built at an angle with wings facing north and east, the structure supported a servant's quarters which sat above its angle like a mock watchtower atop a battlement, and it was there that you now lived.

20   Reached by a flight of outside stairs, it consisted of four small rooms, a bath, and a kitchen. Windows on three of its sides provided a view across the empty frontage to the street, of the back yards behind it, and of the back wall and windows of the building in which your mother worked. It was quite comfortable but you secretly disliked the idea of your mother living in service and missed your friends who now lived far away. Nevertheless, the neighborhood was pleasant, served by a sub-station of the streetcar line, and marked by a variety of activities which challenged your curiosity. Even its affluent alleys were more exciting to explore than those of your old neighborhood, and the one white friend you were to acquire in the area lived nearby.

21   This friend was a brilliant but sickly boy who was tutored at home, and with him you shared your new interest in building radios, a hobby at which he was quite skilled. Your friendship eased your loneliness and helped dispel some of the mystery and resentment imposed by segregation. Through access to his family, headed by an important Episcopalian minister, you learned more about whites and thus about yourself. With him you could make comparisons that were not so distorted by the racial myths which obstructed your thrust toward self-perception; compare their differences in taste, discipline, and manners with those of Negro families of comparable status and income; observe variations between your friend's boyish lore and your own, and measure his intelligence, knowledge, and ambitions against your own. For you this was a most important experience and a rare privilege, because

up to now the prevailing separation of the races had made it impossible to learn how you and your Negro friends compared with boys who lived on the white side of the color line. It was said by word of mouth, proclaimed in newsprint, and dramatized by acts of discriminatory law that you were inferior. You were barred from vying with them in sports and games, competing in the classroom or the world of art. Yet what you saw, heard, and smelled of them left irrepressible doubts. So you ached for objective proof, for a fair field of testing.

22   Even your school's proud marching band was denied participation in the statewide music contests so popular at the time, as though so airy and earth-transcending an art as music would be contaminated if performed by musicians of different races.

23   Which was especially disturbing because after the father of a friend who lived next door in your old neighborhood had taught you the beginner's techniques required to play valved instruments you had decided to become a musician. Then shortly before moving among whites your mother had given you a brass cornet, which in the isolation of the servant's quarters you practiced hours on end. But you yearned to play with other musicians and found none available. Now you lived less than a block from a white school with a famous band, but there was no one in the neighborhood with whom to explore the mysteries of the horn. You could hear the school band's music and watch their marching, but joining in making the thrilling sounds was impossible. Nor did it help that you owned the scores to a few of their marches and could play with a certain facility and fairly good tone. So there, surrounded by sounds but unable to share a sound, you went it alone. You turned yourself into a one-man band.

24   You played along as best you could with the phonograph, read the score to *The Carnival of Venice* while listening to Del Steigers executing triple-tongue variations on its themes; played the trumpet parts of your bandbook's marches while humming in your head the supporting voices of horns and reeds. And since your city was a seedbed of Southwestern jazz you played Kansas City riffs, bugle calls, and wha-wha-muted imitations of blues singers' pleas. But none of this made up for your lack of fellow musicians. And then, late one Saturday afternoon when your mother and brother were away, and when you had dozed off while reading, you awoke to the nearby sound of live music. At first you thought you were dreaming, and then that you were listening to the high school band, but that couldn't be the source because, instead of floating over building tops and bouncing off wall and windowpane, the sounds you heard rose up, somewhat muffled, from below.

25   With that you ran to a window which faced the driveway, and looking down through the high windowpane of the lighted post office you could see the metal glint of instruments. Then you were on your feet and down the stairs, keeping to the shadows as you drew close and peeped below. And there you looked down upon a room full of men and women postal workers who were playing away at a familiar march. It was like the answer to a silent prayer because you could tell by the sound that they were beginners like yourself and the covers of the thicket of bandbooks revealed that they were of the same set as

yours. For a while you listened and hummed along, unseen but shaking with excitement in the dimming twilight. And then, hardly before the idea formed in your head, you were skipping up the stairs to grab your cornet, lyre, and bandbook and hurtling down again to the drive.

26   For a while you listened, hearing the music come to a pause and the sound of the conductor's voice. Then came a rap on a music stand and once again the music. And now turning to the march by the light from the window, you snapped score to lyre, raised horn to lip, and began to play; at first silently tonguing the notes through the mouthpiece and then, carried away with the thrill of stealing a part of the music, you tensed your diaphragm and blew. And as you played, keeping time with your foot on the concrete drive, you realized that you were a better cornetist than some in the band and grew bold in the pride of your sound. Now in your mind you were marching along a downtown street to the flying of flags, the tramping of feet, and the cheering of excited crowds. For at last by an isolated act of brassy cunning you had become a member of the band.

27   Yes, but unfortunately you then let yourself become so carried away that you forgot to listen for the conductor's instructions which you were too high and hidden to see. Suddenly the music faded and you opened your ears to the fact that you were now rendering a lonely solo in the startled quietness. And before you could fully return to reality there came the sound of table legs across a floor and a rustle of movement ending in the appearance of a white startled face in the opened window. Then you heard a man's voice exclaim, "I'll be damn, it's a little nigger!" whereupon you took off like quail at the sound of sudden shotgun fire.

28   Next thing you knew, you were up the stairs and on your bed, crying away in the dark your guilt and embarrassment. You cried and cried, asking yourself how could you have been so lacking in pride as to shame yourself and your entire race by butting in where you weren't wanted. And this just to make some amateur music. To this you had no answers but then and there you made a vow that it would never happen again. And then, slowly, slowly, as you lay in the dark, your earlier lessons in the absurd nature of racial relations came to your aid. And suddenly you found yourself laughing, both at the way you'd run away and the shock you'd caused by joining unasked in the music.

29   Then you could hear yourself intoning in your eight-year-old's imitation of a white Southern accent. "Well, boy, you broke the law, so you have to go, and that means you and your chillun too!"

TOPICS FOR WRITING AND DISCUSSION

1. What is Ellison's purpose in writing this essay? What is his definition of "discrimination"?
2. What is the primary strategy of development used to present this definition? What details make this essay vivid?
3. What is the effect of Ellison's use of second person ("you") in this essay? Does this give an indication of his intended audience?

4. In what way does Ellison's chronological structuring of the essay, as well as the amount of time covered, comment on how discrimination is defined for an individual? Consider, too, Ellison's use of the refrain, "Well, I think you'll have to go now, both you and your chillun too!" How does it affect tone, structure, and theme?

5. In this essay, Ellison presents a series of encounters to show how a child learns the meaning of racial injustice ("It got to you first at the age of six . . ."). In an essay of your own, use Ellison's method to show your reader how you first learned the definition of some sort of racial, ethnic, or gender prejudice or about some important value, such as honesty, responsibility, or generosity.

METAPHORS

Sylvia Plath
(1932–1963)

Born in Jamaica Plain, Massachusetts, poet Sylvia
Plath published her first poem when she was only
eight. By the time she entered Smith College in 1950,
she had a list of published poems, which increased to
more than 400 by the time she graduated *summa cum
laude* in 1955. With a Fulbright scholarship, she studied at Cambridge University, and there married British
poet Ted Hughes in 1956. She received her M.A. in
1957, taught at Smith for a year, and then returned to
England, where her two children were born. In 1960,
her first collection of poems was published, *The Colossus and Other Poems*. In 1963, she published an autobiographical novel, *The Bell Jar* (using the pseudonym
Victoria Lucas). After her suicide in 1963, Hughes
edited and published her remaining works: *Ariel*
(1965), a collection of some of her last poems; *Crossing the Water* (1971); *Winter Trees* (1972); and *The
Collected Poems* (1985). The following poem,
"Metaphors," first appeared in *The Colossus and
Other Poems*.

I'm a riddle in nine syllables
An elephant, a ponderous house,
A melon strolling on two tendrils.
A red fruit, ivory, fine timbers!
5 This loaf's big with its yeasty rising.
Money's new-minted in this fat purse.
I'm a means, a stage, a cow in calf.

I've eaten a bag of green apples,
Boarded the train there's no getting off.

Sylvia Plath (UPI/Corbis-Bettmann)

Topics for Writing and Discussion

1. What is a metaphor?* How does it explain its subject in a way that differs from a dictionary definition?
2. Why is this poem called "Metaphors"? What is the subject of Plath's poem? How did you arrive at this conclusion?
3. Are all the metaphors in this poem equally positive or negative? What is the speaker's attitude toward her "stage"? Is she feeling ripe with life or bloated and bovine—or something else? Does the last line present a woman who is trapped or one who is on a journey?
4. Why is the speaker a "riddle in nine syllables"? (Look closely at the poem. How many lines are there and how many syllables are there in each line? Why?)
5. Try creating some metaphors. Think of several comparisons that might capture your own complex personality or situation at this time. What images would you choose to help others understand your view of yourself?

---

* If you need help with this definition, see the Glossary near the end of this text.

Stephen Crane (UPI/Corbis-Bettmann)

A MYSTERY OF HEROISM

Stephen Crane
(1871–1900)

Born in Newark, New Jersey, Stephen Crane briefly attended Lafayette College and Syracuse University. He worked as a freelance journalist in New York City, at first barely earning a living. His first novel, *Maggie: A Girl of the Streets* (1893), was privately published and was denounced for its sympathetic portrayal of its main character. His next novel, however, *The Red Badge of Courage* (1895), was an immediate success. Even with his literary success, Crane continued his journalistic pursuits, becoming a war correspondent in both Greece and Cuba. He wrote other novels, including *George's Mother* (1896), and several collections of experimental poems and short stories, including "The Open Boat" and "The Blue Hotel." In this 1895 story, Crane invites readers to ponder the meaning of true heroism.

1　THE dark uniforms of the men were so coated with dust from the incessant wrestling of the two armies that the regiment almost seemed a part of the clay bank which shielded them from the shells. On the top of the hill a battery was arguing in tremendous roars with some other guns, and to the eye of the infantry the artillerymen, the guns, the caissons, the horses, were distinctly outlined upon the blue sky. When a piece was fired, a red streak as round as a log flashed low in the heavens, like a monstrous bolt of lightning. The men of the battery wore white duck trousers, which somehow emphasized their legs; and when they ran and crowded in little groups at the bidding of the shouting officers, it was more impressive than usual to the infantry.

2　Fred Collins, of A Company, was saying: "Thunder! I wisht I had a drink. Ain't there any water round here?" Then somebody yelled: "There goes th' bugler!"

3　As the eyes of half the regiment swept in one machinelike movement, there was an instant's picture of a horse in a great convulsive leap of a death wound and a rider leaning back with a crooked arm and spread fingers before his face. On the ground was the crimson terror of an exploding shell, with fibres of flame that seemed like lances. A glittering bugle swung clear of the rider's back as fell headlong the horse and the man. In the air was an odor as from a conflagration.

4   Sometimes they of the infantry looked down at a fair little meadow which spread at their feet. Its long green grass was rippling gently in a breeze. Beyond it was the grey form of a house half torn to pieces by shells and by the busy axes of soldiers who had pursued firewood. The line of an old fence was now dimly marked by long weeds and by an occasional post. A shell had blown the well-house to fragments. Little lines of grey smoke ribboning upward from some embers indicated the place where had stood the barn.

5   From beyond a curtain of green woods there came the sound of some stupendous scuffle, as if two animals the size of islands were fighting. At a distance there were occasional appearances of swift-moving men, horses, batteries, flags, and with the crashing of infantry volleys were heard, often, wild and frenzied cheers. In the midst of it all Smith and Ferguson, two privates of A Company, were engaged in a heated discussion which involved the greatest questions of the national existence.

6   The battery on the hill presently engaged in a frightful duel. The white legs of the gunners scampered this way and that way, and the officers redoubled their shouts. The guns, with their demeanors of stolidity and courage, were typical of something infinitely self-possessed in this clamor of death that swirled around the hill.

7   One of a "swing" team was suddenly smitten quivering to the ground, and his maddened brethren dragged his torn body in their struggle to escape from this turmoil and danger. A young soldier astride one of the leaders swore and fumed in his saddle and furiously jerked at the bridle. An officer screamed out an order so violently that his voice broke and ended the sentence in a falsetto shriek.

8   The leading company of the infantry regiment was somewhat exposed, and the colonel ordered it moved more fully under the shelter of the hill. There was the clank of steel against steel.

9   A lieutenant of the battery rode down and passed them, holding his right arm carefully in his left hand. And it was as if this arm was not at all a part of him, but belonged to another man. His sober and reflective charger went slowly. The officer's face was grimy and perspiring, and his uniform was tousled as if he had been in direct grapple with an enemy. He smiled grimly when the men stared at him. He turned his horse toward the meadow.

10   Collins, of A Company, said: "I wisht I had a drink. I bet there's water in that there ol' well yonder!"

11   "Yes; but how you goin' to git it?"

12   For the little meadow which intervened was now suffering a terrible onslaught of shells. Its green and beautiful calm had vanished utterly. Brown earth was being flung in monstrous handfuls. And there was a massacre of the young blades of grass. They were being torn, burned, obliterated. Some

curious fortune of the battle had made this gentle little meadow the object of the red hate of the shells, and each one as it exploded seemed like an imprecation in the face of a maiden.

13 The wounded officer who was riding across this expanse said to himself: "Why, they couldn't shoot any harder if the whole army was massed here!"

14 A shell struck the grey ruins of the house, and as, after the roar, the shattered wall fell in fragments, there was a noise which resembled the flapping of shutters during a wild gale of winter. Indeed, the infantry paused in the shelter of the bank appeared as men standing upon a shore contemplating a madness of the sea. The angel of calamity had under its glance the battery upon the hill. Fewer white-legged men labored about the guns. A shell had smitten one of the pieces, and after the flare, the smoke, the dust, the wrath of this blow were gone, it was possible to see white legs stretched horizontally upon the ground. And at that interval to the rear where it is the business of battery horses to stand with their noses to the fight, awaiting the command to drag their guns out of the destruction, or into it, or wheresoever these incomprehensible humans demanded with whip and spur—in this line of passive and dumb spectators, whose fluttering hearts yet would not let them forget the iron laws of man's control of them—in this rank of brute-soldiers there had been relentless and hideous carnage. From the ruck of bleeding and prostrate horses, the men of the infantry could see one animal raising its stricken body with its forelegs and turning its nose with mystic and profound eloquence toward the sky.

15 Some comrades joked Collins about his thirst. "Well, if yeh want a drink so bad, why don't yeh go git it?"

16 "Well, I will in a minnet, if yeh don't shut up!"

17 A lieutenant of artillery floundered his horse straight down the hill with as little concern as if it were level ground. As he galloped past the colonel of the infantry, he threw up his hand in swift salute. "We've got to get out of that," he roared angrily. He was a black-bearded officer, and his eyes, which resembled beads, sparkled like those of an insane man. His jumping horse sped along the column of infantry.

18 The fat major, standing carelessly with his sword held horizontally behind him and with his legs far apart, looked after the receding horseman and laughed. "He wants to get back with orders pretty quick, or there'll be no batt'ry left," he observed.

19 The wise young captain of the second company hazarded to the lieutenant-colonel that the enemy's infantry would probably soon attack the hill, and the lieutenant-colonel snubbed him.

20 A private in one of the rear companies looked out over the meadow, and then turned to a companion and said, "Look there, Jim!" It was the wounded officer from the battery, who some time before had started to ride across the meadow, supporting his right arm carefully with his left hand. This man had encountered a shell, apparently, at a time when no one perceived him, and he could now be seen lying face downward with a stirruped foot stretched across the body of his dead horse. A leg of the charger extended slantingly upward, precisely as stiff as a stake. Around this motionless pair the shells still howled.

21   There was a quarrel in A Company. Collins was shaking his fist in the faces of some laughing comrades. "Dern yeh! I ain't afraid t' go. If yeh say much, I will go!"

22   "Of course, yeh will! You'll run through that there medder, won't yeh?"

23   Collins said, in a terrible voice: "You see now!" At this ominous threat his comrades broke into renewed jeers.

24   Collins gave them a dark scowl, and went to find his captain. The latter was conversing with the colonel of the regiment.

25   "Captain," said Collins, saluting and standing at attention—in those days all trousers bagged at the knees—"Captain, I want t' get permission to go git some water from that there well over yonder!"

26   The colonel and the captain swung about simultaneously and stared across the meadow. The captain laughed. "You must be pretty thirsty, Collins?"

27   "Yes, sir, I am."

28   "Well—ah," said the captain. After a moment, he asked, "Can't you wait?"

29   "No, sir."

30   The colonel was watching Collins's face. "Look here, my lad," he said, in a pious sort of voice—"Look here, my lad"—Collins was not a lad—"don't you think that's taking pretty big risks for a little drink of water?"

31   "I dunno," said Collins uncomfortably. Some of the resentment toward his companions, which perhaps had forced him into this affair, was beginning to fade. "I dunno wether 'tis."

32   The colonel and the captain contemplated him for a time.

33   "Well," said the captain finally.

34   "Well," said the colonel, "if you want to go, why, go."

35   Collins saluted. "Much obliged t' yeh."

36   As he moved away the colonel called after him. "Take some of the other boys' canteens with you, an' hurry back, now."

37   "Yes, sir, I will."

38   The colonel and the captain looked at each other then, for it had suddenly occurred that they could not for the life of them tell whether Collins wanted to go or whether he did not.

39   They turned to regard Collins, and as they perceived him surrounded by gesticulating comrades, the colonel said: "Well, by thunder! I guess he's going."

40   Collins appeared as a man dreaming. In the midst of the questions, the advice, the warnings, all the excited talk of his company mates, he maintained a curious silence.

41   They were very busy in preparing him for his ordeal. When they inspected him carefully, it was somewhat like the examination that grooms give a horse before a race; and they were amazed, staggered, by the whole affair. Their astonishment found vent in strange repetitions.

42   "Are yeh sure a-goin'?" they demanded again and again.

43   "Certainly I am," cried Collins at last, furiously.

44   He strode sullenly away from them. He was swinging five or six canteens by their cords. It seemed that his cap would not remain firmly on his head, and often he reached and pulled it down over his brow.

45   There was a general movement in the compact column. The long animal-like thing moved slightly. Its four hundred eyes were turned upon the figure of Collins.

46   "Well, sir, if that ain't th' derndest thing! I never thought Fred Collins had the blood in him for that kind of business."

47   "What's he goin' to do, anyhow?"

48   "He's goin' to that well there after water."

49   "We ain't dying of thirst, are we? That's foolishness."

50   "Well, somebody put him up to it, an' he's doin' it."

51   "Say, he must be a desperate cuss."

52   When Collins faced the meadow and walked away from the regiment, he was vaguely conscious that a chasm, the deep valley of all prides, was suddenly between him and his comrades. It was provisional, but the provision was that he return as a victor. He had blindly been led by quaint emotions, and laid himself under an obligation to walk squarely up to the face of death.

53   But he was not sure that he wished to make a retraction, even if he could do so without shame. As a matter of truth, he was sure of very little. He was mainly surprised.

54   It seemed to him supernaturally strange that he had allowed his mind to manœuvre his body into such a situation. He understood that it might be called dramatically great.

55   However, he had no full appreciation of anything, excepting that he was actually conscious of being dazed. He could feel his dulled mind groping after the form and color of this incident. He wondered why he did not feel some keen agony of fear cutting his sense like a knife. He wondered at this, because human expression had said loudly for centuries that men should feel afraid of certain things, and that all men who did not feel this fear were phenomena— heroes.

56   He was, then, a hero. He suffered that disappointment which we would all have if we discovered that we were ourselves capable of those deeds which we most admire in history and legend. This, then, was a hero. After all, heroes were not much.

57   No, it could not be true. He was not a hero. Heroes had no shames in their lives, and, as for him, he remembered borrowing fifteen dollars from a friend and promising to pay it back the next day, and then avoiding that friend for ten months. When, at home, his mother had aroused him for the early labor of his life on the farm, it had often been his fashion to be irritable, childish, diabolical; and his mother had died since he had come to the war.

58   He saw that, in this matter of the well, the canteens, the shells, he was an intruder in the land of fine deeds.

59   He was now about thirty paces from his comrades. The regiment had just turned its many faces toward him.

60   From the forest of terrific noises there suddenly emerged a little uneven line of men. They fired fiercely and rapidly at distant foliage on which appeared little puffs of white smoke. The spatter of skirmish firing was added to the thunder of the guns on the hill. The little line of men ran forward. A color-sergeant fell flat with his flag as if he had slipped on ice. There was hoarse cheering from this distant field.

61   Collins suddenly felt that two demon fingers were pressed into his ears. He could see nothing but flying arrows, flaming red. He lurched from the shock of this explosion, but he made a mad rush for the house, which he viewed as a man submerged to the neck in a boiling surf might view the shore. In the air little pieces of shell howled, and the earthquake explosions drove him insane with the menace of their roar. As he ran the canteens knocked together with a rhythmical tinkling.

62   As he neared the house, each detail of the scene became vivid to him. He was aware of some bricks of the vanished chimney lying on the sod. There was a door which hung by one hinge.

63   Rifle bullets called forth by the insistent skirmishers came from the far-off bank of foliage. They mingled with the shells and the pieces of shells until the air was torn in all directions by hootings, yells, howls. The sky was full of fiends who directed all their wild rage at his head.

64   When he came to the well, he flung himself face downward and peered into its darkness. There were furtive silver glintings some feet from the surface. He grabbled one of the canteens and, unfastening its cap, swung it down by the cord. The water flowed slowly in with an indolent gurgle.

65   And now, as he lay with his face turned away, he was suddenly smitten with the terror. It came upon his heart like the grasp of claws. All the power faded from his muscles. For an instant he was no more than a dead man.

66   The canteen filled with a maddening slowness, in the manner of all bottles. Presently he recovered his strength and addressed a screaming oath to it. He leaned over until it seemed as if he intended to try to push water into it with his hands. His eyes as he gazed down into the well shone like two pieces of metal, and in their expression was a great appeal and a great curse. The stupid water derided him.

67   There was the blaring thunder of a shell. Crimson light shone through the swift-boiling smoke, and made a pink reflection on part of the wall of the well. Collins jerked out his arm and canteen with the same motion that a man would use in withdrawing his head from a furnace.

68   He scrambled erect and glared and hesitated. On the ground near him lay the old well bucket, with a length of rusty chain. He lowered it swiftly into the well. The bucket struck the water and then, turning lazily over, sank. When, with hand reaching tremblingly over hand, he hauled it out, it knocked often against the walls of the well and spilled some of its contents.

69   In running with a filled bucket, a man can adopt but one kind of gait. So, through this terrible field over which screamed practical angels of death, Collins ran in the manner of a farmer chased out of a dairy by a bull.

70   His face went staring white with anticipating—anticipation of a blow that would whirl him around and down. He would fall as he had seen other men fall, the life knocked out of them so suddenly that their knees were no more quick to touch the ground than their heads. He saw the long blue line of the regiment, but his comrades were standing looking at him from the edge of an impossible star. He was aware of some deep wheel-ruts and hoofprints in the sod beneath his feet.

71   The artillery officer who had fallen in this meadow had been making groans in the teeth of the tempest of sound. These futile cries, wrenched from him by his agony, were heard only by shells, bullets. When wild-eyed Collins came running, this officer raised himself. His face contorted and blanched from pain, he was about to utter some great beseeching cry. But suddenly his face straightened, and he called: "Say, young man, give me a drink of water, will you?"

72   Collins had no room amid his emotions for surprise. He was mad from the threats of destruction.

73   "I can't!" he screamed, and in his reply was a full description of his quaking apprehension. His cap was gone and his hair was riotous. His clothes made it appear that he had been dragged over the ground by the heels. He ran on.

74   The officer's head sank down, and one elbow crooked. His foot in its brass-bound stirrup still stretched over the body of his horse, and the other leg was under the steed.

75   But Collins turned. He came dashing back. His face had now turned grey, and in his eyes was all terror. "Here it is! here it is!"

76   The officer was as a man gone in drink. His arm bent like a twig. His head dropped as if his neck were of willow. He was sinking to the ground, to lie face downward.

77   Collins grabbed him by the shoulder. "Here it is. Here's your drink. Turn over. Turn over, man, for God's sake!"

78   With Collins hauling at his shoulder, the officer twisted his body and fell with his face turned toward that region where lived the unspeakable noises of the swirling missiles. There was the faintest shadow of a smile on his lips as he looked at Collins. He gave a sigh, a little primitive breath like that from a child.

79   Collins tried to hold the bucket steadily, but his shaking hands caused the water to splash all over the face of the dying man. Then he jerked it away and ran on.

80   The regiment gave him a welcoming roar. The grimed faces were wrinkled in laughter.

81   His captain waved the bucket away. "Give it to the men!"

82   The two genial, skylarking young lieutenants were the first to gain possession of it. They played over it in their fashion.

83   When one tried to drink, the other teasingly knocked his elbow. "Don't Billie! You'll make me spill it," said the one. The other laughed.

84   Suddenly there was an oath, the thud of wood on the ground, and a swift murmur of astonishment among the ranks. The two lieutenants glared at each other. The bucket lay on the ground empty.

Topics for Writing and Discussion

1. What motivates Collins to go for water? Is it merely thirst?
2. What internal debate does Collins have with himself over the nature and meaning of "hero"?
3. How does Crane use figurative language to capture the terror Collins feels at the well? Cite some of his most effective imagery.
4. Is Collins a hero? Are any of his actions "heroic"? As you think about your answers, consider both the interaction with the wounded officer and the bucket at the end of the story.
5. Use this story about the "mystery" of heroism to help you formulate your own definition of "hero" or "heroism." In your opinion, what are the origins or motives of heroism? What is the difference between heroic actions and those that are merely daring or skillful? Illustrate your claims by offering some examples of people who are heroic in your eyes.

Writing Assignments for Chapter Six

Definition

1. Poet John Ciardi presents a number of provocative thoughts about the nature of "happiness." Select one of the following statements from "What Is Happiness?" and use it as a basis for your own essay in which you define "happiness" as you have experienced it or hope to experience it in your own life:

   Effort is the gist of it. There is no happiness except as we take on life-engaging difficulties.

   Happiness is never more than partial.

   Happiness . . . is neither in having nor in being, but in becoming.

   A nation is not measured by what it possesses or wants to possess, but by what it wants to become.

2. In "On Self-Respect," Joan Didion writes of a time "in a dry season" when she had lost her sense of self-worth. In contrast, she describes people with self-respect as those who are willing "to accept responsibility for one's own life" and "to recognize that anything worth having has its price." Think of several incidents in which you, or others you have seen, have shown the kind of respect Didion describes; use these as illustrations to clarify and make concrete your own definition of "self-respect."

3. Richard Rodriguez presents a picture of a "marriage" in his essay "Hispanic-American Culture," a blending that will offer change and diversity to both our country and to Hispanic Americans themselves. Consider some aspect of American culture (or popular culture, such as music, movies, fashions, or fads) that has already been greatly influenced by another culture; write an essay defining your subject and explaining its influences. What might we have lost had we not enjoyed such diversity of cultures?

4. Margaret Mead writes about the functions of belief systems in "New Superstitions for Old." Today, some people consider aromatherapy, channeling, astrology, crystal healing, reflexology, tarot-card reading, and other nonscientific practices as new superstitions "generated by our wishes, our fears, and our feelings of helplessness in difficult situations." Others defend them as nontraditional ways to improve our lives. Define a popular alternative technique according to your point of view. Try to convince a skeptical audience that your view is valid.

5. Ralph Ellison's essay "Discrimination" focuses on racial prejudice. Today, we often hear about reverse discrimination. Research the ongoing debate over allocating college scholarships to students who belong to certain groups (ethnic and racial groups, low-income families, first-generation college students, athletes) rather than awarding scholarships based solely on academic strengths. By your own definition, does this practice constitute "discrimination"? Defend your views in an essay.

6. Select a recently coined term that describes some aspect of popular culture. Define and illustrate its meaning as clearly as Stuart Chase does in "Gobbledygook." Will your term become a useful, permanent addition to American vocabulary, or is it merely a trendy one that will fade over time?

7. In her poem "Metaphors," Sylvia Plath uses a number of images to convey a complex view of a situation rich with implications. Think of a particularly meaningful time in your life and the powerful emotion it produced in you; then use the most effective strategies of definition to explain this feeling to your readers. (Some suggestions: first love, thrill of victory, agony of defeat, newly discovered peacefulness, extreme terror, unbridled joy.)

8. In "A Mystery of Heroism," Stephen Crane presents a character who is unsure of the meaning of "hero." Select an abstract word or phrase used today whose definition is new, unclear, in transition, or "mysterious." Define this term for readers who may be confused about its meaning, application, or origin. For example, do your grandparents understand the meanings of "Gen X," "slacker," "virtual reality," or "multiculturalism"? Do your definitions of such words as "success," "failure," "patriotism," or "good marriage" differ from those of previous generations?

CHAPTER SEVEN

ILLUSTRATION

Wʜᴇɴ you state an opinion or a judgment, make a point, or explain something, you may frequently offer some kind of specific detail to support your ideas, to give credibility to your position. Often, that specific support appears in the form of *illustrations* or *examples*. In many cases, well-chosen examples can explain a principle or concept far better than any other method. In "Mankind's Better Moments," Barbara Tuchman uses extensive examples drawn from history to illustrate her belief in "the positive and even admirable capacities of the human race." Brent Staples helps readers to understand his point about African-American men and their unintentional "ability to alter public space in ugly ways" by retelling several incidents he and his friends have experienced. And in "A Dying Art: The Classy Exit Line," Lance Morrow gives numerous examples of "great last words," including those supposedly spoken by Oscar Wilde when he was near death: "Either that wallpaper goes, or I do."

Illustration is also frequently used in combination with other rhetorical strategies. For example, Ralph Ellison's definition of racial prejudice is clearer with his use of examples in "Discrimination" (Chapter Six). And almost all arguments benefit from illustrations; the "Declarations" of both Thomas Jefferson and Elizabeth Cady Stanton are more convincing because the authors give examples of their grievances (Chapter Eleven).

USES OF ILLUSTRATION

1. *Illustration can be used to clarify.*

Illustrations or examples can be used to clarify complex, confusing, or controversial ideas; they may also be used to make abstract ideas more concrete and accessible. Alice Walker ("In Search of Our Mothers' Gardens"), for example, uses real people, including her own mother, to illustrate her point about ancestors passing down a creative spirit.

2. *Illustrations can be used to enliven or provoke interest.*

Almost all ideas can be energized with the use of lively, vivid examples. Generalities can be monotonous, pretentious, or boring without clear examples to catch and hold the reader's interest. William Buckley's use of examples transforms "Why Don't We Complain?" from a potential lecture on our lack of assertiveness into a sly commentary on human nature largely because of the humorous examples Buckley interjects to illustrate our—and his own—helplessness.

3. *Illustrations can be used to persuade.*

The use of illustration can add validity to a thesis or central idea, urging the reader to accept your ideas because they have been tested, proven, or found to exist elsewhere. In "Mankind's Better Moments," Barbara Tuchman presents a convincing argument that humankind has many "positive and even admirable capacities," even though such positive images are often obscured.

WRITING THE ILLUSTRATION ESSAY

When you decide to support a thesis primarily by using examples, you should keep several principles in mind:

1. *Choose accurate examples.*

Certainly, nothing can ruin a discussion more than conclusions based on incorrect or faulty information. When you use an example to illustrate a point, make sure that the example is accurate.

2. *Select examples that are relevant and appropriate to the situation.*

The examples you use should *specifically* support your general statements. Examples that only remotely illustrate your point could confuse your reader, not clarify your ideas.

3. *Use a sufficient number of examples, but resist "overkill."*

Consider how many examples are enough to illustrate your point adequately. If your thesis is that travel abroad is particularly dangerous for Americans, use more than one example of a dangerous or tragic situation to support your assessment. However, be careful not to give too many examples. Choose only those that best serve your purpose. Overuse of examples could be interpreted as padding, which gives your reader the impression that you are merely filling space.

4. *Decide whether or not an extended illustration would best serve your purpose.*

An *extended* illustration could be used when one in-depth example is enough to support your thesis. Alice Walker uses this method to illustrate what she believes it meant for a black woman to be an artist two or three generations ago. In "In Search of Our Mothers' Gardens," Walker uses the example of Phillis Wheatley, a slave in the 1700s, as an example of a woman gifted to write poetry but shackled by slavery to suffer from "malnutrition and neglect and who knows what mental agonies. . . ."

William F. Buckley, Jr. (© Marilynn K. Yoe / NYT Pictures)

WHY DON'T WE COMPLAIN?

William F. Buckley, Jr.
(1925–   )

William F. Buckley, Jr., is one of America's best-known
political commentators. A graduate of Yale University,
he was founder and former editor-in-chief of the
National Review and is host of PBS's *Firing Line*. Buckley is also a prolific writer, publishing several syndicated newspaper columns weekly in addition to
contributing regularly to magazines such as the
*Atlantic Monthly, The New Yorker, Harper's, The New
Republic, Foreign Affairs,* and the *Saturday Evening
Post.* Buckley has written several books, including spy
novels: *God and Man at Yale: The Superstitions of
"Academic Freedom"* (1951), *Saving the Queen*
(1976), *Stained Glass* (1978), *Atlantic High* (1982),
Overdrive: A Personal Documentary (1983), *On the
Firing Line: The Public Life of Our Public Figures*
(1989), *Tucker's Last Stand* (1990), *A Very Private Plot*
(1994), *McCarthy and His Enemies* (1995), and *Brothers No More* (1996). "Why Don't We Complain?" was
first published in *Esquire* in 1961.

1   IT was the very last coach and the only empty seat on the entire train, so
there was no turning back. The problem was to breathe. Outside, the temperature was below freezing. Inside the railroad car the temperature must
have been about 85 degrees. I took off my overcoat, and a few minutes later
my jacket, and noticed that the car was flecked with the white shirts of the
passengers. I soon found my hand moving to loosen my tie. From one end of
the car to the other, as we rattled through Westchester County, we sweated;
but we did not moan.

2   I watched the train conductor appear at the head of the car. "Tickets, all tickets, please!" In a more virile age, I thought, the passengers would seize the conductor and strap him down on a seat over the radiator to share the fate of his patrons. He shuffled down the aisle, picking up tickets, punching commutation cards. *No one addressed a word to him.* He approached my seat, and I drew a deep breath of resolution. "Conductor," I began with a considerable edge to my voice. . . . Instantly the doleful eyes of my seatmate turned tiredly from his newspaper to fix me with a resentful stare: What question could be so important as to justify my sibilant intrusion into his stupor? I was shaken by those eyes. I am incapable of making a discreet fuss, so I mumbled a question about what time we were due in Stamford (I didn't even ask whether it would be before or after dehydration could be expected to set in), got my reply, and went back to my newspaper and to wiping my brow.

3   The conductor had nonchalantly walked down the gauntlet of eighty sweating American freemen, and not one of them had asked him to explain why the passengers in that car had been consigned to suffer. There is nothing to be done when the temperature *outdoors* is 85 degrees, and indoors the air conditioner has broken down; obviously when that happens there is nothing to do, except perhaps curse the day that one was born. But when the temperature outdoors is below freezing, it takes a positive act of will on somebody's part to set the temperature *indoors* at 85. Somewhere a valve was turned too far, a furnace overstocked, a thermostat maladjusted; something that could easily be remedied by turning off the heat and allowing the great outdoors to come indoors. All this is so obvious. What is not obvious is what has happened to the American people.

4   It isn't just the commuters, whom we have come to visualize as a supine breed who have got on to the trick of suspending their sensory faculties twice a day while they submit to the creeping dissolution of the railroad industry. It isn't just they who have given up trying to rectify irrational vexations. It is the American people everywhere.

5   A few weeks ago at a large movie theater I turned to my wife and said, "The picture is out of focus." Be quiet," she answered. I obeyed. But a few minutes later I raised the point again, with mounting impatience. "It will be all right in a minute," she said apprehensively. (She would rather lose her eyesight than be around when I make one of my infrequent scenes.) I waited. It was *just* out of focus—not glaringly out, but out. My vision is 20–20, and I assume that is the vision, adjusted, of most people in the movie house. So, after hectoring my wife throughout the first reel, I finally prevailed upon her to admit that it *was* off, and very annoying. We then settled down, coming to rest on the presumption that: a) someone connected with the management of the theater must soon notice the blur and make the correction; or b) that someone seated near the rear of the house would make the complaint in behalf of those of us up front; or c) that—any minute now—the entire house would explode into catcalls and foot stamping, calling dramatic attention to the irksome distortion.

6   What happened was nothing. The movie ended, as it had begun *just* out of focus, and as we trooped out, we stretched our faces in a variety of contortions to accustom the eye to the shock of normal focus.

7   I think it is safe to say that everybody suffered on that occasion. And I think it is safe to assume that everyone was expecting someone else to take the initiative in going back to speak to the manager. And it is probably true even that if we had supposed the movie would run right through the blurred image, someone surely would have summoned up the purposive indignation to get up out of his seat and file his complaint.

8   But notice that no one did. And the reason no one did is because we are all increasingly anxious in America to be unobtrusive, we are reluctant to make our voices heard, hesitant about claiming our rights; we are afraid that our cause is unjust, or that if it is not unjust, that it is ambiguous; or if not even that, that it is too trivial to justify the horrors of a confrontation with Authority; we will sit in an oven or endure a racking headache before undertaking a head-on, I'm-here-to-tell-you complaint. That tendency to passive compliance, to a heedless endurance, is something to keep one's eyes on—in sharp focus.

9   I myself can occasionally summon the courage to complain, but I cannot, as I have intimated, complain softly. My own instinct is so strong to let the thing ride, to forget about it—to expect that someone will take the matter up, when the grievance is collective, in my behalf—that it is only when the provocation is at a very special key, whose vibrations touch simultaneously a complexus of nerves, allergies, and passions, that I catch fire and find the reserves of courage and assertiveness to speak up. When that happens, I get quite carried away. My blood gets hot, my brow wet, I become unbearably and unconscionably sarcastic and bellicose; I am girded for a total showdown.

10   Why should that be? Why could not I (or anyone else) on that railroad coach have said simply to the conductor, "Sir"—I take that back: that sounds sarcastic—"Conductor, would you be good enough to turn down the heat? I am extremely hot. In fact, I tend to get hot every time the temperature reaches 85 degr—." Strike that last sentence. Just end it with the simple statement that you are extremely hot, and let the conductor infer the cause.

11   Every New Year's Eve I resolve to do something about the Milquetoast in me and vow to speak up, calmly, for my rights, and for the betterment of our society, on every appropriate occasion. Entering last New Year's Eve I was fortified in my resolve because that morning at breakfast I had had to ask the waitress three times for a glass of milk. She finally brought it—after I had finished my eggs, which is when I don't want it any more. I did not have the manliness to order her to take the milk back, but settled instead for a cowardly sulk, and ostentatiously refused to drink the milk—though I later paid for it— rather than state plainly to the hostess, as I should have, why I had not drunk it, and would not pay for it.

12   So by the time the New Year ushered out the Old, riding in on my morning's indignation and stimulated by the gastric juices of resolution that flow so

faithfully on New Year's Eve, I rendered my vow. Henceforward I would conquer my shyness, my despicable disposition to supineness. I would speak out like a man against the unnecessary annoyances of our time.

13   Forty-eight hours later, I was standing in line at the ski repair store in Pico Peak, Vermont. All I needed, to get on with my skiing, was the loan, for one minute, of a small screwdriver, to tighten a loose binding. Behind the counter in the workshop were two men. One was industriously engaged in servicing the complicated requirements of a young lady at the head of the line, and obviously he would be tied up for quite a while. The other—"Jiggs," his workmate called him—was a middle-aged man, who sat in a chair puffing a pipe, exchanging small talk with his working partner. My pulse began its telltale acceleration. The minutes ticked on. I stared at the idle shopkeeper, hoping to shame him into action, but he was impervious to my telepathic reproof and continued his small talk with his friend, brazenly insensitive to the nervous demands of six good men who were raring to ski.

14   Suddenly my New Year's Eve resolution struck me. It was now or never. I broke from my place in line and marched to the counter. I was going to control myself. I dug my nails into my palms. My effort was only partially successful.

15   "If you are not too busy," I said icily, "would you mind handing me a screwdriver?"

16   Work stopped and everyone turned his eyes on me, and I experienced that mortification I always feel when I am the center of centripetal shafts of curiosity, resentment, perplexity.

17   But the worst was yet to come. "I am sorry, sir," said Jiggs deferentially, moving the pipe from his mouth. "I am not supposed to move. I have just had a heart attack." That was the signal for a great whirring noise that descended from heaven. We looked, stricken, out the window, and it appeared as though a cyclone had suddenly focused on the snowy courtyard between the shop and the ski lift. Suddenly a gigantic army helicopter materialized, and hovered down to a landing. Two men jumped out of the plane carrying a stretcher, tore into the ski shop, and lifted the shopkeeper onto the stretcher. Jiggs bade his companion good-bye, was whisked out the door, into the plane, up to the heavens, down—we learned—to a nearby army hospital. I looked up manfully—into a score of man-eating eyes. I put the experience down as a reversal.

18   As I write this, on an airplane, I have run out of paper and need to reach into my briefcase under my legs for more. I cannot do this until my empty lunch tray is removed from my lap. I arrested the stewardess as she passed empty-handed down the aisle on the way to the kitchen to fetch the lunch trays for the passengers up forward who haven't been served yet. "Would you please take my tray?" "Just a *moment*, sir!" she said, and marched on sternly. Shall I tell her that since she is headed for the kitchen *anyway*, it could not delay the feeding of the other passengers by more than two seconds necessary to stash away my empty tray? Or remind her that not fifteen minutes ago she spoke unctuously into the loudspeaker the words undoubtedly devised by the airline's

highly paid public relations counselor: "If there is anything I or Miss French can do for you to make your trip more enjoyable, *please* let us—" I have run out of paper.

19   I think the observable reluctance of the majority of Americans to assert themselves in minor matters is related to our increased sense of helplessness in an age of technology and centralized political and economic power. For generations, Americans who were too hot, or too cold, got up and did something about it. Now we call the plumber, or the electrician, or the furnace man. The habit of looking after our own needs obviously had something to do with the assertiveness that characterized the American family familiar to readers of American literature. With the technification of life goes our direct responsibility for our material environment, and we are conditioned to adopt a position of helplessness not only as regards the broken air conditioner, but as regards the overheated train. It takes an expert to fix the former, but not the latter; yet these distinctions, as we withdraw into helplessness, tend to fade away.

20   Our notorious political apathy is a related phenomenon. Every year, whether the Republican or the Democratic Party is in office, more and more power drains away from the individual to feed vast reservoirs in far-off places; and we have less and less say about the shape of events which shape our future. From this alienation of personal power comes the sense of resignation with which we accept the political dispensations of a powerful government whose hold upon us continues to increase.

21   An editor of a national weekly news magazine told me a few years ago that as few as a dozen letters of protest against an editorial stance of his magazine was enough to convene a plenipotentiary meeting of the board of editors to review policy. "So few people complain, or make their voices heard," he explained to me, "that we assume a dozen letters represent the inarticulated views of thousands of readers." In the past ten years, he said, the volume of mail has noticeably decreased, even though the circulation of his magazine has risen.

22   When our voices are finally mute, when we have finally suppressed the natural instinct to complain, whether the vexation is trivial or grave, we shall have become automatons, incapable of feeling. When Premier Khrushchev first came to this country late in 1959 he was primed, we are informed, to experience the bitter resentment of the American people against his tyranny, against his persecutions, against the movement which is responsible for the great number of American deaths in Korea, for billions in taxes every year, and for life everlasting on the brink of disaster; but Khrushchev was pleasantly surprised, and reported back to the Russian people that he had been met with overwhelming cordiality (read: apathy), except, to be sure, for "a few fascists who followed me around with their wretched posters, and should be horsewhipped."

23   I may be crazy, but I say there would have been lots more posters in a society where train temperatures in the dead of winter are not allowed to climb to 85 degrees without complaint.

Topics for Writing and Discussion

1. What point is Buckley making about modern Americans? Where is this view most clearly stated? Do you agree with his position?

2. Do Buckley's examples adequately support his point? Select two that best illustrate his claims and explain why you chose them.

3. Characterize the tone of this essay. Is it consistent throughout the essay or does it vary according to the point Buckley is making? Is the tone effective? Why or why not?

4. Do you agree with Buckley's claim that the "reluctance of the majority of Americans to assert themselves in minor manners is related to our increased helplessness in an age of technology and centralized political and economic power"? Cite some examples that support or refute this claim. (Your response to this question might also provide the basis for an interesting essay.)

5. Complaints sometimes work—they do bring about necessary changes. Write an essay illustrating a time when someone (you?) lodged a legitimate complaint and caused an important change in behavior, beliefs, or policy.

BLACK MEN AND PUBLIC SPACE

Brent Staples
(1951–   )

Born in Chester, Pennsylvania, Brent Staples earned a
bachelor's degree in behavioral science in 1973 from
Widener University and both a master's degree and a
doctorate in psychology from the University of Chicago.
Staples began his journalistic career as a freelance
reporter and as a music and literary critic. Staples has
written for several publications, including the *Chicago
Sun Times, Harper's,* and *Down Beat* magazine, and he
has served as editor of *The New York Times Review of
Books* and on the editorial board of the *New York
Times.* In 1994, he published his memoir *Parallel Time:
Growing Up in Black and White.* The following essay,
"Black Men and Public Space," first appeared in *Ms.*
magazine in September 1986. In it, he speaks of the
stereotyping of African-American males that results in
their "ability to alter public space in ugly ways."

1   My first victim was a woman—white, well dressed, probably in her late
twenties. I came upon her late one evening on a deserted street in Hyde Park, a
relatively affluent neighborhood in an otherwise mean, impoverished section
of Chicago. As I swung onto the avenue behind her, there seemed to be a
discreet, uninflammatory distance between us. Not so. She cast back a worried
glance. To her, the youngish black man—a broad six feet two inches with a
beard and billowing hair, both hands shoved into the pockets of a bulky military jacket—seemed menacingly close. After a few more quick glimpses, she
picked up her pace and was soon running in earnest. Within seconds she disappeared into a cross street.

2   That was more than a decade ago. I was twenty-two years old, a graduate
student newly arrived at the University of Chicago. It was in the echo of that

Brent Staples in his office at The New York Times *(© Nancy Crampton)*

terrified woman's footfalls that I first began to know the unwieldy inheritance I'd come into—the ability to alter public space in ugly ways. It was clear that she thought herself the quarry of a mugger, a rapist, or worse. Suffering a bout of insomnia, however, I was stalking sleep, not defenseless wayfarers. As a softy who is scarcely able to take a knife to a raw chicken—let alone hold one to a person's throat—I was surprised, embarrassed, and dismayed all at once. Her flight made me feel like an accomplice in tyranny. It also made it clear that I was indistinguishable from the muggers who occasionally seeped into the area from the surrounding ghetto. That first encounter, and those that followed, signified that a vast, unnerving gulf lay between nighttime pedestrians—particularly women—and me. And I soon gathered that being perceived as dangerous is a hazard in itself. I only needed to turn a corner into a dicey situation, or crowd some frightened, armed person in a foyer somewhere, or make an errant move after being pulled over by a policeman. Where fear and weapons meet—and they often do in urban America—there is always the possibility of death.

3   In that first year, my first away from my hometown, I was to become thoroughly familiar with the language of fear. At dark, shadowy intersections, I could cross in front of a car stopped at a traffic light and elicit the *thunk, thunk, thunk, thunk* of the driver—black, white, male, or female—hammering down the door locks. On less traveled streets after dark, I grew accustomed to but never comfortable with people crossing to the other side of the street rather than pass me. Then there were the standard unpleasantries with policemen, doormen, bouncers, cabdrivers, and others whose business it is to screen out troublesome individuals *before* there is any nastiness.

4   I moved to New York nearly two years ago and I have remained an avid night walker. In central Manhattan, the near-constant crowd cover minimizes tense one-on-one street encounters. Elsewhere—in SoHo, for example, where sidewalks are narrow and tightly spaced buildings shut out the sky—things can get very taut indeed.

5   After dark, on the warrenlike streets of Brooklyn where I live, I often see women who fear the worst from me. They seem to have set their faces on neutral, and with their purse straps strung across their chests bandolier-style, they forge ahead as though bracing themselves against being tackled. I understand, of course, that the danger they perceive is not a hallucination. Women are particularly vulnerable to street violence, and young black males are drastically overrepresented among the perpetrators of that violence. Yet these truths are no solace against the kind of alienation that comes of being ever the suspect, a fearsome entity with whom pedestrians avoid making eye contact.

6   It is not altogether clear to me how I reached the ripe old age of twenty-two without being conscious of the lethality nighttime pedestrians attributed to me. Perhaps it was because in Chester, Pennsylvania, the small, angry industrial town where I came of age in the 1960s, I was scarcely noticeable against a backdrop of gang warfare, street knifings, and murders. I grew up one of the

good boys, had perhaps a half-dozen fistfights. In retrospect, my shyness of combat has clear sources.

7   As a boy, I saw countless tough guys locked away; I have since buried several, too. They were babies, really—a teenage cousin, a brother of twenty-two, a childhood friend in his mid-twenties—all gone down in episodes of bravado played out in the streets. I came to doubt the virtues of intimidation early on. I chose, perhaps unconsciously, to remain a shadow—timid, but a survivor.

8   The fearsomeness mistakenly attributed to me in public places often has a perilous flavor. The most frightening of these confusions occurred in the late 1970s and early 1980s, when I worked as a journalist in Chicago. One day, rushing into the office of a magazine I was writing for with a deadline story in hand, I was mistaken for a burglar. The office manager called security and, with an ad hoc posse, pursued me through the labyrinthine halls, nearly to my editor's door. I had no way of proving who I was. I could only move briskly toward the company of someone who knew me.

9   Another time I was on assignment for a local paper and killing time before an interview. I entered a jewelry store on the city's affluent Near North Side. The proprietor excused herself and returned with an enormous red Doberman pinscher straining at the end of a leash. She stood, the dog extended toward me, silent to my questions, her eyes bulging nearly out of her head. I took a cursory look around, nodded, and bade her good night.

10   Relatively speaking, however, I never fared as badly as another black male journalist. He went to nearby Waukegan, Illinois, a couple of summers ago to work on a story about a murderer who was born there. Mistaking the reporter for the killer, police officers hauled him from his car at gunpoint and but for his press credentials would probably have tried to book him. Such episodes are not uncommon. Black men trade tales like this all the time.

11   Over the years, I learned to smother the rage I felt at so often being taken for a criminal. Not to do so would surely have led to madness. I now take precautions to make myself less threatening. I move about with care, particularly late in the evening. I give a wide berth to nervous people on subway platforms during the wee hours, particularly when I have exchanged business clothes for jeans. If I happen to be entering a building behind some people who appear skittish, I may walk by, letting them clear the lobby before I return, so as not to seem to be following them. I have been calm and extremely congenial on those rare occasions when I've been pulled over by the police.

12   And on late-evening constitutionals I employ what has proved to be an excellent tension-reducing measure: I whistle melodies from Beethoven and Vivaldi and the more popular classical composers. Even steely New Yorkers hunching toward nighttime destinations seem to relax, and occasionally they even join in the tune. Virtually everybody seems to sense that a mugger wouldn't be warbling bright, sunny selections from Vivaldi's *Four Seasons*. It is my equivalent of the cowbell that hikers wear when they know they are in bear country.

TOPICS FOR WRITING AND DISCUSSION

1. Why does Staples refer to his "first victim" in his opening paragraph? What effect on the reader is such language intended to have? Who else, according to Staples, is victimized by faulty perceptions?

2. What is Staples' attitude toward "the ability to alter public space in ugly ways"? What is his purpose in writing this essay?

3. Why does Staples retell so many personal experiences? Why include the story of a colleague's experience in Waukegan, Illinois? What details add to the realism of these scenes?

4. What stereotypes does Staples criticize in this essay? Why does he refer to family members and friends, "all gone down in episodes of bravado played out in the streets"?

5. Write an essay exposing a current stereotype of a particular kind of person, using examples drawn from your own experience, from the media, or from advertising. Your exposé might illustrate racial, ethnic, or gender-based prejudice, or perhaps the more subtle stereotyping of a particular class of people (the homeless, the mentally ill, "dumb blondes") or people in certain occupations (the homemaker, the accountant, the athlete).

James Thurber, photographed with his wife returning on the ship Acadia *from Les Revenants, their winter home in Bermuda (AP/Wide World Photos)*

UNIVERSITY DAYS

James Thurber
(1894–1961)

Born in Columbus, Ohio, James Thurber attended
Ohio State University, though he never graduated. An
eye injury made him ineligible for military service in
World War I, so he worked for the State Department in
Washington and in Paris for the *Chicago Tribune*.
When he returned to the United States, he worked as a
reporter for the *Columbus Dispatch*. In 1927, he
joined the staff of *The New Yorker* and began a lifelong association with the magazine. He became well
known for his satiric essays and his witty cartoons. He
produced more than twenty collections of essays, short
stories, autobiographical sketches, and memoirs. Some
of his books include *My World—and Welcome to It*
(1942), *My Life and Hard Times* (1933), *Fables for
Our Time* (1943), and *The Thurber Carnival* (1945).
"University Days" reveals the frustrations, incompetence, and inefficiency he experienced as a student at
Ohio State.

1   I passed all the other courses that I took at my university, but I could never
pass botany. This was because all botany students had to spend several hours a
week in a laboratory looking through a microscope at plant cells, and I could
never see through a microscope. I never once saw a cell through a microscope.
This used to enrage my instructor. He would wander around the laboratory
pleased with the progress all the students were making in drawing the involved
and, so I am told, interesting structure of flower cells, until he came to me.
I would just be standing there. "I can't see anything," I would say. He would
begin patiently enough, explaining how anybody can see through a microscope, but he would always end up in a fury, claiming that I could *too* see
through a microscope but just pretended that I couldn't. "It takes away from

the beauty of flowers anyway," I used to tell him. "We are not concerned with beauty in this course," he would say. "We are concerned solely with what I may call the *mechanics* of flars." "Well," I'd say, "I can't see anything." "Try it just once again," he'd say, and I would put my eye to the microscope and see nothing at all, except now and again a nebulous milky substance—a phenomenon of maladjustment. You were supposed to see a vivid, restless clockwork of sharply defined plant cells. "I see what looks like a lot of milk," I would tell him. This, he claimed, was the result of my not having adjusted the microscope properly, so he would readjust it for me, or rather, for himself. And I would look again and see milk.

2   I finally took a deferred pass, as they called it, and waited a year and tried again. (You had to pass one of the biological sciences or you couldn't graduate.) The professor had come back from vacation brown as a berry, bright-eyed, and eager to explain cell-structure again to his classes. "Well," he said to me, cheerily, when we met in the first laboratory hour of the semester, "we're going to see cells this time, aren't we?" "Yes, sir," I said. Students to right of me and to left of me and in front of me were seeing cells; what's more, they were quietly drawing pictures of them in their notebooks. Of course, I didn't see anything.

3   "We'll try it," the professor said to me grimly, "with every adjustment of the microscope known to man. As God is my witness, I'll arrange this glass so that you see cells through it or I'll give up teaching. In twenty-two years of botany, I—" He cut off abruptly for he was beginning to quiver all over, like Lionel Barrymore, and he genuinely wished to hold onto his temper; his scenes with me had taken a great deal out of him.

4   So we tried it with every adjustment of the microscope known to man. With only one of them did I see anything but blackness or the familiar lacteal opacity, and that time I saw, to my pleasure and amazement, a variegated constellation of flecks, specks, and dots. These I hastily drew. The instructor, noting my activity, came back from an adjoining desk, a smile on his lips and his eyebrows high in hope. He looked at my cell drawing. "What's that?" he demanded, with a hint of a squeal in his voice. "That's what I saw," I said. "You didn't, you didn't, you *didn't!*" he screamed, losing control of his temper instantly, and he bent over and squinted into the microscope. His head snapped up. "That's your eye!" he shouted. "You've fixed the lens so that it reflects! You've drawn your eye!"

5   Another course that I didn't like, but somehow managed to pass, was economics. I went to that class straight from the botany class, which didn't help me any in understanding either subject. I used to get them mixed up. But not as mixed up as another student in my economics class who came there direct from a physics laboratory. He was a tackle on the football team, named Bolenciecwcz. At that time Ohio State University had one of the best football teams in the country, and Bolenciecwcz was one of its outstanding stars. In order to be eligible to play it was necessary for him to keep up in his studies, a very difficult matter, for while he was not dumber than an ox he was not any smarter. Most of his professors were lenient and helped him along. None gave him

more hints in answering questions or asked him simpler ones than the economics professor, a thin, timid man named Bassum. One day when we were on the subject of transportation and distribution, it came Bolenciecwcz's turn to answer a question. "Name one means of transportation," the professor said to him. No light came into the big tackle's eyes. "Just any means of transportation," said the professor. Bolenciecwcz sat staring at him. "That is," pursued the professor, "any medium, agency, or method of going from one place to another." Bolenciecwcz had the look of a man who is being led into a trap. "You may choose among steam, horse-drawn, or electrically propelled vehicles," said the instructor. "I might suggest the one which we commonly take in making long journeys across land." There was a profound silence in which everybody stirred uneasily, including Bolenciecwcz and Mr. Bassum. Mr. Bassum abruptly broke this silence in an amazing manner. "Choo-choo-choo," he said, in a low voice, and turned instantly scarlet. He glanced appealingly around the room. All of us, of course, shared Mr. Bassum's desire that Bolenciecwcz should stay abreast of the class in economics, for the Illinois game, one of the hardest and most important of the season, was only a week off. "Toot, toot, too-toooooot!" some student with a deep voice moaned, and we all looked encouragingly at Bolenciecwcz. Somebody else gave a fine imitation of a locomotive letting off steam. Mr. Bassum himself rounded off the little show. "Ding, dong, ding, dong," he said hopefully. Bolenciecwcz was staring at the floor now, trying to think, his great brow furrowed, his huge hands rubbing together, his face red.

6   "How did you come to college this year, Mr. Bolenciecwcz?" asked the professor. "*Chuffa* chuffa, *chuffa* chuffa."

7   "M'father sent me," said the football player.

8   "What on?" asked Bassum.

9   "I git an 'lowance," said the tackle, in a low, husky voice, obviously embarrassed.

10   "No, no," said Bassum. "Name a means of transportation. What did you *ride* here on?"

11   "Train," said Bolenciecwcz.

12   "Quite right," said the professor. "Now, Mr. Nugent, will you tell us—"

13   If I went through anguish in botany and economics—for different reasons—gymnasium work was even worse. I don't even like to think about it. They wouldn't let you play games or join in the exercises with your glasses on and I couldn't see with mine off. I bumped into professors, horizontal bars, agricultural students, and swinging iron rings. Not being able to see, I could take it but I couldn't dish it out. Also, in order to pass gymnasium (and you had to pass it to graduate) you had to learn to swim if you didn't know how. I didn't like the swimming pool, I didn't like swimming, and I didn't like the swimming instructor, and after all these years I still don't. I never swam but I passed my gym work anyway, by having another student give my gymnasium number (978) and swim across the pool in my place. He was a quiet, amiable blond youth, number 473, and he would have seen through a microscope for me if we could have got away with it, but we couldn't get away with it. Another

thing I didn't like about gymnasium work was that they made you strip the day you registered. It is impossible for me to be happy when I am stripped and being asked a lot of questions. Still, I did better than a lanky agricultural student who was cross-examined just before I was. They asked each student what college he was in—that is, whether Arts, Engineering, Commerce, or Agriculture. "What college are you in?" the instructor snapped at the youth in front of me. "Ohio State University," he said promptly.

14   It wasn't that agricultural student but it was another a whole lot like him who decided to take up journalism, possibly on the ground that when farming went to hell he could fall back on newspaper work. He didn't realize, of course, that that would be very much like falling back full-length on a kit of carpenter's tools. Haskins didn't seem cut out for journalism, being too embarrassed to talk to anybody and unable to use a typewriter, but the editor of the college paper assigned him to the cow barns, the sheep house, the horse pavilion, and the animal husbandry department generally. This was a genuinely big "beat," for it took up five times as much ground and got ten times as great a legislative appropriation as the College of Liberal Arts. The agricultural student knew animals, but nevertheless his stories were dull and colorlessly written. He took all afternoon on each of them, on account of having to hunt for each letter on the typewriter. Once in a while he had to ask somebody to help him hunt. "C" and "L," in particular, were hard letters for him to find. His editor finally got pretty much annoyed at the farmer-journalist because his pieces were so uninteresting. "See here, Haskins," he snapped at him one day, "why is it we never have anything hot from you on the horse pavilion? Here we have two hundred head of horses on this campus—more than any other university in the Western Conference except Purdue—and yet you never get any real lowdown on them. Now shoot over to the horse barns and dig up something lively." Haskins shambled out and came back in about an hour; he said he had something. "Well, start it off snappily," said the editor. "Something people will read." Haskins set to work and in a couple of hours brought a sheet of typewritten paper to the desk; it was a two-hundred-word story about some disease that had broken out among the horses. Its opening sentence was simple but arresting. It read: "Who has noticed the sores on the tops of the horses in the animal husbandry building?"

15   Ohio State was a land grant university and therefore two years of military drill was compulsory. We drilled with old Springfield rifles and studied the tactics of the Civil War even though the World War was going on at the time. At 11 o'clock each morning thousands of freshmen and sophomores used to deploy over the campus, moodily creeping up on the old chemistry building. It was good training for the kind of warfare that was waged at Shiloh but it had no connection with what was going on in Europe. Some people used to think there was German money behind it, but they didn't dare say so or they would have been thrown in jail as German spies. It was a period of muddy thought and marked, I believe, the decline of higher education in the Middle West.

16   As a soldier I was never any good at all. Most of the cadets were glumly indifferent soldiers, but I was no good at all. Once General Littlefield, who

was commandant of the cadet corps, popped up in front of me during regimental drill and snapped, "You are the main trouble with this university!" I think he meant that my type was the main trouble with the university but he may have meant me individually. I was mediocre at drill, certainly—that is, until my senior year. By that time I had drilled longer than anybody else in the Western Conference, having failed at military at the end of each preceding year so that I had to do it all over again. I was the only senior still in uniform. The uniform which, when new, had made me look like an interurban railway conductor, now that it had become faded and too tight made me look like Bert Williams in his bellboy act. This had a definitely bad effect on my morale. Even so, I had become by sheer practice little short of wonderful at squad maneuvers.

17   One day General Littlefield picked our company out of the whole regiment and tried to get it mixed up by putting it through one movement after another as fast as we could execute them: squads right, squads left, squads on right into line, squads right about, squads left front into line, etc. In about three minutes one hundred and nine men were marching in one direction and I was marching away from them at an angle of forty degrees, all alone. "Company, halt!" shouted General Littlefield. "That man is the only man who has it right!" I was made a corporal for my achievement.

18   The next day General Littlefield summoned me to his office. He was swatting flies when I went in. I was silent and he was silent too, for a long time. I don't think he remembered me or why he had sent for me, but he didn't want to admit it. He swatted some more flies, keeping his eyes on them narrowly before he let go with the swatter. "Button up your coat!" he snapped. Looking back on it now I can see that he meant me although he was looking at a fly, but I just stood there. Another fly came to rest on a paper in front of the general and began rubbing its hind legs together. The general lifted the swatter cautiously. I moved restlessly and the fly flew away. "You startled him!" barked General Littlefield, looking at me severely. I said I was sorry. "That won't help the situation!" snapped the General, with cold military logic. I didn't see what I could do except offer to chase some more flies toward his desk, but I didn't say anything. He stared out the window at the faraway figures of co-eds crossing the campus toward the library. Finally, he told me I could go. So I went. He either didn't know which cadet I was or else he forgot what he wanted to see me about. It may have been that he wished to apologize for having called me the main trouble with the university; or maybe he had decided to compliment me on my brilliant drilling of the day before and then at the last minute decided not to. I don't know. I don't think about it much any more.

TOPICS FOR WRITING AND DISCUSSION

1. Why was Thurber unable to pass botany? What two stories does he tell to illustrate his difficulty? Does he explain how he was able to fulfill his requirement in the biological sciences?

2. What two meanings does Thurber suggest for General Littlefield's observation, "You are the main trouble with the university!"? After reading the incidents describing Thurber's performance as a cadet and his various encounters with the general, which interpretation do you think is more plausible?

3. "University Days" includes several short stories, each designed to illustrate some aspect of Thurber's college experience. Look carefully at the sentences that begin paragraphs 5, 13, and 14; then analyze how Thurber connects his stories to form a coherent whole. Note also the beginning of paragraph 15 that introduces the section on military drill. Is this section clearly related to the others?

4. Thurber's essay has no introductory paragraph, no thesis statement, and no concluding paragraph. What would be gained or lost by the addition of a standard opening and closing? How would you state the thesis of the essay?

5. Campus life has changed a great deal since Thurber attended college. Or has it? Write a contemporary "University Days," using a series of examples that illustrate your own difficulties as you pursue higher education.

Mankind's Better Moments

Barbara Tuchman
(1912–1989)

Born in New York City and educated at Radcliffe College, Barbara Tuchman began her career writing for *The Nation* and *The New Statesman* magazines. She served as a war correspondent, covering both the Spanish Civil War and World War II for the London office of *The Nation*. In 1943, she became editor of the U.S. Office of War Information. Two of her books have been awarded the Pulitzer Prize: *The Guns of August* (1962) and *Stillwell and the American Experiment in China: 1911–45* (1971). Tuchman also contributed to magazines such as *Atlantic Monthly, American Scholar, Foreign Affairs,* and *Harper's.* Her last book was *The First Salute* (1989). In "Mankind's Better Moments," from *Practicing History* (1981), Tuchman gives historical illustrations to counteract the negative self-images that characterize people of the twentieth century.

1   For a change from prevailing pessimism, I should like to recall some of the positive and even admirable capacities of the human race. We hear very little of them lately. Ours is not a time of self-esteem or self-confidence—as was, for instance, the nineteenth century, when self-esteem may be seen oozing from its portraits. Victorians, especially the men, pictured themselves as erect, noble, and splendidly handsome. Our self-image looks more like Woody Allen or a character from Samuel Beckett. Amid a mass of worldwide troubles and a poor record for the twentieth century, we see our species—with cause—as functioning very badly, as blunderers when not knaves, as violent, ignoble, corrupt, inept, incapable of mastering the forces that threaten us, weakly subject to our worst instincts; in short, decadent.

Barbara Tuchman (Steve Miller / NYT Pictures)

2   The catalogue is familiar and valid, but it is growing tiresome. A study of history reminds one that mankind has its ups and downs and during the ups has accomplished many brave and beautiful things, exerted stupendous endeavors, explored and conquered oceans and wilderness, achieved marvels of beauty in the creative arts and marvels of science and social progress; has loved liberty with a passion that throughout history has led men to fight and die for it over and over again; has pursued knowledge, exercised reason, enjoyed laughter and pleasures, played games with zest, shown courage, heroism, altruism, honor, and decency; experienced love; known comfort, contentment, and occasionally happiness. All these qualities have been part of human experience, and if they have not had as important notice as the negatives nor exerted as wide and persistent an influence as the evils we do, they nevertheless deserve attention, for they are currently all but forgotten.

3   Among the great endeavors, we have in our own time carried men to the moon and brought them back safely—surely one of the most remarkable achievements in history. Some may disapprove of the effort as unproductive, too costly, and a wrong choice of priorities in relation to greater needs, all of which may be true but does not, as I see it, diminish the achievement. If you look carefully, all positives have a negative underside—sometimes more, sometimes less—and not all admirable endeavors have admirable motives. Some have sad consequences. Although most signs presently point from bad to worse, human capacities are probably what they have always been. If primitive man could discover how to transform grain into bread, and reeds growing by the riverbank into baskets; if his successors could invent the wheel, harness the insubstantial air to turn a millstone, transform sheep's wool, flax, and worms' cocoons into fabric—we, I imagine, will find a way to manage the energy problem.

4   Consider how the Dutch accomplished the miracle of making land out of sea. By progressive enclosure of the Zuider Zee over the last sixty years, they have added half a million acres to their country, enlarging its area by eight percent and providing homes, farms, and towns for close to a quarter of a million people. The will to do the impossible, the spirit of can-do that overtakes our species now and then, was never more manifest than in this earth-altering act by the smallest of the major European nations.

5   A low-lying, windswept, waterlogged land, partly below sea level, pitted with marshes, rivers, lakes, and inlets, sliding all along its outer edge into the stormy North Sea with only fragile sand dunes as nature's barrier against the waves, Holland, in spite of physical disadvantages, has made itself into one of the most densely populated, orderly, prosperous, and, at one stage of its history, dominant nations of the West. For centuries, ever since the first inhabitants, fleeing enemy tribes, settled in the bogs where no one cared to bother them, the Dutch struggled against water and learned how to live with it: building on mounds, constructing and reconstructing seawalls of clay mixed with straw, carrying mud in an endless train of baskets, laying willow mattresses weighted with stones, repairing each spring the winter's damage, draining marshes, channeling streams, building ramps to their attics to save the cattle in

times of flood, gaining dike-enclosed land from the waves in one place and losing as much to the revengeful ocean somewhere else, progressively developing methods to cope with their eternal antagonist.

6   The Zuider Zee was a tidal gulf penetrating eighty miles into the land over an area ten to thirty miles wide. The plan to close off the sea by a dam across the entire mouth of the gulf had long been contemplated but never adopted, for fear of the cost, until a massive flood in 1916, which left saltwater standing on all the farmlands north of Amsterdam, forced the issue. The act for enclosure was passed unanimously by both houses of Parliament in 1918. As large in ambition as the country was small, the plan called for a twenty-mile dike from shore to shore, rising twenty feet above sea level, wide enough at the top to carry an auto road and housing for the hydraulic works, and as much as six hundred feet wide on the sea bottom. The first cartload of gravel was dumped in 1920.

7   The dike was but part of the task. The inland sea it formed had to be drained of its saltwater and transformed from salt to fresh by the inflow from lower branches of the Rhine. Four polders, or areas rising from the shallows, would be lifted by the draining process from under water into the open air. Secondary dikes, pumping stations, sluices, drainage ditches to control the inflow, as well as locks and inland ports for navigation, had to be built, the polder lands restored to fertility, trees planted, roads, bridges, and rural and urban housing constructed, the whole scheduled for completion in sixty years.

8   The best-laid plans of engineers met errors and hazards. During construction, gravel that had been painstakingly dumped within sunken frameworks would be washed away in a night by heavy currents or a capricious storm. Means proved vulnerable, methods sometimes unworkable. Yet slowly the dike advanced from each shore toward the center. As the gap narrowed, the pressure of the tidal current rushing through increased daily in force, carrying away material at the base, undermining the structure, and threatening to prevent a final closing. In the last days a herd of floating derricks, dredges, barges, and every piece of available equipment was mustered at the spot, and fill was desperately poured in before the next return of the tide, due in twelve hours. At this point, gale winds were reported moving in. The check dam to protect the last gap showed signs of giving way; operations were hurriedly moved thirty yards inward. Suspense was now extreme. Roaring and foaming with sand, the tide threw itself upon the narrowing passage; the machines closed in, filled the last space in the dike, and it held. Men stood that day in 1932 where the North Sea's waves had held dominion for seven hundred years.

9   As the dry land appeared, the first comers to take possession were the birds. Gradually, decade by decade, crops, homes, and civilization followed, and unhappily, too, man's destructive intervention. In World War II the retreating Germans blew up a section of the dike, completely flooding the western polder, but by the end of the year the Dutch had pumped it dry, resowed the fields in the spring, and over the next seven years restored the polder's farms

and villages. Weather, however, is never conquered. The disastrous floods of 1953 laid most of coastal Holland under water. The Dutch dried themselves out and, while the work at Zuider Zee continued, applied its lessons elsewhere and lent their hydraulic skills to other countries. Today the *Afsluitdijk,* or Zuider Zee road, is a normal thoroughfare. To drive across it between the sullen ocean on one side and new land on the other is for that moment to feel optimism for the human race.

10   Great endeavor requires vision and some kind of compelling impulse, not necessarily practical as in the case of the Dutch, but sometimes less definable, more exalted, as in the case of the Gothic cathedrals of the Middle Ages. The architectural explosion that produced this multitude of soaring vaults— arched, ribbed, pierced with jeweled light, studded with thousands of figures of the stone-carvers' art—represents in size, splendor, and numbers one of the great, permanent artistic achievements of human hands. What accounts for it? Not religious fervor alone but the zeal of a dynamic age, a desire to outdo, an ambition for the biggest and the best. Only the general will, shared by nobles, merchants, guilds, artisans, and commoners, could command the resources and labor to sustain so great an undertaking. Each group contributed donations, especially the magnates of commerce, who felt relieved thereby from the guilt of money-making. Voluntary work programs involved all classes. "Who has ever seen or heard tell in times past," wrote an observer, "that powerful princes of the world, that men brought up in honors and wealth, that nobles— men and women—have bent their haughty necks to the harness of carts and, like beasts of burden, have dragged to the abode of Christ these wagons loaded with wines, grains, oil, stones, timber and all that is necessary for the construction of the church?"

11   Abbot Suger, whose renovation of St. Denis is considered the start of Gothic architecture, embodied the spirit of the builders. Determined to create the most splendid basilica in Christendom, he supervised every aspect of the work from fund-raising to decoration, and caused his name to be inscribed for immortality on keystones and capitals. He lay awake worrying, as he tells us, where to find trees large enough for the beams, and went personally with his carpenters to the forest to question the woodcutters under oath. When they swore that nothing of the kind he wanted could be found in the area, he insisted on searching for them himself and, after nine hours of scrambling through thorns and thickets succeeded in locating and marking twelve trees of the necessary size.

12   Mainly the compelling impulse lay in the towns, where, in those years, economic and political strengths and wealth were accumulating. Amiens, the thriving capital of Picardy, decided to build the largest church in France, "higher than all the saints, higher than all the kings." For the necessary space, the hospital and bishop's palace had to be relocated and the city walls moved back. At the same time Beauvais, a neighbor town, raised a vault over the crossing of transept and nave to an unprecedented height of 158 feet, the

apogee of architects' daring in its day. It proved too daring, for the height of the columns and spread of the supports caused the vault to collapse after twelve years. Repaired with undaunted purpose, it was defiantly topped by a spire rising 492 feet above ground, the tallest in France. Beauvais, having used up its resources, never built the nave, leaving a structure foreshortened but glorious. The interior is a fantasy of soaring space; to enter is to stand dazed in wonder, breathless in admiration.

13   The higher and lighter grew the buildings and the slenderer the columns, the more new expedients and techniques had to be devised to hold them up. Buttresses flew like angels' wings against the exteriors. This was a period of innovation and audacity, and a limitless spirit of excelsior. In a single century, from 1170 to 1270, six hundred cathedrals and major churches were built in France alone. In England in that period, the cathedral of Salisbury, with the tallest spire in the country, was completed in thirty-eight years. The spire of Freiburg in Germany was constructed entirely of filigree in stone as if spun by some supernatural spider. In the St. Chapelle in Paris the fifteen miraculous windows swallow the walls; they have become the whole.

14   Embellishment was integral to the construction. Reims is populated by five thousand statues of saints, prophets, kings and cardinals, bishops, knights, ladies, craftsmen and commoners, devils, animals and birds. Every type of leaf known in northern France is said to appear in the decoration. In carving, stained glass, and sculpture the cathedrals displayed the art of medieval hands, and the marvel of these buildings is permanent even when they no longer play a central role in everyday life. Rodin said he could feel the beauty and presence of Reims even at night when he could not see it. "Its power," he wrote, "transcends the senses so that the eye sees what it sees not."

15   Explanations for the extraordinary burst that produced the cathedrals are several. Art historians will tell you that it was the invention of the ribbed vault. Religious historians will say it was the product of an age of faith which believed that with God's favor anything was possible; in fact it was not a period of untroubled faith, but of heresies and Inquisition. Rather, one can only say that conditions were right. Social order under monarchy and the towns was replacing the anarchy of the barons, so that existence was no longer merely a struggle to stay alive but allowed a surplus of goods and energies and greater opportunity for mutual effort. Banking and commerce were producing capital, roads were making possible wheeled transport, universities nourishing ideas and communication. It was one of history's high tides, an age of vigor, confidence, and forces converging to quicken the blood.

16   Even when the historical tide is low, a particular group of doers may emerge in exploits that inspire awe. Shrouded in the mists of the eighth century, long before the cathedrals, Viking seamanship was a wonder of daring, stamina, and skill. Pushing relentlessly outward in open boats, the Vikings sailed south, around Spain to North Africa and Arabia, north to the top of the world, west across uncharted seas to American coasts. They hauled their

boats overland from the Baltic to make their way down Russian rivers to the Black Sea. Why? We do not know what engine drove them, only that it was part of the human endowment.

17   What of the founding of our own country, America? We take the *Mayflower* for granted—yet think of the boldness, the enterprise, the determined independence, the sheer grit it took to leave the known and set out across the sea for the unknown where no houses or food, no stores, no cleared land, no crops or livestock, none of the equipment or settlement of organized living awaited.

18   Equally bold was the enterprise of the French in the northern forests of the American continent, who throughout the seventeenth century explored and opened the land from the St. Lawrence to the Mississippi, from the Great Lakes to the Gulf of Mexico. They came not for liberty like the Pilgrims, but for gain and dominion, whether in spiritual empire for the Jesuits or in land, glory, and riches for the agents of the King; and rarely in history have men willingly embraced such hardship, such daunting adventure, and persisted with such tenacity and endurance. They met hunger, exhaustion, frostbite, capture and torture by Indians, wounds and disease, dangerous rapids, swarms of insects, long portages, bitter weather, and hardly ever did those who suffered the experience fail to return, reenter the menacing but bountiful forest, and pit themselves once more against danger, pain, and death.

19   Above all others, the perseverance of La Salle in his search for the mouth of the Mississippi was unsurpassed. While preparing in Quebec, he mastered eight Indian languages. From then on he suffered accidents, betrayals, desertions, losses of men and provisions, fever and snow blindness, the hostility and intrigues of rivals who incited the Indians against him and plotted to ambush or poison him. He was truly pursued, as Francis Parkman wrote, by "a demon of havoc." Paddling through heavy waves in a storm over Lake Ontario, he waded through freezing surf to beach the canoes each night, and lost guns and baggage when a canoe was swamped and sank. To lay the foundations of a fort above Niagara, frozen ground had to be thawed by boiling water. When the fort was at last built, La Salle christened it Crèvecouer—that is, Heartbreak. It earned the name when in his absence it was plundered and deserted by its half-starved mutinous garrison. Farther on, a friendly Indian village, intended as a destination, was found laid waste by the Iroquois with only charred stakes stuck with skulls standing among the ashes, while wolves and buzzards prowled through the remains.

20   When at last, after four months' hazardous journey down the Great River, La Salle reached the sea, he formally took possession in the name of Louis XIV of all the country from the river's mouth to its source and of its tributaries— that is, of the vast basin of the Mississippi from the Rockies to the Appalachians—and named it Louisiana. The validity of the claim, which seems so hollow to us (though successful in its own time), is not the point. What counts is the conquest of fearful adversity by one man's extraordinary exertions and inflexible will.

Topics for Writing and Discussion

1. In the first paragraph, Tuchman gives a list of reasons for the "prevailing pessimism" of the twentieth century. What is her attitude toward these examples of poor performance? How does the rest of the essay respond to this list of negative qualities?

2. What examples from ancient and recent history does Tuchman use to support her belief that we will discover a way to solve the energy crisis? Why does she explain one of her examples in great detail?

3. Tuchman offers several examples to support her premise that the Gothic cathedrals of the Middle Ages represented extraordinary achievement. List several of these examples and explain what positive quality Tuchman ascribes to each.

4. What common activity unites Tuchman's final series of examples? Does that activity have any relevance today? Who might Tuchman add to her final series as representative of the twentieth century?

5. Tuchman uses a series of examples to refute a widely held view. Write a similar essay that refutes a common attitude you find "familiar and valid, but . . . tiresome." For instance, you might argue against the idea that college students are primarily interested in partying. Or you might refute the view that nontraditional families do not provide a stable support system for their members.

IN SEARCH OF OUR MOTHERS' GARDENS

Alice Walker
(1944–   )

*Alice Walker (© F. Capri/
Saga 1991)*

The youngest of eight children born to Georgia
sharecroppers, Alice Malsenior Walker is a novelist,
poet, essayist, and lecturer, widely acclaimed for her
Pulitzer Prize–winning novel, *The Color Purple*
(1983). Following her graduation from Sarah
Lawrence College in 1965, Walker was a voter registration worker in Georgia, a worker in a Mississippi
Head Start program, and a New York City Welfare
Department employee. She has taught and lectured
at colleges, including Wellesley, Yale, Brandeis, and
the University of California at Berkeley. *Possessing
the Secret of Joy,* a novel, was published in 1992;
Anything We Love Can Be Saved, a book of poetry, was published in 1997.
Walker has also published several collections of articles, journal entries,
essays, and other poems. The essay that follows is an excerpt from a collection of essays, articles, and reviews by the same name, *In Search of Our
Mothers' Gardens* (1983). In the essay, Walker pays tribute to women of her
mother's and grandmother's generations for their creative and spiritual energies that flourished despite the barriers confronting them.

1   WHEN the poet Jean Toomer walked through the South in the early twenties, he discovered a curious thing: black women whose spirituality was so intense, so deep, so *unconscious,* they were themselves unaware of the richness
they held. They stumbled blindly through their lives: creatures so abused and
mutilated in body, so dimmed and confused by pain, that they considered
themselves unworthy even of hope. In the selfless abstractions their bodies became to the men who used them, they became more than "sexual objects,"
more even than mere women: they became "Saints." Instead of being perceived as whole persons, their bodies became shrines: what was thought to be
their minds became temples suitable for worship. These crazy Saints stared out

at the world, wildly, like lunatics—or quietly, like suicides; and the "God" that was in their gaze was as mute as a great stone.

2   Who were these Saints? These crazy, loony, pitiful women?

3   Some of them, without a doubt, were our mothers and grandmothers.

4   In the still heat of the post-Reconstruction South, this is how they seemed to Jean Toomer: exquisite butterflies trapped in an evil honey, toiling away their lives in an era, a century, that did not acknowledge them, except as "the *mule* of the world." They dreamed dreams that no one knew—not even themselves, in any coherent fashion—and saw visions no one could understand. They wandered or sat about the countryside crooning lullabies to ghosts, and drawing the mother of Christ in charcoal on courthouse walls.

5   They forced their minds to desert their bodies and their striving spirits sought to rise, like frail whirlwinds from the hard red clay. And when those frail whirlwinds fell, in scattered particles, upon the ground, no one mourned. Instead, men lit candles to celebrate the emptiness that remained, as people do who enter a beautiful but vacant space to resurrect a God.

6   Our mothers and grandmothers, some of them: moving to music not yet written. And they waited.

7   They waited for a day when the unknown thing that was in them would be made known; but guessed, somehow in their darkness, that on the day of their revelation they would be long dead. Therefore to Toomer they walked, and even ran, in slow motion. For they were going nowhere immediate, and the future was not yet within their grasp. And men took our mothers and grandmothers, "but got no pleasure from it." So complex was their passion and their calm.

8   To Toomer, they lay vacant and fallow as autumn fields, with harvest time never in sight: and he saw them enter loveless marriages, without joy; and become prostitutes, without resistance; and become mothers of children, without fulfillment.

9   For these grandmothers and mothers of ours were not Saints, but Artists; driven to a numb and bleeding madness by the springs of creativity in them for which there was no release. They were Creators, who lived lives of spiritual waste, because they were so rich in spirituality—which is the basis of Art— that the strain of enduring their unused and unwanted talent drove them insane. Throwing away this spirituality was their pathetic attempt to lighten the soul to a weight their work-worn, sexually abused bodies could bear.

10   What did it mean for a black woman to be an artist in our grandmothers' time? In our great-grandmothers' day? It is a question with an answer cruel enough to stop the blood.

11   Did you have a genius of a great-great-grandmother who died under some ignorant and depraved white overseer's lash? Or was she required to bake biscuits for a lazy backwater tramp, when she cried out in her soul to paint watercolors of sunsets, or the rain falling on the green and peaceful pasturelands? Or was her body broken and forced to bear children (who were more often than not sold away from her)—eight, ten, fifteen, twenty children—when her one joy was the thought of modeling heroic figures of rebellion, in stone or clay?

12   How was the creativity of the black woman kept alive, year after year and century after century, when for most of the years black people have been in America, it was a punishable crime for a black person to read or write? And the freedom to paint, to sculpt, to expand the mind with action did not exist. Consider, if you can bear to imagine it, what might have been the result if singing, too, had been forbidden by law. Listen to the voices of Bessie Smith, Billie Holiday, Nina Simone, Roberta Flack, and Aretha Franklin, among others, and imagine these voices muzzled for life. Then you may begin to comprehend the lives of our "crazy," "Sainted" mothers and grandmothers. The agony of the lives of women who might have been Poets, Novelists, Essayists, and Short-Story Writers (over a period of centuries), who died with their real gifts stifled within them.

13   And, if this were the end of the story, we would have cause to cry out in my paraphrase of Okot p´Bitek's great poem:

> O, my clanswomen
> Let us all cry together!
> Come,
> Let us mourn the death of our mother,
> The death of a Queen
> The ash that was produced
> By a great fire!
> O, this homestead is utterly dead
> Close the gates
> With *lacari* thorns,
> For our mother
> The creator of the Stool is lost!
> And all the young men
> Have perished in the wilderness!

14   But this is not the end of the story, for all the young women—our mothers and grandmothers, *ourselves*—have not perished in the wilderness. And if we ask ourselves why, and search for and find the answer, we will know beyond all efforts to erase it from our minds, just exactly who, and of what, we black American women are.

15   One example, perhaps the most pathetic, most misunderstood one, can provide a backdrop for our mothers' work: Phillis Wheatley, a slave in the 1700s.

16   Virginia Woolf, in her book *A Room of One's Own*, wrote that in order for a woman to write fiction she must have two things, certainly: a room of her own (with key and lock) and enough money to support herself.

17   What then are we to make of Phillis Wheatley, a slave, who owned not even herself? This sickly, frail black girl who required a servant of her own at times—her health was so precarious—and who, had she been white, would have been easily considered the intellectual superior of all the women and most of the men in the society of her day.

18   Virginia Woolf wrote further, speaking of course not of our Phillis, that "any woman born with a great gift in the sixteenth century [insert "eighteenth century," insert "black woman," insert "born or made a slave"] would certainly have gone crazed, shot herself, or ended her days in some lonely cottage outside the village, half witch, half wizard [insert "Saint"], feared and mocked at. For it needs little skill and psychology to be sure that a highly gifted girl who had tried to use her gift of poetry would have been so thwarted and hindered by contrary instincts [add "chains, guns, the lash, the ownership of one's body by someone else, submission to an alien religion"], that she must have lost her health and sanity to a certainty."

19   The key words, as they relate to Phillis, are "contrary instincts." For when we read the poetry of Phillis Wheatley—as when we read the novels of Nella Larsen or the oddly false-sounding autobiography of that freest of all black women writers, Zora Hurston—evidence of "contrary instincts" is everywhere. Her loyalties were completely divided, as was, without question, her mind.

20   But how could this be otherwise? Captured at seven, a slave of wealthy, doting whites who instilled in her the "savagery" of the Africa they "rescued" her from . . . one wonders if she was even able to remember her homeland as she had known it, or as it really was.

21   Yet, because she did try to use her gift for poetry in a world that made her a slave, she was "so thwarted and hindered by . . . contrary instincts, that she . . . lost her health. . . ." In the last years of her brief life, burdened not only with the need to express her gift but also with a penniless, friendless "freedom" and several small children for whom she was forced to do strenuous work to feed, she lost her health, certainly. Suffering from malnutrition and neglect and who knows what mental agonies, Phillis Wheatley died.

22   So torn by "contrary instincts" was black, kidnapped, enslaved Phillis that her description of "the Goddess"—as she poetically called the Liberty she did not have—is ironically, cruelly humorous. And, in fact, has held Phillis up to ridicule for more than a century. It is usually read prior to hanging Phillis's memory as that of a fool. She wrote:

> The Goddess comes, she moves divinely fair,
> Olive and laurel binds her *golden* hair.
> Wherever shines this native of the skies,
> Unnumber'd charms and recent graces rise. [My italics]

23   It is obvious that Phillis, the slave, combed the "Goddess's" hair every morning; prior, perhaps, to bringing in the milk, or fixing her mistress's lunch. She took her imagery from the one thing she saw elevated above all others.

24   With the benefit of hindsight we ask, "How could she?"

25   But at last, Phillis, we understand. No more snickering when your stiff, struggling, ambivalent lines are forced on us. We know now that you were not an idiot or a traitor; only a sickly little black girl, snatched from your home and country and made a slave; a woman who still struggled to sing the song that was your gift, although in a land of barbarians who praised you for your

bewildered tongue. It is not so much what you sang, as that you kept alive, in so many of our ancestors, *the notion of song.*

26   Black women are called, in the folklore that so aptly identifies one's status in society, "the *mule* of the world," because we have been handed the burdens that everyone else—*everyone* else—refused to carry. We have also been called "Matriarchs," "Superwomen," and "Mean and Evil Bitches." Not to mention "Castraters" and "Sapphire's Mama." When we have pleaded for understanding, our character has been distorted; when we have asked for simple caring, we have been handed empty inspirational appellations, then stuck in the farthest corner. When we have asked for love, we have been given children. In short, even our plainer gifts, our labors of fidelity and love, have been knocked down our throats. To be an artist and a black woman, even today, lowers our status in many respects, rather than raises it: and yet, artists we will be.

27   Therefore we must fearlessly pull out of ourselves and look at and identify with our lives the living creativity some of our great-grandmothers were not allowed to know. I stress *some* of them because it is well known that the majority of our great-grandmothers knew, even without "knowing" it, the reality of their spirituality, even if they didn't recognize it beyond what happened in the singing at church—and they never had any intention of giving it up.

28   How they did it—those millions of black women who were not Phillis Wheatley, or Lucy Terry or Frances Harper or Zora Hurston or Nella Larsen or Bessie Smith; or Elizabeth Catlett, or Katherine Dunham, either—brings me to the title of this essay, "In Search of Our Mothers' Gardens," which is a personal account that is yet shared, in its theme and its meaning, by all of us. I found, while thinking about the far-reaching world of the creative black woman, that often the truest answer to a question that really matters can be found very close.

29   In the late 1920s my mother ran away from home to marry my father. Marriage, if not running away, was expected of seventeen-year-old girls. By the time she was twenty, she had two children and was pregnant with a third. Five children later, I was born. And this is how I came to know my mother: she seemed a large, soft, loving-eyed woman who was rarely impatient in our home. Her quick, violent temper was on view only a few times a year, when she battled with the white landlord who had the misfortune to suggest to her that her children did not need to go to school.

30   She made all the clothes we wore, even my brothers' overalls. She made all the towels and sheets we used. She spent the summers canning vegetables and fruits. She spent the winter evenings making quilts enough to cover all our beds.

31   During the "working" day, she labored beside, not behind—my father in the fields. Her day began before sunup, and did not end until late at night. There was never a moment for her to sit down, undisturbed, to unravel her own private thoughts; never a time free from interruption—by work or the noisy inquiries of her many children. And yet, it is to my mother—and all our

mothers who were not famous—that I went in search of the secret of what has fed that muzzled and often mutilated, but vibrant, creative spirit that the black woman has inherited, and that pops out in wild and unlikely places to this day.

32   But when, you will ask, did my overworked mother have time to know or care about feeding the creative spirit?

33   The answer is so simple that many of us have spent years discovering it. We have constantly looked high, when we should have looked high—and low.

34   For example: in the Smithsonian Institute in Washington, D.C., there hangs a quilt unlike any other in the world. In fanciful, inspired, and yet simple and identifiable figures, it portrays the story of the Crucifixion. It is considered rare, beyond price. Though it follows no known pattern of quilt-making, and though it is made of bits and pieces of worthless rags, it is obviously the work of a person of powerful imagination and deep spiritual feeling. Below this quilt I saw a note that says it was made by "an anonymous Black woman in Alabama, a hundred years ago."

35   If we could locate this "anonymous" black woman from Alabama, she would turn out to be one of our grandmothers—an artist who left her mark in the only materials she could afford, and in the only medium her position in society allowed her to use.

36   As Virginia Woolf wrote further, in *A Room of One's Own*:

> Yet genius of a sort must have existed among women as it must have existed among the working class. [Change this to "slaves" and "the wives and daughters of share-croppers."] Now and again an Emily Brontë or a Robert Burns [change this to "a Zora Hurston or a Richard Wright"] blazes out and proves its presence. But certainly it never got itself on to paper. When, however, one reads of a witch being ducked, of a woman possessed by devils [or "Sainthood"], of a wise woman selling herbs [our root workers], or even a very remarkable man who had a mother, then I think we are on the track of a lost novelist, a suppressed poet, or some mute and inglorious Jane Austen. . . . Indeed, I would venture to guess that Anon, who wrote so many poems without signing them, was often a woman. . . .

37   And so our mothers and grandmothers have, more often than not anonymously, handed on the creative spark, the seed of the flower they themselves never hoped to see: or like a sealed letter they could not plainly read.

38   And so it is, certainly, with my own mother. Unlike "Ma" Rainey's songs, which retained their creator's name even while blasting forth from Bessie Smith's mouth, no song or poem will bear my mother's name. Yet so many of the stories that I write, that we all write, are my mother's stories. Only recently did I fully realize this: that through years of listening to my mother's stories of her life, I have absorbed not only the stories themselves, but something of the manner in which she spoke, something of the urgency that involves the knowledge that her stories—like her life—must be recorded. It is probably for this reason that so much of what I have written is about characters whose counterparts in real life are so much older than I am.

39   But the telling of these stories, which came from my mother's lips as naturally as breathing, was not the only way my mother showed herself as an artist. For stories, too, were subject to being distracted, to dying without conclusions. Dinners must be started, and cotton must be gathered before the big rains. The artist that was and is my mother showed itself to me only after many years. This is what I finally noticed:

40   Like Mem, a character in *The Third Life of Grange Copeland,* my mother adorned with flowers whatever shabby house we were forced to live in. And not just your typical straggly country stand of zinnias, either. She planted ambitious gardens—and still does—with over fifty different varieties of plants that bloom profusely from early March until late November. Before she left home for the fields, she watered her flowers, chopped up the grass, and laid out new beds. When she returned from the fields she might divide clumps of bulbs, dig a cold pit, uproot and replant roses, or prune branches from her taller bushes or trees—until night came and it was too dark to see.

41   Whatever she planted grew as if by magic, and her fame as a grower of flowers spread over three counties. Because of her creativity with her flowers, even my memories of poverty are seen through a screen of blooms—sunflowers, petunias, roses, dahlias, forsythia, spirea, delphiniums, verbena . . . and on and on.

42   And I remember people coming to my mother's yard to be given cuttings from her flowers; I hear again the praise showered on her because whatever rocky soil she landed on, she turned into a garden. A garden so brilliant with colors, so original in its design, so magnificent with life and creativity, that to this day people drive by our house in Georgia—perfect strangers and imperfect strangers—and ask to stand or walk among my mother's art.

43   I notice that it is only when my mother is working in her flowers that she is radiant, almost to the point of being invisible—except as Creator: hand and eye. She is involved in work her soul must have. Ordering the universe in the image of her personal conception of Beauty.

44   Her face, as she prepares the Art that is her gift, is a legacy of respect she leaves to me, for all that illuminates and cherishes life. She has handed down respect for the possibilities—and the will to grasp them.

45   For her, so hindered and intruded upon in so many ways, being an artist has still been a daily part of her life. This ability to hold on, even in very simple ways, is work black women have done for a very long time.

46   This poem is not enough, but it is something, for the woman who literally covered the holes in our walls with sunflowers:

> They were women then
> My mama's generation
> Husky of voice—Stout of
> Step
> With fists as well as
> Hands

How they battered down
Doors
And ironed
Starched white
Shirts
How they led
Armies
Headragged Generals
Across mined
Fields
Booby-trapped
Kitchens
To discover books
Desks
A place for us
How they knew what we
Must know
Without knowing a page
Of it
Themselves.

47   Guided by my heritage of a love of beauty and a respect for strength—in search of my mother's garden, I found my own.

48   And perhaps in Africa over two hundred years ago, there was just such a mother; perhaps she painted vivid and daring decorations in oranges and yellows and greens on the walls of her hut; perhaps she sang—in a voice like Roberta Flack's—*sweetly* over the compounds of her village; perhaps she wove the most stunning mats or told the most ingenious stories of all the village storytellers. Perhaps she was herself a poet—though only her daughter's name is signed to the poems that we know.

49   Perhaps Phillis Wheatley's mother was also an artist.

50   Perhaps in more than Phillis Wheatley's biological life is her mother's signature made clear.

TOPICS FOR WRITING AND DISCUSSION

1. In a symbolic sense, what are the "gardens" Walker speaks of in the essay title?

2. Why, according to Walker, were the "Saints" described by Jean Toomer driven to staring "out at the world wildly, like lunatics—or quietly, like suicides"?

3. For whom is Walker writing this essay? What is her purpose and how do the examples she gives illustrate the dominant idea of the piece?

4. How does Walker's theme transcend the plight of the black woman and speak to the situation of women in general? What problems do black

women face that are not shared by their white counterparts? As part of your response, consider Walker's references to Virginia Woolf's views.

5. Walker's essay describes the tragedy of a group denied expression of self. What other groups, current or past, have lost their "voices" through oppression? Present the story of one such group in a fully developed, illustrative essay. Did this group lose its "voice" but pass on its spirit?

A Dying Art: The Classy Exit Line

Lance Morrow
(1939–   )

Lance Morrow (Courtesy of Lance Morrow, Boston University)

A Harvard graduate, Lance Morrow is best known for his work at *Time* magazine, a career that has spanned over thirty years. Winner of the National Magazine Award in 1981, he has also written *America: A Rediscovery* (1987), *Fishing in the Tiber* (1989), and *The Chief: A Memoir of Fathers and Sons* (1984), which chronicles his relationship with his father Hugh Morrow, former *Saturday Evening Post* writer. His most recent works include *The Heart: A Memoir*, Vol. 1 (1995) and *Mad Genius: The Odyssey, Pursuit, and Capture of the Unibomber Suspect* (1996) which he coauthored. "A Dying Art: The Classy Exit Line" first appeared in *Time* magazine in 1984.

1   THERE was a time when the deathbed was a kind of proscenium, from which the personage could issue one last dramatic utterance, full of the compacted significance of his life. Last words were to sound as if all of the individual's earthly time had been sharpened to that point: he could now etch the grand summation. "More light!" the great Goethe of the Englightenment is said to have cried as he expired. There is some opinion, however, that what he actually said was "Little wife, give me your little paw."

2   In any case, the genre of great last words died quite a few years ago. There are those who think the last genuinely memorable last words were spoken in 1900, when, according to one version, the dying Oscar Wilde said, "Either that wallpaper goes, or I do."

3   Others set the date in 1904, when Chekhov on his deathbed declared, "It's a long time since I drank champagne." Appropriately, his coffin then rode to burial in a freight car marked FRESH OYSTERS.

4   Only now and then does one catch a handsome exit line today. Gary Gilmore, the murderer executed in Utah in 1977, managed a moment of brisk existentialist machismo when he told the warden, "Let's do it." There

was a charm, a mist of the fey overlaying the terror, in the official last words that William Saroyan telephoned to the Associated Press before he died in 1981: "Everybody has got to die, but I have always believed an exception would be made in my case. Now what?" Last fall the British actor John Le Mesurier dictated to his wife his own death announcement, which ran in the *Times* of London. It said, "John Le Mesurier wishes it to be known that he conked out on Nov. 15. He sadly misses family and friends."

5   Last words are a matter of taste, of course, and judgments about them tend to be subjective. A strong though eccentric case might be made for the final utterance of Britain's Lord Chief Justice Gordon Hewart, who died on a spring morning in 1944 with the words "Damn it! There's that cuckoo again!" Tallulah Bankhead used a splendid economy of language at her parting in New York City's St. Luke's Hospital in 1968. "Bourbon," she said. The Irish writer Brendan Behan rose to the occasion in 1964 when he turned to the nun who had just wiped his brow and said, "Ah, bless you, Sister, may all your sons be bishops." Some sort of award for sharp terminal repartee should be bestowed (posthumously) upon an uncle of Oliver Wendell Holmes, Jr., John Holmes, who lay dying in his Boston home in 1899. A nurse kept feeling his feet, and explained to someone in the room, "If his feet are warm, he is alive . . . Nobody ever died with his feet warm." Holmes rose out of his coma long enough to observe, "John Rogers[1] did!" Then he slipped away.

6   The great last words traditionally included in anthologies have usually been more serious than that, and often sound suspiciously perfect. *Le style, c'est l'homme.*[2] General Robert E. Lee is said to have gone in 1870 with just the right military-metaphysical command: "Strike the tent!" The great 18th century classicist and prig Nicolas Boileau managed a sentence of wonderfully plump self-congratulation: "It is a consolation to a poet on the point of death that he has never written a line injurious to good mortals."

7   While such goodbyes are usually retrospective, looking back on the life, they sometimes peer forward. Such lines derive considerable fascination from the fact that they have spoken at a vantage that is the closest that mortals can legitimately come to a glimpse of what lies on the other side. Thomas A. Edison said as he died in 1931, "It's very beautiful over there." (It is also possible, however, that he was referring to the view outside his window.) Voltaire had a mordant premonition. The lamp next to his deathbed flared momentarily, and his last words were "What? The flames already?"

8   Last words are supposed to be a drama of truth-telling, of nothing left to hide, nothing more to lose. Why, then, do they so often have that clunk of the bogus about them? Possibly because the majority of them may have been composed by others—keepers of the flame, hagiologists, busybodies. One hears the little sound of a pious fraud. The last breath is put into service to inflate the larger cause one last time, as with a regret that one has only one life to give for one's country. There is a long-running controversy, for example, over whether

---

[1] An English Protestant divine burned at the stake for heresy in 1555. [Author's note]

[2] *Le Style, c'est l'homme* is a French expression meaning "style makes the man."

the younger Pitt, when departing this life, said, "My country! How I love my country!" or "I think I could eat one of Bellamy's pork pies."

9   As Hamlet says in *his* last words, "the rest is silence." Great terminal summations are a form of theater, really. They demand an audience—someone has to hear them, after all. More than that, they have been traditionally uttered with a high solemnity. Some last words have the irony of inadvertence—as when Civil War General John Sedgwick was heard to say during the battle of Spotsylvania Court House, "Why, they couldn't hit an elephant at this dist—." But premeditated last words—the deathbed equivalent of Neil Armstrong's "One small step for a man, one giant leap for mankind," the canned speech uttered when setting off for other worlds—have a Shakespearean grandiloquence about them.

10   Last words are not a congenial form of theater any more. Suitable stages no longer seem to be available for such death scenes, nor is there much inclination to witness them. People tend either to die suddenly, unexpectedly, without the necessary editorial preparation, or to expire in hospitals, under sedation and probably not during visiting hours. The sedative dusk descends hours or days before the last darkness.

11   Perhaps the demise of great last words has something to do with a decline in the 20th century of the augustness of death. The departure of a single soul was once an imposing occasion. An age of holocausts is less disposed to hear the individual goodbyes.

12   Perhaps some entrepreneur will try to revive the genre of last words by enlisting videotape, a newer form of theater. Customers could write their own final script—or choose appropriate last words from the company's handsome selection ("Pick the goodbye that is you"), and then, well before the actual end, videotape their own official death scenes. The trouble is that most people tend to be windy and predictable when asked to say a few words on an important occasion. Maybe the best way to be memorable at the end is to be enigmatic. When in doubt, simply mutter, "Rosebud."[3]

Topics for Writing and Discussion

1. What is Morrow's thesis about great exit lines of the past? What purposes and characteristics do they share?
2. Characterize the tone of this essay. When did you first realize Morrow's treatment of this subject was different from what you might have expected?
3. What are some of Morrow's best examples of "great last words"? Does he offer enough examples to illustrate his claims?

---

[3] "Rosebud" is the last word (never understood by the movie's characters) in Orson Wells' *Citizen Kane,* arguably the most admired of all American films.

4. Why, in Morrow's opinion, are there fewer outstanding exit lines in modern times? What do Morrow's tongue-in-cheek suggestions for reviving this genre ("Pick the goodbye that is you") say about people today?

5. Morrow uses multiple examples to point out the essence of great exit lines. Write your own essay on classy lines from some other genre. For example, what are some of the most memorable movie lines of all times ("Frankly, my dear, I don't give a damn"), and what do these lines have in common? Or best first or last lines in novels? Or best lines from contemporary song lyrics? Most effective political slogans? Remember that you must have a clear thesis, a point your examples illustrate.

Edwin Arlington Robinson (UPI/Corbis-Bettmann)

RICHARD CORY

Edwin Arlington Robinson
(1869–1935)

Edwin Arlington Robinson grew up in Gardiner, Maine, the model for Tilbury Town, the setting for many of his poems. After a short time at Harvard University, he held various jobs in New York City. In 1902, President Theodore Roosevelt discovered *The Children of the Night* (1897) and *Captain Craig* (1902) and was impressed by Robinson's work. The president arranged a clerk's position in the New York Customs House for the author. This intercession allowed the impoverished Robinson to begin a series of literary projects, and in 1922, Robinson received the first Pulitzer Prize ever awarded for poetry. He later received two more Pulitzer Prizes within a span of seven years. Many of his later poems were long narratives set in the world of King Arthur: *Merlin* (1917), *Lancelot* (1920), and *Tristam* (1927). "Richard Cory" is one of Robinson's best-known poems and presents a clear example of a style that is bitterly realistic and psychologically penetrating.

Whenever Richard Cory went down town,
We people on the pavement looked at him:
He was a gentleman from sole to crown,
Clean favored, and imperially slim.

5 And he was always quietly arrayed,
And he was always human when he talked;
But still he fluttered pulses when he said,
"Good-morning," and he glittered when he walked.

And he was rich—yes, richer than a king—
10 And admirably schooled in every grace:
In fine, we thought that he was everything
To make us wish that we were in his place.

So on we worked, and waited for the light,
And went without the meat, and cursed the bread;
15 And Richard Cory, one calm summer night,
Went home and put a bullet through his head.

TOPICS FOR WRITING AND DISCUSSION

1. Who is speaking in this poem? Who are the "people on the pavement" the speaker mentions in line 2?
2. How do the people regard Richard Cory? Cite some examples the speaker gives to illustrate their opinion of him.
3. How do the people's lives stand in contrast to Richard Cory's? What does the speaker mean in the phrase "[we] waited for the light"?
4. What point about "appearances versus reality" might Robinson be making in the last two lines? About envy?
5. Write about the value of a judgment based on a first impression or an outward appearance. Use a detailed example from your own experience to illustrate your particular claim. Was your judgment ultimately accurate or erroneous?

THE SECRET LIFE OF WALTER MITTY

James Thurber
(1894–1961)

James Thurber (AP/Wide World Photos)

Born in Columbus, Ohio, James Thurber attended Ohio State University, although he never graduated. Due to an eye injury, he was ineligible for military service in World War I, so he worked for the State Department in Washington and in Paris for the *Chicago Tribune*. When he returned to the United States, he worked as a reporter for the *Columbus Dispatch*. In 1927 he joined the staff of *The New Yorker* and began a lifelong association with the magazine where he became well known for his satiric essays and his witty cartoons. He produced more than twenty collections of essays, short stories, autobiographical sketches, and memoirs. Some of his books include *My Life and Hard Times* (1933), *My World—and Welcome to It* (1942), *Fables for Our Time* (1943), and *The Thurber Carnival* (1945). "The Secret Life of Walter Mitty" is perhaps Thurber's best-known story, an affectionate portrait of one man's inner fantasies.

1   "WE'RE going through!" The Commander's voice was like thin ice breaking. He wore his full-dress uniform, with the heavily braided white cap pulled down rakishly over one cold gray eye. "We can't make it, sir. It's spoiling for a hurricane, if you ask me." "I'm not asking you, Lieutenant Berg," said the Commander. "Throw on the power lights! Rev her up to 8,500! We're going through!" The pounding of the cylinders increased; ta-pocketa-pocketa-pocketa-*pocketa-pocketa*. The Commander stared at the ice forming on the pilot window. He walked over and twisted a row of complicated dials. "Switch on No. 8 auxiliary!" he shouted. "Switch on No. 8 auxiliary!" repeated Lieutenant Berg. "Full strength in No. 3 turret!" shouted the Commander. "Full strength in No. 3 turret!" The crew, bending to their various tasks in the huge, hurtling eight-engined Navy hydroplane, looked at each other and grinned.

"The Old Man'll get us through," they said to one another. "The Old Man ain't afraid of Hell!" . . .

2   "Not so fast! You're driving too fast!" said Mrs. Mitty. "What are you driving so fast for?"

3   "Hmm?" said Walter Mitty. He looked at his wife, in the seat beside him, with shocked astonishment. She seemed grossly unfamiliar, like a strange woman who had yelled at him in a crowd. "You were up to fifty-five," she said. "You know I don't like to go more than forty. You were up to fifty-five." Walter Mitty drove on toward Waterbury in silence, the roaring of the SN202 through the worst storm in twenty years of Navy flying fading in the remote, intimate airways of his mind. "You're tensed up again," said Mrs. Mitty. "It's one of your days. I wish you'd let Dr. Renshaw look you over."

4   Walter Mitty stopped the car in front of the building where his wife went to have her hair done. "Remember to get those overshoes while I'm having my hair done," she said. "I don't need overshoes," said Mitty. She put her mirror back into her bag. "We've been all through that," she said, getting out of the car. "You're not a young man any longer." He raced the engine a little. "Why don't you wear your gloves? Have you lost your gloves?" Walter Mitty reached in a pocket and brought out the gloves. He put them on, but after she had turned and gone into the building and he had driven on to a red light, he took them off again. "Pick it up, brother," snapped a cop as the light changed, and Mitty hastily pulled on his gloves and lurched ahead. He drove around the streets aimlessly for a time, and then he drove past the hospital on his way to the parking lot.

5   . . . "It's the millionaire banker, Wellington McMillan," said the pretty nurse. "Yes?" said Walter Mitty, removing his gloves slowly. "Who has the case?" "Dr. Renshaw and Dr. Benbow, but there are two specialists here, Dr. Remington from New York and Dr. Pritchard-Mitford from London. He flew over." A door opened down a long, cool corridor and Dr. Renshaw came out. He looked distraught and haggard. "Hello, Mitty," he said. "We're having the devil's own time with McMillan, the millionaire banker and close personal friend of Roosevelt. Obstreosis of the ductal tract.[1] Tertiary. Wish you'd take a look at him." "Glad to," said Mitty.

6   In the operating room there were whispered introductions: "Dr. Remington, Dr. Mitty. Dr. Pritchard-Mitford, Dr. Mitty." "I've read your book on streptothricosis," said Pritchard-Mitford, shaking hands. "A brilliant performance, sir." "Thank you," said Walter Mitty. "Didn't know you were in the states, Mitty," grumbled Remington. "Coals to Newcastle, bringing Mitford and me up here for a tertiary." "You are very kind," said Mitty. A huge, complicated machine, connected to the operating table, with many tubes and wires, began at this moment to go pocketa-pocketa-pocketa. "The new anaesthetizer is giving away!" shouted an intern. "There is no one in the East who knows how to fix it!" "Quiet, man!" said Mitty, in a low, cool voice. He

---

[1] Obstreosis is a disease found mainly in pigs and cattle.

sprang to the machine, which was now going pocketa-pocketa-queep-pocketa-queep. He began fingering delicately a row of glistening dials. "Give me a fountain pen!" he snapped. Someone handed him a fountain pen. He pulled a faulty piston out of the machine and inserted the pen in its place. "That will hold for ten minutes," he said. "Get on with the operation." A nurse hurried over and whispered to Renshaw, and Mitty saw the man turn pale. "Coreopsis has set in,"[2] said Renshaw nervously. "If you would take over, Mitty?" Mitty looked at him and at the craven figure of Benbow, who drank, and at the grave, uncertain faces of the two great specialists. "If you wish," he said. They slipped a white gown on him; he adjusted a mask and drew on thin gloves; nurses handed him shining . . .

7   "Back it up, Mac! Look out for that Buick!" Walter Mitty jammed on the brakes. "Wrong lane, Mac," said the parking-lot attendant, looking at Mitty closely. "Gee. Yeh," muttered Mitty. He began cautiously to back out of the lane marked "Exit Only." "Leave her sit there," said the attendant. "I'll put her away." Mitty got out of the car. "Hey, better leave the key." "Oh," said Mitty, handing the man the ignition key. The attendant vaulted into the car, backed it up with insolent skill, and put it where it belonged.

8   They're so damn cocky, thought Walter Mitty, walking along Main Street; they think they know everything. Once he had tried to take his chains off, outside New Milford, and he had got them wound around the axles. A man had had to come out in a wrecking car and unwind them, a young, grinning garage man. Since then Mrs. Mitty always made him drive to a garage to have the chains taken off. The next time, he thought, I'll wear my right arm in a sling; they won't grin at me then. I'll have my right arm in a sling and they'll see I couldn't possibly take the chains off myself. He kicked at the slush on the sidewalk. "Overshoes," he said to himself, and he began looking for a shoe store.

9   When he came out into the street again, with the overshoes in a box under his arm, Walter Mitty began to wonder what the other thing was his wife had told him to get. She had told him, twice before they set out from their house for Waterbury. In a way he hated these weekly trips to town—he was always getting something wrong. Kleenex, he thought, Squibb's, razor blades? No. Toothpaste, toothbrush, bicarbonate, carborundum, initiative and referendum? He gave it up. But she would remember it. "Where's the what's-its-name?" she would ask. "Don't tell me you forgot the what's-its-name." A newsboy went by shouting something about the Waterbury trial.

10   . . . "Perhaps this will refresh your memory." The District Attorney suddenly thrust a heavy automatic at the quiet figure on the witness stand. "Have you ever seen this before?" Walter Mitty took the gun and examined it expertly. "This is my Webley-Vickers 50.80," he said calmly. An excited buzz ran around the courtroom. The judge rapped for order. "You are a crack shot with any sort of firearms, I believe?" said the District Attorney, insinuatingly. "Objection!" shouted Mitty's attorney. "We have shown that the defendant could

---

[2] Coreopsis is a plant, not a disease.

not have fired the shot. We have shown that he wore his right arm in a sling on the night of the fourteenth of July." Walter Mitty raised his hand briefly and the bickering attorneys were stilled. "With any known make of gun," he said evenly, "I could have killed Gregory Fitzhurst at three hundred feet *with my left hand.*" Pandemonium broke loose in the courtroom. A woman's scream rose above the bedlam and suddenly a lovely, dark-haired girl was in Walter Mitty's arms. The District Attorney struck at her savagely. Without rising from his chair, Mitty let the man have it on the point of the chin. "You miserable cur!" . . .

11   "Puppy biscuit," said Walter Mitty. He stopped walking and the buildings of Waterbury rose up out of the misty courtroom and surrounded him again. A woman who was passing laughed. "He said 'Puppy biscuit,'" she said to her companion. "That man said 'Puppy biscuit' to himself." Walter Mitty hurried on. He went into an A & P, not the first one he came to but a smaller one farther up the street. "I want some biscuit for small, young dogs," he said to the clerk. "Any special brand, sir?" The greatest pistol shot in the world thought a moment. "It says 'Puppies Bark for It' on the box," said Walter Mitty.

12   His wife would be through at the hairdresser's in fifteen minutes, Mitty saw in looking at his watch, unless they had trouble drying it; sometimes they had trouble drying it. She didn't like to get to the hotel first; she would want him to be there waiting for her as usual. He found a big leather chair in the lobby, facing a window, and he put the overshoes and the puppy biscuit on the floor beside it. He picked up an old copy of *Liberty* and sank down into the chair. "Can Germany Conquer the World through the Air?" Walter Mitty looked at the pictures of bombing planes and of ruined streets.

13   . . . "The cannonading has got the wind up in young Raleigh, sir," said the sergeant. Captain Mitty looked up at him through tousled hair. "Get him to bed," he said wearily, "with the others. I'll fly alone." "But you can't, sir," said the sergeant anxiously. "It takes two men to handle that bomber and the Archies are pounding hell out of the air. Von Richtman's circus is between here and Saulier." "Somebody's got to get that ammunition dump," said Mitty. "I'm going over. Spot of brandy?" He poured a drink for the sergeant and one for himself. War thundered and whined around the dugout and battered at the door. There was a rending of wood and splinters flew through the room. "A bit of a near thing," said Captain Mitty carelessly. "The box barrage is closing in," said the sergeant. "We only live once, sergeant," said Mitty, with his faint, fleeting smile. "Or do we?" He poured another brandy and tossed it off. "I never see a man could hold his brandy like you, sir," said the sergeant. "Begging your pardon, sir." Captain Mitty stood up and strapped on his huge Webley-Vickers automatic. "It's forty kilometers through hell, sir," said the sergeant. Mitty finished one last brandy. "After all," he said softly, "what isn't?" The pounding of the cannon increased; there was the rat-tat-tatting of machine guns, and from somewhere came the menacing pocketa-pocketa-pocketa of the new flame-throwers. Walter Mitty walked to the door of the dugout humming "Auprès de Ma Blonde." He turned and waved to the sergeant. "Cheerio!" he said. . . .

14   Something struck his shoulder. "I've been looking all over this hotel for you," said Mrs. Mitty. "Why do you have to hide in this old chair? How did you expect me to find you?" "Things close in," said Walter Mitty vaguely. "What?" Mrs. Mitty said. "Did you get the what's-its-name? The puppy biscuit? What's in that box?" "Overshoes," said Mitty. "Couldn't you have put them on in the store?" "I was thinking," said Walter Mitty. "Does it ever occur to you that I am sometimes thinking?" She looked at him. "I'm going to take your temperature when I get you home," she said.

15   They went out through the revolving doors that made a faintly derisive whistling sound when you pushed them. It was two blocks to the parking lot. At the drugstore on the corner she said, "Wait here for me. I forgot something. I won't be a minute." She was more than a minute. Walter Mitty lighted a cigarette. It began to rain, rain with sleet in it. He stood up against the wall of the drugstore, smoking. . . . He put his shoulders back and his heels together. "To hell with the handkerchief," said Walter Mitty scornfully. He took one last drag on his cigarette and snapped it away. Then, with that faint, fleeting smile playing about his lips, he faced the firing squad, erect and motionless, proud and disdainful, Walter Mitty the Undefeated, inscrutable to the last.

Topics for Writing and Discussion

1. What kinds of daydreams does Mitty have? What do these daydreams tell readers about his character?

2. How does each fantasy arise? What are the probable sources of these daydreams? What clichés do you see?

3. What pieces of misinformation does Mitty incorporate into his fantasies? How do these details add to our understanding of Mitty's character?

4. Is this story funny or tragic? Is Mitty "undefeated, inscrutable to the last"?

5. Think of three lives you might like to "inhabit." Fantasize about new identities: do you become a rock star, a sports hero, a powerful politician, a generous philanthropist, a popular movie star, an admired spiritual leader? Do these three lives have some trait in common? If so, do your fantasies reveal anything about your own character, as Mitty's do?

WRITING ASSIGNMENTS FOR CHAPTER SEVEN

ILLUSTRATION

1. To address William F. Buckley, Jr.'s complaint that no one complains any-more, write a letter to a company owner or supervisor or to a depart-ment/division head and register your complaint about a product or service. Consider, for example, some of the services provided on your cam-pus. Are there problems associated with the student center, the dorms, the cafeterias? With your school's advising or registration systems or financial aid office? Try to imagine the person to whom you are addressing your complaint; remember that your letter will only be taken seriously if you use the appropriate tone and enough detailed examples to illustrate the na-ture of your complaint thoroughly and persuasively. After you have com-pleted this assignment, send the letter; if you prefer, instead of a letter of complaint, send a letter complimenting some service or product. Such let-ters are rarely received and are always greatly appreciated.

2. Brent Staples' essay "Black Men and Public Space" discusses the dangers of stereotyping and the many kinds of victims it produces. Have you ever been the victim of discrimination? Of someone's preconceived beliefs about you, your family, or your friends? Or have you ever held prejudices that caused you to behave in irrational or even shameful ways? Perhaps you silently participated in acts of discrimination by failing to speak up? Or did you confront prejudice? Write an essay that illustrates your role in one of these situations, making clear how you felt then and how you feel now about the way you or others acted. Did the experience change you in any way? Might your essay change others?

3. Assume that your younger brother or sister is preparing to enter your high school (or your college) and has asked your opinion of that school. Offer several short incidents, as James Thurber did in "University Days," or one extended example that illustrates your attitude toward your school. For in-stance, was your school a playpen for adolescents? A genuinely challeng-ing educational experience? A haven for the athletically endowed? Your essay may be serious or humorous, and you may discover that using some dialogue will help make your essay vivid and persuasive.

4. In her essay, Barbara Tuchman describes some of history's "better mo-ments." Select some important enterprise or discovery that people have successfully accomplished in the past five years. Use this accomplishment as an illustration of people's determination, hard work, independence, or daring. Why should this feat be regarded as one of our "better moments"?

5. In the moving essay "In Search of Our Mothers' Gardens," Alice Walker uses her own mother as the example of black women who, prevented from

becoming recognized artists themselves, passed down creativity, strength of character, and a love of beauty to their daughters and granddaughters. Think of someone you admire—an influential teacher, an older relative, or a close family friend—who was also an unrecognized or underappreciated artist. Write about this person, using him or her to illustrate Walker's points about handing down "respect for the possibilities—and the will to grasp them."

6. Some essays need extended, detailed examples to make their points clearly. Other essays, such as Lance Morrow's "A Dying Art: The Classy Exit Line," profit most from multiple examples. Using Morrow's technique of multiple quotations, write an essay illustrating your insight into someone's sense of humor or folk wisdom or some other skill with language. Your subject could be someone you know well or someone well known, such as Mark Twain, Dorothy Parker, Ambrose Bierce, or Will Rogers.

7. In "Richard Cory," Edwin Arlington Robinson shows people who realize too late that someone they had envied was not the perfectly happy, charmed person they thought. Write an essay presenting a lesson you have learned about envy, using one extended example or several clearly developed examples to illustrate your point.

8. In James Thurber's story "The Secret Life of Walter Mitty," the main character imagines himself as the hero in a variety of exciting situations, some obviously prompted by his choice of reading material. Select a character from literature or history you admire and use this person to illustrate a character trait or heroic action you respect.

CHAPTER EIGHT

COMPARISON AND CONTRAST

COMPARING and contrasting is a natural human behavior that you perform so often you may not even be aware of it. When you walk down the aisle of the supermarket, pick up two packages of chocolate chip cookies, and determine which looks better, you are using your natural talent of contrasting, for you are looking at the differences (size, texture, number, price, etc.). Or, if you walk into a shop to find a shirt to blend with a particular pair of pants, you are comparing the colors because you want them to look alike rather than different. So, simply put, *comparing* means to look for *similarities,* while *contrasting* means to look for *differences.* As you think about the process of comparing or contrasting, you may discover that one seems to suggest the other, and that you often use the two together—considering both the similarities *and* the differences of things being examined.

A special type of comparison is the *analogy.* With analogy, similarities are explored between seemingly dissimilar things. By comparing a herd of stampeding horses to drivers in rush-hour traffic, you can illustrate the wild and dangerous place a highway becomes at five o'clock. However, beware the extent to which you carry the analogy. Eventually, the comparison breaks down, and your intended point may be lost. Analogy is best used in moderation, to enliven the writing and maintain your reader's attention.

As you use the principles of comparison and contrast, you will find that as rhetorical structures they are valuable tools in analysis and evaluation.

WRITING AND ORGANIZING THE COMPARISON/CONTRAST ESSAY

The first step in any writing is selecting a good topic, and in writing a comparison/contrast essay that step is essential. Your goal should be to focus your reader's attention on something important, something interesting. As you choose your subject, avoid the obvious or the "so what" topic. Unless you can present a truly informative or unusual approach to the topic, an essay such as such as one contrasting attending high school with attending college could be boring. Consider the reader: After you have chosen a topic, ask yourself, "Would *I* enjoy reading this? Would *I* learn something from this?" If your answers are "No," presume that would also be your reader's response and select another topic.

The following advice will help you in developing, organizing, and writing a comparison or contrast essay:

1. *Clearly establish the basis of the comparison or contrast.*

Identify the purpose of the writing in a clearly stated (or strongly implied) thesis statement. Suzanne Britt establishes the basis of her contrast right away in "Neat People vs. Sloppy People" by opening her humorous essay with the following:

> I've finally figured out the difference between neat people and sloppy people. The distinction is, as always, moral. Neat people are lazier and meaner than sloppy people. . . . Sloppy people, you see, are not really sloppy. Their sloppiness is merely the unfortunate consequence of their extreme moral rectitude.

On the other hand, in "Grant and Lee: A Study in Contrasts," Bruce Catton takes more space to establish the basis of his contrast between the personalities of the opposing military generals, Robert E. Lee and Ulysses S. Grant. But by providing an appropriate "setting" in the opening two paragraphs, Catton moves smoothly and logically to the essay's thesis in paragraph 3:

> They are two strong men these oddly different generals, and they represented the strengths of two conflicting currents that, through them, had come into final collision.

So, whether your introduction is one paragraph long or more, the reader should be prepared for the discussion that will follow.

2. *Carefully select the points you intend to discuss.*

As you review your thesis statement, determine the best way to emphasize the point of your discussion. Should you focus on similarities, differences, or both? For example, Bruce Catton first contrasts Generals Lee and Grant by noting the differences in their *backgrounds* (Lee, the aristocrat; Grant, the frontiersman), their *personalities* (Lee believed there should be a "pronounced inequality in the social structure"; Grant believed in "privileges each man had won for himself"), and in their *underlying aspirations* (Lee's society "could endure almost anything except change"; Grant fought for a society "tied to growth, expansion, and a constantly widening horizon"). Then, in concluding the essay, Catton draws similarities between the two generals, noting that, aside from their differences, "they were marvelous fighters. . . . Each man had . . . the great virtue of utter tenacity and fidelity . . . daring and resourcefulness . . . and the ability . . . to turn quickly from war to peace once the fighting was over."

3. *Decide if a point-by-point or a subject-by-subject method of development is better for your purpose.*

In the *point-by-point* method, you support your thesis by comparing or contrasting your two subjects first on point 1, then on point 2, then on point 3, and so on. In the *subject-by-subject* method, you would make your comparison or contrast by fully discussing one subject before moving on to another. The key to the comparison or the contrast is in using the same basis of comparison for each subject. When Bruce Catton contrasts the personalities of Grant and Lee, he establishes as his base the two men's personal backgrounds and their attitudes toward society and democracy. Catton develops his study by first exploring Lee's background and attitudes in two paragraphs and then by similarly exploring Grant's in three paragraphs.

The two methods of organization would follow these plans:

POINT-BY-POINT METHOD	SUBJECT-BY-SUBJECT METHOD
Introduction	Introduction
I. Point 1	I. Subject A
A. Subject A	A. Point 1
B. Subject B	B. Point 2
II. Point 2	C. Point 3
A. Subject A	II. Subject B
B. Subject B	A. Point 1
III. Point 3	B. Point 2
A. Subject A	C. Point 3
B. Subject B	Conclusion
Conclusion	

Your purpose and your subject will determine which of the two systems is better for your essay, but consider the advantages and disadvantages of both. The advantage of the point-by-point system is that it allows you to present your ideas side by side. The disadvantage of this approach is the possible back-and-forth "tennis match" effect it may present to the reader.

On the other hand, the subject-by-subject method will allow you to present your ideas as a unit, a whole. This approach is especially effective if only two or three points are being presented. You can, in essence, completely discuss one point and then move on to give a similarly thorough treatment to the other point. Notice how well this approach works in Mark Twain's "Two Ways of Looking at the River." Twain first describes his earlier, emotional response to the beauties of the Mississippi River and then gives a later view from his perspective of a trained river-boat pilot. A problem could arise, however. If there is too much material offered about either of the subjects without adequate reference to the other subject, the essay may begin to resemble two separate essays stuck together in the middle rather than a whole comparison or contrast essay. The reader could get lost and forget the points you are exploring or even, perhaps, the purpose of the essay. To avoid this problem, writers can subtly remind their reader of the essay's purpose by adding connecting phrases. Toni Morrison uses this technique in "A Slow Walk of Trees." She changes the essay's direction with "While my grandparents held opposite views on whether the fortunes of black people were improving, my own parents struck similarly opposed postures, but from another slant." This sentence begins Morrison's discussion of her parents' views.

4. *Describe your subjects clearly and vividly.*

To understand a difference or similarity between two subjects, readers must be able to "see" them as you do. Consequently, use as many details and illustrations as you can to describe both your subjects. Beware a tendency to elaborate on one subject and skimp on the other, especially in a paper that asserts "X" is better than or preferable to "Y." Give each subject a reasonable treatment, as Bruce Catton does in "Grant and Lee: A Study in Contrasts."

5. *Use transitions that indicate comparison or contrast to provide coherence in the development of the essay.*

Transitions such as *however, on the other hand, but, whereas,* and *unlike* will show a contrasting of ideas. Transitions such as *similarly, in addition to, and,* and *likewise* will show a comparing of ideas.

Notice Wendell Barry's use of transitional devices to create a fluid, smooth paragraph contrasting equipment in "A Good Scythe":

> The **other** difference is between kinds of weariness. Using the Marugg scythe causes the simple bodily weariness that comes with exertion. This is a kind of weariness that, when not extreme, can in itself be one of the pleasures of work. The power of the scythe, **on the other hand,** adds to the weariness of exertion the unpleasant and destructive weariness of strain. This is partly because, **in addition to** carrying and handling it, your attention is necessarily clenched to it; if you are to use it effectively and safely, you *must* not look away. **And** partly it is because the power scythe, **like** all motor-driven tools, imposes patterns of endurance that are alien to the body.

As you read the essays that follow, pay close attention to the ways the writers establish the bases of their comparison or contrast, balance their points of discussion, use clear topic sentences to focus each point of discussion, and provide transitions for coherence within and between the paragraphs.

Mark Twain (Library of Congress)

TWO WAYS OF LOOKING
AT THE RIVER

Mark Twain
(1835–1910)

Samuel Langhorne Clemens was born in the town of
Florida, Missouri, and raised in Hannibal, Missouri.
From 1857 to 1861, he served as an apprentice pilot on
a Mississippi riverboat and took his pen name,
Mark Twain, from a riverboat captain's phrase for a
depth of two fathoms, a safe navigating depth. He also
worked as a printer, a journalist, and a writer of comic
sketches and is considered one of America's best writers and humorists. Some of his classic novels include
The Adventures of Tom Sawyer (1876), *The Adventures of Huckleberry Finn* (1885), and *A Connecticut
Yankee at King Arthur's Court* (1889). Some of his
nonfiction books are *A Tramp Abroad* (1880), *Inno-
cents Abroad* (1896), and *Following the Equator*
(1897). "Two Ways of Looking at the River" is an
excerpt from his autobiography *Life on the Mississippi*
(1883).

1   Now when I had mastered the language of this water and had come to
know every trifling feature that bordered the great river as familiarly as I knew
the letters of the alphabet, I had made a valuable acquisition. But I had lost
something, too. I had lost something which could never be restored to me
while I lived. All the grace, the beauty, the poetry, had gone out of the majestic
river! I still kept in mind a certain wonderful sunset which I witnessed when
steamboating was new to me. A broad expanse of the river was turned to
blood; in the middle distance the red hue brightened into gold, through which
a solitary log came floating, black and conspicuous; in one place a long, slanting mark lay sparkling upon the water; in another the surface was broken by
boiling, tumbling rings, that were as many-tinted as an opal; where the ruddy

flush was faintest, was a smooth spot that was covered with graceful circles and radiating lines, ever so delicately traced; the shore on our left was densely wooded and the somber shadow that fell from this forest was broken in one place by a long, ruffled trail that shone like silver; and high above the forest wall a clean-stemmed dead tree waved a single leafy bough that glowed like a flame in the unobstructed splendor that was flowing from the sun. There were graceful curves, reflected images, woody heights, soft distances, and over the whole scene, far and near, the dissolving lights drifted steadily, enriching it every passing moment with new marvels of coloring.

2   I stood like one bewitched. I drank it in, in a speechless rapture. The world was new to me and I had never seen anything like this at home. But as I have said, a day came when I began to cease from noting the glories and the charms which the moon and the sun and the twilight wrought upon the river's face; another day came when I ceased altogether to note them. Then, if that sunset scene had been repeated, I should have looked upon it without rapture, and should have commented upon it inwardly after this fashion: "This sun means that we are going to have wind to-morrow; that floating log means that the river is rising, small thanks to it; that slanting mark on the water refers to a bluff reef which is going to kill somebody's steamboat one of these nights, if it keeps on stretching out like that; those tumbling 'boils' show a dissolving bar and a changing channel there; the lines and circles in the slick water over yonder are a warning that that troublesome place is shoaling up dangerously; that silver streak in the shadow of the forest is the 'break' from a new snag and he has located himself in the very best place he could have found to fish for steamboats; that tall dead tree, with a single living branch, is not going to last long, and then how is a body ever going to get through this blind place at night without the friendly old landmark?"

3   No, the romance and beauty were all gone from the river. All the value any feature of it had for me now was the amount of usefulness it could furnish toward compassing the safe piloting of a steamboat. Since those days, I have pitied doctors from my heart. What does the lovely flush in a beauty's cheek mean to a doctor but a "break" that ripples above some deadly disease? Are not all her visible charms sown thick with what are to him the signs and symbols of hidden decay? Does he ever see her beauty at all, or doesn't he simply view her professionally and comment upon her unwholesome condition all to himself? And doesn't he sometimes wonder whether he has gained most or lost most by learning his trade?

TOPICS FOR WRITING AND DISCUSSION

1. What two views of the river does Twain describe? Can you think of one word or one phrase that would characterize each of these views?
2. What point is Twain making about the two different ways he has looked at the river? What is his thesis? How does his conclusion suggest the way of seeing nature he considers more desirable?

3. In the third paragraph, Twain poses a series of questions. Does he expect the reader to answer these questions? How do you think Twain might respond to his own queries? Would his responses differ from or agree with your own?

4. How does Twain make smooth transitions from his first view of the river to the second and from the second view to the conclusion?

5. Write an essay contrasting the way you looked at an object, a location, or a process before you learned the scientific, mechanical, or practical "truth" about it. For example, you might describe how you as a child viewed the rainbows that form in puddles before and after you learned that they were caused by oil leaking from motor vehicles. Or you might describe your reaction to a magic trick before and after you learned the magician's secret.

Bruce Catton (The Bettmann Archive)

GRANT AND LEE:
A STUDY IN CONTRASTS

Bruce Catton
(1899–1978)

⫸⟍

Considered one of the twentieth century's most outstanding historians of the Civil War, Bruce Catton
worked as a reporter, columnist, and editorial writer
for the *Cleveland Plain Dealer* and other newspapers.
A student at Oberlin College at the onset of World War
I, he abandoned his studies for military service. He
never graduated, but he did go on to write eighteen
books, seventeen of which were written after he was
fifty years old. From 1954 until his death, he was editor and writer for *American Heritage Magazine,* and he
received both the Pulitzer Prize and the National Book
Award for *A Stillness at Appomattox* (1953). His other
books include *Mr. Lincoln's Army* (1951), *The Hallowed Ground* (1956), *Never Call Retreat* (1966), his
autobiography *Waiting for the Morning Train: An
American Boyhood* (1972), and *The Final Fury* (1974).
President Gerald Ford awarded Catton a Medal of
Freedom for the body of his historical works. "Grant
and Lee: A Study in Contrasts" first appeared in *The
American Story* (1956), a collection of essays by eminent historians. In the essay, Catton contrasts not only
two very different men but also the two vastly different
traditions they represent.

1   WHEN Ulysses S. Grant and Robert E. Lee met in the parlor of a modest
house at Appomattox Court House, Virginia, on April 9, 1865, to work out

the terms for the surrender of Lee's Army of Northern Virginia, a great chapter in American life came to a close, and a great new chapter began.

2   These men were bringing the Civil War to its virtual finish. To be sure, other armies had yet to surrender, and for a few days the fugitive Confederate government would struggle desperately and vainly, trying to find some way to go on living now that its chief support was gone. But in effect it was all over when Grant and Lee signed the papers. And the little room where they wrote out the terms was the scene of one of the poignant, dramatic contrasts in American History.

3   They were two strong men these oddly different generals, and they represented the strengths of two conflicting currents that, through them, had come into final collision.

4   Back of Robert E. Lee was the notion that the old aristocratic concept might somehow survive and be dominant in American life.

5   Lee was tidewater Virginia, and in his background were family, culture, and tradition . . . the age of chivalry transplanted to a New World which was making its own legends and its own myths. He embodied a way of life that had come down through the age of knighthood and the English country squire. America was a land that was beginning all over again, dedicated to nothing much more complicated than the rather hazy belief that all men had equal rights and should have an equal chance in the world. In such a land Lee stood for the feeling that it was somehow of advantage to human society to have a pronounced inequality in the social structure. There should be a leisure class, backed by ownership of land; in turn, society itself should be keyed to the land as the chief source of wealth and influence. It would bring forth (according to this ideal) a class of men with a strong sense of obligation to the community; men who lived not to gain advantage for themselves, but to meet the solemn obligations which had been laid on them by the very fact that they were privileged. From them the country would get its leadership; to them it could look for the higher values—of thought, of conduct, or personal deportment—to give it strength and virtue.

6   Lee embodied the noblest elements of this aristocratic ideal. Through him, the landed nobility justified itself. For four years, the Southern states had fought a desperate war to uphold the ideals for which Lee stood. In the end, it almost seemed as if the Confederacy fought for Lee; as if he himself was the Confederacy . . . the best thing that the way of life for which the Confederacy stood could ever have to offer. He had passed into legend before Appomattox. Thousands of tired, underfed, poorly clothed Confederate soldiers, long since past the simple enthusiasm of the early days of the struggle, somehow considered Lee the symbol of everything for which they had been willing to die. But they could not quite put this feeling into words. If the Lost Cause, sanctified by so much heroism and so many deaths, had a living justification, its justification was General Lee.

7   Grant, the son of a tanner on the Western frontier, was everything Lee was not. He had come up the hard way and embodied nothing in particular except the eternal toughness and sinewy fiber of the men who grew up beyond the

mountains. He was one of a body of men who owed reverence and obeisance to no one, who were self-reliant to a fault, who cared hardly anything for the past but who had a sharp eye for the future.

8   These frontier men were the precise opposites of the tidewater aristocrats. Back of them, in the great surge that had taken people over the Alleghenies and into the opening Western country, there was a deep, implicit dissatisfaction with a past that had settled into grooves. They stood for democracy, not from any reasoned conclusion about the proper ordering of human society, but simply because they had grown up in the middle of democracy and knew how it worked. Their society might have privileges, but they would be privileges each man had won for himself. Forms and patterns meant nothing. No man was born to anything, except perhaps to a chance to show how far he could rise. Life was competition.

9   Yet along with this feeling had come a deep sense of belonging to a national community. The Westerner who developed a farm, opened a shop, or set up in business as a trader could hope to prosper only as his own community prospered—and this community ran from the Atlantic to the Pacific and from Canada down to Mexico. If the land was settled, with towns and highways and accessible markets, he could better himself. He saw his fate in terms of the nation's own destiny. As its horizons expanded, so did his. He had, in other words, an acute dollars-and-cents stake in the continued growth and development of his country.

10   And that, perhaps, is where the contrast between Grant and Lee becomes most striking. The Virginia aristocrat, inevitably, saw himself in relation to his own region. He lived in a static society which could endure almost anything except change. Instinctively, his first loyalty would go to the locality in which that society existed. He would fight to the limit of endurance to defend it, because in defending it he was defending everything that gave his own life its deepest meaning.

11   The Westerner, on the other hand, would fight with an equal tenacity for the broader concept of society. He fought so because everything he lived by was tied to growth, expansion, and a constantly widening horizon. What he lived by would survive or fall with the nation itself. He could not possibly stand by unmoved in the face of an attempt to destroy the Union. He would combat it with everything he had, because he could only see it as an effort to cut the ground out from under his feet.

12   So Grant and Lee were in complete contrast, representing two diametrically opposed elements in American life. Grant was the modern man emerging; beyond him, ready to come on the stage, was the great age of steel and machinery, of crowded cities and a restless burgeoning vitality. Lee might have ridden down from the old age of chivalry, lance in hand, silken banner fluttering over his head. Each man was the perfect champion of his cause, drawing both his strengths and his weaknesses from the people he led.

13   Yet it was not all contrast, after all. Different as they were—in background, in personality, in underlying aspiration—these two great soldiers had

much in common. Under everything else, they were marvelous fighters. Furthermore, their fighting qualities were really very much alike.

14   Each man had, to begin with, the great virtue of utter tenacity and fidelity. Grant fought his way down the Mississippi Valley in spite of acute personal discouragement and profound military handicaps. Lee hung on in the trenches at Petersburg after hope itself had died. In each man there was an indomitable quality . . . the born fighter's refusal to give up as long as he can still remain on his feet and lift his two fists.

15   Daring and resourcefulness they had, too: the ability to think faster and move faster than the enemy. These were the qualities which gave Lee the dazzling campaigns of Second Manassas and Chancellorsville and won Vicksburg for Grant.

16   Lastly, and perhaps greatest of all, there was the ability, at the end, to turn quickly from war to peace once the fighting was over. Out of the way these two men behaved at Appomattox came the possibility of a peace of reconciliation. It was a possibility not wholly realized, in the years to come, but which did, in the end, help the two sections to become one nation again . . . after a war whose bitterness might have seemed to make such a reunion wholly impossible. No part of either man's life became him more than the part he played in their brief meeting in the McLean house at Appomattox. Their behavior there put all succeeding generations of Americans in their debt. Two great Americans, Grant and Lee—very different, yet under everything very much alike. Their encounter at Appomattox was one of the great moments of American history.

Topics for Writing and Discussion

1. What qualities and values did Lee and Grant each represent? How did their personal appearance and behavior reflect these qualities and values?
2. Does Catton's essay encourage more admiration for one of the generals than the other? Which details most effectively characterize these two men?
3. Catton's essay is rich in figurative language. Reread paragraphs 1, 3, 5, 7, 8, 9, 10, and 11, noticing the metaphors he uses. How does he use these comparisons to describe the generals and the way of life each represents?
4. Sketch an outline of the essay and use the outline to analyze the structure Catton uses to contrast Grant and Lee. Note the two one-sentence paragraphs, 3 and 4. What do these paragraphs add to the essay? Could they be omitted? Combined with other paragraphs? What would be lost or gained through such changes?
5. While Grant and Lee embodied different ideals, Catton points out that they were also alike in a number of their virtues. Think of two people you admire for some sort of "greatness." In an essay of comparison, show how these two people are similar, even though they may be in different fields or in pursuit of different goals.

A Good Scythe

Wendell Berry
(1934–   )

Born in Henry County, Kentucky, Wendell Berry is a prolific poet, novelist, and essayist. He received his B.A. and M.A. degrees from the University of Kentucky, where he later became a professor of English. His writings, which deal with the preservation of nature, the value of manual labor, and the simple joys of the simple life, have appeared in national literary and popular periodicals. He recently published two collections of short stories—*Fidelity: Five Stories* (1992) and *Watch with M: And Six Other Stories of the Yet-Remembered Ptolemy Proudfoot and His Wife, Miss Minnie, nee Quinch* (1994)—

Wendell Berry (Thomas Victor)

and two collections of poetry, *Entries: Poems* (1994) and *The Farm* (1995). In "A Good Scythe," Berry questions the efficiency of so-called labor-saving agricultural machinery.

1   WHEN we moved to our little farm in the Kentucky River Valley in 1965, we came with a lot of assumptions that we have abandoned or changed in response to the demands of place and time. We assumed, for example, that there would be good motor-powered solutions for all of our practical purposes.

2   One of the biggest problems from the beginning was that our place was mostly on a hillside and included a good deal of ground near the house and along the road that was too steep to mow with a lawn mower. Also, we were using some electric fence, which needed to be mowed out once or twice a year.

3   When I saw that Sears Roebuck sold a "power scythe," it seemed the ideal solution, and I bought one. I don't remember what I paid for it, but it was expensive, considering the relatively small amount of work I needed it for. It consisted of a one-cylinder gasoline engine mounted on a frame with a handlebar, a long metal tube enclosing a flexible drive shaft, and a rotary blade. To use it,

you hung it from your shoulder by a web strap, and swept the whirling blade over the ground at the desired height.

4   It did a fairly good job of mowing, cutting the grass and weeds off clean and close to the ground. An added advantage was that it readily whacked off small bushes and tree sprouts. But this solution to the mowing problem involved a whole package of new problems:

1. The power scythe was heavy.

2. It was clumsy to use, and it got clumsier as the ground got steeper and rougher. The tool that was supposed to solve the problem of steep ground worked best on level ground.

3. It was dangerous. As long as the scythe was attached to you by the shoulder strap, you weren't likely to fall onto that naked blade. But it *was* a naked blade, and it did create a constant threat of flying rock chips, pieces of glass, etc.

4. It enveloped you in noise, and in the smudge and stench of exhaust fumes.

5. In rank growth, the blade tended to choke—in which case you had to kill the engine in a hurry or it would twist the drive shaft in two.

6. Like a lot of small gas engines not regularly used, this one was temperamental and undependable. And dependence on an engine that won't run is a plague and a curse.

5   When I review my own history, I am always amazed at how slow I have been to see the obvious. I don't remember how long I used that "labor-saving" power scythe before I finally donated it to help enlighten one of my friends—but it was too long. Nor do I remember all the stages of my own enlightenment.

6   The turning point, anyhow, was the day when Harlan Hubbard showed me an old-fashioned, human-powered scythe that was clearly the best that I had ever seen. It was light, comfortable to hold and handle. The blade was very sharp, angled and curved precisely to the path of its stroke. There was an intelligence and refinement in its design that made it a pleasure to handle and look and think about. I asked where I could get one, and Harlan gave me an address: The Marugg Company, Tracy City, Tennessee 37387.

7   I wrote for a price list and promptly received a sheet exhibiting the stock in trade of the Marugg Company: grass scythes, bush scythes, snaths, sickles, hoes, stock bells, carry yokes, whetstones, and the hammers and anvils used in beating out the "dangle" cutting edge that is an essential feature of the grass scythes.

8   In due time I became the owner of a grass scythe, hammer and anvil, and whetstone. Learning to use the hammer and anvil properly (the Marugg Company provides a sheet of instructions) takes some effort and some considering. And so does learning to use the scythe. It is essential to hold the point so that it won't dig into the ground, for instance; and you must learn to swing so that you slice rather than hack.

9   Once these fundamentals are mastered, the Marugg grass scythe proves itself an excellent tool. It is the most satisfying hand tool that I have ever used. In tough grass it cuts a little less uniformly than the power scythe. In all other ways, in my opinion it is a better tool:

1. It is light.
2. It handles gracefully and comfortably even on steep ground.
3. It is far less dangerous than the power scythe.
4. It is quiet and makes no fumes.
5. It is much more adaptable to conditions than the power scythe: in ranker growth, narrow the cut and shorten the stroke.
6. It always starts—provided the user will start. Aside from reasonable skill and care in use, there are no maintenance problems.
7. It requires no fuel or oil. It runs on what you ate for breakfast.
8. It is at least as fast as the power scythe. Where the cutting is either light or extra heavy, it can be appreciably faster.
9. It is far cheaper than the power scythe, both to buy and to use.

10   Since I bought my power scythe, a new version has come on the market, using a short length of nylon string in place of the metal blade. It is undoubtedly safer. But I believe the other drawbacks remain. Though I have not used one of these, I have observed them in use, and they appear to me to be slower than the metal-bladed power scythe, and less effective on large-stemmed plants.

11   I have noticed two further differences between the power scythe and the Marugg scythe that are not so practical as those listed above, but which I think are just as significant. The first is that I never took the least pleasure in using the power scythe, whereas in using the Marugg scythe, whatever the weather and however difficult the cutting, I always work with the pleasure that one invariably gets from using a good tool. And because it is not motor driven and is quiet and odorless, the Marugg scythe also allows the pleasure of awareness of what is going on around you as you work.

12   The other difference is between kinds of weariness. Using the Marugg scythe causes the simple bodily weariness that comes with exertion. This is a kind of weariness that, when not extreme, can in itself be one of the pleasures of work. The power scythe, on the other hand, adds to the weariness of exertion the unpleasant and destructive weariness of strain. This is partly because, in addition to carrying and handling it, your attention is necessarily clenched to it; if you are to use it effectively and safely, you *must* not look away. And partly it is because the power scythe, like all motor-driven tools, imposes patterns of endurance that are alien to the body. As long as the motor is running there is a pressure to keep going. You don't stop to consider a rest or look around. You keep on until the motor stops or the job is finished or you have some kind of trouble. (This explains why the tractor soon evolved headlights, and farmers began to do daywork at night.)

13   These differences have come to have, for me, the force of a parable. Once you have mastered the Marugg scythe, what an absurd thing it makes of the power scythe! What possible sense can there be in carrying a heavy weight on your shoulder in order to reduce by a very little the use of your arms? Or to use quite a lot of money as a substitute for a little skill?

14   The power scythe—and it is far from being an isolated or unusual example—is *not* a labor saver or a shortcut. It is a labor maker (you have to work to pay for it as well as to use it) and a long cut. Apologists for such expensive technological solutions love to say that "you can't turn back the clock." But when it makes perfect sense to do so—as when the clock is wrong—of *course* you can!

Topics for Writing and Discussion

1. What two items is Berry contrasting? What is his thesis?
2. In light of this thesis, what is the purpose of this essay? In other words, what larger point is Berry making about modern "labor-saving devices"?
3. What, according to Berry, are the most important differences between the two tools?
4. Describe the organization of Berry's essay. Does he use the block method, point-by-point, or some combination? Is his choice effective? Why or why not?
5. Think of another "modern convenience" in your home or place of work designed to save you time and trouble. Does this piece of technology come with its own set of problems, as did Berry's power scythe?

NEAT PEOPLE VS. SLOPPY PEOPLE

Suzanne Britt

(1946–   )

Born in Winston-Salem, North Carolina, Suzanne Britt received a bachelor's degree from Salem College and a master's degree in English from Washington University. She has taught English at North Carolina State University at Raleigh and has published a textbook, *A Writer's Rhetoric* (1988), and two collections of essays, *Show and Tell* (1982) and *Skinny People Are Dull and Crunchy Like Carrots* (1992). She now works as a columnist and feature writer for various newspapers, including the *New York Times* and the *Boston Globe*, and for *Newsweek* magazine. In "Neat People vs. Sloppy People," she slyly comments on two groups of people: those who are organized and those who are not.

1   I'VE finally figured out the difference between neat people and sloppy people. The distinction is, as always, moral. Neat people are lazier and meaner than sloppy people.

2   Sloppy people, you see, are not really sloppy. Their sloppiness is merely the unfortunate consequence of their extreme moral rectitude. Sloppy people carry in their mind's eye a heavenly vision, a precise plan, that is so stupendous, so perfect, it can't be achieved in this world or the next.

3   Sloppy people live in Never-Never Land. Someday is their **métier**. Someday they are planning to alphabetize all their books and set up home catalogues. Someday they will go through their wardrobes and mark certain items for tentative mending and certain items for passing on to relatives of similar shape and size. Someday sloppy people will make family scrapbooks into which they will put newspaper clippings, postcards, locks of hair, and the fried corsage from their senior prom. Someday they will file everything on the surface of their desks, including the cash receipts from coffee purchases at the snack shop. Someday they will sit down and read all the back issues of *The New Yorker*.

Suzanne Britt (Courtesy of Suzanne Britt)

4   For all these noble reasons and more, sloppy people never get neat. They aim too high and wide. They save everything, planning someday to file, order, and straighten out the world. But while these ambitious plans take clearer and clearer shape in their heads, the books spill from the shelves onto the floor, the clothes pile up in the hamper and closet, the family mementos accumulate in every drawer, the surface of the desk is buried under mounds of paper and the unread magazines threaten to reach the ceiling.

5   Sloppy people can't bear to part with anything. They give loving attention to every detail. When sloppy people say they're going to tackle the surface of the desk, they really mean it. Not a paper will go unturned; not a rubber band will go unboxed. Four hours or two weeks into the excavation, the desk looks exactly the same, primarily because the sloppy person is meticulously creating new piles of papers with new headings and scrupulously stopping to read all the old book catalogs before he throws them away. A neat person would just bulldoze the desk.

6   Neat people are bums and clods at heart. They have cavalier attitudes toward possessions, including family heirlooms. Everything is just another dust-catcher to them. If anything collects dust, it's got to go and that's that. Neat people will toy with the idea of throwing the children out of the house just to cut down on the clutter.

7   Neat people don't care about process. They like results. What they want to do is get the whole thing over with so they can sit down and watch the rasslin' on TV. Neat people operate on two unvarying principles: Never handle any item twice, and throw everything away.

8   The only thing messy in a neat person's house is the trash can. The minute something comes to a neat person's hand, he will look at it, try to decide if it has immediate use and, finding none, throw it in the trash.

9   Neat people are especially vicious with mail. They never go through their mail unless they are standing directly over a trash can. If the trash can is beside the mailbox, even better. All ads, catalogs, pleas for charitable contributions, church bulletins and money-saving coupons go straight into the trash can without being opened. All letters from home, postcards from Europe, bills and paychecks are opened, immediately responded to, then dropped in the trash can. Neat people keep their receipts only for tax purposes. That's it. No sentimental salvaging of birthday cards or the last letter a dying relative ever wrote. Into the trash it goes.

10 Neat people place neatness above everything, even economics. They are incredibly wasteful. Neat people throw away several toys every time they walk through the den. I knew a neat person once who threw away a perfectly good dish drainer because it had mold on it. The drainer was too much trouble to wash. And neat people sell their furniture when they move. They will sell a La-Z-Boy recliner while you are reclining in it.

11 Neat people are no good to borrow from. Neat people buy everything in expensive little single portions. They get their flour and sugar in two-pound bags. They wouldn't consider clipping a coupon, saving a leftover, reusing plastic non-dairy whipped cream containers or rinsing off tin foil and draping it over the

unmoldy dish drainer. You can never borrow a neat person's newspaper to see what's playing at the movies. Neat people have the paper all wadded up and in the trash by 7:05 A.M.

12   Neat people cut a clean swath through the organic as well as the inorganic world. People, animals, and things are all one to them. They are so insensitive. After they've finished with the pantry, the medicine cabinet, and the attic, they will throw out the red geranium (too many leaves), sell the dog (too many fleas), and send the children off to boarding school (too many scuffmarks on the hardwood floors).

Topics for Writing and Discussion

1. What is the purpose of this essay? Is this an entirely serious analysis of these character types? What effects do you think Britt wants to have on her readers?
2. Summarize Britt's attitude toward neat and sloppy people. Which type does she prefer, and why? Do you agree with her on any points?
3. Which method of development did Britt choose to organize her contrast essay? Is it an effective choice? Why or why not?
4. Throughout her essay, Britt uses broad generalizations, highly connotative language, and a host of exaggerated examples. What do these techniques add to the tone of her claims?
5. Sometimes humor helps us see our character traits (and flaws) in a clearer light. What other kinds of people might you contrast in a lighthearted way? Consider, for example, morning people versus night people, athletes versus couch potatoes, computer geniuses versus the technologically impaired, television watchers versus readers, smokers versus nonsmokers. Remember to make a point about your subjects.

MY HORSE

Barry Lopez
(1945–   )

Barry Lopez's works reflect his deep concern for the
environment and its inhabitants. His most ambitious
work about natural history, *Arctic Dreams: Imagination and Desire in a Northern Landscape* (1986), is
widely acclaimed, and he has been compared to naturalist writers such as Loren Eiseley and Edward Abbey.
He has received the Award in Literature from the
American Academy and Institute of Arts and Letters
for the body of his work. His works also include *Crossing Open Ground* (1988), *Crow and Weasel* (1990),
Lessons from the Wolverine (1997), and *About This
Life* (1998). In "My Horse," first published in the
North American Review, Lopez considers the connection between modern-day American road warriors and
their Native-American predecessors.

1   It is curious that Indian warriors on the northern plains in the nineteenth
century, who were almost entirely dependent on the horse for mobility and status, never gave their horses names. If you borrowed a man's horse and went off
raiding for other horses, however, or if you lost your mount in battle and then
jumped on mine and counted coup on an enemy—well, those horses would
have to be shared with the man whose horse you borrowed, and that coup
would be mine, not yours. Because even if I gave him no name, he was my
horse.

2   If you were a Crow warrior and I a young Teton Sioux out after a warrior's
identity and we came over a small hill somewhere in the Montana prairie and
surprised each other, I could tell a lot about you by looking at your horse.

3   Your horse might have feathers tied in his mane, or in his tail, or a medicine bag tied around his neck. If I knew enough about the Crow, and had
looked at you closely, I might make some sense of the decoration, even guess
who you were if you were well-known. If you had painted your horse I could

Barry Lopez (AP/Wide World Photos, Inc.)

tell even more, because we both decorated our horses with signs that meant the same things. Your white handprints high on his flanks would tell me you had killed an enemy in a hand-to-hand fight. Small horizontal lines stacked on your horse's foreleg, or across his nose, would tell me how many times you had counted coup. Horse hoof marks on your horse's rump, or three-sided boxes, would tell me how many times you had stolen horses. If there was a bright red square on your horse's neck I would know you were leading a war party and that there were probably others out there in the coulees behind you.

4   You might be painted all over as blue as the sky and covered with white dots, with your horse painted the same way. Maybe hailstorms were your power—or if I chased you a hailstorm might come down and hide you. There might be lightning bolts on the horse's legs and flanks, and I would wonder if you had lightning power, or a slow horse. There might be white circles around your horse's eyes to help him see better.

5   Or you might be like Crazy Horse, with no decoration, no marks on your horse to tell me anything, only a small lightning bolt on your cheek, a piece of turquoise tied behind your ear.

6   You might have scalps dangling from your rein.

7   I could tell something about you by your horse. All this would come to me in a few seconds. I might decide this was my moment and shout my war cry—*Hoka hey!* Or I might decide you were like the grizzly bear: I would raise my weapon to you in salute and go my way, to see you again when I was older.

8   I do not own a horse. I am attached to a truck, however, and I have come to think of it in a similar way. It has no name; it never occurred to me to give it a name. It has little decoration; neither of us is partial to decoration. I have a piece of turquoise in the truck because I had heard once that some of the southwestern tribes tied a small piece of turquoise in a horse's hock to keep him from stumbling. I like the idea. I also hang sage in the truck when I go on a long trip. But inside, the truck doesn't look much different from others that look just like it on the outside. I like it that way. Because I like my privacy.

9   For two years in Wyoming I worked on a ranch wrangling horses. The horse I rode when I had to have a good horse was a quarter horse and his name was Coke High. The name came with him. At first I thought he'd been named for a soft drink. I'd known stranger names given to horses by whites. Years later I wondered if some deviate Wyoming cowboy wise to cocaine had not named him. Now I think he was probably named after a rancher, an historical figure of the region. I never asked the people who owned him for fear of spoiling the spirit of my inquiry.

10   We were running over a hundred horses on this ranch. They all had names. After a few weeks I knew all the horses and the names too. You had to. No one knew how to talk about the animals or put them in order to tell the wranglers what to do unless they were using the names—Princess, Big Red, Shoshone, Clay.

11   My truck is named Dodge. The name came with it. I don't know if it was named after the town or the verb or the man who invented it. I like it for a

name. Perfectly anonymous, like Rex for a dog, or Old Paint. You can't tell anything with a name like that.

12 The truck is a van. I call it a truck because it's not a car and because "van"
is a suburban sort of consumer word, like "oxford loafer," and I don't like the
sound of it. On the outside it looks like any other Dodge Sportsman 300. It's a
dirty tan color. There are a few body dents, but it's never been in a wreck. I tore
the antenna off against a tree on a pinched mountain road. A boy in Midland,
Texas, rocked one of my rear view mirrors off. A logging truck in Oregon
squeeze-fired a piece of debris off the road and shattered my windshield. The
oil pan and gas tank are pug-faced from high-centering on bad roads. (I remember a horse I rode for a while named Targhee whose hocks were scarred
from tangles in barbed wire when he was a colt and who spooked a lot in high
grass, but these were not like "dents." They were more like bad tires.)

13 I like to travel. I go mostly in the winter and mostly on two-lane roads. I've
driven the truck from Key West to Vancouver, British Columbia, and from
Yuma to Long Island over the past four years. I used to ride Coke High only
about five miles every morning when we were rounding up horses. Hard miles
of twisting and turning. About six hundred miles a year. Then I'd turn him out
and ride another horse for the rest of the day. That's what was nice about having a remuda. You could do all you had to do and not take it all out on your
best horse. Three car family.

14 My truck came with a lot of seats in it and I've never really known what to
do with them. Sometimes I put the seats in and go somewhere with a lot of
people, but most of the time I leave them out. I like riding around with that
empty cavern of space behind my head. I know it's something with a history to
it, that there's truth in it, because I always rode a horse the same way—with
empty saddle bags. In case I found something. The possibility of finding something is half the reason for being on the road.

15 The value of anything comes to me in its use. If I am not using something
it is of no value to me and I give it away. I wasn't always that way. I used to keep
everything I owned—just in case. I feel good about the truck because it gets
used. A lot. To haul hay and firewood and lumber and rocks and garbage and
animals. Other people have used it to haul furniture and freezers and dirt and
recycled newspapers. And to move from one house to another. When I lend it
for things like that I don't look to get anything back but some gas (if we're
going to be friends). But if you go way out in the country to a dump and pick
up the things you can still find out there (once a load of cedar shingles we sold
for $175 to an architect) I expect you to leave some of those things around my
place when you come back—if I need them.

16 When I think back, maybe the nicest thing I ever put in that truck was timber wolves. It was a long night's drive from Oregon up into British Columbia.
We were all very quiet about it; it was like moving clouds across the desert.

17 Sometimes something won't fit in the truck and I think about improving
it—building a different door system, for example. I am forever going to add
better gauges on the dash and a pair of driving lamps and a sunroof, but

I never get around to doing any of it. I remember I wanted to improve Coke High once too, especially the way he bolted like a greyhound through patches of cottonwood on a river flat. But all I could do with him was to try to rein him out of it. Or hug his back.

18   Sometimes, road-stoned in a blur of country like southwestern Wyoming or North Dakota, I talk to the truck. It's like wandering on the high plains under a summer sun, on plains where, George Catlin wrote, you were "out of sight of land." I say what I am thinking out loud, or point at things along the road. It's a crazy, sun-stroked sort of activity, a sure sign it's time to pull over, to go for a walk, to make a fire and have some tea, to lie in the shade of the truck.

19   I've always wanted to pat the truck. It's basic to the relationship. But it never works.

20   I remember when I was on the ranch, just at sunrise, after I'd saddled Coke High, I'd be huddled down in my jacket smoking a cigarette and looking down into the valley, along the river where the other horses had spent the night. I'd turn to Coke and run my hand down his neck and slap-pat him on the shoulder to say I was coming up. It made a bond, an agreement we started the day with.

21   I've thought about that a lot with the truck, because we've gone out together at sunrise on so many mornings. I've even fumbled around trying to do it. But metal won't give.

22   The truck's personality is mostly an expression of two ideas: "with-you" and "alone." When Coke High was "with-you" he and I were the same animal. We could have cut a rooster out of a flock of chickens, we were so in tune. It's the same with the truck: rolling through Kentucky on a hilly two-lane road, three in the morning under a full moon and no traffic. Picture it. You roll like water.

23   There are other times when you are with each other but there's no connection at all. Coke got that way when he was bored and we'd fight each other about which way to go around a tree. When the truck gets like that— "alone"—it's because it feels its Detroit fat-ass design dragging at its heart and making a fool out of it.

24   I can think back over more than a hundred nights I've slept in the truck, sat in it with a lamp burning, bundled up in a parka, reading a book. It was always comfortable. A good place to wait out a storm. Like sleeping inside a buffalo.

25   The truck will go past 100,000 miles soon. I'll rebuild the engine and put a different transmission in it. I can tell from magazine advertisements that I'll never get another one like it. Because every year they take more of the heart out of them. One thing that makes a farmer or a rancher go sour is a truck that isn't worth a shit. The reason you see so many old pickups in ranch country is because these are the only ones with any heart. You can count on them. The weekend rancher runs around in a new pickup with too much engine and not enough transmission and with the wrong sort of tires because he can afford anything, even the worst. A lot of them have names for their pickups too.

26   My truck has broken down, in out of the way places at the worst of times. I've walked away and screamed the foulness out of my system and gotten the tools out. I had to fix a water pump in a blizzard in the Panamint Mountains in California once. It took all day with the Coleman stove burning under the engine block to keep my hands from freezing. We drifted into Beatty, Nevada, that night with it jury-rigged together with—I swear—baling wire, and we were melting snow as we went and pouring it in to compensate for the leaks.

27   There is a dent next to the door on the driver's side I put there one sweltering night in Miami. I had gone to the airport to meet my wife, whom I hadn't seen in a month. My hands were so swollen with poison ivy blisters I had to drive with my wrists. I had shut the door and was locking it when the window fell off its runners and slid down inside the door. I couldn't leave the truck unlocked because I had too much inside I didn't want to lose. So I just kicked the truck a blow in the side and went to work on the window. I hate to admit kicking the truck. It's like kicking a dog, which I've never done.

28   Coke High and I had an accident once. We hit a badger hole at a full gallop. I landed on my back and blacked out. When I came to, Coke High was about a hundred yards away. He stayed a hundred yards away for six miles, all the way back to the ranch.

29   I want to tell you about carrying those wolves, because it was a fine thing. There were ten of them. We had four in the truck with us in crates and six in a trailer. It was a five hundred mile trip. We went at night for the cool air and because there wouldn't be as much traffic. I could feel from the way the truck rolled along that its heart was in the trip. It liked the wolves inside it, the sweet odor that came from the crates. I could feel that same tireless wolf-lope developing in its wheels; it was like you might never have to stop for gas, ever again.

30   The truck gets very self-focused when it works like this; its heart is strong and it's good to be around it. It's good to be *with* it. You get the same feeling when you pull someone out of a ditch. Coke High and I pulled a Volkswagen out of the mud once, but Coke didn't like doing it very much. Speed, not strength, was his center. When the guy who owned the car thanked us and tried to pat Coke, the horse snorted and swung away, trying to preserve his distance, which is something a horse spends a lot of time on.

31   So does the truck.

32   Being distant lets the truck get its heart up. The truck has been cold and alone in Montana at 38 below zero. It's climbed horrible, eroded roads in Idaho. It's been burdened beyond overloading, and made it anyway. I've asked it to do these things because they build heart, and without heart all you have is a machine. You have nothing. I don't think people in Detroit know anything at all about heart. That's why everything they build dies so young.

33   One time in Arizona the truck and I came through one of the worst storms I've ever been in, an outrageous, angry blizzard. But we went down the road, right through it. You couldn't explain our getting through by the sort of tires I had on the truck, or the fact that I had chains on, or was a good driver, or had a lot of weight over my drive wheels or a good engine, because it was more than this. It was a contest between the truck and the blizzard—and the truck

wouldn't quit. I could have gone to sleep and the truck would have just torn a road down Interstate 40 on its own. It scared the hell out of me; but it gave me heart, too.

34   We came off the Mogollon Rim that night and out of the storm and headed south for Phoenix. I pulled off the road to sleep for a few hours, but before I did I got out of the truck. It was raining. Warm rain. I tied a short piece of red avalanche cord into the grill. I left it there for a long time, like an eagle feather on a horse's tail. It flapped and spun in the wind. I could hear it ticking against the grill when I drove.

35   When I have to leave that truck I will just raise up my left arm— *Hoka hey!*—and walk away.

TOPICS FOR WRITING AND DISCUSSION

1. What analogy is Lopez drawing in this essay? What similarities does he see? Differences?
2. How does Lopez make the comparison clear to the reader? What techniques are most persuasive? Why?
3. How does Lopez's use of first-person point of view affect the reader's response to the essay?
4. Consider the essay's structure: is it formal or informal? How does his mention of transporting the wolves (paragraphs 16 and 29) affect essay unity? How does the essay's conclusion help tie the essay together?
5. Using Lopez's essay as a guide, write an essay comparing or contrasting a living creature to a mechanical object (for example, your best friend and your car, your mortal enemy and your computer). Make the point of your essay clear to the reader—why is it important to see your subject in this way?

Toni Morrison in her home along the Hudson River (© Sara Krulwich/The New York Times Pictures)

A Slow Walk of Trees

Toni Morrison
(1931–   )

Born Chloe Anthony Wofford in Lorain, Ohio, Toni
Morrison (she uses a shortened version of her middle
name) was the second of four children of Alabama
sharecroppers who had migrated north. She holds a
bachelor of arts degree in English from Howard University and a master of arts degree from Cornell University. An educator and acclaimed novelist, Morrison has
written seven novels including *Song of Solomon*
(1977), which received the National Book Critics Circle Award, and *Beloved* (1987), winner of the Pulitzer
Prize. Her most recent work is *Paradise* (1998); her
Harvard University lectures are collected in *Playing in
the Dark: Whiteness and the Literary Imagination*
(1992). Her extraordinary work as a writer earned her
the 1993 Nobel Prize for Literature, the first African-
American to receive the award. "A Slow Walk of
Trees," which first appeared in the July 4, 1976, *New
York Times Magazine*, contrasts the way her grandfa-
ther and grandmother viewed the history of African-
American people in America.

---

1   His name was John Solomon Willis, and when at age 5 he heard from the
old folks that "the Emancipation Proclamation was coming," he crawled
under the bed. It was his earliest recollection of what was to be his habitual response to the promise of white people: horror and an instinctive yearning
for safety. He was my grandfather, a musician who managed to hold on to his
violin but not his land. He lost all 88 acres of his Indian mother's inheritance
to legal predators who built their fortunes on the likes of him. He was an un-
reconstructed black pessimist who, in spite of or because of emancipation, was

convinced for 85 years that there was no hope whatever for black people in this country. His rancor was legitimate, for he, John Solomon, was not only an artist but a first-rate carpenter and farmer, reduced to sending home to his family money he made playing the violin because he was not able to find work. And this during the years when almost half the black male population were skilled craftsmen who lost their jobs to white ex-convicts and immigrant farmers.

2   His wife, however, was of a quite different frame of mind and believed that all things could be improved by faith in Jesus and an effort of the will. So it was she, Ardelia Willis, who sneaked her seven children out of the back window into the darkness, rather than permit the patron of their sharecropper's existence to become their executioner as well, and headed north in 1912, when 99.2 percent of all black people in the U.S. were native-born and only 60 percent of white Americans were. And it was Ardelia who told her husband that they could not stay in the Kentucky town they ended up in because the teacher didn't know long division.

3   They have been dead now for 30 years and more and I still don't know which of them came closer to the truth about the possibilities of life for black people in this country. One of their grandchildren is a tenured professor at Princeton. Another, who suffered from what the Peruvian poet called "anger that breaks a man into children," was picked up just as he entered his teens and emotionally lobotomized by the reformatories and mental institutions specifically designed to serve him. Neither John Solomon nor Ardelia lived long enough to despair over one or swell with pride over the other. But if they were alive today each would have selected and collected enough evidence to support the accuracy of the other's original point of view. And it would be difficult to convince either one that the other was right.

4   Some of the monstrous events that took place in John Solomon's America have been duplicated in alarming detail in my own America. There was the public murder of a President in a theater in 1865 and the public murder of another President on television in 1963. The Civil War of 1861 had its encore as the civil-rights movement of 1960. The torture and mutilation of a black West Point Cadet (Cadet Johnson Whittaker) in 1880 had its rerun with the 1970's murders of students at Jackson State College, Texas Southern and Southern University in Baton Rouge. And in 1976 we watch for what must be the thousandth time a pitched battle between the children of slaves and the children of immigrants—only this time, it is not the New York draft riots of 1863, but the busing turmoil in Paul Revere's home town, Boston.

5   Hopeless, he'd said. Hopeless. For he was certain that white people of every political, religious, geographical and economic background would band together against black people everywhere when they felt the threat of our progress. And a hundred years after he sought safety from the white man's "promise," somebody put a bullet in Martin Luther King's brain. And not long before that some excellent samples of the master race demonstrated their courage and virility by dynamiting some little black girls to death. If he were here now, my grandfather, he would shake his head, close his eyes and pull out his violin—too polite to say, "I told you so." And his wife would pay attention

to the music but not to the sadness in her husband's eyes, for she would see what she expected to see—not the occasional historical repetition, but, *like the slow walk of certain species of trees from the flatlands up into the mountains,* she would see the signs of irrevocable and permanent change. She, who pulled her girls out of an inadequate school in the Cumberland Mountains, knew all along that the gentlemen from Alabama who had killed the little girls would be rounded up. And it wouldn't surprise her in the least to know that the number of black college graduates jumped 12 percent in the last three years: 47 percent in 20 years. That there are 140 black mayors in this country; 14 black judges in the District Circuit, 4 in the Courts of Appeals and one on the Supreme Court. That there are 17 blacks in Congress, one in the Senate; 276 in state legislatures—223 in state houses, 53 in state senates. That there are 112 elected black police chiefs and sheriffs, 1 Pulitzer Prize winner; 1 winner of the Prix de Rome; a dozen or so winners of the Guggenheim; 4 deans of predominantly white colleges. . . . Oh, her list would go on and on. But so would John Solomon's sweet sad music.

6   While my grandparents held opposite views on whether the fortunes of black people were improving, my own parents struck similarly opposed postures, but from another slant. They differed about whether the moral fiber of white people would ever improve. Quite a different argument. The old folks argued about how and if black people could improve themselves, who could be counted on to help us, who would hinder us and so on. My parents took issue over the question of whether it was possible for white people to improve. They assumed that black people were the humans of the globe, but had serious doubts about the quality and existence of white humanity. Thus my father, distrusting every word and every gesture of every white man on earth, assumed that the white man who crept up the stairs one afternoon had come to molest his daughters and threw him down the stairs and then our tricycle after him. (I think my father was wrong, but considering what I have seen since, it may have been very healthy for me to have witnessed that as my first black-white encounter.) My mother, however, *believed* in them—their possibilities. So when the meal we got on relief was bug-ridden, she wrote a long letter to Franklin Delano Roosevelt. And when white bill collectors came to our door, it was she who received them civilly and explained in a sweet voice that we were people of honor and that the debt would be taken care of. Her message to Roosevelt got through—our meal improved. Her message to the bill collectors did not always get through and there was occasional violence when my father (self-exiled to the bedroom for fear he could not hold his temper) would hear that her reasonableness had failed. My mother was always wounded by these scenes, for she thought the bill collector knew that she loved good credit more than life and that being in arrears on a payment horrified her probably more than it did him. So she thought he was rude because he was white. For years she walked to utility companies and department stores to pay bills in person and even now she does not seem convinced that checks are legal tender. My father loved excellence, worked hard (he held three jobs at once for 17 years) and was so outraged by the suggestion of personal slackness that he could explain

it to himself only in terms of racism. He was a fastidious worker who was frightened of one thing: unemployment. I can remember now the doomsday-cum-graveyard sound of "laid off" and how the minute school was out he asked us, "Where you workin'?" Both my parents believed that all succor and aid came from themselves and their neighborhood, since "they"—white people in charge and those not in charge but in obstructionist positions—were in some way fundamentally, genetically corrupt.

7   So I grew up in a basically racist household with more than a child's share of contempt for white people. And for each white friend I acquired who made a small crack in that contempt, there was another who repaired it. For each one who related to me as a person, there was one who in my presence at least, became actively "white." And like most black people of my generation, I suffer from racial vertigo that can be cured only by taking what one needs from one's ancestors. John Solomon's cynicism and his deployment of his art as both weapon and solace, Ardelia's faith in the magic that can be wrought by sheer effort of the will; my mother's open-mindedness in each new encounter and her habit of trying reasonableness first; my father's temper, his impatience and his efforts to keep "them" (throw them) out of his life. And it is out of these learned and selected attitudes that I look at the quality of life for my people in this country now. These widely disparate and sometimes conflicting views, I suspect, were held not only by me, but by most black people. Some I know are clearer in their positions, have not sullied their anger with optimism or dirtied their hope with despair. But most of us are plagued by a sense of being worn shell-thin by constant repression and hostility as well as the impression of being buoyed by visible testimony of tremendous strides. There *is* repetition of the grotesque in our history. And there *is* the miraculous walk of trees. The question is whether our walk is progress or merely movement. O. J. Simpson leaning on a Hertz car *is* better than the Gold Dust Twins on the back of a soap box. But is "Good Times" better than Stepin Fetchit? Has the first order of business been taken care of? Does the law of the land work for us?

8   Are white people who murder black people punished with at least the same dispatch that sends black teen-age truants to Coxsackie? Can we relax now and discuss "The Jeffersons" instead of genocide? Or is the difference between the two only the difference between a greedy pointless white lifestyle and a messy pointless black death? Now that Mr. Poitier and Mr. Belafonte have shot up all the racists in "Buck and the Preacher," have they all gone away? Can we really move into better neighborhoods and not be set on fire? Is there anybody who will lay me a $5 bet on it?

9   The past decade is a fairly good index of the odds at which you lay your money down.

10   Ten years ago in Queens, as black people like me moved into a neighborhood 20 minutes away from the Triborough Bridge, "for sale" signs shot up in front of white folks' houses like dandelions after a hot spring rain. And the black people smiled. "Goody, goody," said my neighbor. "Maybe we can push them on out to sea. You think?"

11   Now I live in another neighborhood, 20 minutes away from the George Washington Bridge, and again the "for sale" signs are pushing up out of the ground. Fewer, perhaps, and for different reasons, perhaps. Still the Haitian lady and I smile at each other. "My, my," she says "they goin' on up to the hills? Seem like they just come from there." "The woods," I say. "They like to live in the woods." She nods with infinite understanding, then shrugs. The Haitians have already arranged for one mass in the church to be said in French, already have their own newspaper, stores, community center. That's not movement. That's progress.

12   But the decade has other revelations. Ten years ago, young, bright, energetic blacks were sought out, pursued and hired into major corporations, major networks, and onto the staffs of newspapers and national magazines. *Many survived that courtship, some even with their souls intact.* Newscasters, corporate lawyers, marketing specialists, journalists, production managers, plant foremen, college deans. But many more spend a lot of time on the telephone these days, or at the typewriter preparing résumés, which they send out (mostly to friends now) with little notes attached: "Is there anything you know of?" Or they think there is a good book in the story of what happened to them, the great hoax that was played on them. They are right, of course, about the hoax, for many of them were given elegant executive jobs with the work drained out. Work minus power. Work minus decision-making. Work minus dominion. Affirmative Action Make Believe that a lot of black people *did* believe because they also believed that the white people in those nice offices were not like the ones in the general store or in the plumbers' union—that they were fundamentally kind, or fair, or something. Anything but the desperate prisoners of economics they turned out to be, holding on to their dominion with a tenacity and sang-froid that can only be described as Nixonian. So the bright and the black (architects, reporters, vice-presidents in charge of public relations) walk the streets right along with that astounding 38 percent of the black teen-aged female work force that does not have and never has had a job. So the black female college graduate earns two-thirds of what a white male high-school dropout earns. So the black people who put everything into community-action programs supported by Government funds have found themselves bereft of action, bereft of funds and all but bereft of community.

13   This decade has been rife with disappointment in practically every place where we thought we saw permanent change: Hostos, CUNY, and the black-studies departments that erupted like minivolcanoes on campuses all over the nation; easy integrations of public-school systems; acceleration of promotion in factories and businesses. But now when we describe what has happened we cannot do it without using the verbs of upheaval and destruction: Open admission *closes;* minority-student quotas *fall* or *discontinue;* salary gaps between blacks and whites *widen;* black-studies departments *merge.* And the only growth black people can count on is in the prison population and the unemployment line. Even busing, which used to be a plain, if emotional, term at best, has now taken on an adjective normally reserved for rape and burglary—it is now called "forced" busing.

14   All of that counts, but I'm not sure that in the long haul it matters. Maybe
Ardelia Willis had the best idea. One sees signs of her vision and the fruits of
her prophecy in spite of the dread-lock statistics. The trees *are* walking, albeit
slowly and quietly and without the fanfare of a cross-country run. It seems
that at last black people have abandoned our foolish dependency on the
Government to do the work that we once thought all of its citizenry would be
delighted to do. Our love affair with the Federal Government is over. We mis-
judged the ardor of its attention. We thought its majority constituency would
prefer having their children grow up among happy, progressive, industrious,
contented black children rather than among angry, disenchanted and dangerous ones. That the profit motive of industry alone would keep us employed and
therefore spending, and that our poverty was bad for business. We thought
landlords wanted us to have a share in our neighborhoods and therefore love
and care for them. That city governments wanted us to control our schools
and therefore preserve them.

15   We were wrong. And now, having been eliminated from the lists of urgent
national priorities, from TV documentaries and the platitudes of editorials,
black people have chosen, or been forced to seek safety from the white man's
promise, but happily not under a bed. More and more, there is the return of
Ardelia's ways: the exercise of the will, the recognition of obstacles as only
that—obstacles, not fixed stars. Black judges are fixing appropriate rather than
punitive bail for black "offenders" and letting the rest of the community of ju-
risprudence scream. Young black women are leaving plush Northern jobs to sit
in their living rooms and teach black children, work among factory women
and spend months finding money to finance the college education of young
blacks. Groups of blacks are buying huge tracts of land in the South and cutting off entirely the dependency of whole communities on grocery chains. For
the first time, significant numbers of black people are returning or migrating
to the South to focus on the acquisition of land, the transferral of crafts and
skills, and the sharing of resources, the rebuilding of neighborhoods.

16   In the shambles of closing admissions, falling quotas, widening salary gaps
and merging black-studies departments, builders and healers are working quietly among us. They are not like the heroes of old, the leaders we followed
blindly and upon whom we depended for everything, or the blacks who had
accumulated wealth for its own sake, fame, medals or some public acknowl-
edgment of success. These are the people whose work is real and pointed and
clear in its application to the race. Some are old and have been at work for a
long time in and out of the public eye. Some are new and just finding out what
their work is. But they are unmistakably the natural aristocrats of the race.
The ones who refuse to imitate, to compromise, and who are indifferent to
public accolade. Whose work is free or priceless. They take huge risks economically and personally. They are not always popular, even among black
people, but they are the ones whose work black people respect. They are the
healers. Some are nowhere near the public eye: Ben Chavis, preacher and political activist languishing now in North Carolina prisons; Robert Moses, a

pioneering activist; Sterling Brown, poet and teacher; Father Al McKnight, land reformer; Rudy Lombard, urban sociologist; Lerone Bennett, historian; C.L.R. James, scholar; Alyce Gullattee, psychologist and organizer. Others are public legends: Judge Crockett, Judge Bruce Wright, Stevie Wonder, Ishmael Reed, Miles Davis, Richard Pryor, Muhammad Ali, Fannie Lou Hamer, Eubie Blake, Angela Davis, Bill Russell. . . .

17   But a complete roll-call is neither fitting nor necessary. They know who they are and so do we. They clarify our past, make livable our present and are certain to shape our future. And since the future is where our immortality as a race lies, no overview of the state of black people at this time can ignore some speculation on the only ones certain to live it—the children.

18   They are both exhilarating and frightening, those black children, and a source of wonderment to me. Although statistics about black teen-age crime and the "failure" of the courts to gut them are regularly printed and regularly received with outrage and fear, the children I know and see, those born after 1960, do not make such great copy. They are those who have grown up with nothing to prove to white people, whose perceptions of themselves are so new, so different, so focused they appear to me to be either magnificent hybrids or throwbacks to the time when our ancestors were called "royal." They are the baby sisters of the sit-in generation, the sons of the neighborhood blockbusters, the nephews of jailed revolutionaries, and a huge number who have had college graduates in their families for three and four generations. I thought we had left them nothing to love and nothing to want to know. I thought that those who exhibited some excitement about their future had long ago looked into the eyes of their teachers and were either saddened or outraged by the death of possibility they found there. I thought that those who were interested in the past had looked into the faces of their parents and seen betrayal. I thought the state had deprived them of a land and the landlords and banks had deprived them of a turf. So how is it that, with nothing to love, nothing they need to know, landless, turfless, minus a future and a past, these black children look us dead in the eye? They seem not to know how to apologize. And even when they are wrong they do not ask for forgiveness. It is as though they are waiting for us to apologize to them, to get their pardon, to seek their approval. What species of black is this that not only does not choose to grovel, but doesn't know how? How will they keep jobs? How will they live? Won't they be killed before they reproduce? But they are unafraid. Is it because they refuse to see the world as we did? Is it because they have rejected both land and turf to seek instead a world? Maybe they finally got the message that we had been shouting into their faces; that they *live* here, *belong* here on this planet earth and that it is *theirs*. So they watch us with the eyes of poets and carpenters and musicians and scholars and other people who know who they are because they have invented themselves and know where they are going because they have envisioned it. All of which would please Ardelia—and John Solomon, too, I think. After all, he did hold on to his violin.

Topics for Writing and Discussion

1. How did Morrison's grandfather view the future of African-Americans in the United States? How did her grandmother view that same future? List five details from the essay that could be used to support her grandfather's view and five details that could be used to support her grandmother's.
2. What is Morrison's main idea in this essay? Does she ever directly state her thesis? With whose ideas does she seem to identify most closely, those of her grandmother or of her grandfather?
3. Read the section of the essay comparing the situations of African-Americans ten years before the essay was written to the situations of African-Americans living at the time Morrison was writing. How does that comparison relate to the main comparison of the essay?
4. What kind of details, reasons, and examples does Morrison use to develop her ideas? Note, for instance, her use of statistics as well as her use of personal anecdotes.
5. Morrison uses the analogy of "the slow walk of certain species of trees from the flatlands up into the mountains" to describe the way her grandmother saw the progress of African-Americans. Develop your own analogy to describe the way you see changes in the course of your own life.

SONNET 130

William Shakespeare
(1564–1616)

William Shakespeare is considered by many as the
greatest writer in the English language. His father may
have been a glovemaker, merchant, and, at one time,
mayor of Stratford-upon-Avon, Shakespeare's birthplace. Young William probably attended grammar
school there and studied literature and Latin. In 1582,
when he was eighteen, he married twenty-six-year-old
Anne Hathaway, who bore him three children. By
1592, he was well known as an actor and playwright in
London. His theater company, the King's Men (named
in honor of their patron, James I), was eventually
housed in the Globe Theater, and in 1608 he bought
the Blackfriars as well. Shakespeare's legacy includes 36
plays, 154 sonnets, and 5 long narrative poems. In this
sonnet, the speaker uses comparison and contrast to
present a realistic, but ultimately affectionate, picture
of his "mistress" rather than a false, flattering one typical of love poems at that time.

My mistress' eyes are nothing like the sun;
Coral is far more red than her lips' red;
If snow be white, why then her breasts are dun;[1]
If hairs be wires, black wires grow on her head.
5 I have seen roses damask'd,[2] red and white,
But no such roses see I in her cheeks,
And in some perfumes there is more delight

---

[1] dull grayish brown
[2] patterned, richly decorated

William Shakespeare (Corbis-Bettmann)

Than in the breath that from my mistress reeks.
I love to hear her speak, yet well I know
10 That music hath a far more pleasing sound.
I grant I never saw a goddess go;
My mistress, when she walks, treads on the ground:
And yet, by heaven, I think my love as rare
As any she belied[3] with false compare.[4]

Topics for Writing and Discussion

1. What comparisons and contrasts do you find in this poem? What sort of picture of his "mistress" does the speaker create?
2. How is this poem different from a traditional love poem in which overstated compliments often play a major role?
3. This poem is written in the form of the English sonnet, also called the Shakespearean sonnet, named after its greatest practitioner. Look up this poetic term in the Glossary at the back of this text and identify its elements in this poem. Does this poem fit the definition in all respects?
4. The Shakespearean sonnet concludes with a couplet, two rhyming lines that often sum up the poem's main idea with a clear or memorable statement. What is the speaker's main point in this sonnet? Is this a love poem, after all?
5. Describe a person you know well by using several vivid comparisons or contrasts. Consider, as did Shakespeare, such features as this person's eyes, lips, hair, complexion, breath, voice, and walk.

---

[3] misrepresented

[4] comparison

Katherine Anne Porter (Archive Photos)

ROPE

Katherine Anne Porter
(1890–1980)

Born Callie Russell Porter in a log cabin in Indian
Creek, Texas, near San Antonio, Katherine Anne Porter
was raised by her father and her paternal grandmother
after the death of her mother in 1892. In 1918, she
moved to Denver and worked as a reporter and theater
critic for the *Rocky Mountain News*. Porter traveled
extensively in the United States and abroad; she lived for
periods of time in Mexico, Belgium, Switzerland, France,
and Germany. Though Porter was interested in writing
even as a child, she did not publish her first story until
she was in her thirties. She wrote essays and one novel,
Ship of Fools (1962), but she is best known for her
finely crafted short stories. Her first collection of stories,
Flowering Judas (1930), won immediate critical acclaim
and earned her a Guggenheim Fellowship. In 1965, her
Collected Stories won the Pulitzer Prize and the
National Book Award. Her story "Rope" exposes a relationship viewed from very different perspectives.

1   ON the third day after they moved to the country he came walking back
from the village carrying a basket of groceries and a twenty-four-yard coil of
rope. She came out to meet him, wiping her hands on her green smock. Her
hair was tumbled, her nose was scarlet with sunburn; he told her that already
she looked like a born country woman. His gray flannel shirt stuck to him, his
heavy shoes were dusty. She assured him he looked like a rural character in
a play.

2   Had he brought the coffee? She had been waiting all day long for coffee.
They had forgot it when they ordered at the store the first day.

3   Gosh, no, he hadn't. Lord, now he'd have to go back. Yes, he would if it
killed him. He thought, though, he had everything else. She reminded him it

was only because he didn't drink coffee himself. If he did he would remember it quick enough. Suppose they ran out of cigarettes? Then she saw the rope. What was that for? Well, he thought it might do to hang clothes on, or something. Naturally she asked him if he thought they were going to run a laundry? They already had a fifty-foot line hanging right before his eyes? Why, hadn't he noticed it, really? It was a blot on the landscape to her.

4   He thought there were a lot of things a rope might come in handy for. She wanted to know what, for instance. He thought a few seconds, but nothing occurred. They could wait and see, couldn't they? You need all sorts of strange odds and ends around a place in the country. She said, yes, that was so; but she thought just at that time when every penny counted, it seemed funny to buy more rope. That was all. She hadn't meant anything else. She hadn't just seen, not at first, why he felt it was necessary.

5   Well, thunder, he had bought it because he wanted to, and that was all there was to it. She thought that was reason enough, and couldn't understand why he hadn't said so, at first. Undoubtedly it would be useful, twenty-four yards of rope, there were hundreds of things, she couldn't think of any at the moment, but it would come in. Of course. As he had said, things always did in the country.

6   But she was a little disappointed about the coffee, and oh, look, look, look at the eggs! Oh, my, they're all running! What had he put on top of them? Hadn't he known eggs mustn't be squeezed? Squeezed, who had squeezed them, he wanted to know. What a silly thing to say. He had simply brought them along in the basket with the other things. If they got broke it was the grocer's fault. He should know better than to put heavy things on top of eggs.

7   She believed it was the rope. That was the heaviest thing in the pack, she saw him plainly when he came in from the road, the rope was a big package on top of everything. He desired the whole wide world to witness that this was not a fact. He had carried the rope in one hand and the basket in the other, and what was the use of her having eyes if that was the best they could do for her?

8   Well, anyhow, she could see one thing plain: no eggs for breakfast. They'd have to scramble them now, for supper. It was too damned bad. She had planned to have steak for supper. No ice, meat wouldn't keep. He wanted to know why she couldn't finish breaking the eggs in a bowl and set them in a cool place.

9   Cool place! if he could find one for her, she'd be glad to set them there. Well, then, it seemed to him they might very well cook the meat at the same time they cooked the eggs and then warm up the meat for tomorrow. The idea simply choked her. Warmed-over meat, when they might as well have had it fresh. Second best and scraps and makeshifts, even to the meat! He rubbed her shoulder a little. It doesn't really matter so much, does it, darling? Sometimes when they were playful, he would rub her shoulder and she would arch and purr. This time she hissed and almost clawed. He was getting ready to say that they could surely manage somehow when she turned on him and said, if he told her they could manage somehow she would certainly slap his face.

10   He swallowed the words red hot, his face burned. He picked up the rope and started to put it on the top shelf. She would not have it on the top shelf, the jars and tins belonged there; positively she would not have the top shelf cluttered up with a lot of rope. She had borne all the clutter she meant to bear in the flat in town, there was space here at least and she meant to keep things in order.

11   Well, in that case, he wanted to know what the hammer and nails were doing up there? And why had she put them there when she knew very well he needed that hammer and those nails upstairs to fix the window sashes? She simply slowed down everything and made double work on the place with her insane habit of changing things around and hiding them.

12   She was sure she begged his pardon, and if she had had any reason to believe he was going to fix the sashes this summer she would have left the hammer and nails right where he put them; in the middle of the bedroom floor where they could step on them in the dark. And now if he didn't clear the whole mess out of there she would throw them down the well.

13   Oh, all right, all right—could he put them in the closet? Naturally not, there were brooms and mops and dustpans in the closet, and why couldn't he find a place for his rope outside her kitchen? Had he stopped to consider there were seven God-forsaken rooms in the house, and only one kitchen?

14   He wanted to know what of it? And did she realize she was making a complete fool of herself? And what did she take him for, a three-year-old idiot? The whole trouble with her was she needed something weaker than she was to heckle and tyrannize over. He wished to God now they had a couple of children she could take it out on. Maybe he'd get some rest.

15   Her face changed at this, she reminded him he had forgot the coffee and had bought a worthless piece of rope. And when she thought of all the things they actually needed to make the place even decently fit to live in, well, she could cry, that was all. She looked so forlorn, so lost and despairing he couldn't believe it was only a piece of rope that was causing all the racket. What *was* the matter, for God's sake?

16   Oh, would he please hush and go away, and *stay* away, if he could, for five minutes? By all means, yes, he would. He'd stay away indefinitely if she wished. Lord, yes, there was nothing he'd like better than to clear out and never come back. She couldn't for the life of her see what was holding him, then. It was a swell time. Here she was, stuck, miles from a railroad, with a half-empty house on her hands, and not a penny in her pocket, and everything on earth to do; it seemed the God-sent moment for him to get out from under. She was surprised he hadn't stayed in town as it was until she had come out and done the work and got things straightened out. It was his usual trick.

17   It appeared to him that this was going a little far. Just a touch out of bounds, if she didn't mind his saying so. Why the hell had he stayed in town the summer before? To do a half-dozen extra jobs to get the money he had sent her. That was it. She knew perfectly well they couldn't have done it otherwise. She had agreed with him at the time. And that was the only time so help him he had ever left her to do anything by herself.

18   Oh, he could tell that to his great-grandmother. She had her notion of what had kept him in town. Considerably more than a notion, if he wanted to know. So, she was going to bring all that up again, was she? Well, she could just think what she pleased. He was tired of explaining. It may have looked funny but he had simply got hooked in, and what could he do? It was impossible to believe that she was going to take it seriously. Yes, yes, she knew how it was with a man: if he was left by himself a minute, some woman was certain to kidnap him. And naturally he couldn't hurt her feelings by refusing!

19   Well, what was she raving about? Did she forget she had told him those two weeks alone in the country were the happiest she had known in four years? And how long had they been married when she said that? All right, shut up! If she thought that hadn't stuck in his craw.

20   She hadn't meant she was happy because she was away from him. She meant she was happy getting the devilish house nice and ready for him. That was what she had meant, and now look! Bringing up something she had said a year ago simply to justify himself for forgetting her coffee and breaking the eggs and buying a wretched piece of rope they couldn't afford. She really thought it was time to drop the subject, and now she wanted only two things in the world. She wanted him to get that rope from underfoot, and go back to the village and get her coffee, and if he could remember it, he might bring a metal mitt for the skillets, and two more curtain rods, and if there were any rubber gloves in the village, her hands were simply raw, and a bottle of milk of magnesia from the drugstore.

21   He looked out at the dark blue afternoon sweltering on the slopes, and mopped his forehead and sighed heavily and said, if only she could wait a minute for *anything,* he was going back. He had said so, hadn't he, the very instant they found he had overlooked it?

22   Oh, yes, well . . . run along. She was going to wash windows. The country was so beautiful! She doubted they'd have a moment to enjoy it. He meant to go, but he could not until he had said that if she wasn't such a hopeless melancholiac she might see that this was only for a few days. Couldn't she remember anything pleasant about the other summers? Hadn't they ever had any fun? She hadn't time to talk about it, and now would he please not leave that rope lying around for her to trip on? He picked it up, somehow it had toppled off the table, and walked out with it under his arm.

23   Was he going this minute? He certainly was. She thought so. Sometimes it seemed to her he had second sight about the precisely perfect moment to leave her ditched. She had meant to put the mattresses out to sun, if they put them out this minute they would get at least three hours, he must have heard her say that morning she meant to put them out. So of course he would walk off and leave her to it. She supposed he thought the exercise would do her good.

24   Well, he was merely going to get her coffee. A four-mile walk for two pounds of coffee was ridiculous, but he was perfectly willing to do it. The habit was making a wreck of her, but if she wanted to wreck herself there was nothing he could do about it. If he thought it was coffee that was making a wreck of her, she congratulated him: he must have a damned easy conscience.

25   Conscience or no conscience, he didn't see why the mattresses couldn't very well wait until tomorrow. And anyhow, for God's sake, were they living *in* the house, or were they going to let the house ride them to death? She paled at this, her face grew livid about the mouth, she looked quite dangerous, and reminded him that housekeeping was no more her work than it was his: she had other work to do as well, and when did he think she was going to find time to do it at this rate?

26   Was she going to start on that again? She knew as well as he did that his work brought in the regular money, hers was only occasional, if they depended on what *she* made—and she might as well get straight on this question once for all!

27   That was positively not the point. The question was, when both of them were working on their own time, was there going to be a division of the house-work, or wasn't there? She merely wanted to know, she had to make her plans. Why, he thought that was all arranged. It was understood that he was to help. Hadn't he always, in summers?

28   Hadn't he, though? Oh, just hadn't he? And when, and where, and doing what? Lord, what an uproarious joke!

29   It was such a very uproarious joke that her face turned slightly purple, and she screamed with laughter. She laughed so hard she had to sit down, and finally a rush of tears spurted from her eyes and poured down into the lifted corners of her mouth. He dashed towards her and dragged her up to her feet and tried to pour water on her head. The dipper hung by a string on a nail and he broke it loose. Then he tried to pump water with one hand while she strug-gled in the other. So he gave it up and shook her instead.

30   She wrenched away, crying out for him to take his rope and go to hell, she had simply given him up: and ran. He heard her high-heeled bedroom slippers clattering and stumbling on the stairs.

31   He went out around the house and into the lane; he suddenly realized he had a blister on his heel and his shirt felt as if it were on fire. Things broke so suddenly you didn't know where you were. She could work herself into a fury about simply nothing. She was terrible, damn it: not an ounce of reason. You might as well talk to a sieve as that woman when she got going. Damned if he'd spend his life humoring her! Well, what to do now? He would take back the rope and exchange it for something else. Things accumulated, things were mountainous, you couldn't move them or sort them out or get rid of them. They just lay and rotted around. He'd take it back. Hell, why should he? He wanted it. What was it anyhow? A piece of rope. Imagine anybody caring more about a piece of rope than about a man's feelings. What earthly right had she to say a word about it? He remembered all the useless, meaningless things she bought for herself: Why? because I wanted it, that's why! He stopped and selected a large stone by the road. He would put the rope behind it. He would put it in the tool-box when he got back. He'd heard enough about it to last him a life-time.

32   When he came back she was leaning against the post box beside the road waiting. It was pretty late, the smell of broiled steak floated nose high in the cooling air. Her face was young and smooth and fresh-looking. Her unman-ageable funny black hair was all on end. She waved to him from a distance, and

he speeded up. She called out that supper was ready and waiting, was he starved?

33   You bet he was starved. Here was the coffee. He waved it at her. She looked at his other hand. What was that he had there?

34   Well, it was the rope again. He stopped short. He had meant to exchange it but forgot. She wanted to know why he should exchange it, if it was something he really wanted. Wasn't the air sweet now, and wasn't it fine to be here?

35   She walked beside him with one hand hooked into his leather belt. She pulled and jostled him a little as he walked, and leaned against him. He put his arm clear around her and patted her stomach. They exchanged wary smiles. Coffee, coffee for the Ootsum-Wootsums! He felt as if he were bringing her a beautiful present.

36   He was a love, she firmly believed, and if she had had her coffee in the morning, she wouldn't have behaved so funny . . . There was a whippoorwill still coming back, imagine, clear out of season, sitting in the crab-apple tree calling all by himself. Maybe his girl stood him up. Maybe she did. She hoped to hear him once more, she loved whippoorwills . . . He knew how she was, didn't he?

37   Sure, he knew how she was.

Topics for Writing and Discussion

1.   Why is this story called "Rope"? Is this story really about rope? What very common human interaction does Porter capture here?

2.   What contrasting views are presented in this story? How might you briefly summarize each person's view of their relationship? Do you feel Porter sides with one of the characters?

3.   What are some of the problems in this relationship that seem more serious than others? How do you interpret the ending of this story? Do these two people really "know" and understand each other, or have they, in your opinion, only temporarily restored their relationship?

4.   Take note of Porter's style. How does she use sentence structure and unconventional presentation of dialogue to give readers a sense of "being there"?

5.   Have you ever been involved in a quarrel and later, in a calmer state, compared your view of the problem with that of the person with whom you argued? Were you surprised at how differently each of you interpreted the event or conversation that was the source of the trouble?

WRITING ASSIGNMENTS FOR CHAPTER EIGHT

COMPARISON AND CONTRAST

1. In "Two Ways of Looking at the River," Samuel Clemens describes the differences in his point of view before and after he became a riverboat pilot. Write an essay in which you contrast an earlier view of a scene with a later view. For instance, you might think of a visit to a childhood haunt or family vacation spot or even your room at home since you've been away at college. Has the place itself changed or has only your perception of it altered?

2. Contrast two towns (or two tourist attractions or two schools) you know well for an out-of-state friend who's considering a short visit. Is one place more inviting than the other? You might consider giving each place a personality to help you develop your contrast for your reader.

3. In "Grant and Lee: A Study in Contrasts," Bruce Catton contrasts two famous Civil War antagonists. Select two famous rivals from your field of study or from current politics, sports, or some social controversy. Familiarize yourself with each person's beliefs and present your readers with a clear contrast. You may either take a position that argues support for one person over the other, or you may make your essay an objective look at both parties that will allow your readers to decide a preference for themselves.

4. In "My Horse," Barry Lopez praises his truck, even though it is old, worn, and dented. According to Lopez, his truck has "heart" and gives this quality to its owner, too. Similarly, in "A Good Scythe," Wendell Berry concludes that sometimes newer is not always better. Think about an older possession, product, or service that you believe is far superior to its current or modern version. Is the older product better because it is more reliable, durable, or aesthetically pleasing? (For example, do you secretly prefer records to CDs? Fans to air conditioners? Typewriters to computers?) Write an essay defending your choice of old-over-new, making your standards for judgment clear to your readers. (You may, of course, take the opposite position: the good old days never were!)

5. In "A Slow Walk of Trees," Toni Morrison contrasts her grandparents' views "on the possibilities of life for black people in this country." That contrast, in turn, helps her clarify her own point of view. Select an important social or political belief and make your attitude toward this subject clear by contrasting your opinion with that of your parents, grandparents, or older friends.

6. In her essay "Neat People vs. Sloppy People," Suzanne Britt uses overstatement and generalizations for comic effect. Write an essay in which you use the opposite technique; that is, using as many appropriate specific examples

and details as you can, contrast two products or businesses to make a serious point about important differences you see.

7. In Sonnet 130, Shakespeare's speaker contrasts the real woman he loves with the romantic ideal of the "Beloved Lady," who is described as goddess-like in her beauty and grace. Write an essay in which you compare/contrast the reality of someone, some place, or some event to its romanticized or too-perfect ideal. Was the reality you experienced better or worse than the romanticized expectation? Why? Make a clear point about the contrast in your thesis, as Shakespeare did in his concluding couplet.

8. The couple in Katherine Anne Porter's story "Rope" sees a number of issues in different ways. Draft an essay on a controversial topic about which you and someone close to you (a friend or family member, perhaps) hold dramatically different views. Does your draft show some common ground after all, or does your essay reveal a contrast so great that any sort of agreement on this subject is unlikely?

CHAPTER NINE

DIVISION AND CLASSIFICATION

Division and classification are rhetorical structures that will help you make large or complex subjects easier to understand. *Division* is the act of separating one thing into its component parts so that you can grasp, understand, or better comprehend its makeup. For example, consider a subject such as the cost of attending college. Perhaps you have seen a picture on television or in a newspaper or magazine of the average student's budget represented by a circle or pie that has been *divided* into "slices" and labeled. Room and board might represent one slice; tuition and books, another slice; food, still another slice; and so on. By dividing the budget into parts and by studying those parts, students may have a better sense of how their money is being spent.

DIVISION

The principle of division is also at work in many of your college courses. Your anthropology professor, for instance, might lecture on the Mesa Verde Indian Era by dividing it into its important time periods—Basket Maker (A.D. 1–450), Modified Basket Maker (A.D. 450–750), and Pueblo (A.D. 750–1300)—so that your class can analyze and thereby clearly understand the characteristics of the era. Your chemistry lab-instructor may ask you to break down a substance into its components to learn how the parts interact to form the chemical. Even this textbook is divided into chapters to make it easier for you to use. When you think of *division,* then, think of dividing or separating one subject (often a large or complex or unfamiliar one) into its parts so that the subject can be more easily understood.

CLASSIFICATION

While division calls for separating one thing into its parts, *classification* systematically groups a number of things into categories to make the information easier to grasp. The categories of classification are generally based on similarities or differences. For example, you might classify restaurants according to price—very expensive, expensive, moderately expensive, and so on—or perhaps according to cuisine—Chinese, French, Italian, German, and so on. The chief purpose of the classification essay is to *explain*. Without some imposed system of order, a body of information could be a jumble of facts and figures. At some point, for instance, you've probably turned to the classified ads in the newspaper; if the ads were not grouped (classified) into categories such as "cars for sale" or "help wanted," you would have to search through countless ads to find the service or item you wanted.

Classification occurs everywhere around you. As a student, you may be classified as a freshman, sophomore, junior, or senior; you may also be classified by your major. If you have registered to vote, you may be classified as a Democrat, Republican, Libertarian, or something else; if you attend religious services, you may be classified as Baptist, Catholic, Jewish, Methodist, and so on. Even the books you buy are grouped and shelved by the bookstore into mysteries, biographies, romance, reference, travel, and other categories. Professionals classify almost every kind of knowledge: ornithologists classify birds; etymologists classify words by origin; botanists classify plants; zoologists classify animals.

Just remember that when you use division, you move from *the whole to its parts*:

A book	→	Chapters
Your college	→	Departments
The United States	→	The fifty states

When you classify, you move from *specific examples* to the *common characteristic* that the examples share:

William Faulkner, Flannery O'Connor, Reynolds Price, Eudora Welty, Zora Neale Hurston	→	Southern writers
Freshmen, sophomores, juniors, seniors	→	College students
Democrats, Republicans, Libertarians, Independents	→	Voters
Westerns, biographies, adventure stories, mysteries	→	Books

USES OF DIVISION AND CLASSIFICATION

Although division and classification are processes that often work together, it is important to understand the purpose of each and how each works. *Division* begins with one thing and separates it into its parts; *classification* sorts and organizes many things into appropriate groups or categories.

Writers, then, use division and classification to explain, to analyze, to organize, to clarify. In "College Pressures," William Zinsser classifies into four types the pressures he sees weighing on today's college students. In "Friends, Good Friends, and Such Good Friends," Judith Viorst classifies her friends into a variety of categories to show the roles they play in her life. The mother in Amy Tan's story "Two Kinds" divides daughters into two distinct types, according to their behavior. Sometimes, authors divide or classify to give us a new way of looking at something. Many classification essays, especially those that appear in popular magazines and newspapers, often are used to entertain or evaluate, as well as to inform, hence such articles as "Five Blind Dates to Avoid," "The Four Best Restaurants in New Orleans," or "The Three Biggest Mistakes in Buying a Used Car."

WRITING THE DIVISION OR CLASSIFICATION ESSAY

Once you have determined that your topic should be developed using division or classification, you will need some guidelines to help in planning your essay. The following hints should help:

1. *Select one principle of classification or division and apply it consistently.*

If you are classifying all the students at your school by major, for instance, don't suddenly switch to classification by college: French, economics, psychology, *arts and sciences*, math, and chemistry. A similar error occurs in the classification of dogs by breeds because it includes a physical characteristic: spaniels, terriers, *long-haired hounds*, and retrievers. Decide on what basis you will classify or divide your subject and then be consistent throughout the essay.

2. *Make the purpose of your division or classification clear to your audience.*

Don't just announce that "There are four kinds of 'X' or that 'Z' has three important parts." Why does the audience need to know the information? Consider the following thesis statements:

> By recognizing the three kinds of poisonous snakes in this area, campers and backpackers may be able to take the proper medical steps if they are bitten.

> Knowing the four types of spinning reels will enable novice fishermen to purchase the equipment best suited to their needs.

> While karate has become a popular form of exercise as well as of self-defense, few people know what the six levels of achievement—or "belts" as they are called—actually are.

Organize your material for a particular purpose and then explain to your readers what that purpose is.

3. *After you have selected the principle you will use to divide or classify your topic, decide how you will discuss the parts or categories.*

A classification or division essay is not a mechanical list; each category or part should contain enough specific details to make it clearly recognizable and interesting. To present each category or part, you may draw upon the methods of development you already know, such as illustration, description, comparison and contrast, and definition. Try to use the same techniques in each category so that no one category or part of your essay seems underdeveloped or unclear.

4. *Make sure that the categories you establish are mutually exclusive.*

Make sure the items in your categories don't overlap. For example, if you were classifying college students into categories, you might use undergraduates, graduate students, and postgraduate students, but you could not include commuter students and resident students because the latter two types probably also belong to one of the former groups. Similarly, in a classification of soft drinks by flavor, to include sugar-free with cola, root beer, orange, grape, and so on, is misleading because sugar-free drinks come in many different flavors. In other words, make each category distinct.

5. *Account for all the parts in your division or classification.*

Your division or classification must be complete. Don't, for instance, claim to classify all the trees native to your home state and then leave out one or more species. For a short essay, narrow your ruling principle rather than omit categories. You couldn't, for example, classify all the architectural styles in America in a short paper, but you might be able to discuss the major styles on your campus. In the same manner, the enormous task of classifying all types of mental illness might be narrowed to the most common forms of schizophrenia in children under twelve.

As you read the essays that follow, carefully examine the authors' use of division or classification and note the ways that their use of the strategy helps to clarify, organize, or give insight into their subjects.

THE PLOT AGAINST PEOPLE

Russell Baker
(1925–   )

Journalist Russell Baker began his career at the *Baltimore Sun* in 1947. In 1954, he left the *Sun* to become a reporter for the *New York Times*. There he wrote his "Observer" column for which he was awarded the George Polk Award for Distinguished Commentary in 1972 and in 1979 his first Pulitzer Prize. His columns have been collected into several books, including *All Things Considered* (1965), *So This Is Depravity* (1983), *The Good Times* (1989), and *Russell Baker's Book of American Humor* (1993). Baker was awarded his second Pulitzer Prize for *Growing Up* (1982), a chronicle of his childhood in the Depression. He has recently appeared as the host of Masterpiece Theater on PBS. "The Plot Against People" originally appeared in the *New York Times* in 1968. In the essay, Baker classifies three categories of annoying inanimate objects.

1   INANIMATE objects are classified into three major categories—those that don't work, those that break down and those that get lost.

2   The goal of all inanimate objects is to resist man and ultimately to defeat him, and the three major classifications are based on the method each object uses to achieve its purpose. As a general rule, any object capable of breaking down at the moment when it is most needed will do so. The automobile is typical of the category.

3   With the cunning typical of its breed, the automobile never breaks down while entering a filling station with a large staff of idle mechanics. It waits until it reaches a downtown intersection in the middle of the rush hour, or until it is fully loaded with family and luggage on the Ohio Turnpike.

Russell Baker in his office at The New York Times *in Washington, D.C.*
(Alan MacWeeney/Archive Pictures)

4   Thus it creates maximum misery, inconvenience, frustration and irritability among its human cargo, thereby reducing its owner's life span.

5   Washing machines, garbage disposals, lawn mowers, light bulbs, automatic laundry dryers, water pipes, furnaces, electrical fuses, television tubes, hose nozzles, tape recorders, slide projectors—all are in league with the automobile to take their turn at breaking down whenever life threatens to flow smoothly for their human enemies.

6   Many inanimate objects, of course, find it extremely difficult to break down. Pliers, for example, and gloves and keys are almost totally incapable of breaking down. Therefore, they have had to evolve a different technique for resisting man.

7   They get lost. Science has still not solved the mystery of how they do it, and no man has ever caught one of them in the act of getting lost. The most plausible theory is that they have developed a secret method of locomotion which they are able to conceal the instant a human eye falls upon them.

8   It is not uncommon for a pair of pliers to climb all the way from the cellar to the attic in its single-minded determination to raise its owner's blood pressure. Keys have been known to burrow three feet under mattresses. Women's purses, despite their great weight, frequently travel through six or seven rooms to find hiding space under a couch.

9   Scientists have been struck by the fact that things that break down virtually never get lost, while things that get lost hardly ever break down.

10   A furnace, for example, will invariably break down at the depth of the first winter cold wave, but it will never get lost. A woman's purse, which after all does have some inherent capacity for breaking down, hardly ever does; it almost invariably chooses to get lost.

11   Some persons believe this constitutes evidence that inanimate objects are not entirely hostile to man, and that a negotiated peace is possible. After all, they point out, a furnace could infuriate a man even more thoroughly by getting lost than by breaking down, just as a glove could upset him far more by breaking down than by getting lost.

12   Not everyone agrees, however, that this indicates a conciliatory attitude among inanimate objects. Many say it merely proves that furnaces, gloves, and pliers are incredibly stupid.

13   The third class of objects—those that don't work—is the most curious of all. These include such objects as barometers, car clocks, cigarette lighters, flashlights and toy-train locomotives. It is inaccurate, of course, to say that they never work. They work once, usually for the first few hours after being brought home, and then quit. Thereafter, they never work again.

14   In fact, it is widely assumed that they are built for the purpose of not working. Some people have reached advanced ages without ever seeing some of these objects—barometers, for example—in working order.

15   Science is utterly baffled by the entire category. There are many theories about it. The most interesting holds that the things that don't work have attained the highest state possible for an inanimate object, the state to which things that break down and things that get lost can still only aspire.

16   They have truly defeated man by conditioning him never to expect anything of them, and in return they have given man the only peace he receives from inanimate society. He does not expect his barometer to work, his electric locomotive to run, his cigarette lighter to light or his flashlight to illuminate, and when they don't, it does not raise his blood pressure.

17   He cannot attain that peace with furnaces and keys and cars and women's purses as long as he demands that they work for their keep.

TOPICS FOR WRITING AND DISCUSSION

1. What is Baker's thesis? Can you identify Baker's categories and principle of classification?
2. Why does Baker give examples of items belonging to each category? Do these specifics strengthen his essay? Why or why not?
3. Describe the tone of this essay. What role does personification play in creating this tone?
4. What does Baker's title contribute to the tone of this essay and also to his readers' understanding of his classifying principle?
5. Consider writing your own humorous essay about annoying inanimate objects in your home, school, or workplace. What categories would you create? What items would you include in these categories?

THREE BOYS

John Updike
(1932–   )

Born in Reading, Pennsylvania (the model for his fictional Brewer), John Hoyer Updike grew up in Shillington, Pennsylvania (Olinger in his stories and novels). He graduated from Harvard in 1954 and immediately began his career as a writer, contributing poems, essays, and short stories to national publications including *The New Yorker*. Updike is a prolific writer whose work includes many novels and short story collections: *The Centaur* (1964), winner of the National Book Award; *Rabbit, Run* (1960); *Rabbit Redux* (1971); *Rabbit Is Rich* (1981), winner of both the Pulitzer Prize and the American Book Award; *Rabbit at Rest* (1990), winner of a second Pulitzer Prize and the National Book Critics Award; and *Pigeon Feathers and Other Stories* (1962). He recently published *In the Beauty of the Lilies* (1996), which received the Ambassador Book Award; *Toward the End of Time* (1997), and *Beck at Bay* (1998). He was awarded the National Medal of Arts in 1989 and 1997. In "Three Boys," Updike categorizes his childhood acquaintances, showing each boy's unique qualities and influences.

1   A, B, and C, I'll say, in case they care. A lived next door; he *loomed* next door, rather. He seemed immense—a great wallowing fatso stuffed with possessions; he was the son of a full-fashioned knitter. He seemed to have a beer-belly; after several generations beer-bellies may become congenital. Also his face had no features. It was just a blank ball on his shoulders. He used to call me "Ostrich," after Disney's Ollie Ostrich. My neck was not very long; the

John Updike in his publisher's office (© Nancy Crampton)

name seemed horribly unfair; it was its injustice that made me cry. But nothing I could say, or scream, would make him stop, and I still, now and then—in reading, say, a book review by one of the apple-cheeked savants of the quarterlies or one of the pious gremlins who manufacture puns for *Time*—get the old sensations: my ears close up, my eyes go warm, my chest feels thin as an eggshell, my voice churns silently in my stomach. From A I received my first impression of the smug, chinkless, irresistible *power* of stupidity; it is the most powerful force on earth. It says "Ostrich" often enough, and the universe crumbles.

2   A was more than a boy, he was a force-field that could manifest itself in many forms, that could take the wiry, disconsolate shape of wide-mouthed, tiny-eared boys who would now and then beat me up on the way back from school. I did not greatly mind being beaten up, though I resisted it. For one thing, it firmly involved me, at least during the beating, with the circumambient humanity that so often seemed evasive. Also, the boys who applied the beating were misfits, periodic flunkers, who wore corduroy knickers with threadbare knees and men's shirts with the top button buttoned—this last an infallible sign of deep poverty. So that I felt there was some justice, some condonable revenge, being applied with their fists to this little teacher's son. And then there was the delicious alarm of my mother and grandmother when I returned home bloody, bruised, and torn. My father took the attitude that it was making a boy of me, an attitude I dimly shared. He and I both were afraid of me becoming a sissy—he perhaps more afraid than I.

3   When I was eleven or so I met B. It was summer and I was down at the playground. He was pushing a little tank with moving rubber treads up and down the hills in the sandbox. It was a fine little toy, mottled with camouflage green; patriotic manufacturers produced throughout the war millions of such authentic miniatures which we maneuvered with authentic, if miniature, militance. Attracted by the toy, I spoke to him; though taller and a little older than I, he had my dull straight brown hair and a look of being also alone. We became fast friends. He lived just up the street—toward the poorhouse, the east part of the street, from which the little winds of tragedy blew. He had just moved from the Midwest, and his mother was a widow. Beside wage war, we did many things together. We played marbles for days at a time, until one of us had won the other's entire coffee-canful. With jigsaws we cut out of plywood animals copied from comic books. We made movies by tearing the pages from Big Little Books and coloring the drawings and pasting them in a strip and winding them on toilet-paper spools, and making a cardboard carton a theatre. We rigged up telephones, and racing wagons, and cities of the future, using orange crates and cigar boxes and peanut-butter jars and such potent debris. We loved Smokey Stover and were always saying "Foo." We had an intense spell of Monopoly. He called me "Uppy"—the only person who ever did. I remember once, knowing he was coming down that afternoon to my house to play Monopoly, in order to show my joy I set up the board elaborately, with the Chance and Community Chest cards fanned painstakingly, like spiral staircases. He came into the room, groaned, "Uppy, what are you doing?" and

impatiently scrabbled the cards together in a sensible pile. The older we got, the more the year between us told, and the more my friendship embarrassed him. We fought. Once, to my horror, I heard myself taunting him with the fact that he had no father. The unmentionable, the unforgivable. I suppose we patched things up, children do, but the fabric had been torn. He had a long, pale, serious face, with buckteeth, and is probably an electronics engineer somewhere now, doing secret government work.

4   So through B I first experienced the pattern of friendship. There are three stages. First, acquaintance: we are new to each other, make each other laugh in surprise, and demand nothing beyond politeness. The death of the one would startle the other, no more. It is a pleasant stage, a stable stage; on austere rations of exposure it can live a lifetime, and the two parties to it always feel a slight gratification upon meeting, will feel vaguely confirmed in their human state. Then comes intimacy: now we laugh before two words of the joke are out of the other's mouth, because we know what he will say. Our two beings seem marvelously joined, from our toes to our heads, along tingling points of agreement; everything we venture is right, everything we put forth lodges in a corresponding socket in the frame of the other. The death of one would grieve the other. To be together is to enjoy a mounting excitement, a constant echo and amplification. It is an ecstatic and unstable stage, bound of its own agitation to tip into the third: revulsion. One or the other makes a misjudgment; presumes; puts forth that which does not meet agreement. Sometimes there is an explosion; more often the moment is swallowed in silence, and months pass before its nature dawns. Instead of dissolving, it grows. The mind, the throat, are clogged; forgiveness, forgetfulness, that have arrived so often, fail. Now everything jars and is distasteful. The betrayal, perhaps a tiny fraction in itself, has inverted the tingling column of agreement, made all pluses minuses. Everything about the other is hateful, despicable; yet he cannot be dismissed. We have confided in him too many minutes, too many words; he has those minutes and words as hostages, and his confidences are embedded in us where they cannot be scraped away, and even rivers of time cannot erode them completely, for there are indelible stains. Now—though the friends may continue to meet, and smile, as if they had never trespassed beyond acquaintance—the death of the one would please the other.

5   An unhappy pattern to which C is an exception. He was my friend before kindergarten, he is my friend still. I go to his home now, and he and his wife serve me and my wife with alcoholic drinks and slices of excellent cheese on crisp crackers, just as twenty years ago he served me with treats from his mother's refrigerator. He was a born host, and I a born guest. Also he was intelligent. If my childhood's brain, when I look back at it, seems a primitive mammal, a lemur or shrew, his brain was an angel whose visitation was widely hailed as wonderful. When in school he stood to recite, his cool rectangular forehead glowed. He tucked his right hand into his left armpit and with his left hand mechanically tapped a pencil against his thigh. His answers were always correct. He beat me at spelling bees and, in another sort of competition, when we both collected Big Little Books, he outbid me for my supreme find (in the

attic of a third boy), the first Mickey Mouse. I can still see that book, I wanted it so badly, in paper tan with age and its drawings done in Disney's primitive style, when Mickey's black chest is naked like a child's and his eyes are two nicked oblongs. Losing it was perhaps a lucky blow; it helped wean me away from hope of ever having possessions.

6   C was fearless. He deliberately set fields on fire. He engaged in rock-throwing duels with tough boys. One afternoon he persisted in playing quoits with me although—as the hospital discovered that night—his appendix was nearly bursting. He was enterprising. He peddled magazine subscriptions door-to-door; he mowed neighbors' lawns; he struck financial bargains with his father. He collected stamps so well his collection blossomed into a stamp company that filled his room with steel cabinets and mimeograph machinery. He collected money—every time I went over to his house he would get out a little tin box and count the money in it for me: $27.50 one week, $29.95 the next, $30.90 the next—all changed into new bills nicely folded together. It was a strange ritual, whose meaning for me was: since he was doing it, I didn't have to. His money made me richer. We read Ellery Queen and played chess and invented board games and discussed infinity together. In later adolescence, he collected records. He liked the Goodman quintets but loved Fats Waller. Sitting there in that room so familiar to me, where the machinery of the Shilco Stamp Company still crowded the walls and for that matter the tin box of money might still be stashed, while my thin friend grunted softly along with that dead dark angel on "You're Not the Only Oyster in the Stew," I felt, in the best sense, patronized: the perfect guest of the perfect host. What made it perfect was that we had both spent our entire lives in Shillington.

Topics for Writing and Discussion

1. Describe A and explain what Updike means when he says that "A was more than a boy, he was a force-field that could manifest itself in many forms. . . ." What group of individuals does he represent to Updike?

2. Updike divides his friendship with B into three stages. What are those stages? Do you agree with this definition of friendship?

3. How does Updike's attitude toward owning things change as he comes to know A, B, and C? What does he learn from C that neither A nor B could teach him? How does C teach Updike this lesson?

4. Compare Updike's attitude toward and definition of friendship with Judith Viorst's attitude and definition in "Friends, Good Friends, and Such Good Friends." Do you agree with one or the other? Why?

5. Write an essay tracing the growth of a friendship. Divide your life into a series of time periods that will help the reader see how the relationship developed.

COLLEGE PRESSURES

William Zinsser
(1922–   )

Born in New York, William Zinsser was educated at Princeton and worked for *Life* and *Look* magazines as well as the *New York Herald Tribune* after his graduation. He is the author of the highly acclaimed book *On Writing Well: An Informal Guide to Writing Nonfiction* (1976). In 1970, Zinsser joined the faculty at Yale University and created the first nonfiction writing course ever offered at the university. His *On Writing Well* is based not only on his own experiences as a writer, but also on his observations of his students' writing processes. He has written and edited numerous books, including *Pop Goes America* (1966), *Writing with a Word Processor* (1982), *Paths of Resistance: The Art and Craft of the Political Novel* (1989), *Worlds of Childhood: The Art and Craft of Writing for Children* (1990), and *Inventing the Truth: The Art and Craft of Memoir* (1998). In the following excerpt from the April 1979 issue of *Country Journal*, Zinsser categorizes the pressures faced by college students and then analyzes their impact on both the students and the college community.

William Zinsser
(© Nancy Crampton)

---

1 *D*EAR *Carlos: I desperately need a dean's excuse for my chem midterm which will begin in about 1 hour. All I can say is that I totally blew it this week. I've fallen incredibly, inconceivably behind.*

2 **CARLOS:**   *Help! I'm anxious to hear from you. I'll be in my room and won't leave it until I hear from you. Tomorrow is the last day for . . .*

3 **CARLOS:**   *I left town because I started bugging out again. I stayed up all night to finish a take home make-up exam & am typing it to hand in on the 10th. It was due on the 5th. P.S. I'm going to the dentist. Pain is pretty bad.*

4 **CARLOS:**   *Probably by Friday I'll be able to get back to my studies. Right now I'm going to take a long walk. This whole thing has taken a lot out of me.*

5 **CARLOS:** *I'm really up the proverbial creek. The problem is I really* bombed *the history final. Since I need that course for my major . . .*

6 **CARLOS:** *Here follows a tale of woe. I went home this weekend, had to help my Mom, & caught a fever so didn't have much time to study. My professor . . .*

7 **CARLOS:** *Aargh! Nothing original but everything's piling up at once. To be brief, my job interview . . .*

8 *Hey Carlos, good news! I've got mononucleosis.*

9   Who are these wretched supplicants, scribbling notes so laden with anxiety, seeking such miracles of postponement and balm? They are men and women who belong to Branford College, one of the twelve residential colleges at Yale University, and the messages are just a few of the hundreds that they left for their dean, Carlos Hortas—often slipped under his door at 4 A.M.—last year.

10   But students like the ones who wrote those notes can also be found on campuses from coast to coast—especially in New England and at many other private colleges across the country that have high academic standards and highly motivated students. Nobody could doubt that the notes are real. In their urgency and their gallows humor they are authentic voices of a generation that is panicky to succeed.

11   My own connection with the message writers is that I am master of Branford College. I live in its Gothic quadrangle and know the students well. (We have 485 of them.) I am privy to their hopes and fears—and also to their stereo music and their piercing cries in the dead of night ("Does anybody *ca-a-are?*"). If they went to Carlos to ask how to get through tomorrow, they come to me to ask how to get through the rest of their lives.

12   Mainly I try to remind them that the road ahead is a long one and that it will have more unexpected turns than they think. There will be plenty of time to change jobs, change careers, change whole attitudes and approaches. They don't want to hear such liberating news. They want a map—right now—that they can follow unswervingly to career security, financial security, Social Security and, presumably, a prepaid grave.

13   What I wish for all students is some release from the clammy grip of the future. I wish them a chance to savor each segment of their education as an experience in itself and not as a grim preparation for the next step. I wish them the right to experiment, to trip and fall, to learn that defeat is as instructive as victory and is not the end of the world.

14   My wish, of course, is naive. One of the few rights that America does not proclaim is the right to fail. Achievement is the national god, venerated in our media—the million-dollar athlete, the wealthy executive—and glorified in our praise of possessions. In the presence of such a potent state religion, the young are growing up old.

15   I see four kinds of pressure working on college students today: economic pressure, parental pressure, peer pressure, and self-induced pressure. It is easy to look around for villains—to blame the colleges for charging too much money, the professors for assigning too much work, the parents for pushing their children too far, the students for driving themselves too hard. But there are no villains; only victims.

16   "In the late 1960s," one dean told me, "the typical question that I got from students was 'Why is there so much suffering in the world?' or 'How can I make a contribution?' Today it's 'Do you think it would look better for getting into law school if I did a double major in history and political science, or just majored in one of them?'" Many other deans confirmed this pattern. One said "They're trying to find an edge—the intangible something that will look better on paper if two students are about equal."

17   Note the emphasis on looking better. The transcript has become a sacred document, the passport to security. How one appears on paper is more important than how one appears in person. *A* is for Admirable and *B* is for Borderline, even though, in Yale's official system of grading, *A* means "excellent" and *B* means "very good." Today, looking very good is no longer good enough, especially for students who hope to go on to law school or medical school. They know that entrance into the better schools will be an entrance into the better law firms and better medical practices where they will make a lot of money. They also know that the odds are harsh. Yale Law School, for instance, matriculates 170 students from an applicant pool of 3,700; Harvard enrolls 550 from a pool of 7,000.

18   It's all very well for those of us who write letters of recommendation for our students to stress the qualities of humanity that will make them good lawyers or doctors. And it's nice to think that admission officers are really reading our letters and looking for the extra dimension of commitment or concern. Still, it would be hard for a student not to visualize these officers shuffling so many transcripts studded with *A*s that they regard a *B* as positively shameful.

19   The pressure is almost as heavy on students who just want to graduate and get a job. Long gone are the days of the "gentleman's *C*," when students journeyed through college with a certain relaxation, sampling a wide variety of courses—music, art, philosophy, classics, anthropology, poetry, religion—that would send them out as liberally educated men and women. If I were an employer I would rather employ graduates who have this range and curiosity than those who narrowly pursued safe subjects and high grades. I know countless students whose inquiring minds exhilarate me. I like to hear the play of their ideas. I don't know if they are getting *A*s or *C*s, and I don't care. I also like them as people. The country needs them, and they will find satisfying jobs. I tell them to relax. They can't.

20   Nor can I blame them. They live in a brutal economy. Tuition, room, and board at most private colleges now comes to at least $7,000, not counting books and fees. This might seem to suggest that the colleges are getting rich. But they are equally battered by inflation. Tuition covers only 60 percent of what it costs to educate a student, and ordinarily the remainder comes from what colleges receive in endowments, grants, and gifts. Now the remainder

keeps being swallowed by the cruel costs—higher every year—of just opening the doors. Heating oil is up. Insurance is up. Postage is up. Health-premium costs are up. Everything is up. Deficits are up. We are witnessing in America the creation of a brotherhood of paupers—colleges, parents, and students, joined by the common bond of debt.

21   Today it is not unusual for a student, even if he works part time at college and full time during the summer, to accrue $5,000 in loans after four years—loans that he must start to repay within one year after graduation. Exhorted at commencement to go forth into the world, he is already behind as he goes forth. How could he not feel under pressure throughout college to prepare for this day of reckoning? I have used "he," incidentally, only for brevity. Women at Yale are under no less pressure to justify their expensive education to themselves, their parents, and society. In fact, they are probably under more pressure. For although they leave college superbly equipped to bring fresh leadership to traditionally male jobs, society hasn't yet caught up with this fact.

22   Along with economic pressure goes parental pressure. Inevitably, the two are deeply intertwined.

23   I see many students taking pre-medical courses with joyless tenacity. They go off to their labs as if they were going to the dentist. It saddens me because I know them in other corners of their life as cheerful people.

24   "Do you want to go to medical school?" I ask them.

25   "I guess so," they say, without conviction, or "Not really."

26   "Then why are you going?"

27   "Well, my parents want me to be a doctor. They're paying all this money and . . ."

28   Poor students, poor parents. They are caught in one of the oldest webs of love and duty and guilt. The parents mean well; they are trying to steer their sons and daughters toward a secure future. But the sons and daughters want to major in history or classics or philosophy—subjects with no "practical" value. Where's the payoff on the humanities? It's not easy to persuade such loving parents that the humanities do indeed pay off. The intellectual faculties developed by studying subjects like history and classics—an ability to synthesize and relate, to weigh cause and effect, to see events in perspective—are just the faculties that make creative leaders in business or almost any general field. Still, many fathers would rather put their money on courses that point toward a specific profession—courses that are pre-law, pre-medical, pre-business, or, as I sometimes heard it put, "pre-rich."

29   But the pressure on students is severe. They are truly torn. One part of them feels obligated to fulfill their parents' expectations; after all, their parents are older and presumably wiser. Another part tells them that the expectations that are right for their parents are not right for them.

30   I know a student who wants to be an artist. She is very obviously an artist and will be a good one—she has already had several modest local exhibits. Meanwhile she is growing as a well-rounded person and taking humanistic subjects that will enrich the inner resources out of which her art will grow. But her father is strongly opposed. He thinks that an artist is a "dumb" thing to be. The student vacillates and tries to please everybody. She keeps up with her

art somewhat furtively and takes some of the "dumb" courses her father wants her to take—at least they are dumb courses for her. She is a free spirit on a campus of tense students—no small achievement in itself—and she deserves to follow her muse.

31   Peer pressure and self-induced pressure are also intertwined, and they begin almost at the beginning of freshman year.

32   "I had a freshman student I'll call Linda," one dean told me, "who came in and said she was under terrible pressure because her roommate, Barbara, was much brighter and studied all the time. I couldn't tell her that Barbara had come in two hours earlier to say the same thing about Linda."

33   The story is almost funny—except that it's not. It's symptomatic of all the pressures put together. When every student thinks every other student is working harder and doing better, the only solution is to study harder still. I see students going off to the library every night after dinner and coming back when it closes at midnight. I wish they could sometimes forget about their peers and go to a movie. I hear the clacking of typewriters in the hours before dawn. I see the tension in their eyes when exams are approaching and papers are due: *"Will I get everything done?"*

34   Probably they won't. They will get sick. They will get "blocked." They will sleep. They will oversleep. They will bug out. *Hey Carlos, help!*

35   Part of the problem is that they do more than they are expected to do. A professor will assign five-page papers. Several students will start writing ten-page papers to impress him. Then more students will write ten-page papers, and a few will raise the ante to fifteen. Pity the poor student who is still just doing the assignment.

36   "Once you have twenty or thirty percent of the student population deliberately overexerting," one dean points out, "it's bad for everybody. When a teacher gets more and more effort from his class, the student who is doing normal work can be perceived as not doing well. The tactic works, psychologically."

37   Why can't the professor just cut back and not accept longer papers? He can, and he probably will. But by then the term will be half over and the damage done. Grade fever is highly contagious and not easily reversed. Besides, the professor's main concern is with his course. He knows his students only in relation to the course and doesn't know that they are also overexerting in their other courses. Nor is it really his business. He didn't sign up for dealing with the student as a whole person and with all the emotional baggage the student brought along from home. That's what deans, masters, chaplains, and psychiatrists are for.

38   To some extent this is nothing new: a certain number of professors have always been self-contained islands of scholarship and shyness, more comfortable with books than with people. But the new pauperism has widened the gap still further, for professors who actually like to spend time with students don't have as much time to spend. They also are overexerting. If they are young, they are busy trying to publish in order not to perish, hanging by their finger nails onto a shrinking profession. If they are old and tenured, they are buried under the

duties of administering departments—as departmental chairmen or members of committees—that have been thinned out by the budgetary axe.

39   Ultimately it will be the students' own business to break the circles in which they are trapped. They are too young to be prisoners of their parents' dreams and their classmates' fears. They must be jolted into believing in themselves as unique men and women who have the power to shape their own future.

40   "Violence is being done to the undergraduate experience," says Carlos Hortas. "College should be open-ended: at the end it should open many, many roads. Instead, students are choosing their goal in advance, and their choices narrow as they go along. It's almost as if they think that the country has been codified in the type of jobs that exist—that they've got to fit into certain slots. Therefore, fit into the best-paying slot.

41   "They ought to take chances. Not taking chances will lead to a life of colorless mediocrity. They'll be comfortable. But something in the spirit will be missing."

42   I have painted too drab a portrait of today's students, making them seem a solemn lot. That is only half of their story; if they were so dreary I wouldn't so thoroughly enjoy their company. The other half is that they are easy to like. They are quick to laugh and to offer friendship. They are not introverts. They are usually kind and are more considerate of one another than any student generation I have known.

43   Nor are they so obsessed with their studies that they avoid sports and extracurricular activities. On the contrary, they juggle their crowded hours to play on a variety of teams, perform with musical and dramatic groups, and write for campus publications. But this in turn is one more cause of anxiety. There are too many choices. Academically, they have 1,300 courses to select from; outside class they have to decide how much spare time they can spare and how to spend it.

44   This means that they engage in fewer extracurricular pursuits than their predecessors did. If they want to row on the crew and play in the symphony they will eliminate one; in the '60s they would have done both. They also tend to choose activities that are self-limiting. Drama, for instance, is flourishing in all twelve of Yale's residential colleges as it never has before. Students hurl themselves into these productions—as actors, directors, carpenters, and technicians—with a dedication to create the best possible play, knowing that the day will come when the run will end and they can get back to their studies.

45   They also can't afford to be the willing slave of organizations like the *Yale Daily News.* Last spring at the one-hundredth anniversary banquet of that paper—whose past chairmen include such once and future kings as Potter Stewart, Kingman Brewster, and William F. Buckley, Jr.—much was made of the fact that the editorial staff used to be small and totally committed and that "newsies" routinely worked fifty hours a week. In effect they belonged to a club; newsies is how they defined themselves at Yale. Today's student will write one or two articles a week, when he can, and he defines himself as a student. I've never heard the word newsie except at the banquet.

46   If I have described the modern undergraduate primarily as a driven creature who is largely ignoring the blithe spirit inside who keeps trying to come
out and play, it's because that's where the crunch is, not only at Yale but
throughout American education. It's why I think we should all be worried
about the values that are nurturing a generation so fearful of risk and so goal-
obsessed at such an early age.

47   I tell students that there is no one "right" way to get ahead—that each of
them is a different person, starting from a different point and bound for a different destination. I tell them that change is a tonic and that all the slots are
not codified nor the frontiers closed. One of my ways of telling them is to invite men and women who have achieved success outside the academic world to
come and talk informally with my students during the year. They are heads of
companies or ad agencies, editors of magazines, politicians, public officials,
television magnates, labor leaders, business executives, Broadway producers,
artists, writers, economists, photographers, scientists, historians—a mixed bag
of achievers.

48   I ask them to say a few words about how they got started. The students assume that they started in their present profession and knew all along that it
was what they wanted to do. Luckily for me, most of them got into their field
by a circuitous route, to their surprise, after many detours. The students are
startled. They can hardly conceive of a career that was not pre-planned. They
can hardly imagine allowing the hand of God or chance to nudge them down
some unforeseen trail.

Topics for Writing and Discussion

1. Zinsser begins his essay with a series of notes college students at Yale
   wrote to their dean. What are the common thoughts and feelings that
   unite these examples? How do they serve as an introduction to Zinsser's
   thesis?

2. What four major categories does Zinsser establish as he discusses college
   pressures? How does he see these categories in relationship to each other?
   Is each category clearly defined as separate and distinct?

3. What is Zinsser's main purpose? Does he use the categories primarily as a
   way of explaining the pressures? Does he see college pressures as mostly
   positive? Mostly negative? Inevitable? Does he hope to encourage changes
   on college campuses?

4. This essay was first published in 1979. Do Zinsser's categories still hold
   true today? Do college students face fewer pressures now? More? About
   the same? Have some of the 1979 pressures been replaced by new forces?

5. Think about your own need to succeed and explain the three or four main
   kinds of pressures you feel. Are your sources of anxiety the same as those
   described by Zinsser?

FRIENDS, GOOD FRIENDS, AND SUCH GOOD FRIENDS

Judith Viorst
(1936–   )

Born in Newark, New Jersey, Judith Viorst is an essayist, poet, columnist, and contributing editor to *Redbook* magazine. Her poetic monologues written for the CBS special "Annie, the Woman in the Life of a Man" won her an Emmy Award in 1970. She has published collections of both poetry and prose, including *It's Hard to Be Hip Over Thirty, and Other Tragedies of Married Life* (1970); *Yes, Married: A Saga of Love and Complaint* (1972); *Necessary Losses* (1987); *Forever Fifty* (1989); *Earrings!* (1990); *Murdering Mr. Monti* (1994); and her most recent work *Imperfect Control: Our Lifelong Struggles with Power Surrender* (1998). In "Friends, Good Friends, and Such Good Friends," which first appeared in 1997 in *Redbook* magazine, Viorst uses the rhetorical mode of classification to describe her past and present friends and the changing nature of friendship.

Judith Viorst
(© David Morowitz)

---

1   WOMEN are friends, I once would have said, when they totally love and support and trust each other, and bare to each other the secrets of their souls, and run—no questions asked—to help each other, and tell harsh truths to each other (no, you can't wear that dress unless you lose ten pounds first) when harsh truths must be told.

2   Women are friends, I once would have said, when they share the same affection for Ingmar Bergman, plus train rides, cats, warm rain, charades, Camus, and hate with equal ardor Newark and Brussels sprouts and Lawrence Welk and camping.

3   In other words, I once would have said that a friend is a friend all the way, but now I believe that's a narrow point of view. For the friendships I have and the friendships I see are conducted at many levels of intensity, serve many different functions, meet different needs and range from those as all-the-way as

the friendship of the soul sisters mentioned above to that of the most nonchalant and casual playmates.

4   Consider these varieties of friendship:

5   1. Convenience friends. These are the women with whom, if our paths weren't crossing all the time, we'd have no particular reason to be friends: a next-door neighbor, a woman in our car pool, the mother of one of our children's closest friends or maybe some mommy with whom we serve juice and cookies each week at the Glenwood Co-op Nursery.

6   Convenience friends are convenient indeed. They'll lend us their cups and silverware for a party. They'll drive our kids to soccer when we're sick. They'll take us to pick up our car when we need a lift to the garage. They'll even take our cats when we go on vacation. As we will for them.

7   But we don't, with convenience friends, ever come too close or tell too much; we maintain our public face and emotional distance. "Which means," says Elaine, "that I'll talk about being overweight but not about being depressed. Which means I'll admit being mad but not blind with rage. Which means I might say that we're pinched this month but never that I'm worried sick over money."

8   But which doesn't mean that there isn't sufficient value to be found in these friendships of mutual aid, in convenience friends.

9   2. Special-interest friends. These friendships aren't intimate, and they needn't involve kids or silverware or cats. Their value lies in some interest jointly shared. And so we may have an office friend or a yoga friend or a tennis friend or a friend from the Women's Democratic Club.

10   "I've got one woman friend," says Joyce, "who likes, as I do, to take psychology courses. Which makes it nice for me—and nice for her. It's fun to go with someone you know and it's fun to discuss what you've learned, driving back from the classes." And for the most part, she says, that's all they discuss.

11   "I'd say that what we're doing is *doing* together, not being together," Suzanne says of her Tuesday-doubles friends. "It's mainly a tennis relationship, but we play together well. And I guess we all need to have a couple of playmates."

12   I agree.

13   *My* playmate is a shopping friend, a woman of marvelous taste, a woman who knows exactly *where* to buy *what*, and furthermore is a woman who always knows beyond a doubt what one ought to be buying. I don't have the time to keep up with what's new in eyeshadow, hemlines and shoes and whether the smock look is in or finished already. But since (oh, shame!) I care a lot about eyeshadow, hemlines and shoes, and since I don't *want* to wear smocks if the smock look is finished, I'm very glad to have a shopping friend.

14   3. Historical friends. We all have a friend who knew us when . . . maybe way back in Miss Meltzer's second grade, when our family lived in that three-room flat in Brooklyn, when our dad was out of work for seven months, when our brother Allie got in that fight where they had to call the police, when our sister married the endodontist from Yonkers and when, the morning after we lost our virginity, she was the first, the only, friend we told.

15   The years have gone by and we've gone separate ways and we've little in common now, but we're still an intimate part of each other's past. And so whenever we go to Detroit we always go to visit this friend of our girlhood. Who knows how we looked before our teeth were straightened. Who knows how we talked before our voice got un-Brookyned. Who knows what we ate before we learned about artichokes. And who, by her presence, puts us in touch with an earlier part of ourself, a part of ourself it's important never to lose.

16   "What this friend means to me and what I mean to her," says Grace, "is having a sister without sibling rivalry. We know the texture of each other's lives. She remembers my grandmother's cabbage soup. I remember the way her uncle played the piano. There's simply no other friend who remembers those things."

17   4. Crossroads friends. Like historical friends, our crossroads friends are important for *what was*—for the friendship we shared at a crucial, now past, time of life. A time, perhaps, when we roomed in college together; or worked as eager young singles in the Big City together; or went together, as my friend Elizabeth and I did, through pregnancy, birth and that scary first year of new motherhood.

18   Crossroads friends forge powerful links, links strong enough to endure with not much more contact than once-a-year letters at Christmas. And out of respect for those crossroads years, for those dramas and dreams we once shared, we will always be friends.

19   5. Cross-generational friends. Historical friends and crossroads friends seem to maintain a special kind of intimacy—dormant but always ready to be revived—and though we may rarely meet, whenever we do connect, it's personal and intense. Another kind of intimacy exists in the friendships that form across generations in what one woman calls her daughter-mother and her mother-daughter relationships.

20   Evelyn's friend is her mother's age—"but I share so much more than I ever could with my mother"—a woman she talks to of music, of books and of life. "What I get from her is the benefit of her experience. What she gets—and enjoys—from me is a youthful perspective. It's a pleasure for both of us."

21   I have in my own life a precious friend, a woman of 65 who has lived very hard, who is wise, who listens well; who has been where I am and can help me understand it; and who represents not only an ultimate ideal mother to me but also the person I'd like to be when I grow up.

22   In our daughter role we tend to do more than our share of self-revelation; in our mother role we tend to receive what's revealed. It's another kind of pleasure—playing wise mother to a questing younger person. It's another very lovely kind of friendship.

23   6. Part-of-a-couple friends. Some of the women we call our friends we never see alone—we see them as part of a couple at couples' parties. And though we share interests in many things and respect each other's views, we aren't moved to deepen the relationship. Whatever the reason, a lack of time or—and this is more likely—a lack of chemistry, our friendship remains in the

context of a group. But the fact that our feeling on seeing each other is always, "I'm so glad she's here" and the fact that we spend half the evening talking together says that this too, in its own way, counts as a friendship.

24   (Other part-of-a-couple friends are the friends that came with the marriage, and some of these are friends we could live without. But sometimes, alas, she married our husband's best friend; and sometimes, alas, she *is* our husband's best friend. And so we find ourself dealing with her, somewhat against our will, in a spirit of what I'll call *reluctant* friendship.)

25   7. Men who are friends. I wanted to write just of women friends, but the women I've talked to won't let me—they say I must mention man-woman friendships too. For these friendships can be just as close and as dear as those that we form with women. Listen to Lucy's description of one such friendship:

26   "We've found we have things to talk about that are different from what he talks about with my husband and different from what I talk about with his wife. So sometimes we call on the phone or meet for lunch. There are similar intellectual interests—we always pass on to each other the books that we love—but there's also something tender and caring too."

27   In a couple of crises, Lucy says, "he offered himself, for talking and for helping. And when someone died in his family he wanted me there. The sexual, flirty part of our friendship is very small, but *some*—just enough to make it fun and different." She thinks—and I agree—that the sexual part, though small is always *some*, is always there when a man and a woman are friends.

28   It's only in the past few years that I've made friends with men, in the sense of a friendship that's *mine*, not just part of two couples. And achieving with them the ease and the trust I've found with women friends has value indeed. Under the dryer at home last week, putting on mascara and rouge, I comfortably sat and talked with a fellow named Peter. Peter, I finally decided, could handle the shock of me minus mascara under the dryer. Because we care for each other. Because we're friends.

29   8. There are medium friends, and pretty good friends, and very good friends indeed, and these friendships are defined by their level of intimacy. And what we'll reveal at each of these levels of intimacy is calibrated with care. We might tell a medium friend, for example, that yesterday we had a fight with our husband. And we might tell a pretty good friend that this fight with our husband made us so mad that we slept on the couch. And we might tell a very good friend that the reason we got so mad in that fight that we slept on the couch had something to do with that girl who works in his office. But it's only to our very best friends that we're willing to tell all, to tell what's going on with that girl in his office.

30   The best of friends, I still believe, totally love and support and trust each other, and bare to each other the secrets of their souls, and run—no questions asked—to help each other, and tell harsh truths to each other when they must be told.

31   But we needn't agree about everything (only 12-year-old girl friends agree about *everything*) to tolerate each other's point of view. To accept without judgment. To give and to take without ever keeping score. And to *be* there, as

I am for them and as they are for me, to comfort our sorrows, to celebrate our joys.

Topics for Writing and Discussion

1. How does Viorst describe her earlier views of women's friendships? What single sentence sums up those views? How do those earlier views serve as an introduction to her thesis? What single sentence states that thesis?
2. What are the categories of friends Viorst describes? Do your own friendships fall neatly into these categories? If you were writing about your own friendships, would you eliminate some of Viorst's groups? Would you add some of your own?
3. Viorst originally published this essay in *Redbook* magazine, which defines its readers as primarily women between the ages of 25 and 35. What elements of the essay reflect Viorst's sensitivity to this audience? Would she need to revise the essay if she were submitting it to *Esquire* magazine, which has a primarily male audience? What if she were submitting it to a magazine read mainly by older Americans, both male and female?
4. Are Viorst's categories distinct and clearly presented? Does Viorst use enough examples and details to explain each category? Support your answer with reference to the essay.
5. Write an essay classifying into categories the people at your place of work or the people who are members of a club or organization to which you belong. In your essay, explain how the people in each of these categories contribute to your attitude toward your job or your club or organization.

Lewis Thomas at Lincoln Center in New York City after winning a National Book Award (© 1991 by Jill Krementz)

NOTES ON PUNCTUATION

Lewis Thomas
(1913–1993)

Educated at Princeton University and Harvard Medical
School, Lewis Thomas practiced medicine in Boston
and New York and taught at several American universities. In 1971, he began contributing a regular column,
"Notes of a Biology Watcher," to the *New England
Journal of Medicine.* His columns were collected into
The Lives of a Cell: Notes of a Biology Watcher
(1974), for which he won the National Book Award for
Arts and Letters. A second collection, *The Medusa and
the Snail: More Notes of a Biology Watcher,* was published in 1979. His last works include *Late Night
Thoughts on Listening to Mahler's Ninth Symphony*
(1983) and *Et Cetera, Et Cetera: Notes of a Wordwatcher* (1990). In the following essay, Lewis cleverly
categorizes punctuation marks and gives his suggestions on their use—and misuse.

1 THERE are no precise rules about punctuation (Fowler* lays out some general advice (as best he can under the complex circumstances of English prose
(he points out, for example, that we possess only four stops (the comma, the
semicolon, the colon and the period (the question mark and exclamation point
are not, strictly speaking, stops; they are indicators of tone (oddly enough, the
Greeks employed the semicolon for their question mark (it produces a strange
sensation to read a Greek sentence which is a straightforward question: Why

---

* H. W. Fowler was the author of widely used reference books on language, including *A Dictionary of Modern English Usage* and *The King's English.*

weepest thou; (instead of Why weepest thou? (and, of course, there are parentheses (which are surely a kind of punctuation making this whole matter much more complicated by having to count up the left-handed parentheses in order to be sure of closing with the right number (but if the parentheses were left out, with nothing to work with but the stops, we would have considerably more flexibility in the deploying of layers of meaning than if we tried to separate all the clauses by physical barriers (and in the latter case, while we might have more precision and exactitude for our meaning, we would lose the essential flavor of language, which is its wonderful ambiguity))))))))))).

2   The commas are the most useful and usable of all the stops. It is highly important to put them in place as you go along. If you try to come back after doing a paragraph and stick them in the various spots that tempt you you will discover that they tend to swarm like minnows into all sorts of crevices whose existence you hadn't realized and before you know it the whole long sentence becomes immobilized and lashed up squirming in commas. Better to use them sparingly, and with affection, precisely when the need for each one arises, nicely, by itself.

3   I have grown fond of semicolons in recent years. The semicolon tells you that there is still some question about the preceding full sentence; something needs to be added; it reminds you sometimes of the Greek usage. It is almost always a greater pleasure to come across a semicolon than a period. The period tells you that that is that; if you didn't get all the meaning you wanted or expected, anyway you got all the writer intended to parcel out and now you have to move along. But with a semicolon there you get a pleasant little feeling of expectancy; there is more to come; read on; it will get clearer.

4   Colons are a lot less attractive, for several reasons: firstly, they give you the feeling of being rather ordered around, or at least having your nose pointed in a direction you might not be inclined to take if left to yourself, and, secondly, you suspect you're in for one of those sentences that will be labeling the points to be made: firstly, secondly and so forth, with the implication that you haven't sense enough to keep track of a sequence of notions without having them numbered. Also, many writers use this system loosely and incompletely, starting out with number one and number two as though counting off on their fingers but then going on and on without the succession of labels you've been led to expect, leaving you floundering about searching for the ninethly or seventeenthly that ought to be there but isn't.

5   Exclamation points are the most irritating of all. Look! they say, look at what I just said! How amazing is my thought! It is like being forced to watch someone else's small child jumping up and down crazily in the center of the living room shouting to attract attention. If a sentence really has something of importance to say, something quite remarkable, it doesn't need a mark to point it out. And if it is really, after all, a banal sentence needing more zing, the exclamation point simply emphasizes its banality!

6   Quotation marks should be used honestly and sparingly, when there is a genuine quotation at hand, and it is necessary to be very rigorous about the

words enclosed by the marks. If something is to be quoted, the *exact* words must be used. If part of it must be left out because of space limitations, it is good manners to insert three dots to indicate the omission, but it is unethical to do this if it means connecting two thoughts which the original author did not intend to have tied together. Above all, quotation marks should not be used for ideas that you'd like to disown, things in the air so to speak. Nor should they be put in place around clichés; if you want to use a cliché you must take full responsibility for it yourself and not try to fob it off on anon., or on society. The most objectionable misuse of quotation marks, but one which illustrates the dangers of misuse in ordinary prose, is seen in advertising, especially in advertisement for small restaurants, for example "just around the corner," or "a good place to eat." No single, identifiable, citable person ever really said, for the record, "just around the corner," much less "a good place to eat," least likely of all for restaurants of the type that use this type of prose.

7   The dash is a handy device, informal and essentially playful, telling you that you're about to take off on a different tack but still in some way connected with the present course—only you have to remember that the dash is there, and either put a second dash at the end of the notion to let the reader know that he's back on course, or else end the sentence, as here, with a period.

8   The greatest danger in punctuation is for poetry. Here it is necessary to be as economical and parsimonious with commas and periods as with the words themselves, and any marks that seem to carry their own subtle meanings, like dashes and little rows of periods, even semicolons and question marks, should be left out altogether rather than inserted to clog up the thing with ambiguity. A single exclamation point in a poem, no matter what else the poem has to say, is enough to destroy the whole work.

9   The things I like best in T. S. Eliot's poetry, especially in the *Four Quartets*, are the semicolons. You cannot hear them, but they are there, laying out the connections between the images and the ideas. Sometimes you get a glimpse of a semicolon coming, a few lines farther on, and it is like climbing a steep path through woods and seeing a wooden bench just at a bend in the road ahead, a place where you can expect to sit for a moment, catching your breath.

10   Commas can't do this sort of thing; they can only tell you how the different parts of a complicated thought are to be fitted together, but you can't sit, not even take a breath, just because of a comma,

TOPICS FOR WRITING AND DISCUSSION

1. What subject is categorized in this essay? What is Thomas' main point about his subject and the uses of language?
2. Look carefully at each punctuation mark's description. How does Thomas cleverly illustrate his own subject? (If you are confused about this question, look closely at paragraph 3, for example.)
3. What are some of the techniques Thomas uses to make each of his categories distinct from the others?

4. Characterize Thomas' tone in this essay. How does it compare to one of the punctuation or grammar handbooks you may have used in high school or college? Consider, too, Thomas' use of figurative language, such as the similes in paragraphs 2 and 5. What do they add to the reader's understanding and enjoyment of Thomas' points?

5. The first paragraph in the essay is, technically, one extremely long and complex sentence. How might you rewrite it for clarity and ease of reading, using the various marks of punctuation discussed in this essay? Why do you think Thomas introduces his essay with such a paragraph?

THINKING AS A HOBBY

William Golding
(1911–1993)

Born in Cornwall, English novelist, essayist, and poet
William Gerald Golding is perhaps best known for his
first novel, *Lord of the Flies* (1954), an allegorical
work about the conflict between humankind's innate
barbarism and the civilizing effect of reason. He studied physics and English literature at Marlborough
Grammar School and Brasenose College at Oxford,
and served in the British Navy during World War II.
Many of Golding's works use allusions to classical literature, mythology, and Christian symbolism and also
reflect his rejection of society's norms and the status
quo. His works include *The Inheritors* (1955), *Pincher
Martin* (1956), *Free Fall* (1959), *The Spire* (1964),
Darkness Visible (1979), *Rites of Passage* (1981),
Close Quarters (1987), and *Fire Down Below* (1989).
His last novel was *Double Tongue* (1993). In addition
to his novels, Golding published one play, *The Brass
Butterfly* (1958); a book of verse, *Poems* (1934); and
two collections of essays, *The Hot Gates* (1965) and *A
Moving Target* (1984). He was awarded the Nobel
Prize for literature in 1983. In "Thinking as a Hobby,"
Golding provides illustrations of what he classifies as
grade-three, grade-two, and grade-one thinking.

1   WHILE I was still a boy, I came to the conclusion that there were three
grades of thinking; and since I was later to claim thinking as my hobby, I came
to an even stranger conclusion—namely, that I myself could not think at all.

2   I must have been an unsatisfactory child for grownups to deal with. I remember how incomprehensible they appeared to me at first, but not, of

William Golding at age 72 at his home near Salisbury, England, on the day he received the Nobel Prize for literature. (AP/Wide World Photos)

course, how I appeared to them. It was the headmaster of my grammar school who first brought the subject of thinking before me—though neither in the way, nor with the result he intended. He had some statuettes in his study. They stood on a high cupboard behind his desk. One was a lady wearing nothing but a bath towel. She seemed frozen in an eternal panic lest the bath towel slip down any farther; and since she had no arms, she was in an unfortunate position to pull the towel up again. Next to her, crouched the statuette of a leopard, ready to spring down at the top drawer of a filing cabinet labeled A–AH. My innocence interpreted this as the victim's last, despairing cry. Beyond the leopard was a naked, muscular gentleman, who sat, looking down, with his chin on his fist and his elbow on his knee. He seemed utterly miserable.

3   Some time later, I learned about these statuettes. The headmaster had placed them where they would face delinquent children, because they symbolized to him the whole of life. The naked lady was the Venus of Milo. She was Love. She was not worried about the towel. She was just busy being beautiful. The leopard was Nature, and he was being natural. The naked, muscular gentleman was not miserable. He was Rodin's Thinker, an image of pure thought. It is easy to buy small plaster models of what you think life is like.

4   I had better explain that I was a frequent visitor to the headmaster's study, because of the latest thing I had done or left undone. As we now say, I was not integrated. I was, if anything, disintegrated; and I was puzzled. Grownups never made sense. Whenever I found myself in a penal position before the headmaster's desk, with the statuettes glimmering whitely above him, I would sink my head, clasp my hands behind my back and writhe one shoe over the other.

5   The headmaster would look opaquely at me through flashing spectacles.

6   "What are we going to do with you?"

7   Well, what *were* they going to do with me? I would writhe my shoe some more and stare down at the worn rug.

8   "Look up, boy! Can't you look up?"

9   Then I would look up at the cupboard, where the naked lady was frozen in her panic and the muscular gentleman contemplated the hindquarters of the leopard in endless gloom. I had nothing to say to the headmaster. His spectacles caught the light so that you could see nothing human behind them. There was no possibility of communication.

10   "Don't you ever think at all?"

11   No, I didn't think, wasn't thinking, couldn't think—I was simply waiting in anguish for the interview to stop.

12   "Then you'd better learn—hadn't you?"

13   On one occasion the headmaster leaped to his feet, reached up and plonked Rodin's masterpiece on the desk before me.

14   "That's what a man looks like when he's really thinking."

15   I surveyed the gentleman without interest or comprehension.

16   "Go back to your class."

17   Clearly there was something missing in me. Nature had endowed the rest of the human race with a sixth sense and left me out. This must be so, I mused,

on my way back to the class, since whether I had broken a window, or failed to remember Boyle's Law, or been late for school, my teachers produced me one, adult answer: "Why can't you think?"

18 As I saw the case, I had broken the window because I had tried to hit Jack Arney with a cricket ball and missed him; I could not remember Boyle's Law because I had never bothered to learn it; and I was late for school because I preferred looking over the bridge into the river. In fact, I was wicked. Were my teachers, perhaps, so good that they could not understand the depths of my depravity? Were they clear, untormented people who could direct their every action by this mysterious business of thinking? The whole thing was incomprehensible. In my earlier years, I found even the statuette of the Thinker confusing. I did not believe any of my teachers were naked, ever. Like someone born deaf, but bitterly determined to find out about sound, I watched my teachers to find out about thought.

19 There was Mr. Houghton. He was always telling me to think. With a modest satisfaction, he would tell me that he had thought a bit himself. Then why did he spend so much time drinking? Or was there more sense in drinking than there appeared to be? But if not, and if drinking were in fact ruinous to health—and Mr. Houghton was ruined, there was no doubt about that—why was he always talking about the clean life and the virtues of fresh air? He would spread his arms wide with the action of a man who habitually spent his time striding along mountain ridges.

20 "Open air does me good, boys—I know it!"

21 Sometimes, exalted by his own oratory, he would leap from his desk and hustle us outside into a hideous wind.

22 "Now boys! Deep breaths! Feel it right down inside you—huge draughts of God's good air!"

23 He would stand before us, rejoicing in his perfect health, an open-air man. He would put his hands on his waist and take a tremendous breath. You could hear the wind, trapped in the cavern of his chest and struggling with all the unnatural impediments. His body would reel with shock and his ruined face go white at the unaccustomed visitation. He would stagger back to his desk and collapse there, useless for the rest of the morning.

24 Mr. Houghton was given to high-minded monologues about the good life, sexless and full of duty. Yet in the middle of one of these monologues, if a girl passed the window, tapping along on her neat little feet, he would interrupt his discourse, his neck would turn of itself and he would watch her out of sight. In this instance, he seemed to me ruled not by thought but by an invisible and irresistible spring in his nape.

25 His neck was an object of great interest to me. Normally it bulged a bit over his collar. But Mr. Houghton had fought in the First World War alongside both Americans and French, and had come—by who knows what illogic?—to a settled detestation of both countries. If either country happened to be prominent in current affairs, no argument could make Mr. Houghton think well of it. He would bang the desk, his neck would bulge still further and go red. "You

can say what you like," he would cry, "but I've thought about this—and I know what I think!"

26   Mr. Houghton thought with his neck.

27   There was Miss Parsons. She assured us that her dearest wish was our welfare, but I knew even then, with the mysterious clairvoyance of childhood, that what she wanted most was the husband she never got. There was Mr. Hands—and so on.

28   I have dealt at length with my teachers because this was my introduction to the nature of what is commonly called thought. Through them I discovered that thought is often full of unconscious prejudice, ignorance and hypocrisy. It will lecture on disinterested purity while its neck is being remorselessly twisted toward a skirt. Technically, it is about as proficient as most businessmen's golf, as honest as most politicians' intentions, or—to come near my own preoccupation—as coherent as most books that get written. It is what I came to call grade-three thinking, though more properly, it is feeling, rather than thought.

29   True, often there is a kind of innocence in prejudices, but in those days I viewed grade-three thinking with an intolerant contempt and an incautious mockery. I delighted to confront a pious lady who hated the Germans with the proposition that we should love our enemies. She taught me a great truth in dealing with grade-three thinkers; because of her, I no longer dismiss lightly a mental process which for nine-tenths of the population is the nearest they will ever get to thought. They have immense solidarity. We had better respect them, for we are outnumbered and surrounded. A crowd of grade-three thinkers, all shouting the same thing, all warming their hands at the fire of their own prejudices, will not thank you for pointing out the contradictions in their beliefs. Man is a gregarious animal, and enjoys agreement as cows will graze all the same way on the side of a hill.

30   Grade-two thinking is the detection of contradictions. I reached grade two when I trapped the poor, pious lady. Grade-two thinkers do not stampede easily, though often they fall into the other fault and lag behind. Grade-two thinking is a withdrawal, with eyes and ears open. It became my hobby and brought satisfaction and loneliness in either hand. For grade-two thinking destroys without having the power to create. It set me watching the crowds cheering His Majesty the King and asking myself what all the fuss was about, without giving me anything positive to put in the place of that heady patriotism. But there were compensations. To hear people justify their habit of hunting foxes and tearing them to pieces by claiming that the foxes liked it. To hear our Prime Minister talk about the great benefit we conferred on India by jailing people like Pandit Nehru and Gandhi. To hear American politicians talk about peace in one sentence and refuse to join the League of Nations in the next. Yes, there were moments of delight.

31   But I was growing toward adolescence and had to admit that Mr. Houghton was not the only one with an irresistible spring in his neck. I, too, felt the compulsive hand of nature and began to find that pointing out contradiction could be costly as well as fun. There was Ruth, for example, a serious and attractive

girl. I was an atheist at the time. Grade-two thinking is a menace to religion and knocks down sects like skittles. I put myself in a position to be converted by her with an hypocrisy worthy of grade three. She was a Methodist—or at least, her parents were, and Ruth had to follow suit. But, alas, instead of relying on the Holy Spirit to convert me, Ruth was foolish enough to open her pretty mouth in argument. She claimed that the Bible (King James Version) was literally inspired. I countered by saying that the Catholics believed in the literal inspiration of Saint Jerome's *Vulgate,* and the two books were different. Argument flagged.

32   At last she remarked that there were an awful lot of Methodists, and they couldn't be wrong, could they—not all those millions? That was too easy, said I restively (for the nearer you were to Ruth, the nicer she was to be near to) since there were more Roman Catholics than Methodists anyway; and they couldn't be wrong, could they—not all those hundreds of millions? An awful flicker of doubt appeared in her eyes. I slid my arm round her waist and murmured breathlessly that if we were counting heads, the Buddhists were the boys for my money. But Ruth had *really* wanted to do me good, because I was so nice. She fled. The combination of my arm and those countless Buddhists was too much for her.

33   That night her father visited my father and left, red-cheeked and indignant. I was given the third degree to find out what had happened. It was lucky we were both of us only fourteen. I lost Ruth and gained an undeserved reputation as a potential libertine.

34   So grade-two thinking could be dangerous. It was in this knowledge, at the age of fifteen, that I remember making a comment from the heights of grade two, on the limitations of grade three. One evening I found myself alone in the schoolhall, preparing it for a party. The door of the headmaster's study was open. I went in. The headmaster had ceased to thump Rodin's Thinker down on the desk as an example to the young. Perhaps he had not found any more candidates, but the statuettes were still there, glimmering and gathering dust on top of the cupboard. I stood on a chair and rearranged them. I stood Venus in her bath towel on the filing cabinet, so that now the top drawer caught its breath in a gasp of sexy excitement. "A-ah!" The portentous Thinker I placed on the edge of the cupboard so that he looked down at the bath towel and waited for it to slip. Grade-two thinking, though it filled life with fun and excitement, did not make for content. To find out the deficiencies of our elders bolsters the young ego but does not make for personal security. I found that grade two was not only the power to point out contradictions. It took the swimmer some distance from the shore and left him there, out of his depth. I decided that Pontius Pilate was a typical grade-two thinker. "What is truth?" he said, a very common grade-two thought, but one that is used always as the end of an argument instead of the beginning. There is a still higher grade of thought which says, "What is truth?" and sets out to find it.

35   But these grade-one thinkers were few and far between. They did not visit my grammar school in the flesh though they were there in books. I aspired to them, partly because I was ambitious and partly because I now saw my hobby

as an unsatisfactory thing if it went no further. If you set out to climb a mountain, however high you climb, you have failed if you cannot reach the top.

36   I *did* meet an undeniably grade-one thinker in my first year at Oxford. I was looking over a small bridge in Magdalen Deer Park, and a tiny mustached and hatted figure came and stood by my side. He was a German who had just fled from the Nazis to Oxford as a temporary refuge. His name was Einstein.

37   But Professor Einstein knew no English at that time and I knew only two words of German. I beamed at him, trying wordlessly to convey by my bearing all the affection and respect that the English felt for him. It is possible—and I have to make the admission—that I felt here were two grade-one thinkers standing side by side; yet I doubt if my face conveyed more than a formless awe. I would have given my Greek and Latin and French and a good slice of my English for enough German to communicate. But we were divided; he was as inscrutable as my headmaster. For perhaps five minutes we stood together on the bridge, undeniable grade-one thinker and breathless aspirant. With true greatness, Professor Einstein realized that any contact was better than none. He pointed to a trout wavering in midstream.

38   He spoke: *"Fisch."*

39   My brain reeled. Here I was, mingling with the great, and yet helpless as the veriest grade-three thinker. Desperately I sought for some sign by which I might convey that I, too, revered pure reason. I nodded vehemently. In a brilliant flash I used up half of my German vocabulary. *"Fisch. Ja. Ja."*

40   For perhaps another five minutes we stood side by side. Then Professor Einstein, his whole figure still conveying good will and amiability, drifted away out of sight.

41   I, too, would be a grade-one thinker. I was irreverent at the best of times. Political and religious systems, social customs, loyalties and traditions, they all came tumbling down like so many rotten apples off a tree. This was a fine hobby and a sensible substitute for cricket, since you could play it all the year round. I came up in the end with what must always remain the justification for grade-one thinking, its sign, seal and charter. I devised a coherent system for living. It was a moral system, which was wholly logical. Of course, as I readily admitted, conversion of the world to my way of thinking might be difficult, since my system did away with a number of trifles, such as big business, centralized government, armies, marriage. . . .

42   It was Ruth all over again. I had some very good friends who stood by me, and still do. But my acquaintances vanished, taking the girls with them. Young women seemed oddly contented with the world as it was. They valued the meaningless ceremony with a ring. Young men, while willing to concede the chaining sordidness of marriage, were hesitant about abandoning the organizations which they hoped would give them a career. A young man on the first rung of the Royal Navy, while perfectly agreeable to doing away with big business and marriage, got as rednecked as Mr. Houghton when I proposed a world without any battleships in it.

43   Had the game gone too far? Was it a game any longer? In those prewar days, I stood to lose a great deal, for the sake of a hobby.

44   Now you are expecting me to describe how I saw the folly of my ways and came back to the warm nest, where prejudices are so often called loyalties, where pointless actions are hallowed into custom by repetition, where we are content to say we think when all we do is feel.

45   But you would be wrong. I dropped my hobby and turned professional.

46   If I were to go back to the headmaster's study and find the dusty statuettes still there, I would arrange them differently. I would dust Venus and put her aside, for I have come to love her and know her for the fair thing she is. But I would put the Thinker, sunk in his desperate thought, where there were shadows before him—and at his back, I would put the leopard, crouched and ready to spring.

TOPICS FOR WRITING AND DISCUSSION

1. Why did Golding as a boy come to the conclusion that he could not think at all? What examples does he give to explain how he reached that conclusion? What irony does an adult, reading Golding's examples, see in his claim that he could not think?

2. Why does Golding call grade-two thinking dangerous? How does his adventure with Rodin's Thinker and Venus (paragraph 34) in the headmaster's office illustrate what he believes to be one of the primary limitations of grade-two thinking?

3. Golding describes the negative aspects of grade-three and grade-two thinking. Does he see grade-one thinking as entirely desirable? What sacrifices does grade-one thinking require? Would these sacrifices, in your opinion, be justified by a world full of Golding's grade-one thinkers?

4. What does Golding's meeting with Einstein illustrate? Why does this meeting confirm his decision to be a grade-one thinker? How does the final paragraph, with its references to the Thinker, Venus, and the leopard, relate to Golding's decision to be a "professional"?

5. Using Golding's categories in "Thinking as a Hobby," write an essay in which you offer current illustrations of grade-one, -two, and -three thinking. Consider using as examples some of the popular social or political controversies or trends today.

THE UNKNOWN CITIZEN

W. H. Auden
(1907–1973)

English born and Oxford educated, Wystan Hugh
Auden was one of the most important poets of the
twentieth century. His first book of poetry was
accepted by T. S. Eliot, then the editor at the London
publisher responsible for its publication. After World
War II, Auden became an American citizen and spent
much of his life in New York City. Some of his collections include *The Orators* (1932); *Look Stranger!*
(1936); *The Age of Anxiety* (1947), for which he won a
Pulitzer Prize; *Homage to Clio* (1960); and *Collected
Poems* (1974). Additionally, he collaborated with
dramatist Christopher Isherwood on several plays,
including *The Dance of Death* (1933) and *The Ascent
of F6* (1936), and his texts have been used for Benjamin Britten's *Paul Bunyan* (1941) and for Igor
Stravinski's *The Rake's Progress* (1951). His poetry
often contains simple language, and his subjects range
from politics to psychology. This well-known poem
illustrates Auden's satire on the witless conformity and
bureaucracy he saw thriving in the modern age.

To JS/07/M378

He was found by the Bureau of Statistics to be
One against whom there was no official complaint,
And all the reports on his conduct agree
That, in the modern sense of an old-fashioned word, he was a
    saint,
5 For in everything he did he served the Greater Community,
Except for the War till the day he retired
He worked in a factory and never got fired,
But satisfied his employers, Fudge Motors Inc.

W. H. Auden (AP/Wide World Photos, Inc.)

Yet he wasn't a scab or odd in his views,

10 For his Union reports that he paid his dues,
(Our report on his Union shows it was sound)
And our Social Psychology workers found
That he was popular with his mates and liked a drink.
The Press are convinced that he bought a paper every day

15 And that his reactions to advertisements were normal in every
way.
Policies taken out in his name prove that he was fully insured.
And his Health-card shows he was once in hospital but left it
cured.
Both Producers Research and High-Grade Living declare
He was fully sensible to the advantages of the Installment Plan

20 And had everything necessary to the Modern Man,
A phonograph, radio, a car and a frigidaire.
Our researchers into Public Opinion are content
That he held the proper opinions for the time of year;
When there was peace, he was for peace; when there was war,
he went.

25 He was married and added five children to the population,
Which our Eugenist says was the right number for a parent of
his generation,
And our teachers report that he never interfered with their
education.
Was he free? Was he happy? The question is absurd:
Had anything been wrong, we should certainly have heard.

TOPICS FOR WRITING AND DISCUSSION

1. In what ways has the life of the citizen in this essay been classified by several bureaucratic agencies?

2. Describe in a few sentences this person. What are his distinguishing personality traits?

3. Are readers meant to admire this person? What do lines such as "he held the proper opinions for the time of year" suggest about the man's ability to think for himself? Why is the dedication "To JS/07/M378" especially appropriate for this well-documented but "unknown" citizen?

4. Why do the "we" of the last line think the questions "Was he free? Was he happy?" are absurd? What is Auden satirizing about contemporary society and its citizens?

5. Look at the students on your campus. Do you see certain types of conformists—or nonconformists—in identifiable categories? Make a serious or satirical point about the types of people you see. In comparison to Auden's poem, what does your classification say about individuality in modern life today?

Amy Tan (Reuters/Corbis-Bettmann)

TWO KINDS

Amy Tan
(1952–   )

≈≈≈≈≈⟩

Though born in Oakland, California, of then recently
emigrated Chinese parents, Amy Tan's clear perspective of her identity as a Chinese-American began when
she and her mother moved to Switzerland after the
death of her brother and father. After returning to the
United States, Tan completed bachelor's and master's
degrees from San Jose State University and began writing fiction in 1984. A few years later, she traveled with
her mother to China to visit relatives. Soon after the
trip, she published *The Joy Luck Club* (1989), a collection of interwoven stories about four Chinese mothers and their four American daughters. The novel
became an immediate bestseller, was nominated for a
National Book Award, and was made into a popular
film. Her other novels include *The Kitchen God's Wife*
(1991), *The Hundred Secret Senses* (1995), and *The
Year of No Flood* (1995). "Two Kinds," one of the stories from *The Joy Luck Club*, examines the tensions
between an American-born daughter and her Chinese-
born mother.

1   My mother believed you could be anything you wanted to be in America.
You could open a restaurant. You could work for the government and get good
retirement. You could buy a house with almost no money down. You could
become rich. You could become instantly famous.

2   "Of course you can be prodigy, too," my mother told me when I was nine.
"You can be best anything. What does Auntie Lindo know? Her daughter, she
is only best tricky."

3   America was where all my mother's hopes lay. She had come here in 1949 after losing everything in China: her mother and father, her family home, her first husband, and two daughters, twin baby girls. But she never looked back with regret. There were so many ways for things to get better.

4   We didn't immediately pick the right kind of prodigy. At first my mother thought I could be a Chinese Shirley Temple. We'd watch Shirley's old movies on TV as though they were training films. My mother would poke my arm and say, *"Ni kan"*—You watch. And I would see Shirley tapping her feet, or singing a sailor song, or pursing her lips into a very round O while saying, "Oh my goodness."

5   *"Ni kan,"* said my mother as Shirley's eyes flooded with tears. "You already know how. Don't need talent for crying!"

6   Soon after my mother got this idea about Shirley Temple, she took me to a beauty training school in the Mission district and put me in the hands of a student who could barely hold the scissors without shaking. Instead of getting big fat curls, I emerged with an uneven mass of crinkly black fuzz. My mother dragged me off to the bathroom and tried to wet down my hair.

7   "You look like Negro Chinese," she lamented, as if I had done this on purpose.

8   The instructor of the beauty training school had to lop off these soggy clumps to make my hair even again. "Peter Pan is very popular these days," the instructor assured my mother. I now had hair the length of a boy's, with straight-across bangs that hung at a slant two inches above my eyebrows. I liked the haircut and it made me actually look forward to my future fame.

9   In fact, in the beginning, I was just as excited as my mother, maybe even more so. I pictured this prodigy part of me as many different images, trying each one on for size. I was a dainty ballerina girl standing by the curtains, waiting to hear the right music that would send me floating on my tiptoes. I was like the Christ child lifted out of the straw manger, crying with holy dignity. I was Cinderella stepping from her pumpkin carriage with sparkly cartoon music filling the air.

10   In all of my imaginings, I was filled with a sense that I would soon become *perfect.* My mother and father would adore me. I would be beyond reproach. I would never feel the need to sulk for anything.

11   But sometimes the prodigy in me became impatient. "If you don't hurry up and get me out of here, I'm disappearing for good," it warned. "And then you'll always be nothing."

12   Every night after dinner, my mother and I would sit at the Formica kitchen table. She would present new tests, taking her examples from stories of amazing children she had read in *Ripley's Believe It or Not,* or *Good Housekeeping, Reader's Digest,* and a dozen other magazines she kept in a pile in our bathroom. My mother got these magazines from people whose houses she cleaned. And since she cleaned many houses each week, we had a great assortment. She would look through them all, searching for stories about remarkable children.

13   The first night she brought out a story about a three-year-old boy who knew the capitals of all the states and even most of the European countries. A teacher was quoted as saying the little boy could also pronounce the names of the foreign cities correctly.

14   "What's the capital of Finland?" my mother asked me, looking at the magazine story.

15   All I knew was the capital of California, because Sacramento was the name of the street we lived on in Chinatown. "Nairobi!" I guessed, saying the most foreign word I could think of. She checked to see if that was possibly one way to pronounce "Helsinki" before showing me the answer.

16   The tests got harder—multiplying numbers in my head, finding the queen of hearts in a deck of cards, trying to stand on my head without using my hands, predicting the daily temperatures in Los Angeles, New York, and London.

17   One night I had to look at a page from the Bible for three minutes and then report everything I could remember. "Now Jehoshaphat had riches and honor in abundance and . . . that's all I remember, Ma," I said.

18   And after seeing my mother's disappointed face once again, something inside of me began to die. I hated the tests, the raised hopes and failed expectations. Before going to bed that night, I looked in the mirror above the bathroom sink and when I saw only my face staring back—and that it would always be this ordinary face—I began to cry. Such a sad, ugly girl! I made high-pitched noises like a crazed animal, trying to scratch out the face in the mirror.

19   And then I saw what seemed to be the prodigy side of me—because I had never seen that face before. I looked at my reflection, blinking so I could see more clearly. The girl staring back at me was angry, powerful. This girl and I were the same. I had new thoughts, willful thoughts, or rather thoughts filled with lots of won'ts. I won't let her change me, I promised myself. I won't be what I'm not.

20   So now on nights when my mother presented her tests, I performed listlessly, my head propped on one arm. I pretended to be bored. And I was. I got so bored I started counting the bellows of the foghorns out on the bay while my mother drilled me in other areas. The sound was comforting and reminded me of the cow jumping over the moon. And the next day, I played a game with myself, seeing if my mother would give up on me before eight bellows. After a while I usually counted only one, maybe two bellows at most. At last she was beginning to give up hope.

21   Two or three months had gone by without any mention of my being a prodigy again. And then one day my mother was watching *The Ed Sullivan Show* on TV. The TV was old and the sound kept shorting out. Every time my mother got halfway up from the sofa to adjust the set, the sound would go back on and Ed would be talking. As soon as she sat down, Ed would go silent again. She got up, the TV broke into loud piano music. She sat down. Silence. Up and down, back and forth, quiet and loud. It was like a stiff embraceless

dance between her and the TV set. Finally she stood by the set with her hand on the sound dial.

22   She seemed entranced by the music, a little frenzied piano piece with this mesmerizing quality, sort of quick passages and then teasing lilting ones before it returned to the quick playful parts.

23   "*Ni kan,*" my mother said, calling me over with hurried hand gestures. "Look here."

24   I could see why my mother was fascinated by the music. It was being pounded out by a little Chinese girl, about nine years old, with a Peter Pan haircut. The girl had the sauciness of a Shirley Temple. She was proudly modest like a proper Chinese child. And she also did this fancy sweep of a curtsy, so that the fluffy skirt of her white dress cascaded slowly to the floor like the petals of a large carnation.

25   In spite of these warning signs, I wasn't worried. Our family had no piano and we couldn't afford to buy one, let alone reams of sheet music and piano lessons. So I could be generous in my comments when my mother bad-mouthed the little girl on TV.

26   "Play note right, but doesn't sound good! No singing sound," complained my mother.

27   "What are you picking on her for?" I said carelessly. "She's pretty good. Maybe she's not the best, but she's trying hard." I knew almost immediately I would be sorry I said that.

28   "Just like you," she said. "Not the best. Because you not trying." She gave a little huff as she let go of the sound dial and sat down on the sofa.

29   The little Chinese girl sat down also to play an encore of "Anitra's Dance" by Grieg. I remember the song, because later on I had to learn how to play it.

30   Three days after watching *The Ed Sullivan Show,* my mother told me what my schedule would be for piano lessons and piano practice. She had talked to Mr. Chong, who lived on the first floor of our apartment building. Mr. Chong was a retired piano teacher and my mother had traded house-cleaning services for weekly lessons and a piano for me to practice on every day, two hours a day, from four until six.

31   When my mother told me this, I felt as though I had been sent to hell. I whined and then kicked my foot a little when I couldn't stand it anymore.

32   "Why don't you like me the way I am? I'm *not* a genius! I can't play the piano. And even if I could, I wouldn't go on TV if you paid me a million dollars!" I cried.

33   My mother slapped me. "Who ask you be genius?" she shouted. "Only ask you be your best. For you sake. You think I want you be genius? Hnnh! What for! Who ask you!"

34   "So ungrateful," I heard her mutter in Chinese. "If she had as much talent as she has temper, she would be famous now."

35   Mr. Chong, whom I secretly nicknamed Old Chong, was very strange, always tapping his fingers to the silent music of an invisible orchestra. He looked

ancient in my eyes. He had lost most of the hair on top of his head and he wore thick glasses and had eyes that always looked tired and sleepy. But he must have been younger than I thought, since he lived with his mother and was not yet married.

36   I met Old Lady Chong once and that was enough. She had this peculiar smell like a baby that had done something in its pants. And her fingers felt like a dead person's, like an old peach I once found in the back of the refrigerator; the skin just slid off the meat when I picked it up.

37   I soon found out why Old Chong had retired from teaching piano. He was deaf. "Like Beethoven!" he shouted to me. "We're both listening only in our head!" And he would start to conduct his frantic silent sonatas.

38   Our lessons went like this. He would open the book and point to different things, explaining their purpose: "Key! Treble! Bass! No sharps or flats! So this is C major! Listen now and play after me!"

39   And then he would play the C scale a few times, a simple chord, and then, as if inspired by an old, unreachable itch, he gradually added more notes and running trills and a pounding bass until the music was really something quite grand.

40   I would play after him, the simple scale, the simple chord, and then I just played some nonsense that sounded like a cat running up and down on top of garbage cans. Old Chong smiled and applauded and then said, "Very good! But now you must learn to keep time!"

41   So that's how I discovered that Old Chong's eyes were too slow to keep up with the wrong notes I was playing. He went through the motions in half-time. To help me keep rhythm, he stood behind me, pushing down on my right shoulder for every beat. He balanced pennies on top of my wrists so I would keep them still as I slowly played scales and arpeggios. He had me curve my hand around an apple and keep that shape when playing chords. He marched stiffly to show me how to make each finger dance up and down, staccato like an obedient little soldier.

42   He taught me all these things, and that was how I also learned I could be lazy and get away with mistakes, lots of mistakes. If I hit the wrong notes because I hadn't practiced enough, I never corrected myself. I just kept playing in rhythm. And Old Chong kept conducting his own private reverie.

43   So maybe I never really gave myself a fair chance. I did pick up the basics pretty quickly, and I might have become a good pianist at that young age. But I was so determined not to try, not to be anybody different that I learned to play only the most ear-splitting preludes, the most discordant hymns.

44   Over the next year, I practiced like this, dutifully in my own way. And then one day I heard my mother and her friend Lindo Jong both talking in a loud bragging tone of voice so others could hear. It was after church, and I was leaning against the brick wall wearing a dress with stiff white petticoats. Auntie Lindo's daughter, Waverly, who was about my age, was standing farther down the wall about five feet away. We had grown up together and shared all the closeness of two sisters squabbling over crayons and dolls. In other words,

for the most part, we hated each other. I thought she was snotty. Waverly Jong had gained a certain amount of fame as "Chinatown's Littlest Chinese Chess Champion."

45 "She bring home too many trophy," lamented Auntie Lindo that Sunday. "All day she play chess. All day I have no time do nothing but dust off her winnings." She threw a scolding look at Waverly, who pretended not to see her.

46 "You lucky you don't have this problem," said Auntie Lindo with a sigh to my mother.

47 And my mother squared her shoulders and bragged: "Our problem worser than yours. If we ask Jing-mei wash dish, she hear nothing but music. It's like you can't stop this natural talent."

48 And right then, I was determined to put a stop to her foolish pride.

49 A few weeks later, Old Chong and my mother conspired to have me play in a talent show which would be held in the church hall. By then, my parents had saved up enough to buy me a secondhand piano, a black Wurlitzer spinet with a scarred bench. It was the showpiece of our living room.

50 For the talent show, I was to play a piece called "Pleading Child" from Schumann's *Scenes from Childhood*. It was a simple, moody piece that sounded more difficult than it was. I was supposed to memorize the whole thing, playing the repeat parts twice to make the piece sound longer. But I dawdled over it, playing a few bars and then cheating, looking up to see what notes followed. I never really listened to what I was playing. I daydreamed about being somewhere else, about being someone else.

51 The part I liked to practice best was the fancy curtsy: right foot out, touch the rose on the carpet with a pointed foot, sweep to the side, left leg bends, look up and smile.

52 My parents invited all the couples from the Joy Luck Club to witness my debut. Auntie Lindo and Uncle Tin were there. Waverly and her two older brothers had also come. The first two rows were filled with children both younger and older than I was. The littlest ones got to go first. They recited simple nursery rhymes, squawked out tunes on miniature violins, twirled Hula Hoops, pranced in pink ballet tutus, and when they bowed or curtsied, the audience would sigh in unison, "Awww," and then clap enthusiastically.

53 When my turn came, I was very confident. I remember my childish excitement. It was as if I knew, without a doubt, that the prodigy side of me really did exist. I had no fear whatsoever, no nervousness. I remember thinking to myself, This is it! This is it! I looked out over the audience, at my mother's blank face, my father's yawn, Auntie Lindo's stiff-lipped smile, Waverly's sulky expression. I had on a white dress layered with sheets of lace, and a pink bow in my Peter Pan haircut. As I sat down I envisioned people jumping to their feet and Ed Sullivan rushing up to introduce me to everyone on TV.

54 And I started to play. It was so beautiful. I was so caught up in how lovely I looked that at first I didn't worry how I would sound. So it was a surprise to me when I hit the first wrong note and I realized something didn't sound quite right. And then I hit another and another followed that. A chill started at the

top of my head and began to trickle down. Yet I couldn't stop playing, as though my hands were bewitched. I kept thinking my fingers would adjust themselves back, like a train switching to the right track. I played this strange jumble through two repeats, the sour notes staying with me all the way to the end.

55   When I stood up, I discovered my legs were shaking. Maybe I had just been nervous and the audience, like Old Chong, had seen me go through the right motions and had not heard anything wrong at all. I swept my right foot out, went down on my knee, looked up and smiled. The room was quiet, except for Old Chong, who was beaming and shouting, "Bravo! Bravo! Well done!" But then I saw my mother's face, her stricken face. The audience clapped weakly, and as I walked back to my chair, with my whole face quivering as I tried not to cry, I heard a little boy whisper loudly to his mother, "That was awful," and the mother whispered back, "Well, she certainly tried."

56   And now I realized how many people were in the audience, the whole world it seemed. I was aware of eyes burning into my back. I felt the shame of my mother and father as they sat stiffly throughout the rest of the show.

57   We could have escaped during intermission. Pride and some strange sense of honor must have anchored my parents to their chairs. And so we watched it all: the eighteen-year-old boy with a fake mustache who did a magic show and juggled flaming hoops while riding a unicycle. The breasted girl with white makeup who sang from *Madama Butterfly* and got honorable mention. And the eleven-year-old boy who won first prize playing a tricky violin song that sounded like a busy bee.

58   After the show, the Hsus, the Jongs, and the St. Clairs from the Joy Luck Club came up to my mother and father.

59   "Lots of talented kids," Auntie Lindo said vaguely, smiling broadly.

60   "That was somethin' else," said my father, and I wondered if he was referring to me in a humorous way, or whether he even remembered what I had done.

61   Waverly looked at me and shrugged her shoulders. "You aren't a genius like me," she said matter-of-factly. And if I hadn't felt so bad, I would have pulled her braids and punched her stomach.

62   But my mother's expression was what devastated me: a quiet, blank look that said she had lost everything. I felt the same way, and it seemed as if everybody were now coming up, like gawkers at the scene of an accident, to see what parts were actually missing. When we got on the bus to go home, my father was humming the busy-bee tune and my mother was silent. I kept thinking she wanted to wait until we got home before shouting at me. But when my father unlocked the door to our apartment, my mother walked in and then went to the back, into the bedroom. No accusations. No blame. And in a way, I felt disappointed. I had been waiting for her to start shouting, so I could shout back and cry and blame her for all my misery.

63   I assumed my talent-show fiasco meant I never had to play the piano again. But two days later, after school, my mother came out of the kitchen and saw me watching TV.

64   "Four clock," she reminded me as if it were any other day. I was stunned, as though she were asking me to go through the talent-show torture again. I wedged myself more tightly in front of the TV.

65   "Turn off TV," she called from the kitchen five minutes later.

66   I didn't budge. And then I decided. I didn't have to do what my mother said anymore. I wasn't her slave. This wasn't China. I had listened to her before and look what happened. She was the stupid one.

67   She came out from the kitchen and stood in the arched entryway of the living room. "Four clock," she said once again, louder.

68   "I'm not going to play anymore," I said nonchalantly. "Why should I? I'm not a genius."

69   She walked over and stood in front of the TV. I saw her chest was heaving up and down in an angry way.

70   "No!" I said, and I now felt stronger, as if my true self had finally emerged. So this was what had been inside me all along.

71   "No! I won't!" I screamed.

72   She yanked me by the arm, pulled me off the floor, snapped off the TV. She was frighteningly strong, half pulling, half carrying me toward the piano as I kicked the throw rugs under my feet. She lifted me up and onto the hard bench. I was sobbing by now, looking at her bitterly. Her chest was heaving even more and her mouth was open, smiling crazily as if she were pleased I was crying.

73   "You want me to be someone that I'm not!" I sobbed. "I'll never be the kind of daughter you want me to be!"

74   "Only two kinds of daughters," she shouted in Chinese. "Those who are obedient and those who follow their own mind! Only one kind of daughter can live in this house. Obedient daughter!"

75   "Then I wish I wasn't your daughter. I wish you weren't my mother," I shouted. As I said these things I got scared. I felt like worms and toads and slimy things were crawling out of my chest, but it also felt good, as if this awful side of me had surfaced, at last.

76   "Too late change this," said my mother shrilly.

77   And I could sense her anger rising to its breaking point. I wanted to see it spill over. And that's when I remembered the babies she had lost in China, the ones we never talked about. "Then I wish I'd never been born!" I shouted. "I wish I were dead! Like them."

78   It was as if I had said the magic words. Alakazam!—and her face went blank, her mouth closed, her arms went slack, and she backed out of the room, stunned, as if she were blowing away like a small brown leaf, thin, brittle, lifeless.

79   It was not the only disappointment my mother felt in me. In the years that followed, I failed her so many times, each time asserting my own will, my right to fall short of expectations. I didn't get straight As. I didn't become class president. I didn't get into Stanford. I dropped out of college.

80   For unlike my mother, I did not believe I could be anything I wanted to be. I could only be me.

81   And for all those years, we never talked about the disaster at the recital or my terrible accusations afterward at the piano bench. All that remained unchecked, like a betrayal that was now unspeakable. So I never found a way to ask her why she had hoped for something so large that failure was inevitable.

82   And even worse, I never asked her what frightened me the most: Why had she given up hope?

83   For after our struggle at the piano, she never mentioned my playing again. The lessons stopped. The lid to the piano was closed, shutting out the dust, my misery, and her dreams.

84   So she surprised me. A few years ago, she offered to give me the piano, for my thirtieth birthday. I had not played in all those years. I saw the offer as a sign of forgiveness, a tremendous burden removed.

85   "Are you sure?" I asked shyly. "I mean, won't you and Dad miss it?"

86   "No, this your piano," she said firmly. "Always your piano. You only one can play."

87   "Well, I probably can't play anymore," I said. "It's been years."

88   "You pick up fast," said my mother, as if she knew this was certain. "You have natural talent. You could been genius if you want to."

89   "No I couldn't."

90   "You just not trying," said my mother. And she was neither angry nor sad. She said it as if to announce a fact that could never be disproved. "Take it," she said.

91   But I didn't at first. It was enough that she had offered it to me. And after that, every time I saw it in my parents' living room, standing in front of the bay windows, it made me feel proud, as if it were a shiny trophy I had won back.

92   Last week I sent a tuner over to my parents' apartment and had the piano reconditioned, for purely sentimental reasons. My mother had died a few months before and I had been getting things in order for my father, a little bit at a time. I put the jewelry in special silk pouches. The sweaters she had knitted in yellow, pink, bright orange—all the colors I hated—I put those in moth-proof boxes. I found some old Chinese silk dresses, the kind with little slits up the sides. I rubbed the old silk against my skin, then wrapped them in tissue and decided to take them home with me.

93   After I had the piano tuned, I opened the lid and touched the keys. It sounded even richer than I remembered. Really, it was a very good piano. Inside the bench were the same exercise notes with handwritten scales, the same secondhand music books with their covers held together with yellow tape.

94   I opened up the Schumann book to the dark little piece I had played at the recital. It was on the left-hand side of the page, "Pleading Child." It looked more difficult than I remembered. I played a few bars, surprised at how easily the notes came back to me.

95   And for the first time, or so it seemed, I noticed the piece on the right-hand side. It was called "Perfectly Contented." I tried to play this one as well. It had a lighter melody but the same flowing rhythm and turned out to be quite easy. "Pleading Child" was shorter but slower; "Perfectly Contented" was longer but faster. And after I played them both a few times, I realized they were two halves of the same song.

TOPICS FOR WRITING AND DISCUSSION

1. The mother in this story divides "daughters" into which two kinds? Which kind does she obviously prefer?
2. Which kind of daughter is the narrator in this story determined to be? Why? Why is Waverly included in this story?
3. Why do you think it is so important to the mother that her daughter succeed? How has her past shaped her hopes? Do you sympathize with her at all?
4. How does the piano function as a symbolic "shiny trophy" for the daughter in her adult life? Why does she mention the two songs in the last paragraph?
5. Think about your own family. Were there, according to your family's expectations, different kinds of "acceptable" or "unacceptable" sons and daughters?

WRITING ASSIGNMENTS FOR CHAPTER NINE

DIVISION AND CLASSIFICATION

1. After reading Judith Viorst's essay "Friends, Good Friends, and Such Good Friends" and John Updike's "Three Boys," write an essay categorizing the kinds of friends you had during a specific period in your life—during part of your childhood or your first year of college, for example. Which friends were the best and why? Make your categories clear, as Viorst and Updike did, by using vivid details.

2. The anxieties William Zinsser describes in "College Pressures" often contribute to students becoming "stressed-out" or physically ill. Write an article for your school newspaper that identifies some good ways to cope with the stress of classes and exams. Make your suggestions concrete by illustrating them from your own experience or from that of your friends. Or, if you prefer, present one way you cope with stress (running or shopping or listening to music, perhaps) and explain the main reasons your method works for you.

3. Write an essay classifying the primary pressures motivating people in some group other than college students (for instance, members of a specific sports team). Explain whether you think these pressures are a positive or negative force in the lives of the individuals you are discussing.

4. After reading William Golding's essay "Thinking as a Hobby," write an essay establishing your own "grades of thinking." Use examples from your childhood, adolescence, and adulthood to illustrate your categories.

5. Using Russell Baker's essay "The Plot Against People" as a guide, write a humorous or satiric classification essay about other kinds of "plots" aimed at a specific group of people. Consider, for example, "the plot against freshmen," "the plot against bicycle riders," "the plot against chain smokers," or some other group that often grouses about unjust treatment.

6. In "Notes on Punctuation," Lewis Thomas has fun with his subject while also giving his readers much useful advice. Write a classification or division essay of your own in which you, the expert, tackle a subject that many readers find difficult or confusing. For example, if you are knowledgeable about computers or popular software, write an essay for beginners who need to choose among the various kinds. Or help someone understand kinds or uses of equipment in a hobby, sport, or professional specialty. Focus on a particular audience and include a thesis that tells why your advice is important to these readers.

7. In the poem "The Unknown Citizen," W. H. Auden satirizes a bureaucratic society of conformist citizens. Write an essay in which you criticize

a specific bureaucracy or business that has given you trouble. Classify its problem areas or your complaints in distinct categories that make clear to the reader why you consider this agency so difficult to deal with.

8. The daughter in Amy Tan's story "Two Kinds" is determined not to become the person her mother wants her to be. Analyze the various kinds of family influences on your character by organizing them into three main categories that show their effects on you as an adult.

CHAPTER TEN

CAUSE AND EFFECT

As you have seen in previous chapters, some essays are developed around specific questions: process essays answer the question *how* something is done or made; definition essays tell *what* an idea or concept is; narratives address *who, when, where, what happened* (and sometimes *how* and *why*). An essay developed by using *cause and effect* specifically addresses the question *why*.

Like the very natural behavior of comparing and contrasting, *causal analysis* is our way of investigating the reasons behind, and the results of, events, attitudes, or actions. For example, whenever we hear of an unfortunate event such as a plane crash in which many were killed, we automatically want to know why—what *caused* the tragedy. By using causal analysis, complex as well as simple questions often can be answered.

Rhetorically, *cause* often concerns reasons, actions, or events while *effect* concerns the consequences of those reasons, actions, or events. Therefore, by using cause and effect, you can focus a discussion either on an analysis of the cause of something or on the outcome of something. For example, officials could determine that faulty wing design (the cause) led to a plane crash (the effect). They could then use that information to prevent a similar occurrence. Causal analysis allows you to examine a question by moving from the cause to the effect or from the effect to the cause.

Establishing cause-and-effect relationships can be a complicated endeavor, for not all causes are equal in their ability to provoke response. You must weigh the significance of the cause in its relation to the effect, and you must also determine the appropriate sequence of causes that logically leads to the effect. The first step, then, in organizing your thoughts for a cause-and-effect essay is to examine the various types of causes and how those causes relate to or produce a given effect.

TYPES OF CAUSES

There are four types of causes: necessary (or main), sufficient, contributing, and remote.

- A *necessary* cause is just that—necessary for the effect to occur. This cause *must* be present; without it, the effect will not happen. It is possible, however (and, perhaps, probable), that the necessary cause alone could not produce the effect. For example, some type of fuel or energy is absolutely necessary for an automobile to operate; however, fuel or energy alone will not put a car in motion. Of course, sometimes there may be more than one necessary cause needed to produce an effect. An automobile may have fuel but will still not travel anywhere if it has no wheels. Both wheels and fuel are necessary to get the vehicle moving.

- A *contributing* cause contributes to or aids in bringing about the effect. It does not work alone, but is an important factor in producing the effect. For example, in "My Wood," E. M. Forster states that "a cheque to the author was the result" of Americans' eager consumption of one of his books. With that cheque, Forster bought his "wood." Thus, by purchasing his book, Americans contributed to his acquiring the property.

- A *sufficient* cause could by itself produce an effect, but other factors might also play a role. Excessive absenteeism could (is sufficient to) cause a person to lose a job, but the employee might also be unproductive or poorly skilled; that is, many other factors could also produce the same effect.

- A *remote* cause is not an impossible or unlikely one, as the term might suggest. Instead, it is a cause so far removed in time and, perhaps, distance from the effect that its role in producing the effect is often overlooked. Ignoring remote causes can be a serious mistake, though, for failure to recognize their importance could lead to flawed predicted outcomes or oversimplified cause-and-effect relationships. Seeking the remote cause for an effect is, therefore, a logical way to analyze a problem, but you should be careful not to go too far afield. For instance, to argue that a man would not have had a fatal heart attack at age 40 if he had not eaten foods high in saturated fat when he was a child is not convincing. However, medical science has established a cause-effect relationship with some skin cancers in adults who, as children, at one time suffered a severe sunburn.

The Cause-Effect Chain

Exploring remote causes can often lead to a sequence of causes and effects called a *cause-and-effect chain,* where cause A produces cause B, which in turn produces cause C, which produces cause D, and so on. Causal analyses of historical events often take this form; for example, one might show the connection between the Stamp Act, the Boston Tea Party, and other events leading to the American Revolution.

Writing the Cause-and-Effect Essay

The following advice will help you in preparing a cause-and-effect essay:

1. *Choose a subject that you can manage.*

Narrow your thesis to accommodate the scope of the assignment. If the assigned length of your essay is 500 words, don't try to discuss the causes of World War I. Volumes have been written about that conflict; it is probably not possible to explain the causes of the Great War in "500 words or less."

2. *Carefully examine the evidence you will use to base your ideas.*

Make sure the information you plan to use is adequate. Determine if your own experience or expertise is enough or if research will be necessary. Make sure your evidence is logical and accurate. Remember, any essay based on faulty evidence will be weak.

3. *Decide if you should focus on the cause, the effect, or both.*

Ask yourself, "What exactly *is* the cause-and-effect relationship of my topic? What is my point?" Once you have answered these questions, you can decide on the focus. If you decide that your essay should concentrate on the causes, your essay will show how X, Y, and Z caused (or will cause) some stated effect. If your essay will focus on the effects, it will show how certain results were (or will be) brought about by certain causes. Perhaps you will decide that your subject would be better served if you looked at both the cause and the effect. If you choose to discuss both, limit your topic so that your analysis will not be skimpy or underdeveloped.

4. *Use the essay's introduction to lay the foundation of your case and present a clear thesis that specifically states or strongly suggests the major idea of the essay.*

In "Politics and the English Language," for example, writer George Orwell begins his essay by setting up a problem: the decline of the English language and people's assumption that nothing can be done about it. In his second paragraph Orwell presents the main ideas of his essay. He dismisses the notion that faulty language is the product of a few bad writers and argues that it has political and economic causes and effects. According to Orwell, sloppy language is not only ugly but also "makes it easier for us to have foolish thoughts." But bad habits can be reversed, and doing so "is clearly a necessary first step toward political regeneration." Orwell then goes on to devote the rest of his well-known essay to illustrate this cause-and-effect relationship between language and thought.

5. *Though your thesis should be clear, do not overstate it and run the danger of oversimplifying a possibly complex cause-and-effect relationship.*

Remember that for most subjects there are many causes that often are determined by the perspective from which those causes are viewed. Furthermore, some cause-and-effect relationships just cannot be proved conclusively, especially those that predict future outcomes. Therefore, when you present your cause-and-effect ideas, avoid words that leave no room for exceptions. Words such as *must, will,* and *all* are restrictive and deny other possibilities. Instead, use words such as *may, many,* and *probably* that leave room for alternative connections between the cause and the effect.

6. *Review the types of causes you are using to support your thesis.*

If your essay will focus on the causes of something, begin by attempting to pinpoint the necessary cause, that is, the condition that must be present. Then, distinguish between sufficient and contributing causes. Could one (or more) of the causes you present have created the result all by itself? Next, review the sequence of causes to see if you need to include a remote cause or if you are dealing with a causal chain.

7. *Make your analysis convincing.*

It is not enough merely to state that "X caused Y"; you must prove your case by showing the reader the steps of the causal relationship in a convincing manner. Your essay is successful when your reader can say, "Yes, I can see how and why this happened" or "I can clearly see the effects or results of this." For instance, in "'This Is the End of the World': The Black Death," historian Barbara Tuchman convinces her readers of the terrible effects of the plague that devastated Europe in the fourteenth century by presenting numerous statistics, chilling eyewitness reports, and vivid descriptions.

8. *Avoid* post hoc *reasoning.*

Do not automatically assume that because A precedes B in time, A *caused* B. In other words, do not mistake coincidence for causality. For example, if you found a $100 bill lying on the ground moments after a black cat had crossed your path, it would be *post hoc* reasoning to believe that each time a black cat crossed your path you would find a $100 bill.

THE DECISIVE ARREST

Martin Luther King, Jr.
(1929–1968)

Martin Luther King, Jr., was born in Atlanta, Georgia. A product of the Atlanta public schools (where he skipped both the ninth and twelfth grades), he graduated from Morehouse College in 1948, just after he followed his father's example by being ordained as a Baptist minister. He was just 18. By 1951, he had earned a divinity degree from Crozer Theological Seminary in Pennsylvania, and in 1955 he received his doctorate in systematic theology from Boston University. His efforts in demanding justice for all people, regardless of race or economic status, contributed to the 1956 Supreme Court decision declaring the segregated bus system in Alabama unconstitutional; the passing of the Civil Rights Act of 1964, which prohibited discrimination in public places and demanded equal opportunity in education and employment; the Civil Rights Act of 1968 (after his death), which banned discrimination in the sale and renting of housing; and the landmark Voting Rights Act of 1965. In 1964, King was awarded the Nobel Peace Prize (at 35, he was the youngest person ever to win the prize). Four years later, he was assassinated.

In "The Decisive Arrest," excerpted from *Stride Toward Freedom* (1987), King clarifies the reasons behind the actions of Rosa Parks, whose refusal to give up her bus seat helped ignite the Civil Rights Movement of the 1960s.

1   ON December 1, 1955, an attractive Negro seamstress, Mrs. Rosa Parks, boarded the Cleveland Avenue Bus in downtown Montgomery. She was

Rosa Parks, pictured here on a Montgomery bus (UPI/Corbis-Bettmann)

returning home after her regular day's work in the Montgomery Fair—a leading department store. Tired from long hours on her feet, Mrs. Parks sat down in the first seat behind the section reserved for whites. Not long after she took her seat, the bus operator ordered her, along with three other Negro passengers, to move back in order to accommodate boarding white passengers. By this time every seat in the bus was taken. This meant that if Mrs. Parks followed the driver's command she would have to stand while a white male passenger, who had just boarded the bus, would sit. The other three Negro passengers immediately complied with the driver's request. But Mrs. Parks quietly refused. The result was her arrest.

2   There was to be much speculation about why Mrs. Parks did not obey the driver. Many people in the white community argued that she had been "planted" by the NAACP in order to lay the groundwork for a test case, and at first glance that explanation seemed plausible, since she was a former secretary of the local branch of the NAACP. So persistent and persuasive was this argument that it convinced many reporters from all over the country. Later on, when I was having press conferences three times a week—in order to accommodate the reporters and journalists who came to Montgomery from all over the world—the invariable first question was: "Did the NAACP start the bus boycott?"

3   But the accusation was totally unwarranted, as the testimony of both Mrs. Parks and the officials of the NAACP revealed. Actually, no one can understand the action of Mrs. Parks unless he realizes that eventually the cup of endurance runs over, and the human personality cries out, "I can take it no longer." Mrs. Parks's refusal to move back was her intrepid affirmation that she had had enough. It was an individual expression of a timeless longing for human dignity and freedom. She was not "planted" there by the NAACP, or any other organization; she was planted there by her personal sense of dignity and self-respect. She was anchored to that seat by the accumulated indignities of days gone by and the boundless aspirations of generations yet unborn. She was a victim of both the forces of history and the forces of destiny. She had been tracked down by the *Zeitgeist*—the spirit of the time.

Topics for Writing and Discussion

1. What cause-effect relationship does King explain in this short excerpt from his book *Stride Toward Freedom*?
2. What is King's purpose in explaining his view of this event? Historically, why was this event so important, so "decisive"?
3. What, according to King, is the true or root cause of Rosa Parks' action?
4. How does the tone of the last paragraph differ from the first one? Is this shift in tone and diction appropriate? Persuasive? Why or why not?
5. Many times the action of one individual or one group becomes the recognizable symbol in a fight against injustice. Can you think of any other cases in which someone's "cup of endurance" ran over, thus causing an event that contributed to social change?

E. M. Forster, working on the libretto of Benjamin Britten's opera Billy Budd *for the 1951 Festival of Britain (The Bettmann Archive)*

MY WOOD

E. M. Forster
(1879–1970)

Edward Morgan Forster was born in London and spent
his early years in England. He attended Tonbridge
School at Kent and King's College at Cambridge.
Forster began his literary career in 1903 as a writer for
The Independent Review, a periodical that fostered his
anti-imperialist ideas. He published several books
within a few years: *Where Angels Fear to Tread* (1905),
The Longest Journey (1907), *A Room with a View*
(1908), and *Howards End* (1910). Much of the inspiration for his writings came from his travels. His observations of the British colonialists' attitudes toward the
people of India became the subject of *A Passage to
India* (1924), the book to which he refers in the first
paragraph of "My Wood." Later in his life, his work
included short stories, essays, literary criticism, and
biographies. A collection of his essays, *Two Cheers for
Democracy,* was published in 1951. "My Wood" is
taken from *Abinger Harvest* (1936). In the essay,
Forster light-heartedly explains the effects produced by
owning property, suggesting that purchasing land may
not bring the uncomplicated happiness one might
expect.

1 A few years ago I wrote a book which dealt in part with the difficulties of
the English in India. Feeling that they would have had no difficulties in India
themselves, the Americans read the book freely. The more they read it the better it made them feel, and a cheque to the author was the result. I bought a
wood with the cheque. It is not a large wood—it contains scarcely any trees,

and it is intersected, blast it, by a public footpath. Still, it is the first property that I have owned, so it is right that other people should participate in my shame, and should ask themselves, in accents that will vary in horror, this very important question: What is the effect of property upon the character? Don't let's touch economics; the effect of private ownership upon the community as a whole is another question—a more important question, perhaps, but another one. Let's keep to psychology. If you own things, what's their effect on you? What's the effect on me of my wood?

2   In the first place, it makes me feel heavy. Property does have this effect. Property produces men of weight, and it was a man of weight who failed to get into the Kingdom of Heaven. He was not wicked, that unfortunate millionaire in the parable, he was only stout; he stuck out in front, not to mention behind, and as he wedged himself this way and that in the crystalline entrance and bruised his well-fed flanks, he saw beneath him a comparatively slim camel passing through the eye of a needle and being woven into the robe of God. The Gospels all through couple stoutness and slowness. They point out what is perfectly obvious, yet seldom realized: that if you have a lot of things you cannot move about a lot, that furniture requires dusting, dusters require servants, servants require insurance stamps, and the whole tangle of them makes you think twice before you accept an invitation to dinner or go for a bathe in the Jordan. Sometimes the Gospels proceed further and say with Tolstoy that property is sinful; they approach the difficult ground of asceticism here, where I cannot follow them. But as to the immediate effects of property on people, they just show straightforward logic. It produces men of weight. Men of weight cannot, by definition, move like the lightning from the East unto the West, and the ascent of a fourteen-stone bishop into a pulpit is thus the exact antithesis of the coming of the Son of Man. My wood makes me feel heavy.

3   In the second place, it makes me feel it ought to be larger.

4   The other day I heard a twig snap in it. I was annoyed at first, for I thought that someone was blackberrying, and depreciating the value of the undergrowth. On coming nearer, I saw it was not a man who had trodden on the twig and snapped it, but a bird, and I felt pleased. My bird. The bird was not equally pleased. Ignoring the relation between us, it took fright as soon as it saw the shape of my face, and flew straight over the boundary hedge into a field, the property of Mrs. Henessy, where it sat down with a loud squawk. It had become Mrs. Henessy's bird. Something seemed grossly amiss here, something that would not have occurred had the wood been larger. I could not afford to buy Mrs. Henessy out, I dared not murder her, and limitations of this sort beset me on every side. Ahab did not want that vineyard—he only needed it to round off his property, preparatory to plotting a new curve—and all the land around my wood has become necessary to me in order to round off the wood. A boundary protects. But—poor little thing—the boundary ought in its turn to be protected. Noises on the edge of it. Children throw stones. A little more, and then a little more, until we reach the sea. Happy Canute! Happier Alexander! And after all, why should even the world be the limit of possession? A rocket containing a Union Jack, will, it is hoped, be shortly fired at

the moon. Mars. Sirius. Beyond which . . . But these immensities ended by saddening me. I could not suppose that my wood was the destined nucleus of universal dominion—it is so very small and contains no mineral wealth beyond the blackberries. Nor was I comforted when Mrs. Henessy's bird took alarm for the second time and flew clean away from us all, under the belief that it belonged to itself.

5   In the third place, property makes its owner feel that he ought to do something to it. Yet he isn't sure what. A restlessness comes over him, a vague sense that he has a personality to express—the same sense which, without any vagueness, leads the artist to an act of creation. Sometimes I think I will cut down such trees as remain in the wood, at other times I want to fill up the gaps between them with new trees. Both impulses are pretentious and empty. They are not honest movements toward money-making or beauty. They spring from a foolish desire to express myself and from an inability to enjoy what I have got. Creation, property, enjoyment form a sinister trinity in the human mind. Creation and enjoyment are both very, very good, yet they are often unattainable without a material basis, and at such moments property pushes itself in as a substitute, saying, "Accept me instead—I'm good enough for all three." It is not enough. It is, as Shakespeare said of lust, "The expense of spirit in a waste of shame": it is "Before, a joy proposed; behind, a dream." Yet we don't know how to shun it. It is forced on us by our economic system as the alternative to starvation. It is also forced on us by an internal defect in the soul, by the feeling that in property may lie the germs of self-development and of exquisite or heroic deeds. Our life on earth is, and ought to be, material and carnal. But we have not yet learned to manage our materialism and carnality properly; they are still entangled with the desire for ownership, where (in the words of Dante) "Possession is one with loss."

6   And this brings us to our fourth and final point: the blackberries.

7   Blackberries are not plentiful in this meagre grove, but they are easily seen from the public footpath which traverses it, and all too easily gathered. Foxgloves, too—people will pull up the foxgloves, and ladies of an educational tendency even grub for toadstools to show them on the Monday in class. Other ladies, less educated, roll down the bracken in the arms of their gentlemen friends. There is paper, there are tins. Pray, does my wood belong to me or doesn't it? And, if it does, should I not own it best by allowing no one else to walk there? There is a wood near Lyme Regis, also cursed by a public footpath, where the owner has not hesitated on this point. He had built high stone walls each side of the path, and has spanned it by bridges, so that the public circulate like termites while he gorges on the blackberries unseen. He really does own his wood, this able chap. Dives in Hell did pretty well, but the gulf dividing him from Lazarus could be traversed by vision, and nothing traverses it here. And perhaps I shall come to this in time. I shall wall in and fence out until I really taste the sweets of property. Enormously stout, endlessly avaricious, pseudocreative, intensely selfish, I shall weave upon my forehead the quadruple crown of possession until those nasty Bolshies come and take it off again and thrust me aside into the outer darkness.

Topics for Writing and Discussion

1. What are the four effects Forster describes as resulting from his purchase of the wood? Explain briefly some of the details Forster uses to explain each of these four effects.

2. In the opening section of the essay, Forster describes the response of Americans to a book he wrote. Why does he emphasize the reaction of Americans? What relationship does the opening paragraph have to the rest of the essay?

3. Forster uses many allusions (references to works or events outside the essay itself) to explain his ideas. Research several of these allusions and explain how these contribute to the central idea of the essay. (For example, in the second paragraph Forster refers to the Gospel of Matthew 19:24 and to Leo Tolstoy's views on property.)

4. In the fifth paragraph, Forster begins with specific examples from his own wood and his response to it and ends with generalizations. As he moves from the concrete to the abstract, his tone changes. Analyze the change in tone and explain how it relates to Forster's thesis.

5. Think of something you have purchased after wanting it for a long time. In an essay explain the two or three main ways in which owning this item has affected your life.

THE VIOLENCE IS FAKE,
THE IMPACT IS REAL

Ellen Goodman
(1941–   )

Born in 1941 in Newton, Massachusetts, Ellen Goodman is a journalist who has worked for *Newsweek*,
CBS, NBC, and a number of newspapers, including the
Detroit Free Press and the *Boston Globe*, her home
newspaper since 1967. Goodman's Pulitzer Prize–
winning "At Large" column is syndicated in more than
440 newspapers across the country. She has published
several volumes of her column, including *Close to
Home* (1975), *Turning Points* (1979), *At Large* (1981),
Keeping in Touch (1985), *Making Sense* (1989), and
most recently, *Value Judgments* (1993). Goodman's
writing has earned her numerous awards, including the
Pulitzer Prize for distinguished commentary (1980), the
American Society of Newspaper Editors Distinguished
Writing Award (1980), the Hubert H. Humphrey Civil
Rights Award (1988), the President's Award from the
National Women's Political Caucus (1993), and the
American Woman Award, presented by the Women's
Research & Education Institute (1994). "The Violence
Is Fake, the Impact Is Real" first appeared in 1977.
In the essay, Goodman looks at the impact of television
violence on children.

1   I don't usually think of television executives as being modest, shy and retir-
ing. But for a decade or two, the same souls who have bragged about their
success in selling products have been positively humble about their success in
selling messages.

2   Yes indeed, they would tell advertisers, children see, children do . . . do buy
candy bars and cereals and toys. But no, no, they would tell parents, children
see, but children don't . . . imitate mangling and mayhem.

Ellen Goodman (© William Huber)

3   But now the government has released another study on TV and violence. The predictable conclusion is that "violence on television does lead to aggressive behavior by children and teenagers who watch the programs." After analyzing 2500 studies and publications since 1970, the "overwhelming" scientific evidence is that "excessive" violence on the screen produces violence off the screen.

4   Somehow or other, I feel like I have been here before. By now, the protestations of the networks sound like those of the cigarette manufacturers who will deny the link between cigarettes and lung disease to their (and our) last breath. By now, studies come and go, but the problem remains.

5   Today the average kid sits in front of the tube for 26 hours a week. The kids don't begin with a love of violence. Even today, one runaway favorite in the Saturday morning line-up is about the benign "Smurfs." But eventually they learn from grown-ups.

6   In the incredible shrinking world of kidvid, there is no regularly scheduled program for kids on any of the three networks between the hours of 7 A.M. and 6 P.M. A full 80 percent of the programs kids watch are adult television. For those who choose adventures, the broadcasters offer endless sagas of terror, chase, murder, rescue.

7   As Peggy Charren, who has watched this scene for a long time as head of Action for Children's Television, puts it: "Broadcasters believe that the more violent the problems, the more attractive the adventure to audiences in terms of sitting there and not turning it off. The ultimate adventure is doing away with someone's life. The ultimate excitement is death."

8   The government, in its report, listed some theories about why there is this link between violence on TV and violence in kids' behavior. One theory was that TV is a how-to lesson in aggression. Children learn "how to" hit and hurt from watching the way they learn how to count and read. Another theory is that kids who see a world full of violence accept it as normal behavior.

9   But I wonder whether violence isn't accepted because it is normalized— sanitized and packaged. We don't see violence on television in terms of pain and suffering, but in terms of excitement. In cartoons, characters are smashed with boulders, and dropped from airplanes only to get up unscathed. In adventure shows, people are killed all the time, but they are rarely "hurt."

10   As Charren put it, "There is no feeling badly about violence on television." We don't bear witness to the pain of a single gunshot wound. We don't see the broken hand and teeth that come from one blow to the jaw. We don't share the blood or the guilt, the anguish or the mourning. We don't see the labor of rebuilding a car, a window, a family.

11   Our television stars brush themselves off and return same time, same situation, next week without a single bruise. Cars are replaced. The dead are carted off and forgotten.

12   In Japan, I am told, there is an unwritten rule that if you show violence on television, you show the result of that violence. Such a program is, I am sure, much more disturbing. But maybe it should be. Maybe that's what's missing.

13   In the real world, people repress aggression because they know the consequences. But on television, there are no consequences. In the end kids may be
less affected by the presence of violence than by the absence of pain. They
learn that violence is okay. That nobody gets hurt.

14   So, if the broadcasters refuse to curb their profitable adventures in hurting,
their national contribution to violence, then let them add something to the
mix: equal time for truth and consequences.

Topics for Writing and Discussion

1. What cause-effect relationship is Goodman exploring? What is her thesis?
2. What point is Goodman making in her introduction about the success of
    advertising products on television? Is this an effective way to start her
    essay? Why or why not?
3. Evaluate Goodman's use of the government study and her quotes from
    Peggy Charren. What do these add to Goodman's essay?
4. What does Goodman want the television industry to change, in light of its
    reluctance to decrease the amount of violence on the screen? Why?
5. Goodman's essay is over twenty years old. One recent study claims chil-
    dren are watching even more television than ever, twenty-eight or more
    hours per week; another study, quoted in a 1997 *Time* article, asserts that
    the average family has the TV on seven hours a day, or nearly half of the
    family's waking hours. Do you think Goodman's claims are outdated, or
    are they still important today? Do you agree or disagree with Goodman?
    Why or why not?

"THIS IS THE END OF THE WORLD": THE BLACK DEATH

Barbara Tuchman
(1912–1989)

Barbara Tuchman
(© 1988 Jill Krementz)

Born in New York City and educated at Radcliffe College, Barbara Tuchman began her career as a journalist writing for *The Nation* and *The New Statesman* magazines. She served as a war correspondent, covering both the Spanish Civil War and World War II for the London office of *The Nation*. In 1943, she became editor of the U.S. Office of War Information. Two of her books have been awarded the Pulitzer Prize: *The Guns of August* (1962) and *Stillwell and the American Experiment in China: 1911–45* (1971). Tuchman also contributed to magazines such as the *Atlantic Monthly, American Scholar, Foreign Affairs,* and *Harper's.* Her last book was *The First Salute* (1989). "'This Is the End of the World': The Black Death" was taken from *A Distant Mirror* (1978). Here Tuchman explains both the causes and effects of the devastating plague that swept through Europe in the fourteenth century.

1   IN October 1347, two months after the fall of Calais, Genoese trading ships put into the harbor of Messina in Sicily with dead and dying men at the oars. The ships had come from the Black Sea port of Caffa (now Feodosiya) in the Crimea, where the Genoese maintained a trading post. The diseased sailors showed strange black swellings about the size of an egg or an apple in the armpits and groin. The swellings oozed blood and pus and were followed by spreading boils and black blotches on the skin from internal bleeding. The sick suffered severe pain and died quickly within five days of the first symptoms. As the disease spread, other symptoms of continuous fever and spitting of blood appeared instead of the swelling or buboes. These victims coughed and

sweated heavily and died even more quickly, within three days or less, sometimes in 24 hours. In both types everything that issued from the body—breath, sweat, blood from the buboes and lungs, bloody urine, and blood-blackened excrement—smelled foul. Depression and despair accompanied the physical symptoms, and before the end "death is seen seated on the face."

2   The disease was bubonic plague, present in two forms: one that infected the bloodstream, causing the buboes and internal bleeding, and was spread by contact; and a second, more virulent pneumonic type that infected the lungs and was spread by respiratory infection. The presence of both at once caused the high mortality and speed of contagion. So lethal was the disease that cases were known of persons going to bed well and dying before they woke, of doctors catching the illness at a bedside and dying before the patient. So rapidly did it spread from one to another that to a French physician, Simon de Covino, it seemed as if one sick person "could infect the whole world." The malignity of the pestilence appeared more terrible because its victims knew no prevention and no remedy.

3   The physical suffering of the disease and its aspect of evil mystery were expressed in a strange Welsh lament which saw "death coming into our midst like black smoke, a plague which cuts off the young, a rootless phantom which has no mercy for fair countenance. Woe is me of the shilling in the armpit! It is seething, terrible . . . a head that gives pain and causes a loud cry . . . a painful angry knob . . . Great is its seething like a burning cinder . . . a grievous thing of ashy color." Its eruption is ugly like the "seeds of black peas, broken fragments of brittle sea-coal . . . the early ornaments of black death, cinders of the peelings of the cockle weed, a mixed multitude, a black plague like halfpence, like berries. . . ."

4   Rumors of a terrible plague supposedly arising in China and spreading through Tartary (Central Asia) to India and Persia, Mesopotamia, Syria, Egypt, and all of Asia Minor had reached Europe in 1346. They told of a death so devastating that all of India was said to be depopulated, whole territories covered by dead bodies, other areas with no one left alive. As added up by Pope Clement VI at Avignon, the total of reported dead reached 23,840,000. In the absence of a concept of contagion, no serious alarm was felt in Europe until the trading ships brought their black burden of pestilence into Messina while other infected ships from the Levant carried it to Genoa and Venice.

5   By January 1348 it penetrated France via Marseille, and North Africa via Tunis. Shipborne along coasts and navigable rivers, it spread westward from Marseille through the ports of Languedoc to Spain and northward up the Rhône to Avignon, where it arrived in March. It reached Narbonne, Montpellier, Carcassonne, and Toulouse between February and May, and at the same time in Italy spread to Rome and Florence and their hinterlands. Between June and August it reached Bordeaux, Lyon, and Paris, spread to Burgundy and Normandy, and crossed the Channel from Normandy into southern England. From Italy during the same summer it crossed the Alps into Switzerland and reached eastward to Hungary.

6   In a given area the plague accomplished its kill within four to six months and then faded, except in the larger cities, where, rooting into the close-quartered population, it abated during the winter, only to reappear in spring and rage for another six months.

7   In 1349 it resumed in Paris, spread to Picardy, Flanders, and the Low Countries, and from England to Scotland and Ireland as well as to Norway, where a ghost ship with a cargo of wool and a dead crew drifted offshore until it ran aground near Bergen. From there the plague passed into Sweden, Denmark, Prussia, Iceland, and as far as Greenland. Leaving a strange pocket of immunity in Bohemia, and Russia unattacked until 1351, it had passed from most of Europe by mid-1350. Although the mortality rate was erratic, ranging from one fifth in some places to nine tenths or almost total elimination in others, the overall estimate of modern demographers has settled—for the area extending from India to Iceland—around the same figure expressed in Froissart's casual words: "a third of the world died." His estimate, the common one at the time, was not an inspired guess but a borrowing of St. John's figure for mortality from plague in Revelation, the favorite guide to human affairs of the Middle Ages.

8   A third of Europe would have meant about 20 million deaths. No one knows in truth how many died. Contemporary reports were an awed impression, not an accurate count. In crowded Avignon, it was said, 400 died daily; 7,000 houses emptied by death were shut up; a single graveyard received 11,000 corpses in six weeks; half the city's inhabitants reportedly died, including 9 cardinals or one third of the total, and 70 lesser prelates. Watching the endlessly passing death carts, chroniclers let normal exaggeration take wings and put the Avignon death toll at 62,000 and even at 120,000, although the city's total population was probably less than 50,000.

9   When graveyards filled up, bodies at Avignon were thrown into the Rhône until mass burial pits were dug for dumping the corpses. In London in such pits corpses piled up in layers until they overflowed. Everywhere reports speak of the sick dying too fast for the living to bury. Corpses were dragged out of homes and left in front of doorways. Morning light revealed new piles of bodies. In Florence the dead were gathered up by the Compagnia della Misericordia—founded in 1244 to care for the sick—whose members wore red robes and hoods masking the face except for the eyes. When their efforts failed, the dead lay putrid in the streets for days at a time. When no coffins were to be had, the bodies were laid on boards, two or three at once, to be carried to graveyards or common pits. Families dumped their own relatives into the pits, or buried them so hastily and thinly "that dogs dragged them forth and devoured their bodies."

10   Amid accumulating death and fear of contagion, people died without last rites and were buried without prayers, a prospect that terrified the last hours of the stricken. A bishop in England gave permission to laymen to make confession to each other as was done by the Apostles, "or if no man is present then even to a woman," and if no priest could be found to administer extreme unction, "then faith must suffice." Clement VI found it necessary to grant

remissions of sin to all who died of the plague because so many were unattended by priests. "And no bells tolled," wrote a chronicler of Siena, "and nobody wept no matter what his loss because almost everyone expected death. . . . And people said and believed, 'this is the end of the world.'"

11   In Paris, where the plague lasted through 1349, the reported death rate was 800 a day, in Pisa 500, in Vienna 500 to 600. The total dead in Paris numbered 50,000 or half the population. Florence, weakened by the famine of 1347, lost three to four fifths of its citizens, Venice two thirds, Hamburg and Bremen, though smaller in size, about the same proportion. Cities, as centers of transportation, were more likely to be affected than villages, although once a village was infected, its death rate was equally high. At Givry, a prosperous village in Burgundy of 1,200 to 1,500 people, the parish register records 615 deaths in the space of fourteen weeks, compared to an average of thirty deaths a year in the previous decade. In three villages of Cambridgeshire, manorial records show a death rate of 47 percent, 57 percent, and in one case 70 percent. When the last survivors, too few to carry on, moved away, a deserted village sank back into the wilderness and disappeared from the map altogether, leaving only a grass-covered ghostly outline to show where mortals once had lived.

12   In enclosed places such as monasteries and prisons, the infection of one person usually meant that of all, as happened in the Franciscan convents of Carcassonne and Marseille, where every inmate without exception died. Of the 140 Dominicans at Montpellier only seven survived. Petrarch's brother Gherardo, member of a Carthusian monastery, buried the prior and 34 fellow monks one by one, sometimes three a day, until he was left alone with his dog and fled to look for a place that would take him in. Watching every comrade die, men in such places could not but wonder whether the strange peril that filled the air had not been sent to exterminate the human race. In Kilkenny, Ireland, Brother John Clyn of the Friars Minor, another monk left alone among dead men, kept a record of what had happened lest "things which should be remembered perish with time and vanish from the memory of those who come after us." Sensing "the whole world, as it were, placed within the grasp of the Evil One," and waiting for death to visit him too, he wrote, "I leave parchment to continue this work, if perchance any man survive and any of the race of Adam escape this pestilence and carry on the work which I have begun." Brother John, as noted by another hand, died of the pestilence, but he foiled oblivion.

13   The largest cities of Europe, with populations of about 100,000, were Paris and Florence, Venice and Genoa. At the next level, with more than 50,000, were Ghent and Bruges in Flanders, Milan, Bologna, Rome, Naples, and Palermo, and Cologne. London hovered below 50,000, the only city in England except York with more than 10,000. At the level of 20,000 to 50,000 were Bordeaux, Toulouse, Montpellier, Marseille, and Lyon in France, Barcelona, Seville, and Toledo in Spain, Siena, Pisa, and other secondary cities in Italy, and the Hanseatic trading cities of the Empire. The plague raged

through them all, killing anywhere from one third to two thirds of their inhabitants. Italy, with a total population of 10 to 11 million, probably suffered the heaviest toll. Following the Florentine bankruptcies, the crop failures and workers' riots of 1346–47, the revolt of Cola di Rienzi that plunged Rome into anarchy, the plague came as the peak of successive calamities. As if the world were indeed in the grasp of the Evil One, its first appearance on the European mainland in January 1348 coincided with a fearsome earthquake that carved a path of wreckage from Naples up to Venice. Houses collapsed, church towers toppled, villages were crushed, and the destruction reached as far as Germany and Greece. Emotional response, dulled by horrors, underwent a kind of atrophy epitomized by the chronicler who wrote, "And in these days was burying without sorrowe and wedding without friendschippe."

14   In Siena, where more than half of the inhabitants died of the plague, work was abandoned on the great cathedral, planned to be the largest in the world, and never resumed, owing to loss of workers and master masons and "the melancholy and grief" of the survivors. The cathedral's truncated transept still stands in permanent witness to the sweep of death's scythe. Agnolo di Tura, a chronicler of Siena, recorded the fear of contagion that froze every other instinct. "Father abandoned child, wife husband, one brother another," he wrote, "for this plague seemed to strike through the breath and sight. And so they died. And no one could be found to bury the dead for money or friendship. . . . And I, Angolo di Tura, called the Fat, buried my five children with my own hands, and so did many others likewise."

15   There were many to echo his account of inhumanity and few to balance it, for the plague was not the kind of calamity that inspired mutual help. Its loathsomeness and deadliness did not herd people together in mutual distress, but only prompted their desire to escape each other. "Magistrates and notaries refused to come and make the wills of the dying," reported a Franciscan friar of Piazza in Sicily; what was worse, "even the priests did not come to hear their confessions." A clerk of the Archbishop of Canterbury reported the same of English priests who "turned away from the care of their benefices from fear of death." Cases of parents deserting children and children their parents were reported across Europe from Scotland to Russia. The calamity chilled the hearts of men, wrote Boccaccio in his famous account of the plague in Florence that serves as introduction to the *Decameron*. "One man shunned another . . . kinsfolk held aloof, brother was forsaken by brother, oftentimes husband by wife; nay, what is more, and scarcely to be believed, fathers and mothers were found to abandon their own children to their fate, untended, unvisited as if they had been strangers." Exaggeration and literary pessimism were common in the 14th century, but the Pope's physician, Guy de Chauliac, was a sober, careful observer who reported the same phenomenon: "A father did not visit his son, nor the son his father. Charity was dead."

16   Yet not entirely. In Paris, according to the chronicler Jean de Venette, the nuns of the Hôtel Dieu or municipal hospital, "having no fear of death, tended the sick with all sweetness and humility." New nuns repeatedly took the places

of those who died, until the majority "many times renewed by death now rest in peace with Christ as we may piously believe."

17   When the plague entered northern France in July 1348, it settled first in Normandy and, checked by winter, gave Picardy a deceptive interim until the next summer. Either in mourning or warning, black flags were flown from church towers of the worst-stricken villages of Normandy. "And in that time," wrote a monk of the abbey of Fourcarment, "the mortality was so great among the people of Normandy that those of Picardy mocked them." The same un-neighborly reaction was reported of the Scots, separated by a winter's immu-nity from the English. Delighted to hear of the disease that was scourging the "southrons," they gathered forces for an invasion, "laughing at their enemies." Before they could move, the savage mortality fell upon them too, scattering some in death and the rest in panic to spread the infection as they fled.

18   In Picardy in the summer of 1349 the pestilence penetrated the castle of Coucy to kill Enguerrand's mother,[1] Catherine, and her new husband. Whether her nine-year-old son escaped by chance or was perhaps living else-where with one of his guardians is unrecorded. In nearby Amiens, tannery workers, responding quickly to losses in the labor force, combined to bargain for higher wages. In another place villagers were seen dancing to drums and trumpets, and on being asked the reason, answered that, seeing their neigh-bors die day by day while their village remained immune, they believed that they could keep the plague from entering "by the jollity that is in us. That is why we dance." Further north in Tournai on the border of Flanders, Gilles li Muisis, Abbot of St. Martin's, kept one of the epidemic's most vivid ac-counts. The passing bells rang all day and all night, he recorded, because sex-tons were anxious to obtain their fees while they could. Filled with the sound of mourning, the city became oppressed by fear, so that the authorities forbade the tolling of bells and the wearing of black and restricted funeral services to two mourners. The silencing of funeral bells and of criers' announcements of deaths was ordained by most cities. Siena imposed a fine on the wearing of mourning clothes by all except widows.

19   Flight was the chief recourse of those who could afford it or arrange it. The rich fled to their country places like Boccaccio's young patricians of Flo-rence, who settled in a pastoral palace "removed on every side from the road" with "wells of cool water and vaults of rare wines." The urban poor died in their burrows, "and only the stench of their bodies informed neigh-bors of their death." That the poor were more heavily afflicted than the rich was clearly remarked at the time, in the north as in the south. A Scottish chronicler, John of Fordun, stated flatly that the pest "attacked especially the meaner sort and common people—seldom the magnates." Simon de Covino of Montpellier made the same observation. He ascribed it to the misery and

---

[1] To unify and personalize *A Distant Mirror*, the study of the fourteenth century from which this excerpt is taken, Tuchman shows how events affected the life of one individual, a French nobleman named Enguerrand de Coucy. [Editor's note]

want and hard lives that made the poor more susceptible, which was half the truth. Close contact and lack of sanitation was the unrecognized other half. It was noticed too that the young died in greater proportion than the old; Simon de Covino compared the disappearance of youth to the withering of flowers in the fields.

20   In the countryside peasants dropped dead on the roads, in the fields, in their houses. Survivors in growing helplessness fell into apathy, leaving ripe wheat uncut and livestock untended. Oxen and asses, sheep and goats, pigs and chickens ran wild and they too, according to local reports, succumbed to the pest. English sheep, bearers of the precious wool, died throughout the country. The chronicler Henry Knighton, canon of Leicester Abbey, reported 5,000 dead in one field alone, "their bodies so corrupted by the plague that neither beast nor bird would touch them," and spreading an appalling stench. In the Austrian Alps wolves came down to prey upon sheep and then, "as if alarmed by some invisible warning, turned and fled back into the wilderness." In remote Dalmatia bolder wolves descended upon a plague-stricken city and attacked human survivors. For want of herdsmen, cattle strayed from place to place and died in hedgerows and ditches. Dogs and cats fell like the rest.

21   The dearth of labor held a fearful prospect because the 14th century lived close to the annual harvest both for food and for next year's seed. "So few servants and laborers were left," wrote Knighton, "that no one knew where to turn for help." The sense of a vanishing future created a kind of dementia of despair. A Bavarian chronicler of Neuberg on the Danube recorded that "Men and women . . . wandered around as if mad" and let their cattle stray "because no one had any inclination to concern themselves about the future." Fields went uncultivated, spring seed unsown. Second growth with nature's awful energy crept back over cleared land, dikes crumbled, salt water reinvaded and soured the lowlands. With so few hands remaining to restore the work of centuries, people felt, in Walsingham's words, that "the world could never again regain its former prosperity."

22   Though the death rate was higher among the anonymous poor, the known and the great died too. King Alfonso XI of Castile was the only reigning monarch killed by the pest, but his neighbor King Pedro of Aragon lost his wife, Queen Leonora, his daughter Marie, and a niece in the space of six months. John Cantacuzene, Emperor of Byzantium, lost his son. In France the lame Queen Jeanne and her daughter-in-law Bonne de Luxemburg, wife of the Dauphin, both died in 1349 in the same phase that took the life of Enguer-rand's mother. Jeanne, Queen of Navarre, daughter of Louis X, was another victim. Edward III's second daughter, Joanna, who was on her way to marry Pedro, the heir of Castile, died in Bordeaux. Women appear to have been more vulnerable than men, perhaps because, being more housebound, they were more exposed to fleas. Boccaccio's mistress Fiammetta, illegitimate daughter of the King of Naples, died, as did Laura, the beloved—whether real or fictional—of Petrarch. Reaching out to us in the future, Petrarch cried, "Oh

happy posterity who will not experience such abysmal woe and will look upon our testimony as a fable."

23   In Florence Giovanni Villani, the great historian of his time, died at 68 in the midst of an unfinished sentence: . . . "*e dure questo pistolenza fino a . . .* (in the midst of this pestilence there came to an end . . .)." Siena's master painters, the brothers Ambrogio and Pietro Lorenzetti, whose names never appear after 1348, presumably perished in the plague, as did Andrea Pisano, architect and sculptor of Florence. William of Ockham and the English mystic Richard Rolle of Hampole both disappear from mention after 1349. Francisco Datini, merchant of Prato, lost both his parents and two siblings. Curious sweeps of mortality afflicted certain bodies of merchants in London. All eight wardens of the Company of Cutters, all six wardens of the Hatters, and four wardens of the Goldsmiths died before July 1350. Sir John Pulteney, master draper and four times Mayor of London, was a victim, likewise Sir John Montgomery, Governor of Calais.

24   Among the clergy and doctors the mortality was naturally high because of the nature of their professions. Out of 24 physicians in Venice, 20 were said to have lost their lives in the plague, although, according to another account, some were believed to have fled or to have shut themselves up in their houses. At Montpellier, site of the leading medieval medical school, the physician Simon de Covino reported that, despite the great number of doctors, "hardly one of them escaped." In Avignon, Guy de Chauliac confessed that he performed his medical visits only because he dared not stay away for fear of infamy, but "I was in continual fear." He claimed to have contracted the disease but to have cured himself by his own treatment; if so, he was one of the few who recovered.

25   Clerical mortality varied with rank. Although the one-third toll of cardinals reflects the same proportion as the whole, this was probably due to their concentration in Avignon. In England, in strange and almost sinister procession, the Archbishop of Canterbury, John Stratford, died in August 1348, his appointed successor died in May 1349, and the next appointee three months later, all three within a year. Despite such weird vagaries, prelates in general managed to sustain a higher survival rate than the lesser clergy. Among bishops the deaths have been estimated at about one in twenty. The loss of priests, even if many avoided their fearful duty of attending the dying, was about the same as among the population as a whole.

26   Government officials, whose loss contributed to the general chaos, found, on the whole, no special shelter. In Siena four of the nine members of the governing oligarchy died, in France one third of the royal notaries, in Bristol 15 out of the 52 members of the Town Council or almost one third. Tax-collecting obviously suffered, with the result that Philip VI was unable to collect more than a fraction of the subsidy granted him by the Estates in the winter of 1347–48.

27   Lawlessness and debauchery accompanied the plague as they had during the great plague of Athens of 430 B.C., when according to Thucydides, men grew bold in the indulgence of pleasure: "For seeing how the rich died in a

moment and those who had nothing immediately inherited their property, they reflected that life and riches were alike transitory and they resolved to enjoy themselves while they could." Human behavior is timeless. When St. John had his vision of plague in Revelation, he knew from some experience or race memory that those who survived "repented not of the work of their hands. . . . Neither repented they of their murders, nor of their sorceries, nor of their fornication, nor of their thefts."

NOTES[2]

1. "Death Is Seen Seated": Simon de Covino, q. Campbell, 80.
2. "Could Infect the World": q. Gasquet, 41.
3. Welsh Lament: q. Ziegler, 190.
9. "Dogs Dragged Them Forth": Agnolo di Tura, q. Ziegler, 58.
10. "Or If No Man Is Present": Bishop of Bath and Wells, q. Ziegler, 125. "No Bells Tolled": Agnolo di Tura, q. Schevill, *Siena,* 211. The same observation was made by Gabriel de Muisis, notary of Piacenza, q. Crawfurd, 113.
11. Givry Parish Register: Renouard, III. Three Villages of Cambridgeshire: Saltmarsh.
12. Petrarch's Brother: Bishop, 273. Brother John Clyn: q. Ziegler, 195.
13. Atrophy; "and in These Days": q. Deaux, 143, citing only "an old northern chronicle."
14. Agnolo Di Tura, "Father Abandoned Child": q. Ziegler, 58.
15. "Magistrates and Notaries": q. Deaux, 49. English Priests Turned away: Ziegler, 261. Parents Deserting Children: Hecker, 30. Guy De Chauliac, "A Father": q. Gasquet, 50–51.
16. Nuns of the Hotel Dieu: *Chron. Jean de Venette,* 49.
17. Picards and Scots Mock Mortality of Neighbors: Gasquet, 53, and Ziegler, 198.
18. Catherine de Coucy: *L'Art de vérifier,* 237. Amiens Tanners: Gasquet, 57. "By the Jollity That Is in Us": *Grandes Chrons.,* VI, 486–87.
19. John of Fordun: q. Ziegler, 199. Simon de Covino on the Poor: Gasquet, 42. On Youth: Cazelles, *Peste.*
20. Knighton on Sheep: q. Ziegler, 175. Wolves of Austria and Dalmatia: ibid., 84, III. Dogs and Cats: Muisis, q. Gasquet, 44, 61.
21. Bavarian Chronicler of Neuberg: q. Ziegler, 84. Walsingham, "The World Could Never": Denifle, 273.
22. "Oh Happy Posterity": q. Ziegler, 45.
23. Giovanni Villani, *"e dure questo"*: q. Snell, 334.

---

[2] In *A Distant Mirror* Tuchman chooses to document all the sources of her information at the end of her book, rather than to use hundreds of footnotes throughout her study. For this excerpt, however, we have listed Tuchman's sources by the paragraph in which they appear in this text. A bibliography of the works cited follows these notes. [Editor's note]

24. Physicians of Venice: Campbell, 98. Simon de Covino: ibid., 31. Guy de Chauliac, "I Was in Fear": q. Thompson, *Ec. and Soc.,* 379.

27. Thucydides: q. Crawfurd, 30–31.

BIBLIOGRAPHY

L'Art de vérifier les dates des faits historiques, par un Religieux de la Congregation de St.-Maur, vol. XII. Paris, 1818.

Bishop, Morris, *Petrarch and His World.* Indiana University Press, 1963.

Campbell, Anna M., *The Black Death and Men of Learning.* Columbia University Press, 1931.

Cazelles, Raymond. *"La Peste de 1348–49 en Langue d'oil; épidémie prolitarienne et enfantine." Bull. philologique et historique,* 1962, pp. 293–305.

Chronicle of Jean de Venette. Trans. Jean Birdsall. Ed. Richard A. Newhall. Columbia University Press, 1853.

Crawfurd, Raymond, *Plague and Pestilence in Literature and Art.* Oxford, 1914.

Deaux, George. *The Black Death, 1347.* London, 1969.

Denifle, Henri, *La Désolation des églises, monastères et hopitaux en France pendant la guerre de cent ans,* vol. I. Paris, 1899.

Gasquet, Francis Aidan, Abbot, *The Black Death of 1348 and 1349,* 2nd ed. London, 1908.

Grandes Chroniques de France, vol. VI (to 1380). Ed. Paulin Paris. Paris, 1838.

Hecker, J. F. C., *The Epidemics of the Middle Ages.* London, 1844.

Renouard, Yves. *"La Peste noirs de 1348–50." Rev. de Paris,* March, 1950.

Saltmarsh, John, "Plague and Economic Decline in England in the Later Middle Ages," *Cambridge Historical Journal,* vol. VII, no. 1, 1941.

Schevill, Ferdinand, *Siena: The History of a Medieval Commune.* New York, 1909.

Snell, Frederick, *The Fourteenth Century.* Edinburgh, 1899.

Thompson, James Westfall, *Economic and Social History of Europe in the Later Middle Ages.* New York, 1931.

Ziegler, Philip, *The Black Death.* New York, 1969. (The best modern study.)

TOPICS FOR WRITING AND DISCUSSION

1. According to Tuchman's account, where did the bubonic plague originate and how did it spread to Europe?

2. Tuchman describes a complex scene as she explains the responses of groups and of individuals to the plague. Make a list of these responses and then divide them into negative, positive, and neutral categories. How did these responses affect the spread of the plague?

3. Tuchman cites many statistics to support her ideas. How does she keep these statistics from being simply a dull list of numbers?

4. How does Tuchman use cause-and-effect structure in this essay? Does she first explain the causes of the plague and then describe its effects? Or does

she describe first effects and then causes? Or is the structure more complex than either of these choices?

5. Research and argue either the primary causes or effects of some well-known disaster, such as the 1918 influenza epidemic, the 1906 San Francisco earthquake, the 1929 stock-market crash, or the 1986 *Challenger* explosion. Try to incorporate your facts, figures, and quotations as smoothly as Tuchman did, so your readers will experience the event you describe.

Marya Mannes (Courtesy of David Blow)

How Do You Know It's Good?

Marya Mannes
(1904–1990)

Marya Mannes was well known as a journalist in New York. She was a feature editor for *Vogue* and *Glamour* magazines and a staff writer for *Reporter* magazine; she wrote a column for the *New York Times* and contributed essays to *The New Republic*. Her many essay collections include a look at television, *Who Owns the Air?* (1960); a study of divorce, *Uncoupling: The Art of Coming Apart* (1972); and an examination of euthanasia, *Last Rights* (1974). She also wrote several novels, including *Message from a Stranger* (1948), and a volume of poems, *Subverse* (1964). The essay "How Do You Know It's Good?" appeared in *But Will It Sell?* (1964). In the essay, Mannes challenges people to make their own judgments about artistic quality.

---

1   SUPPOSE there were no critics to tell us how to react to a picture, a play, or a new composition of music. Suppose we wandered innocent as the dawn into an art exhibition of unsigned paintings. By what standards, by what values would we decide whether they were good or bad, talented or untalented, successes or failures? How can we ever know that what we think is right?

2   For the last fifteen or twenty years the fashion in criticism or appreciation of the arts has been to deny the existence of any valid criteria and to make the words "good" or "bad" irrelevant, immaterial, and inapplicable. There is no such thing, we are told, as a set of standards, first acquired through experience and knowledge and later imposed on the subject under discussion. This has been a popular approach, for it relieves the critic of the responsibility of judgment and the public of the necessity of knowledge. It pleases those resentful of disciplines, it flatters the empty-minded by calling them open-minded, it comforts the confused. Under the banner of democracy and the kind of equality which our forefathers did *not* mean, it says, in effect, "Who are you to tell us what *is* good or bad?" This is the same cry used so long and so effectively

by the producers of mass media who insist that it is the public, not they, who decides what it wants to hear and see, and that for a critic to say that *this* program is bad and *this* program is good is purely a reflection of personal taste. Nobody recently has expressed this philosophy more succinctly than Dr. Frank Stanton, the highly intelligent president of CBS television. At a hearing before the Federal Communications Commission, this phrase escaped him under questioning: "One man's mediocrity is another man's good program."

3   There is no better way of saying "No values are absolute." There is another important aspect to this philosophy of *laissez faire:* It is the fear, in all observers of all forms of art, of guessing wrong. This fear is well come by, for who has not heard of the contemporary outcries against artists who later were called great? Every age has its arbiters who do not grow with their times, who cannot tell evolution from revolution or the difference between frivolous faddism, amateurish experimentation, and profound and necessary change. Who wants to be caught *flagrante delicto* with an error of judgment as serious as this? It is far safer, and certainly easier, to look at a picture or a play or a poem and to say "This is hard to understand, but it may be good," or simply to welcome it as a new form. The word "new"—in our country especially—has magical connotations. What is new must be good; what is old is probably bad. And if a critic can describe the new in language that nobody can understand, he's safer still. If he has mastered the art of saying nothing with exquisite complexity, nobody can quote him later as saying anything.

4   But all these, I maintain, are forms of abdication from the responsibility of judgment. In creating, the artist commits himself; in appreciating, you have a commitment of your own. For after all, it is the audience which makes the arts. A climate of appreciation is essential to its flowering, and the higher the expectations of the public, the better the performance of the artist. Conversely, only a public ill-served by its critics could have accepted as art and as literature so much in these last years that has been neither. If anything goes, everything goes; and at the bottom of the junkpile lie the discarded standards too.

5   But what are these standards? How do you get them? How do you know they're the right ones? How can you make a clear pattern out of so many intangibles, including that greatest one, the very private I?

6   Well for one thing, it's fairly obvious that the more you read and see and hear, the more equipped you'll be to practice that art of association which is at the basis of all understanding and judgment. The more you live and the more you look, the more aware you are of a consistent pattern—as universal as the stars, as the tides, as breathing, as night and day—underlying everything. I would call this pattern and this rhythm an order. Not order—*an* order. Within it exists an incredible diversity of forms. Without it lies chaos—the wild cells of destruction—sickness. It is in the end up to you to distinguish between the diversity that is health and the chaos that is sickness, and you can't do this without a process of association that can link a bar of Mozart with the corner of a Vermeer painting, or a Stravinsky score with a Picasso abstraction; or that can relate an aggressive act with a Franz Kline painting and a fit of coughing with a John Cage composition.

7   There is no accident in the fact that certain expressions of art live for all time and that others die with the moment, and although you may not always define the reasons, you can ask the questions. What does an artist say that is timeless; how does he say it? How much is fashion, how much is merely reflection? Why is Sir Walter Scott so hard to read now, and Jane Austen not? Why is baroque right for one age and too effulgent for another?

8   Can a standard of craftsmanship apply to art of all ages, or does each have its own, and different, definitions? You may have been aware, inadvertently, that craftsmanship has become a dirty word these years because, again, it implies standards—something done well or done badly. The result of this convenient avoidance is a plenitude of actors who can't project their voices, singers who can't phrase their songs, poets who can't communicate emotion, and writers who have no vocabulary—not to speak of painters who can't draw. The dogma now is that craftsmanship gets in the way of expression. You can do better if you don't know *how* you do it, let alone *what* you're doing.

9   I think it is time you helped reverse this trend by trying to rediscover craft: the command of the chosen instrument, whether it is a brush, a word, or a voice. When you begin to detect the difference between freedom and sloppiness, between serious experimentation and egotherapy, between skill and slickness, between strength and violence, you are on your way to separating the sheep from the goats, a form of segregation denied us for quite a while. All you need to restore it is a small bundle of standards and a Geiger counter that detects fraud, and we might begin our tour of the arts in an area where both are urgently needed: contemporary painting.

10   I don't know what's worse: to have to look at acres of bad art to find the little good, or to read what the critics say about it all. In no other field of expression has so much double-talk flourished, so much confusion prevailed, and so much nonsense been circulated: further evidence of the close interdependence between the arts and the critical climate they inhabit. It will be my pleasure to share with you some of this double-talk so typical of our times.

11   Item one: preface for a catalogue of an abstract painter:

12   "Time-bound meditation experiencing a life; sincere with plastic piety at the threshold of hallowed arcana; a striving for pure ideation giving shape to inner drive; formalized patterns where neural balances reach a fiction." End of quote. Know what this artist paints like now?

13   Item two: a review in the *Art News:*

14   ". . . a weird and disparate assortment of material, but the monstrosity which bloomed into his most recent cancer of aggregations is present in some form everywhere. . . ." Then, later, "A gluttony of things and processes terminated by a glorious constipation."

15   Item three, same magazine, review of an artist who welds automobile fragments into abstract shapes:

16   "Each fragment . . . is made an extreme of human exasperation, torn at and fought all the way, and has its rightness of form as if by accident. *Any technique that requires order or discipline would just be the human ego.* No,

these must be egoless, uncontrolled, undesigned and different enough to give you a bang—fifty miles an hour around a telephone pole. . . ."

17   "Any technique that requires order or discipline would just be the human ego." What does he mean—"just be"? What are they really talking about? Is this journalism? Is it criticism? Or is it that other convenient abdication from standards of performance and judgment practiced by so many artists and critics that they, like certain writers who deal only in sickness and depravity, "reflect the chaos about them"? Again, whose chaos? Whose depravity?

18   I had always thought that the prime function of art was to create order *out* of chaos—again, not the order of neatness or rigidity or convention or artifice, but the order of clarity by which one will and one vision could draw the essential truth out of apparent confusion. I still do. It is not enough to use parts of a car to convey the brutality of the machine. This is as slavishly representative, and just as easy, as arranging dried flowers under glass to convey nature.

19   Speaking of which, i.e., the use of real materials (burlap, old gloves, bottletops) in lieu of pigment, this is what one critic had to say about an exhibition of Assemblage at the Museum of Modern Art last year: .

> Spotted throughout the show are indisputable works of art, accounting for a quarter or even a half of the total display. But the remainder are works of non-art, anti-art, and art substitutes that are the aesthetic counterparts of the social deficiencies that land people in the clink on charges of vagrancy. These aesthetic bankrupts . . . have no legitimate ideological roof over their heads and not the price of a square intellectual meal, much less a spiritual sandwich, in their pockets.

20   I quote these words of John Canaday of *The New York Times* as an example of the kind of criticism which puts responsibility to an intelligent public above popularity with an intellectual coterie. Canaday has the courage to say what he thinks and the capacity to say it clearly: two qualities notably absent from his profession.

21   Next to art, I would say that appreciation and evaluation in the field of music is the most difficult. For it is rarely possible to judge a new composition at one hearing only. What seems confusing or fragmented at first might well become clear and organic a third time. Or it might not. The only salvation here for the listener is, again, an instinct born of experience and association which allows him to separate intent from accident, design from experimentation, and pretense from conviction. Much of contemporary music is, like its sister art, merely a reflection of the composer's own fragmentation: an absorption in self and symbols at the expense of communication with others. The artist, in short, says to the public: If you don't understand this, it's because you're dumb. I maintain that you are not. You may have to go part way or even halfway to meet the artist, but if you must go the whole way, it's his fault, not yours. Hold fast to that. And remember it too when you read new poetry, that estranged sister of music.

A multitude of causes, unknown to former times, are now acting with a combined force to blunt the discriminating powers of the mind, and, unfitting it for all voluntary exertion, to reduce it to a state of almost savage torpor. The most effective of these causes are the great national events which are daily taking place and the increasing accumulation of men in cities, where the uniformity of their occupations produces a craving for extraordinary incident, which the rapid communication of intelligence hourly gratifies. To this tendency of life and manners, the literature and theatrical exhibitions of the country have conformed themselves.

22   This startlingly applicable comment was written in the year 1800 by William Wordsworth in the preface to his "Lyrical Ballads"; and it has been cited by Edwin Muir in his recently published book "The Estate of Poetry." Muir states that poetry's effective range and influence have diminished alarmingly in the modern world. He believes in the inherent and indestructible qualities of the human mind and the great and permanent objects that act upon it, and suggests that the audience will increase when "poetry loses what obscurity is left in it by attempting greater themes, for great themes have to be stated clearly." If you keep that firmly in mind and resist, in Muir's words, "the vast dissemination of secondary objects that isolate us from the natural world," you have gone a long way toward equipping yourself for the examination of any work of art.

23   When you come to theatre, in this extremely hasty tour of the arts, you can approach it on two different levels. You can bring to it anticipation and innocence, giving yourself up, as it were, to the life on the stage and reacting to it emotionally, if the play is good, or listlessly, if the play is boring; a part of the audience organism that expresses its favor by silence or laughter and its disfavor by coughing and rustling. Or you can bring to it certain critical faculties that may heighten, rather than diminish, your enjoyment.

24   You can ask yourselves whether the actors are truly in their parts or merely projecting themselves; whether the scenery helps or hurts the mood; whether the playwright is honest with himself, his characters, and you. Somewhere along the line you can learn to distinguish between the true creative act and the false arbitrary gesture; between fresh observation and stale cliché; between the avant-garde play that is pretentious drivel and the avant-garde play that finds new ways to say old truths.

25   Purpose and craftsmanship—end and means—these are the keys to your judgment in all the arts. What is this painter trying to say when he slashes a broad band of black across a white canvas and lets the edges dribble down? Is it a statement of violence? Is it a self-portrait? If it is *one* of these, has he made you believe it? Or is this a gesture of the ego or a form of therapy? If it shocks you, what does it shock you into?

26   And what of this tight little painting of bright flowers in a vase? Is the painter saying anything new about flowers? Is it different from a million other canvases of flowers? Has it any life, any meaning, beyond its statement? Is there any pleasure in its forms or texture? The question is not whether a thing

is abstract or representational, whether it is "modern" or conventional. The question, inexorably, is whether it is good. And this is a decision which only you, on the basis of instinct, experience, and association, can make for yourself. It takes independence and courage. It involves, moreover, the risk of wrong decision and the humility, after the passage of time, of recognizing it as such. As we grow and change and learn, our attitudes can change too, and what we once thought obscure or "difficult" can later emerge as coherent and illuminating. Entrenched prejudices, obdurate opinions are as sterile as no opinions at all.

27   Yet standards there are, timeless as the universe itself. And when you have committed yourself to them, you have acquired a passport to that elusive but immutable realm of truth. Keep it with you in the forests of bewilderment. And never be afraid to speak up.

TOPICS FOR WRITING AND DISCUSSION

1. According to Mannes, what has happened to critical "standards" in recent years, and what effects has this change had on the art community? On critics? On the general public?

2. Note that Mannes' essay was first printed in 1962. Are her claims still applicable to our culture over thirty years later? Cite examples of current art forms, and the ways they are received by the public and reviewed by critics, to support your response.

3. Review the essay and consider the point of view used by Mannes. At what point does she shift from emphasis on first person ("I") to second person ("you")? How does this shift affect the audience? What does this change tell the reader about her purpose in writing?

4. Describe Mannes' tone. Is it consistent throughout the essay?

5. Write a critical review of a piece of art you consider first-rate. You may choose a painting, a piece of literature, a film, a photograph, a sculpture, or some other artistic creation. Keep in mind Mannes' guidelines: "Purpose and craftsmanship—end and means—these are the keys to your judgment in all the arts." Show your readers clearly why you think the subject of your review is "good," avoiding the vague or pretentious language Mannes often finds in reviews.

Politics and the English Language

George Orwell
(1903–1950)

George Orwell is the pseudonym of Eric Arthur Blair,
born in Motihari, India, to parents who were members
of the Indian Civil Service. Orwell completed his education at Eaton College in England and then returned
to India to join the Indian Imperial Police in Burma.
His first nonfiction book, *Down and Out in Paris and
London* (1933), is an account of his three years of self-
imposed poverty after leaving Burma. His first novel,
Burmese Days (1934), reflects his experiences as a
police official there. In 1938, he published *Homage to
Catalonia,* which tells of his experiences fighting for
the Loyalists in the Spanish Civil War.

Orwell is best known for the books that reflect
his hatred of tyranny, his distrust of autocratic governments, his commitment to independence, and his
sympathy for the oppressed: *Animal Farm* (1945), an
allegory attacking Stalin, and *1984* (1949), a disturbing novel warning against an intrusive, autocratic government system. In "Politics and the English
Language," taken from the collection *Shooting an
Elephant and Other Essays* (1950), Orwell shows the
cause-and-effect relationship among thought, language, and politics.

1 Most people who bother with the matter at all would admit that the
English language is in a bad way, but it is generally assumed that we cannot by
conscious action do anything about it. Our civilization is decadent and our language—so the argument runs—must inevitably share in the general collapse.
It follows that any struggle against the abuse of language is a sentimental

George Orwell, in an undated photograph (AP/Wide World)

archaism, like preferring candles to electric light or hansom cabs to aero-planes. Underneath this lies the half-conscious belief that language is a natural growth and not an instrument which we shape for our own purpose.

2   Now, it is clear that the decline of a language must ultimately have politi-cal and economic causes: it is not due simply to the bad influence of this or that individual writer. But an effect can become a cause, reinforcing the origi-nal cause and producing the same effect in an intensified form, and so on in-definitely. A man may take to drink because he feels himself to be a failure, and then fail all the more completely because he drinks. It is rather the same thing that is happening to the English language. It becomes ugly and inaccurate because our thoughts are foolish, but the slovenliness of our language makes it easier for us to have foolish thoughts. The point is that the process is re-versible. Modern English, especially written English, is full of bad habits which spread by imitation and which can be avoided if one is willing to take the necessary trouble. If one gets rid of these habits one can think more clearly, and to think clearly is a necessary first step toward political regeneration: so that the fight against bad English is not frivolous and is not the exclusive con-cern of professional writers. I will come back to this presently, and I hope that by that time the meaning of what I have said here will have become clearer. Meanwhile, here are five specimens of the English language as it is now habit-ually written.

3   These five passages have not been picked out because they are especially bad—I could have quoted far worse if I had chosen—but because they illus-trate various of the mental vices from which we now suffer. They are a little below the average, but are fairly representative samples. I number them so that I can refer back to them when necessary:

> (1) I am not, indeed, sure whether it is not true to say that the Milton who once seemed not unlike a seventeenth-century Shelley had not become, out of an expe-rience ever more bitter in each year, more alien *[sic]* to the founder of that Jesuit sect which nothing could induce him to tolerate.
>
>   Professor Harold Laski (Essay in *Freedom of Expression*)

> (2) Above all, we cannot play ducks and drakes with a native battery of idioms which prescribes such egregious collocations of vocables as the Basic *put up with* for *tolerate* or *put at a loss* for *bewilder.*
>
>   Professor Lancelot Hogben *(Interglossa)*

> (3) On the one side we have the free personality: by definition it is not neurotic, for it has neither conflict nor dream. Its desires, such as they are, are transparent, for they are just what institutional approval keeps in the forefront of consciousness; an-other institutional pattern would alter their number and intensity; there is little in them that is natural, irreducible, or culturally dangerous. But *on the other side,* the social bond itself is nothing but the mutual reflection of these self-secure integrities. Recall the definition of love. Is not this the very picture of a small academic? Where is there a place in this hall of mirrors for either personality or fraternity?
>
>   Essay on psychology in *Politics* (New York)

(4) All the "best people" from the gentlemen's clubs, and all the frantic fascist captains, united in common hatred of Socialism and bestial horror of the rising tide of the mass revolutionary movement, have turned to acts of provocation, to foul incendiarism, to medieval legends of poisoned wells, to legalize their own destruction of proletarian organizations, and rouse the agitated petty-bourgeoisie to chauvinistic fervor on behalf of the fight against the revolutionary way out of the crisis.

Communist pamphlet

(5) If a new spirit *is* to be infused into this old country, there is one thorny and contentious reform which must be tackled, and that is the humanization and galvanization of the B.B.C. Timidity here will bespeak cancer and atrophy of the soul. The heart of Britain may be sound and of strong beat, for instance, but the British lion's roar at present is like that of Bottom in Shakespeare's *Midsummer Night's Dream*—as gentle as any sucking dove. A virile new Britain cannot continue indefinitely to be traduced in the eyes or rather ears, of the world by the effete languors of Langham Place, brazenly masquerading as "standard English." When the Voice of Britain is heard at nine o'clock, better far and infinitely less ludicrous to hear aitches honestly dropped than the present priggish, inflated, inhibited, schoolma'amish arch braying of blameless bashful mewing maidens!

Letter in *Tribune*

4   Each of these passages has faults of its own, but, quite apart from avoidable ugliness, two qualities are common to all of them. The first is staleness of imagery; the other is lack of precision. The writer either has a meaning and cannot express it, or he inadvertently says something else, or he is almost indifferent as to whether his words mean anything or not. The mixture of vagueness and sheer incompetence is the most marked characteristic of modern English prose, and especially of any kind of political writing. As soon as certain topics are raised, the concrete melts into the abstract and no one seems to think of turns of speech that are not hackneyed: prose consists less and less of *words* chosen for the sake of their meaning, and more and more of *phrases* tacked together like the sections of a prefabricated henhouse. I list below, with notes and examples, various of the tricks by means of which the work of prose-construction is habitually dodged:

Dying Metaphors

5 A newly invented metaphor assists thought by evoking a visual image, while on the other hand a metaphor which is technically "dead" (e.g., *iron resolution*) has in effect reverted to being an ordinary word and can generally be used without loss of vividness. But in between these two classes there is a huge dump of worn-out metaphors which have lost all evocative power and are merely used because they save people the trouble of inventing phrases for themselves. Examples are: *ring the changes on, take up the cudgels for, toe the line, ride roughshod over, stand shoulder to shoulder with, play into the hands of, no axe to grind, grist to the mill, fishing in troubled waters, rift within the*

lute, on the order of the day, Achilles' heel, swan song, hotbed. Many of these are used without knowledge of their meaning (what is a "rift," for instance?), and incompatible metaphors are frequently mixed, a sure sign that the writer is not interested in what he is saying. Some metaphors now current have been twisted out of their original meaning without those who use them even being aware of the fact. For example, *toe the line* is sometimes written *tow the line.* Another example is *the hammer and the anvil,* now always used with the implication that the anvil gets the worst of it. In real life it is always the anvil that breaks the hammer, never the other way about: a writer who stopped to think what he was saying would be aware of this, and would avoid perverting the original phrase.

OPERATORS OR VERBAL FALSE LIMBS

6 These save the trouble of picking out appropriate verbs and nouns, and at the same time pad each sentence with extra syllables which give it an appearance of symmetry. Characteristic phrases are: *render inoperative, militate against, make contact with, be subjected to, give rise to, give grounds for, have the effect of, play a leading part (role) in, make itself felt, take effect, exhibit a tendency to, serve the purpose of,* etc., etc. The keynote is the elimination of simple verbs. Instead of being a single word, such as *break, stop, spoil, mend, kill,* a verb becomes a *phrase,* made up of a noun or adjective tacked on to some general-purpose verb such as *prove, serve, form, play, render.* In addition, the passive voice is wherever possible used in preference to the active, and noun constructions are used instead of gerunds (*by examination of* instead of *by examining*). The range of verbs is further cut down by means of the *-ize* and *de-* formation, and the banal statements are given an appearance of profundity by means of the *not un-* formation. Simple conjunctions and prepositions are replaced by such phrases as *with respect to, having regard to, the fact that, by dint of, in view of, in the interests of, on the hypothesis that;* and the ends of sentences are saved from anticlimax by such resounding commonplaces as *greatly to be desired, cannot be left out of account, a development to be expected in the near future, deserving of serious consideration, brought to a satisfactory conclusion,* and so on and so forth.

PRETENTIOUS DICTION

7 Words like *phenomenon, element, individual* (as noun), *objective, categorical, effective, virtual, basic, primary, promote, constitute, exhibit, exploit, utilize, eliminate, liquidate,* are used to dress up simple statements and give an air of scientific impartiality to biased judgments. Adjectives like *epoch-making, epic, historic, unforgettable, triumphant, age-old, inexorable, inevitable, veritable,* are used to dignify the sordid processes of international politics, while writing that aims at glorifying war usually takes on an archaic color, its characteristic words being: *realm, throne, chariot, mailed fist, trident, sword, shield, buckler, banner, jackboot, clarion.* Foreign words and expressions such

as *cul de sac, ancien régime, deus ex machina, mutatis mutandis, status quo, gleich-shaltung, weltanschauung,* are used to give an air of culture and elegance. Except for the useful abbreviations *i.e., e.g.,* and *etc.,* there is no real need for any of the hundreds of foreign phrases now current in English. Bad writers, and especially scientific, political and sociological writers, are nearly always haunted by the notion that Latin or Greek words are grander than Saxon ones, and unnecessary words like *expedite, ameliorate, predict, extraneous, deracinated, clandestine, subaqueous* and hundreds of others constantly gain ground from their Anglo-Saxon opposite numbers.[1] The jargon peculiar to Marxist writing (*hyena, hangman, cannibal, petty bourgeois, these gentry, lacquey, flunkey, mad dog, White Guard,* etc.) consists largely of words and phrases translated from Russian, German, or French; but the normal way of coining a new word is to use a Latin or Greek root with the appropriate affix and, where necessary, the *-ize* formation. It is often easier to make up words of this kind (*deregionalize, impermissible, extramarital, nonfragmentatory* and so forth) than to think up the English words that will cover one's meaning. The result, in general, is an increase in slovenliness and vagueness.

MEANINGLESS WORDS

8 In certain kinds of writing, particularly in art criticism and literary criticism, it is normal to come across long passages which are almost completely lacking in meaning.[2] Words like *romantic, plastic, values, human, dead, sentimental, natural, vitality,* as used in art criticism, are strictly meaningless in the sense that they not only do not point to any discoverable object, but are hardly ever expected to do so by the reader. When one critic writes, "The outstanding feature of Mr. X's work is its living quality," while another writes, "The immediately striking thing about Mr. X's work is its peculiar deadness," the reader accepts this as a simple difference of opinion. If words like *black* and *white* were involved, instead of the jargon words *dead* and *living,* he would see at once that language was being used in an improper way. Many political words are similarly abused. The word *Fascism* has now no meaning except in so far as it signifies "something not desirable." The words *democracy, socialism, freedom, patriotic, realistic, justice,* have each of them several different meanings which cannot be reconciled with one another. In the case of a word like *democracy,* not only is there no agreed definition, but the attempt to make one

---

[1] An interesting illustration of this is the way in which the English flower names which were in use till very recently are being ousted by Greek ones, *snapdragon* becoming *antirrhinum, forget-me-not* becoming *myosotis,* etc. It is hard to see any practical reason for this change of fashion: it is probably due to an instinctive turning-away from the more homely word and a vague feeling that the Greek word is scientific.

[2] Example: "Comfort's catholicity of perception and image, strangely Whitmanesque in range, almost the exact opposite in aesthetic compulsion, continues to evoke that trembling atmospheric accumulative hinting at a cruel, an inexorably serene timelessness . . . Wrey Gardiner scores by aiming at simple bull's-eyes with precision. Only they are not so simple, and through this contended sadness runs more than the surface bitter-sweet of resignation." *(Poetry Quarterly)*

is resisted from all sides. It is almost universally felt that when we call a country democratic we are praising it: consequently the defenders of every kind of régime claim that it is a democracy, and fear that they might have to stop using the word if it were tied down to any one meaning. Words of this kind are often used in a consciously dishonest way. That is, the person who uses them has his own private definition, but allows his hearer to think he means something quite different. Statements like *Marshall Pétain was a true patriot, The Soviet Press is the freest in the world, The Catholic Church is opposed to persecution,* are almost always made with intent to deceive. Other words used in variable meanings, in most cases more or less dishonestly, are: *class, totalitarian, science, progressive, reactionary, bourgeois, equality.*

9   Now that I have made this catalogue of swindles and perversions, let me give another example of the kind of writing that they lead to. This time it must of its nature be an imaginary one. I am going to translate a passage of good English into modern English of the worst sort. Here is a well-known verse from *Ecclesiastes:*

> I returned and saw the sun, that the race is not to the swift, nor the battle to the strong, neither yet bread to the wise, nor yet riches to men of understanding, nor yet favour to men of skill; but time and chance happeneth to them all.

Here it is in modern English:

> Objective consideration of contemporary phenomena compels the conclusion that success or failure in competitive activities exhibits no tendency to be commensurate with innate capacity, but that a considerable element of the unpredictable must invariably be taken into account.

10   This is a parody, but not a very gross one. Exhibit (3), above, for instance, contains several patches of the same kind of English. It will be seen that I have not made a full translation. The beginning and ending of the sentence follow the original meaning fairly closely, but in the middle the concrete illustrations—race, battle, bread—dissolve into the vague phrase "success or failure in competitive activities." This had to be so, because no modern writer of the kind I am discussing—no one capable of using phrases like "objective consideration of contemporary phenomena"—would ever tabulate his thoughts in that precise and detailed way. The whole tendency of modern prose is away from concreteness. Now analyze these two sentences a little more closely. The first contains forty-nine words but only sixty syllables, and all its words are those of everyday life. The second contains thirty-eight words of ninety syllables: eighteen of its words are from Latin roots, and one from Greek. The first sentence contains six vivid images, and only one phrase ("time and chance") that could be called vague. The second contains not a single fresh, arresting phrase, and in spite of its ninety syllables it gives only a shortened version of the meaning contained in the first. Yet without a doubt it is the second kind of sentence that is gaining ground in modern

English. I do not want to exaggerate. This kind of writing is not yet universal; and outcrops of simplicity will occur here and there in the worst-written page. Still, if you or I were told to write a few lines on the uncertainty of human fortunes, we should probably come much nearer to my imaginary sentence than to the one from *Ecclesiastes.*

11   As I have tried to show, modern writing at its worst does not consist in picking out words for the sake of their meaning and inventing images in order to make the meaning clearer. It consists in gumming together long strips of words which have already been set in order by someone else, and making the results presentable by sheer humbug. The attraction of this way of writing is that it is easy. It is easier—even quicker once you have the habit—to say *In my opinion it is a not unjustifiable assumption that* than to say *I think.* If you use ready-made phrases, you not only don't have to hunt about for words; you also don't have to bother with the rhythms of your sentences, since these phrases are generally so arranged as to be more or less euphonious. When you are composing in a hurry—when you are dictating to a stenographer, for instance, or making a public speech—it is natural to fall into a pretentious, Latinized style. Tags like *a consideration which we should do well to bear in mind* or *a conclusion to which all of us would readily assent* will save many a sentence from coming down with a bump. By using stale metaphors, similes and idioms, you save much mental effort, at the cost of leaving your meaning vague, not only for your reader but for yourself. This is the significance of mixed metaphors. The sole aim of a metaphor is to call up a visual image. When these images clash—as in *The Fascist octopus has sung its swan song, the jackboot is thrown into the melting pot*—it can be taken as certain that the writer is not seeing a mental image of the objects he is naming; in other words he is not really thinking. Look again at the examples I gave at the beginning of this essay. Professor Laski (1) uses five negatives in fifty-three words. One of these is superfluous, making nonsense of the whole passage, and in addition there is the slip *alien* for *akin,* making further nonsense, and several avoidable pieces of clumsiness which increase the general vagueness. Professor Hogben (2) plays ducks and drakes with a battery which is able to write prescriptions, and, while disapproving of the everyday phrase *put up with,* is unwilling to look *egregious* up in the dictionary and see what it means. (3), if one takes an uncharitable attitude towards it, is simply meaningless. Probably one could work out its intended meaning by reading the whole of the article in which it occurs. In (4), the writer knows more or less what he wants to say, but an accumulation of stale phrases chokes him like tea leaves blocking a sink. In (5), words and meaning have almost parted company. People who write in this manner usually have a general emotional meaning—they dislike one thing and want to express solidarity with another—but they are not interested in the detail of what they are saying. A scrupulous writer, in every sentence that he writes, will ask himself at least four questions, thus: What am I trying to say? What words will express it? What image or idiom will make it clearer? Is this image fresh enough to have an effect? And he will probably ask himself two more: Could I put it more shortly? Have I said anything that is avoidably ugly? But

you are not obliged to go to all this trouble. You can shirk it by simply throwing your mind open and letting the ready-made phrases come crowding in. They will construct your sentences for you—even think your thoughts for you, to a certain extent—and at need they will perform the important service of partially concealing your meaning even from yourself. It is at this point that the special connection between politics and the debasement of language becomes clear.

12   In our times it is broadly true that political writing is bad writing. Where it is not true, it will generally be found that the writer is some kind of rebel, expressing his private opinions and not a "party line." Orthodoxy, of whatever color, seems to demand a lifeless, imitative style. The political dialects to be found in pamphlets, leading articles, manifestos, White Papers and the speeches of under-secretaries do, of course, vary from party to party, but they are all alike in that one almost never finds in them a fresh, vivid, home-made turn of speech. When one watches some tired hack on the platform mechanically repeating the familiar phrases—*bestial atrocities, iron heel, bloodstained tyranny, free peoples of the world, stand shoulder to shoulder*—one often has a curious feeling that one is not watching a live human being but some kind of dummy, a feeling which suddenly becomes stronger at moments when the light catches the speaker's spectacles and turns them into blank discs which seem to have no eyes behind them. And this is not altogether fanciful. A speaker who uses that kind of phraseology has gone some distance towards turning himself into a machine. The appropriate noises are coming out of his larynx, but his brain is not involved as it would be if he were choosing his words from himself. If the speech he is making is one that he is accustomed to make over and over again, he may be almost unconscious of what he is saying, as one is when one utters the responses in church. And this reduced state of consciousness, if not indispensable, is at any rate favorable to political conformity.

13   In our time, political speech and writing are largely the defense of the indefensible. Things like the continuance of British rule in India, the Russian purges and deportations, the dropping of the atom bombs on Japan, can indeed be defended, but only by arguments which are too brutal for most people to face, and which do not square with the professed aims of political parties. Thus political language has to consist largely of euphemism, question-begging and sheer cloudy vagueness. Defenseless villages are bombarded from the air, the inhabitants driven out into the countryside, the cattle machine-gunned, the huts set on fire with incendiary bullets: this is called *pacification*. Millions of peasants are robbed of their farms and sent trudging along the roads with no more than they can carry: this is called *transfer of population* or *rectification of frontiers*. People are imprisoned for years without trial, or shot in the back of the neck or sent to die of scurvy in Arctic lumber camps: this is called *elimination of unreliable elements*. Such phraseology is needed if one wants to name things without calling up mental pictures of them. Consider for instance some comfortable English professor defending Russian totalitarianism. He cannot say outright, "I believe in killing off your opponents when you can get good results by doing so." Probably, therefore, he will say something like this:

14   "While freely conceding that the Soviet régime exhibits certain features which the humanitarian may be inclined to deplore, we must, I think, agree that a certain curtailment of the right to political opposition is an unavoidable concomitant of transitional periods, and that the rigors which the Russian people have been called upon to undergo have been amply justified in the sphere of concrete achievement."

15   The inflated style is itself a kind of euphemism. A mass of Latin words falls upon the facts like soft snow, blurring the outlines and covering up all the details. The great enemy of clear language is insincerity. Where there is a gap between one's real and one's declared aims, one turns as it were instinctively to long words and exhausted idioms, like a cuttlefish squirting out ink. In our age there is no such thing as "keeping out of politics." All issues are political issues, and politics itself is a mass of lies, evasions, folly, hatred and schizophrenia. When the general atmosphere is bad, language must suffer. I should expect to find—this is a guess which I have not sufficient knowledge to verify—that the German, Russian and Italian languages have all deteriorated in the last ten or fifteen years, as a result of dictatorship.

16   But if thought corrupts language, language can also corrupt thought. A bad usage can spread by tradition and imitation, even among people who should and do know better. The debased language that I have been discussing is in some ways very convenient. Phrases like *a not unjustifiable assumption, leaves much to be desired, would serve no good purpose, a consideration which we should do well to bear in mind,* are a continuous temptation, a packet of aspirins always at one's elbow. Look back through this essay, and for certain you will find that I have again and again committed the very faults I am protesting against. By this morning's post I have received a pamphlet dealing with conditions in Germany. The author tells me that he "felt impelled" to write it. I open it at random, and here is almost the first sentence that I see: "(The Allies) have an opportunity not only of achieving a radical transformation of Germany's social and political structure in such a way as to avoid a nationalistic reaction in Germany itself, but at the same time of laying the foundations of a co-operative and unified Europe." You see, he "feels impelled" to write—feels, presumably, that he has something new to say—and yet his words, like cavalry horses answering the bugle, group themselves automatically into the familiar dreary pattern. This invasion of one's mind by ready-made phrases *(lay the foundations, achieve a radical transformation)* can only be prevented if one is constantly on guard against them, and every such phrase anaesthetizes a portion of one's brain.

17   I said earlier that the decadence of our language is probably curable. Those who deny this would argue, if they produced an argument at all, that language merely reflects existing social conditions, and that we cannot influence its development by any direct tinkering with words and constructions. So far as the general tone or spirit of a language goes, this may be true, but it is not true in detail. Silly words and expressions have often disappeared, not through any evolutionary process but owing to the conscious action of a minority. Two

recent examples were *explore every avenue* and *leave no stone unturned,* which were killed by the jeers of a few journalists. There is a long list of fly-blown metaphors which could similarly be got rid of if enough people would interest themselves in the job; and it should also be possible to laugh the *not un-* formation out of existence,[3] to reduce the amount of Latin and Greek in the average sentence, to drive out foreign phrases and strayed scientific words, and, in general, to make pretentiousness unfashionable. But all these are minor points. The defense of the English language implies more than this, and perhaps it is best to start by saying what it does *not* imply.

18   To begin with it has nothing to do with archaism, with the salvaging of obsolete words and turns of speech, or with the setting up of a "standard English" which must never be departed from. On the contrary, it is especially concerned with the scrapping of every word or idiom which has outworn its usefulness. It has nothing to do with correct grammar and syntax, which are of no importance so long as one makes one's meaning clear, or with the avoidance of Americanisms, or with having what is called a "good prose style." On the other hand, it is not concerned with fake simplicity and the attempt to make written English colloquial. Nor does it even imply in every case preferring the Saxon word to the Latin one, though it does imply using the fewest and shortest words that will cover one's meaning. What is above all needed is to let the meaning choose the word, and not the other way about. In prose, the worst thing one can do with words is to surrender to them. When you think of a concrete object, you think wordlessly, and then, if you want to describe the thing you have been visualizing you probably hunt about till you find the exact words that seem to fit. When you think of something abstract, you are more inclined to use words from the start, and unless you make a conscious effort to prevent it, the existing dialect will come rushing in and do the job for you, at the expense of blurring or even changing your meaning. Probably it is better to put off using words as long as possible and get one's meaning as clear as one can through pictures or sensations. Afterwards one can choose—not simply *accept*—the phrases that will best cover the meaning, and then switch round and decide what impression one's words are likely to make on another person. This last effort of the mind cuts out all stale or mixed images, all prefabricated phrases, needless repetitions, and humbug and vagueness generally. But one can often be in doubt about the effect of a word or a phrase, and one needs rules that one can rely on when instinct fails. I think the following rules will cover most cases:

(i)   Never use a metaphor, simile or other figure of speech which you are used to seeing in print.

(ii)   Never use a long word where a short one will do.

---

[3] One can cure oneself of the *not un-* formation by memorizing this sentence: *A not unblack dog was chasing a not unsmall rabbit across a not ungreen field.*

(iii) If it is possible to cut a word out, always cut it out.

(iv) Never use the passive where you can use the active.

(v) Never use a foreign phrase, a scientific word or jargon word if you can think of an everyday English equivalent.

(vi) Break any of these rules sooner than say anything outright barbarous.

These rules sound elementary, and so they are, but they demand a deep change in attitude in anyone who has grown used to writing in the style now fashionable. One could keep all of them and still write bad English, but one could not write the kind of stuff that I quoted in those five specimens at the beginning of this article.

19   I have not here been considering the literary use of language, but merely language as an instrument for expressing and not for concealing or preventing thought. Stuart Chase and others have come near to claiming that all abstract words are meaningless, and have used this as a pretext for advocating a kind of political quietism. Since you don't know what Fascism is, how can you struggle against Fascism? One need not swallow such absurdities as this, but one ought to recognize that the present political chaos is connected with the decay of language; and that one can probably bring about some improvement by starting at the verbal end. If you simplify your English, you are freed from the worst follies of orthodoxy. You cannot speak any of the necessary dialects, and when you make a stupid remark, its stupidity will be obvious, even to yourself. Political language—and with variations this is true of all political parties, from Conservatives to Anarchists—is designed to make lies sound truthful and murder respectable, and to give an appearance of solidity to pure wind. One cannot change this all in a moment, but one can at least change one's own habits, and from time to time one can even, if one jeers loudly enough, send some worn-out and useless phrase—some *jackboot, Achilles' heel, hotbed, melting pot, acid test, veritable inferno* or other lump of verbal refuse—into the dustbin where it belongs.

TOPICS FOR WRITING AND DISCUSSION

1. What does Orwell mean when he says in paragraph 2 that "an effect can become a cause, reinforcing the original cause and producing the same effect in an intensified form"? How does he illustrate this assertion? How does he apply the illustration to his beliefs concerning the decline of the English language?

2. According to Orwell, what are the four main "tricks" writers of political English use to dodge "the work of prose construction"? What *is* "the work of prose construction"? Why do writers use "tricks" to keep language from doing its intended work? (See paragraphs 11 through 14.)

3. In the first part of the essay, Orwell argues that "thought corrupts language," but in paragraph 16 he turns his thesis around and proposes that

"language can also corrupt thought." What does he mean by this? How can use of language affect the way a person thinks? Do you find Orwell's examples convincing?

4. What does Orwell believe must be done to cure what he sees as the decadence of the English language? Do you think he would make the same recommendations today?

5. Using Orwell's advice in "Politics and the English Language" as a guide, analyze a piece of ineffective writing, clearly explaining the causes and effects of its "bad habits." Do you agree that "the slovenliness of our language makes it easier for us to have foolish thoughts"?

Elizabeth Bishop (Special Collections, Vassar College Libraries, Poughkeepsie, NY)

THE FISH

Elizabeth Bishop
(1911–1979)

After graduating from Vassar, Elizabeth Bishop
planned to attend Cornell Medical School and pursue a
career in medicine. However, she was persuaded by
poet Marianne Moore to become a writer. After years
of traveling in Europe, Canada, and both North and
South America, Bishop settled in Rio de Janeiro, where
she lived for twenty years. In 1966, she returned to the
United States to teach at the University of Washington
and later at Harvard. Her writing output was modest,
comprising only four volumes of poetry and one of
prose. However, her first collection, *North and South*
(1946), was later expanded into *North and South—A
Cold Spring* (1955), which won her the Pulitzer Prize
for poetry in 1956. Another volume, *Geography III*
(1976), received the National Book Critics Award. The
other two volumes containing her work—*Complete
Poems 1927–1979* (1983) and *Collected Prose*
(1984)—were published after her death. In "The Fish,"
Bishop employs vivid imagery as she explains a personal decision made in the middle of a lake.

I caught a tremendous fish
and held him beside the boat
half out of water, with my hook
fast in a corner of his mouth.
5 He didn't fight.
He hadn't fought at all.
He hung a grunting weight,
battered and venerable

and homely. Here and there
10 his brown skin hung in strips
like ancient wallpaper,
and its pattern of darker brown
was like wallpaper:
shapes like full-blown roses
15 stained and lost through age.
He was speckled with barnacles,
fine rosettes of lime,
and infested
with tiny white sea-lice,
20 and underneath two or three
rags of green weed hung down.
While his gills were breathing in
the terrible oxygen
—the frightening gills,
25 fresh and crisp with blood,
that can cut so badly—
I thought of the coarse white flesh
packed in like feathers,
the big bones and the little bones,
30 the dramatic reds and blacks
of his shiny entrails,
and the pink swim-bladder
like a big peony.
I looked into his eyes
35 which were far larger than mine
but shallower, and yellowed,
the irises backed and packed
with tarnished tinfoil
seen through the lenses
40 of old scratched isinglass.
They shifted a little, but not
to return my stare.
—It was more like the tipping
of an object toward the light.
45 I admired his sullen face,
the mechanism of his jaw,
and then I saw
that from his lower lip
—if you could call it a lip—
50 grim, wet, and weaponlike,
hung five old pieces of fish-line,
or four and a wire leader
with the swivel still attached,
with all their five big hooks

55 grown firmly in his mouth.
    A green line, frayed at the end
    where he broke it, two heavier lines,
    and a fine black thread
    still crimped from the strain and snap
60 when it broke and he got away.
    Like medals with their ribbons
    frayed and wavering,
    a five-haired beard of wisdom
    trailing from his aching jaw.
65 I stared and stared
    and victory filled up
    the little rented boat,
    from the pool of bilge
    where oil had spread a rainbow
70 around the rusted engine
    to the bailer rusted orange,
    the sun-cracked thwarts,
    the oarlocks on their strings,
    the gunnels—until everything
75 was rainbow, rainbow, rainbow!
    And I let the fish go.

TOPICS FOR WRITING AND DISCUSSION

1. What is the cause-effect relationship presented in this poem?
2. Why does the speaker take the action she does? How does she ultimately feel about the fish and the sense of "victory" (line 66) that fills the boat?
3. What does the simile comparing the hooks and lines to medals and ribbons (line 61) add to the reader's understanding of the speaker's decision? The image of a "five-haired beard of wisdom" (line 63)?
4. What other details and images provide the reader with a vivid picture of this fish?
5. Have you ever suddenly seen beauty or strength in something commonplace, a realization that caused a change in your attitude or behavior? How might you explain this change in an essay of causal analysis?

Kate Chopin (Courtesy of Louisiana State University Press)

THE STORY OF AN HOUR

Kate Chopin
(1851–1904)

The daughter of an Irish immigrant father and a French Creole mother, Katherine O'Flaherty was born in St. Louis. Her father died when she was four, and she was raised by her mother, grandmother, and great-grandmother, descendants of early colonizers of Louisiana. In 1870, following her graduation from Sacred Heart Convent school, she married Oscar Chopin, a New Orleans cotton broker. In 1880, after his business failed, Oscar moved his wife and six children to a plantation he owned near Cloutierville, a town in central Louisiana. Two years later he died, and Kate returned with her children to her mother's home in St. Louis. There, at age thirty-seven, she began to write. She was well read in French literature and especially admired the work of Guy de Maupassant, whose work she translated. Many of her stories were published in national magazines such as *Vogue,* the *Century,* and the *Atlantic Monthly.* She published her first novel, *At Fault,* in 1890, and then collected her stories into two books, *Bayou Folk* (1894) and *A Night in Acadie* (1897). These collections gained her a reputation as an accomplished chronicler of Creole life. In 1899, she published her second novel, *The Awakening,* the story of a woman's disillusionment with her role as wife and mother and her attempts to achieve self-fulfillment. *The Awakening* produced a storm of controversy that virtually ended Chopin's literary career. "The Story of an Hour" (1894) is an ironic commentary on one woman's all-too-brief hopes for self-assertion.

1   Knowing that Mrs. Mallard was afflicted with a heart trouble, great care was taken to break to her as gently as possible the news of her husband's death.

2   It was her sister Josephine who told her, in broken sentences, veiled hints that revealed in half concealing. Her husband's friend Richards was there, too, near her. It was he who had been in the newspaper office when intelligence of the railroad disaster was received, with Brently Mallard's name leading the list of "killed." He had only taken the time to assure himself of its truth by a second telegram, and had hastened to forestall any less careful, less tender friend in bearing the sad message.

3   She did not hear the story as many women have heard the same, with a paralyzed inability to accept its significance. She wept at once, with sudden, wild abandonment, in her sister's arms. When the storm of grief had spent itself she went away to her room alone. She would have no one follow her.

4   There stood, facing the open window, a comfortable, roomy armchair. Into this she sank, pressed down by a physical exhaustion that haunted her body and seemed to reach into her soul.

5   She could see in the open square before her house the tops of trees that were all aquiver with the new spring life. The delicious breath of rain was in the air. In the street below a peddler was crying his wares. The notes of a distant song which some one was singing reached her faintly, and countless sparrows were twittering in the eaves.

6   There were patches of blue sky showing here and there through the clouds that had met and piled each above the other in the west facing her window.

7   She sat with her head thrown back upon the cushion of the chair quite motionless, except when a sob came up into her throat and shook her, as a child who has cried itself to sleep continues to sob in its dreams.

8   She was young, with a fair, calm face, whose lines bespoke repression and even a certain strength. But now there was a dull stare in her eyes, whose gaze was fixed away off yonder on one of those patches of blue sky. It was not a glance of reflection, but rather indicated a suspension of intelligent thought.

9   There was something coming to her and she was waiting for it, fearfully. What was it? She did not know; it was too subtle and elusive to name. But she felt it, creeping out of the sky, reaching toward her through the sounds, the scents, the color that filled the air.

10 Now her bosom rose and fell tumultuously. She was beginning to recognize this thing that was approaching to possess her, and she was striving to beat it back with her will—as powerless as her two white slender hands would have been.

11 When she abandoned herself a little whispered word escaped her slightly parted lips. She said it over and over under her breath: "Free, free, free!" The vacant stare and the look of terror that had followed it went from her eyes. They stayed keen and bright. Her pulses beat fast, and the coursing blood warmed and relaxed every inch of her body.

12   She did not stop to ask if it were not a monstrous joy that held her. A clear and exalted perception enabled her to dismiss the suggestion as trivial.

13   She knew that she would weep again when she saw the kind, tender hands folded in death; the face that had never looked save with love upon her, fixed and gray and dead. But she saw beyond that bitter moment a long procession of years to come that would belong to her absolutely. And she opened and spread her arms out to them in welcome.

14   There would be no one to live for during those coming years; she would live for herself. There would be no powerful will bending her in that blind persistence with which men and women believe they have a right to impose a private will upon a fellow creature. A kind intention or a cruel intention made the act seem no less a crime as they looked upon it in that brief moment of illumination.

15   And yet she had loved him—sometimes. Often she had not. What did it matter! What could love, the unsolved mystery, count for in face of this possession of self-assertion which she suddenly recognized as the strongest impulse of her being.

16   "Free! Body and soul free!" she kept whispering.

17   Josephine was kneeling before the closed door with her lips to the keyhole, imploring for admission. "Louise, open the door! I beg; open the door—you will make yourself ill. What are you doing, Louise? For heaven's sake open the door."

18   "Go away. I am not making myself ill." No; she was drinking in a very elixir of life through that open window.

19   Her fancy was running riot along those days ahead of her. Spring days, and summer days, and all sorts of days that would be her own. She breathed a quick prayer that life might be long. It was only yesterday she had thought with a shudder that life might be long.

20   She arose at length and opened the door to her sister's importunities. There was a feverish triumph in her eyes, and she carried herself unwittingly like a goddess of Victory. She clasped her sister's waist, and together they descended the stairs. Richards stood waiting for them at the bottom.

21   Some one was opening the front door with a latchkey. It was Brently Mallard who entered, a little travel-stained, composedly carrying his gripsack and umbrella. He had been far from the scene of accident, and did not even know there had been one. He stood amazed at Josephine's piercing cry; at Richards' quick motion to screen him from this view of his wife.

22   But Richards was too late.

23   When the doctors came they said she had died of heart disease—of joy that kills.

Topics for Writing and Discussion

1. According to her doctors, what is the cause of Mrs. Mallard's death? Do you agree with their diagnosis?

2. What is the feeling Mrs. Mallard senses "creeping out of the sky" (paragraph 9)? Describe the revelation she has about the nature of the coming years. How is her attitude toward the future changed?

3. During what season is this story set? Why did Chopin select this season? What other details in the setting of this story add to its meaning? Consider, for example, the use of the closed room, the open window, and the irony of her sister Josephine's pleas.

4. What kind of imagery describes Mrs. Mallard after her revelation? Why? Does Chopin describe Mr. Mallard as a villain? What, in your opinion, is Chopin criticizing in this story, written more than 100 years ago?

5. Chopin's story describes Mrs. Mallard's relief upon thinking she had escaped the role 1894 society had prescribed for her. Can you think of a time when someone stereotyped you unfairly because of your gender, race, religion, or ethnic heritage? Write an essay explaining the effects of this situation on your sense of self.

WRITING ASSIGNMENTS FOR CHAPTER TEN

CAUSE AND EFFECT

1. In "My Wood," E. M. Forster discusses the effects of ownership. Think of your most prized material possession. What one item would you save if your house, apartment, or dorm were on fire? Write an essay that clearly explains the reasons for, or causes of, your attachment to this object.

2. Barbara Tuchman vividly captures the devastation of the plague in "'This Is the End of the World': The Black Death." If you have ever experienced a life-threatening illness or accident, write about its effects on you. Are you different for having survived your ordeal? (Or, if you prefer, write an essay explaining the effects of someone else's illness or accident on you, your family, or circle of friends.)

3. Marya Mannes concludes her essay "How Do You Know It's Good?" by noting that there are standards for critical judgment and exhorts the reader to "never be afraid to speak up." Consider the standards by which you judge the artistic worth of literature, painting, theater, music, film, or other visual and performing arts. Choose one art form as your focus and narrow your subject to a particular type, genre, or style (for example, literature might be narrowed to science fiction; film might be narrowed to Westerns; painting might be narrowed to pop art, and so on). Write an essay in which you present your own definition of "quality" for the kind of art you have chosen; use sufficient examples to illustrate your definition and to convince the reader that your opinion is accurate.

4. Select a paragraph from another essay in this text that you think is clear and well written. As George Orwell did with the verse from *Ecclesiastes* in "Politics and the English Language," rewrite the passage, using as many vague, clichéd abstractions as possible. Exchange papers with a classmate and see how many of Orwell's rules you can apply to the murky prose.

5. In "The Decisive Arrest," Martin Luther King, Jr., tries to clarify the cause of an event he feels was misunderstood by a number of people at the time. Write an essay with a similar purpose, one that shows why the cause people first took up was not the accurate or most important one, as you persuasively explain the true source of the action or event.

6. In "The Violence Is Fake, the Impact Is Real," columnist Ellen Goodman argues that children are adversely affected by television that teaches "violence is okay." According to the American Psychological Association, a child watches more than one hundred thousand acts of violence on television before he or she finishes elementary school. Read the current research on this subject and write your own causal analysis of the effects of TV violence on children. Do you agree or disagree with Goodman's position?

Does the new television rating system make a difference? (Or, if you prefer, consider the treatment of violence in contemporary movies or music. Write an essay in which you argue their effects on those watching or listening today.)

7. The speaker in Elizabeth Bishop's poem "The Fish" sees a part of nature in a new, meaningful way. Write an essay in which you explain how a particular place or experience in the outdoors significantly affected or changed you. If appropriate, consider using some vivid figurative language, as Bishop did, to help your readers understand your feelings.

8. In Kate Chopin's "The Story of an Hour," Mrs. Mallard, under the impression that her husband has been killed, experiences a revelation that dictates a dramatic change in her view of her future. Write an essay explaining a dramatic change in your own life following a major insight of some kind. Make the cause-effect relationship clear to your readers so that they will understand both the motivation for, and the extent of, your change.

CHAPTER ELEVEN

PERSUASION AND ARGUMENT

PERSUASION and argument are frequently used interchangeably as terms describing the attempt to shape or change someone's opinion or to move someone to action. The words, however, are not synonymous. *Persuasion* often refers to shaping or changing people's opinions by appealing to their emotions or to their sense of self-interest. *Argument* often refers to shaping or changing people's opinions by appealing to their sense of reason and logic. Many writers, though, employ principles of both argument and persuasion in their attempt to convince their readers that what they have to say is valid. The purpose of your writing and your audience will ultimately determine which of the appeals you should use; however, in most of the writing you will do in college, argument—an appeal to reason—will be the more appropriate form.

As you plan the structure of your essay, consider the following:

1. *Audience.* Your audience will probably fall into one or more of these four categories:

   - those who have formed opinions, hold tightly to those opinions, and are hesitant to acknowledge the validity of another view
   - those who have formed opinions but realize that another view may be equally valid
   - those who have not formed opinions but are interested in learning more about the issue
   - those who have not formed opinions because they are uninterested in the issue

Once you recognize the attitudes of your audience, you can decide which methods of development—appeal to emotions, appeal to logic, or appeal to self-interest, or some combination—will be the most effective in swaying your readers to your side. To prepare your case, consider these questions:

   - Does your audience *already* agree with you? If so, the presentation of your case may be primarily ceremonial, providing encouragement, reinforcement, or inspiration, like a "pep talk" or a "rallying cry" rather than a genuine attempt at persuasion. In addressing this audience, you might couch reason and logic in an appeal to the audience's emotions. (Emotional appeals often speak to people's pride, vanity, fears, prejudices, or loyalties. For instance, a candidate might stir an audience by constantly referring to his or her plan as the "American Way.").

- Is your audience interested but perhaps poorly informed? If so, rely heavily on evidence and logic, because this audience is looking for information upon which to *base* an opinion. It's up to you to provide that solid base.

- Is your audience neutral or is the audience ambivalent on the issue? If so, take great care in organizing your material in a logical, reasonable manner, for there may be many reasons why this audience has not formed an opinion or has developed conflicting feelings toward the issue. Give this audience solid, well-documented evidence; however, be aware that their neutrality or ambivalence may be emotionally based, so an appropriate emotional appeal might also be effective.

- Is your audience *uninterested* in the issue? Unless you can establish a strong basis for your case that would be beneficial to the audience, you may not succeed.

- Does your audience hold a view entirely different from yours? If so, establishing your credibility as one who is an authority or as one who has done considerable research on the issue is essential, even crucial, because this audience will present the strongest resistance to persuasion. Here, it is especially necessary to state and refute opposing arguments to show your audience that you clearly understand all sides of the issue.

2. *Topic.* Your topic should be one you really care about.

Your essay will be more convincing if the reader believes that you have a genuine interest (though not one of personal gain) in it. Your approach to the topic may be serious or humorous, but it must be sincere.

3. *Position.* Your position on the issue must be clearly stated.

Once you begin to write, the first and most important step is stating your position, taking a firm stand. Of course, you should come to that firm stand only after you have given the issue considerable thought and, if necessary, done considerable research. When you are comfortable in your own position, you will be better able to plan the strategy necessary to persuade your audience.

Once you have carefully thought about your own position, you can express that position in the form of a *thesis.* Your thesis must be one that is debatable, addressing an issue that has two or more sides.

4. *Opposition.* The next step in determining your plan of persuasion will be to decide what evidence you will need.

As you gather the material to support your own case, keep in mind that you must also deal effectively with opposing views. Though *refuting* or answering all arguments against your position may be impossible, certainly you must address the most obvious ones. Discover the most notable objections to your thesis and straightforwardly address them. By doing this, you will go far in convincing your audience that your position is sound.

Prepare your strategy by carefully considering the kinds of evidence you will need to support your argument and watch for any fallacies you might encounter as you gather your evidence and organize your thoughts.

Types of Evidence

Evidence is the information you use to persuade your audience to accept your ideas and to agree with your position on an issue. It is also the material you must present to refute the major opposing views. So, in argumentation, the judicious selection of evidence is essential.

As you consider your choice of evidence upon which to base your argument, notice the types of information at your disposal. *Facts* will provide evidence based on information whose verification is not affected by the source. No matter who says it, a fact is a fact. It is a fact, for example, that President John F. Kennedy was killed on November 22, 1963, in Dallas, Texas, while riding in a motorcade. The source of that information does not affect the truth of the information. However, even though much investigation and debate have been focused on the assassination, the question of who was ultimately responsible for the murder is, for many people, still a matter of opinion—that is, depending on the speaker, a lone gunman named Lee Harvey Oswald committed the crime; Oswald and another assailant were responsible; the Mafia ordered the killing; the Cuban government was involved; or perhaps some other persons or groups were part of a conspiracy. *Opinions,* then, are often based on personal feelings or beliefs or on one's interpretations of facts.

Facts are primary sources of information. They may be cited and documented in your essay directly or they may be presented by experts in the field of the issue you are discussing. When readers feel that the information they receive is from a knowledgeable, credible, and reliable source, they will be more likely to accept your view.

Another type of evidence is judgment. *Judgments* are secondary sources derived from the synthesizing of primary sources. The strength of judgments you might use in your argument will be largely based upon the source of the judgment. An expert in the field, someone with a good reputation, could present judgments that your audience may readily accept; however, realize that judgments are interpretations. For your readers to accept the judgment, they must accept the source.

Statistics can play a role similar to that of expert testimony. They can provide solid evidence on which to base an argument, and we seem to be a society with a respect for numbers. If we hear that 99 out of 100 physicians who treat patients suffering from tension headaches recommend a particular pain reliever, we may be tempted to try that medication if we become afflicted with a tension headache.

For statistics to be reliable evidence in persuasion, however, they must be unambiguous. For instance, if we hear that 10 out of 100 drivers are involved in automobile accidents each day, we may not be convinced to be more careful drivers or to take better care of our vehicles because we know so little about the accidents. However, if we are told that 10 of 100 drivers are involved in traffic accidents *because of faulty brakes,* we might be more inclined to have our car brakes checked. The statistics are more convincing because we know specifically what they address.

It also is important to use statistics from a reliable source. You would probably accept statistically based evidence that suggests you should have your brakes checked if the report came from the National Highway Safety Commission. However, if that same information came from a spokesperson for a chain of brake and muffler shops, the evidence would be suspect.

Types of Reasoning

Two types of reasoning may be used to present an argument: inductive and deductive. In *inductive* reasoning, specific facts or individual cases or observations lead to a general conclusion, one that appears to be true or appears to be better than any other conclusion. In *deductive* reasoning, one begins with a general premise or assumption and moves to a specific conclusion. Deductive reasoning tells us that if all the premises are true, the conclusion must be true. Inductive reasoning tells us that the conclusion must be true if the evidence points to it.

Inductive Reasoning

In form, the inductive argument begins with a *hypothesis* stating the conclusion you will try to impress upon your reader. For the reader to accept your hypothesis, you must present evidence that leads directly to it; thus, the reader can conclude that your hypothesis is valid.

Hypothesis: Donald has the flu.

Evidence: He has a fever.

               He has aches and pains in his muscles.

He has a sore throat.

He is sniffling and sneezing and has a persistent cough.

Conclusion: Donald has the flu.

This is a simple example, but it serves to demonstrate how a hypothesis can lead to a probable conclusion (called an *inference*) if the evidence is convincing. However, if any piece of the evidence does not fit in with the hypothesis, the conclusion would be invalid.

Remember, conclusions drawn from inductive reasoning are often *probable* conclusions drawn from incomplete evidence, so the evidence you choose should be selected carefully. For example, you may think that all people who wear glasses, excel in science and mathematics, and would rather work on a computer than watch a sporting event are nerds (hypothesis). You base your logic on a couple of movies you have seen and a guy you knew in high school (evidence). Therefore, you conclude that science and math majors are nerds who have no social skills (conclusion). The truth is, you don't know many math and science majors very well because you have a different circle of friends and you have had little opportunity to get to know anyone from those departments. Your conclusion would be made from an *inductive leap,* a specific conclusion drawn from a limited sample and then turned into a general conclusion. True, conclusions made from inductive reasoning are common; in fact, most of what we "know" is known by induction. But because induction can lead to conclusions that may not be valid, it often contributes to untrue, and sometimes unfair, assumptions about people, places, and ideas. These assumptions can later become the basis of stereotypes, which in turn may lead to misunderstandings, misconceptions, and perhaps even distrust and hatred. Therefore, for a conclusion based on inductive reasoning to be creditable, the sample from which the conclusions are drawn must be known, sufficient, and representative.

A *known* sample is literally one you know, one you can examine for yourself to test its reliability. Suppose you were about to book a vacation to an exotic spot in the South Pacific—say, Tasmania—and your best friend tried to dissuade you by saying that Tasmania is a terrible place for a vacation because the hotels are poorly run, the people are arrogant and unfriendly, and the beaches are littered and covered with seaweed. You respond by asking the source of his information and find that he just "heard it somewhere." Your friend's conclusions about Tasmania were made with an absent sample, and therefore his conclusions may be invalid.

In addition to a known sample, a *sufficient* sample is also necessary to make sound judgments. Consider the following statements:

Sure, I'm over 35; I love french fries, potato chips, and chocolate bars; my body's carrying a few extra pounds; and I smoke and drink. So what? I'll still live to be 100 because my grandfather lived to be 105, and my grandmother is now 92.

That professor must be really tough. My two best friends took her class, and both failed.

A Hispanic family in the neighborhood spells trouble. My cousin has been in dispute with his Hispanic neighbors ever since they moved in.

Statements like the ones above are all founded on insufficient evidence. The truth is that many doctors maintain that diet and lifestyle do play a role in determining not only the quality of our life but also the probable length of our life. Though heredity is important, it is not a guarantee of a long life. Similarly, the trouble that two friends had in a certain professor's class does not indicate all students believe the professor's course is difficult. The two friends who failed may have done so for a variety of reasons. Likewise, the racial background of a person will not be an indicator of the type of neighbor that person will be. Neighborhood disputes can arise from a number of causes. It is possible that the cousin's disagreement with his Hispanic neighbors stemmed from their meticulous house- and lawn-keeping habits that made the cousin's own habits seem bad in comparison.

It is in this area of induction that stereotypes leading to prejudices are born. Simplistic, negative, descriptions of ethnic, racial, religious, political, and other groups often stem from insufficient samples.

In addition to a known sample and a sufficient sample, one needs a *representative* sample before a sound conclusion can be drawn. A representative sample is a sample typical of the entire class of things being discussed. A city could not decide on its policy toward the treatment of transients by polling only those hostile to the transients' plight. Nor could that city gauge the attitudes of its citizens toward adult entertainment by polling only the owners of adult-entertainment businesses. Such polls would be unrepresentative of the city's population. Or, if you were to discover that students at your school ranked fifth out of five schools on a standardized test given to students at the end of their sophomore year, the news would be quite distressing. But if you found out that the test from which the statistics were derived was given to only 2 students at your school and to 150, 100, 230, and 89 students, respectively, at the other schools, any conclusions suggesting a poor quality of education at your institution would be invalid.

Sometimes, drawing conclusions from limited information is difficult to avoid. We do it every day. The important point: be aware of the possible flaws in the conclusions that have been drawn.

DEDUCTIVE REASONING

The intellectual method used to come to a conclusion in deductive reasoning is the opposite of the method used in inductive reasoning. As stated before, deduction moves from general assumptions, called *premises,* to a specific conclusion about the general assumptions or to a specific application of the general assumptions. The organizational form of this type of reasoning is the *syllogism,* in which two premises are made and a conclusion is drawn from them.

For a syllogism to be useful in constructing an argument, its premises must be true, its language must be clear and unambiguous, and its form must be valid. First, remember that your conclusion will be valid only if the premises upon which you base it are themselves valid. The classic example of a syllogism is this:

Major Premise:	All men are mortal.
Minor Premise:	Socrates is a man.
Conclusion:	Socrates is a mortal.

Another example is this:

Major Premise:	All students pay tuition.
Minor Premise:	Adam is a student.
Conclusion:	Adam pays tuition.

Notice that the conclusion is drawn directly from the premises and depends on their accuracy for its own accuracy. Your premises will most likely be accurate if they are drawn from known, sufficient, or representative samples—the same conditions needed to draw a solid conclusion by inductive reasoning.

Translated into its basic form, the syllogism would look like this:

Major Premise:	All A are B.
Minor Premise:	C is A.
Conclusion:	C is B.

Now, notice what happens to the conclusion when one or both of the premises are *inaccurate:*

Major Premise:	All Americans are wealthy and drive luxury cars.
Minor Premise:	Donald is an American.
Conclusion:	Donald is wealthy and drives a luxury car.

Reduced, the form is this:

Major Premise:	All A (Americans) are B (wealthy and drive luxury cars).
Minor Premise:	C (Donald) is A (an American).
Conclusion:	C (Donald) is B (wealthy and drives a luxury car).

Because the major premise is not accurate, the conclusion is not necessarily valid either. Thus, an argument can be *valid* in form, but not *sound.*

Here is another form:

Major Premise:	If A then B	If (first sentence) then (second sentence)
Minor Premise:	A	The first sentence
Conclusion:	Then B	Then, the second sentence

Example:

Major Premise:	If it's autumn, then the leaves are changing.
Minor Premise:	It's autumn.
Conclusion:	The leaves are changing.

Next, the language of your premises must be clear and unambiguous if the conclusion is going to be sound. For example:

Major Premise:	Only good citizens should have the right to free speech.
Minor Premise:	Travis is a good citizen.
Conclusion:	Travis should have the right to free speech.

Here, the term "good citizen" is unclear. What constitutes a good citizen? Does Travis fit the definition? Until we know how the term is specifically used, we cannot accept the conclusion as true, that Travis should be allowed free speech.

Finally, the structure—or form—of the syllogism must be valid. This means that (1) the subject or general topic (or condition) of the major premise must appear in the minor premise but (2) the subject or general topic (or condition) of the minor premise must not be equal to the major premise. For example:

Major Premise:	All college students eat food.
Minor Premise:	All criminals eat food.
Conclusion:	All college students are criminals.

The problem with this syllogism is that the minor premise does not repeat the subject (college students) of the main premise. What results is an invalid—and ridiculous—conclusion. Reduced, it would look like this:

Major Premise:	All A eat B.
Minor Premise:	All C eat B.
Conclusion:	All A are C.

Or, consider this example:

Major Premise:	Roses are flowers.	A are B.
Minor Premise:	Daisies are flowers.	C are B.
Conclusion:	Daisies are roses.	C are A.

The problem with this syllogism is twofold: The word *roses* does not recur in the minor premise, and daisies are not a subclass—or division—of roses. When the minor premise is revised to repeat the subject of the major premise and to be a subclass of the major premise, the conclusion becomes valid—and sound:

Major Premise:	Roses are flowers.	A are B.
Minor Premise:	The American Beauty is a rose.	C is A.
Conclusion:	The American Beauty is a flower.	C is B.

Types of Fallacies

Fallacies are flawed statements in arguments. They may sound reasonable, but upon close scrutiny, you will discover that they cannot be defended logically. Generally, reasoning will be fallacious if it does not adhere to the patterns of sound, cogent thinking. If you accept a premise that is doubtful, if you neglect pertinent or relevant evidence, or if you draw conclusions from insufficient evidence, you are guilty of fallacious reasoning.

Whether fallacies are used intentionally or unintentionally, a reader's detection of these statements can cast the writer in a poor light indeed, making the writer seem ignorant or, even worse, dishonest. Often, you may not recognize fallacious statements in your essay's first draft. However, when you are ready to revise, watch out for the following common flaws in logic.

False Analogy.   This fallacy is based on presumption. To base an argument on analogy means to base the argument on the comparison of two things you know to be alike in certain aspects. The fallacy occurs when that analogy is presumed to extend into other aspects. For example, you might hear someone argue that antismoking laws of the 1980s won't work because they are just like Prohibition reforms of the 1920s. But are the programs so alike? Antismoking laws today have popular support as well as support from the medical profession and government health officials. Remember also that while the best of analogies may sound persuasive, they cannot *prove* anything.

Equivocation.   This fallacy occurs when you shift the meaning of a key term or terms in the midst of the argument to make your conclusion appear to follow logically from your premise. Read the following carefully:

> In the realm of human experience we all find ourselves presented with difficult choices to make. It is, then, a very human experience to make the mistake that our client did.

The use of "human experience" in the first sentence refers to the *experience* of being human. The second sentence refers to an *act* that a person committed.

Begging the Question. This fallacy results when you present a debatable premise as if it were a fact. For example, notice this premise:

> An immoral book such as *The Adventures of Huckleberry Finn* must be removed from our school's library because it will corrupt young minds.

This statement begs the question because it presents as fact an idea that must be proven—that *Huckleberry Finn* is an immoral book. Such a statement cannot be used as a premise.

Post Hoc, Ergo Propter Hoc (After this, therefore because of this). This fallacy occurs when the writer establishes a false cause-effect relationship. The *post hoc* fallacy presumes that because one thing happened first in time, it caused the second happening. The problem with this reasoning is that it ignores some of the complex factors that actually contribute to an outcome. Using this kind of reasoning, one might conclude that finding a lucky horseshoe in the morning caused one to win an election that afternoon.

Non Sequitur (It does not follow). This fallacy occurs when the writer suggests that a given fact has already led to or must eventually lead to a particular result. For example, to suggest that a famous scientist will deliver a brilliant lecture is not necessarily true. Knowing a subject well does not automatically mean one can communicate it; hence, the conclusion is not necessarily valid.

Circular Argument. In circular argument, the writer argues that something is true simply by restating the idea in different words. For example, to suggest that freeways are too crowded because people drive too many cars is simply repetition. Such an argument is a dead-end topic.

Either/Or Fallacy. This fallacy assumes that an issue or argument has only two sides when it actually could have many facets. For example, if a friend told you that she failed a math examination that you considered easy, you would commit an either/or fallacy by responding, "Well, either you didn't study or you don't have an aptitude for understanding math." Of course, either (or both) of those things might be true, but there are also several other possible reasons for her failing grade: perhaps she felt ill and found she could not concentrate on the exam; perhaps she did not finish the test (for a variety of reasons); perhaps she suffers from test anxiety, and no matter how prepared she is for a test, she "freezes" whenever an exam is placed in front of her. The point is that there could be many other reasons why your friend failed the exam.

Argument ad Hominem (Argument to the man). Arguments of this type attack a person rather than an issue. For example:

> The Governor supports raising taxes. What else would you expect from a multi-millionaire who inherited all his money?

On occasion, you may find that raising questions about a person's character is justified, that the person's character really may be one of the issues. For example, if a political candidate for a high national office belonged to a club that restricted women or minorities, one might ask if the candidate's membership might be an issue by which the person should be judged—that is, if his choice suggests a character trait or flaw that would affect his ability to function fairly in office. But *argument ad hominem* appeals only to passions and prejudices rather than to reason and logic. We often use the term "mud slinging" to describe the practice.

A variation of this is *guilt by association*, where someone might be judged not by her actions but by the company she keeps. The fairness of this type of judgment often depends on the particular facts surrounding each case.

Similar to *argument ad hominem* is *argument ad populum* (argument to the people). Here, the writer defends, "sells," or attacks an ideology, a group, or a product by asking the reader to associate one idea that appeals to people's emotions or prejudices with another idea, regardless of whether the two are logically connected. An example would be suggesting that all Southerners are racists in order to sway support away from a Southern political candidate. Like *argument ad hominem,* the attack is not on the issue; instead, the reader's attention is transferred to something else, a perception about Southerners. Consider the use of pretty female models, cute animals, and American symbols in commercials for products having nothing whatsoever to do with gender, nature, or nationalism.

Still another type of "argument to" is *argument ad verecundiam* (argument to authority). This is a technique of transferring prestige from one area to another. Here, the reader's attention is focused upon an authority who shares the same ideas with the writer. The reader acknowledges the authority and thus is persuaded to accept the idea. For instance, when manufacturers advertise that their product is the one most used by doctors, the idea is, "Well, if doctors use it, it must be good." Many television commercials use this tactic. Beware the false authority. Do football players know any more about popcorn poppers than anyone else?

One more type of "argument to" is *argumentum ad ignoratiam* (appeal, or argument, to ignorance). This fallacy takes the position that the absence of evidence is proof that the evidence does not exist. An example would be to suggest that there is no life elsewhere in the galaxy because no one has proven that there is.

Consensus Genitum (Consensus [agreement] of the people).   This is the concept of "going along with the crowd." The fallacy attempts to establish that something is true or worthwhile simply because many people believe it is or because "everybody's doing it." This fallacy is sometimes called "the bandwagon."

The validity of the point to be made is based on majority vote. To argue that the speed limit along a certain stretch of road should be raised because everybody exceeds it anyway, argues the point based on *consensus genitum.*

Hasty Generalization. This fallacy presumes that a general principle is applicable to any specific case. To assume that because Nancy lost 20 pounds in one week on an artichoke and banana diet, everyone else would also lose 20 pounds in one week on the same diet is making a hasty generalization. There are many factors that might have contributed to Nancy's dramatic weight loss, factors that might not be present in any other case.

Red Herring. This fallacy represents a move of desperation. It occurs when the writer changes the subject to divert the reader's attention away from the issue at hand. Such a ploy is used when the writer finds that the position he or she is supporting is so weak that something is needed to obscure the issue. For example, "Yes, this man has admitted to brutally killing two people, but he only turns mean when he's had too much to drink; otherwise, he is a kind, considerate, generous man who has financially supported many of the cultural endeavors of this town."

Tu Quoque (You're another). This fallacy occurs when you avoid the issue or hostile charge by making a similar charge against your opponent. For example:

> Don't tell me to take better care of myself; you smoke.
>
> How can you tell me I need a good education when you dropped out of school in the eleventh grade?

Weaknesses in inductive reasoning or deductive reasoning or in the careless use of words usually lead to the fallacies you have read about in this chapter. Be careful when you form your argument based on syllogism, for a flawed syllogistic form will result in a false analogy. Likewise, an inductive leap can result in a *post hoc* error. Remember that if you must wittingly use a fallacy to support your argument, the argument is weak or the information from which you support the argument is insufficient. In either case, choose another topic or reexamine your position.

USE OF RHETORICAL STRATEGIES IN ARGUMENT AND PERSUASION

Many of the rhetorical strategies discussed earlier in the text may be used in persuasion and argument essays.

Writers often include examples to *illustrate* hypotheses or premises, thereby leading the reader to accept their views. For instance, Jonathan Swift ironically proposes examples of ways children can be used to bring about prosperity in Ireland in "A Modest Proposal." Both Thomas Jefferson and Elizabeth Cady Stanton present many examples of grievances in their respective "Declarations."

The principles of *causal analysis* also appear frequently in arguments, especially when writers are trying to convince their readers that something needs to be done to prevent or to create something in the future. Rachel Carson, for example, argues the effects of pesticides on nature in "The Obligation to Endure," and in his "I Have a Dream" speech, Martin Luther King, Jr., calls for action that will assure a better future for all children, regardless of race.

Richard Rodriguez uses *narrative* techniques in "None of This Is Fair" as he recounts the story of his academic job search, a process that shaped his views on affirmative action. Virginia Woolf makes extensive use of *descriptive* details in "Professions for Women" as she confesses to a metaphorical murder.

Process, definition, comparison and contrast, division and classification, and *cause and effect* can also use the principles of persuasion and argument.

What should be clear by this time is that rhetorical strategies are seldom used in isolation. One or more strategies often are used in developing an essay primarily organized by another strategy. Good writers recognize and use all of the tools available to them.

Rachel Carson at her home in Washington in March 1963 (AP/Wide World Photos)

THE OBLIGATION TO ENDURE

Rachel Carson
(1907–1964)

Born in the rural river town of Springfield, Pennsylvania, Rachel Carson was a writer, a scientist, and an ecologist. She graduated from Pennsylvania College for Women (now Chatham College) and later received an M.A. in zoology from Johns Hopkins University. During the Great Depression, she began working for the U.S. Fish and Wildlife Service and for the *Baltimore Sun* as a feature writer of articles on natural history. Her passion was marine biology, and she wrote a variety of works on conservation and natural resources. In 1941, she published *Under the Sea-Wind: A Naturalist's Picture of Ocean Life*. It was followed in 1945 with *Fish and Shellfish of the Middle Atlantic Coast*. She was awarded the National Book Award in 1951 for *The Sea Around Us*. In 1952, Carson resigned from her government position to devote herself to writing full time. In 1962, she published her most well-known work, *Silent Spring,* in which she challenges the practice of indiscriminate use of pesticides. The book caused tremendous controversy, and she was unfairly attacked by the chemical industry as an alarmist. She testified before Congress in 1964 to call for new policies to protect humans and the environment. "The Obligation to Endure" is an excerpt from *Silent Spring.* In the essay, Carson explains her reasons for urging careful study of the threat that chemical insecticides pose to the environment.

---

1   THE history of life on earth has been a history of interaction between living things and their surroundings. To a large extent, the physical form and

the habits of the earth's vegetation and its animal life have been molded by the environment. Considering the whole span of earthly time, the opposite effect, in which life actually modifies its surroundings, has been relatively slight. Only within the moment of time represented by the present century has one species—man—acquired significant power to alter the nature of his world.

2   During the past quarter century this power has not only increased to one of disturbing magnitude but it has changed in character. The most alarming of all man's assaults upon the environment is the contamination of air, earth, rivers, and sea with dangerous and even lethal materials. This pollution is for the most part irrecoverable; the chain of evil it initiates not only in the world that must support life but in living tissues is for the most part irreversible. In this now universal contamination of the environment, chemicals are the sinister and little-recognized partners of radiation in changing the very nature of the world—the very nature of its life. Strontium 90, released through nuclear explosions into the air, comes to earth in rain or drifts down in fallout, lodges in soil, enters into the grass or corn or wheat grown there, and in time takes up its abode in the bones of a human being, there to remain until his death. Similarly, chemicals sprayed on croplands or forests or gardens lie long in soil, entering into living organisms, passing from one to another in a chain of poisoning and death. Or they pass mysteriously by underground streams until they emerge and, through the alchemy of air and sunlight, combine into new forms that kill vegetation, sicken cattle, and work unknown harm on those who drink from once pure wells. As Albert Schweitzer has said, "Man can hardly even recognize the devils of his own creation."

3   It took hundreds of millions of years to produce the life that now inhabits the earth—eons of time in which that developing and evolving and diversifying life reached a state of adjustment and balance with its surroundings. The environment, rigorously shaping and directing the life it supported, contained elements that were hostile as well as supporting. Certain rocks gave out dangerous radiation; even within the light of the sun, from which all life draws its energy, there were short-wave radiations with power to injure. Given time— time not in years but in millennia—life adjusts, and a balance has been reached. For time is the essential ingredient; but in the modern world there is no time.

4   The rapidity of change and the speed with which new situations are created follow the impetuous and heedless pace of man rather than the deliberate pace of nature. Radiation is no longer merely the background radiation of rocks, the bombardment of cosmic rays, the ultraviolet of the sun that have existed before there was any life on earth; radiation is now the unnatural creation of man's tampering with the atom. The chemicals to which life is asked to make its adjustment are no longer merely the calcium and silica and copper and all the rest of the minerals washed out of the rocks and carried in rivers to the sea; they are the synthetic creations of man's inventive mind, brewed in his laboratories, and having no counterparts in nature.

5   To adjust to these chemicals would require time on the scale that is nature's; it would require not merely the years of a man's life but the life of generations.

And even this, were it by some miracle possible, would be futile, for the new chemicals come from our laboratories in an endless stream; almost five hundred annually find their way into actual use in the United States alone. The figure is staggering and its implications are not easily grasped—500 new chemicals to which the bodies of men and animals are required somehow to adapt each year, chemicals totally outside the limits of biologic experience.

6   Among them are many that are used in man's war against nature. Since the mid-1940's over 200 basic chemicals have been created for use in killing insects, weeds, rodents, and other organisms described in the modern vernacular as "pests"; and they are sold under several thousand different brand names.

7   These sprays, dusts, and aerosols are now applied almost universally to farms, gardens, forests, and homes—nonselective chemicals that have the power to kill every insect, the "good" and the "bad," to still the songs of birds and the leaping of fish in the streams, to coat the leaves with a deadly film, and to linger on in soil—all this though the intended target may be only a few weeds or insects. Can anyone believe it is possible to lay down such a barrage of poisons on the surface of the earth without making it unfit for all life? They should not be called "insecticides," but "biocides."

8   The whole process of spraying seems caught up in an endless spiral. Since DDT was released for civilian use, a process of escalation has been going on in which ever more toxic materials must be found. This has happened because insects, in a triumphant vindication of Darwin's principle of the survival of the fittest, have evolved super races immune to the particular insecticide used, hence a deadlier one has always to be developed—and then a deadlier one than that. It has happened also because, for reasons to be described later, destructive insects often undergo a "flareback" or resurgence, after spraying in numbers greater than before. Thus the chemical war is never won, and all life is caught in its violent crossfire.

9   Along with the possibility of the extinction of mankind by nuclear war, the central problem of our age has therefore become the contamination of man's total environment with such substances of incredible potential for harm—substances that accumulate in the tissues of plants and animals and even penetrate the germ cells to shatter or alter the very material of heredity upon which the shape of the future depends.

10   Some would-be architects of our future look toward a time when it will be possible to alter the human germ plasm by design. But we may easily be doing so now by inadvertence, for many chemicals, like radiation, bring about gene mutations. It is ironic to think that man might determine his own future by something so seemingly trivial as the choice of an insect spray.

11   All this has been risked—for what? Future historians may well be amazed by our distorted sense of proportion. How could intelligent beings seek to control a few unwanted species by a method that contaminated the entire environment and brought the threat of disease and death even to their own kind? Yet this is precisely what we have done. We have done it, moreover, for reasons that collapse the moment we examine them. We are told that the enormous and expanding use of pesticides is necessary to maintain farm production. Yet

is our real problem not one of *overproduction?* Our farms, despite measures to remove acreages from production and to pay farmers *not* to produce, have yielded such a staggering excess of crops that the American taxpayer in 1962 is paying out more than one billion dollars a year as the total carrying cost of the surplus-food storage program. And is the situation helped when one branch of the Agriculture Department tries to reduce production while another states, as it did in 1958, "It is believed generally that reduction of crop acreages under provisions of the Soil Bank will stimulate interest in use of chemicals to obtain maximum production on the land retained in crops."

12   All this is not to say there is no insect problem and no need of control. I am saying, rather, that control must be geared to realities, not to mythical situations, and that the methods employed must be such that they do not destroy us along with the insects.

13   The problem whose attempted solution has brought such a train of disaster in its wake is an accompaniment of our modern way of life. Long before the age of man, insects inhabited the earth—a group of extraordinarily varied and adaptable beings. Over the course of time since man's advent, a small percentage of the more than half a million species of insects have come into conflict with human welfare in two principal ways: as competitors for the food supply and as carriers of human disease.

14   Disease-carrying insects become important where human beings are crowded together, especially under conditions where sanitation is poor, as in time of natural disaster or war or in situations of extreme poverty and deprivation. Then control of some sort becomes necessary. It is a sobering fact, however, as we shall presently see, that the method of massive chemical control has had only limited success, and also threatens to worsen the very conditions it is intended to curb.

15   Under primitive agricultural conditions the farmer had few insect problems. These arose with the intensification of agriculture—the devotion of immense acreages to a single crop. Such a system set the stage for explosive increases in specific insect populations. Single-crop farming does not take advantage of the principles by which nature works; it is agriculture as an engineer might conceive it to be. Nature has introduced great variety into the landscape, but man has displayed a passion for simplifying it. Thus he undoes the built-in checks and balances by which nature holds the species within bounds. One important natural check is a limit on the amount of suitable habitat for each species. Obviously then, an insect that lives on wheat can build up its population to much higher levels on a farm devoted to wheat than on one in which wheat is intermingled with other crops to which the insect is not adapted.

16   The same thing happens in other situations. A generation or more ago, the towns of large areas of the United States lined their streets with the noble elm tree. Now the beauty they hopefully created is threatened with complete destruction as disease sweeps through the elms, carried by a beetle that would have only limited chance to build up large populations and to spread

from tree to tree if the elms were only occasional trees in a richly diversified planting.

17   Another factor in the modern insect problem is one that must be viewed against a background of geologic and human history: the spreading of thousands of different kinds of organisms from their native homes to invade new territories. This worldwide migration has been studied and graphically described by the British ecologist Charles Elton in his recent book *The Ecology of Invasions*. During the Cretaceous Period, some hundred million years ago, flooding seas cut many land bridges between continents and living things found themselves confined in what Elton calls "colossal separate nature reserves." There, isolated from others of their kind, they developed many new species. When some of the land masses were joined again, about 15 million years ago, these species began to move out into new territories—a movement that is not only still in progress but is now receiving considerable assistance from man.

18   The importation of plants is the primary agent in the modern spread of species, for animals have almost invariably gone along with the plants, quarantine being a comparatively recent and not completely effective innovation. The United States Office of Plant Introduction alone has introduced almost 200,000 species and varieties of plants from all over the world. Nearly half of the 180 or so major insect enemies of plants in the United States are accidental imports from abroad, and most of them have come as hitchhikers on plants.

19   In new territory, out of reach of the restraining hand of the natural enemies that kept down its numbers in its native land, an invading plant or animal is able to become enormously abundant. Thus it is no accident that our most troublesome insects are introduced species.

20   These invasions, both the naturally occurring and those dependent on human assistance, are likely to continue indefinitely. Quarantine and massive chemical campaigns are only extremely expensive ways of buying time. We are faced, according to Dr. Elton, "with a life-and-death need not just to find new technological means of suppressing this plant or that animal"; instead we need the basic knowledge of animal populations and their relations to their surroundings that will "promote an even balance and damp down the explosive power of outbreaks and new invasions."

21   Much of the necessary knowledge is now available but we do not use it. We train ecologists in our universities and even employ them in our governmental agencies but we seldom take their advice. We allow the chemical death rain to fall as though there were no alternative, whereas in fact there are many, and our ingenuity could soon discover many more if given opportunity.

22   Have we fallen into a mesmerized state that makes us accept as inevitable that which is inferior or detrimental, as though having lost the will or the vision to demand that which is good? Such thinking, in the words of the ecologist Paul Shepard, "idealizes life with only its head out of water, inches above the limits of toleration of the corruption of its own environment . . . Why should we tolerate a diet of weak poisons, a home in insipid surroundings, a circle of acquaintances who are not quite our enemies, the noise of motors

with just enough relief to prevent insanity? Who would want to live in a world which is just not quite fatal?"

23   Yet such a world is pressed upon us. The crusade to create a chemically sterile, insect-free world seems to have engendered a fanatic zeal on the part of many specialists and most of the so-called control agencies. On every hand there is evidence that those engaged in spraying operations exercise a ruthless power. "The regulatory entomologists . . . function as prosecutor, judge and jury, tax assessor and collector and sheriff to enforce their own orders," said Connecticut entomologist Neely Turner. The most flagrant abuses go unchecked in both state and federal agencies.

24   It is not my contention that chemical insecticides must never be used. I do contend that we have put poisonous and biologically potent chemicals indiscriminately into the hands of persons largely or wholly ignorant of their potentials for harm. We have subjected enormous numbers of people to contact with these poisons, without their consent and often without their knowledge. If the Bill of Rights contains no guarantee that a citizen shall be secure against lethal poisons distributed either by private individuals or by public officials, it is surely only because our forefathers, despite their considerable wisdom and foresight, could conceive of no such problem.

25   I contend, furthermore, that we have allowed these chemicals to be used with little or no advance investigation of their effect on soil, water, wildlife, and man himself. Future generations are unlikely to condone our lack of prudent concern for the integrity of the natural world that supports all life.

26   There is still very limited awareness of the nature of the threat. This is an era of specialists, each of whom sees his own problem and is unaware of or intolerant of the larger frame into which it fits. It is also an era dominated by industry, in which the right to make a dollar at whatever cost is seldom challenged. When the public protests, confronted with some obvious evidence of damaging results of pesticide applications, it is fed little tranquilizing pills of half truth. We urgently need an end to these false assurances, to the sugar coating of unpalatable facts. It is the public that is being asked to assume the risks that the insect controllers calculate. The public must decide whether it wishes to continue on the present road, and it can do so only when in full possession of the facts. In the words of Jean Rostand, "The obligation to endure gives us the right to know."

Topics for Writing and Discussion

1. The essay's title is taken from a quotation by noted French biologist Jean Rostand, cited by Carson in the final paragraph. How do Rostand's words suggest Carson's main purpose and the thesis of her argument?
2. Does Carson seem to be writing to a hostile or a friendly audience? For example, does she assume that her readers will share many of her concerns? Does she seem to blame her readers for the pollution of the environment or does she identify those who are responsible as someone other than her audience?

3. How does Carson try to convince her audience of her views? Is her approach mainly rational or mainly emotional? Or is it a combination? How does she use statistics, reference to authority, and anecdotal examples to support her ideas?

4. What changes have taken place in the manufacture and use of pesticides since Carson wrote this essay in 1962? Has the situation she describes improved or worsened? Explain the reasons for your opinion.

5. Both Rachel Carson in "The Obligation to Endure" and Gretel Ehrlich in "Life at Close Range" (Chapter 2) write about nature. Contrast the way each uses aspects of nature to fulfill the purpose of her essay. Which author is more effective in achieving her purpose? Why do you think so?

Martin Luther King, Jr., delivering his "I Have a Dream" speech at the March on Washington demonstration, August 28, 1963 (AP/Wide World)

I Have a Dream

Martin Luther King, Jr.
(1929–1968)

Martin Luther King, Jr., was born in Atlanta, Georgia.
A product of the Atlanta public schools (where he
skipped both the ninth and twelfth grades), he graduated from Morehouse College in 1948, just after he
followed his father's example by being ordained as a
Baptist minister. He was just 18. By 1951, he had
earned a divinity degree from Crozer Theological Seminary in Pennsylvania, and in 1955 he received his doctorate in systematic theology from Boston University.
His efforts in demanding justice for all people, regardless of race or economic status, contributed to the 1956
Supreme Court decision declaring the segregated bus
system in Alabama unconstitutional; the passing of the
Civil Rights Act of 1964, which prohibited discrimination in public places and demanded equal opportunity
in education and employment; the Civil Rights Act of
1968 (after his death), which banned discrimination
in the sale and renting of housing; and the landmark
Voting Rights Act of 1965. In 1964, King was awarded
the Nobel Peace Prize (at 35, he was the youngest person ever to win the prize). Four years later, he was
assassinated.

On August 28, 1963, King led a march of over
200,000 people to the Lincoln Memorial where he
delivered his now-famous "I Have a Dream" speech to
commemorate the centennial of the Emancipation
Proclamation, which declared all slaves to be free.

1   Five score years ago, a great American, in whose symbolic shadow we stand, signed the Emancipation Proclamation. This momentous decree came as a great beacon light of hope to millions of Negro slaves who had been seared in the flames of withering injustice. It came as a joyous daybreak to end the long night of captivity.

2   But one hundred years later, we must face the tragic fact that the Negro is still not free. One hundred years later, the life of the Negro is still sadly crippled by the manacles of segregation and the chains of discrimination. One hundred years later, the Negro lives on a lonely island of poverty in the midst of a vast ocean of material prosperity. One hundred years later, the Negro is still languishing in the corners of American society and finds himself an exile in his own land. So we have come here today to dramatize an appalling condition.

3   In a sense we have come to our nation's capital to cash a check. When the architects of our republic wrote the magnificent words of the Constitution and the Declaration of Independence, they were signing a promissory note to which every American was to fall heir. This note was a promise that all men would be guaranteed the unalienable rights of life, liberty, and the pursuit of happiness.

4   It is obvious today that America has defaulted on this promissory note insofar as her citizens of color are concerned. Instead of honoring this sacred obligation, America has given the Negro people a bad check; a check which has come back marked "insufficient funds." But we refuse to believe that the bank of justice is bankrupt. We refuse to believe that there are insufficient funds in the great vaults of opportunity of this nation. So we have come to cash this check—a check that will give us upon demand the riches of freedom and the security of justice. We have also come to this hallowed spot to remind America of the fierce urgency of *now*. This is no time to engage in the luxury of cooling off or to take the tranquilizing drugs of gradualism. *Now* is the time to make real the promises of Democracy. *Now* is the time to rise from the dark and desolate valley of segregation to the sunlit path of racial justice. *Now* is the time to open the doors of opportunity to all of God's children. *Now* is the time to lift our nation from the quicksands of racial injustice to the solid rock of brotherhood.

5   It would be fatal for the nation to overlook the urgency of the moment and to underestimate the determination of the Negro. This sweltering summer of the Negro's legitimate discontent will not pass until there is an invigorating autumn of freedom and equality. 1963 is not an end, but a beginning. Those who hope that the Negro needed to blow off steam and will now be content will have a rude awakening if the nation returns to business as usual. There will be neither rest nor tranquility in America until the Negro is granted his citizenship rights. The whirlwinds of revolt will continue to shake the foundations of our nation until the bright day of justice emerges.

6   But there is something that I must say to my people who stand on the warm threshold which leads into the palace of justice. In the process of gaining

our rightful place we must not be guilty of wrongful deeds. Let us not seek to satisfy our thirst for freedom by drinking from the cup of bitterness and hatred. We must forever conduct our struggle on the high plane of dignity and discipline. We must not allow our creative protest to degenerate into physical violence. Again and again we must rise to the majestic heights of meeting physical force with soul force. The marvelous new militancy which has engulfed the Negro community must not lead us to a distrust of all white people, for many of our white brothers, as evidenced by their presence here today, have come to realize that their destiny is tied up with our destiny and their freedom is inextricably bound to our freedom. We cannot walk alone.

7   And as we walk, we must make the pledge that we shall march ahead. We cannot turn back. There are those who are asking the devotees of civil rights, "When will you be satisfied?" We can never be satisfied as long as the Negro is the victim of the unspeakable horrors of police brutality. We can never be satisfied as long as our bodies, heavy with the fatigue of travel, cannot gain lodging in the motels of the highways and the hotels of the cities. We cannot be satisfied as long as the Negro's basic mobility is from a smaller ghetto to a larger one. We can never be satisfied as long as a Negro in Mississippi cannot vote and a Negro in New York believes he has nothing for which to vote. No, no, we are not satisfied, and we will not be satisfied until justice rolls down like waters and righteousness like a mighty stream.

8   I am not unmindful that some of you have come here out of great trials and tribulations. Some of you have come fresh from narrow jail cells. Some of you have come from areas where your quest for freedom left you battered by the storms of persecution and staggered by the winds of police brutality. You have been the veterans of creative suffering. Continue to work with the faith that unearned suffering is redemptive.

9   Go back to Mississippi, go back to Alabama, go back to South Carolina, go back to Georgia, go back to Louisiana, go back to the slums and ghettos of our northern cities, knowing that somehow this situation can and will be changed. Let us not wallow in the valley of despair.

10   I say to you today, my friends, that in spite of the difficulties and frustrations of the moment I still have a dream. It is a dream deeply rooted in the American dream.

11   I have a dream that one day this nation will rise up and live out the true meaning of its creed: "We hold these truths to be self-evident; that all men are created equal."

12   I have a dream that one day on the red hills of Georgia the sons of former slaves and the sons of former slaveowners will be able to sit down together at the table of brotherhood.

13   I have a dream that one day even the state of Mississippi, a desert state sweltering with the heat of injustice and oppression, will be transformed into an oasis of freedom and justice.

14   I have a dream that my four little children will one day live in a nation where they will not be judged by the color of their skin but by the content of their character.

15   I have a dream today.

16   I have a dream that one day the state of Alabama, whose governor's lips are presently dripping with the words of interposition and nullification, will be transformed into a situation where little black boys and black girls will be able to join hands with little white boys and white girls and walk together as sisters and brothers.

17   I have a dream today.

18   I have a dream that one day every valley shall be exalted, every hill and mountain shall be made low, the rough places will be made plain, and the crooked places will be made straight, and the glory of the Lord shall be revealed, and all flesh shall see it together.

19   This is our hope. This is the faith with which I return to the South. With this faith we will be able to hew out of the mountain of despair a stone of hope. With this faith we will be able to transform the jangling discords of our nation into a beautiful symphony of brotherhood. With this faith we will be able to work together, to pray together, to struggle together, to go to jail together, to stand up for freedom together, knowing that we will be free one day.

20   This will be the day when all of God's children will be able to sing with new meaning

> My country, 'tis of thee,
> Sweet land of liberty,
> Of thee I sing:
> Land where my fathers died,
> Land of the pilgrims' pride,
> From every mountain-side
> Let freedom ring.

21   And if America is to be a great nation this must become true. So let freedom ring from the prodigious hilltops of New Hampshire. Let freedom ring from the mighty mountains of New York. Let freedom ring from the heightening Alleghenies of Pennsylvania!

22   Let Freedom ring from the snowcapped Rockies of Colorado!

23   Let freedom ring from the curvaceous peaks of California!

24   But not only that; let freedom ring from Stone Mountain of Georgia!

25   Let freedom ring from Lookout Mountain of Tennessee!

26   Let freedom ring from every hill and molehill of Mississippi. From every mountainside, let freedom ring.

27   When we let freedom ring, when we let it ring from every village and every hamlet, from every state and every city, we will be able to speed up that day when all of God's children, black men and white men, Jews and Gentiles, Protestants and Catholics, will be able to join hands and sing in the words of the old Negro spiritual, "Free at last! free at last! thank God almighty, we are free at last!"

Topics for Writing and Discussion

1. What is King's thesis? How does he establish that idea in the first four paragraphs? How does he use Lincoln's words and sentiments to lead to his own?

2. What problems and injustices suffered by African Americans does King list? How does he believe these wrongs can best be addressed? What examples does he use to inspire his audience to the actions he sees as most appropriate and most effective?

3. King's speech is rich with metaphors and allusions. Find several examples of each and explain what they contribute to the essay's thesis and how they serve to make his argument convincing.

4. Identify examples of repetition and parallel structure. How does King use these devices to emphasize his beliefs and to urge his audience to share his vision?

5. Write an argument either for or against the following proposition: the essential elements of Martin Luther King, Jr.'s dream have become reality today.

The Health-Care System

Lewis Thomas
(1913–1993)

Educated at Princeton University and Harvard Medical School, Lewis Thomas practiced medicine in Boston and New York and taught at several American universities. In 1971, he began contributing a regular column, "Notes of a Biology Watcher," to the *New England Journal of Medicine*. His columns were collected into *The Lives of a Cell: Notes of a Biology Watcher* (1974), for which he won the National Book Award for Arts and Letters. A second collection, *The Medusa and the Snail: More Notes of a Biology Watcher,* was published in 1979. Later works include *Late Night Thoughts on Listening to Mahler's Ninth Symphony* (1983) and *Et Cetera, Et Cetera: Notes of a Wordwatcher* (1990). *The Youngest Science: Notes of a Medicine Watcher* was reprinted in 1995. The second edition of his work, *The Fragile Species,* was published posthumously in 1997. "The Health-Care System" looks at the dangers of living in a society of people who believe that they are "fundamentally fragile, always on the verge of mortal disease." Instead, Thomas says we should be celebrating the reality of longer, healthier lifespans that those of previous generations.

Lewis Thomas
(© Nancy Crampton)

1   THE health-care system of this country is a staggering enterprise, in any sense of the adjective. Whatever the failures of distribution and lack of coordination, it is the gigantic scale and scope of the total collective effort that first catches the breath, and its cost. The dollar figures are almost beyond grasping. They vary from year to year, always upward, ranging from something like $10 billion in 1950 to an estimated $140 billion in 1978, with much more to come in the years just ahead, whenever a national health-insurance program is installed. The official guess is that we are now investing around 8 percent of the GNP in Health; it could soon rise to 10 or 12 percent.

2   Those are the official numbers, and only for the dollars that flow in an authorized way—for hospital charges, physician's fees, prescribed drugs, insurance premiums, the construction of facilities, research, and the like.

3   But these dollars are only part of it. Why limit the estimates to the strictly professional costs? There is another huge marketplace, in which vast sums are exchanged for items designed for the improvement of Health.

4   The television and radio industry, no small part of the national economy, feeds on Health, or, more precisely, on disease, for a large part of its sustenance. Not just the primarily medical dramas and the illness or surgical episodes threaded through many of the nonmedical stories, in which the central human dilemma is illness; almost all the commercial announcements, in an average evening, are pitches for items to restore failed health: things for stomach gas, constipation, headaches, nervousness, sleeplessness or sleepiness, arthritis, anemia, disquiet, and the despair of malodorousness, sweat, yellowed teeth, dandruff, furuncles, piles. The food industry plays the role of surrogate physician, advertising breakfast cereals as though they were tonics, vitamins, restoratives; they are now out-hawked by the specialized Health-food industry itself, with its nonpolluted, organic, "naturally" vitalizing products. Chewing gum is sold as a tooth cleanser. Vitamins have taken the place of prayer.

5   The publishing industry, hardcover, paperbacks, magazines, and all, seems to be kept alive by Health, new techniques for achieving mental health, cures for arthritis, and diets mostly for the improvement of everything.

6   The transformation of our environment has itself become an immense industry, costing rather more than the moon, in aid of Health. Pollution is supposed to be primarily a medical problem; when the television weatherman tells whether New York's air is "acceptable" or not that day, he is talking about human lungs, he believes. Pollutants which may be impairing photosynthesis by algae in the world's oceans, or destroying all the life in topsoil, or killing all the birds are being worried about lest they cause cancer in us, for heaven's sake.

7   Tennis has become more than the national sport; it is a rigorous discipline, a form of collective physiotherapy. Jogging is done by swarms of people, out onto the streets each day in underpants, moving in a stolid sort of rapid trudge, hoping by this to stay alive. Bicycles are cures. Meditation may be good for the soul but it is even better for the blood pressure.

8   As a people, we have become obsessed with Health.

9   There is something fundamentally, radically unhealthy about all this. We do not seem to be seeking more exuberance in living as much as staving off failure, putting off dying. We have lost all confidence in the human body.

10   The new consensus is that we are badly designed, intrinsically fallible, vulnerable to a host of hostile influences inside and around us, and only precariously alive. We live in danger of falling apart at any moment, and are therefore always in need of surveillance and propping up. Without the professional attention of a health-care system, we would fall in our tracks.

11   This is a new way of looking at things, and perhaps it can only be accounted for as a manifestation of spontaneous, undirected, societal *propaganda*. We

keep telling each other this sort of thing, and back it comes on television or in the weekly newsmagazines, confirming all the fears, instructing us, as in the usual final paragraph of the personal-advice columns in the daily paper, to "seek professional help." Get a checkup. Go on a diet. Meditate. Jog. Have some surgery. Take two tablets, with water. *Spring* water. If pain persists, if anomie persists, if boredom persists, see your doctor.

12   It is extraordinary that we have just now become convinced of our bad health, our constant jeopardy of disease and death, at the very time when the facts should be telling us the opposite. In a more rational world, you'd think we would be staging bicentennial ceremonies for the celebration of our general good shape. In the year 1976, out of a population of around 220 million, only 1.9 million died, or just under 1 percent, not at all a discouraging record once you accept the fact of mortality itself. The life expectancy for the whole population rose to seventy-two years, the longest stretch ever achieved in this country. Despite the persisting roster of still-unsolved major diseases—cancer, heart disease, stroke, arthritis, and the rest—most of us have a clear, unimpeded run at a longer and healthier lifetime than could have been foreseen by any earlier generation. The illnesses that plague us the most, when you count up the numbers in the U.S. Vital Statistics reports, are respiratory and gastrointestinal infections, which are, by and large, transient, reversible affairs needing not much more than Grandmother's advice for getting through safely. Thanks in great part to the improved sanitary engineering, nutrition, and housing of the past century, and in real but less part to contemporary immunization and antibiotics, we are free of the great infectious diseases, especially tuberculosis and lobar pneumonia, which used to cut us down long before our time. We are even beginning to make progress in our understanding of the mechanisms underlying the chronic illnesses still with us, and sooner or later, depending on the quality and energy of biomedical research, we will learn to cope effectively with most of these, maybe all. We will still age away and die, but the aging, and even the dying, can become a healthy process. On balance, we ought to be more pleased with ourselves than we are, and more optimistic for the future.

13   The trouble is, we are being taken in by the propaganda, and it is bad not only for the spirit of society; it will make any health-care system, no matter how large and efficient, unworkable. If people are educated to believe that they are fundamentally fragile, always on the verge of mortal disease, perpetually in the need of support by health-care professionals at every side, always dependent on an imagined discipline of "preventive" medicine, there can be no limit to the numbers of doctors' offices, clinics, and hospitals required to meet the demand. In the end, we would all become doctors, spending our days screening each other for disease.

14   We are, in real life, a reasonably healthy people. Far from being ineptly put together, we are amazingly tough, durable organisms, full of health, ready for most contingencies. The new danger to our well-being, if we continue to listen to all the talk, is in becoming a nation of healthy hypochondriacs, living gingerly, worrying ourselves half to death.

15   And we do not have time for this sort of thing anymore, nor can we afford such a distraction from our other, considerably more urgent problems. Indeed, we should be worrying that our preoccupation with personal health may be a symptom of copping out, an excuse for running upstairs to recline on a couch, sniffing the air for contaminants, spraying the room with deodorants, while just outside, the whole of society is coming undone.

TOPICS FOR WRITING AND DISCUSSION

1. Thomas titled his essay "The Health-Care System." What "system" is he referring to? What role does the American consumer play in it?
2. Consider Thomas' tone and word choice, particularly his use of "we." What effect does this have on his audience?
3. Note the structure of the essay. At what point does Thomas' focus become clear? Is there one—or more than one—dominant idea that he communicates to the reader?
4. In paragraphs 4, 7, and 11, Thomas offers a cataloguing of ills, cures, and advice. How does the mention of these specifics, rather than general description, change the impact of the essay? Which items would you add to each of these lists?
5. Test Thomas' claim that our health paranoia is fed by mass media. Choose a popular weekly magazine to review or watch television during prime time and keep a log of the type of products you see advertised. Do your findings confirm or call into question Thomas' viewpoint? Present your findings in an essay responding to "The Health-Care System," using your own perspective to either refute Thomas or agree with, and extend, his argument.

None of This Is Fair

Richard Rodriguez
(1944–   )

Richard Rodriguez
(© James Wilson/Woodfin Camp and Associates, Inc.)

Born in San Francisco, the son of Mexican-American immigrants, Richard Rodriguez is a prolific writer who has published his work in numerous publications, including *Time, Harper's* and *Mother Jones*. Much of his writing focuses on affirmative action and on bilingualism. He spoke only Spanish until he entered school at age five, and reacted so strongly to his early school experiences that for a while he refused to speak Spanish at home. He actually learned his parents' native language by studying Spanish in school as a foreign language. Rodriguez went on to study at Stanford University, Columbia University, the Warburg Institute in London, and the University of California at Berkeley, where he earned a Ph.D. in English literature. Among his writings are *Hunger of Memory: The Education of Richard Rodriguez* (1982), *Mexico's Children* (1990), and *Days of Obligation: An Argument with My Father* (1992). His most recent work, *Justice: A Question of Race,* was published in 1997. In "None of This Is Fair," Rodriguez recounts the numerous job offers he received after earning his doctorate. He felt uncomfortable about the motives behind the offers, doubting that his academic credentials were the sole reason for those offers. Such doubts ultimately led him to question the applications of affirmative-action programs.

1   Mʏ plan to become a professor of English—my ambition during long years in college at Stanford, then in graduate school at Columbia and Berkeley—was complicated by feelings of embarrassment and guilt. So many times I would see other Mexican-Americans and know we were alike only in race. And yet, simply because our race was the same, I was, during the last years of my schooling, the beneficiary of their situation. Affirmative Action programs

had made it all possible. The disadvantages of others permitted my promotion; the absence of many Mexican-Americans from academic life allowed my designation as a "minority student."

2   For me opportunities had been extravagant. There were fellowships, summer research grants, and teaching assistantships. After only two years in graduate school, I was offered teaching jobs by several colleges. Invitations to Washington conferences arrived and I had the chance to travel abroad as a "Mexican-American representative." The benefits were often, however, too gaudy to please. In three published essays, in conversations with teachers, in letters to politicians and at conferences, I worried the issue of Affirmative Action. Often I proposed contradictory opinions. Though consistent was the admission that—because of an early, excellent education—I was no longer a principal victim of racism or any other social oppression. I said that but still I continued to indicate on applications for financial aid that I was a Hispanic-American. It didn't really occur to me to say anything else, or to leave the question unanswered.

3   Thus I complied with and encouraged the odd bureaucratic logic of Affirmative Action. I let government officials treat the disadvantaged condition of many Mexican-Americans with my advancement. Each fall my presence was noted by Health, Education, and Welfare department statisticians. As I pursued advanced literary studies and learned the skill of reading Spenser and Wordsworth and Emerson, I would hear myself numbered among the culturally disadvantaged. Still, silent, I didn't object.

4   But the irony cut deep. And guilt would not be evaded by averting my glance when I confronted a face like my own in a crowd. By late 1975, nearing the completion of my graduate studies at Berkeley, I was so wary of the benefits of Affirmative Action that I feared my inevitable success as an applicant for a teaching position. The months of fall—traditionally that time of academic job-searching—passed without my applying to a single school. When one of my professors chanced to learn this in late November, he was astonished, then furious. He yelled at me: Did I think that because I was a minority student jobs would just come looking for me? What was I thinking? Did I realize that he and several other faculty members had already written letters on my behalf? Was I going to start acting like some other minority students he had known? They struggled for success and then, when it was almost within reach, grew strangely afraid and let it pass. Was that it? Was I determined to fail?

5   I did not respond to his questions. I didn't want to admit to him, and thus to myself, the reason I delayed.

6   I merely agreed to write to several schools. (In my letter I wrote: "I cannot claim to represent disadvantaged Mexican-Americans. The very fact that I am in a position to apply for this job should make that clear.") After two or three days, there were telegrams and phone calls, invitations to interviews, then airplane trips. A blur of faces and the murmur of their soft questions. And, over someone's shoulder, the sight of campus buildings shadowing pictures I had seen years before when I leafed through Ivy League catalogues with great expectations. At the end of each visit, interviewers would smile and wonder if I

had any questions. A few times I quietly wondered what advantage my race had given me over other applicants. But that was an impossible question for them to answer without embarrassing me. Quickly, several persons insisted that my ethnic identity had given me no more than a "foot inside the door"; at most, I had a "slight edge" over other applicants. "We just looked at your dossier with extra care and we like what we saw. There was never any question of having to alter our standards. You can be certain of that."

7   In the early part of January, offers arrived on stiffly elegant stationery. Most schools promised terms appropriate for any new assistant professor. A few made matters worse—and almost more tempting—by offering more: the use of university housing; an unusually large starting salary; a reduced teaching schedule. As the stack of letters mounted, my hesitation increased. I started calling department chairmen to ask for another week, then 10 more days— "more time to reach a decision"—to avoid the decision I would need to make.

8   At school, meantime, some students hadn't received a single job offer. One man, probably the best student in the department, did not even get a request for his dossier. He and I met outside a classroom one day and he asked about my opportunities. He seemed happy for me. Faculty members beamed. They said they had expected it. "After all, not many schools are going to pass up getting a Chicano with a Ph.D. in Renaissance literature," somebody said laughing. Friends wanted to know which of the offers I was going to accept. But I couldn't make up my mind. February came and I was running out of time and excuses. (One chairman guessed my delay was a bargaining ploy and increased his offer with each of my calls.) I had to promise a decision by the 10th; the 12th at the very latest.

9   On the 18th of February, late in the afternoon, I was in the office I shared with several other teaching assistants. Another graduate student was sitting across the room at his desk. When I got up to leave, he looked over to say in an uneventful voice that he had some big news. He had finally decided to accept a position at a faraway university. It was not a job he especially wanted, he admitted. But he had to take it because there hadn't been any other offers. He felt trapped, and depressed, since his job would separate him from his young daughter.

10   I tried to encourage him by remarking that he was lucky at least to have found a job. So many others hadn't been able to get anything. But before I finished speaking I realized that I had said the wrong thing. And I anticipated his next question.

11   "What are your plans?" he wanted to know. "Is it true you've gotten an offer from Yale?"

12   I said that it was. "Only, I still haven't made up my mind."

13   He stared at me as I put on my jacket. And smiling, then unsmiling, he asked if I knew that he too had written to Yale. In his case, however, no one had bothered to acknowledge his letter with even a postcard. What did I think of that?

14   He gave me no time to answer.

15   "Damn!" he said sharply and his chair rasped the floor as he pushed himself back. Suddenly, it was to *me* that he was complaining. "It's just not right, Richard. None of this is fair. You've done some good work, but so have I. I'll bet our records are just about equal. But when we look for jobs this year, it's a different story. You get all of the breaks."

16   To evade his criticism, I wanted to side with him. I was about to admit the injustice of Affirmative Action. But he went on, his voice hard with accusation. "It's all very simple this year. You're a Chicano. And I am a Jew. That's the only real difference between us."

17   His words stung me: there was nothing he was telling me that I didn't know. I had admitted everything already. But to hear someone else say these things, and in such an accusing tone, was suddenly hard to take. In a deceptively calm voice, I responded that he had simplified the whole issue. The phrases came like bubbles to the tip of my tongue: "new blood"; "the importance of cultural diversity"; "the goal of racial integration." These were all the arguments I had proposed several years ago—and had long since abandoned. Of course the offers were unjustifiable. I knew that. All I was saying amounted to a frantic self-defense. I tried to find an end to a sentence. My voice faltered to a stop.

18   "Yeah, sure," he said. "I've heard all that before. Nothing you say really changes the fact that Affirmative Action is unfair. You see that, don't you? There isn't any way for me to compete with you. Once there were quotas to keep my parents out of certain schools; now there are quotas to get you in and the effect on me is the same as it was for them."

19   I listened to every word he spoke. But my mind was really on something else. I knew at that moment that I would reject all of the offers. I stood there silently surprised by what an easy conclusion it was. Having prepared for so many years to teach, having trained myself to do nothing else, I had hesitated out of practical fear. But now that it was made, the decision came with relief. I immediately knew I had made the right choice.

20   My colleague continued talking and I realized that he was simply right. Affirmative Action programs *are* unfair to white students. But as I listened to him assert his rights, I thought of the seriously disadvantaged. How different they were from white, middle-class students who come armed with the testimony of their grades and aptitude scores and self-confidence to complain about the unequal treatment they now receive. I listen to them. I do not want to be careless about what they say. Their rights are important to protect. But inevitably when I hear them or their lawyers, I think about the most seriously disadvantaged, not simply Mexican-Americans, but of all those who do not ever imagine themselves going to college or becoming doctors: white, black, brown. Always poor. Silent. They are not plaintiffs before the court or against the misdirection of Affirmative Action. They lack the confidence (my confidence!) to assume their right to a good education. They lack the confidence and skills a good primary and secondary education provides and which are prerequisites for informed public life. They remain silent.

21   The debate drones on and surrounds them in stillness. They are distant, faraway figures like the boys I have seen peering down from freeway overpasses in some other part of town.

TOPICS FOR WRITING AND DISCUSSION

1. Explain what Rodriguez means by Affirmative Action. Why does he believe that Affirmative Action represents a form of discrimination?

2. Rodriguez explains that he turned down a number of very good job offers. Why did he turn them down? Does he convince you that his reasons for refusing these positions are valid?

3. How do the two concluding paragraphs relate to the rest of Rodriguez's argument? Would the thesis of the essay be different if the final two paragraphs were omitted? Explain why or why not.

4. In some paragraphs Rodriguez uses directly recorded conversation while in others he simply describes his discussions with others. (See, for instance, his conversation with his officemate in paragraphs 11–18 and his reported discussion with his professor in paragraph 4.) Why does he choose to use indirect quotation in some instances and direct quotation in others? What effect does each conversation have on the argument?

5. Write an argument defending or refuting the following statement: Richard Rodriguez unfairly attacks Affirmative-Action programs because he fails to consider many of the complexities of this issue.

Professions for Women

Virginia Woolf
(1882–1941)

Virginia Woolf photographed in the 30s by Man Ray (The Granger Collection)

Born in London, the daughter of a respected biographer and scholar Sir Leslie Stephen, Virginia Woolf was informally educated and never attended a university. However, her extraordinary inquisitiveness, keen mind, and voracious appetite for reading and learning provided her with an ample education. As a teenager, she began the habit of keeping a journal and matured into a prolific essayist and novelist. In 1912, she married author and publisher Leonard Woolf. She and her husband formed the "Bloomsbury Group" with her sister Vanessa and brother-in-law, the art critic Clive Bell, economist John Maynard Keynes, painter Roger Frye, biographer Lytton Strachey, and novelist E. M. Forster. The Bloomsbury Group, named after a section of London near the British Museum, committed themselves to excellence in literature and art and rebelled against the traditions of the Victorians.

Woolf's novels *To the Lighthouse* (1927) and *Orlando* (1929) were well received and helped to establish her as a major writer. She has been particularly acclaimed for her character studies and for her experimental use of point of view. Other novels include *Jacob's Room* (1922), *Mrs. Dalloway* (1925), and *The Waves* (1931). Although Woolf is best known for her novels, she was also a distinguished literary and social critic. Among her best-known nonfiction is *A Room of One's Own* (1929), a collection of lectures exploring the questions and pressures faced by women.

1   WHEN your secretary invited me to come here, she told me that your Society is concerned with the employment of women and she suggested that I might tell you something about my own professional experiences. It is true that

I am a woman; it is true I am employed; but what professional experiences have I had? It is difficult to say. My profession is literature; and in that profession there are fewer experiences for women than in any other, with the exception of the stage—fewer, I mean, that are peculiar to women. For the road was cut many years ago—by Fanny Burney, by Aphra Behn, by Harriet Martineau, by Jane Austen, by George Eliot—many famous women, and many more unknown and forgotten, have been before me, making the path smooth, and regulating my steps. Thus, when I came to write, there were very few material obstacles in my way. Writing was a reputable and harmless occupation. The family peace was not broken by the scratching of a pen. No demand was made upon the family purse. For ten and sixpence one can buy paper enough to write all the plays of Shakespeare—if one has a mind that way. Pianos and models, Paris, Vienna and Berlin, masters and mistresses, are not needed by a writer. The cheapness of writing paper is, of course, the reason why women have succeeded as writers before they have succeeded in the other professions.

2   But to tell you my story—it is a simple one. You have only got to figure to yourselves a girl in a bedroom with a pen in her hand. She had only to move that pen from left to right—from ten o'clock to one. Then it occurred to her to do what is simple and cheap enough after all—to slip a few of those pages into an envelope, fix a penny stamp in the corner, and drop the envelope into the red box at the corner. It was thus that I became a journalist; and my effort was rewarded on the first day of the following month—a very glorious day it was for me—by a letter from an editor containing a cheque for one pound ten shillings and sixpence. But to show you how little I deserve to be called a professional woman, how little I know of the struggles and difficulties of such lives, I have to admit that instead of spending that sum upon bread and butter, rent, shoes and stockings, or butcher's bills, I went out and bought a cat—a beautiful cat, a Persian cat, which very soon involved me in bitter disputes with my neighbours.

3   What could be easier than to write articles and to buy Persian cats with the profits? But wait a moment. Articles have to be about something. Mine, I seem to remember, was about a novel by a famous man. And while I was writing this review, I discovered that if I were going to review books I should need to do battle with a certain phantom. And the phantom was a woman, and when I came to know her better I called her after the heroine of a famous poem, The Angel in the House.* It was she who used to come between me and my paper when I was writing reviews. It was she who bothered me and wasted my time and so tormented me that at last I killed her. You who come of a younger and happier generation may not have heard of her—you may not know what I mean by the Angel in the House. I will describe her as shortly as

---

* *The Angel in the House* is a long poem by Coventry Patmore, which was originally published in four volumes (1854–62). He was a friend of Tennyson and his poem was very popular in the nineteenth century.

I can. She was intensely sympathetic. She was immensely charming. She was utterly unselfish. She excelled in the difficult arts of family life. She sacrificed herself daily. If there was chicken, she took the leg; if there was a draught she sat in it—in short she was so constituted that she never had a mind or a wish of her own, but preferred to sympathize always with the minds and wishes of others. Above all—I need not say it—she was pure. Her purity was supposed to be her chief beauty—her blushes, her great grace. In those day—the last of Queen Victoria—every house had its Angel. And when I came to write I encountered her with the very first words. The shadow of her wings fell on my page; I heard the rustling of her skirts in the room. Directly, that is to say, I took my pen in hand to review that novel by a famous man, she slipped behind me and whispered: "My dear, you are a young woman. You are writing about a book that has been written by a man. Be sympathetic; be tender; flatter; deceive; use all the arts and wiles of our sex. Never let anybody guess that you have a mind of your own. Above all, be pure." And she made as if to guide my pen. I now record the one act for which I take some credit to myself, though the credit rightly belongs to some excellent ancestors of mine who left me a certain sum of money—shall we say five hundred pounds a year?—so that it was not necessary for me to depend solely on charm for my living. I turned upon her and caught her by the throat. I did my best to kill her. My excuse, if I were to be had up in a court of law, would be that I acted in self-defence. Had I not killed her she would have killed me. She would have plucked the heart out of my writing. For, as I found, directly I put pen to paper, you cannot review even a novel without having a mind of your own, without expressing what you think to be the truth about human relations, morality, sex. And all these questions, according to the Angel in the House, cannot be dealt with freely and openly by women; they must charm, they must conciliate, they must—to put it bluntly—tell lies if they are to succeed. Thus, whenever I felt the shadow of her wing or the radiance of her halo upon my page, I took up the inkpot and flung it at her. She died hard. Her fictitious nature was of great assistance to her. It is far harder to kill a phantom than a reality. She was always creeping back when I thought I had despatched her. Though I flatter myself that I killed her in the end, the struggle was severe; it took much time that had better have been spent upon learning Greek grammar; or in roaming the world in search of adventures. But it was a real experience; it was an experience that was bound to befall all women writers at that time. Killing the Angel in the House was part of the occupation of a woman writer.

4   But to continue my story. The Angel was dead; what then remained? You may say that what remained was a simple and common object—a young woman in a bedroom with an inkpot. In other words, now that she had rid herself of falsehood, that young woman had only to be herself. Ah, but what is "herself"? I mean, what is a woman? I assure you, I do not know. I do not believe that you know. I do not believe that anybody can know until she has expressed herself in all the arts and professions open to human skill. That indeed is one of the reasons why I have come here—out of respect for you, who are in process of showing us by your experiments what a woman is, who are in

process of providing us, by your failures and successes, with that extremely important piece of information.

5 But to continue the story of my professional experiences. I made one pound ten and six by my first review; and I bought a Persian cat with the proceeds. Then I grew ambitious. A Persian cat is all very well, I said; but a Persian cat is not enough. I must have a motor car. And it was thus that I became a novelist—for it is a very strange thing that people will give you a motor car if you will tell them a story. It is a still stranger thing that there is nothing so delightful in the world as telling stories. It is far pleasanter than writing reviews of famous novels. And yet, if I am to obey your secretary and tell you my professional experiences as a novelist, I must tell you about a very strange experience that befell me as a novelist. And to understand it you must try first to imagine a novelist's state of mind. I hope I am not giving away professional secrets if I say that a novelist's chief desire is to be as unconscious as possible. He has to induce in himself a state of perpetual lethargy. He wants life to proceed with the utmost quiet and regularity. He wants to see the same faces, to read the same books, to do the same things day after day, month after month, while he is writing, so that nothing may break the illusion in which he is living—so that nothing may disturb or disquiet the mysterious nosings about, feelings round, darts, dashes and sudden discoveries of that very shy and illusive spirit, the imagination. I suspect that this state is the same both for men and women. Be that as it may, I want you to imagine me writing a novel in a state of trance. I want you to figure to yourself a girl sitting with a pen in her hand, which for minutes, and indeed for hours, she never dips into the inkpot. The image that comes to my mind when I think of this girl is the image of a fisherman lying sunk in dreams on the verge of a deep lake with a rod held out over the water. She was letting her imagination sweep unchecked round every rock and cranny of the world that lies submerged in the depths of our unconscious being. Now came the experience, the experience that I believe to be far commoner with women writers than with men. The line raced through the girl's fingers. Her imagination had rushed away. It had sought the pools, the depths, the dark places where the largest fish slumber. And then there was a smash. There was an explosion. There was foam and confusion. The imagination had dashed itself against something hard. The girl was roused from her dream. She was indeed in a state of the most acute and difficult distress. To speak without figure she had thought of something, something about the body, about the passions which it was unfitting for her as a woman to say. Men, her reason told her, would be shocked. The consciousness of what men will say of a woman who speaks the truth about her passions had roused her from her artist's state of unconsciousness. She could write no more. The trance was over. Her imagination could work no longer. This I believe to be a very common experience with women writers—they are impeded by the extreme conventionality of the other sex. For though men sensibly allow themselves great freedom in these respects, I doubt that they realize or can control the extreme severity with which they condemn such freedom in women.

6   These then were two very genuine experiences of my own. These were two of the adventures of my professional life. The first—killing the Angel in the House—I think I solved. She died. But the second, telling the truth about my own experiences as a body, I do not think I solved. I doubt that any woman has solved it yet. The obstacles against her are still immensely powerful—and yet they are very difficult to define. Outwardly, what is simpler than to write books? Outwardly, what obstacles are there for a woman rather than for a man? Inwardly, I think, the case is very different: she has still many ghosts to fight, many prejudices to overcome. Indeed it will be a long time still, I think, before a woman can sit down to write a book without finding a phantom to be slain, a rock to be dashed against. And if this is so in literature, the freest of all professionals for women, how is it in the new professions which you are now for the first time entering?

7   Those are the questions that I should like, had I time, to ask you. And indeed, if I have laid stress upon these professional experiences of mine, it is because I believe that they are, though in different forms, yours also. Even when the path is nominally open—when there is nothing to prevent a woman from being a doctor, a lawyer, a civil servant—there are many phantoms and obstacles, as I believe, looming in her way. To discuss and define them is I think of great value and importance; for thus only can the labour be shared, the difficulties be solved. But besides this, it is necessary also to discuss the ends and the aims for which we are fighting, for which we are doing battle with these formidable obstacles. Those aims cannot be taken for granted; they must be perpetually questioned and examined. The whole position, as I see it—here in this hall surrounded by women practising for the first time in history I know not how many different professions—is one of extraordinary interest and importance. You have won rooms of your own in the house hitherto exclusively owned by men. You are able, though not without great labour and effort, to pay the rent. You are earning your five hundred pounds a year. But this freedom is only a beginning; the room is your own, but it is still bare. It has to be furnished; it has to be decorated; it has to be shared. How are you going to furnish it, how are you going to decorate it? With whom are you going to share it, and upon what terms? These, I think are questions of the utmost importance and interest. For the first time in history you are able to ask them; for the first time you are able to decide for yourselves what the answers should be. Willingly would I stay and discuss those questions and answers—but not tonight. My time is up; and I must cease.

TOPICS FOR WRITING AND DISCUSSION

1. Woolf's essay is titled "Professions for Women." Which profession does she discuss in detail? Why does she say women have been successful in this profession before they have succeeded in other professions?
2. What difficulties did Woolf face in following her chosen work? How does she use the figure of the Angel in the House to explain her struggles as a writer? What were the Angel's characteristics? What advice did Woolf

imagine the angel giving her? How did Woolf respond to this advice? What does she mean when she says that she killed the angel?

3. How does Woolf use the analogy of the "fisherman lying sunk in dreams" to explain another difficulty she faced? Who does the fisherman represent? The line racing through the girl's fingers? The smash? What is the "something hard" that the imagination smashes against?

4. How does Woolf relate her own experiences as a writer to the problems faced by women entering professions traditionally considered to be male? What effects does she suggest might result from choosing these careers?

5. Woolf uses several analogies to describe difficulties she faced in achieving success in her chosen profession. Develop your own analogy to explain a problem you (or someone you know) face or have faced in pursuing a chosen career.

A Scientist: "I Am the Enemy"

Ron Kline
(1961–   )

Ron Kline was born in 1961 in Los Angeles, California. He is currently an assistant professor at the University of Louisville and director of the pediatric bone
marrow transplant program. His area of interest is in
the immunotherapy of cancer and he has published on
this topic. At the time of this essay, Dr. Kline was a
biotechnology fellow in the Experimental Immunology
Branch of the National Cancer Institute in Washington
D.C. The following essay, which appeared in the "My
Turn" column of *Newsweek* magazine in 1989, argues
that the use of animals is sometimes necessary for medical research that may ultimately save human lives.

1   I am the enemy! One of those vilified, inhumane physician-scientists involved
in animal research. How strange, for I have never thought of myself as an evil
person. I became a pediatrician because of my love for children and my desire
to keep them healthy. During medical school and residency, however, I saw
many children die of leukemia, prematurity and traumatic injury—circumstances against which medicine has made tremendous progress, but still has
far to go. More important, I also saw children, alive and healthy, thanks to
advances in medical science such as infant respirators, potent antibiotics, new
surgical techniques and the entire field of organ transplantation. My desire
to tip the scales in favor of the healthy, happy children drew me to medical
research.

2   My accusers claim that I inflict torture on animals for the sole purpose of
career advancement. My experiments supposedly have no relevance to medicine
and are easily replaced by computer simulation. Meanwhile, an apathetic public
barely watches, convinced that the issue has no significance, and publicity-
conscious politicians increasingly give way to the demands of the activists.

3   We in medical research have also been unconscionably apathetic. We
have allowed the most extreme animal-rights protesters to seize the initiative

Ron Kline (© 1989 Wally McNamee/Woodfin Camp and Associates)

and frame the issue as one of "animal fraud." We have been complacent in our belief that a knowledgeable public would sense the importance of animal research to the public health. Perhaps we have been mistaken in not responding to the emotional tone of the argument created by those sad posters of animals by waving equally sad posters of children dying of leukemia or cystic fibrosis.

4   Much is made of the pain inflicted on these animals in the name of medical science. The animal-rights activists contend that this is evidence of our malevolent and sadistic nature. A more reasonable argument, however, can be advanced in our defense. Life is often cruel, both to animals and human beings. Teenagers get thrown from the back of a pickup truck and suffer severe head injuries. Toddlers, barely able to walk, find themselves at the bottom of a swimming pool while a parent checks the mail. Physicians hoping to alleviate the pain and suffering these tragedies cause have but three choices: create an animal model of the injury or disease and use that model to understand the process and test new therapies; experiment on human beings—some experiments will succeed, most will fail—or finally, leave medical knowledge static, hoping that accidental discoveries will lead us to the advances.

5   Some animal-rights activists would suggest a fourth choice, claiming that computer models can simulate animal experiments, thus making the actual experiments unnecessary. Computers can simulate, reasonably well, the effects of well-understood principles on complex systems, as in the application of the laws of physics to airplane and automobile design. However, when the principles themselves are in question, as is the case with the complex biological systems under study, computer modeling alone is of little value.

6   One of the terrifying effects of the effort to restrict the use of animals in medical research is that the impact will not be felt for years and decades: drugs that might have been discovered will not be; surgical techniques that might have been developed will not be, and fundamental biological processes that might have been understood will remain mysteries. There is the danger that politically expedient solutions will be found to placate a vocal minority, while the consequences of those decisions will not be apparent until long after the decisions are made and the decision makers forgotten.

7   Fortunately, most of us enjoy good health, and the trauma of watching one's child die has become a rare experience. Yet our good fortune should not make us unappreciative of the health we enjoy or the advances that make it possible. Vaccines, antibiotics, insulin and drugs to treat heart disease, hypertension and stroke are all based on animal research. Most complex surgical procedures, such as coronary-artery bypass and organ transplantation, are initially developed in animals. Presently undergoing animal studies are techniques to insert genes in humans in order to replace the defective ones found to be the cause of so much disease. These studies will effectively end if animal research is severely restricted.

8   In America today, death has become an event isolated from our daily existence—out of the sight and thoughts of most of us. As a doctor who has watched many children die, and their parents grieve, I am particularly angered

by people capable of so much compassion for a dog or a cat, but with seemingly so little for a dying human being. These people seem so insulated from the reality of human life and death and what it means.

9   Make no mistake, however: I am not advocating the needlessly cruel treatment of animals. To the extent that the animal-rights movement has made us more aware of the needs of these animals, and made us search harder for suitable alternatives, they have made a significant contribution. But if the more radical members of this movement are successful in limiting further research, their efforts will bring about a tragedy that will cost many lives. The real question is whether an apathetic majority can be aroused to protect its future against a vocal, but misdirected, minority.

Topics for Writing and Discussion

1. Why does Kline begin his essay "I am the enemy!"? Why does he talk about himself in his introductory paragraph?
2. What is Kline's position on using animals in medical research? What two groups does he criticize for their apathy?
3. How does Kline advance his argument by addressing the opposition's arguments? What is Kline's major point for his side of this controversy?
4. What tone does Kline maintain in this essay? For example, what is the effect of Kline's comment on the contribution of the animal-rights movement in his last paragraph?
5. Overall, were you persuaded by Kline's argument? If so, what points or evidence might you add to make an even stronger essay? If not, how would you organize an essay to refute his claims?

I WANT A WIFE

Judy Brady
(1937–   )

Born in San Francisco where she now lives, Judy Brady
received her degree in fine arts from the University of
Iowa. She has published articles on union organizing,
Cuban politics and education, abortion, and other
women's issues. She served as the editor for *Women and
Cancer* (1990) and *One in Three: Women with Cancer
Confront an Epidemic* (1991), both of which are collections of writings by women. "I Want a Wife" appeared
in the first issue of *Ms.* magazine in Spring 1972, and
has been reprinted there as one of the best-known
essays of the modern women's movement. With finely
tuned irony, Brady criticizes the excessive and often
unreasonable demands made on many wives.

1   I belong to that classification of people known as wives. I am A Wife. And,
not altogether incidentally, I am a mother.

2   Not too long ago a male friend of mine appeared on the scene fresh from
a recent divorce. He had one child, who is, of course, with his ex-wife. He is
looking for another wife. As I thought about him while I was ironing one
evening, it suddenly occurred to me that I, too, would like to have a wife. Why
do I want a wife?

3   I would like to go back to school so that I can become economically independent, support myself, and, if need be, support those dependent upon me. I
want a wife who will work and send me to school. And while I am going to
school I want a wife to take care of my children. I want a wife to keep track of
the children's doctor and dentist appointments. And to keep track of mine, too.
I want a wife to make sure my children eat properly and are kept clean. I want
a wife who will wash the children's clothes and keep them mended. I want a
wife who is a good nurturant attendant to my children, who arranges for their
schooling, makes sure that they have an adequate social life with their peers,
takes them to the park, the zoo, etc. I want a wife who takes care of the children when they are sick, a wife who arranges to be around when the children

Judy Brady (Courtesy of Judy Brady)

need special care, because, of course, I cannot miss classes at school. My wife must arrange to lose time at work and not lose the job. It may mean a small cut in my wife's income from time to time, but I guess I can tolerate that. Needless to say, my wife will arrange and pay for the care of the children while my wife is working.

4   I want a wife who will take care of *my* physical needs. I want a wife who will keep my house clean. A wife who will pick up after my children, a wife who will pick up after me. I want a wife who will keep my clothes clean, ironed, mended, replaced when need be, and who will see to it that my personal things are kept in their proper place so that I can find what I need the minute I need it. I want a wife who cooks the meals, a wife who is a *good* cook. I want a wife who will plan the menus, do the necessary grocery shopping, prepare the meals, serve them pleasantly, and then do the cleaning up while I do my studying. I want a wife who will care for me when I am sick and sympathize with my pain and loss of time from school. I want a wife to go along when our family takes a vacation so that someone can continue to care for me and my children when I need a rest and change of scene.

5   I want a wife who will not bother me with rambling complaints about a wife's duties. But I want a wife who will listen to me when I feel the need to explain a rather difficult point I have come across in my course of studies. And I want a wife who will type my papers for me when I have written them.

6   I want a wife who will take care of the details of my social life. When my wife and I are invited out by my friends, I want a wife who will take care of the babysitting arrangements. When I meet people at school that I like and want to entertain, I want a wife who will have the house clean, will prepare a special meal, serve it to me and my friends, and not interrupt when I talk about things that interest me and my friends. I want a wife who will have arranged that the children are fed and ready for bed before my guests arrive so that the children do not bother us. I want a wife who takes care of the needs of my guests so that they feel comfortable, who makes sure that they have an ashtray, that they are passed the hors d'oeuvres, that they are offered a second helping of the food, that their wine glasses are replenished when necessary, that their coffee is served to them as they like it. And I want a wife who knows that sometimes I need a night out by myself.

7   I want a wife who is sensitive to my sexual needs, a wife who makes love passionately and eagerly when I feel like it, a wife who makes sure that I am satisfied. And, of course, I want a wife who will not demand sexual attention when I am not in the mood for it. I want a wife who assumes the complete responsibility for birth control, because I do not want more children. I want a wife who will remain sexually faithful to me so that I do not have to clutter up my intellectual life with jealousies. And I want a wife who understands that *my* sexual needs may entail more than strict adherence to monogamy. I must, after all, be able to relate to people as fully as possible.

8   If, by chance, I find another person more suitable as a wife than the wife I already have, I want the liberty to replace my present wife with another one.

Naturally, I will expect a fresh, new life; my wife will take the children and be solely responsible for them so that I am left free.

9   When I am through with school and have a job, I want my wife to quit working and remain at home so that my wife can more fully and completely take care of a wife's duties.

10   My God, who *wouldn't* want a wife?

Topics for Writing and Discussion

1. Read paragraphs 3 through 9 carefully and then summarize the six qualities of a wife as Brady sees them.

2. How does Brady use these categories to argue the plight of wives? Do any of her descriptions seem fair and literal or are they all exaggerated? Are some more exaggerated than others? Do some of her descriptions of wives make you more sympathetic to her argument than do others?

3. What event caused Brady to start thinking about a wife's duties? How does that event relate to the main idea of the essay? Where else in the essay does Brady allude to this event?

4. How much have times (and people) changed since this essay was first published? Would most wives today assume the roles that Brady describes? Would most husbands expect their wives (or want their wives) to take on these roles? Could Brady publish this essay today with no revisions and expect the same response she got in 1971? Can you suggest changes she might make?

5. Write your own satiric argument explaining why you want a secretary, a mother, a husband, a housekeeper, or someone else. Remember that your purpose is to reveal how difficult it is to be a secretary, husband, or mother and to argue that people's expectations for those who fill that role should be changed.

DRUGS

Gore Vidal
(1925–   )

Born at the U.S. Military Academy at West Point, Gore
Vidal is the son of Eugene Vidal, the Academy's first avi-
ation instructor and later the director of air commerce
under Franklin Delano Roosevelt. His grandfather was
Oklahoma Senator Thomas P. Gore. At the age of 10,
Vidal became the youngest person ever to pilot a plane,
a feat recorded in *Screening History* (1992); at seventeen
he enlisted in the U.S. Army, and at nineteen he wrote
his first novel, *Williwaw* (1946). Among his other
twenty-plus novels are a series of historical novels and
novelized histories, including *Washington, D.C.* (1967),
Burr (1973), *1876* (1976), *Lincoln* (1984), *Empire*
(1987), and *Hollywood* (1990). One of his collections of
essays, *The Second American Revolution and Other
Essays* (1982), was awarded the National Book Critics
Award for Criticism. In addition to writing for magazines such as the *New York Review of Books,* he has
written plays and screenplays and has run for Congress
twice. Recent works include his memoir *Palimpsest*
(1995) and his latest novel, *The Smithsonian Institute*
(1998). The following essay, "Drugs," first appeared in
1970 on the *New York Times* op-ed page. It argues a
position that is attracting renewed interest as America
wages the "war on drugs."

1   IT is possible to stop most drug addiction in the United States within a very
short time. Simply make all drugs available and sell them at cost. Label each
drug with a precise description of what effect—good and bad—the drug will
have on the taker. This will require heroic honesty. Don't say that marijuana is
addictive or dangerous when it is neither, as millions of people know—unlike

Gore Vidal (© Nancy Crampton)

"speed," which kills most unpleasantly, or heroin, which is addictive and difficult to kick.

2 For the record, I have tried—once—almost every drug and liked none, disproving the popular Fu Manchu theory that a single whiff of opium will enslave the mind. Nevertheless many drugs are bad for certain people to take and they should be told why in a sensible way.

3 Along with exhortation and warning, it might be good for our citizens to recall (or learn for the first time) that the United States was the creation of men who believed that each man has the right to do what he wants with his own life as long as he does not interfere with his neighbor's pursuit of happiness. (That his neighbor's idea of happiness is persecuting others does confuse matters a bit.)

4 This is a startling notion to the current generation of Americans. They reflect a system of public education which has made the Bill of Rights, literally, unacceptable to a majority of high school graduates (see the annual Purdue reports) who now form the "silent majority"—a phrase which that underestimated wit Richard Nixon took from Homer who used it to describe the dead.

5 Now one can hear the warning rumble begin: If everyone is allowed to take drugs everyone will and the GNP will decrease, the Commies will stop us from making everyone free, and we shall end up a race of zombies, passively murmuring "groovy" to one another. Alarming thought. Yet it seems most unlikely that any reasonably sane person will become a drug addict if he knows in advance what addiction is going to be like.

6 Is everyone reasonably sane? No. Some people will always become drug addicts just as some people will always become alcoholics, and it is just too bad. Every man, however, has the power (and should have the legal right) to kill himself if he chooses. But since most men don't, they won't be mainliners either. Nevertheless, forbidding people things they like or think they might enjoy only makes them want those things all the more. This psychological insight is, for some mysterious reason, perennially denied our governors.

7 It is a lucky thing for the American moralist that our country has always existed in a kind of time-vacuum: We have no public memory of anything that happened before last Tuesday. No one in Washington today recalls what happened during the years alcohol was forbidden to the people by a Congress that thought it had a divine mission to stamp out Demon Rum—launching, in the process, the greatest crime wave in the country's history, causing thousands of deaths from bad alcohol, and creating a general (and persisting) contempt among the citizenry for the laws of the United States.

8 The same thing is happening today. But the government has learned nothing from past attempts at prohibition, not to mention repression.

9 Last year when the supply of Mexican marijuana was slightly curtailed by the Feds, the pushers got the kids hooked on heroin and deaths increased dramatically, particularly in New York. Whose fault? Evil men like the Mafiosi? Permissive Dr. Spock? Wild-eyed Dr. Leary? No.

10 The government of the United States was responsible for those deaths. The bureaucratic machine has a vested interest in playing cops and robbers. Both

the Bureau of Narcotics and the Mafia want strong laws against the sale and use of drugs because if drugs are sold at cost there would be no money in it for anyone.

11   If there was no money in it for the Mafia, there would be no friendly playground pushers, and addicts would not commit crimes to pay for the next fix. Finally, if there was no money in it, the Bureau of Narcotics would wither away, something they are not about to do without a struggle.

12   Will anything sensible be done? Of course not. The American people are as devoted to the idea of sin and its punishment as they are to making money—and fighting drugs is nearly as big a business as pushing them. Since the combination of sin and money is irresistible (particularly to the professional politician), the situation will only grow worse.

TOPICS FOR WRITING AND DISCUSSION

1. What is Vidal's solution for the drug problem in America?
2. What strategies does Vidal use to argue his position? Are all his arguments equally persuasive? Critique what you believe are his strongest and his weakest points.
3. How does Vidal try to refute his critics? Is he, in your opinion, successful? Why or why not?
4. Characterize Vidal's "voice" in this essay. How might such comments as Americans "have no public memory of anything that happened before last Tuesday" and "American people are as devoted to the idea of sin and its punishment as they are to making money" affect Vidal's readers?
5. This essay appeared as an editorial in 1970; since that time the debate has continued as drug use and drug trafficking have escalated. Write an editorial of your own, arguing for a sensible drug policy for today.

THE RIGHT TO DIE

Norman Cousins
(1915–1990)

Born in Union City, New Jersey, Norman Cousins graduated from Columbia University's Teachers College. He
began his long career in journalism as a writer for the
New York Evening Post. Later, he joined the staff of the
Saturday Review and served as the magazine's editor for
over thirty-five years. His life was drastically changed in
1964 when he was stricken with ankylotic spondylitis, a
severe connective tissue disease. Dealing with the life-
threatening condition provided an opportunity of profound growth for Cousins, as he shared his journey of
healing with a multitude of readers. In 1979, he published *Anatomy of an Illness*, which chronicled his way
to recovery. Also in the late 1970s, he became affiliated
with the UCLA School of Medicine, and his writings
turned to examining the effects of positive thinking as a
means to combat illnesses. His works include *The Celebration of Life* (1974), *Healing and Belief* (1982), *The
Healing Heart: Antidotes to Panic and Helplessness*
(1983), *The Pathology of Power* (1987), and *Head
First: The Biology of Hope* (1989), which examines the
effect of emotions on the body's resistance to disease. In
the following essay, first published in the *Saturday
Review* in 1975, Cousins argues for people's right to
choose death with dignity.

1   THE world of religion and philosophy was shocked recently when Henry P.
Van Dusen and his wife ended their lives by their own hands. Dr. Van Dusen
had been president of Union Theological Seminary; for more than a quarter-
century he had been one of the luminous names in Protestant theology. He enjoyed world status as a spiritual leader. News of the self-inflicted death of the

Norman Cousins (Steve Shapiro/Sygma)

Van Dusens, therefore, was profoundly disturbing to all those who attach a moral stigma to suicide and regard it as a violation of God's laws.

2   Dr. Van Dusen had anticipated this reaction. He and his wife left behind a letter that may have historic significance. It was very brief, but the essential point it made is now being widely discussed by theologians and could represent the beginning of a reconsideration of traditional religious attitudes toward self-inflicted death. The letter raised a moral issue: does an individual have the obligation to go on living even when the beauty and meaning and power of life are gone?

3   Henry and Elizabeth Van Dusen had lived full lives. In recent years, they had become increasingly ill, requiring almost continual medical care. Their infirmities were worsening, and they realized they would soon become completely dependent for even the most elementary needs and functions. Under these circumstances, little dignity would have been left in life. They didn't like the idea of taking up space in a world with too many mouths and too little food. They believed it was a misuse of medical science to keep them technically alive.

4   They therefore believed they had the right to decide when to die. In making that decision, they weren't turning against life as the highest value; what they were turning against was the notion that there were no circumstances under which life should be discontinued.

5   An important aspect of human uniqueness is the power of free will. In his books and lectures, Dr. Van Dusen frequently spoke about the exercise of this uniqueness. The fact that he used his free will to prevent life from becoming a caricature of itself was completely in character. In their letter, the Van Dusens sought to convince family and friends that they were not acting solely out of despair or pain.

6   The use of free will to put an end to one's life finds no sanction in the theology to which Pitney Van Dusen was committed. Suicide symbolizes discontinuity; religion symbolizes continuity, represented as its quintessence by the concept of the immortal soul. Human logic finds it almost impossible to come to terms with the concept of nonexistence. In religion, the human mind finds a larger dimension and is relieved of the ordeal of a confrontation with nonexistence.

7   Even without respect to religion, the idea of suicide has been abhorrent throughout history. Some societies have imposed severe penalties on the families of suicides in the hope that the individual who sees no reason to continue his existence may be deterred by the stigma his self-destruction would inflict on loved ones. Other societies have enacted laws prohibiting suicide on the grounds that it is murder. The enforcement of such laws, of course, has been an exercise in futility.

8   Customs and attitudes, like individuals themselves, are largely shaped by the surrounding environment. In today's world, life can be prolonged by science far beyond meaning or sensibility. Under these circumstances, individuals who feel they have nothing more to give to life, or to receive from it, need not be applauded, but they can be spared our condemnation.

9   The general reaction to suicide is bound to change as people come to understand that it may be a denial, not an assertion, of moral or religious ethics to allow life to be extended without regard to decency or pride. What moral or religious purpose is celebrated by the annihilation of the human spirit in the triumphant act of keeping the body alive? Why are so many people more readily appalled by an unnatural form of dying than by an unnatural form of living?

10   "Nowadays," the Van Dusens wrote in their last letter, "it is difficult to die. We feel that this way we are taking will become more usual and acceptable as the years pass.

11   "Of course, the thought of our children and our grandchildren makes us sad, but we still feel that this is the best way and the right way to go. We are both increasingly weak and unwell and who would want to die in a nursing home?

12   "We are not afraid to die. . . ."

13   Pitney Van Dusen was admired and respected in life. He can be admired and respected in death. "Suicide," said Goethe, "is an incident in human life which, however much disputed and discussed, demands the sympathy of every man, and in every age must be dealt with anew."

14   Death is not the greatest loss in life. The greatest loss is what dies inside us while we live. The unbearable tragedy is to live without dignity or sensitivity.

TOPICS FOR WRITING AND DISCUSSION

1. What is Cousins' thesis? According to Cousins, what is the "greatest loss in life"?

2. Why does this essay focus on the action of the Van Dusens? Why does Cousins use them as an example to argue his view?

3. What are Cousins' main points supporting his view of suicide? How does he address objections to his view?

4. Why does Cousins quote the Van Dusens' letter and the philosopher Goethe? Note, too, Cousins' word choice: what, for example, do phrases such as "technically alive" (paragraph 3) and "unnatural form of living" (paragraph 9) add to his argument?

5. Suicide, and "assisted suicide," continue to be controversial. Do you agree with Cousins? Should Cousins' argument be extended to those who are not aged, infirm, or rational? For instance, should teenagers, who have one of the highest suicide rates, be accorded "the right to die"? Write an essay arguing your own view of this troubling issue.

DECLARATION OF INDEPENDENCE

Thomas Jefferson
(1743–1826)

After graduating from William and Mary College, Thomas Jefferson became a lawyer. Later, he was elected to the Virginia House of Burgesses, and in 1775 he became a delegate to the Continental Congress. In this capacity and in that of governor of Virginia, he wielded great power in forming and molding the new republic. Following the Revolutionary War, he served under George Washington as secretary of state. He was subsequently elected vice-president and then third president of the United States. Jefferson, along with several others, wrote and revised the Declaration of Independence, which was later amended by the Continental Congress and finally accepted by that body on July 4, 1776. Although the document had several framers and went through many drafts, it reflects Jefferson's clear, direct style and his logical process of developing an argument.

1   WHEN in the course of human events, it becomes necessary for one people to dissolve the political bands which have connected them with another, and to assume among the Powers of the earth, the separate and equal station to which the Laws of Nature and of Nature's God entitle them, a decent respect to the opinions of mankind requires that they should declare the causes which impel them to the separation.

2   We hold these truths to be self-evident, that all men are created equal, that they are endowed by their Creator with certain unalienable Rights, that among these are Life, Liberty, and the pursuit of Happiness. That to secure these rights, Governments are instituted among Men, deriving their just powers from the consent of the governed. That whenever any Form of Government becomes destructive of these ends, it is the Right of the People to alter or

Thomas Jefferson (The Bettmann Archive)

to abolish it, and to institute a new Government, laying its foundation on such principles and organizing its powers in such form, as to them shall seem most likely to effect their Safety and Happiness. Prudence, indeed, will dictate that Governments long established should not be changed for light and transient causes; and accordingly all experience hath shown that mankind are more disposed to suffer, while evils are sufferable, than to right themselves by abolishing the forms to which they are accustomed. But when a long train of abuses and usurpations pursuing invariably the same Object evinces a design to reduce them under absolute Despotism, it is their right, it is their duty, to throw off such government, and to provide new Guards for their future security. Such has been the patient sufferance of these Colonies; and such is now the necessity which constrains them to alter their former Systems of Government. The history of the present King of Great Britain is a history of repeated injuries and usurpations, all having in direct object the establishment of an absolute Tyranny over these States. To prove this, let Facts be submitted to a candid world.

3   He has refused his Assent to Laws, the most wholesome and necessary for the public good.

4   He has forbidden his Governors to pass Laws of immediate and pressing importance, unless suspended in their operation till his Assent should be obtained; and when so suspended, he has utterly neglected to attend to them.

5   He has refused to pass other Laws for the accommodation of large districts of people, unless those people would relinquish the right of Representation in the Legislature, a right inestimable to them and formidable to tyrants only.

6   He has called together legislative bodies at places unusual, uncomfortable, and distant from the depository of their Public Records, for the sole purpose of fatiguing them into compliance with his measures.

7   He has dissolved Representative Houses repeatedly, for opposing with manly firmness his invasions on the rights of the people.

8   He has refused for a long time, after such dissolutions, to cause others to be elected; whereby the Legislative Powers, incapable of Annihilation, have returned to the People at large for their exercise; the State remaining in the mean time exposed to all the dangers of invasion from without, and convulsions within.

9   He has endeavored to prevent the population of these States; for that purpose obstructing the Laws of Naturalization of Foreigners; refusing to pass others to encourage their migration hither, and raising the conditions of new Appropriations of Lands.

10   He has obstructed the Administration of Justice, by refusing his Assent to Laws for establishing Judiciary Powers.

11   He has made Judges dependent on his Will alone, for the tenure of their offices, and the amount and payment of their salaries.

12   He has erected a multitude of New Offices, and sent hither swarms of Officers to harass our People, and eat out their substance.

13   He has kept among us, in time of peace, Standing Armies without the consent of our Legislature.

14   He has affected to render the Military independent of and superior to the Civil Power.

15   He has combined with others to subject us to jurisdictions foreign to our constitution, and unacknowledged by our laws; giving his Assent to their acts of pretended Legislation:

16   For quartering large bodies of armed troops among us:

17   For protecting them, by a mock Trial, from Punishment for any Murders which they should commit on the Inhabitants of these States:

18   For cutting off our Trade with all parts of the world:

19   For imposing Taxes on us without our Consent:

20   For depriving us in many cases, of the benefits of Trial by Jury:

21   For transporting us beyond Seas to be tried for pretended offenses:

22   For abolishing the free System of English Laws in a Neighbouring Province, establishing therein an Arbitrary government, and enlarging its boundaries so as to render it at once an example and fit instrument for introducing the same absolute rule into these Colonies:

23   For taking away our Charters, abolishing our most valuable Laws, and altering fundamentally the Forms of our Governments:

24   For suspending our own Legislatures, and declaring themselves invested with Power to legislate for us in all cases whatsoever.

25   He has abdicated Government here, by declaring us out of his Protection and waging War against us.

26   He has plundered our seas, ravaged our Coasts, burnt our towns and destroyed the Lives of our people.

27   He is at this time transporting large Armies of foreign Mercenaries to compleat the works of death, desolution and tyranny, already begun with circumstances of Cruelty & perfidy scarcely paralleled in the most barbarous ages, and totally unworthy the Head of a civilized nation.

28   He has constrained our fellow Citizens taken Captive on the high Seas to bear Arms against their Country, to become the executioners of their friends and Brethren, or to fall themselves by their Hands.

29   He has excited domestic insurrections amongst us, and has endeavored to bring on the inhabitants of our frontiers, the merciless Indian Savages, whose known rule of warfare, is an undistinguished destruction of all ages, sexes and conditions.

30   In every stage of these Oppressions We Have Petitioned for Redress in the most humble terms: Our repeated petitions have been answered only by repeated injury. A Prince, whose character is thus marked by every act which may define a Tyrant, is unfit to be the ruler of a free People.

31   Nor have We been wanting in attention to our British brethren. We have warned them from time to time of attempts by their legislature to extend an unwarrantable jurisdiction over us. We have reminded them of the circumstances of our emigration and settlement here. We have appealed to their native

justice and magnanimity and we have conjured them by the ties of our common kindred to disavow these usurpations, which would inevitably interrupt our connections and correspondence. They too have been deaf to the voice of justice and of consanguinity. We must, therefore, acquiesce in the necessity, which denounces our Separation, and hold them, as we hold the rest of mankind, Enemies in War, in Peace Friends.

32   We, therefore, the Representatives of the United States of America, in General Congress, Assembled, appealing to the Supreme Judge of the world for the rectitude of our intentions, do, in the Name, and by Authority of the good People of these Colonies, solemnly publish and declare, That these United Colonies are, and of Right ought to be, Free and Independent States; that they are Absolved from all Allegiance to the British Crown, and that all political connection between them and the State of Great Britain, is and ought to be totally dissolved; and that as Free and Independent States, they have full power to levy War, conclude Peace, contract Alliances, establish Commerce, and do all other Acts and Things which Independent States may of right do. And for the support of this Declaration, with a firm reliance on the protection of Divine Providence, we mutually pledge to each other our lives, our Fortunes and our sacred Honor.

TOPICS FOR WRITING AND DISCUSSION

1. The Declaration of Independence exemplifies the deductive argument at its best. What is the major premise of the Declaration? What is the minor premise? What is the conclusion that readers must reach if they are convinced that the major and minor premises are valid?
2. How is the major premise supported? How is the minor premise supported? Do you find the inductive evidence for one more convincing than the assumptions that underlie the other?
3. Describe the original audience for the Declaration. What parts of the document seem particularly aimed at special segments of that audience? Why did the framers of the Declaration need to explain in such detail their reasons for declaring independence?
4. What is the tone of the Declaration? Examine the language used by Jefferson and the other writers of the document to determine their attitude toward the subject of independence.
5. Write your own "Declaration of Independence" from someone or something you feel has compiled "a history of injuries" toward you. Make your case as clearly and as forcefully as did Jefferson.

Elizabeth Cady Stanton (© The Bettmann Archive)

DECLARATION OF SENTIMENTS AND RESOLUTIONS

Elizabeth Cady Stanton
(1815–1902)

Elizabeth Cady Stanton was an early and powerful advocate for women's rights and suffrage. She attended Johnstown Academy and studied Greek and mathematics, and in 1830 convinced her father, a successful New York lawyer and judge, to allow her to attend Troy Female Seminary, where she studied logic, physiology, and natural rights philosophy. After reading many of her father's law books and watching him handle cases, she saw firsthand how women suffered legal discrimination. At the same time, she became involved with the abolitionist movement; she married journalist and abolitionist Henry Stanton in 1840. In addition to collaborating with Susan B. Anthony on *Revolution*, a weekly forum for discussion of women's rights, Cady Stanton wrote *The Women's Bible* (1895) and an autobiography, *Eighty Years and More (1815–1897): Reminiscences of Elizabeth Cady Stanton* (1898). She presented the "Declaration of Sentiments and Resolutions" at the First Women's Rights Convention, held in Seneca Fall, New York, in 1848. Despite a life-long fight for American women's right to vote, she died 18 years before women were enfranchised in 1920.

1 WHEN, in the course of human events, it becomes necessary for one portion of the family of man to assume among the people of the earth a position different from that which they have hitherto occupied, but one to which the laws of nature and of nature's God entitle them, a decent respect to the opinions

of mankind requires that they should declare the causes that impel them to such a course.

2   We hold these truths to be self-evident: that all men and women are created equal; that they are endowed by their Creator with certain inalienable rights; that among these are life, liberty, and the pursuit of happiness; that to secure these rights governments are instituted, deriving their just powers from the consent of the governed. Whenever any form of government becomes destructive of these ends, it is the right of those who suffer from it to refuse allegiance to it, and to insist upon the institution of a new government, laying its foundation on such principles, and organizing its powers in such form, as to them shall seem most likely to effect their safety and happiness. Prudence, indeed, will dictate that governments long established should not be changed for light and transient causes; and accordingly all experience hath shown that mankind are more disposed to suffer, while evils are sufferable, than to right themselves by abolishing the forms to which they were accustomed. But when a long train of abuses and usurpations, pursuing invariably the same object, evinces a design to reduce them under absolute despotism, it is their duty to throw off such government, and to provide new guards for their future security. Such has been the patient sufferance of the women under this government, and such is now the necessity which constrains them to demand the equal station to which they are entitled.

3   The history of mankind is a history of repeated injuries and usurpations on the part of man toward woman, having in direct object the establishment of an absolute tyranny over her. To prove this, let facts be submitted to a candid world.

4   He has never permitted her to exercise her inalienable right to the elective franchise.

5   He has compelled her to submit to laws, in the formation of which she had no voice.

6   He has withheld from her rights which are given to the most ignorant and degraded men—both natives and foreigners.

7   Having deprived her of this first right of a citizen, the elective franchise, thereby leaving her without representation in the halls of legislation, he has oppressed her on all sides.

8   He has made her, if married, in the eye of the law, civilly dead.

9   He has taken from her all right in property, even to the wages she earns.

10   He has made her, morally, an irresponsible being, as she can commit many crimes with impunity, provided they be done in the presence of her husband. In the covenant of marriage, she is compelled to promise obedience to her husband, he becoming to all intents and purposes, her master—the law giving him power to deprive her of her liberty, and to administer chastisement.

11   He has so framed the laws of divorce, as to what shall be the proper causes, and in case of separation, to whom the guardianship of the children shall be given, as to be wholly regardless of the happiness of women—the law, in all cases, going upon a false supposition of the supremacy of man, and giving all power into his hands.

12 After depriving her of all rights as a married woman, if single, and the owner of property, he has taxed her to support a government which recognizes her only when her property can be made profitable to it.

13 He has monopolized nearly all the profitable employments, and from those she is permitted to follow, she receives but a scanty remuneration. He closes against her all the avenues to wealth and distinction which he considers most honorable to himself. As a teacher of theology, medicine, or law, she is not known.

14 He has denied her the facilities for obtaining a thorough education, all colleges being closed against her.

15 He allows her in Church, as well as State, but a subordinate position, claiming Apostolic authority for her exclusion from the ministry, and, with some exceptions, from any public participation in the affairs of the Church.

16 He has created a false public sentiment by giving to the world a different code of morals for men and women, by which moral delinquencies which exclude women from society, are not only tolerated, but deemed of little account in man.

17 He has usurped the prerogative of Jehovah himself, claiming it as his right to assign for her a sphere of action, when that belongs to her conscience and to her God.

18 He has endeavored, in every way that he could, to destroy her confidence in her own powers, to lessen her self-respect, and to make her willing to lead a dependent and abject life.

19 Now, in view of this entire disfranchisement of one-half the people of this country, their social and religious degradation—in view of the unjust laws above mentioned, and because women do feel themselves aggrieved, oppressed, and fraudulently deprived of their most sacred rights, we insist that they have immediate admission to all the rights and privileges which belong to them as citizens of the United States.

20 In entering upon the great work before us, we anticipate no small amount of misconception, misrepresentation, and ridicule; but we shall use every instrumentality within our power to effect our object. We shall employ agents, circulate tracts, petition the State and National legislatures, and endeavor to enlist the pulpit and the press in our behalf. We hope this Convention will be followed by a series of Conventions embracing every part of this country.

21 [The following resolutions were discussed by Lucretia Mott, Thomas and Mary Ann McClintock, Amy Post, Catharine A. F. Stebbins, and others, and were adopted:]

22 Whereas, The great precept of nature is conceded to be, that "man shall pursue his own true and substantial happiness." Blackstone in his Commentaries remarks, that this law of Nature being coeval with mankind, and dictated by God himself, is of course superior in obligation to any other. It is binding over all the globe, in all countries, and at all times; no human laws are of any validity if contrary to this, and such of them as are valid, derive all their

force, and all their validity, and all their authority, mediately and immediately, from this original; therefore,

23   *Resolved,* That such laws as conflict, in any way, with the true and substantial happiness of woman, are contrary to the great precept of nature and of no validity, for this is "superior in obligation to any other."

24   *Resolved,* That all laws which prevent woman from occupying such a station in society as her conscience shall dictate, or which place her in a position inferior to that of man, are contrary to the great precept of nature, and therefore of no force or authority.

25   *Resolved,* That woman is man's equal—was intended to be so by the Creator, and the highest good of the race demands that she should be recognized as such.

26   *Resolved,* That the women of this country ought to be enlightened in regard to the laws under which they live, that they may no longer publish their degradation by declaring themselves satisfied with their present position, nor their ignorance, by asserting that they have all the rights they want.

27   *Resolved,* That inasmuch as man, while claiming for himself intellectual superiority, does accord to woman moral superiority, it is preeminently his duty to encourage her to speak and teach, as she has an opportunity, in all religious assemblies.

28   *Resolved,* That the same amount of virtue, delicacy, and refinement of behavior that is required of woman in the social state, should also be required of man, and the same transgressions should be visited with equal severity on both man and woman.

29   *Resolved,* That the objection of indelicacy and impropriety, which is so often brought against woman when she addresses a public audience, comes with a very ill-grace from those who encourage, by their attendance, her appearance on the stage, in the concert, or in feats of the circus.

30   *Resolved,* That woman has too long rested satisfied in the circumscribed limits which corrupt customs and a perverted application of the Scriptures have marked out for her, and that it is time she should move in the enlarged sphere which her great Creator has assigned her.

31   *Resolved,* That it is the duty of the women of this country to secure to themselves their sacred right to the elective franchise.

32   *Resolved,* That the equality of human rights results necessarily from the fact of the identity of the race in capabilities and responsibilities.

33   *Resolved, therefore,* That, being invested by the Creator with the same capabilities, and the same consciousness of responsibility for their exercise, it is demonstrably the right and duty of woman, equally with man, to promote every righteous cause by every righteous means; and especially in regard to the great subjects of morals and religion, it is self-evidently her right to participate with her brother in teaching them, both in private and in public, by writing and by speaking, by any instrumentalities proper to be used, and in any assemblies proper to be held; and this being a self-evident truth growing out of the divinely implanted principles of human nature, any custom or authority

adverse to it, whether modern or wearing the hoary sanction of antiquity, is to be regarded as a self-evident falsehood, and at war with mankind.

34   [At the last session Lucretia Mott offered and spoke to the following resolution:]

35   *Resolved,* That the speedy success of our cause depends upon the zealous and untiring efforts of both men and women, for the overthrow of the monopoly of the pulpit, and for the securing to woman an equal participation with men in the various trades, professions, and commerce.

TOPICS FOR WRITING AND DISCUSSION

1. Describe Cady Stanton's tone and purpose. How are the two interrelated?
2. Given that Cady Stanton's "Declaration" was written for the First Woman's Rights Convention, in what ways is Cady Stanton's language and word choice appropriate for this specific audience? Who might Cady Stanton's larger intended audience be? Is her style equally appropriate for them?
3. Compare Cady Stanton's essay to Jefferson's Declaration of Independence, noting key parallels and specific contrasts between the two documents. What effect does her purposeful allusion to Jefferson's Declaration have on the reader? What is the significance of Cady Stanton's "revision" of key words and phrases, as well as additions to and deletions from Jefferson's work?
4. In the nearly 150 years since Cady Stanton wrote, "The great precept of nature is conceded to be, that 'man shall pursue his own true and substantial happiness,'" has this goal been met for all people? Describe a current group you believe has either made great gains since Cady Stanton's time, or continues to struggle against "a long train of abuses and usurpations."
5. Review Cady Stanton's "resolutions." Which of these have been achieved? Choose one resolution as the focus of an essay arguing either that the resolution has been fulfilled or that it has not. Use current events as well as your own perspective to support your stance.

*Jonathan Swift, as painted by Charles Jervas, National Portrait Gallery, London
(The Bettmann Archive)*

A MODEST PROPOSAL

Jonathan Swift
(1667–1745)

Born in Dublin, Ireland, to English parents, Jonathan Swift studied at Trinity College and Oxford University. After college, he worked as a secretary to Sir William Temple, and in 1699 he was ordained as an Anglican priest and eventually made dean of St. Patrick's Cathedral in Dublin. He is best known for his satires, including *A Tale of a Tub* (published anonymously in 1704), a vicious attack on government abuses and on the divisions within Christianity. After the death of Queen Anne in 1714, Swift spent most of his life in Ireland. There he continued to write satirical pieces to address English exploitation and repression of the Irish. His *Drapier's Letters* (1724) attacked the English for their plans to debase Irish coinage, and his masterpiece *Gulliver's Travels* (1726) alerted readers to the tyranny of the English. Originally published as a pamphlet, "A Modest Proposal" appeared in 1729. Written at the height of a terrible famine and at a time when the English were proposing a severe tax on the Irish citizens, the essay uses irony and satiric exaggeration to emphasize the desperate living conditions of the Irish peasants and the callousness and greed of the English.

**For Preventing the Children of
Poor People in Ireland
from Being a Burden to Their Parents
or Country,
and for Making Them Beneficial to the Public**

1   It is a melancholy object to those who walk through this great town or travel in the country, when they see the streets, the roads, and cabin doors, crowded with beggars of the female sex, followed by three, four, or six children, all in

rags and importuning every passenger for an alms. These mothers, instead of being able to work for their honest livelihood, are forced to employ all their time in strolling to beg sustenance for their helpless infants, who, as they grow up, either turn thieves for want of work, or leave their dear native country to fight for the Pretender in Spain, or sell themselves to the Barbadoes.

2   I think it is agreed by all parties that this prodigious number of children in the arms, or on the backs, or at the heels of their mothers, and frequently of their fathers, is in the present deplorable state of the kingdom a very great additional grievance; and therefore whoever could find out a fair, cheap, and easy method of making these children sound, useful members of the commonwealth would deserve so well of the public as to have his statue set up for a preserver of the nation.

3   But my intention is very far from being confined to provide only for the children of professed beggars; it is of a much greater extent, and shall take in the whole number of infants at a certain age who are born of parents in effect as little able to support them as those who demand our charity in the streets.

4   As to my own part, having turned my thoughts for many years upon this important subject, and maturely weighed the several schemes of other projectors, I have always found them grossly mistaken in their computation. It is true, a child just dropped from its dam may be supported by her milk for a solar year, with little other nourishment; at most not above the value of two shillings, which the mother may certainly get, or the value in scraps, by her lawful occupation of begging; and it is exactly at one year old that I propose to provide for them in such a manner as instead of being a charge upon their parents or the parish, or wanting food and raiment for the rest of their lives, they shall on the contrary contribute to the feeding, and partly to the clothing, of many thousands.

5   There is likewise another great advantage in my scheme, that it will prevent those voluntary abortions, and that horrid practice of women murdering their bastard children, alas, too frequent among us, sacrificing the poor innocent babes, I doubt, more to avoid the expense than the shame, which would move tears and pity in the most savage and inhuman breast.

6   The number of souls in this kingdom being usually reckoned one million and a half, of these I calculate there may be about two hundred thousand couples whose wives are breeders; from which number I subtract thirty thousand couples who are able to maintain their own children, although I apprehend there cannot be so many under the present distress of the kingdom; but this being granted, there will remain an hundred and seventy thousand breeders. I again subtract fifty thousand for those women who miscarry, or whose children die by accident or disease within the year. There only remain an hundred and twenty thousand children of poor parents annually born. The question therefore is, how this number shall be reared and provided for, which, as I have already said, under the present situation of affairs, is utterly impossible by all the methods hitherto proposed. For we can neither employ them in handicraft nor agriculture; we neither build houses (I mean in the country) nor cultivate

land. They can very seldom pick up a livelihood by stealing till they arrive at six years old, except where they are of towardly parts; although I confess they learn the rudiments much earlier, during which time they can however be looked upon only as probationers, as I have been informed by a principal gentleman in the country of Cavan, who protested to me that he never knew above one or two instances under the age of six, even in a part of the kingdom so renowned for the quickest proficiency in that art.

7   I am assured by our merchants that a boy or a girl before twelve years old is no salable commodity; and even when they come to this age, they will not yield above three pounds, or three pounds and half a crown at most on the Exchange; which cannot turn to account either to the parents or the kingdom, the charge of nutriment and rags having been at least four times that value.

8   I shall now therefore humbly propose my own thoughts, which I hope will not be liable to the least objection.

9   I have been assured by a very knowing American of my acquaintance in London, that a young healthy child well nursed is at a year old a most delicious, nourishing, and wholesome food, whether stewed, roasted, baked, or boiled; and I make no doubt that it will equally serve in a fricassee or a ragout.

10   I do therefore humbly offer it to public consideration that of the hundred and twenty thousand children, already computed, twenty thousand may be reserved for breed, whereof only one fourth part to be males, which is more than we allow to sheep, black cattle, or swine; and my reason is that these children are seldom the fruits of marriage, a circumstance not much regarded by our savages, therefore one male will be sufficient to serve four females. That the remaining hundred thousand may at a year old be offered in sale to the persons of quality and fortune through the kingdom, always advising the mother to let them suck plentifully in the last month, so as to render them plump and fat for a good table. A child will make two dishes at an entertainment for friends; and when the family dines alone, the fore or hind quarter will make a reasonable dish, and seasoned with a little pepper or salt will be very good boiled on the fourth day, especially in winter.

11   I have reckoned upon a medium that a child just born will weigh twelve pounds, and in a solar year if tolerably nursed increaseth to twenty-eight pounds.

12   I grant this food will be somewhat dear, and therefore very proper for landlords, who, as they have already devoured most of the parents, seem to have the best title to the children.

13   Infant's flesh will be in season throughout the year, but more plentiful in March, and a little before and after. For we are told by a grave author, an eminent French physician, that fish being a prolific diet, there are more children born in Roman Catholic countries about nine months after Lent, than at any other season; therefore, reckoning a year after Lent, the markets will be more glutted than usual, because the number of popish infants is at least three to one in this kingdom; and therefore it will have one other collateral advantage, by lessening the number of Papists among us.

14   I have already computed the charge of nursing a beggar's child (in which list I reckon all cottagers, laborers, and four fifths of the farmers) to be about two shillings per annum, rags included; and I believe no gentleman would repine to give ten shillings for the carcass of a good fat child, which, as I have said, will make four dishes of excellent nutritive meat, when he hath only some particular friend or his own family to dine with him. Thus the squire will learn to be a good landlord, and grow popular among the tenants; the mother will have eight shillings net profit, and be fit for work till she produces another child.

15   Those who are more thrifty (as I must confess the times require) may flay the carcass; the skin of which artificially dressed will make admirable gloves for ladies, and summer boots for fine gentlemen.

16   As to our city of Dublin, shambles may be appointed for this purpose in the most convenient parts of it, and butchers we may be assured will not be wanting; although I rather recommend buying the children alive, and dressing them hot from the knife as we do roasting pigs.

17   A very worthy person, a true lover of his country, and whose virtues I highly esteem, was lately pleased in discoursing on this matter to offer a refinement upon my scheme. He said that many gentlemen of his kingdom, having of late destroyed their deer, he conceived that the want of venison might be well supplied by the bodies of young lads and maidens, not exceeding fourteen years of age nor under twelve, so great a number of both sexes in every county being now ready to starve for want of work and service; and these to be disposed of by their parents, if alive, or otherwise by their nearest relations. But with due deference to so excellent a friend and so deserving a patriot, I cannot be altogether in his sentiments; for as to the males, my American acquaintance assured me from frequent experience that their flesh was generally tough and lean, like that of our schoolboys, by continual exercise, and their taste disagreeable; and to fatten them would not answer the charge. Then as to the females, it would, I think with humble submission, be a loss to the public, because they soon would become breeders themselves; and besides, it is not improbable that some scrupulous people might be apt to censure such a practice (although indeed very unjustly) as a little bordering upon cruelty; which, I confess, hath always been with me the strongest objection against any project, how well soever intended.

18   But in order to justify my friend, he confessed that this expedient was put into his head by the famous Psalmanazar, a native of the island Formosa, who came from thence to London above twenty years ago, and in conversation told my friend that in his country when any young person happened to be put to death, the executioner sold the carcass to the persons of quality as a prime dainty; and that in his time the body of a plump girl of fifteen, who was crucified for an attempt to poison the emperor, was sold to his Imperial Majesty's prime minister of state, and other great mandarins of the court, in joints from the gibbet, at four hundred crowns. Neither indeed can I deny that if the same use were made of several plump young girls in this town, who without one single groat to their fortunes cannot stir abroad without a chair, and appear at

the playhouse and assemblies in foreign fineries which they never will pay for, the kingdom would not be the worse.

19   Some persons of a desponding spirit are in great concern about that vast number of poor people who are aged, diseased, or maimed, and I have been desired to employ my thoughts what course may be taken to ease the nation of so grievous an encumbrance. But I am not in the least pain upon that matter, because it is very well known that they are every day dying and rotting by cold and famine, and filth and vermin, as fast as can be reasonably expected. And as to the younger laborers, they are now in almost as hopeful a condition. They cannot get work, and consequently pine away for want of nourishment to a degree that if any time they are accidentally hired to common labor, they have not strength to perform it; and thus the country and themselves are happily delivered from the evils to come.

20   I have too long digressed, and therefore shall return to my subject. I think the advantages by the proposal which I have made are obvious and many, as well as of the highest importance.

21   For first, as I have already observed, it would greatly lessen the number of Papists, with whom we are yearly overrun, being the principal breeders of the nation as well as our most dangerous enemies; and who stay at home on purpose to deliver the kingdom to the Pretender, hoping to take their advantage by the absence of so many good Protestants, who have chosen rather to leave their country than to stay at home and pay tithes against their conscience to an Episcopal curate.

22   Secondly, the poorer tenants will have something valuable of their own, which by law may be made liable to distress, and help to pay their landlord's rent, their corn and cattle being already seized and money a thing unknown.

23   Thirdly, whereas the maintenance of an hundred thousand children, from two years old and upwards, cannot be computed at less than ten shillings a piece per annum, the nation's stock will be thereby increased fifty thousand pounds per annum, besides the profit of a new dish introduced to the tables of all gentlemen of fortune in the kingdom who have any refinement in taste. And the money will circulate among ourselves, the goods being entirely of our own growth and manufacture.

24   Fourthly, the constant breeders, besides the gain of eight shillings sterling per annum by the sale of their children, will be rid of the charge for maintaining them after the first year.

25   Fifthly, this food would likewise bring great custom to taverns, where the vintners will certainly be so prudent as to procure the best receipts for dressing it to perfection, and consequently have their houses frequented by all the fine gentlemen, who justly value themselves upon their knowledge in good eating; and a skillful cook, who understands how to oblige his guests, will contrive to make it as expensive as they please.

26   Sixthly, this would be a great inducement to marriage, which all wise nations have either encouraged by rewards or enforced by laws and penalties. It would increase the care and tenderness of mothers toward their children, when they were sure of a settlement for life to the poor babes, provided in some sort

by the public, to their annual profit instead of expense. We should see an honest emulation among the married women, which of them could bring the fattest child to the market. Men would become as fond of their wives during the time of their pregnancy as they are now of their mares in foal, their cows in calf, or sows when they are ready to farrow; nor offer to beat or kick them (as is too frequent a practice) for fear of a miscarriage.

27   Many other advantages might be enumerated. For instance, the addition of some thousand carcasses in our exportation of barreled beef, the propagation of swine's flesh, and improvements in the art of making good bacon, so much wanted among us by the great destruction of pigs, too frequent at our tables, which are no way comparable in taste or magnificence to a well-grown, fat, yearling child, which roasted whole will make a considerable figure at a lord mayor's feast or any other public entertainment. But this and many others I omit, being studious of brevity.

28   Supposing that one thousand families in this city would be constant customers for infants' flesh, besides others who might have it at merry meetings, particularly weddings and christenings, I compute that Dublin would take off annually about twenty thousand carcasses, and the rest of the kingdom (where probably they will be sold somewhat cheaper) the remaining eighty thousand.

29   I can think of no one objection that will possibly be raised against this proposal, unless it should be urged that the number of people will be thereby much lessened in the kingdom. This I freely own, and it was indeed one principal design in offering it to the world. I desire the reader will observe, that I calculate my remedy for this one individual kingdom of Ireland and for no other that ever was, is, or I think ever can be upon earth. Therefore, let no man talk to me of other expedients: of taxing our absentees at five shillings a pound: of using neither clothes nor household furniture except what is of our own growth and manufacture: of utterly rejecting the materials and instruments that promote foreign luxury: of curing the expensiveness of pride, vanity, idleness, and gaming in our women: of introducing a vein of parsimony, prudence, and temperance: of learning to love our country, in the want of which we differ even from Laplanders and the inhabitants of Topinamboo: of quitting our animosities and factions, nor acting any longer like the Jews, who were murdering one another at the very moment their city was taken: of being a little cautious not to sell our country and conscience for nothing: of teaching landlords to have at least one degree of mercy toward their tenants: lastly, of putting a spirit of honesty, industry, and skill into our shopkeepers; who, if a resolution could now be taken to buy only our native goods, would immediately unite to cheat and exact upon us in the price, the measure, and the goodness, nor could ever yet be brought to make one fair proposal of just dealing, though often and earnestly invited to it.

30   Therefore, I repeat, let no man talk to me of these and the like expedients, till he hath at least some glimpse of hope that there will ever be some hearty and sincere attempt to put them in practice.

31   But as to myself, having been wearied out for many years with offering vain, idle, visionary thoughts, and at length utterly despairing of success, I

fortunately fell upon this proposal, which, as it is wholly new, so it hath something solid and real, of no expense and little trouble, full in our own power, and whereby we can incur no danger in disobliging England. For this kind of commodity will not bear exportation, the flesh being of too tender a consistence to admit a long continuance in salt, although perhaps I could name a country which would be glad to eat up our whole nation without it.

32   After all, I am not so violently bent upon my own opinion as to reject any offer proposed by wise men, which shall be found equally innocent, cheap, easy, and effectual. But before something of that kind shall be advanced in contradiction to my scheme, and offering a better, I desire the author or authors will be pleased maturely to consider two points. First, as things now stand, how they will be able to find food and raiment for an hundred thousand useless mouths and backs. And secondly, there being a round million of creatures in human figure throughout this kingdom, whose sole subsistence put into a common stock would leave them in debt two millions of pounds sterling, adding those who are beggars by profession to the bulk of farmers, cottagers, and laborers, with their wives and children who are beggars in effect; I desire those politicians who dislike my overture, and may perhaps be so bold to attempt an answer, that they will first ask the parents of these mortals whether they would not at this day think it a great happiness to have been sold for food at a year old in this manner I prescribe, and thereby have avoided such a perpetual scene of misfortunes as they have since gone through by the oppression of landlords, the impossibility of paying rent without money or trade, the want of common sustenance, with neither house nor clothes to cover them from the inclemencies of the weather, and the most inevitable prospect of entailing the like or greater miseries upon their breed forever.

33   I profess, in the sincerity of my heart, that I have not the least personal interest in endeavoring to promote this necessary work, having no other motive than the public good of my country, by advancing our trade, providing for infants, relieving the poor, and giving some pleasure to the rich. I have no children by which I can propose to get a single penny; the youngest being nine years old, and my wife past childbearing.

Topics for Writing and Discussion

1. When does it first become obvious that "A Modest Proposal" is written ironically? What hints do you have in earlier paragraphs that the proposal you are reading is not to be taken literally? Notice particularly both the denotations and connotations of words Swift chooses to describe the Irish people.

2. Swift uses the persona of a "projector" (a person who suggests plans for social or economic change) to put forth the "modest proposal." How would you characterize the projector? How do his views differ from the views of Swift? Where do you find Swift's voice (and beliefs) breaking through the voice of the persona?

3. How does Swift use statistics and other facts to promote his own argument while remaining in the character of his projector?

4. Swift condemns the English for their oppression and exploitation of the Irish, but he also condemns the Irish for certain social practices and beliefs. Analyze and give examples of his criticism of both the English and the Irish.

5. Write your own "modest proposal," adopting a persona and using irony to argue for better treatment of a particular group of people in your community or in this country.

TO HIS COY MISTRESS

Andrew Marvell
(1621–1678)

One of the major metaphysical poets of the seventeenth century, Andrew Marvell was educated at Cambridge. Though he was not a Puritan, Marvell supported the Puritan cause during the Civil Wars of 1642–1649 and held posts during the Interregnum (1649–1660), including that of assistant to poet John Milton (at the time, Oliver Cromwell's Latin Secretary). In 1659, Marvell was elected to Parliament, where he served until his death. After the Restoration, Marvell expressed his strong disagreements with the government in a series of satires (printed anonymously). Many of his poems were published only after his death. In "To His Coy Mistress," Marvell's speaker playfully argues the need to pursue immediate pleasures while there is still time.

Had we but world enough, and time,
This coyness,[1] Lady, were no crime.
We would sit down and think which way
To walk and pass our long love's day.
5 Thou by the Indian Ganges'[2] side
Shouldst rubies find; I by the tide
Of Humber[3] would complain. I would
Love you ten years before the Flood,
And you should, if you please, refuse
10 Till the conversion of the Jews.

---

[1] *coyness:* shyness, reserve

[2] *Ganges:* a river in India

[3] *Humber:* an English estuary that flows to the North Sea

Andrew Marvell (Archive Photos)

My vegetable love should grow
Vaster than empires, and more slow;
An hundred years should go to praise
Thine eyes and on thy forehead gaze;
15 Two hundred to adore each breast,
But thirty thousand to the rest;
An age at least to every part,
And the last age should show your heart.
For, Lady, you deserve this state,
20 Nor would I love at lower rate.
    But at my back I always hear
Time's wingéd chariot hurrying near;
And yonder all before us lie
Deserts of vast eternity.
25 Thy beauty shall no more be found,
Nor, in thy marble vault, shall sound
My echoing song; then worms shall try
That long preserved virginity,
And your quaint honor turn to dust,
30 And into ashes all my lust:
The grave's a fine and private place,
But none, I think, do there embrace.
    Now therefore, while the youthful hue
Sits on thy skin like morning dew,
35 And while thy willing soul transpires
At every pore with instant fires,
Now let us sport us while we may,
And now, like amorous birds of prey,
Rather at once our time devour
40 Than languish in his slow-chapped⁴ power.
Let us roll all our strength and all
Our sweetness up into one ball,
And tear our pleasures with rough strife
Through the iron gates of life:
45 Thus, though we cannot make our sun
Stand still, yet we will make him run.

Topics for Writing and Discussion

1. Who is speaking in this poem? To whom is the poem addressed? What was
    the seventeenth-century meaning of "mistress"?
2. What has been the attitude of the lady toward the speaker? For what
    change is the speaker arguing?

---

⁴ *slow-chapped:* slow-jawed, devouring slowly

3. What main point does the speaker use to advance his argument? Whose "winged chariot" (line 21) does he hear and why does he talk about "a fine and private place"?

4. Describe the three sections of this poem as parts of a structured argument. How is exaggeration in the first section contrasted with more realistic details in the second section? Which imagery presents the call to action?

5. What sort of rebuttal might the "coy mistress" write to the speaker of this poem today? What main points would you include if you were writing an essay in response to this poem?

HILLS LIKE WHITE ELEPHANTS

Ernest Hemingway
(1899–1961)

⁓⁓⁓⁓

Born in Oak Park, Illinois, Ernest Hemingway began work for the Kansas City *Star* in 1917, after his high school graduation. He left the *Star* to serve as an ambulance driver for the American Red Cross with the Italian Army during World War I, but was soon wounded. After a six-month convalescence, he returned to the United States and then found work as a foreign correspondent in Paris for the Toronto *Star.* In 1922, he settled in Paris, where he associated with a group of expatriate Americans, including Ezra Pound, Gertrude Stein, and F. Scott Fitzgerald. While in Paris, Hemingway wrote about the "lost generation" of disillusioned, seemingly rootless young Americans who were traveling and living in Europe at the time. In 1928, he returned to the United States and enjoyed popular acclaim as a novelist and short story writer. He worked as a war correspondent during the Spanish Civil War and World War II and received the Nobel Prize for Literature in 1954. Some of his most famous novels include *The Sun Also Rises* (1926), *Farewell to Arms* (1929), *For Whom the Bell Tolls* (1940), and *The Old Man and the Sea* (1952). "Hills Like White Elephants" presents an argument between a couple facing a serious decision, told in Hemingway's typically sparse, realistic style.

---

1   THE hills across the valley of the Ebro* were long and white. On this side there was no shade and no trees and the station was between two lines of rails

---

*A river in Spain.

Ernest Hemingway (Springer/Corbis-Bettmann)

in the sun. Close against the side of the station there was the warm shadow of the building and a curtain, made of strings of bamboo beads, hung across the open door into the bar, to keep out flies. The American and the girl with him sat at a table in the shade, outside the building. It was very hot and the express from Barcelona would come in forty minutes. It stopped at this junction for two minutes and went on to Madrid.

2   "What should we drink?" the girl asked. She had taken off her hat and put it on the table.

3   "It's pretty hot," the man said.

4   "Let's drink beer."

5   "Dos cervezas," the man said into the curtain.

6   "Big ones?" a woman asked from the doorway.

7   "Yes. Two big ones."

8   The woman brought two glasses of beer and two felt pads. She put the felt pads and the beer glasses on the table and looked at the man and the girl. The girl was looking off at the line of hills. They were white in the sun and the country was brown and dry.

9   "They look like white elephants," she said.

10   "I've never seen one," the man drank his beer.

11   "No, you wouldn't have."

12   "I might have," the man said. "Just because you say I wouldn't have doesn't prove anything."

13   The girl looked at the bead curtain. "They've painted something on it," she said. "What does it say?"

14   "Anis del Toro. It's a drink."

15   "Could we try it?"

16   The man called "Listen" through the curtain. The woman came out from the bar.

17   "Four reales."

18   "We want two Anis del Toro."

19   "With water?"

20   "Do you want it with water?"

21   "I don't know," the girl said. "Is it good with water?"

22   "It's all right."

23   "You want them with water?" asked the woman.

24   "Yes, with water."

25   "It tastes like licorice," the girl said and put the glass down.

26   "That's the way with everything."

27   "Yes," said the girl. "Everything tastes of licorice. Especially all the things you've waited so long for, like absinthe."

28   "Oh, cut it out."

29   "You started it," the girl said. "I was being amused. I was having a fine time."

30   "Well, let's try and have a fine time."

31   "All right. I was trying. I said the mountains looked like white elephants. Wasn't that bright?"

32   "That was bright."

33   "I wanted to try this new drink. That's all we do, isn't it—look at things and try new drinks?"

34   "I guess so."

35   The girl looked across at the hills.

36   "They're lovely hills," she said. "They don't really look like white elephants. I just meant the coloring of their skin through the trees."

37   "Should we have another drink?"

38   "All right."

39   The warm wind blew the bead curtain against the table.

40   "The beer's nice and cool," the man said.

41   "It's lovely," the girl said.

42   "It's really an awfully simple operation, Jig," the man said. "It's not really an operation at all."

43   The girl looked at the ground the table legs rested on.

44   "I know you wouldn't mind it, Jig. It's really not anything. It's just to let the air in."

45   The girl did not say anything.

46   "I'll go with you and I'll stay with you all the time. They just let the air in and then it's all perfectly natural."

47   "Then what will we do afterward?"

48   "We'll be fine afterward. Just like we were before."

49   "What makes you think so?"

50   "That's the only thing that bothers us. It's the only thing that's made us unhappy."

51   The girl looked at the bead curtain, put her hand out and took hold of two of the strings of beads.

52   "And you think then we'll be all right and be happy."

53   "I know we will. You don't have to be afraid. I've known lots of people that have done it."

54   "So have I," said the girl. "And afterward they were all so happy."

55   "Well," the man said, "if you don't want to you don't have to. I wouldn't have you do it if you didn't want to. But I know it's perfectly simple."

56   "And you really want to?"

57   "I think it's the best thing to do. But I don't want you to do it if you don't really want to."

58   "And if I do it you'll be happy and things will be like they were and you'll love me?"

59   "I love you now. You know I love you."

60   "I know. But if I do it, then it will be nice again if I say things are like white elephants, and you'll like it?"

61   "I'll love it. I love it now but I just can't think about it. You know how I get when I worry."

62   "If I do it you won't ever worry?"

63   "I won't worry about that because it's perfectly simple."

64 "Then I'll do it. Because I don't care about me."

65 "What do you mean?"

66 "I don't care about me."

67 "Well, I care about you."

68 "Oh, yes. But I don't care about me. And I'll do it and then everything will be fine."

69 "I don't want you to do it if you feel that way."

70 The girl stood up and walked to the end of the station. Across, on the other side, were fields of grain and trees along the banks of the Ebro. Far away, beyond the river, were mountains. The shadow of a cloud moved across the field of grain and she saw the river through the trees.

71 "And we could have all this," she said. "And we could have everything and every day we make it more impossible."

72 "What did you say?"

73 "I said we could have everything."

74 "We can have everything."

75 "No, we can't."

76 "We can have the whole world."

77 "No, we can't."

78 "We can go everywhere."

79 "No, we can't. It isn't ours any more."

80 "It's ours."

81 "No, it isn't. And once they take it away, you never get it back."

82 "But they haven't taken it away."

83 "We'll wait and see."

84 "Come on back in the shade," he said. "You mustn't feel that way."

85 "I don't feel any way," the girl said. "I just know things."

86 "I don't want you to do anything that you don't want to do—"

87 "Nor that isn't good for me," she said. "I know. Could we have another beer?"

88 "All right. But you've got to realize—"

89 "I realize," the girl said. "Can't we maybe stop talking?"

90 They sat down at the table and the girl looked across at the hills on the dry side of the valley and the man looked at her and at the table.

91 "You've got to realize," he said, "that I don't want you to do it if you don't want to. I'm perfectly willing to go through with it if it means anything to you."

92 "Doesn't it mean anything to you? We could get along."

93 "Of course it does. But I don't want anybody but you. I don't want any one else. And I know it's perfectly simple."

94 "Yes, you know it's perfectly simple."

95 "It's all right for you to say that, but I do know it."

96 "Would you do something for me now?"

97 "I'd do anything for you."

98 "Would you please please please please please please please stop talking?"

99   He did not say anything but looked at the bags against the wall of the station. There were labels on them from all the hotels where they had spent nights.

100   "But I don't want you to," he said, "I don't care anything about it."

101   "I'll scream," the girl said.

102   The woman came out through the curtains with two glasses of beer and put them down on the damp felt pads. "The train comes in five minutes," she said.

103   "What did she say?" asked the girl.

104   "That the train is coming in five minutes."

105   The girl smiled brightly at the woman, to thank her.

106   "I'd better take the bags over to the other side of the station," the man said. She smiled at him.

107   "All right. Then come back and we'll finish the beer."

108   He picked up the two heavy bags and carried them around the station to the other tracks. He looked up the tracks but could not see the train. Coming back, he walked through the barroom, where people waiting for the train were drinking. He drank an Anis at the bar and looked at the people. They were all waiting reasonably for the train. He went out through the bead curtain. She was sitting at the table and smiled at him.

109   "Do you feel better?" he asked.

110   "I feel fine," she said. "There's nothing wrong with me. I feel fine."

Topics for Writing and Discussion

1. Although it remains unnamed, what choice is this couple debating? What effect on the reader is produced through Hemingway's use of dialogue rather than description?

2. What is the man advocating, and why? Do you find his argument sincere and persuasive? Is he presented sympathetically or not?

3. How would you characterize the woman's reactions to her companion's wishes? Is this choice "perfectly simple" for her?

4. How are the details about the setting of this story (the hills, sides of the valley, train station, etc.) used symbolically? Why is it called "Hills Like White Elephants"?

5. Readers often disagree about the ending of this story, especially the last line. What decision has been made? Do you think the woman is honest when she says she feels "fine"? Compare your reading to those of your classmates and then write an essay arguing your interpretation.

WRITING ASSIGNMENTS FOR CHAPTER ELEVEN

PERSUASION AND ARGUMENT

1. In a popular song of the 1960s, Joni Mitchell claimed that we'd "paved paradise and put up a parking lot." She called on farmers to put away their chemicals and "give me spots on my apples but leave me the birds and bees." Research the use of some chemical agent, industrial process, or food additive that you believe seriously threatens our health or environment today and write an argumentative essay calling for its investigation or prohibition. Think of your congressional representative as your audience and try to maintain a concerned, reasonable tone as does Rachel Carson in "The Obligation to Endure."

2. On August 28, 1963, when Martin Luther King, Jr., delivered his "I Have a Dream" speech, he faced a formidable task. He had to turn some of his audience away from anger and thoughts of violence while, at the same time, inspire them to continue the nonviolent fight for civil rights. Select a social problem that arouses controversy today and designate an audience whose sympathies are not firmly aligned with yours. Write a speech that will convince them to adopt your point of view.

3. In "The Health-Care System," Lewis Thomas declares that "we have become obsessed with Health." According to Thomas, we are worrying ourselves to death because we are "being taken in by the propaganda." Focus on some specific health issue and write an essay arguing for or against Thomas' position that we spend too much time and energy becoming a nation of healthy hypochondriacs. For instance, is our attitude toward thinness and dieting a product of mass media? Or does Thomas overstate his case? Are jogging and bicycling more than fads of people preoccupied with disease and death?

4. Thomas argues that the health obsession he describes will make any health-care system unworkable. Research the issue of national health care in this country and write an essay arguing for or against some specific plan or proposal you discover in your reading. What are the primary arguments for and against this plan? Who is for or against such a plan, and why? Is Thomas' complaint one of the major reasons some people oppose such a plan or proposal?

5. In "None of This Is Fair," Richard Rodriguez uses his own experience and that of his classmate to argue the disadvantages of Affirmative Action. Select a controversial law or social action and, similarly, use your personal experience to point out one of its main strengths or weaknesses. You may wish, as Rodriguez did, to experiment with dialogue as well as narrative.

6. In his essay "Drugs," Gore Vidal calls for the truthful, not exaggerated, description of illegal drugs' effects on people, and he mentions, to establish his credibility, his own experimentation with drugs. Have you or someone you know well been adversely affected by illegal drug use? Has the experience shaped or changed your attitude toward drug sale or use? Write an essay using your experience to argue your views on the sale or use of a particular drug popular on the streets today.

7. Vidal claims that prohibition of alcohol from 1920 to 1933 and today's laws aimed at drug use are similar in their promotion of violence and crime. Research the Prohibition era in this country and write an essay that argues for or against similarities of either the problems or their solutions.

8. In "I Want a Wife," Judy Brady describes the many roles a wife has often been expected to play. Using Brady's essay as your inspiration, write an essay about a role you do *not* want to play, a role that perhaps has been dictated by other people's expectations or by certain traditions or even by your family. Why do you reject this role? Do you see, as Brady did, something inherently unfair about it?

9. Consider Martin Luther King, Jr.'s "I Have a Dream" speech and Thomas Jefferson's "Declaration of Independence." Draft a letter King might have written to Jefferson, urging him to make important changes in the famous document. You may draw on twentieth-century events to make your arguments persuasive.

10. In 1848 when Elizabeth Cady Stanton drafted the "Declaration of Sentiments and Resolutions," she obviously felt the original Declaration did not speak adequately to both sexes. Research one of the grievances Cady Stanton lists (for example, no right to vote, no property rights, few educational or employment opportunities) and write an editorial advocating change that might have appeared in a local newspaper in 1848. What specific arguments might Cady Stanton have offered to support any one of the "tyrannies" she mentions in her "Declaration"?

11. As a writer, Virginia Woolf had to overcome some serious obstacles, including the Angel in the House whose "murder" she describes in "Professions for Women." Think of an obstacle that you have faced in your pursuit of an important personal or professional goal and argue one means of conquering that problem. Consider writing your paper as an address to people who are just beginning to face the obstacle you successfully overcame.

12. Compare and contrast Virginia Woolf's essay "Professions for Women" with her other essay in this text, "If Shakespeare Had Had a Sister." How do the two selections compare in terms of purpose, audience, organizational techniques, language, and tone? In effectiveness? If you were to select only one of these two essays to give to a friend interested in Virginia Woolf or in women's issues, which would you select? Support your answer with ample illustrations from the two essays.

13. Choose some regulation, requirement, or plan currently in effect on your campus that you think is unwise. Using Jonathan Swift's famous essay as a model, write your own satire that acquaints your readers with this unjust or ineffective situation. Consider sending your essay to your campus or local newspaper.

14. After reading Ron Kline's essay "A Scientist: 'I Am the Enemy,'" investigate the possibility of experimentation on animals at your college or in your community. Do any local industries, farms, or hatcheries maintain animals in controversial production processes? Investigate a specific scientific or agricultural use of animals in your area and then write an essay that defends or attacks this procedure.

15. In "The Right to Die," Norman Cousins notes that medical science can now prolong life "far beyond meaning or sensibility." A series of court cases in the 1990s, often focused on Dr. Jack Kevorkian, questioned whether physicians have the right to assist in the suicide of someone who requests their help. Investigate one of these court cases and then write an essay arguing your response had you been one of the jurors.

16. "To His Coy Mistress" may be included in a group of literary works with a *carpe diem* (seize the day) theme. Can you think of any contemporary works of literature or music that also present this theme? Select one example and analyze its argument and persuasive techniques. Do you find it more or less effective than Andrew Marvell's seventeenth-century poem?

17. In "Hills Like White Elephants" by Ernest Hemingway, a couple confronts a difficult decision. Think of a difficult choice you faced in the past and write an essay that presents the choice you made. Explain the two or three strongest points that ultimately persuaded you.

Glossary of Rhetorical and Literary Terms

Ad Hominem Attack   An ad hominem argument attacks an opponent's character rather than his or her ideas and beliefs.

Alliteration   Alliteration is the repetition of the initial consonant sounds of two or more neighboring words: wild and woolly, "The Woman Warrior," tea for two.

Analogy   An analogy shows a similarity between two otherwise dissimilar things. For example, music is analogous to the wind—strong and loud at some times, gentle and quiet at others. A false analogy distorts the points of similarity and results in an invalid conclusion.

Analysis   Analysis breaks a subject into parts in order to clarify the whole.

Antithesis   An antithesis is an idea directly opposite to the thesis of an essay.

Argument   Argument is a mode of writing whose purpose is to persuade the reader to act or agree. (See Chapter 11.)

Audience   Audience is the expected readership for an essay that helps to determine the writing strategy and evidence the writer will use.

Brainstorming   Brainstorming means writing down anything that comes to mind in an unstructured way in order to generate ideas for writing. (See Chapter 2.)

Cause and Effect   Cause and effect is a strategy of development used by a writer to explain the reasons for, or the results of, a particular action or event. (See Chapter 10.)

Characterization   Characterization refers to the ways a writer depicts and develops the characters in an essay.

Chronological Order   Chronological order refers to presenting the events in an essay in the same time sequence in which they occurred or are occurring.

Cliché   A cliché is a trite, overused expression, such as "old as the hills" or "up the creek without a paddle."

Climactic Order   Climactic order refers to arranging the parts of a composition from the least important to the most important or from smallest to largest.

Coherence   Coherence is the clear and logical connection of the thesis and all parts of an essay, achieved by a logical sequence, transitions, and repetition of key words or synonyms.

Comparison and Contrast   Comparison and contrast is a strategy of development used by a writer to examine the similarities and differences between people, ideas, and things. (See Chapter 8.)

Connotation   Connotation refers to the feelings and memories associated with a word, such as moonlight suggesting romance and mystery. See also *Denotation*.

Controlling Idea   The controlling idea, or thesis, of an essay is the central meaning or message that the writer is trying to convey to the reader.

Deduction   Deduction is the method of logical reasoning that moves from the general to the specific, such as "All men are mortal" and "Socrates is a man" producing the conclusion "Therefore, Socrates is mortal."

Definition   Definition refers both to the explanation of the meaning of a word and the strategy of development used by a writer to explore the meaning of a word or concept in an essay. (See Chapter 6.)

Denotation   Denotation is the literal and explicit meaning of a word independent of any emotional association, such as moonlight being "the rays of light reflected by the moon." See also *Connotation*.

Description   Description is the mode of writing in which a writer uses concrete details to create a representation of what something is or appears to be. (See Chapter 4.)

Division and Classification   Division and classification are strategies of development used to explain a general category that is sorted into smaller groups on the basis of some selected principle. (See Chapter 9.)

Essay   An essay is a short, nonfiction composition on one topic, often written from a personal point of view.

Evidence   Evidence is the material used to support an opinion, argument, or explanation.

Exposition   Exposition refers to a mode of writing that explains a subject by supplying information through the strategies of illustration, comparison and contrast, division and classification, process analysis, definition, and cause and effect.

Figurative Language   Figurative language is the use of comparisons and associations to communicate meaning and to achieve emphasis. Common figures of speech are the metaphor, simile, personification, and hyperbole.

Freewriting   Freewriting means writing down whatever thoughts occur in order to stimulate ideas and generate material for writing an essay.

Hyperbole   Hyperbole is an expression that uses deliberate exaggeration rather than a literal statement to make a point: He's the most handsome man this side of the Mississippi.

Illustration   Illustration is a strategy of development used by a writer to prove the validity of the thesis of an essay by supporting or clarifying it with examples. (See Chapter 7.)

Image   An image is a vivid description that appeals to the reader's sense of sight, sound, smell, taste, or touch.

Induction   Induction is the method of logical reasoning that derives a conclusion about an entire group by examining some of its members.

Irony   Irony is the use of language to convey a meaning that is the opposite of what is intended.

Jargon   Jargon is the special vocabulary of a specific group such as doctors, film directors, or anthropologists. Jargon should be avoided when it obscures meaning or overburdens style.

Metaphor   A metaphor is a figure of speech that conveys information by comparing two dissimilar things in order to show or clarify an unexpected similarity: Her eyes were stars shining in the midnight sky.

Narration   Narration is a mode of writing wherein the writer tells a story or recounts events. (See Chapter 3.)

Non Sequitur   A non sequitur is a logical fallacy in which the conclusion does not follow from the evidence: If one brownie tastes good, two must taste twice as good.

Paradox   A paradox is an idea or statement that seems contradictory but which expresses a truth: arming for peace, spending money to make money.

Parody   Parody is a humorous or satirical imitation, often used to make fun of or criticize a literary style.

Persona   Persona refers to the voice and character an author creates in a piece of fiction or nonfiction.

Personification   Personification is a figure of speech that assigns human characteristics to nonhuman things: The car waited patiently in the driveway. The vacuum cleaner devoured the dust.

Point of View   Point of view refers to the way the narrator presents the subject in a piece of writing. Points of view for the same subject may differ, depending on the opinion of each different writer.

Process   Process is a strategy of development used by a writer to trace the steps of an event or operation. (See Chapter 5.)

Purpose   Purpose is the writer's reason for writing—to entertain, to explain, to win an argument, to move the audience to action.

Rhetoric   Rhetoric is the study and effective use of language. The rhetorical modes (narration, description, exposition, and argument) present different organizational strategies for achieving an author's purpose in an essay.

Satire   A satire is a piece of writing that may use wit, irony, and ridicule to expose the folly of its subject matter.

Simile   A simile is a figure of speech in which a comparison is made between two dissimilar things by using the words *like* or *as:* as jumpy as a cat on a hot tin roof, children sprouting up like weeds.

Sonnet, Shakespearean   A Shakespearean sonnet is a single-stanza poem of fourteen lines arranged in three quatrains (abab, cdcd, efef) and a concluding couplet (gg), written in regular iambic pentameter pattern (five lightly stressed syllables, each followed by a stressed syllable).

Spatial Order   Spatial order refers to arranging details in a description so that readers can follow the eye's path.

Symbol   A symbol is an image or an object that stands for an idea or complex of ideas. An eagle may symbolize freedom; a heart may symbolize love.

Synonym   A synonym is a word with approximately the same meaning as another word: "fright" is a synonym for fear; "bravery" is a synonym for courage.

Thesis   The thesis is the central or controlling idea of an essay. The content of the essay should support and develop the thesis.

Tone   Tone refers to the general attitude of the writer toward the essay's subject or audience: The tone of the movie review was hostile.

Topic Sentence   The topic sentence is the statement of the main idea in a paragraph.

LITERARY CREDITS

Index